DIGITAL FILTERS

Edited by **Fausto Pedro García Márquez**

INTECHOPEN.COM

Digital Filters

Edited by Fausto Pedro García Márquez

CBS, Edition **2016**

Published by InTech

Janeza Trdine 9, 51000 Rijeka, Croatia

Publishing Process Manager Katarina Lovrecic

Technical Editor Teodora Smiljanic

Cover Designer InTech Design Team

Image Copyright Prudkov, 2010. Used under license from Shutterstock.com

Additional hard copies can be obtained from orders@intechopen.com

Digital Filters, Edited by Fausto Pedro García Márquez
p. cm.
ISBN 978-953-307-190-9

Contents

Preface

The new technologies and communications systems are being set up in all areas. It leads to treating data from different sources and for several proposes. But it is necessary to obtain only the information that is required. Digital filters, together with analogue filters, are used for these objectives. The main advantage of the digital filters is that they can be applied at zero cost and with a great flexibility. The mathematical models where they are created have different complexity and computational cost. In this book the most relevant filters are described, and with different applications. The material covered in this text is crucial for getting a general idea about digital filters. This book also presents some best options for each case study considered.

In spite of the mathematical complexity of the digital filters, the text is presented for any reader with a motivation for learning about digital filters. The high level contents are shown with an exhaust introduction, where the most important works in the literature are referenced and it completed with various examples.

A discrete filter is presented within a well-known and common framework, namely the State Space with the help of the Kalman Filter (KF) and/or complementary Fixed Interval Smoother (FIS) algorithms. It is presented in several case studies for detecting faults where these models can be adapted to external and internal conditions to the mechanism. All of these models are developed within a well-known common framework, namely the State Space (SS). The KF is a powerful algorithm, because it supports estimations of past, present and future states. In this case, it is used for filtering with Integrated Random Walks by setting up a bivariate model composed of two time series, i.e. the reference curve on one hand and each one of the empirical curves obtained on line on the other hand. Other options are to use a model VARMA (Vector autoregressive moving-average) class or a local level plus noise but set up in continuous time. Finally, due to the nature of the data, a pertinent class is a Dynamic Harmonic Regression, similar to a Fourier analysis, but with advanced features included to incorporate a time varying period observed in the data.

In the case of a linear circuit and frequency filter analysis for sinusoidal and periodical input signals, the spectral representations employing Fourier transform are studied. In that case, Laplace's transformations are employed in order to consider a complex frequency. The compound finite signal representations are done in the form of the set of damped oscillatory components. It is an efficient method for filtering and it can work with a complex coordinate. In the case of Infinite Impulse Response (IIR) filter impulse functions the representation uses this set of damped oscillatory components. Impulse functions of Finite Impulse Response (FIR) filters representation are also based on this set of damped oscillatory components, but with the difference of a finite duration of the impulse functions. It considers the stationary and non stationary modes, where it can be calculated easily in the spectral representation context. It is possible considering the application of spectral representations in complex frequency coordinates. It leads to consider both spectral approach and the state space method for frequency filter analysis and synthesis. The filter synthesis problem comes to dependence composition for filter transfer function on complex frequencies of input signal components.

Complex filters can be namely digital filters with complex coefficients. They are employed in complex signal processing compared to the real signal processing (e.g. telecommunications). This can imply real and imaginary inputs and outputs, and these signals need to be separated into real and imaginary parts for being studied as complex signals. The first- and second-order IIR orthogonal complex sections are synthesized as filters in designing cascade structures or as single filter structures. It leads delay-free loops and has a canonical number of elements. The low-sensitivity 1 and 2 variable complex sections can be used in narrowband band-pass / band-stop structures. The main advantages of these models are the higher freedom of tuning, reduced complexity and lower stop-band sensitivity.

The response dela in digital circuits should be adjusted to a fraction of the sampling interval and it should be fixed or variable in order to control the fractional delay (FD). These circuits are used in telecommunications applications that require speech synthesis and processing, image interpolation, sigma-delta modulators, time-delay estimation, in some biomedical applications and for modeling of musical instruments. Considering the phase-sensitivity minimization of each individual first- and second-order allpass section in the filter cascade realization, fixed and variable allpass-based fractional delay filters are developed and adjusted through sensitivity minimizations. The real and complex-conjugate poles combinations for different values of the FD parameter D and of the transfer function (TF) order N are analyzed trying to minimize the overall sensitivity.

A two-dimensional (2D) digital filter is employed to attain the desired cut-off frequency and the stable monotonic amplitude-frequency responses of this filter. It is developed in accordance with monotonic amplitude-frequency responses employing Darlington-type gyrator networks and doubly-terminated RLC-networks by the application of Generalized Bilinear Transformation (GBT). The doubly terminated RLC networks are adjusted as second-order Butterworth and Gargour & Ramachandran. It leads low-pass, high-pass, band-pass and band-elimination filters. The transformation between these filters is done by the value and sign of the parameter called g and GBT. It is useful in digital image (video and audio), and for enhancement and restoration in different fields, as medical science, geographical science and environment, space and robotic engineering, etc.

From a 1D filter (low-pass and maximally-flat or very selective), a 2D filter can be developed. These are essentially spectral transformations (frequency transformations) via bilinear or Euler transformations followed by mappings. This book analyzes the case of recursive filter approaches in the frequency domain applied in image processing: directional selective filters, oriented wedge filters, fan filters, diamond-shaped filters, etc. The zero-phase case is also considered. All the models are mainly analytical, and in some cases, numerical optimization is employed, in particular - rational approximations. The reason to choose the analytical approach is that the 2D parameters can be controlled by adjusting the prototype. An analytical design method in polar coordinates is proposed and defined by a periodic function expressed in polar coordinates in the frequency plane. It can yield selective two or multi-directional filters, and also fan and diamond filters. Finally, two-lobe filters are analysed, selective four-lobe filters with an arbitrary orientation angle, fan filters and diamond filters.

Single correction filters or ensembles of correction filters, sensitivity filters, lumbar spine filter, banks of vehicle filters, and road texture filters are presented. They are studied in two examples on safety of traffic: road hump analysis and determination of road texture. Digital filters are recommended for low robustness, and this originates from the definition of the feature and/or its incomplete specification instead of a feature which is not robust and questionable. The digital filters employed fit into the above mentioned standard linear-in-response finite/infinite impulse response (FIR/IIR) form for direct implementation. In this case any filter may be transferred to a state-space form for generalization into a KF.

Carry-Save Arithmetic is employed in order to achieve an optimal design of single constant multipliers for coefficients with up to 19 bits wordlength. The non-redundant representation is also considered. The proposed techniques are useful when a high-speed realization is required. It is demonstrated in the multiple constant multiplication problems suitable for transposed direct form FIR filters using carry-save representation of intermediate results but non-redundant input.

Lattice wave digital (LWD) filter (parallel connections of all-pass filters) is a structure implemented in the recursive digital filters. Three cases are considered in this book: primarily the overall filter, constructed as a cascade of low-order LWD filters. Secondly, approximately linear-phase LWD filters are constructed as a single block. The reason for this is the lack of benefits for the direct-form LWD filter design in the usage of a cascade of several filter blocks. Finally, it is focused on the design of special recursive single-stage and multistage Nth-band decimators and interpolators. The coefficient optimization is performed with following steps: an initial infinite-precision filter is designed such that it exceeds the given criteria in order to provide some tolerance for coefficient quantization; then, a nonlinear optimization algorithm is employed for determining a parameter space of the infinite-precision coefficients including the feasible space where the filter meets the given criteria; and finally, the filter parameters are found in this space so that the resulting filter meets the given criteria with the simplest coefficient representation forms. The realization of these filters does not require the use of a costly general multiplier element. It leads to the fact that the filters are goods in very large-scale integration (VLSI).

The sampled-data and digital filters (i.e. "memory transistor" or "memory transconductor" approaches) are both studied for their effectivity. This case is about biquadratic sections used in cascade design. The switched-current (SI) circuits are also one of the case studies employed, where it can be extended to cases as digital VLSI-CMOS technologies, lower supply voltage and wide dynamic range, considering an SI as "analog counterpart" of the digital filters. The biquadratic realization structures are developed from the first and second direct forms of the 2nd-order digital filter. The continuous-time biquadratic sections design is also considered. Finally, the optimization of sampled-data and digital filters design is solved by using the heuristic algorithm as the differential evolutionary algorithm.

Fausto Pedro García Márquez
University of Castilla-La Mancha (UCLM)
Spain

Digital Filters for Maintenance Management

Fausto Pedro García Márquez and Diego José Pedregal Tercero
Ingenium Research Group, University of Castilla-La Mancha
Spain

1. Abstract

Faults in mechanisms must be detected quickly and reliably in order to avoid important losses. Detection systems should be developed to minimize maintenance costs and are generally based on consistent models, but as simple as possible. Also, the models for detecting faults must adapt to external and internal conditions to the mechanism. The present chapter deals with three particular maintenance algorithms for turnouts in railway infrastructure by means of discrete filters that comply with these general objectives. All of them have the virtue of being developed within a well-known and common framework, namely the State Space with the help of the Kalman Filter (KF) and/or complementary Fixed Interval Smoother (FIS) algorithms. The algorithms are tested on real applications and thorough results are shown.

2. Introduction

Faults in any important mechanisms must be detected quickly and reliably if the information is to be useful. Generally such mechanisms may be modeled as discrete dynamic systems, where data must be processed on line. When feasible, the detection system should use a model as simple as possible for detecting faults quickly by analyzing data in real time. The models for detecting faults must adapt to external and internal conditions to the mechanism, since both of them may affect the system as a whole.

The present chapter deals with maintenance systems for turnouts in railway infrastructure by means of discrete filters. Turnouts are assembled from switches and a crossing where the moving parts are often described as the "points" move by the point mechanism. The standard railway point mechanism is a complex electro-mechanical device with many potential failure modes.

Several approaches for maintenance of such devices are shown in this chapter and briefly described in this introduction. All of them have the virtue of being developed within a well-known common framework, namely the State Space (SS) with the help of the Kalman Filter (KF) and/or complementary Fixed Interval Smoother (FIS) algorithms, exposed in general terms in the following section.

Based on this common framework, the following subsections in this introduction show the particular applications shown in later sections of the chapter.

2.1. Filtering with Integrated Random Walks (IRW)

One possible way to analyze faults on line is to work with a reference dynamic system for their analysis. If the absolute value of the difference between the actual data and the reference data (i.e. the profile without any fault) is analyzed, the majority of faults may be detected by means of a simplified univariate dynamic system, like the one explored in [9]. The dynamic system and the use of the SS framework and the KF in this study allow increasing the reliability of the model presented that is the basic input to a rule-based decision mechanism. When applied to the linear discrete data filtering problem, the KF is a powerful algorithm, because it supports estimations of past, present and, most importantly, future states. It can therefore be used in predictive maintenance applications where data collected from sensors is affected by measurement and transmission line noise [12].

The previous approach may be exploited by setting up a bivariate model composed of two time series, i.e. the reference curve on one hand and each one of the empirical curves obtained on line on the other hand. More specifically (see section 4.2 below) a tentative model consists of a bivariate trend plus noise structure. The correlation between either trends or signals free from noise is considered as an indication of similarity between the curves and therefore the inexistence of failures. As long as the new incoming data is free from fault, the correlation parameter is close to one, but as a failure starts to develop this parameter tends to differ from one. The cut-off value of the correlation coefficient relevant to discern 'good' and 'bad' curves is selected on practical grounds based on past experience with this kind of data, but refined formal statistical criteria may be used as well [19]. Even forecasts of the curve that is being studied may be produced at any point in time, based on the current parameter values and the future data of the reference curve [14]. Therefore the fault may be detected ahead of time.

2.2. Random Walks and smoothing

Similar measurement data were collected from sensors mounted on a UK type M63 point machine at the Carillion Rail (formerly GTRM) Training Centre in Stafford (UK). It is difficult to compare the measurements taken during induced failure conditions with those from the fault-free condition because of noise in the measurements. The measurement data needed to be filtered in order to reduce the noise before comparisons may be made. Filtering using a SS model and the KF was an option (like in [9], [19] and [20]). Assuming the noisy data is a signal plus noise model, the KF reduces the power of the 100 and 200 Hz interfering signals. Rather than augmenting the SS models to express the additional knowledge of the interfering signals, a much simpler smoothing seems more convenient because of the relationship between the sample rate and the frequencies of the interfering signals, and provides excellent results for the data collected during this series of experiments [10].

2.3. Advance Dynamic Harmonic Regression (DHR)

A different case study was based on data collected from point mechanisms at Abbotswood Junction (UK). Three electro-mechanical and four electro-hydraulic point machines were monitored by a RCM system. Processed information was sent remotely from the trackside data-collection units to a personal computer located in a local relay room.

A fault is detected by comparing the forecasts of the model, considered as the expected signal in the case of no faults, with the actual data coming from the point mechanism when a movement is in progress. If the error is too large, measured by its standard deviation, a fault alarm is issued. The limit at which an error is considered too large is a design parameter that is fixed by experimentation. The system adapts to the changes experienced by the point machine. There are internal alterations (like friction, wear, etc.) and external as well (like environmental conditions, impacts, obstacles, etc.). The adaptability of the system is accomplished by continuous estimation of the models as new information becomes available and by discarding the oldest information. Models are always estimated on fault-free data [13].

The key point in this application is that the expected shape is computed as the forecast of a combination of two models that work interactively on historical data coming from signals free from any fault. The first of the models forecasts the time span a movement would take in case of absence of faults (an appropriate model used in this case was of the VARMA class or a local level plus noise but set up in continuous time). The second model is run to forecast the signal itself (due to the nature of the data a pertinent class is a Dynamic Harmonic Regression, DHR, similar to a Fourier analysis, but with advanced features included to incorporate a time varying period observed in the data).

The outline of the chapter is as follows. Section 3 reports a brief explanation of the general framework on which all the models in this chapter are set up, namely the State Space systems. Section 4 shows the first of the applications, i.e. in the point mechanisms. Finally section 5 shows how a fault detection algorithm may be implemented on seven point machines at Abbotswood junction (UK).

3. State Space systems

The general framework on which all models in this chapter are cast, is the so called State Space systems, that have experienced a remarkable attention during the last decades, as the extended literature about it reveals [3], [7], [13], [15], [16], [17], [21], [24], [26] and [27].

A stochastic discrete-time State Space system (SS) is a model composed of two sets of equations, the *Observation Equations*, and *State Equations*. The former relates the output to the states of the system, while the latter reflects the dynamic behavior of the system by relating the current value of the states to their past values. There are a number of different formulations of these equations, but one fairly general representation is given by equations (1) (see [3] and [21]). In general, much simpler models are sufficient, as later case studies show.

$$
\begin{aligned}
\text{State Equations} \quad &: \quad \mathbf{x}_{t+1} = \mathbf{\Phi}_t \mathbf{x}_t + \mathbf{E}_t \mathbf{w}_t \quad &\text{(i)} \\
\text{Observation Equations} \quad &: \quad \mathbf{z}_t = \mathbf{H}_t \mathbf{x}_t + \mathbf{C}_t \mathbf{v}_t \quad &\text{(ii)}
\end{aligned}
\tag{1}
$$

In (1) $\mathbf{z}_t$ is the m dimensional vector of observed variables for $t = 1,2,\ldots,N$; $\mathbf{X}_t$ is an n dimensional stochastic state vector; $\mathbf{w}_t$ is an r dimensional vector of (to be Gaussian) system disturbances, i.e. zero mean white noise inputs with a covariance matrix $\mathbf{Q}_t$; and $\mathbf{v}_t$ is a s dimensional vector of zero mean white noise variables (measurement noise: again assumed to be Gaussian) with a covariance matrix $\mathbf{R}_t$. In general, the vector $\mathbf{v}_t$ is assumed to be independent of $\mathbf{w}_t$ (not necessarily), and these two noise vectors are independent of the initial state vector $\mathbf{x}_0$. $\boldsymbol{\Phi}_t, \mathbf{E}_t, \mathbf{H}_t, \mathbf{C}_t, \mathbf{Q}_t,$ and $\mathbf{R}_t$ are, respectively, the $n \times n$, $n \times r$, $m \times n$, and $m \times s$, $r \times r$ and $s \times s$ system matrices, some elements of which are known and others that need to be estimated in some way.

Given the general SS form (1), the estimation problem consists of finding the first and second order moments (mean and covariance) of the state vector, conditional on all the data in a sample. Provided that all disturbances in the model are Gaussian, a *Kalman Filter* (KF) produces the optimal estimates of such moments in the sense of minimizing the Mean Squared Errors (MSE). An algorithm that is used in parallel with the KF and is not so well-known in certain contexts is the *Fixed Interval Smoothing* (FIS) algorithm, which allows for an operation similar to that of the KF but with a different set of information. The KF used in this chapter is:

$$\mathbf{F}_t = \left[\mathbf{C}_t \mathbf{R}_t \mathbf{C}_t^T + \mathbf{H}_t \hat{\mathbf{P}}_{t\,t-1} \mathbf{H}_t^T \right]$$

$$\mathbf{K}_t = \left[\boldsymbol{\Phi}_{t+1} \hat{\mathbf{P}}_{t\,t-1} \mathbf{H}_t^T \right] \mathbf{F}_t^{-1}$$

$$\hat{\mathbf{x}}_{t+1|t} = \left[\boldsymbol{\Phi}_{t+1} - \mathbf{K}_t \mathbf{H}_t^T \right] \hat{\mathbf{x}}_{t\,t-1} + \mathbf{K}_t \mathbf{z}_t$$

$$\hat{\mathbf{P}}_{t+1\,t} = \boldsymbol{\Phi}_{t+1} \hat{\mathbf{P}}_{t|t-1} \boldsymbol{\Phi}_{t+1}^T - \mathbf{K}_t \left[\boldsymbol{\Phi}_{t+1} \hat{\mathbf{P}}_{t\,t-1} \mathbf{H}_t^T \right]^T + \mathbf{E}_t \mathbf{Q}_t \mathbf{E}_t^T$$

The backward FIS recursions are:

$$\hat{\mathbf{x}}_{t|N} = \hat{\mathbf{x}}_{t\,t-1} + \hat{\mathbf{P}}_{t|t-1} \mathbf{s}_{t-1}$$

$$\hat{\mathbf{P}}_{t|N} = \hat{\mathbf{P}}_{t\,t-1} - \hat{\mathbf{P}}_{t|t-1} \mathbf{S}_{t-1} \hat{\mathbf{P}}_{t\,t-1}$$

$$\mathbf{s}_{t-1} = \mathbf{H}_t^T \mathbf{F}_t^{-1}\left(\mathbf{z}_t - \mathbf{H}_t \hat{\mathbf{x}}_{t\,t-1}\right) + \overline{\boldsymbol{\Phi}}_t^T \mathbf{s}_t \qquad \text{with } \mathbf{s}_N = \mathbf{0}$$

$$\mathbf{S}_{t-1} = \mathbf{H}_t^T \mathbf{F}_t^{-1} \mathbf{H}_t + \overline{\boldsymbol{\Phi}}_t^T \mathbf{S}_t \overline{\boldsymbol{\Phi}}_t \qquad\qquad \text{with } \mathbf{S}_N = \mathbf{0}$$

$$\overline{\boldsymbol{\Phi}}_t = \boldsymbol{\Phi}_t - \boldsymbol{\Phi}_t \hat{\mathbf{P}}_{t|t-1} \mathbf{H}_t^T \mathbf{F}_t^{-1} \mathbf{H}_t$$

This general SS formulation is capable of handling many nonstationary linear dynamical systems; also it can model nonlinear systems but conditionally Gaussian; general heteroscedastic systems; time-varying systems; etc. In addition, many kinds of extensions of model have been proposed in the literature, such as linear approximations of functionally nonlinear dynamic systems; non-Gaussian disturbances; etc. Missing data is not a problem given the recursive nature of the algorithms, because such data are replaced by their expectations based on the model and the data. Then, if such data is at the end of the sample the KF produces forecasts of the signal, while if they are in the middle or at the beginning both algorithms produce interpolation or forecasts from the beginning of the series backwards.

The application of the recursive KF/FIS algorithms requires values for all the system matrices $\mathbf{\Phi}_t, \mathbf{E}_t, \mathbf{H}_t, \mathbf{C}_t, \mathbf{Q}_t,$ and $\mathbf{R}_t$. Most of the elements of these matrices must be estimated by efficient methods. The Maximum Likelihood (ML) method in the time domain by means of 'prediction error decomposition' ([24] and [15]) is the most common because of its generality and good theoretical properties.

4. Filtering with Integrated Random Walks (IRW)

4.1. Data

Approximately 55 % of railway infrastructure component failures on high speed lines are due to signalling equipment and turnouts. "Signalling equipment" covers signals, track circuits, interlockings, automatic train protection (ATP) or LZB (track loop based ATP), and the traffic control centre. From another point of view, the annual cost of maintaining points is rather high compared to other infrastructure elements, about 3.4 million UKP (United Kingdom Pound) per year for about 1000 km of railway. TC-TCR trade circuits, for example, cost 2.1 million UKP per year for the same area. Of the points expenditure, 1.2 million UKP is for clamp lock type (hydraulic) turnout and 1.4 UPK million for electrically operated turnouts (data provided by a British asset manager). Turnouts can also be used to implement flank protection for a train route allocated to another train. This is achieved by positioning the blades of the turnout in such a way that a train driving through the turnout is not directed into a track segment belonging to the route of another train.

Most standard point machines (see Fig. 1) contain a switch actuating and a locking mechanism which includes a hand-throw lever and a selector lever to allow operation by power or hand. The mechanism is normally divided into three major subsystems: (i) the motor unit which may includes a contactor control arrangement and a terminal area; (ii) a gearbox comprising spur-gears and a worm reduction unit with overload clutch; and (iii) the dual control mechanism as well as a controller subsystem with motor cut-off and detection contacts. Generally, there are also mechanical linkages for the detection and locking of the point. The standard railway point is therefore a complex electro-mechanical device with many potential failure modes.

The circuit controller includes detection switches and a pair of snap-action switches to stop the machine at the end of its stroke and to brake the motor electrically so that the mechanism is not subject to impacts. The detection switches have high pressure wiping contacts made of silver/cadmium oxide or gold and they are operated by both the lockbox and the detection rod. The detection switches have additional contacts to allow mid-stroke short circuiting of the detection relays to avoid wrong indications in the signal box or electronic interlocking.

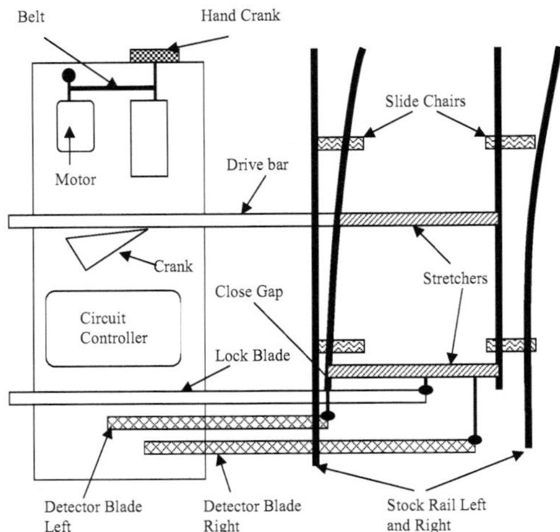

Fig. 1. Point Mechanism

476 experiments (point moves or attempted point moves) were carried out while collecting time, force and operating current data. The data from the point mechanism is initially classified in terms of direction of movement, i.e., either reverse to normal direction or normal to reverse direction. For both directions, faults have been detected with "current (A) vs. time (s)" curves and "force (N) vs. (s)" curves (see some examples in Fig. 2(a) and 2(b)). It was observed that "current (A) vs. time (s)" curves are not the best choice for detecting faults in point mechanisms. The final classification of faults employs only the magnitude and the moment when they change with respect to the reference curves.

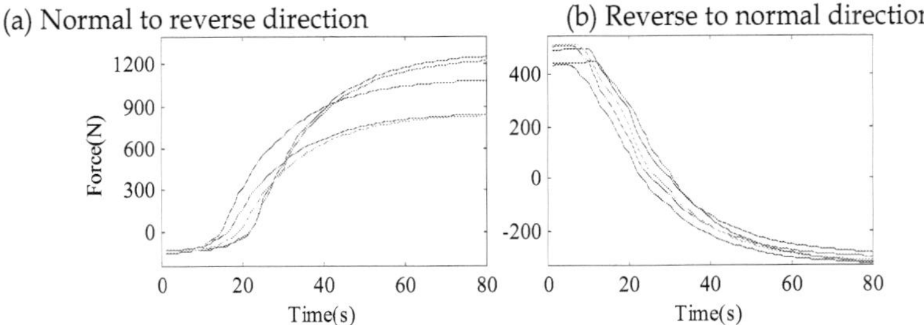

Fig. 2. Operating force curves for a point mechanism

For detecting faults in point mechanisms, a model was employed that can determine the dynamic character of the system. For instance, the reference signals or curves for detecting faults depend on the environmental conditions (temperature, humidity, etc.), and on the in service time of the system, because the friction forces are larger at the beginning than once the system has worn in. The available data consists of 79 curves for the reverse to normal direction, including 4 curves "as commissioned", and 72 curves for the normal to reverse direction, with 3 curves "as commissioned" (some of them may be seen in Fig. 2). A reference dynamic system has to be applied to all of these variables. The data collected refers to force (N) versus time (s). The first conclusion after studying these curves is that we can detect only a few faults by analyzing the signal directly but, if we analyze the differences between the current data x^j and the reference data x^i in the form of absolute values d^j (1), we can detect the majority of faults as they develop.

$$d_t^j = \left| x_t^j - x_t^i \right|, \quad \forall t \tag{1}$$

Some of these curves are shown in Fig. 3(a) and 3(b) for reverse to normal direction and normal to reverse direction respectively. The 'x' axis is time [s] and the 'y' axis is the difference between the dynamic mean geometric and the current curve as an absolute value [N].

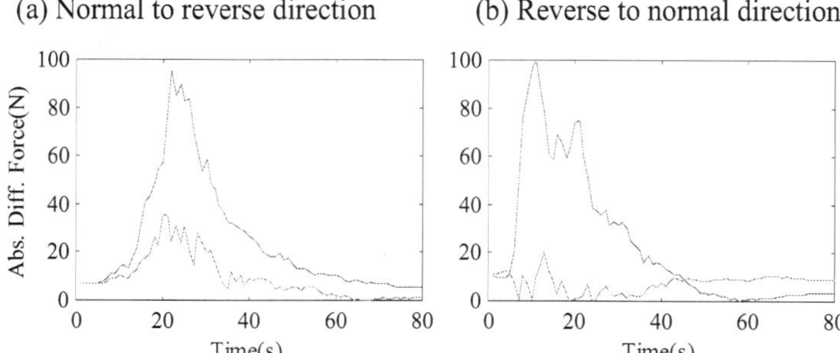

Fig. 3. Difference between the reference signal for the point and the newly acquired data in absolute values

4.2. The model

One feasible model written in SS form (1) for this application is of the type local mean plus noise for two signals simultaneously, where the local means are modeled by the dynamics implied by the state equations, i.e.

$$\mathbf{x}_{t+1} = \begin{pmatrix} \mathbf{I} & \mathbf{I} \\ \mathbf{0} & \mathbf{I} \end{pmatrix} \mathbf{x}_t + \begin{pmatrix} \mathbf{0} \\ \mathbf{I} \end{pmatrix} \begin{pmatrix} w_{1t} \\ w_{2t} \end{pmatrix}$$

$$\mathbf{z}_t = \text{signal} + \text{noise} = (\mathbf{I} \quad \mathbf{0})\mathbf{x}_t + \mathbf{v}_t \tag{2}$$

$$\mathbf{Q} = \begin{pmatrix} \sigma_{w_1}^2 & \rho\sqrt{\sigma_{w_1}^2 \sigma_{w_2}^2} \\ \rho\sqrt{\sigma_{w_1}^2 \sigma_{w_2}^2} & \sigma_{w_2}^2 \end{pmatrix}; \quad \mathbf{R} = \begin{pmatrix} \sigma_{v_1}^2 & \sigma_{v_1 v_2} \\ \sigma_{v_1 v_2} & \sigma_{v_2}^2 \end{pmatrix}$$

In model (2) all the system matrices are time invariant: $\mathbf{I}$ is a two dimensional identity matrix; $\mathbf{0}$ is a two by two matrix of zeros; $\sigma_{\bullet}^2$ are the variances of the noise signals or disturbances either in the state or observation equations; $\sigma_{\bullet\bullet}$ is the covariance between two disturbances; and ρ is the correlation coefficient between the two noise signals in the state equation.

By comparing systems (2) and (1) it is easy to see the system matrices values in this particular case, i.e.

$$\mathbf{\Phi}_t = \begin{pmatrix} \mathbf{I} & \mathbf{I} \\ \mathbf{0} & \mathbf{I} \end{pmatrix}; \quad \mathbf{E}_t = \begin{pmatrix} \mathbf{0} \\ \mathbf{I} \end{pmatrix}; \quad \mathbf{w}_t = \begin{pmatrix} w_{1t} \\ w_{2t} \end{pmatrix}; \quad \mathbf{H}_t = \begin{pmatrix} \mathbf{I} & \mathbf{0} \end{pmatrix}; \quad \mathbf{C}_t = 1$$

The unknown *hyper-parameters* to be estimated by ML in this model are $\mathbf{Q}$ and $\mathbf{R}$. It should be noted that $\mathbf{Q}$ is parameterized in the way shown above in order to force the appearance of the correlation coefficient between the state disturbances explicitly. The following points must be taken into account when interpreting model (2):

- The observation equation implies that the series are composed of a local mean level or trend with added noise.
- The first two states in the model are the local mean level (or trends) of each series. In other words, they are the signals free from noise;
- Given the structure of the model, it is easy to show that the third and fourth states are the gradients of the trends. The slopes are modelled here as stochastic and therefore changing as a function of time according to the variance of the state disturbances;
- If the correlation coefficient is 1, both trends are proportional to each other, meaning that the dynamic behaviour of both trends is the same. This is an important point that the authors wanted to test later;
- By definition, $\sigma_\bullet^2$ must be positive; $-1 \leq \rho \leq 1$; and $\mathbf{R}$ must be positive definite. Since all these are parameters to be estimated, it may be advantageous constrained search algorithms;
- The asymptotic distribution of the ML estimates are Gaussian if all the disturbances in model (2) are Gaussian. Then, since ρ is estimated explicitly, the confidence intervals and statistical hypothesis tests for this parameter may be easily constructed.

In fact, the parameter ρ is proposed here as a way to discriminate between "faulty" and "as commissioned" curves (see below), where the "faulty" curve is caused by wear as described above. Strictly speaking, the two curves are behaving in the same way when $\rho = 1$, but previous experience with point mechanisms of a similar kind must be incorporated here, because it is, difficult, in general to find those values in practical situations. Then, a cut-off value of ρ must be considered in order to discriminate between 'good' and 'bad' curves.

The modeling strategy outlined above may be applied to both off-line and on-line situations. In this latter case it would be possible to get an estimated time series for ρ (with confidence bands) and the time of wear assessment detected on-line very quickly when parameters start to move away from their initial values. Even forecasts of the current curve may be produced at any point in time, based on the current parameter values and the future data of the reference curve.

Very fast algorithms have been developed for ML estimation of SS systems in which all the unknowns are some elements of the covariance matrices $\mathbf{Q}$ and $\mathbf{R}$, such as in model (4).

The problem of initializing the KF and hence ML needs to be resolved. One of the most important tools is the use of the *exact likelihood function* [5] and[6].

4.3. Experimental Results

The model described in the previous subsection was employed in an off-line mode with data collected during laboratory tests (see Fig. 2). The model output (shown in Fig. 4, based in signals from Fig. 3) was then used to classify the curves as either "as commissioned" or "faulty". This step may be achieved several ways. The approach compares ρ with the individual points in time with a relating high threshold value. A value of ρ below the threshold is an indication of a lack of correlation with the current reference curve and therefore is classified as "faulty"[i]. A more refined and somewhat more formal criterion is based on such single point estimate and its 95% confidence band. In this case, a curve is considered to be "as commissioned" if the upper limit of the confidence band is close to target value or equal to 1.

For point operation in both directions, with a value of $\rho = 0.99$ the totality of faulty curves could be detected. In the NR direction, since the highest value of ρ for faulty curves was 0.92 and the 95% confidence interval uses (0.77, 0.98). In the RN direction, the highest value of ρ for faulty curves was 0.97 and the 95% confidence interval was (0.93, 0.99).

The results achieved with the same reference curve, but different test results are shown in Fig. 4, one "as commissioned" curve (top panel) and one faulty curve (bottom).

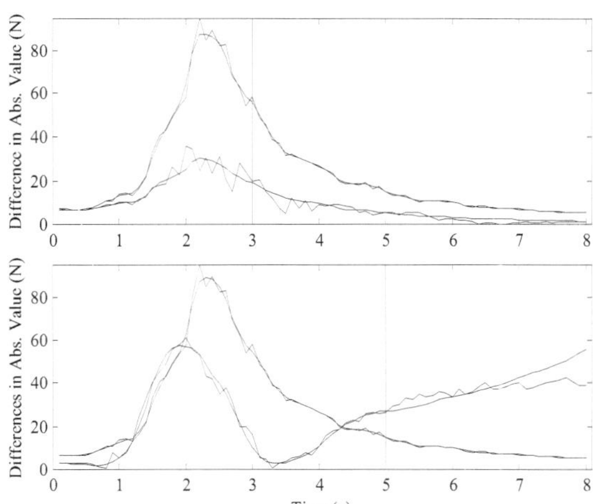

Fig. 4. Two examples of forecasts based on model (4) at different forecast origins. One "as commissioned" curve (top) and one "faulty" curve (bottom). Forecast origins are marked by the vertical line.

In both cases the reference curve was available for the whole time span (based on previous curves taken from the system) and the information to test each curves was set up to the

---

[i] Alternatively, the estimated correlation coefficient may be tuned so that the number of curves correctly classified is maximised.

forecast origin (vertical line). The objective of obtaining a forecast for the behavior of the system based on such incomplete information was thus using model (4). In an on-line situation, the parameters and the forecasts are updated each time a new observation is available.

Fig. 5 shows the recursive estimate of ρ with its 95% confidence intervals (assuming gaussian noises) for an "as commissioned" curve (top) and a "faulty" one (bottom). In both cases the confidence on the estimate tends to increase as more information becomes available.

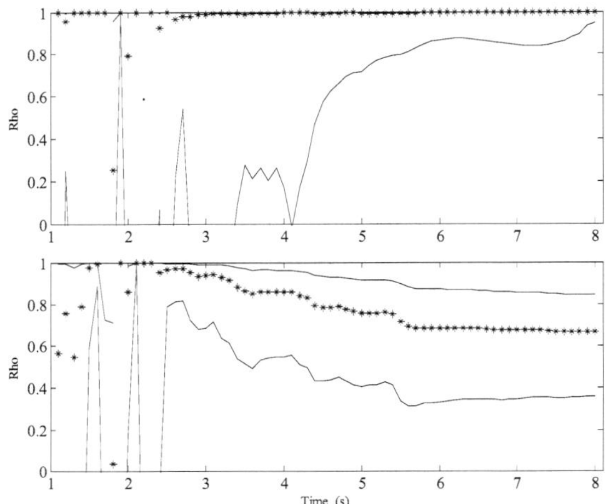

Fig. 5. Recursive estimation of ρ (stars) and 95% confidence bands (solid) for one "as commissioned" curve (top) and one "faulty" curve (bottom).

5. Random Walks and smoothing

5.1. Device and data

Following successful implementation on a level crossing mechanism (Roberts 2002) [23], the authors adapted the methods to detect faults in seven point machines at Abbotswood junction, shown in Fig. 6 as boxes 638, 639, 640, 641A, 641B, 642A and 642B.

The configuration deployed at Abbotswood junction was developed in collaboration with Carillion Rail (formerly GTRM), Network Rail (formerly RailTrack) and Computer Controlled Solutions Ltd. The junction consists of four electro-mechanical M63 and three electro-hydraulic point machines, shown in Figure 2. Each M63 machine is fitted with a load pin and Hall-effect current clamps. The electric-hydraulic point machines are instrumented with two hydraulic pressure transducers, namely an oil level transducer and a current transducer. A 1 Mb/sec WorldFIP network, compatible with the Fieldbus standard EN50170 (CENELEC EN50170 2002) [4], connects the trackside data-collection units to a PC located in the local relay room. Data acquisition software was written to collect data with a sampling rate of 200 Hz. Processed results can be observed on the local PC and also remotely.

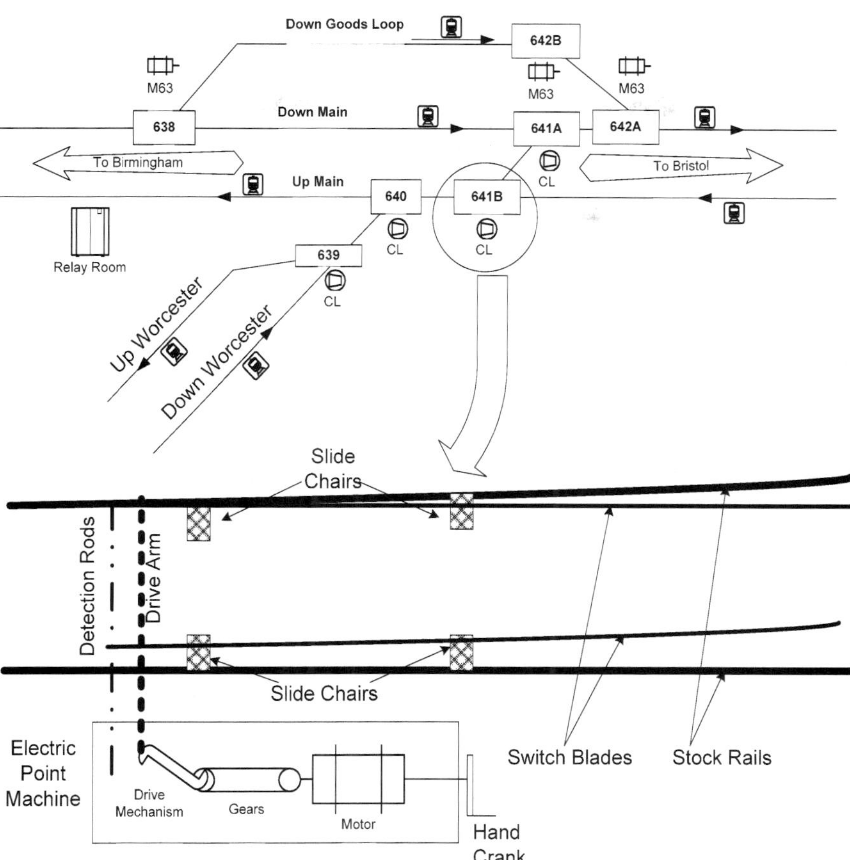

Fig. 6. Set of points and the relevant components/sub-units at Abbotswood junction.

The supply voltage of the point machine was measured (Fig. 7a), as well as the current drawn by the electric motor (Fig. 7b) and the system as a whole (Fig. 7d). In addition, the force in the drive bar was measured with a load pin introduced into the bolted connection between the drive bar and the drive rod (Fig. 7c). Fig. 7 shows the raw measurement signals taken in the fault-free (control or "as commissioned") condition for normal to reverse and reverse to normal operation, respectively. Note that the currents and voltages begin and end at zero for both directions of operation, but a static force remains following the reverse to normal throw and a different force remains after the normal to reverse throw.

It is difficult to compare the measurements taken during induced failure conditions with those from the fault-free condition because of noise in the measurements.

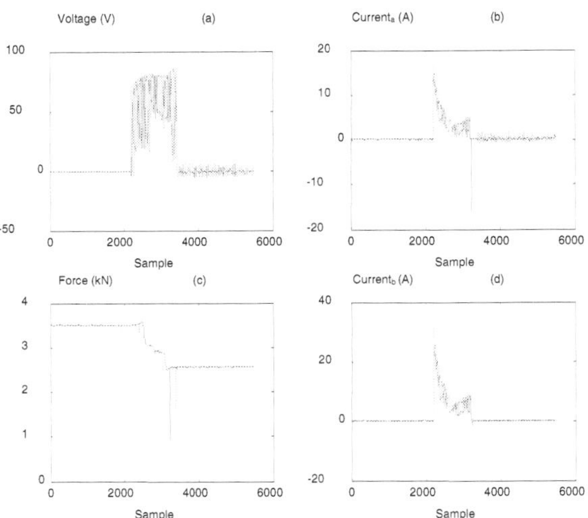

Fig. 7. 'As commissioned' measured signals for the normal to reverse throw

5.2. Filtering the signal

One possibility to reduce the noise is by using the SS formulation in (1) as a digital filter capable of reducing observation noise when the measured quantity varies slowly, but additive measurement noise covers a broad spectrum [8], [9]. In this particular case the signal being measured is modeled as a random walk, i.e. it tends to change by small amounts in a short time but can change by larger amounts over longer periods of time. The SS model used for each signal is described by equations (3).

$$\left. \begin{aligned} x_{t+1} &= x_t + w_t \\ z_t &= x_t + v_t \end{aligned} \right\} \tag{3}$$

$$Q = E\!\left(w_t^2\right), \quad R = E\!\left(v_t^2\right)$$

Comparing with the general SS equations (1) we have:

- Variables x_t, z_t, Q, R, w_t and v_t are all scalars.
- $\Phi_t = 1;\ \mathbf{E}_t = 1;\ \mathbf{w}_t = w_t;\ \mathbf{H}_t = 1;\ \mathbf{C}_t = 1\cdot$
- The initial value given to $\hat{x}_0$ is: $\hat{x}_0 = 0$.
- The initial value of P_0 is chosen to reflect uncertainty in the initial estimate. Here P_0 is initialised as $P_0 = 10^6$.
- The remaining quantities to be specified are Q, the variance of the noise driving the random walk, and R, the variance of the observation noise.

By empirical methods using simulation, the best filtering is achieved with $Q = 0.03$ and $R = 0.5$. Note that the ratio Q/R defines the filter behavior.

The power spectral density of the filtered motor current (computed only while the motor is running) shows significant energy peaks at 100 and 200 Hz (Fig. 8, where the normalized frequency of 1 corresponds to a frequency of 250 Hz).

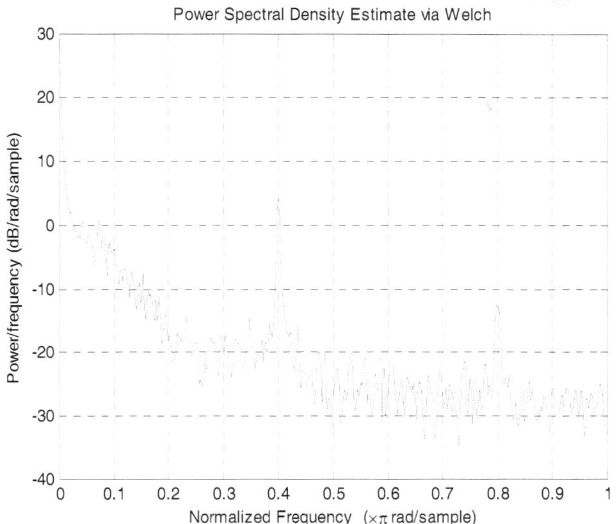

Fig. 8. Motor current power spectral density following Kalman filtering

The dynamic model used can be augmented to model the observed interfering signals as narrow band disturbances centred at 100 and 200 Hz. The spectrum of the motor current signal is examined next before a decision on the most appropriate filtering is taken.

A spectral analysis of the motor current signal against time (or sample) shows that the characteristic of the noise varies with the operating condition of the motor. From the spectrogram one can identify a small 50 Hz interference signal before the motor begins to turn (samples 1 to 1100). In the second stage, where the motor is turning, the interfering signal has strong 100 Hz and 200 Hz components but no 50 Hz component. In the final stage, the motor current does not have identifiable 50, 100, or 200 Hz components, but is affected by general wideband noise.

Power spectral densities (psds) were computed for data selected from each of the three distinct operating regions. There is a 50 Hz interference signal during the first region and wideband noise during the last. Fig. 9 shows the psd for the middle phase, which is the noisiest region. It is possible to augment the SS model to describe the observed interfering signals, using different models for each of the three distinct phases. However, a simpler yet effective smoothing scheme exists, as described in the next section.

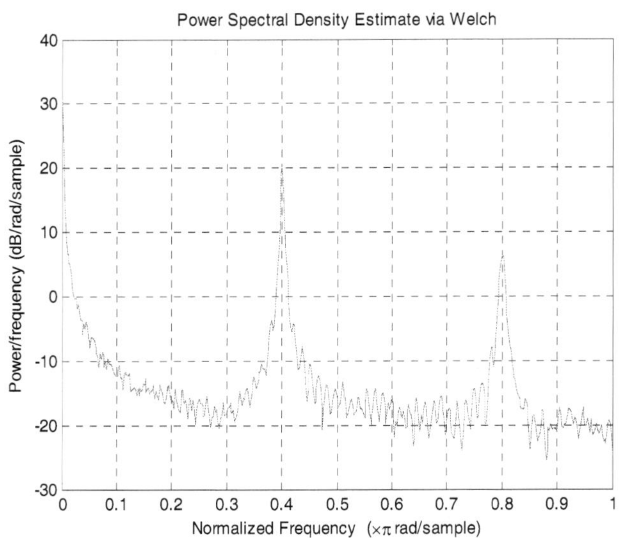

Fig. 9. Power Spectral Density estimate (samples 1000 to 4000).

5.3. Smoothing

Noting that the sampling rate is 500 Hz and the interfering signals appear at 50, 100 and 200 Hz, an alternative filtering method, or, more correctly, smoothing method, is to compute a moving average of the original signal over a suitable number of samples. For example, computing the moving average with 10 samples has zero response to signals at 50 Hz. However, a 100 Hz signal, with only 5 samples per cycle, is not necessarily removed, depending on the relative phase of the 100 Hz signal and the samples. Removal of the 50 Hz, 100 Hz and 200 Hz interfering signals is guaranteed by computing a moving average over 40 samples, i.e. over a time window of 80 ms. This moving average also spreads an instantaneous motor current change over 80 ms, but this is not a problem in practice as the motor current does not change instantaneously. A moving average computed over 40 samples (80 ms) removes information at 12.5 Hz (and integer multiples thereof) and in addition acts as a general first-order low pass filter with a –3 dB point at 5.5 Hz. Losing information around 12.5 Hz is not important as long as comparisons are made between identically processed signals. By suitable alignment of the moving average result, filtering becomes smoothing. The smoothed signals are delayed by 40 ms, but this is of no concern for comparison with similarly processed fault-free signals. There is still some residual 100 and 200 Hz interference, but it is much reduced. Identical smoothing has been applied to all measurement channels, even though they are not equally affected by 50 Hz noise and its harmonics. A comparison of the smoothed signals with the corresponding signals obtained in the fault-free condition is now possible.

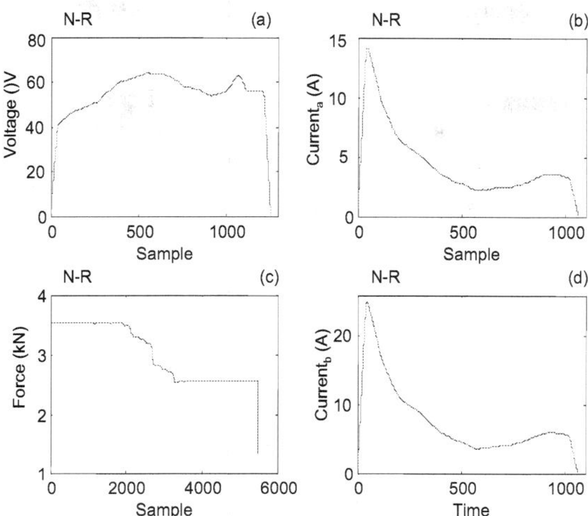

Fig. 10. Average control curves. N-R: Normal to Reverse Direction

5.4. Results

The failure modes listed are identified using a pattern recognition method. The signals obtained in the fault-free condition, smoothed as described above and averaged over five throws, are shown in Fig. 10. The smoothed signals obtained under induced failure modes have been compared to the reference (or control) signals.

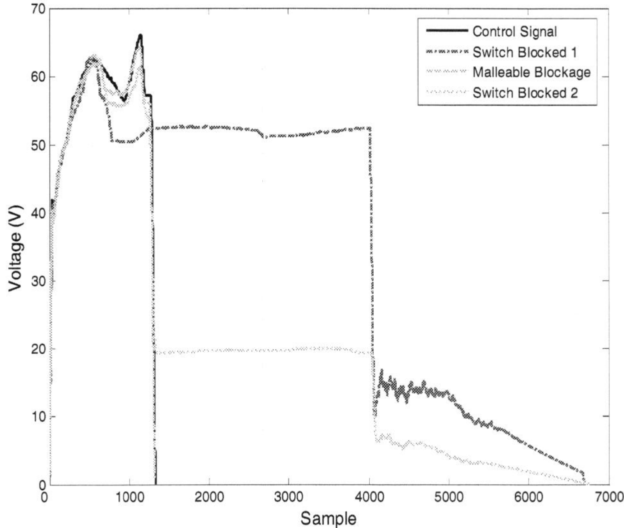

Fig. 11. A Control signal and Switch Blocked and Malleable Blockage failure modes signals

Fig. 11 shows the voltage signals for the failure modes Switch Blocked 1, Switch Blocked 2 and Malleable Blockage, in the normal to reverse direction.

Every failure can potentially be detected from signals a, b and c for normal to reverse transitions, and using signals b and c for reverse to normal transitions. Therefore, employing only signal b or c it potentially is possible to detect every fault in both operating directions.

6. Advanced Dynamic Harmonic Regression (DHR)

The system developed in this section detects faults by means of comparing what can be considered a "normal" or "expected" shape of a signal with respect to the actual shape observed as new data become available. One important feature of this system is that it adapts gradually to the changes experienced in the state of the point mechanism. The forecasts are always computed by including into the estimation sample the last point movements and discarding the older ones. In this way, time varying properties of the system due to a number of factors, like wear, are included, and hence the forecasts are adaptive.

The data is a signal with long periods of inactivity, mixed up with other short periods where a point movement is being produced. Fig. 12 shows one small part of the dataset in the later case study, where the time axis has been truncated in order to show the movements of the signal. The real picture is one in which the inactivity periods are much longer that those shown in the figure, in a way that the movement periods would appear as thin lines.

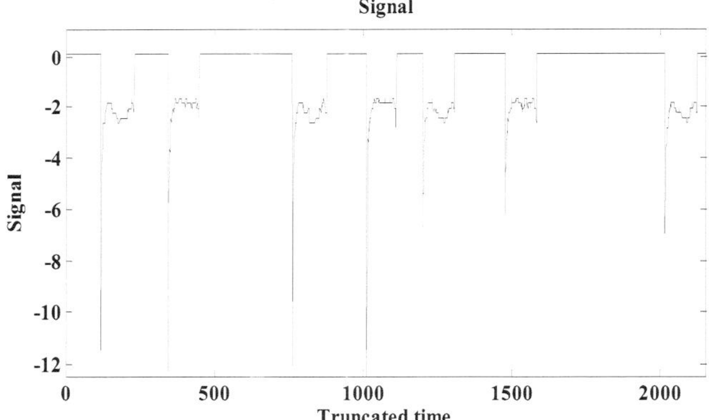

Fig. 12. Signal used by the fault detection algorithm.

A new signal can be composed exclusively of those time intervals where the point mechanism is actually working. Looking at Fig. 12 it can be devised that even movements (normal to reverse move) have a slightly different pattern than uneven movements (reverse to normal). Therefore, two signals may be formed by concatenating the normal to reverse movements of the point mechanism in one hand, and the reverse to normal moves in the other. Fig. 13 shows one portion of the normal to reverse signal.

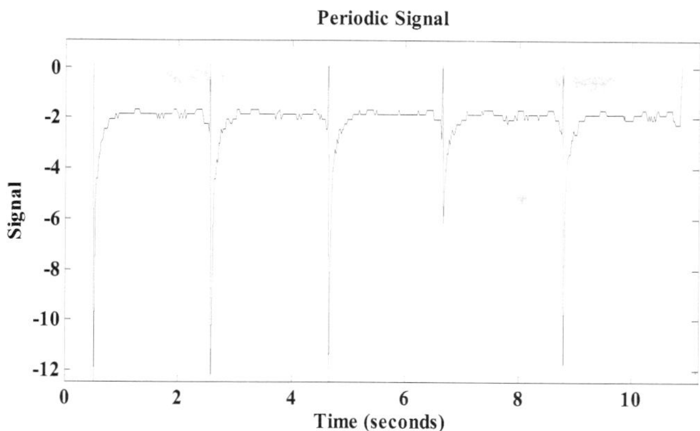

Fig. 13. Signal obtained by concatenation of portions of data where the point mechanism is working.

As it is clearly shown in Figure 13, the signal to analyse has strong periodicity and can be then modelled and forecast by a statistical model capable of replicating such behaviour. The period of the signal is exactly the time it takes to the point mechanism to produce a complete movement. Two difficulties arise that should be considered by the model: (i) the sampling interval of the data is not constant, it has small variations produced by the measurement equipment that should be taken into account; and (ii) the frequency or period of the waves changes over time. As a matter of fact, the changes of the period may be considered as a measurement of the wear in the system, as illustrated in Figure 14.

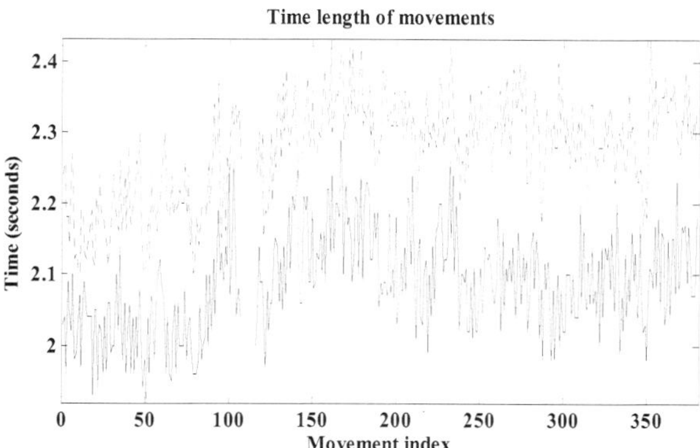

Fig. 14. Time the point mechanism spend to produce movements in normal to reverse direction (solid) and reverse to normal (dotted).

Fig. 14 shows the 380 time varying periods (or time to produce a complete movement of the mechanism) for the "normal to reverse" and "reverse to normal" signals (the first five data points corresponds to the signal shown in Fig. 13) that constitutes the full data set in the later case study. There were several sudden increases of the period at some points in time due to faults that have been removed from the figure, in order to avoid distortions of the vertical axis. The time axis is on an irregular sampling interval, in order to take into account the moment at which each movement has taken place. It is clear that the period is lower at the beginning of the sample with a rapid increase that tends to come down from the middle of the sample. A similar behaviour is devised in the reverse to normal signal.

The fault detection algorithm proposed here in essence would be composed of the following steps:
1. Forecasting next period on the basis of the signal in Figure 14.
2. Forecasting the signal in Figure 13 by a Dynamic Harmonic Regression model that uses the period forecast of the previous step.

Assessing forecasts by comparing the forecast of step 2 with the actual signal coming from the sensors installed in the point mechanism. If the forecasts generated in step 2 are too bad (measured by the variance of the forecast error), a fault is detected. The way to assess whether a failure has been produced is by checking the variance of the forecast error above a certain level fixed for each specific point mechanism.

6.1. Step 1: Modeling and forecasting the period

Two procedures have been considered: i) VARMA models in discrete time with two signals (the periods for normal to reverse and reverse to normal) modeled jointly; ii) once again a univariate local level model plus noise, but in continuous time.

6.1.1. VARMA model

The VARMA (Vector Auto-Regressive Moving-Average) models (see e.g. [1], [18] and [25]) are natural extensions of the ARIMA (Auto-Regressive Integrated Moving Average) models to the multivariate case. One of the simplest but general formulations of a VARMA(p, q) model is

$$\mathbf{P}_t = \boldsymbol{\varphi}_1 \mathbf{P}_{t-1} + \ldots + \boldsymbol{\varphi}_p \mathbf{P}_{t-p} + \mathbf{v}_t + \boldsymbol{\Theta}_1 \mathbf{v}_{t-1} + \boldsymbol{\Theta}_q \mathbf{v}_{t-q} \tag{4}$$

where $\mathbf{P}_t = \begin{bmatrix} p_{1,t} & p_{2,t} \end{bmatrix}^T$ is a bivariate signal; $\mathbf{v}_t$ is a bivariate white noise, i.e. purely random signal with no serial correlation and covariance matrix $\mathbf{R}$; and $\boldsymbol{\varphi}_i$ $(i=1,2,\ldots,p)$ and $\boldsymbol{\Theta}_j$ $(j=1,2,\ldots,q)$ are squared blocks of coefficients of dimension 2×2.

VARMA models admit several SS representation according to equation (1). The one prefered here is (with $r = \max(p,q)$)

$$\mathbf{x}_{t+1} = \begin{pmatrix} \varphi_1 & \mathbf{I} & 0 & \cdots & 0 \\ \varphi_2 & 0 & \mathbf{I} & \cdots & 0 \\ \vdots & \vdots & \vdots & \ddots & \vdots \\ \varphi_{r-1} & 0 & 0 & \cdots & \mathbf{I} \\ \varphi_r & 0 & 0 & \cdots & 0 \end{pmatrix} \mathbf{x}_t + \begin{pmatrix} \varphi_1 + \Theta_1 \\ \varphi_2 + \Theta_2 \\ \vdots \\ \varphi_{r-1} + \Theta_{r-1} \\ \varphi_r + \Theta_r \end{pmatrix} \mathbf{v}_t$$

$$\mathbf{z}_t = \begin{pmatrix} \mathbf{I} & 0 & 0 & \cdots & 0 \end{pmatrix} \mathbf{x}_t + \mathbf{v}_t$$

The model orders p and q can be identified using multivariate autocorrelation and multivariate partial autocorrelation functions. The block parameters, as well as the covariance matrix of the noise, are estimated using Maximum Likelihood. Forecasts are then computed on the basis of the actual data and the estimates of the model parameters, once the model passes a validation process. One of the most important validation tests is the absence of serial correlation in the perturbation vector noise $\mathbf{v}_t$ (see e.g. [1], [18] and [25]).

It is vital that the signals $\mathbf{P}_t$ on which all the VARMA methodology is applied should have stationary mean and variance.

6.1.2. Local level model in continuous time
The model used for forecasting the period of the next movement (in a particular direction) in this case represents the observation, i.e. the period drifts over time, as wear varies simply because of usage (increases) or by preventive maintenance (decreases). Since the point movements are not produced at equally spaced intervals of time, a continuous-time model should be used. Formally, the continuous time SS model is given by

$$\frac{d}{dt}\begin{bmatrix} l(t) \\ s(t) \end{bmatrix} = \begin{bmatrix} 0 & 1 \\ 0 & 0 \end{bmatrix}\begin{bmatrix} l(t) \\ s(t) \end{bmatrix} + \begin{bmatrix} w_1(t) \\ w_2(t) \end{bmatrix}$$
$$P(t) = l(t) + v(t) \tag{5}$$

with

$$\mathbf{Q} = \begin{bmatrix} q_1 & 0 \\ 0 & q_2 \end{bmatrix}.$$

where $P(t)$ stands for the time varying period that is decomposed into the local level $l(t)$ and a noise term $v(t)$ assumed to be white Gaussian noise; $w_1(t)$ and $w_2(t)$ are independent white noises.

One way to treat the continuous system above is by finding a *discrete-time* SS equivalent to it (see e.g. Harvey 1989) [15], by means of the solution to the differential equation implied by the system. A change in notation is necessary to convert the system to discrete-time: denote the k th observation of the series z_k (for $k = 1, 2, \ldots, N$) and assume that this observation is made at time t_k. Let $t_0 = 0$ and $\delta_k = t_k - t_{k-1}$, i.e. the time interval between two consecutive measurements. System (3) may be represented by the *discrete-time* SS system in (5).

$$\begin{bmatrix} l_k \\ s_k \end{bmatrix} = \begin{bmatrix} 1 & \delta_k \\ 0 & 1 \end{bmatrix} \begin{bmatrix} l_{k-1} \\ s_{k-1} \end{bmatrix} + \begin{bmatrix} w_{1,k} \\ w_{2,k} \end{bmatrix}$$

$$P_k = l_k + v_k \tag{6}$$

In order to make systems (6) and (5) equivalent, the variances of observational noise is unchanged as R, but the covariance matrix of the process noise in the state equations becomes

$$\mathbf{Q}_k = \delta_k \begin{bmatrix} 1/3\delta_k^2 q_2 + q_1 & 1/2 q_2 \delta_k \\ 1/2 q_2 \delta_k & q_2 \end{bmatrix}$$

(see Harvey 1989, page 487) [15]. If all the data are sampled at regular time intervals, then $\delta_k = \delta$ and the noise variances are all constant; but if the data is irregularly spaced, as it is in our case, δ_k would take into account the irregularities of the sampling process. It is worth noting that the continuous-time model (5) involved system matrices that are all constant and the state noises were all independent of each other with constant variances. Beware that system (6) is written in form (1) and is the only case in this chapter that involves a time variable transition matrix $\mathbf{\Phi}_k$ and time variable variance noises that are correlated to each other according to the expression of $\mathbf{Q}_k$.

6.2. Step 2: Modeling and forecasting the signal

Once the period or the time length of the next movement of the point mechanism is forecast by any of the models in section 5.1., it is necessary to produce the forecast of the signal itself for the next occurrence, in order to produce what should be expected in case of no faults.

This is done by a Dynamic Harmonic Regression model (DHR) set up as described below. This model is very convenient in the present situation because it can easily handle the time-varying nature of the movement period. Obviously, the model can also be written in the form of a SS system as in (1).

The formula of a DHR with the required properties is shown in equation (7).

$$z_{k,t} = \sum_{i=1}^{M} \left[a_{i,k} \sin\left(\omega_{i,k,t} t^*\right) + b_{i,k} \cos\left(\omega_{i,k,t} t^*\right)\right] + e_{k,t} \tag{7}$$

Here, $z_{k,t}$ is the periodic signal in which the subscript k indicates whether the normal to reverse ($k = 1$) or the reverse to normal ($k = 2$) signals are being considered; M is the number of harmonics that should be included in the regression to achieve an adequate representation of the signal $z_{k,t}$; $a_{i,k}$ and $b_{i,k}$ are $2M$ parameters to be estimated, representing the amplitudes of the co-sinusoidal waves; $\omega_{i,k,t}$ are frequencies at which the sinusoids are evaluated, with $\omega_{i,k,t} = 2i\pi/p_{k,t}$ for $i = 1,2,\ldots,M$ and $M \geq p_{k,t}/2$ and $k = 1,2$; $e_{k,t}$ is a pure random white noise with constant variance. Separate Harmonic Regression models are used for the normal to reverse and reverse to normal signals.

There are two key points for the model (7) to be an adequate representation of $z_{k,t}$:

1. $p_{k,t}$ and $\omega_{i,k,t}$ have time varying period/frequency. The nature of such variation is dependent on the signal itself. For one full movement of the point mechanism $p_{k,t}$ is maintained constant and is equal to the time it takes to produce the full movement. This value will be different in the next movement and is modified accordingly.

2. The time index t^* is a variable linked to $p_{k,t}$ that varies from 0 to $p_{k,t}$ in each movement. Therefore, this variable is reset to 0 as soon as a movement finishes (see Fig. 15.

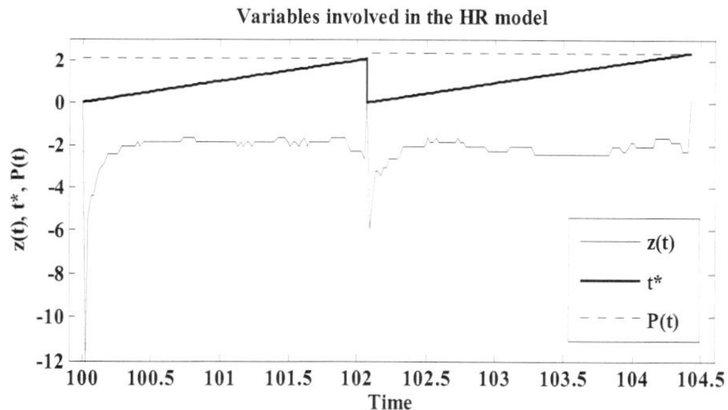

Fig. 15. Two full movements of the point mechanism, with their associated period and time index according to model (7).

Model (7) is then a regression of a signal on a set of deterministic functions of time and therefore all the standard regression theory can be applied, in particular estimates and forecasts can be made quickly. Model (7) have been generalized further by allowing parameters $a_{i,k}$ and $b_{i,k}$ to be time varying, producing a more flexible model, known as a Dynamic Harmonic Regression (DHR; see [21] [26]), but such complications are not found necessary in the case study described later.

6.3. The full fault detection algorithm

The full algorithm for fault detection comprises the following steps:

1. Determine which historical data to use. In the later case study the previous 50 free-from-faults movements of the point mechanism are used to estimate models (4) (5) and (7) at each new movement.

2. A point forecast of the time that it would take the next movement is produced by means of model (4) or (5), together with its 95% confidence interval. In this way, a range of lengths or periods of the next movement are considered. Then, a different forecast of the signal $z_{k,t}$ is produced for each period forecast in the previous step.

    Following this a full set of forecasts become available for a time horizon long enough to cover a full movement of the point mechanism.

3. The new data points measured by the system are compared to all the forecasts produced in the previous step. The forecast closer to the actual data measured by the minimum of the standard deviation of the error is then considered to be the best forecast of the signal.

4. If the best forecast is systematically bad, a fault has occurred and the system issues a warning. If the best errors are always low, no faults are detected. The boundary is measured in terms of standard deviation of the errors and such a value has to be adjusted for each particular point mechanism.

5. If no fault is detected, then the data of the latest movement is incorporated into the historical data to be used next time, the oldest movement data being dropped. However, if a fault is detected, the historical data used to perform step 1 for the next movement is unchanged for the next movement.

The algorithm can be used in on-line or off-line contexts. For on-line use, step 3 can be repeated as each measurement data point becomes available. For off-line use the algorithm is applied to all the data collected for a full movement of the mechanism.

The system requires a couple of values to be fixed by experimentation, namely the alarm limit that can be calculated from the standard deviation of signal $z_{k,t}$, and also the number of harmonics to include in the Harmonic Regression (M in model (7)). Experiments carried out on logged data have been performed to set these two design parameters of the algorithm. The final setting for the standard deviation is 0.4 for the standard deviation, found to give the best discrimination between faulty and non-faulty events; and $M = 62$ harmonics for model (7) produces accurate fit and forecasts to the signal.

6.4. Results

Standard identification techniques on VARMA models suggested a VARMA(0, 1). Estimation of such a model for the full data set was

$$\begin{bmatrix} p_1 \\ p_2 \end{bmatrix}_t = \begin{bmatrix} p_1 \\ p_2 \end{bmatrix}_{t-1} + \begin{bmatrix} -0.89 & 0.13 \\ 0 & -0.71 \end{bmatrix} \begin{bmatrix} v_1 \\ v_2 \end{bmatrix}_{t-1} + \begin{bmatrix} v_1 \\ v_2 \end{bmatrix}_t$$

$$\mathbf{R} = \begin{bmatrix} 3.3 & 0.9 \\ 0.9 & 2.5 \end{bmatrix} \times 10^{-3}$$

The correlation between the components of the noise vector is 0.3. The relation between the output variables can be more easily seen if the model is written in the form of difference equations,

$$p_{1,t} = p_{1,t-1} - 0.89v_{1,t-1} + 0.13v_{2,t-1} + v_{1,t}$$
$$p_{2,t} = p_{2,t-1} \qquad\qquad - 0.71v_{2,t-1} + v_{2,t}$$

The correlation of each variable with its own past is more important that the relation to each other, judging by the coefficients relating both variables and the correlation of noises. Nevertheless, the relation between them is significant and should be taken into account in order to forecast the output variables. The model is adequate in the sense that no serial correlation left in the residuals.

One example is shown in Fig. 16. The top panels show the forecast of the periods to use in the DHR models, with the 95% confidence intervals. Such period is the expected length of the next movement, that is the value introduced into the DHR model to forecast the signal itself. The forecast of the signal is shown in the bottom panels, where the dotted lines are the actual values and the solid lines are the final forecast of the system. It is clear that the left case is free from any fault, since the forecast matches perfectly the actual data, while the expected behavior in the right panel is very different to the actual data, implying that a fault has occurred.

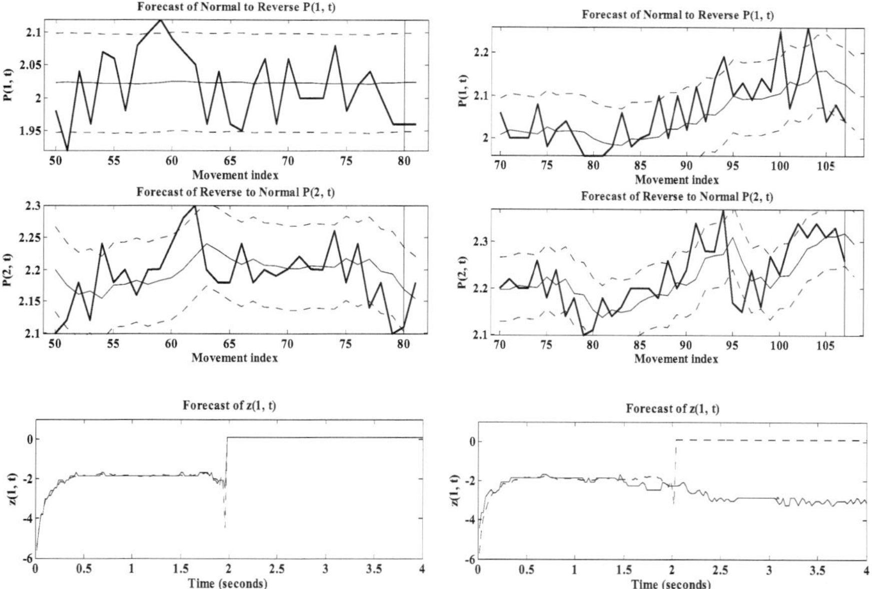

Fig. 16. Left panels shows results for fault free data. Right panels show results for a faulty signal. Panels in the two first rows show the forecast of VARMA model (from the vertical line on); solid lines show the actual periods and the forecast (smoother line). Panels in bottom row show the forecast of the DHR model with the period forecast in the top panels; solid lines are the actual data, dashed lines are the forecast.

Similar results are achieved when the local level model set up in continuous time is used instead (see Fig. 17).

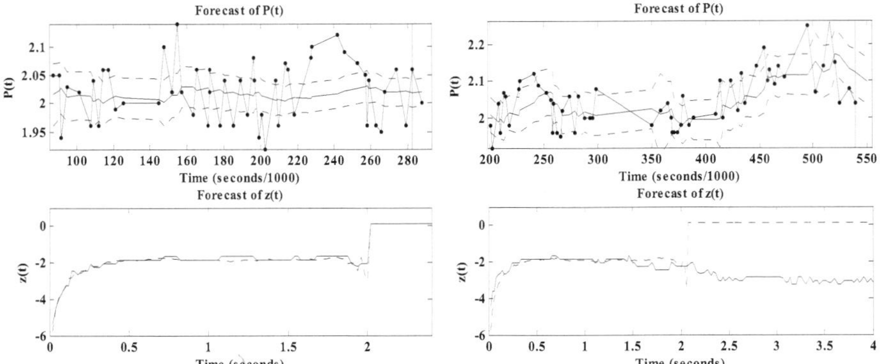

Fig. 17. Left panels shows results for fault free data. Right panels show results for a faulty signal. Panels in the first row show the forecast of the local level model (from the vertical line on); solid lines show the actual periods and the forecast (smoother line). Panels in bottom row show the forecast of the DHR model with the period forecast in the top panels; solid lines are the actual data, dashed lines are the forecast.

This algorithm was applied to the full dataset (380 movements in either directions). From normal to reverse movements 8 were abnormal due to faults similar to the one shown in Figure 17. No faults were registered in the reverse to normal direction data. Selecting a standard deviation of 0.4 as the boundary of faults detection we get that all the faults were detected and not a single false alarm was produced in any of the cases.

7. References

[1] Box G.E.P., Jenkins G.M., Reinsel G.C. 1994. Time Series Analysis, Forecasting and Control. Englewood Cliffs, New Jersey, Prentice Hall International.
[2] Bryson A.E., Ho Y.C. (1969). Applied optimal control, optimization, estimation and control. Waltham, Mass.: Blaisdell Publising Company.
[3] Casals J., Jerez M., Sotoca S., Exact Smoothing for stationary and non-stationary time series, International Journal of Forecasting, 16 (2000), 59-69.
[4] CENELEC EN50170 (2002), General purpose field communication system.
[5] de Jong P., Stable algorithms for the state space model, Journal of Time Series Analysis, 12, (2)(1991) 143-157.
[6] de Jong P., The likelihood for a state space model, Biometrika, 75, (1)(1988) 165-169.
[7] Durbin J., Koopman S.J., Time series analysis by state space methods. Oxford University Press, Oxford, 2001.
[8] García Márquez F.P., Schmid F. and Collado J.C., 2003. "Wear Assessment Employing Remote Condition Monitoring: A Case Study". Wear, Vol. 255, Issue 7-12, pp. 1209-1220.

[9]   García Márquez F.P., Schmid F. and Conde J.C., 2003. A Reliability Centered Approach to Remote Condition Monitoring. A Railway Points Case Study. Reliability Engineering and System Safety, Vol. 80 No. 1, pp 33-40.

[10] Garcia Marquez, F.P and Pedregal D.J. (2004). Failure Analysis and Diagnostics for Railway Trackside Equipment. *Engineering Failure Analysis*, Vol. 14(8), pp. 1411-1426.

[11] Garcia Marquez, F.P and Pedregal D.J. (2007). Applied RCM^2 Algorithms Based on Statistical Methods. *International Journal of Automation and Computing*, Vol. 4, pp. 109-116.

[12] Garcia Marquez, F.P and Schmid F. (2007). Digital Filter Based Approach to the Remote Condition Monitoring of Railway Turnouts. *Reliability Engineering & System Safety*, Vol. 92, pp. 830-840.

[13]   Garcia Marquez, F.P, Pedregal D.J. and Roberts C. (2010). Time Series Methods Applied to Failure Prediction and Detection. *Reliability Engineering & System Safety*. Vol. 95(6), pp. 698-703.

[14] Garcia Marquez, F.P, Pedregal D.J.and Schmid F. (2007). Unobserved Component Models Applied To The Assessment Of Wear In Railway Points: A Case Study. *European Journal of Operational Research*, Vol. 176, pp. 1703-1702.

[15] Harvey, A.C. (1989). Forecasting structural time series models and the Kalman filter. Cambridge: Cambridge University Press.

[16] Kalman R.E., A new approach to linear filtering and prediction problems, ASME Trans., Journal Basic Eng., 83-D (1960) 95-108.

[17] Koopman S.J., Disturbance smoother for state-space models, Biometrika, 76 (1993) 65-79.

[18] Lütkepohl H. 1991. Introduction to Multiple Time Series Analysis. Berlin, Springer-Verlag.

[19] Pedregal D.J., Garcia Marquez, F.P and Schmid F. (2004). Predictive Maintenance of Railway Systems Based on Unobserved Components Model. *Reliability Engineering & System Safety*, Vol. 8(1), pp. 53-62.

[20] Pedregal D.J., Garcia Marquez, F.P, Roberts C. (2009). An Algorithmic Approach for Maintenance Management". *Annals of Operations Research*. Vol. 166, pp. 109-124.

[21] Pedregal D.J., Young P.C., Statistical approaches to modelling and forecasting time series. In Clements M., Hendry D. (eds.), Companion to Economic Forecasting, Blackwell Publishers, 2002.

[22] Proctor P., Infrastructure Risk Modelling – Electric Machine Point Operating Mechanism: HW Type. EE&CS Railtrack H.Q. 2000.

[23]   Roberts, C., Dassanayake, H.P.B., Lehrasab, N., Goodman, C.J. (2002). Distributed quantitative and qualitative fault diagnosis: railway junction case study. Control Engineering Practice, 10, 419-429.

[24] Schweppe F., Evaluation of likelihood function for Gaussian signals, I.E.E.E. Trans. on Inf. Theory, 11 (1965) 61-70.

[25] Tiao G.C., Box G.E.P., 1981, Modelling multiple time series with applications, Journal of the American Statistical Association, 76, 802-816.

[26] Young P.C., Pedregal D.J., Tych W., Dynamic harmonic regression, Journal of Forecasting, 18, (1999) 369-394.

[27] Young P.C., Recursive estimation and time-series analysis, Berlin: Springer-Verlag, 1984.

2

The application of spectral representations in coordinates of complex frequency for digital filter analysis and synthesis

Alexey Mokeev
Northern (Arctic) Federal University
Russian Federation

1. Introduction

The suitability of using one or another spectral representation depends on the type of signal to be analysed and problem to be solved, etc. (Kharkevich, 1960, Jenkins, 1969). Thus, the spectral representations, based on Fourier transform, are widely applied for linear circuit and frequency filter analysis for sinusoidal and periodical input signals (Siebert, 1986, Atabekov, 1978). However, using these spectral representations for a filter analysis of non-stationary signals would not be so simple and visually advantageous (Kharkevich, 1960).

In the majority of cases input signals of automation and measurement devices have an analogue nature, and can be represented as a set of semi-infinite or finite damped oscillatory components. In the case of IIR filter impulse functions the representation uses this set of damped oscillatory components. Impulse functions of FIR filters representation are also based on this set of damped oscillatory components, but with the difference of a finite duration of the impulse functions. Thus, the generalized signal and impulse function of analog filters have similar mathematical expressions. In this case it is reasonable to use the Laplace transform instead of the Fourier transform, because the Laplace transform operates with complex frequency, and its damped oscillatory component is a base function of the transform (Mokeev, 2006, 2007, 2009a).

The application of the spectral representations based on Laplace transform, or in other words, the spectral representations in complex frequency coordinates, enables to simplify significantly calculations of stationary and non-stationary modes and get efficient methods of filter synthesis (Mokeev, 2006). It also extends the application area of the complex amplitude method, including use of this method for analysis of stationary and non-stationary modes of analog and digital filters (Mokeev, 2007, 2008b, 2009a).

2. Mathematical description of filters

2.1 Mathematical description of input signals

It should be considered in frequency filter simulation, that input signals of digital automation and measurement devices have an analogue nature. Therefore, an analog filter-prototype is theoretically perfect. In the majority of cases filter signals and impulse functions can be described by a set of semi-infinite or finite damped oscillatory components.

The mathematical expression of the generalized complex continuous and discrete input signal can be briefly represented in the following way

$$\dot{x}(t) = \dot{\mathbf{X}}^{\mathrm{T}} e^{\mathbf{P}(\mathbf{C}t - \mathbf{t})} - \dot{\mathbf{X}}'^{\mathrm{T}} e^{\mathbf{P}(\mathbf{C}t - \mathbf{t}')} , \tag{1}$$

$$\dot{x}(k) = \dot{\mathbf{X}}^{\mathrm{T}} Z(\mathbf{P}, \mathbf{C}k - \mathbf{K}) - \dot{\mathbf{X}}'^{\mathrm{T}} Z(\mathbf{P}, \mathbf{C}k - \mathbf{K}') , \tag{2}$$

where $\dot{\mathbf{X}} = \left[\dot{X}_n \right]_N = \left[X_{m_n} e^{-j\varphi_n} \right]_N$ and $\dot{\mathbf{X}}' = \left[\dot{X}'_n \right]_N = \left[\dot{X}_n e^{p_n(t'_n - t_n)} \right]_N$ – are complex amplitude vectors of two input signal components, $\mathbf{p} = \left[p_n \right]_N = \left[-\beta_n + j\omega_n \right]_N$ – is complex frequency vector, $\mathbf{t} = \left[t_n \right]_N$, $\mathbf{t}' = \left[t'_n \right]_N$, $\mathbf{K} = \left[K_n \right]_N$, $\mathbf{K}' = \left[K'_n \right]_N$ – are vectors, which elements define a time delay of input signal components, $\mathbf{P} = \mathrm{diag}(\mathbf{p})$ – is square matrix $N \times N$ with the vector $\mathbf{p}$ on the main diagonal, $\mathbf{C}$ – is unit vector, T – is discrete sampling step, $Z(p, k) = e^{pkT}$.

The use of the complex generalized input signal (1) enables to get more compact form of the signal expression. The transition to real signal

$$x(t) = \mathrm{Re}\left(\dot{x}(t) \right), \ x(k) = \mathrm{Re}\left(\dot{x}(k) \right) .$$

When $\dot{\mathbf{X}}' = 0$ и $\mathbf{t} = 0$ ($\mathbf{K} = 0$), the input signal is represented by a set of continuous (discrete) semi-infinite damped oscillatory components.

Particular cases of n-th damped oscillatory component at $t_n = 0$

$$\dot{x}_n(t) = \dot{X}_n e^{p_n t}, \ x_n(t) = \mathrm{Re}\left(\dot{x}_n(t) \right) = X_{m_n} e^{-\beta_n t} \cos(\omega_n t - \varphi_n) ,$$

are semi-infinite sinusoidal ($p_n = j\omega_n$) and constant ($p_n = 0$) components, exponential component ($p_n = -\beta_n$), component in the form of a delta function ($X_{mn} = \beta_n$, $p_n = -\beta_n$, $\beta_n \to \infty$).

Compound signals of different forms, including compound periodical and quasi-periodic signals, non-stationary signals and signals with compound envelopes can be synthesized on the basis of the collection of components mentioned above.

The most frequently used semi-infinite or finite signals with compound envelopes in radio engineering are described by the following model

$$\dot{x}(t) = \dot{X}(t) e^{p_1 t}, \ x(t) = \mathrm{Re}\left(\dot{x}(t) \right),$$

or in general case it would be

$$\dot{x}(t) = \dot{\mathbf{X}}(t)^{\mathrm{T}} e^{\mathbf{P}(\mathbf{C}t - \mathbf{t})}, \ x(t) = \mathrm{Re}\left(\dot{x}(t) \right). \tag{3}$$

Examples of signal mathematical expression, represented by mathematical model (3) and model (1), are shown in the Table 1. In this case signal models (1) and (3) enable to describe not only radio signal (item 1 and 2), but real signals of measurement and automation devices. The example for a signal of intellectual electronic devices of electric power systems as the set of sequentially adjacent finite component groups, each one of those corresponds to defined operation mode of the electric power system, is represented in the item 3, Table 1.

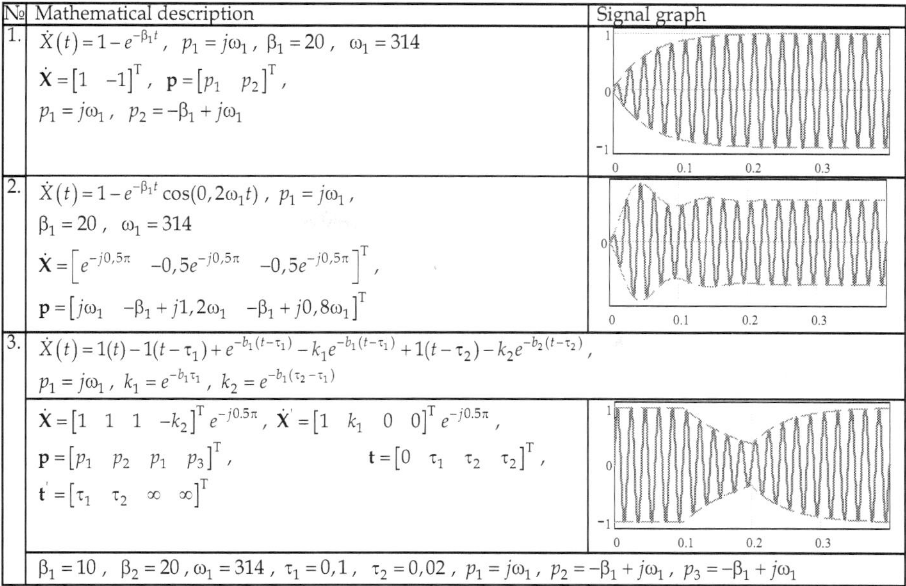

№	Mathematical description	Signal graph
1.	$\dot{X}(t) = 1 - e^{-\beta_1 t}$, $p_1 = j\omega_1$, $\beta_1 = 20$, $\omega_1 = 314$ $\dot{\mathbf{X}} = \begin{bmatrix} 1 & -1 \end{bmatrix}^T$, $\mathbf{p} = \begin{bmatrix} p_1 & p_2 \end{bmatrix}^T$, $p_1 = j\omega_1$, $p_2 = -\beta_1 + j\omega_1$	
2.	$\dot{X}(t) = 1 - e^{-\beta_1 t} \cos(0,2\omega_1 t)$, $p_1 = j\omega_1$, $\beta_1 = 20$, $\omega_1 = 314$ $\dot{\mathbf{X}} = \begin{bmatrix} e^{-j0,5\pi} & -0,5e^{-j0,5\pi} & -0,5e^{-j0,5\pi} \end{bmatrix}^T$, $\mathbf{p} = \begin{bmatrix} j\omega_1 & -\beta_1 + j1,2\omega_1 & -\beta_1 + j0,8\omega_1 \end{bmatrix}^T$	
3.	$\dot{X}(t) = 1(t) - 1(t - \tau_1) + e^{-b_1(t-\tau_1)} - k_1 e^{-b_1(t-\tau_1)} + 1(t - \tau_2) - k_2 e^{-b_2(t-\tau_2)}$, $p_1 = j\omega_1$, $k_1 = e^{-b_1\tau_1}$, $k_2 = e^{-b_1(\tau_2-\tau_1)}$	
	$\dot{\mathbf{X}} = \begin{bmatrix} 1 & 1 & 1 & -k_2 \end{bmatrix}^T e^{-j0.5\pi}$, $\dot{\mathbf{X}}' = \begin{bmatrix} 1 & k_1 & 0 & 0 \end{bmatrix}^T e^{-j0.5\pi}$, $\mathbf{p} = \begin{bmatrix} p_1 & p_2 & p_1 & p_3 \end{bmatrix}^T$, $\mathbf{t} = \begin{bmatrix} 0 & \tau_1 & \tau_2 & \tau_2 \end{bmatrix}^T$, $\mathbf{t}' = \begin{bmatrix} \tau_1 & \tau_2 & \infty & \infty \end{bmatrix}^T$	
	$\beta_1 = 10$, $\beta_2 = 20$, $\omega_1 = 314$, $\tau_1 = 0,1$, $\tau_2 = 0,02$, $p_1 = j\omega_1$, $p_2 = -\beta_1 + j\omega_1$, $p_3 = -\beta_1 + j\omega_1$	

Table 1. Input signal models

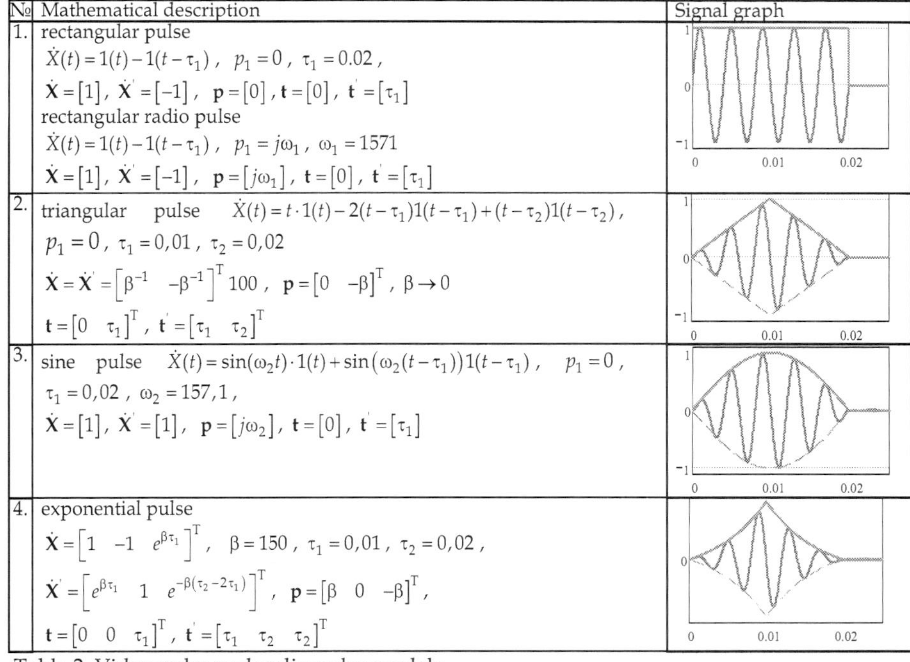

№	Mathematical description	Signal graph
1.	rectangular pulse $\dot{X}(t) = 1(t) - 1(t - \tau_1)$, $p_1 = 0$, $\tau_1 = 0.02$, $\dot{\mathbf{X}} = [1]$, $\dot{\mathbf{X}}' = [-1]$, $\mathbf{p} = [0]$, $\mathbf{t} = [0]$, $\mathbf{t}' = [\tau_1]$ rectangular radio pulse $\dot{X}(t) = 1(t) - 1(t - \tau_1)$, $p_1 = j\omega_1$, $\omega_1 = 1571$ $\dot{\mathbf{X}} = [1]$, $\dot{\mathbf{X}}' = [-1]$, $\mathbf{p} = [j\omega_1]$, $\mathbf{t} = [0]$, $\mathbf{t}' = [\tau_1]$	
2.	triangular pulse $\dot{X}(t) = t \cdot 1(t) - 2(t - \tau_1)1(t - \tau_1) + (t - \tau_2)1(t - \tau_2)$, $p_1 = 0$, $\tau_1 = 0,01$, $\tau_2 = 0,02$ $\dot{\mathbf{X}} = \dot{\mathbf{X}}' = \begin{bmatrix} \beta^{-1} & -\beta^{-1} \end{bmatrix}^T 100$, $\mathbf{p} = \begin{bmatrix} 0 & -\beta \end{bmatrix}^T$, $\beta \to 0$ $\mathbf{t} = \begin{bmatrix} 0 & \tau_1 \end{bmatrix}^T$, $\mathbf{t}' = \begin{bmatrix} \tau_1 & \tau_2 \end{bmatrix}^T$	
3.	sine pulse $\dot{X}(t) = \sin(\omega_2 t) \cdot 1(t) + \sin(\omega_2(t - \tau_1))1(t - \tau_1)$, $p_1 = 0$, $\tau_1 = 0,02$, $\omega_2 = 157,1$, $\dot{\mathbf{X}} = [1]$, $\dot{\mathbf{X}}' = [1]$, $\mathbf{p} = [j\omega_2]$, $\mathbf{t} = [0]$, $\mathbf{t}' = [\tau_1]$	
4.	exponential pulse $\dot{\mathbf{X}} = \begin{bmatrix} 1 & -1 & e^{\beta\tau_1} \end{bmatrix}^T$, $\beta = 150$, $\tau_1 = 0,01$, $\tau_2 = 0,02$, $\dot{\mathbf{X}}' = \begin{bmatrix} e^{\beta\tau_1} & 1 & e^{-\beta(\tau_2-2\tau_1)} \end{bmatrix}^T$, $\mathbf{p} = \begin{bmatrix} \beta & 0 & -\beta \end{bmatrix}^T$, $\mathbf{t} = \begin{bmatrix} 0 & 0 & \tau_1 \end{bmatrix}^T$, $\mathbf{t}' = \begin{bmatrix} \tau_1 & \tau_2 & \tau_2 \end{bmatrix}^T$	

Table 2. Video pulse and radio pulse models

The model (1) also makes it possible to describe the majority of impulse signals, which are widely applicable in radio engineering. Examples of some impulse signals are shown it the Table 2. Therefore, the generalized mathematical model (1) enables to describe a big variety of semi-infinite or finite signals.

As it is shown below, the compound finite signal representations in the form of the set of damped oscillatory components significantly simplifies the problem solving of the signal passage analysis through the frequency filters, by using the analysis methods based on signal and filter spectral representations in complex frequency coordinates (Mokeev, 2007, 2008b).

2.2 Mathematical description of filters

Analysis and synthesis of filters of digital automation and measurement devices are primarily carried out for analog filter-prototypes. The transition to digital filters is implemented by using the known synthesis methods. However, this method can only be applied for IIR filters, as a pure analog FIR filter does not exist because of complications of its realization. Nevertheless, implementation of this type of analog filters is rational exclusively as they are considered "perfect" filters for analog signal processing and as filter-prototypes for digital FIR filters (Mokeev, 2007, 2008b).

When solving problems of digital filters analysis and synthesis, one will not take into account the AD converter errors, including the errors due to signal amplitude quantization. This gives the opportunity to use simpler discrete models instead of digital signal and filter models (Ifeachor, 2002, Smith, 2002). These types of errors are only taken into consideration during the final design phase of digital filters. In case of DSP with high digit capacity, these types of errors are not taken into account at all.

The mathematical description of analog filter-prototypes and digital filters can be expressed with the following generalized forms of impulse functions:

$$\dot{g}(t) = \dot{\mathbf{G}}^{\mathrm{T}} e^{\mathbf{q}t} - \dot{\mathbf{G}}^{'\mathrm{T}} e^{\mathbf{Q}(\mathbf{C}t - \mathbf{T})} \,, \quad g(t) = \mathrm{Re}\big(\dot{g}(t)\big), \tag{4}$$

$$\dot{g}(k) = \dot{\mathbf{G}}^{\mathrm{T}} Z(\mathbf{q}, k) - \dot{\mathbf{G}}^{'\mathrm{T}} Z(\mathbf{Q}, \mathbf{C}k - \mathbf{N}) \,, \quad g(k) = \mathrm{Re}\big(\dot{g}(k)\big). \tag{5}$$

Therefore, for analog and digital filter description it is sufficient to use vectors of complex amplitudes of two parts of complex function:

$\dot{\mathbf{G}} = \big[\dot{G}_m\big]_M = \big[k_m e^{-j\phi_m}\big]_M$ and $\dot{\mathbf{G}}' = \big[\dot{G}'_m\big]_M = \big[\dot{G}_m e^{\rho_m T_m}\big]_M$, vector of complex frequencies $\mathbf{q} = \big[\rho_m\big]_M = \big[-\alpha_m + jw_m\big]_M$ and vectors $\mathbf{T} = \big[T_m\big]_M$ и $\mathbf{N} = \big[N_m\big]_M$, which define the duration (length) of the filter pulse function components; $\mathbf{Q} = \mathrm{diag}(\mathbf{q})$ – is a square matrix $M{\times}M$ with the vector $\mathbf{q}$ on the main diagonal.

Adhering to the mathematical description of the FIR filter impulse function mentioned above (4), the IIR filter impulse functions are a special case of analogous functions of FIR filters at $\dot{\mathbf{G}}' = 0$.

Recording the mathematical description of filters in such a complex form has advantages: firstly, the expression density, and secondly, correlation to two filters at the same time, which allows for ensured calculation of instant spectral density module and phase on given complex frequency (Smith, 2002).

The transfer function of the filter (4) with the complex coefficients is

$$\underline{K}(p) = \dot{\mathbf{G}}^{\mathrm{T}} \left[\frac{1}{p - \rho_m} \right]_M - \dot{\mathbf{G}}^{'\mathrm{T}} \left[\frac{1}{p - \rho_m} e^{-pT_m} \right]_M , \qquad (6)$$

The transfer function $\underline{K}(p)$ is an expression of the complex impulse function (6), therefore it has along with the complex variable p complex coefficients, defined by the vectors $\dot{\mathbf{G}}$, $\dot{\mathbf{G}}'$ and $\mathbf{q}$. A filter with the transfer function $\underline{K}(p)$ correlates with two ordinary filters, which transfer functions are $\mathrm{Re}(\underline{K}(p))$ and $\mathrm{Im}(\underline{K}(p))$. In this case the extraction of the real and imaginary parts of $\underline{K}(p)$ can be applied only to complex coefficients of the transfer function and has no relevance for the complex variable p.

As it appears from the input signal models (1) and filter impulse functions (4), there is a similarity between their expressions of time and frequency domains. Filter impulse functions based on the model (4) may have a compound form, including the analogous ones referred to above in Tables 1 and 2.

The similarity of mathematical signal and filter expressions: firstly, allow to use one compact form for their expression as a set of complex amplitudes, complex frequencies and temporary parameters. Secondly, it significantly simplifies solving problems of mathematical simulation and frequency filter analysis.

The digital filter description (5) can be considered as a discretization result of analog filter impulse function (4). Another known transition (synthesis) methods can be also applied, if they are revised for use with analogue filters-prototypes with a finite-impulse response (Mokeev, 2008b).

2.3 Methods of the transition from an analog FIR filter to a digital filter

The mathematical description of digital FIR filters at $M = 1$ is given in the Table 3, these filters were obtained on the basis of the analog FIR filter (item 0) by use of three transformed known synthesis methods: the discrete sampling method of the differential equation (item 1), as well as the method of invariant impulse responses (item 2) and the method of bilinear transformation (item 3).

№	Differential or difference equation	Impulse function	Transfer or system function
0.	$\dfrac{d\dot{y}(t)}{dt} - \rho_1 \dot{y}(t) = \dot{G}_1 x(t) - \dot{G}_1' x(t - T_1)$	$\dot{g}(t) = \dot{G}_1 e^{\rho_1 t} - \dot{G}_1' e^{\rho_1 (t - T_1)}$	$\underline{K}(p) = \dfrac{1}{p - \rho_1}\left(\dot{G}_1 - \dot{G}_1' e^{-pT_1}\right)$
1.	$\nabla \dot{y}_k - \rho_1 \dot{y}_k = \dot{G}_1 x_k - \dot{G}_2 x_{k-N_1}$	$g_k = k_{11}\left(\dot{G}_1 z_{11}^k - \dot{G}_1 z_{11}^{k-N_1}\right)$	$K(z) = \dfrac{k_{11} z}{z - z_{11}}\left(\dot{G}_1 - \dot{G}_2 z^{-N_1}\right)$
2.	$\nabla \dot{y}_k - a_0 \dot{y}_k = \dot{G}_1 x_k - \dot{G}_2 x_{k-N_1}$	$g_k = k_{12}\left(\dot{G}_1 z_1^k - \dot{G}_1 z_1^{k-N_1}\right)$	$K(z) = \dfrac{k_{12} z}{z - z_1}\left(\dot{G}_1 - \dot{G}_2 z^{-N_1}\right)$
3.	-	-	$K(z) = k_{13}\dfrac{z+1}{z - z_{13}}\left(\dot{G}_1 - \dot{G}_2 z^{-N_1}\right)$

Table 3. Methods of the transition from an analog FIR filter to a digital FIR filter

Note: The double subscripts are given for the parameters that do not coincide. The second number means the sequence number of the transition method.

1. $k_{11} = T$, $z_{11} = 1/(1 - T\rho_1)$, $N_1 = T_1/T$, complex frequency $\rho_{11} = \ln(z_{11})/T$;

2. $z_1 = e^{\rho_1 T}$, $a_0 = (z_1 - 1) / T$, $k_{12} = T$;

3. $k_{13} = T / (2 - \rho_1 T)$, $z_{13} = (2 + \rho_1 T) / (2 - \rho_1 T)$, complex frequency $\rho_{13} = \ln(z_{13}) / T$.

In cases of the first and third methods the coincidence of impulse function complex frequencies of digital filter and analog filter-prototype is possible only if $T \to 0$. The second method ensures the entire concurrence of complex frequencies of an analogue filter-prototype and a digital filter in all instances. The later is very important, when the filter is supposed to be used as a spectrum analyzer in coordinates of complex frequency.

The features of transition from a digital (discrete) filter, considering finite digit capacity influence of microprocessor, including cases for filters with integer-valued coefficients, are considered by the author in the research .

One of the most important advantages of the considered above approach to mathematical description of FIR filters is obtaining FIR filter fast algorithms (Mokeev, 2008a, 2008b).

2.4 Overlapping the spectral and time approach

The impulse function (3) corresponds to the following differential equation

$$\frac{d\dot{\mathbf{y}}(t)}{dt} = \mathbf{A}\dot{\mathbf{y}}(t) + \mathbf{B}x(t) + \mathbf{D}x(Ct - \mathbf{T}), \tag{7}$$

where $\mathbf{A} = \mathrm{diag}(\mathbf{q})$, $\mathbf{B} = \dot{\mathbf{G}}$, $\mathbf{D} = \mathrm{diag}(\dot{\mathbf{G}})$; $y(t) = \mathrm{Re}\left(\mathbf{C}^{\mathrm{T}}\dot{\mathbf{y}}(t)\right)$ is a output signal of the filter.

In case of FIR filter ($\mathbf{D} = 0$) the expression (7) is conform to one of known forms of state space method. Thus, the application of mentioned spectral representations allows to combine the spectral approach with the state space method for frequency filter analysis and synthesis (Mokeev, 2008b, 2009b).

If one places the expression of generalized impulse characteristic (4) to the expression of convolution integral, one will get the following expression of the filter output signal

$$\dot{y}(t) = \int\limits_{Ct-T}^{t} x(\tau)\dot{\mathbf{G}}^{\mathrm{T}}e^{\mathbf{q}(t-\tau)}d\tau . \tag{8}$$

If a generalized input signal (1) is fed into the filter input, simple input-output relations (Mokeev, 2008b) can be gained on the base of the expression (8).

The expression (8) can be transformed into the following form

$$\dot{y}(t) = \sum_{m=1}^{M} \dot{G}_m X_T(\rho_m) e^{\rho_m t} ,$$

where $X_T(p,t) = \int\limits_{t-T}^{t} x(\tau)e^{-p\tau}d\tau$ - is the instant spectrum of input signal in coordinates of complex frequency.

Therefore, the elements of the vector $\dot{y}(t)$ are defined by solving M-number of independent equations (7), each one of those can be interpreted as a value of instant (FIR filter) or current (IIR filter) Laplace spectrum in corresponding complex frequency of filter impulse function component.

The expression (7) is a generalization of one of state space method forms, and at the same time directly connected with the Laplace spectral representations. So, one can view the overlapping time approach (state space method) and frequency approach in complex frequency coordinates.

On the base of analogue filter-prototype (7) descriptions, a mathematical expression of digital filters can be obtained, by use of the known transition (synthesis) methods, applied to FIR filters (Mokeev, 2008b). In this case fast algorithms for FIR filters are additionally synthesized.

2.5 Features of signal spectrum and filter frequency responses in complex frequency coordinates

To illustrate the features of signal spectrums and filter frequency responses in coordinates of complex frequency, the fig. 1 shows amplitude-frequency response schematics of IIR filter and a spectral density module of input signal, if the following conditions apply: the filter represents a series of low-pass second-order and first-order filters, and can be described by complex amplitude vector $\dot{\mathbf{G}} = \begin{bmatrix} 9{,}63e^{-j2{,}336} & 6{,}67 \end{bmatrix}^{\mathrm{T}}$ and complex frequency vector $\mathbf{q} = \begin{bmatrix} -150 + j640 & -400 \end{bmatrix}^{\mathrm{T}}$; the input signal consists of an additive mixture of an unit step, exponential component, semi-infinite sinusoidal component and damped oscillatory component, and can be compactly described by complex amplitude vector $\dot{\mathbf{X}} = \begin{bmatrix} 1 & e^{j\pi} & 2e^{j0{,}25\pi} & 2 \end{bmatrix}^{\mathrm{T}}$ and complex frequency vector $\mathbf{p} = \begin{bmatrix} 0 & -120 & j300 & -40 + j500 \end{bmatrix}^{\mathrm{T}}$.

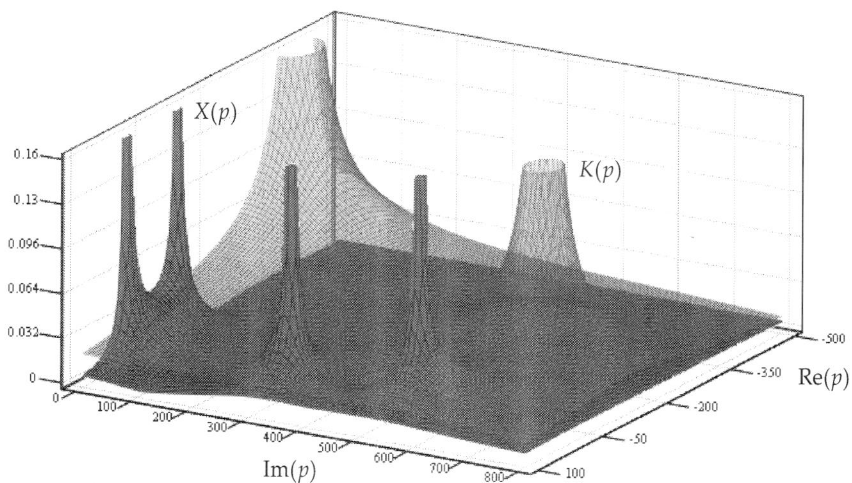

Fig. 1. 3D amplitude signal spectrum and filter amplitude-frequency response

The 3D amplitude-frequency response (fig. 1) of the filter and signal spectrum module shows, that complex frequencies of filter and input signal impulse functions have clearly defined peaks.

This means, a 3D signal spectrum in complex frequency coordinates contains a continuous spectrum along with four discrete lines on complex frequencies of input signal components. The signal spectral densities on the mentioned complex frequencies are proportional to delta function. Values of the transfer function on the mentioned complex frequencies of input signal define a variation law of forced filter output signal components concerning input signal components (Mokeev, 2007, 2008b). The rest of spectral regions characterize the transient process in the filter due to step-by-step change of the input signal at the time zero.

A filters amplitude-frequency response is also three-dimensional and is represented by a continuous spectrum and two discrete lines on complex frequencies of impulse function components. In this case the values of the input signal representation of the above mentioned complex frequencies, define a variation law of free components in relation to filter impulse function components (Mokeev, 2007).

3. Filter analysis

3.1 Analysis methods based on features of signal and filter
spectral representations in complex frequency coordinates

Three methods of frequency filter analysis are suggested from the time-and-frequency representations positions of signals and linear systems in coordinates of complex frequency (Mokeev, 2007, 2008b).

The first method is based on the above considered features of signal spectrums and filter frequency responses in complex frequency coordinates, and it allows for the determination of forces and free filter components, by the use of simple arithmetic operations.

The other two methods are based on applied time-and-frequency representations of signals or filters in coordinates of complex frequency. In this case instead of determining forced and free components of the output filter signal, it is enough to consider the filter dynamic properties by using only one of the mentioned component groups.

Based on time-and-frequency representations of signals and linear systems in coordinates of complex frequency, the known definition by Charkevich A.A. (Kharkevich, 1960) for accounting the dynamic properties of linear system is generalized:

1. the signal is considered as current or instantaneous spectrum, and the system (filter) – only as discrete components of frequency responses in coordinates of complex frequency;

2. the signal is characterized only by discrete components of spectrum, and the system (filter) – by time dependence frequency responses.

Analysis methods for analog and digital IIR filters in case of semi-infinite input signals, similar to (1), are considered below. These methods of filter analysis can be simply applied to more complicated cases, for instance, to FIR filter (4) analysis at finite input signals (Mokeev, 2008b).

3.2 The first method of filter analysis: complex amplitude method generalization

The first method is a complex amplitude method generalization for definition of forced and free components for filter reaction at semi-infinite or finite input signals.

The advantages of this method are related to simple algebraic operations, which are used for determining the parameters of linear system reaction (filter, linear circuit) components to input action described by a set of semi-infinite or finite damped oscillatory components.

Here, the expressions for determining forced and free components of analog and digital IIR filter reaction to a signal, fed to filter input as a set of continuous or discrete damped oscillatory components, i.e. for the generalized signal (1) and (2) at $\dot{\mathbf{X}}' = \mathbf{0}$, are given as examples on fig. 2 and 3.

$$
\begin{array}{c|c|c}
\dot{\mathbf{X}}, \ \mathbf{x}(t) = \mathrm{Re}\left(\dot{\mathbf{X}}^{\mathrm{T}} e^{\mathbf{p}t}\right) & K(p) & \dot{\mathbf{Y}} = K(\mathbf{P})\dot{\mathbf{X}}, \ y_1(t) = \mathrm{Re}\left(\dot{\mathbf{Y}}^{\mathrm{T}} e^{\mathbf{p}t}\right) \\
\hline
\dot{\mathbf{X}}, \ \mathbf{x}(k) = \mathrm{Re}\left(\dot{\mathbf{X}}^{\mathrm{T}} Z(\mathbf{P},k)\right) & K(z) & \dot{\mathbf{Y}} = K(\mathbf{Z})\dot{\mathbf{X}}, \ y_1(k) = \mathrm{Re}\left(\dot{\mathbf{Y}}^{\mathrm{T}} Z(\mathbf{P},k)\right)
\end{array}
$$

Fig. 2. Determining the forced components of an IIR filter output signal

$$
\begin{array}{c|c|c}
\dot{\mathbf{G}}, \ g(t) = \mathrm{Re}\left(\dot{\mathbf{G}}^{\mathrm{T}} e^{\mathbf{q}t}\right) & X(p) & \dot{\mathbf{V}} = X(\mathbf{q})\dot{\mathbf{G}}, \ y_2(t) = \mathrm{Re}\left(\dot{\mathbf{V}}^{\mathrm{T}} e^{\mathbf{Q}(C t - t)}\right) \\
\hline
\dot{\mathbf{G}}, \ g(k) = \mathrm{Re}\left(\dot{\mathbf{G}}^{\mathrm{T}} Z(\mathbf{Q},k)\right) & X(z) & \dot{\mathbf{V}} = X(\mathbf{Q})\dot{\mathbf{G}}, \ y_2(k) = \mathrm{Re}\left(\dot{\mathbf{V}}^{\mathrm{T}} Z(\mathbf{Q},k)\right)
\end{array}
$$

Fig. 3. Determining the free components of an IIR filter output signal

The following notations are used in the expressions on fig. 2 and fig. 3: $X(p)$ or $X(z)$, that are the representations of the input signal without regard for phase shift of signal components $\mathbf{Z} = e^{\mathbf{q}T}$.

The example for determining the reaction (curve 1) of analog and digital (discrete) third-order filter (condition in item 3.1), and the total forced (curve 2) and free (curve 3) components is shown on the fig. 4. Using Matlab and Mathcad for determining the forced and free components of an output signal, only complex amplitude vectors of an input signal and filter impulse function , as well as the complex frequency vectors of an input signal and filter are needed to be specified. The remaining calculations are carried out automatically.

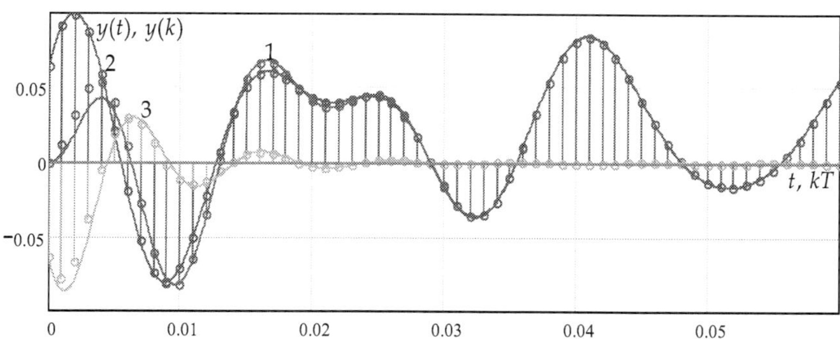

Fig. 4. Determining the forced and free components of an output signal

The input-output expressions presented on fig. 2 and fig. 3 can be applied also to FIR filters and finite signals (Mokeev, 2008b).

3.3 The second method: filter as a spectrum analyzer

The second method is based on interpreting a filter as an analyzer of current or instantaneous spectrum of an input signal in coordinates of complex frequency (Mokeev, 2007, 2008b).

If one converts the expression for an IIR filter complex impulse function (4) into an expression of convolution integral, the result will be the dependence for a filter output signal:

$$\dot{y}(t) = \int_0^t x(\tau)\dot{g}(t-\tau)d\tau = \dot{\mathbf{G}}^T X(\mathbf{Q},t)e^{qt}\,,\tag{9}$$

where $X(p,t) = \int_0^t x(\tau)e^{-p\tau}d\tau$ - is the current spectral density of an input signal, using Laplace transform.

On the base of the expression (9) the calculations for determining a filter output signal components are gained and represented on the fig. 5.

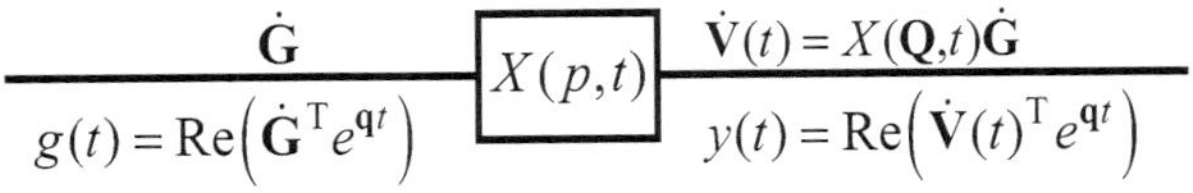

$$\frac{\dot{\mathbf{G}}}{g(t) = \mathrm{Re}\left(\dot{\mathbf{G}}^T e^{qt}\right)} \boxed{X(p,t)} \frac{\dot{V}(t) = X(\mathbf{Q},t)\dot{\mathbf{G}}}{y(t) = \mathrm{Re}\left(\dot{V}(t)^T e^{qt}\right)}$$

Fig. 5. Determining the IIR filter reaction

As concluded from the expression above, an IIR filter output signal depends on values of the current Laplace spectrum of an input signal on filter impulse function complex frequencies. Thus, a FIR filter is an analyzer of a signal instantaneous spectrum in a coordinates of complex frequency.

3.4 The third method: diffusion of time-and-frequency approach to transfer function

The time-and-frequency approach in the third analysis method applies to a filter transfer function, i.e. time dependent transfer function of the filter is used.

If one places the expression for a complex semi-infinite input signal (1) into the expression for convolution integral, one will obtain the following dependence

$$\dot{y}(t) = \int_0^t \dot{x}(\tau)g(t-\tau)d\tau = \dot{\mathbf{X}}^T K(\mathbf{P},t)e^{\mathbf{p}t}\,,$$

where $K(p,t) = \int_0^t g(\tau)e^{-p\tau}d\tau$ - is time dependent transfer function of filter.

Then the input-output dependence for an IIR filter (4), when it is fed to semi-infinite input signal, can be compactly presented in the following way (fig. 6).

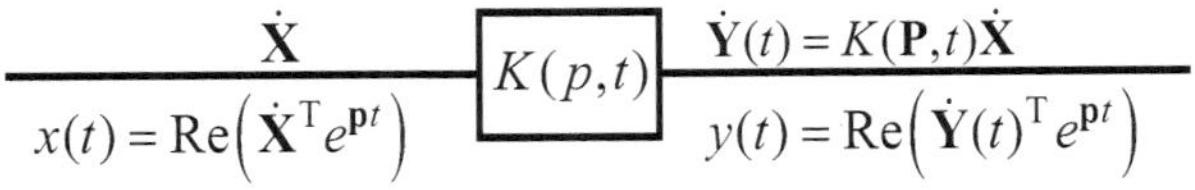

$$\frac{\dot{\mathbf{X}}}{x(t) = \mathrm{Re}\left(\dot{\mathbf{X}}^T e^{\mathbf{p}t}\right)} \boxed{K(p,t)} \frac{\dot{\mathbf{Y}}(t) = K(\mathbf{P},t)\dot{\mathbf{X}}}{y(t) = \mathrm{Re}\left(\dot{\mathbf{Y}}(t)^T e^{\mathbf{p}t}\right)}$$

Fig. 6. Filter reaction determination

Thus, a function modulus $K(p_n,t)$ value on the complex frequency of n-th input signal component describes the variation law of n-th component envelope of filter output signal.

The function argument characterizes phase change of the later mentioned output signal component. Since the transient processes in filter are completed, the complex amplitude $\dot{Y}_n(t)$ will coincide with the complex amplitude of the forced component $\dot{Y}_n$.

In that case, filter amplitude-frequency and phase-frequency functions will be a three-variable functions, i.e. it is necessary to represent responses in 4D space. For practical visualization of frequency responses the approach, based on use of three-dimensional frequency responses at complex frequency real or imaginary partly fixed value, can be applied.

Let us consider the example from the item 3.1. The plot, shown on fig. 7 , is proportional to the product $\left|K(-\beta_4 + j\omega, t)\right| e^{-\beta_4 t}$. This plot on the complex frequency $p_4 = -\beta_4 + j\omega_4$ is equal to the envelope (curve 1 and 2) of filter reaction (curve 3) on the fourth component's input action for the filter input signal.

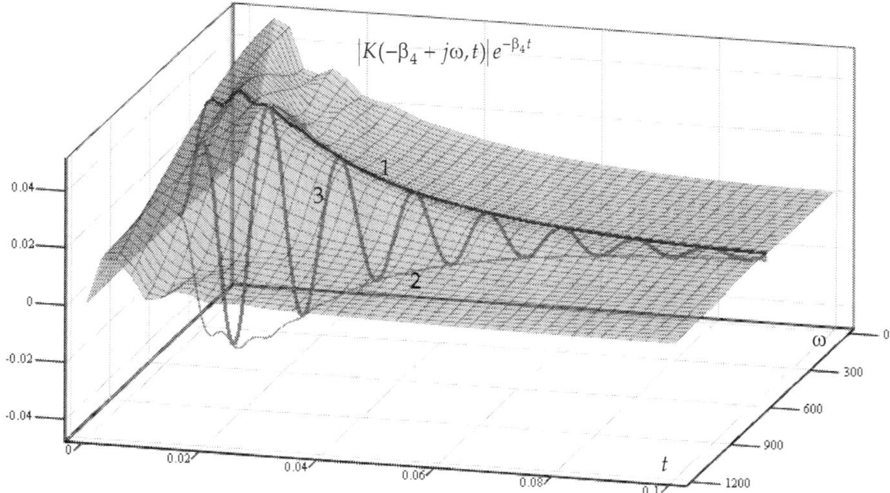

Fig. 7. Plot of the function $\left|K(-\beta_4 + j\omega, t)\right| e^{-\beta_4 t}$

The advantages of these suggested analysis methods, comparing to the existing ones for specified generalized models of input signals and frequency filters, consist in calculation simplicity, including solving problems of determining the performance parameters of signal processing by frequency filters.

4. Filter synthesis

4.1 IIR filter synthesis
The application of spectral representations in complex frequency coordinates allows to simplify significantly solving problems of filter synthesis for generalized signal model (1).

Let us consider robust filter synthesis, which have low sensitivity to change of useful signal and disturbance parameters (Sánchez Peña, 1998). In other words, robust filters must ensure the required signal performance factors at any possible variation of useful signal and disturbance parameters, influencing on their spectrums. If one takes into account only two main performance factors of signals: speed and accuracy, it will be enough to assure fulfillment of requirements, connected to limitations for filter transfer function module on complex frequency of useful signal and disturbance components (Mokeev, 2009c).

Thus, filter synthesis problem, instead of setting the requirements to particular frequency response domains (pass band and rejection band), comes to form the dependences for filter transfer function on complex frequencies of input signal components. To ensure the required performance signal factors, it is necessary to consider possible variation ranges of mentioned complex frequencies.

The synthesis will be carried out with increasing numbers of impulse function components (4) till the achievement of the specified performance signal factors.

The block diagram, shown on fig. 8, illustrates the synthesis of optimal analogue filter-prototype.

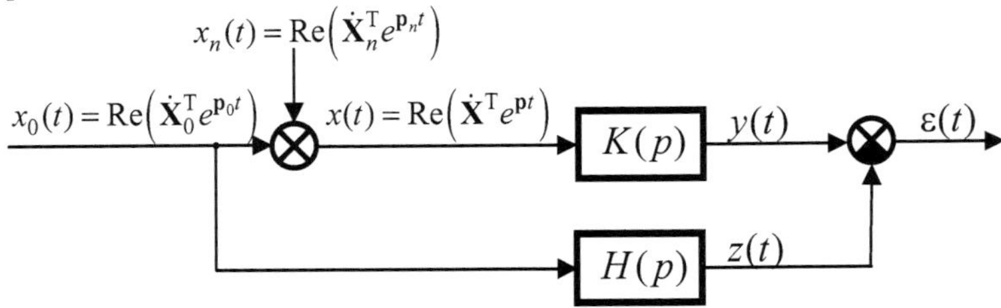

Fig. 8. Block diagram of optimal filter

The useful signal $x_0(t)$ and the disturbance $x_n(t)$ on the graph _ are completely determined by complex amplitude vectors $\dot{\mathbf{X}}_0$, $\dot{\mathbf{X}}_n$ and complex frequency vectors $\mathbf{p}_0$, $\mathbf{p}_n$. The vectors of complex amplitudes and input signal frequencies are characterized as $\dot{\mathbf{X}} = \begin{bmatrix} \dot{\mathbf{X}}_0 & \dot{\mathbf{X}}_n \end{bmatrix}^{\mathrm{T}}$, $\mathbf{p} = \begin{bmatrix} \mathbf{p}_0 & \mathbf{p}_n \end{bmatrix}^{\mathrm{T}}$. In case of the value of the transformation operator $H(p) = 1$, the error vector-function is $\varepsilon(t) = y(t) - x_0(t)$, in the rest of cases : $\varepsilon(t) = y(t) - z(t)$.

Limitations on forced component level for IIR filter are set by the limitations on filter amplitude-frequency response in complex frequency coordinates. Therefore, the problem of fulfillment of signal processing accuracy requirements in filter operation stationary mode is completely solved, and the filter speed τ will be determined by transient process duration in the filter, i.e. by free component damping below the permissible level (less than acceptable error of signal processing). Free components damping can be approximately determined by the sum of their envelopes. Thus, filter synthesis at specified structure comes to determination of its parameters, at which the specified requirements to frequency responses in complex frequency coordinates are ensured, and to ascertain the minimum time for signal processing performance requirements guaranteeing. One more suggested method, that enables to simplify optimal filter estimation, is related to use of time dependent filter transfer function $K(p,t)$.

For searching the optimal solution it is reasonable to apply the realization in Optimization Toolbox package, a part of MATLAB system of nonlinear optimization procedure methods with the limitations to a filter transfer function value on specified complex frequencies of input signal components and filter speed.

Order of filter synthesis, according to specified block diagram (fig. 8), consists in the following. Type and filter order are given on the basis of features of solving problem, target function and restrictions on filter frequency response values in complex frequency coordinates are formed based on ensuring of signal processing performance required parameters. Then filter parameters are calculated with use of optimization procedures. In case of the found solution does not meet signal processing performance requirements, the order of filter should be raised and filter parameters should be found again.

Let us consider an example of analogue filter-prototype synthesis to separate the sine signal against a disturbance background in the exponential component form.

To extract the useful signal and eliminate the disturbance, acceptable speed can be only be obtained with use of second-order and higher order filters. Let us consider second-order high-pass filter synthesis.

The main phases of IIR filter synthesis for selection industrial frequency useful signal against a background of exponential disturbance are presented in table 4.

№	Name	Conditions
1.	Input signal $x(t) = X_{m1}\cos\omega_1 t - X_2 e^{-\beta_2 t}$	limits of useful signal frequency variation $\omega_1 = 2\pi(45 \div 55)$ rad/s, maximum disturbance level $X_2 = X_{m1}$, changing size of damping coefficient $\beta_2 = 0 \div 200$ s^{-1}

2.	Signal processing performance requirements	1. acceptable error in signal processing:
		  automation function $\varepsilon_1 \le 0,1$ (5 %),
		  metering function $\varepsilon_2 \le 0,01$ (1 %),
		2. speed: $\tau_1 \le 20$ мс (5%), $\tau_2 \le 40$ ms (1%),
		3. acceptable overshoot level: $\le 10\%$

3.	Requirements to filter amplitude-frequency response in complex frequency coordinates	1. section $p = j\omega$: $\quad\left\|K(j\omega_0)\right\| = 1$, $\quad\omega_0 = 100\pi$ rad/s, $\quad 1 - \varepsilon_2 \le \left\|K\left(j(\omega_0 \pm \Delta\omega)\right)\right\| \le 1 + \varepsilon_2$, $\quad\Delta\omega = 10\pi$ rad/s 2. section $p = -\gamma$: $\left\|K(-\gamma)\right\|e^{-\gamma\tau_1} \le \varepsilon_1$, $\left\|K(-\gamma)\right\|e^{-\gamma\tau_2} \le \varepsilon_2$
4.	Transfer function of second-order high-pass filter	$K(p) = \dfrac{0,874p^2}{p^2 + 224p + 221^2}$

Table 4. IIR filter synthesis

The amplitude-frequency responses in the sections $p = j\omega$ and $p = -\gamma$ (at $\tau_1 = 0,02$ s) are represented on fig. 9. On fig. 9 along with filter amplitude-frequency response the limitations on filter amplitude-frequency response values, according to the requirements in table 4 item 3, are shown. Amplitude-frequency response value out of mentioned restrictions zone conventionally is ≤ 1. As follows from the fig. 9, the synthesized filter completely meets the requirements of signal processing accuracy at frequency change ± 5 Hz in power system.

The plot of transient process in second-order high-pass filter at signal feeding (table 4 point 1) is presented on fig. 10. The transient process durations are 11 ms (that is 10% of acceptable error), 15 ms (5%) and 33 ms (1%) at any exponential component damping coefficient value from the specified range $\beta = 0 \div 200$ s⁻¹.

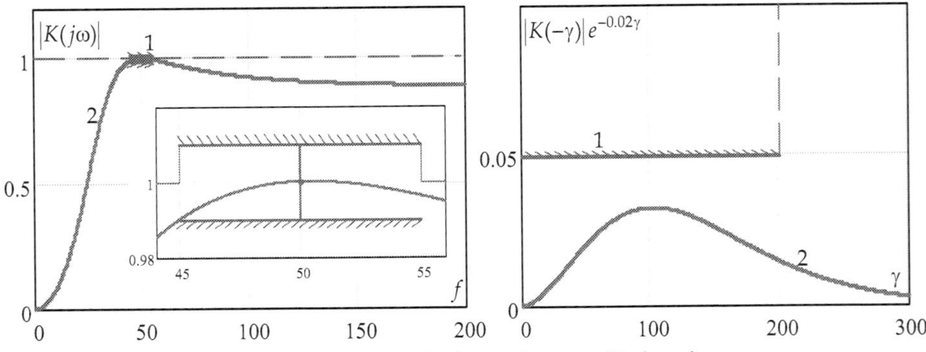

Fig. 9. Filter amplitude-frequency response in the sections $p = j2\pi f$ and $p = -\gamma$

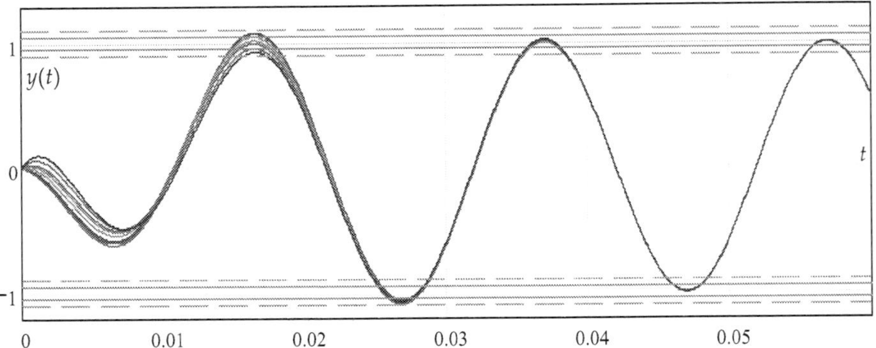

Fig. 10. Filter output signal

Therefore, synthesized second-order high-pass filter has low sensitivity to exponential component damping coefficient variation and to power system frequency deviation.

This example clearly illustrates the advantages of using the Laplace transform spectral representations for frequency filter synthesis. Applying these representations in combination with multidimensional optimization methods with the contingencies enables to perform frequency filter synthesis for problems, that were unsolvable at traditional spectral representations usage (Mokeev, 2008b). For instance, for the problem of filter synthesis for separation of the following signals: constant and exponential signals, two exponential signals with non-overlapping damping coefficient change ranges, sinusoidal and damped oscillatory components with equal or similar frequencies.

The mentioned above synthesis method can be also effectively apply for typical signal filtering problems, including problems of useful signal extraction against the white noise. In that, the white noise realizations can be described by the special case of generalized signal model (1) as a set of time-shifted fast damping exponents of different digits. Initial values and appearance time of the mentioned exponential components are random variables, which variation law ensures the white noise specified spectral characteristics. This white noise model allows to approach filter synthesis on the basis of the signal spectral representation features (1) in complex frequency coordinates and to guarantee the required combinations of signal processing speed and accuracy (Mokeev, 2008b).

4.2 FIR filter synthesis

Comparing to IIR filter synthesis, synthesis of FIR filters is significantly simpler due to easier control over transient processes duration in filter. In case of compliance with the restrictions on amplitude-frequency response values on input signal complex frequencies (1), filter speed will be determined by the length of its impulse response.

As examples of synthesis, let us consider averaging FIR filter synthesis for intellectual electronic devices (IED) of electric power systems. Block diagram of the most widespread signal processing algorithm is given on Fig. 11.

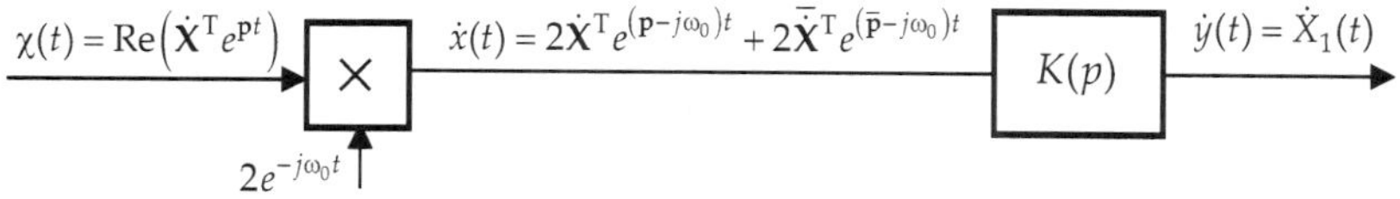

$$\chi(t) = \mathrm{Re}\left(\dot{\mathbf{X}}^{\mathrm{T}} e^{\mathbf{p}t}\right) \quad\boxed{\times}\quad \dot{x}(t) = 2\dot{\mathbf{X}}^{\mathrm{T}} e^{(\mathbf{p}-j\omega_0)t} + 2\overline{\dot{\mathbf{X}}}^{\mathrm{T}} e^{(\overline{\mathbf{p}}-j\omega_0)t} \quad\boxed{K(p)}\quad \dot{y}(t) = \dot{X}_1(t)$$

$$2e^{-j\omega_0 t}$$

Fig. 11. Block diagram for signal processing

There is the input-output dependence for the considered algorithm

$$\dot{X}_1(t) = \int_{t-T}^{t} \chi(\tau) e^{j\omega_0 \tau} w(t-\tau) d\tau = \int_{t-T}^{t} \dot{x}(\tau) w(t-\tau) d\tau .$$

This expression corresponds to short-time Fourier transform on the frequency ω_0.

Frequency filtering efficiency depends much to a large extent on the choice (synthesis) of time window $w(t)$, or on filter impulse function, that is equivalent for averaging filter.

Let us consider input signal as a set of complex amplitudes and exponential disturbance frequencies, industrial frequency useful signal ω_1 and higher harmonics

$$\dot{\mathbf{X}} = \begin{bmatrix} X_0 & \dot{X}_1 & \dot{X}_2 & \dot{X}_3 & \dots & \dot{X}_N \end{bmatrix}^{\mathrm{T}}, \quad \mathbf{p} = \begin{bmatrix} -\beta_0 & j\omega_1 & j2\omega_1 & j3\omega_1 & \dots & j4\omega_1 \end{bmatrix}^{\mathrm{T}} . \tag{10}$$

If one separates the exponential component and denotes the vector for harmonic complex amplitudes by $\dot{\mathbf{X}}_1$, the filter input signal can be presented in the following way

$$\dot{x}(t) = 2X_0 e^{(-\beta - j\omega_0)t} + 2\dot{\mathbf{X}}_1^{\mathrm{T}} e^{j(\mathbf{n}\omega_1 - \omega_0)t} + 2\overline{\dot{\mathbf{X}}}_1^{\mathrm{T}} e^{-j(\mathbf{n}\omega_1 + \omega_0)t} ,$$

where the vector $\overline{\dot{\mathbf{X}}}_1$ consists of conjugate to the vector $\dot{\mathbf{X}}_1$ elements.

When nominal frequency of power system is $\omega_1 = \omega_0$,

$$\dot{x}(t) = 2X_0 e^{(-\beta - j\omega_0)t} + \dot{X}_1 + \overline{\dot{X}}_1 e^{j2\omega_0 t} + \sum_{n=2}^{N} \left(\dot{X}_n e^{j(n-1)\omega_0 t} + \overline{\dot{X}}_n e^{-j(n+1)\omega_0 t} \right) .$$

Thus, averaging FIR filter at $\omega_1 = \omega_0$ must ensure the separation of constant component $\dot{X}_1$ and elimination of damped oscillatory component, sinusoidal component with double to industrial frequency, related to useful signal transform , and also of higher harmonics with frequencies multiple of ω_0. In case of $\omega_1 \neq \omega_0$, useful input signal of averaging filter will be a low-frequency sine signal with the frequency $\omega_1 - \omega_0$.

In filter synthesis the following signal parameters should be taken into account: the exponential disturbance damping coefficient changes in signal $x(t)$, power system frequency and related to it useful signal and disturbance changes, which influence on signal spectral composition and useful signal-disturbance ratio.

Let us consider averaging FIR filters synthesis for PMU (Phasor Measurement Units) devices and compare the gained results with averaging FIR filters, applied in one of the best PMU – Model 1133A Power Sentinel, made by American company Arbiter (Gustafson, 2009).

In this PMU one of the following time windows can be implemented: Raised cosine, Hann, Hamming, Blackman, Bartlett, Rectangular, Flat Top, Kaiser, Nutall 4-term, at any filter length, which can be from one to several periods of industrial frequency $T_0 = 2\pi / \omega_0$.

First let us find the solutions without consideration of exponential disturbance elimination, as it is accepted in the most of PMU (Phadke, 2008). The filter must guarantee less than 40 ms speed and 0.2 accuracy class.

Let us accept the following parameters for FIR filter generalized impulse function:

$$\dot{\mathbf{G}} = \dot{\mathbf{G}}' = \begin{bmatrix} G_0 & G_1 & G_2 & G_3 & G_4 \end{bmatrix}^T, \quad \mathbf{q} = \begin{bmatrix} 0 & jw_1 & j2w_1 & j3w_1 & j4w_1 \end{bmatrix}^T,$$

$$\mathbf{T} = \begin{bmatrix} T_1 & T_1 & T_1 & T_1 & T_1 \end{bmatrix}^T, \quad T_1 = 2\pi / w_1 .$$

This special case corresponds to so-called generalized cosine time window (Smith, 2002). This type of window will be further described by the set of only two parameters: $\dot{\mathbf{G}}$ and T_1.

Optimization procedure and target function choice of is a nontrivial problem. In general, in case of several synthesis purposes (criteria), it is complicated to get a rigorous optimal solution. Therefore, the found solutions for averaging FIR filters, should be considered as suboptimal.

Let us consider averaging FIR filters synthesis with use of nonlinear multivariable method, based on function of The Optimization Toolbox extends of MATLAB system. The found solutions at different filter lengths are given in table 5 and on fig. 12.

№	$\dot{\mathbf{G}}$	T_1, c
1.	$98,8842 \begin{bmatrix} 0,2601 & -0,4843 & 0,2325 & -0,0231 & 0 \end{bmatrix}^T$	0,0401
2.	$101,0814 \begin{bmatrix} 0,2827 & -0,5148 & 0,1983 & -0,0058 & -0,0016 \end{bmatrix}^T$	0,0350
3.	$70,027 \begin{bmatrix} 0,3989 & -0,4976 & 0,1015 & -0,0021 & -0,0001 \end{bmatrix}^T$	0,0358
4.	$73,505 \begin{bmatrix} 0,4535 & -0,4953 & 0,0547 & 0 & -0,0034 \end{bmatrix}^T$	0,0300
5.	$77,691 \begin{bmatrix} 0,5108 & -0,4819 & 0,0204 & 0,0014 & -0,0145 \end{bmatrix}^T$	0,0252
6.	$82,7152 \begin{bmatrix} 0,5397 & -0,4651 & 0,0072 & 0 & -0,0121 \end{bmatrix}^T$	0,0224

Table 5. Averaging FIR filter parameters

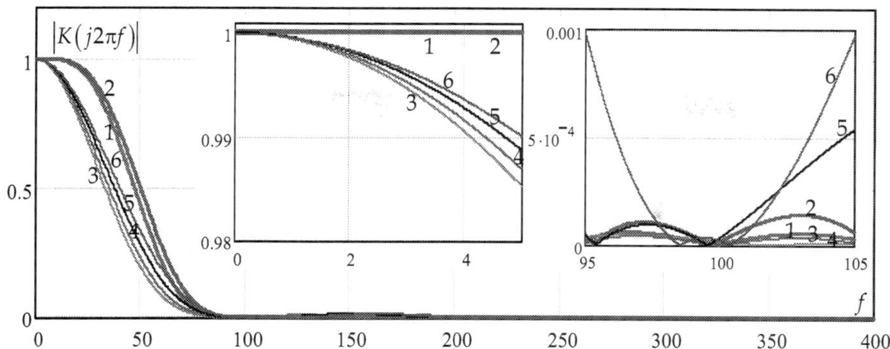

Fig. 12. Amplitude-frequency responses of FIR filters

The impulse functions (time windows) of synthesized filters are presented on fig. 13.

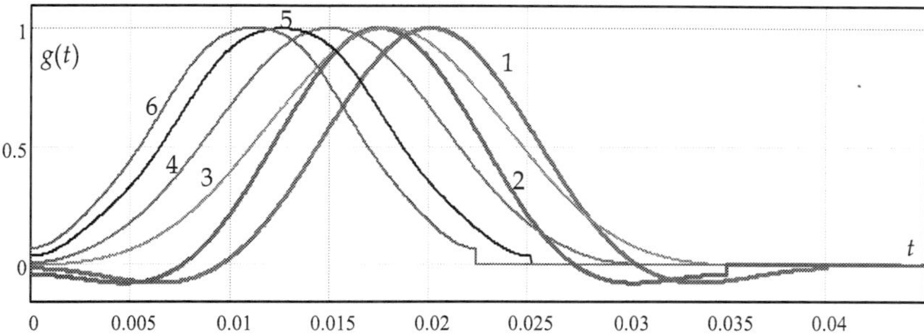

Fig. 13. Time windows of averaging FIR filters

As follows from the fig. 12, filters 1 and 2 have significantly better metrological performances, than averaging FIR filters PMU 1133A.

Filters 3÷6 are used in algorithms of IED signal processing, which do not need ensuring of amplitude-frequency responses stability over the range 0÷5 Hz, according to specified accuracy class (Mokeev, 2009c). Besides that, the more amplitude-frequency responses will be reduced with the frequency growth and the more harmonic elimination with the frequency about 100 Hz there will be, the more exactly the power system frequency will be determined

$$\omega_1(t) = \omega_0 - \frac{\dfrac{dX_{c1}(t)}{dt}X_{s1}(t) - \dfrac{dX_{s1}(t)}{dt}X_{c1}(t)}{X_{m1}^2(t)}, \tag{11}$$

where $\dot{X}_1(t) = X_{c1}(t) + jX_{s1}(t)$.

Although the mentioned algorithms of signal processing are adaptive, stationary filters are used in them. Signal processing error, connected to amplitude-frequency response deviation from 1 over the range from 0 to 5 Hz, can be easily compensated due to frequency measurement according to (11).

Let us do synthesis of averaging filter with use of FIR filter generalized model (4) at $M = 2$, according to the requirements in table 6.

№	Name	Conditions	
1.	Changing sizes of filter input signal parameters (10)	$\omega_1 = 2\pi(45 \div 55)$ rad/s, $\varphi_1 = 0 \div 2\pi$, $X_0 = (0 \div 1)X_{m1}$, $\beta_0 = 20 \div 200$ s^{-1}, $X_0 = (0 \div 1)X_{m1}$, $X_n = (0 \div 0,5)X_{m1}$, $n \geq 2$	
2.	Signal processing performance requirements	1.	Acceptable error: $\varepsilon_1 \leq 0,001$, $\varepsilon_2 \leq 0,0015$ (0,15 %), additional error at power system frequency deviation: $\varepsilon_2 \leq 0,0015$ (0.15 %), additional error at $X_0 = X_{m1}$, $\beta_0 = 20 \div 200$ s^{-1} and $t \geq T_1$: $\varepsilon_3 \leq 0,03$ (3 %),
		2.	speed: $T_1 \leq 0,06$ s, $\tau_1 \leq 0,04$ s
		3.	acceptable overshoot level: $\leq 10\%$
3.	Requirements to filter amplitude-frequency responses in complex frequency coordinates	1.	section $p = j\omega$: $\|K(0)\| = 1$, $1 - \varepsilon_{12} < \|K(j\Delta\omega)\| < 1 + \varepsilon_{12}$, $\|K(j2\omega_0)\| \leq \varepsilon_1$, $\|K(j(2\omega_0 \pm \Delta\omega))\| < \varepsilon_{12}$, $\|K(j(2\omega_0 \pm \Delta\omega)n)\| < 0,5\varepsilon_{12}$, $n \geq 3$ where $\Delta\omega = 10\pi$ rad/s, $\varepsilon_{12} = \varepsilon_1 + \varepsilon_2$
		2.	section $p = -\gamma + j\omega_0$: $2\|K(-\gamma + j\omega_0)\|e^{-\gamma T_1} \leq \varepsilon_3$, $2\|K(-\gamma + j\omega_0)\|e^{-\gamma\tau_1} \leq 0.05$

Table 6. Averaging FIR filter synthesis

The lengths of all finite damped oscillatory components of filter impulse functions will be considered as equal. Using different efficiency functions, two averaging FIR filters with practically identical frequency responses were obtained:

$$\dot{\mathbf{G}}_1 = \begin{bmatrix} 80,48e^{j4,232} & 37,93e^{j0,5887} \end{bmatrix}^T, \quad \mathbf{q}_1 = \begin{bmatrix} -22,99 + j62,30 & -23,26 + j186,9 \end{bmatrix}^T,$$

$$\mathbf{T}_1 = \begin{bmatrix} T_{11} & T_{11} \end{bmatrix}^T, \quad T_{11} = 0,051 \text{ c}, \quad g_1(t) = \text{Re}\left(\dot{\mathbf{G}}_1^T e^{\mathbf{q}_1 t} - \dot{\mathbf{G}}_1^{'T} e^{\mathbf{q}_1(t - T_{11})} \right); \tag{12}$$

$$\dot{\mathbf{G}}_2 = \begin{bmatrix} 42,26e^{j6,024} & 38,36e^{j2,938} \end{bmatrix}^T, \quad \mathbf{q}_2 = \begin{bmatrix} -4,668 + j42,69 & -23,28 + j178,7 \end{bmatrix}^T,$$

$$\mathbf{T}_2 = \begin{bmatrix} T_{21} & T_{21} \end{bmatrix}^T, \quad T_{21} = 0,050 \text{ c}, \quad g_2(t) = \text{Re}\left(\dot{\mathbf{G}}_2^T e^{\mathbf{q}_2 t} - \dot{\mathbf{G}}_2^{'T} e^{\mathbf{q}_2(t - T_{21})} \right). \tag{13}$$

Filter amplitude-frequency responses and their impulse responses (curve 1 and 2) are shown on the fig. 14 and fig. 15. The averaging filters impulse responses as opposed to ones, considered above (fig. 13), are asymmetrical. Therefore, the filters with mirror-inverse impulse responses (curve 3 and 4) will have the same amplitude-frequency responses in the sections $p = j2\pi f$, i.e. $g_3(t) = g_1(T_{11} - t)$ and $g_4(t) = g_2(T_{21} - t)$. However, filter amplitude-frequency responses with the numbers 3 and 4 in the section $p = -\gamma + j\omega_0$ significantly differ from the analogous amplitude-frequency responses of filters – ancestors (filters 1 and 2).

Thus, the principal conclusion follows from the above: the use of filter traditional amplitude-frequency responses (the section $p = j2\pi f$) for aperiodic signals analysis is not effective.

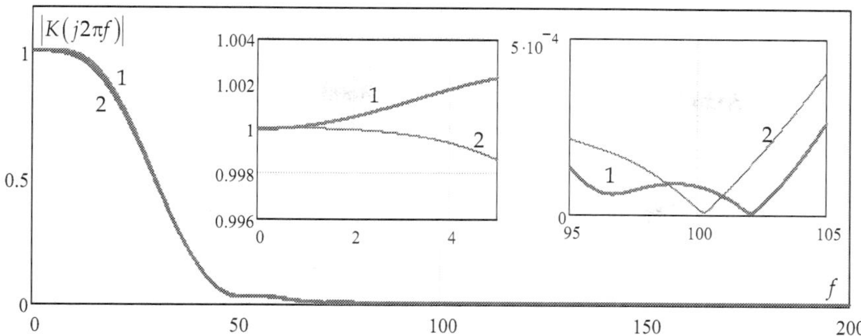

Fig. 14. Filter amplitude-frequency response in the section $p = j2\pi f$

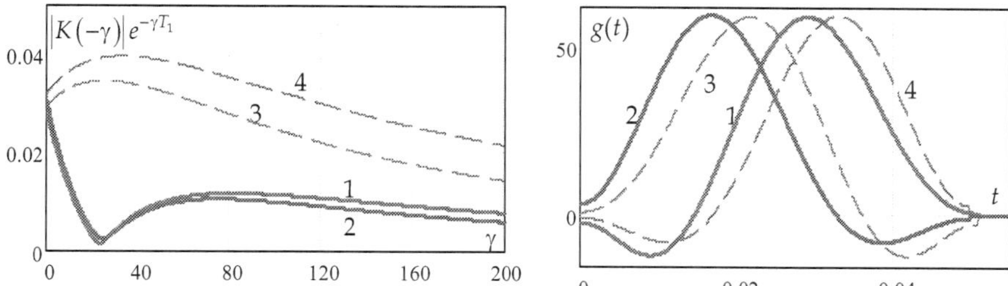

Fig. 15. Amplitude-frequency response in the section $p = -\gamma + j\omega_0$ and impulse responses

The principal difference filter 1 from filter 2 consists in the following: in the first case (filter 1) oscillatory nature of transient process will be observed in the beginning, in the second case it will occur after transient process completes in the filter. As it follows from the fig. 16, the combined use of filters 1 and 2 with practically identical amplitude-frequency response enables to reveal the transient processes in filters (curve 3).

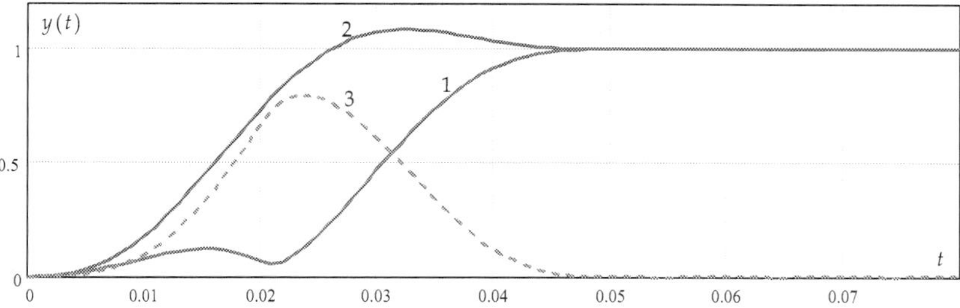

Fig. 16. Output signals of FIR filter

Synthesized filters ensure the combination of signal processing high speed and accuracy, have a low sensitivity to power system frequency deviation and to disturbance spectrum change, and significantly exceed filters, used in PMU 1133A.

The following regularities of time windows for averaging FIR filters can be defined on example of filter synthesis for special case
1. in case of using the cosine time windows and/or time windows (4) at harmonic input signals the form of the synthesized windows is similar to symmetrical "bell-shaped" or in the form of "hat" (fig. 13);
2. in case of using the general time windows (4) at necessity of aperiodic disturbance elimination the windows with clearly defined asymmetrical form (fig. 15) are obtained.
Therefore, the fact can be stated, that for processing of compound semi-infinite or finite aperiodic input signals it is reasonable to use the FIR filter impulse functions (4). Considering the relation between filters and wavelet transforms Koronovskii, 2005, Lyons, 2004), the conclusion about reasonability of mother and father wavelets synthesis, based on the expression (4), can be made. The transition from the mathematical description of analogue filter-prototype to digital filter is carried out by one of the following known methods with the consideration of analog FIR filter specifics (Mokeev, 2008b).

5. Fast algorithms synthesis of FIR filters and spectrum analyzers

5.1 FIR filter fast algorithms synthesis, based on generalized model of analogue filter-prototype impulse function

The advantage of using the analogue filter-prototypes with finite impulse response is direct synthesis of FIR filter realization fast (recursive) algorithms, according to the chosen modified transition method under the table 3.

The fast (recursive) algorithm for general case, using the first or second synthesis methods, is given below

$$\dot{\mathbf{y}}(k) = \mathbf{A}x(k) - \mathbf{B}x(\mathbf{C}k - \mathbf{N}) + \mathbf{D}\dot{\mathbf{y}}(k-1), \; y(k) = \mathrm{Re}\left(\mathbf{C}^\mathrm{T}\dot{\mathbf{y}}(k)\right). \tag{14}$$

where for the first method $\mathbf{A} = \left[\dot{G}_m T \left(1 - T\rho_m\right)^{-1}\right]_M$, $\mathbf{B} = \left[\dot{G}'_m T \left(1 - T\rho_m\right)^{-1}\right]_M$, $\mathbf{D} = \left[\left(1 - T\rho_m\right)^{-1}\right]_M$, $\mathbf{C} = \left[1\right]_M$, $\mathbf{N} = \left[N_m\right]_M$; for the second method $\mathbf{A} = \left[\dot{G}_m T\right]_M$, $\mathbf{B} = \left[\dot{G}'_m T\right]_M$, $\mathbf{D} = \left[e^{\rho_m T}\right]_M$.

The block scheme of FIR filter (14) fast (recursive) algorithm is represented on the fig. 17, where $\mathbf{Z} = \left[z^{-N_m}\right]_M$.

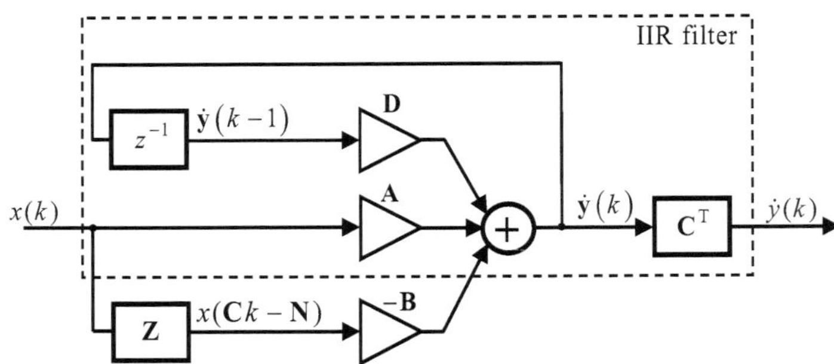

Fig. 17. FIR filter fast algorithm

The fast algorithm (14) expression form, using matrixes, is a compact way of algorithm expression, however, there is a system of M-number independent equations in case of practical realization.

$$\dot{y}_m(k) = a_m x(k) - b_m x(k - N_m) + d_m \dot{y}(k-1),$$ (15)

where a_m, b_m, d_m - are complex coefficients, which are the m-th elements of **A**, **B**, **D** vectors.

The fast algorithm (14) or (15) can be directly realized by using DSPs, which include the instructions to multiplication with accumulation. At other cases, it is necessary to divide the algorithm (15) into two algorithms, which conform to real and imaginary components, i.e. two common filters will be realized (Mokeev, 2008b). Another method consists in algorithm forming, based on the operation fulfillment $y(k) = \mathrm{Re}\big(\dot{y}(k)\big)$.

In the first case

$$y_{mc}(k) = a_{mc} x(k) - b_{mc} x(k - N) + d_{mc} y_{mc}(k-1) - d_{ms} y_{ms}(k-1),$$

$$y_{ms}(k) = a_{ms} x(k) - b_{ms} x(k - N) + d_{mc} y_{ms}(k-1) + d_{ms} y_{mc}(k-1),$$

where $\dot{y}_m(k) = y_{mc}(k) + j y_{ms}(k)$, $a_m = a_{mc} + j a_{ms}$, $b_m = b_{mc} + j b_{ms}$, $d_m = d_{mc} + j d_{ms}$.
The second method demands by one multiplication operation less

$$y_m(k) = c_{m0} x(k) + c_{m1} x(k-1) - c_{m2} x(k - N_m) - c_{m3} x(k - N_m - 1) + h_{m1} y_m(k-1) - h_{m2} y_m(k-2) .$$

The fast algorithms synthesis for digital filters with integer coefficients, based on analogue filter-prototype descriptions, is considered in item 5.3.

5.2 Averaging FIR filter fast algorithms synthesis
One of the most extended problems of digital signal processing in measuring technology is connected to FIR filter use, realizing moving-average algorithm (Rabiner, 1975, Vanin, 1991). For reducing the computing expenditures, the digital filtering fast algorithms are applied at FIR filter implementation, including moving-average filters (Blahut, 1985, Nussbaumer, 1981, Yaroslavsky, 1984).

Averaging FIR filters are the special cases for FIR filters. Thus, the fast algorithm synthesis method, considered above, should be used for that kind of filter.
Let us contemplate the most elementary case – rectangular time window. The mathematical expression of analog filter-prototype will be

$$g(t) = k_1\big(1(t) - 1(t - T_1)\big), \quad K(p) = \frac{k_1}{p}\big(1 - e^{-pT_1}\big), \quad y(t) = k_1 \int_{t-T_1}^{t} x(\tau)d\tau ,$$

T_1 - is averaging time (window length).
Using the transition methods from an analog filter-prototype to a digital filter, shown in the table 3 , in cases of first and second methods at $k_1 = 1/T$ the following known (Myasnikov, 2005) fast algorithm of moving-average will be obtained

$$y(k) = x(k) - x(k - N_1) + y(k-1) ,$$

where $N_1 = T_1 / T$.

In case of bilinear transformation method application, there will be the following fast algorithm

$$y(k) = x(k) + x(k-1) - x(k-N_1) - x(k-N_1-1) + y(k-1),$$

At usage of triangle time window, the following fast algorithm of averaging FIR filter realization will be obtained

$$y(k) = x(k) + x(k-1) - 2x(k-N_1-1) + x(k-2N_1-1) + 2y(k-1) - y(k-2).$$

The considered moving-average realization algorithms involve recursive computations, as IIR filters do. However, the principal difference between them is a finite length of filter impulse function. This approach can be also applied to more complicated types of digital filters, including filters, which assure the moving-average computation in case of using different kinds of time windows (Mokeev, 2008a, 2008b, 2009c). The issues about averaging digital filter fast algorithms synthesis, based on given analog filter-prototype (13), considering the microprocessor finite digit capacity influence (Mokeev, 2008a), are investigated.

5.3 FIR filter fast algorithms synthesis, considering microprocessor finite digit capacity

The stability requirements for the discrete filter (5) at any value of FIR filter system function poles $K(z)$ are always ensured. The situation can be changed in case of filter coefficients quantization - at failed coefficient selection, instead of FIR filter IIR filter will be obtained. At negative real components of filter impulse function complex frequencies it is important to assure the filter impulse function level being out of its length is less than a value, specified before.

During the digital FIR filters designing, particular attention should be given to ensuring the impulse response finiteness and filter stability in case, that at least one complex frequency of filter impulse function has a positive real component, as an unstable filter can be obtained at filter coefficients quantization.

Let us consider an example of digital FIR filter synthesis for DSP with the support to fixed point data operations (four numbers to the left of the decimal point). In case of using the method of invariant impulse responses, based on the analogue filter-prototype (13) at $T = 500$ microseconds, the following fast algorithm will be obtained

$$\begin{bmatrix} \dot{y}_1(k) \\ \dot{y}_2(k) \end{bmatrix} = \begin{bmatrix} -0,0171 - j0,0364 \\ 0,0158 + j0,0105 \end{bmatrix} x(k) - \begin{bmatrix} 0,0049 + j0,0115 \\ -0,0045 - j0,0037 \end{bmatrix} x(k-102) + \begin{bmatrix} (0,9881 + j0,0308)\dot{y}_1(k-1) \\ (0,9841 + j0,0922)\dot{y}_2(k-1) \end{bmatrix}.$$

The fast algorithm efficiency is 17 times higher, than algorithm, based on discrete convolution realization with DSP support of complex multiplication/accumulation operations has, and 9 times higher in case of using the ordinary DSPs.

Fast algorithm synthesis for digital filters with integer coefficients is an ambiguous problem, which can be simpler solved by several iterations on the basis of the following expression

$$\dot{y}_n(k) = \frac{\mathbf{A}_n x_n(k) - \mathbf{B}_n x(\mathbf{C}k-\mathbf{N}) + \mathbf{D}_n \dot{y}_n(k-1)}{m_3},$$

where $\mathbf{A}_n = \text{Int}(m_1\mathbf{A})$, $\mathbf{B}_n = \text{Int}(m_2\mathbf{B})$, $\mathbf{D}_n = \text{Int}(m_1\mathbf{D})$, Int - is an operator, taking an integral part of the number, $x_n(k)$ - is an input signal, considering amplitude quantization, m_1, m_2, m_3 - are scale integer coefficients.

To assure the finite duration of impulse response, the following conditions are required to
be fulfilled

$$\mathrm{Int}\left(m_1 \mathbf{A}^\mathrm{T} \mathbf{z}^N\right) - \mathrm{Int}\left(m_2 \mathbf{B}^\mathrm{T} \mathbf{C}\right) \to 0 \,.$$

The following averaging filter fast algorithm with the integer coefficients is obtained for the
considered synthesis problem

$$\begin{bmatrix} \dot{y}_{n1}(k) \\ \dot{y}_{n2}(k) \end{bmatrix} = \begin{bmatrix} \dfrac{(-1711 - j3642)x_n(k) - (489 + j1146)x_n(k-102) + (9881 + j308)\dot{y}_{n1}(k-1)}{10000} \\ \dfrac{(1577 + j1053)x_n(k) - (-445 - j371)x_n(k-102) + (9841 + j922)\dot{y}_{n2}(k-1)}{10000} \end{bmatrix} \,.$$

The output signals for analog and digital signal processing system (fig. 11), using the
averaging FIR filters, mentioned above (two filters for real and imaginary signal components
$\dot{y}(t)$ or $\dot{y}(k)$ processing), for first harmonic module measuring $\left|\dot{X}_1(t)\right|$ and $\left|\dot{X}_1(k)\right|$ are shown
on the fig 18. Digital and analog signal graphs are reduced to digital signal scale.

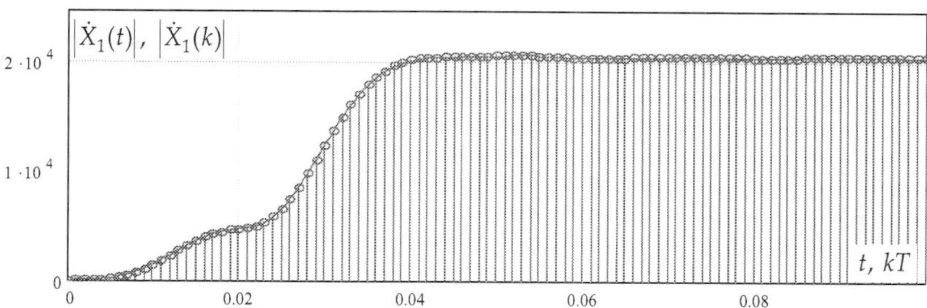

Fig. 18. Output signal

5.4 Fast algorithms synthesis of non-stationary FIR filter with using of the state space method

The expression for FIR filter (14) fast algorithm along with the mathematical description of
analogue filter-prototype (7) can be interpreted as a definition, based on filter spectral
representations in complex frequency coordinates, and as exposition on the basis of the state
space method (Mokeev, 2008b). As is known, the advantage of the state space method
consists in mathematical descriptions similarity of stationary and non-stationary systems.
Thus, the expression for non-stationary filters can be obtained and interpreted by analogy
on the basis of this approach. At that, the matrixes $\mathbf{A}$, $\mathbf{B}$ and $\mathbf{D}$ will be time dependent

$$\dot{\mathbf{y}}(k) = \mathbf{A}(k)x(k) - \mathbf{B}(k)x(\mathbf{C}k - \mathbf{N}) + \mathbf{D}(k)\dot{\mathbf{y}}(k-1)\,. \tag{16}$$

The algorithm for non-stationary filter with periodic coefficients, which is used for fast Fourier
transform realization (Mokeev, 2008b), can be obtained on the basis of the expression above (16)

$$\dot{\mathbf{X}}(k) = \mathbf{W}(k)x(k) - \mathbf{W}(k-N)x(k-N) + \dot{\mathbf{X}}(k-1)\,, \tag{17}$$

where $\mathbf{W}(k) = T\left[e^{-j\omega_m kT}\right]_M$, $\omega_m = m\omega_0$, $N = \dfrac{2\pi}{\omega_0 T}$, $\dot{X}_m(k)$ - is spectral density of the signal

$x(t)$ on the basis of short-time Fourier transform application on the frequency $m\omega_0$, using rectangular time window.

Each component of the equation (17) is an analyzer of instantaneous signal spectrum on the specified frequency ω_m.

The fast algorithm of spectrum analyzer (17) has incontestable advantages over the FFT at $N > 5$ (Mokeev, 2008b). At that, it should be noted, that spectral density computation algorithm, as opposed to FFT, is not connected to the number of spectral density values and to uniform frequency scale.

The non-stationary filter algorithm with the periodic coefficients (17) is a special case of more general algorithm (16), which can be applied to describe more complicated types of filters, including adaptive digital filters.

5.5 Synthesis of spectrum analyzer fast algorithms

The spectrum analyzers, based on short-time Fourier transform, can be realized in different ways, including using the fast Fourier transform algorithms (Rabiner, 1975, Blahut, 1985, Nussbaumer, 1981).

The fast algorithms of mentioned spectrum analyzers can be also obtained on the basis of the approaches, considered in this chapter, including the non-stationary filter algorithm (17) with the periodic coefficients, which was contemplated above.

Another approach is based on subdividing the expression for the short-time Fourier transform on the specified frequency into two main operations: multiplication by complex exponent and further using the averaging filter. The issues of averaging FIR filter fast algorithms synthesis were considered in items 5.1 and 5.3.

The third approach is connected to using FIR filter fast algorithms with the orthogonal impulse functions (Mokeev, 2008b).

Let us consider the problems of fast spectrum analyzers synthesis in complex frequency coordinates. Two methods of fast spectrum analyzers realization on complex frequency coordinates, overcoming the difficulties of direct short-time Laplace transform implementation, are offered by the author in this paper (Mokeev, 2008b). The first method is based on using the FIR filter fast algorithms (4), as each finite component of filter with generalized impulse function makes spectrum analysis on the specified complex frequency. The second method is connected to partitioning the expression for short-time Laplace transform on the given frequency into two basic operations: multiplication by complex exponent and further using the averaging filter with the transfer of exponential window to averaging filter (Mokeev, 2008b).

Considered approaches to FIR filter fast algorithms synthesis can be apply also for the case of wavelet transform fast algorithms, as is known, that wavelet transform is identical with the reconstructed FIR filter with the frequency responses, similar to band pass filter (Mokeev, 2008b).

6. Conclusion

It is shown in this chapter, that for many practical tasks it is reasonable to use the similar generalized mathematical models of analog and digital filter input signals and impulse functions in the form of a set of continuous/discrete semi-infinite or finite damped oscillatory components. To express signals and filters, it is sufficient to exercise the vectors of complex amplitudes and complex frequencies, and also time delay vectors.

For the signal and filter models, mentioned above, it is rational to use the spectral representations of the Laplace transform, in which the damped oscillatory component is a base transform function. Three new methods of analog and digital IIR and FIR filters analysis at semi-infinite and finite input signals were presented on the basis of the research into the spectral representations features of signal and filter frequency responses in complex frequency coordinates. The advantages of offered analysis methods consist in calculation simplicity, including solving problems of direct determination the performance of signal processing by frequency filters.

The application of spectral representations in complex frequency coordinates enables to combine the spectral approach and the state space method for frequency filter analysis and synthesis.

Spectral representations and linear system usage, based on Laplace transform, allow to ensure the effective solution of robust IIR and FIR filters synthesis problems. The filter synthesis problem instead of setting the requirements to separate areas of frequency response (pass band and rejection band) comes to dependence composition for filter transfer function on complex frequencies of input signal components. The synthesis is carried out with the growth of impulse function components number till the specified signal processing performance will be achieved.

7. References

Atabekov, G. I. (1978). *Theoretical Foundations of Electrical Engineering*, Part 1, Energiya, Moscow.

Blahut, R. E. (1985). *Fast Algorithms for Digital Signal Processing*, MA, Addison-Wesley Publishing Company.

Gustafson, J. A. (2009). Model 1133A Power Sentinel. Power Quality. Revenue Standard. Operation manual. Arbiter Systems, Inc., Paso Robles, CA 93446. U.S.A.

Ifeachor, E. C. & Jervis, B. W. (2002). *Digital Signal Processing: A Practical Approach*, 2nd edition, Pearson Education.

Jenkins, G. M. & Watts D. G. (1969). *Spectral analisis and its applications*, Holden-day.

Kharkevich, A. A. (1960). *Spectra and Analysis*, New York, Consultants Bureau.

Koronovskii, A. A. & Hramov, A. E. (2003). *Continuous Wavelet Analysis and Its Applications*, Fizmatlit, Moscow.

Lyons, R .G. (2004). *Understanding Digital Signal Processing*, 2th ed. Prentice Hall PTR.

Mokeev, A. V. (2006). Signal and system spectral expansion application based on Laplace transform to analyse linear systems. In *International Conference DSPA-2006*, Moscow, vol.1, pp. 43-47.

Mokeev, A.V. (2007). Spectral expansion in coordinates of complex frequency application to analysis and synthesis filters. In *International TICSP Workshop Spectral Methods and Multirate Signal Processing*, Moscow, pp. 159-167.

Mokeev, A. V. (2008a). Fast algorithms' synthesis for fir filters, Fourier and Laplace transforms. In *International Conference DSPA-2008*, Moscow, vol. 1, pp. 43-47.

Mokeev, A. V. (2008b). *Signal processing in intellectual electronic devices of electric power systems*, Arkhangelsk, ASTU.

Mokeev, A. V. (2009a). Frequency filters analysis on the basis of features of signal spectral representations in complex frequency coordinates. *Scientific and Technical Bulletin of SPbSPU*, vol. 2, pp. 61-68.

Mokeev, A. V. (2009b). Description of the digital filter by the state space method. In *IEEE International Siberian Conference on Control and Communications*, Tomsk, pp. 128-132.

Mokeev, A. V. (2009c). Intellectual electronic devices design for electric power systems based on phasor measurement technology. In *International Conference Relay Protection and Substation Automation of Modern Power Systems*, CIGRE-2009, Moskow, pp. 523-530.

Myasnikov, V. V. (2005). On recursive computation of the convolution of image and 2-D inseparable FIR filter. *Computer optics*, vol. 27, pp.117-122.

Nussbaumer, H. J. (1981). *Fast Fourier Transform and Convolution Algorithms*, 2th ed., Springer-Verlag.

Phadke, A. G. & Thorp, J. S. (2008). *Synchronized Phasor Measurements And Their Applications*, Springer.

Rabiner, L. R. & Gold, B. (1975) *The Theory and Application of Digital Signal Processing*, Prentice-Hall, Englewood Cliffs, New Jersey.

Sánchez Peña, R .S. & Sznaier, M. (1998). *Robust systems theory and applications*, Wiley, New York.

Siebert, W. M. (1986). *Circuits, signal and system*, The MIT Press.

Smith, S. W. (2002). *Digital Signal Processing: A Practical Guide for Engineers and Scientists* Newnes.

Vanin, V. K. & Pavlov, G. M. (1991). *Relay Protection of Computer Components*, Énergoatomizdat, Moscow.

Yaroslavsky, L. P. (1984). *About a Possibility of the Parallel and Recursive Organization of Digital Filters*, Radiotechnika, no. 3.

3

Design of Two-Dimensional Digital Filters Having Variable Monotonic Amplitude-Frequency Responses Using Darlington-type Gyrator Networks

Muhammad Tariqus Salam and Venkat Ramachandran, *Fellow, IEEE*
Department of Electrical and Computer Engineering
Concordia University
Montreal, Canada

Abstract

This paper develops a design of two-dimensional (2D) digital filter with monotonic amplitude-frequency responses using Darlington-type gyrator networks by the application of Generalized Bilinear Transformation (GBT). The proposed design provides the stable monotonic amplitude-frequency responses and the desired cutoff frequency of the 2D digital filters. This 2D recursive digital filter design includes 2D digital low-pass, high-pass, band-pass and band-elimination filters. Design examples are given to illustrate the usefulness of the proposed technique.
Index Terms — Stability, monotonic response, GBT, gyrator network.

1. Introduction

Because of recent growth in the 2D signal processing activities, a significant amount of research work has been done on the 2D filter design [1] and it is seen that monotonic characteristics in frequency response of a filter is getting more popular. The filters with the monotonic characteristics are one of the best filters for the digital image, video and audio (enhancement and restoration) [2]. The filters are widely accepted in the applications of medical science, geographical science and environment, space and robotic engineering [1]. For example, medical applications are concerned with processing of chest X-Ray, cine angiogram, projection of frame axial tomography and other medical images that occurs in radiology, nuclear magnetic resonance (NMR), ultrasonic scanning and magnetic resonance imaging (MRI) etc. and the restoration and enhancement of these images are done by the 2D digital filters [3].

The design of 2D recursive filters is difficult due to the non-existence of the fundamental theorem of algebra in that the factorization of 2D polynomials into lower order polynomials and the testing for stability of a 2D transfer function (recursive) requires a large number of computations. But, the major drawbacks of the recursive filters are their lower-order realizations and computational intensive design techniques. Several design techniques of 2D recursive filter have been reported in the literature [2], [4] – [9] and most of these designs have problems of computational complexity, stability and unable to provide variable magnitude monotonic characteristic. A design technique of 2D recursive filters have been shown which met simultaneously magnitude and group delay specifications [4], although the technique has the advantage of always ensuring the filter stability, the difficulties to be encountered are computational complexity and convergence [5]. In [6], 2D filter design as a linear programming problem has been proposed, but, this tends to require relatively long computation time. In [7], a filter design has been shown using the two specifications as the problem of minimizing the total length of modified complex errors and minimized it by an iterative procedure. Difficulties of the design obtain for two-dimensional stability testing at each iteration during the minimization procedure.

One way to ensure a 2D transfer function is stable is if the denominator of the transfer function is satisfied to be a Very Strict Hurwitz Polynomial (VSHP) [8] and that can ensure a transfer function that there is no singularity in the right half of the biplane, which can make a system unstable. In [9]-[11], stable 2D recursive filters have been designed by generation of Very Strict Hurwitz Polynomial (VSHP), but it is not guaranteed to provide the stable monotonic amplitude-frequency responses. Several filter designs with monotonic amplitude frequency response has been reported [12] – [16], but to the best of our knowledge, filter design with variable monotonic amplitude frequency response is not proposed yet.

In this paper, 2-D digital filters with variable monotonic amplitude frequency responses are designed starting from Darlington-type networks containing gyrators and doubly-terminated RLC-networks. The extension of Darlington-synthesis to two-variable positive real functions is given in [17], [18]; but they do not contain gyrators. From the 2-D stable transfer functions so obtained, the GBT [19] is applied to obtain 2-D digital functions and their properties are studied. The designed filters are used in the image processing application.

2. THE TWO BASIC STRUCTURES CONSIDERED

Two filter structures are considered for 2D digital recursive filters design and both structures are taken from Darlington-synthesis [20]. Figures 1(a) and (b) show the two structures considered in this paper.

The impedances of the filters are replaced by doubly-terminated RLC filters and the overall transfer function will be of the form

$$H(s_1, s_2, g) = \frac{\displaystyle\sum_{\rho=0}^{M_n}\sum_{\nu=0}^{N_n} N_{\rho\nu}(g) s_1^{\rho} s_2^{\nu}}{\displaystyle\sum_{\kappa=0}^{M_d}\sum_{\ell=0}^{N_d} D_{\kappa\ell}(g) s_1^{\kappa} s_2^{\ell}} \tag{1}$$

where the coefficients of $H(s_1, s_2, g)$ are functions of g.

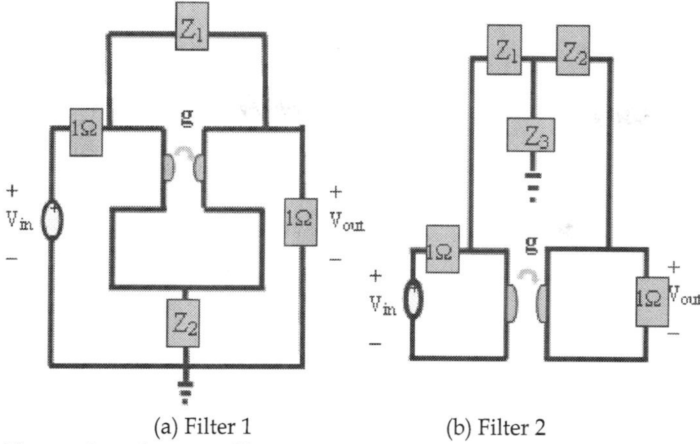

(a) Filter 1   (b) Filter 2
Fig. 1. Doubly terminated gyrator filters.

In this paper, second-order Butterworth and Gargour & Ramachandran filters [19] are considered as doubly terminated RLC networks. For simplicity, each gyrator network is classified into three cases, such as the impedances of gyrator network are replaced by the second-order Butterworth filter and Gargour & Ramachandran filter are called case-I and case-II respectively. The impedances of gyrator network are replaced by second-order Butterworth and Gargour & Ramachandran filters is called case-III.

3. Filter 1

Transfer functions of case-I, case-II and case-III of Filter 1 (Figure 1(a)) provide stable functions, when denominators of the cases are VSHPs. This can be verified easily by the method of Inners [21]. The impedances of the cases are modified by first applying the GBT given by

$$s_i = k_i \frac{z_i + a_i}{z_i + b_i}, \ i = 1, 2$$

(2)

To ensure stability, the conditions to be satisfied are:

$$k_i > 0, \ |a_i| \leq 1, \ |b_i| \leq 1, \ a_i b_i < 0$$

(3)

and then applying the inverse bilinear transformation [22]. In such a case, the inductor impedance becomes

$$s_i L \rightarrow k_i L \frac{(1 - a_i) + s_i(1 + a_i)}{(1 + b_i) + s_i(1 - b_i)}$$

(4a)

and the impedance of a capacitor becomes

$$\frac{1}{s_i C} \rightarrow \frac{1}{k_i C} \frac{(1+b_i) + s_i(1-b_i)}{(1-a_i) + s_i(1+a_i)} \tag{4b}$$

For example, the transfer function of the case-I represents as

$$H_{G1}(s_1, s_2, g) = \frac{\mathbf{S_1} \, \mathbf{R_1} \, \mathbf{S}_2^{T}}{\mathbf{S_1} \, \mathbf{R_2} \, \mathbf{S}_2^{T}} \tag{5}$$

where,

$$\mathbf{S_1} = \begin{bmatrix} 1 & s_1 & s_1^2 \end{bmatrix}, \quad \mathbf{S_2} = \begin{bmatrix} 1 & s_2 & s_2^2 \end{bmatrix},$$

$$\mathbf{R_1} = \begin{bmatrix} 2\,(1+g+g^2) & 0.7 + 0.7\,g + 4.2\,g^2 & 1.5\,g^2 \\ 0.7 + 4.2\,(g+g^2) & 0.23 + 1.5\,g + 9.1\,g^2 & 3\,g^2 \\ 1.5\,g + 1.5\,g^2 & 3.1\,g + 0.5\,g^2 & g^2 \end{bmatrix},$$

$$\mathbf{R_2} = \begin{bmatrix} 3\,(1+g^2) & 1 + 4.4\,g^2 & 1.4\,g^2 \\ 2.8 + 6.4\,g^2 & 0.92 + 9.6\,g^2 & 3\,g^2 \\ 0.72 + 2.1\,g^2 & 0.24 + 3.2\,g^2 & g^2 \end{bmatrix}$$

The coefficients are dependent on the value and sign of 'g'.

The GBT [19] is applied to the transfer function (5) and it is shown that the 2D digital low-pass filters are obtained for the lower values of g and the 2D digital high-pass filters are obtained for the higher values of g. But the amplitude-frequency response of the Filter 1 is constant for g = 1.

If monotonicity in the magnitude response is desired, the values of a_i, b_i and k_i have to be adjusted and these are given in Table 1. Figure 2 shows the 3-D magnitude plot of such a low-pass filter.

g	a_i	b_i	Case-I	Case-II	Case-III
0.001	-0.9	0.9	$0.09 > k_i > 0$	$82 > k_i > 0$	$0.1 > k_i > 0$
0.001	-0.9	0.5	$0.4 > k_i > 0$	$1.5 > k_i > 0$	$0.9 > k_i > 0$
0.001	-0.5	0.9	$205 > k_i > 0$	$95 > k_i > 0$	$100 > k_i > 0$

Table 1. The ranges of k_i satisfy the monotonic characteristics in the amplitude-frequency response of 2D Low-passFilter (Filter 1).

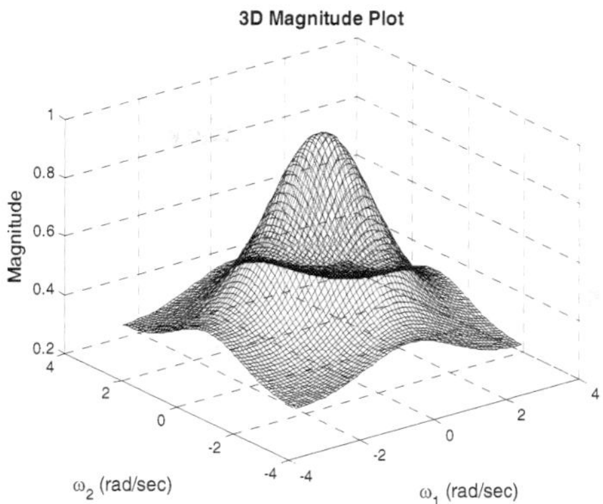

Fig. 2. 3D magnitude plot and contour plot of the 2D digital low-pass filter (Filter 1) when
g = 0.01.

4. Filter 2

The impedances Z_1, Z_2 and Z_3 of Filter 2 (Fig.1(b)) are replaced by impedances of the second-
order RLC filters. The resultant transfer function is unstable, because, the denominator is
indeterminate [8].

In order to generate a stable analog transfer function $H_{MB2}(s_1,s_2,g)$, the impedances Z_1 and Z_2
of Filter 2 (Figure 1(b)) are replaced by the impedances of the second-order RLC filters and
the third impedance (Z_3) is replaced by a resistive element. As a result, the denominator of
the case-I, case-II and case-III of Filter 2 are VSHPs.

Transfer function of the case-I (Filter 2) is represented as

$$H_{MB2}(s_1,s_2,g) = \frac{S_1 R_3 S_2^T}{S_1 R_4 S_2^T} \tag{6}$$

where,

$$R_3 = \begin{bmatrix} 2+6g & 0.68+8.8g & 2.8g \\ 0.68+8.8g & 0.22+12g & 3.4g \\ 2.8g & 3.4g & g \end{bmatrix},$$

$$R_4 = \begin{bmatrix} 1.6+6g^2 & 16+8.8g^2 & 4.4+2.8g^2 \\ 16+8.8g^2 & 15+12g^2 & 3.9+3.4g^2 \\ 4.4+2.8g^2 & 3.4+3.9g^2 & 1+g^2 \end{bmatrix}.$$

The coefficients of numerator are dependent on the value and sign of 'g', but the coefficients
of denominator are dependent only the value of 'g'.

The GBT [19] is applied to (6) and it is shown that the 2D digital low-pass filters are obtained for the lower values of g, the 2D digital high-pass filters are obtained for the higher values of g and inverse filter responses are obtained for the opposite sign of g.

If monotonicity in the magnitude response is desired, the values of g, a_i, b_i and k_i have to be adjusted and these are given in Table 2 and Table 3. Figure 3 shows the 3-D magnitude plot of such a high-pass filter.

g	a_i	b_i	Case-I	Case-II	Case-III
0.01	-0.9	0.9	$0.2 > k_i > 0$	$0.2 > k_i > 0$	$0.2 > k_i > 0$
0.01	-0.9	0.5	$0.7 > k_i > 0$	$0.6 > k_i > 0$	$0.5 > k_i > 0$
0.01	-0.5	0.9	$4 > k_i > 0$	$3 > k_i > 0$	$3.2 > k_i > 0$

Table 2. The ranges of k_i satisfy the monotonic characteristics in the amplitude-frequency response of 2D Low-passFilter (Filter2).

a_i	b_i	k_i	Case-I (Filter 1)	Case-I (Filter 2)
-0.1	0.1	1	$0.3 > g \geq 0$	$\infty > g \geq 0, 0.4 > g \geq -0.1$
-0.1	0.1	5	$0.1 > g \geq 0$	$\infty > g \geq 9, 0.2 > g \geq -0.01$
-0.1	0.1	10	$0.05 > g \geq 0$	$\infty > g \geq 13, 0.08 > g \geq -0.005$
-0.5	0.5	1	$0.7 > g \geq 0$	$\infty > g \geq 3.2, 0.5 > g \geq -0.1$
-0.5	0.5	5	$0.4 > g \geq 0$	$\infty > g \geq 4.8, 0.3 > g \geq -0.04$
-0.5	0.5	10	$0.18 > g \geq 0$	$\infty > g \geq 7, 0.2 > g \geq -0.04$
-0.9	0.9	1	$\infty > g \geq 0$	$\infty > \vert g \vert > 0$
-0.9	0.9	5	$4.6 > g \geq -1.5$	$\infty > g \geq 3.2, 0.5 > g \geq -0.1$
-0.9	0.9	10	$1 > g \geq -0.67$	$\infty > g \geq 3.4, 0.41 > g \geq -0.09$

Table 3. The ranges of g for the various parameter-values of the GBT, where the 2D digital high-pass filter contains the monotonic characteristics.

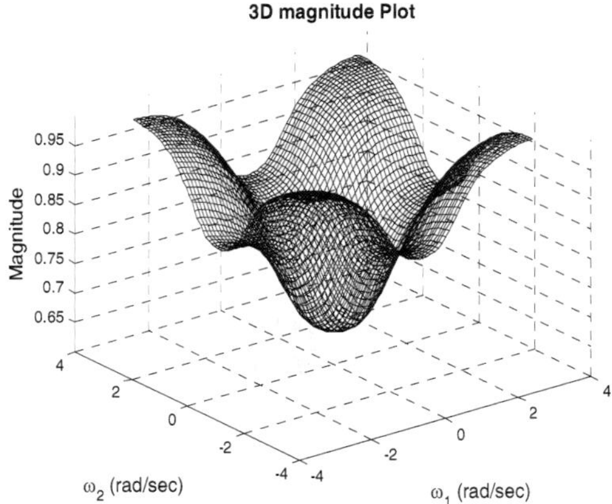

Fig. 3. 3D magnitude plot and contour plot of the 2D digital high-pass filter (Filter 2) when $g = -0.7$.

5. Band-pass and band-elimination filters

In order to design the 2D digital band-pass and band-elimination filter, the following GBT [23] is applied to a stable analog transfer function.

$$s_i = k_{1i} \frac{(z_i + a_{1i})}{(z_i + b_{1i})} + k_{2i} \frac{(z_i + a_{2i})}{(z_i + b_{2i})} \tag{7}$$

To ensure stability, the conditions to be satisfied are:

$$k_{1i} > 0, \; k_{1i} > 0, \; |a_{1i}| \leq 1, \; |a_{2i}| \leq 1, \tag{8}$$
$$|b_{1i}| \leq 1, \; |b_{1i}| \leq 1, \; a_{1i}b_{1i} < 0, \; a_{2i}b_{2i} < 0$$

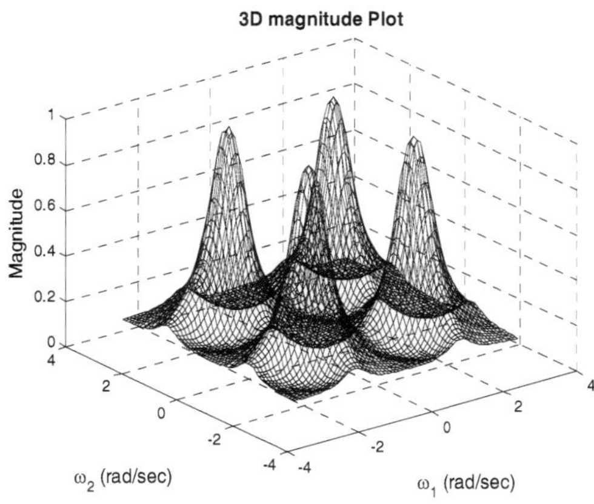

Fig. 4. 3D magnitude plot 2D digital band-pass filter (g =-001).

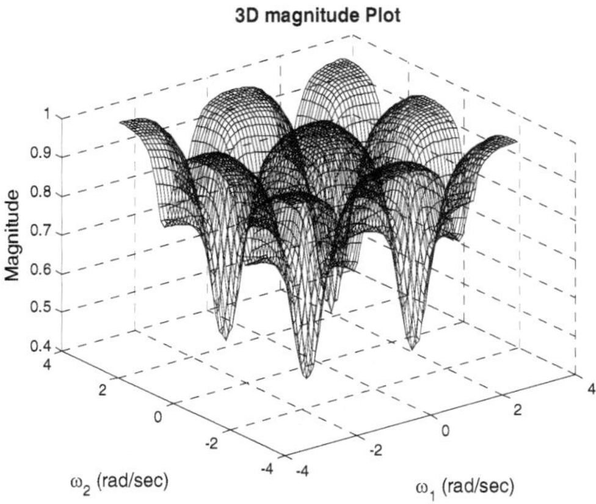

Fig. 5. 3D magnitude plot of the 2D digital band-elimination filter (g = -0.5)

The 2D digital band-pass filters and the 2D digital band-elimination filters are obtained depending on the values and sign of g which is shown in Table 4. Figures 4 and 5 show the 3D magnitude plots of the digital band-pass and band-elimination filter respectively, which are obtained from Case-I (Filter1) and case-I (Filter2).

6. Digital filter Transformation

The proposed digital filter transformation provides the low-pass to high-pass filter (Table 5) or the band-pass to band-elimination filter (Table 6) or vice-versa transformation by regulating the value or sign of g. However, the low-pass to band-pass or the high-pass to band-elimination filter or vice versa transformation is obtained by regulating the value or sign of g and the parameters of the GBT as shown in Figure 6. In Filter 1, the digital filter transformations are obtained by regulating the value of g. However, in Filter 2, the digital filter transformations are obtained by regulating the value or sign of g.

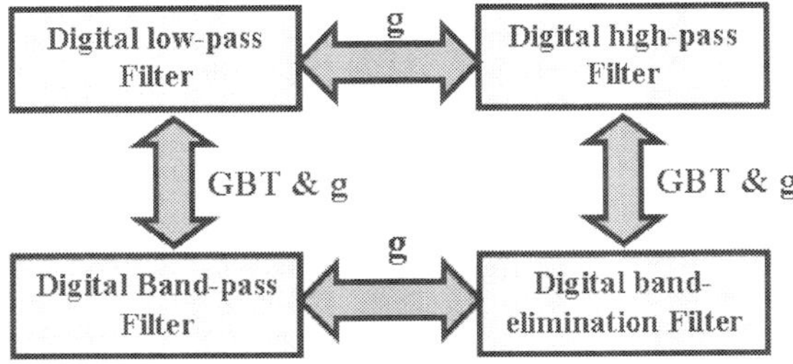

Fig. 6. Block diagram of the digital filter transformation

	a_{1i}	b_{1i}	a_{2i}	b_{2i}	k_{ii}	g	Filter type
Filter 1	-0.1	0.9	0.1	-0.9	1	$0.08 > \mid g \mid \geq 0$	Band-pass Filter
	-0.1	0.9	0.1	-0.9	1	$\infty > \mid g \mid \geq 0.2$	Band-elimination Filter
Filter 2	-0.1	0.9	0.1	-0.9	1	$0.1 > g \geq 0, \quad \infty > g \geq 8$ $0 > g \geq -0.02$	Band-pass Filter
	-0.1	0.9	0.1	-0.9	1	$4.5 > g \geq 0.3$ $-0.1 \geq g > \infty$	Band-elimination Filter

Table 4. The ranges of g of the case-I To obtain the 2D digital band-pass and band-elimination filters.

Filter	Low-pass Filter	High-Pass Filter
Case-I (Filter 1)	g = 0.01	g =50
Case-II (Filter 1)	g =0.03	g =100
Case-III (Filter 1)	g =0.01	g =115
Case-I (Filter 2)	g = 10	g = -10
Case-II (Filter 2)	g = 8	g = -8
Case-III (Filter 2)	g = 9	g = -9

Table 5. Digital filter transformation from 2D low-pass filter to high-pass filter.

Filter	Band-pass Filter	Band-stop Filter
Case-I (Filter 1)	g = 0.01	g =100
Case-II (Filter 1)	g =0.03	g =150
Case-III (Filter 1)	g =0.05	g = 50
Case-I (Filter 2)	g = 5	g = -5
Case-II (Filter 2)	g = 25	g = -25
Case-III (Filter 2)	g = 100	g = -100

Table 6. Digital filter transformation from 2D band-pass filter to band-elimination filter.

7. Applications

The designed 2D digital filters can use in the various image processing applications, such as image restoration, image enhancement. The band-width of the designed digital filter can be controlled by the magnitude of g and the parameters of the GBT. As a result, the 2d digital filter provides facilities as required in the image processing applications.

For illustration, a standard image (Lena) (Figure 7 (a)) [1] is corrupted by gaussian noises and the degraded image (Figure 7 (b)) is passed through the 2D digital low-pass filters for de-noising purposes. Table 7 shows the quality of the reconstructed images is measured in term of mean squared error (*MSE*) [24] and peak signal-to-noise ratio (*PSNR*) [24] in decibels (dB) for the most common gray image [3]. Average PSNR of the reconstructed images are obtained by Filter2 is higher than Filter1, but, some cases, Filter1 provides better performance than Filter2. Overall, it is seen that the significant amount of noise is reduced from a degraded image by the both filters

Filter	g	*MSEns*	*PSNRns(dB)*	*MSEout*	*PSNRout(dB)*
Case-I (Filter1)	0.001	629.9926	20.1374	257.3906	24.0249
Case-II (Filter1)	0.001	636.2678	20.0944	257.7424	24.0189
Case-III (Filter1)	0.001	636.3893	20.0936	273.4251	23.7624
Case-I (Filter2)	0.001	630.9419	20.1309	256.4292	24.0411
Case-II (Filter2)	0.001	634.0169	20.1098	244.2690	24.2521
Case-III (Filter2)	0.001	639.1828	20.0746	253.6035	24.0893

Table 7. DENOISING EXPERIMENT ON LENA IMAGE (GAUSSIAN NOISE WITH mean = 0, variance = 0.01 IS ADDED INTO THE IMAGE)

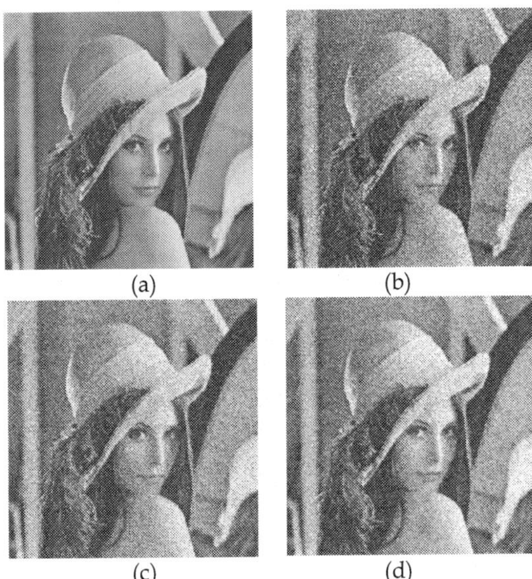

(a)   (b)

(c)   (d)

Fig. 7.(a) The original image of Lena, (b) the noisy image with Gaussian noise (variance =0.01), (c) the reconstructed image by case I (Filter 1) when g = 0.001 ($PSNR_{out}$ = 24.3337 dB), (f) the reconstructed image by case I (Filter 2) when g =0.001 ($PSNR_{out}$ = 24.2287 dB)

8. Conclusion

A new design of 2-D recursive digital filters has been proposed and it includes low-pass, high-pass, band-pass and band-elimination filters using Darlington-type gyrator network. It is seen that the behavior of the gyrator filter is changed not only for the values of resistance, capacitance and inductance of the filter, but also the value and sign of g. The coefficients of the transfer functions of Filter 1 and Filter 2 are function of g. The ranges of g are defined for attaining stable monotonic characteristics in the pass-band region, because g has control over the frequency responses of the filters.

9. References

A. K. Jain, Fundamentals of digital image processing, Prentice-Hall, 1989.

A. S. Sandhu, Generation of 1-D and 2-D analog and digital lowpass filters with monotonic amplitude-frequency response, Concordia University, Montreal, QC: M.A.Sc. Thesis, 2005.

R. C. Gonzalez and R. E. Woods, Digital image processing, Prentice-Hall, 2002.

G. A. Maria and M. M. Fahmy, "lp approximation of the group delay response of one and two-dimensional filters," IEEE Trans. Circuits Syst., vol. CAS-21, pp. 431-436, May 1974.

S. A. H. Aly and M. M. Fahmy, "Design of two-dimensional recursive digital filters with specified magnitude and group delay characteristics," IEEE Trans. Circuits Syst., vol. CAS-25, pp. 908-916, Nov. 1978.

A. T. Chottera and G. A. Jullien, "Design of two-dimensional recursive digital filters using linear programming," IEEE Trans. Circuits Syst., vol. CAS-29,, pp. 417-826, Dec. 1982.

S. Fallah, Generation of polynominal for application in the design of stable 2-D Filter, Concordia Unversity, QC: Ph.D Thesis, June 1988.

V. Ramachandran and C. S. Gargour, Generation of Very Strict Hurwitz Polynomials and Applications in 2-D Filter Design, Multidiemsnional Systems: Signal Processing and Modeling Techniques, Academic Press, Inc., Vol.60, 1995.

V. Ramachandran and M. Ahmadi, "Design of stable 2-D recursive filters by generation of VSHP using terminated n-port gyrator networks", Journal of Franklin Institute, Vol.316, pp.373-380, 1983.

A. U. Haque and V. Ramachandran "A study of designing recursive 2D digiatl filter from an analog bridged T-network", Canadian Conference on Electrical and Computer Engineering, pp. 312-315, 2005.

K. K. Sundaram; V. Ramachandran, "Analysis of the coefficients of generalized bilinear transformation in the design of 2D band-pass and band-stop filters and an application in image processing", Canadian Conference on Electrical and Computer Engineering, pp. 1233-1236, 2005.

T. Ueda, N. Aikawa, and Masamitsu, "Design method of analog low-pass filters with monotonic characteristics and arbitary flatness", Electronics and Communications in Japan, Vol. 82, No.2, pp. 21-29, 1999.

V. Ramachandran, C. S. Gargour and Ravi P. Ramachandran, "Generation of analog and digital transfer functions having a monotonic magnitude response", IEEE Canadian Conference on Electrical and Computer Engineering, Vol. 1, pp. 319-322, 2004.

I. M. Filanovsky, "A generalization of filters with monotonic magnitude-frequency response", IEEE Transactiond on Circuits and System I : Fundamental Theory and Applications, Vol. 46, No. 11, pp. 1382 – 1385, 1999.

A. Papoulis, "Optimum filter with monotonic response", Proc IRE, Vol. 46, pp. 606-609, 1958.

M. Fukada, "Optimum even order with monotonic response", IRE Trans. Circuit Theory, Vol. CT-6, pp. 277-281, 1959.

M. Ahmad, H. C. Reddy, V. Ramachandran and M. N. S. Swamy, "Cascade synthesis of a class of muiltivariable positive real function", IEEE Trans. Circuits and Systems, Vol.CAS-25, pp.871-878, 1978.

M. O. Ahmad, K. V. V. Murthy and V. Ramachandran, "Doubly-terminated two-variable lossless networks", Journal of Frankin Institute, Vol.314, Issue 6, pp.381-392, 1982.

C. S. Gargour, V. Ramachandran, R. P. Ramachandran and F. Awad, "Variable magnitude characteristics of 1-D IIR filters by a generalized bilinear transformation", 43rd Midwest Symposium on Circuits and Systems, Michigan State University, U.S.A., Session FAP-2, Four pages, August 8-11, 2000.

D. Hazony, Elements of network synthesis, New York: Reinhold Pub., 1963.

E. I. Jury, Inners and Stability of Dynamic Systems, John Wiley and Sons, 1984.

A. Oppenheim and Schafer, Discrete-Time Signal Processing, Englewood Cliffs, NJ: Prentice-Hall, 1989.

C. S. Gargour, V. Ramachandran, and R. P. Ramachandran, "Modification of filter responses by the generalized bilinear transformations and the inverse bilinear transformations", IEEE Trans. Circuits Syst., pp. 2043–2046, May 2003.

A. Netravali and B. Haskell, Digital Pictures: Representation, Compression, and Standards (2nd Ed). New York, NY: Plenum Press, 1995.

4

Common features of analog sampled-data and digital filters design

Pravoslav Martinek and Jiří Hospodka
Czech Technical University in Prague
Czech Republic

Daša Tichá
University of Žilina
Slovak Republic

1. Introduction

Cascade realization of the analog ARC- and digital filters shows more common features. These relationships are especially evident in comparison of sampled-data and digital filters, namely biquadratic sections used in cascade design. Aim of this chapter is thus to show, how to effectively use the mentioned relationships in the optimized design of both the sampled-data and digital filters.

Here the most important role play possible transformations between sampled-data and digital biquadratic section structures, application of the sensitivity concept in digital filter design and optimization of dynamic properties in the digital and sampled-data filters.

The switched-current (SI) circuits were chosen as an "analog counterpart" of the digital filters, with respect to their full compatibility to the digital VLSI-CMOS technologies, lower supply voltage and wide dynamic range. In addition, principle of SI-circuit signal processing is rather similar to the digital ones, therefore arises possibility to use a "digital prototype" for the SI filter design. On the other hand, some procedures applied in SI filter design can be successfully applied in the optimized design of digital filters, especially digital biquadratic sections.

Content of the chapter is divided into the following parts:

A short introduction to SI circuit theory and principles of operation. Although the theory of SI circuits has been described in detail in several publications – see e.g. Toumazou et al. (1993), Toumazou et al. (1996), we consider appropriate to shortly introduce the basic of operation of SI circuits for better understanding. The dynamic current mirror, memory cell, integrator and differentiator are presented as the main building blocks – i.e. blocks indispensable in filter design.

The next section presents a new universal algorithm suitable for symbolic analysis of all types of sampled-data filters. The original approach using "memory transistor" or "memory transconductor" has been introduced in Bičák et al. (1999), Martinek et al. (2003), Bičák & Hospodka (2006) and was applied in newly developed libraries for symbolic analysis PraSCan and PraCAn of the MAPLE program.

The main part of this chapter is an overview of possible biquad realization structures and follows the previous work Martinek & Tichá (2007). We turn attention to some aspects of the "digital prototype" approach in sampled-data biquads design. Here the first and second direct forms of the 2nd-order digital filter were chosen as the prototypes. As a generalization of this approach the replacement of the memory cells in the basic structure by a simple BD integrator and differentiator is discussed. The structures obtained were compared in according to their sensitivity properties, an influence of SI building blocks losses and element values spread. The results obtained are demonstrated on the examples of the 2nd-order biquad realizations. The following section of the chapter is devoted to some auxiliary tools, suitable for digital- and sampled-data filters design.

The first concerns an application of sensitivity approach, a powerful tool in continuous-time biquadratic sections design. With respect to the discrete-time character of SI- and digital filters, the "equivalent sensitivities" are derived and used. A more detailed explanation of this approach has been published in Tichá (2006). The relevance of sensitivity computation in digital filter design can be more obvious, if we are aware of the correspondence between rounding errors in "digital area" and tolerances of element values in the "continuous-time area". Therein the sensitivities represent the measure for possible rounding without loss of the accuracy of the filter frequency response.

The second useful tool for filter optimized design is a symbolic analysis. The prospective approach leads via mathematical programs oriented to the symbolic mathematics. A suitable program for this purpose seems to be MAPLE, especially developed for symbolic computations. The symbolic analysis of analog circuits is supported in MAPLE by SYRUP library Riel (2007) and newly developed libraries PraSCan and PraCAn – see Bičák et al. (1999) and Bičák & Hospodka (2006). All the libraries represent simple, but very efficient universal tool for circuit analysis, similar to the SPICE program in numerical area. The mentioned libraries allow simple modeling of the basic building blocks of digital filters - i.e. memory cells, summers and multipliers. Usage of the extended library is demonstrated on the analysis of some typical examples of digital filters, represented by block diagrams. It is important to say, that the obtained transfer functions $H(z)$ can be easily post-processed in MAPLE environment and used for the optimized design of the simulated subsystems.

The final section summarizes the results achieved and the usefulness of the presented principles of optimized analog filter design usage in "digital area".

2. The basic of Switched-Currents technique

Switched-currents (SI), as the latest technique for sampled-data analogue circuits, play an important role in modern electronic system design. In comparison to switched-capacitor circuits, SI have some important advantages, particularly full compatibility to the digital VLSI-CMOS technologies, lower supply voltage and wider dynamic range, as mentioned in the previous section.

The basic SI-cell is shown in Fig 1. Switches $S_1 - S_3$ are controlled by 2-phase switching signal. A principle of operation corresponds to the current mirror - during phase ϕ_1 are switched S_1 and S_2 and circuit operates as the input of current mirror with low input resistance (input current $i_{in(nT)}$). The second phase ϕ_2 is a storage (or output) phase – S_3 is closed and output current $i_{out(nT+1/2)}$ flows into load. The function is characterized by equations Eq. (1) and (2). To obtain transfer function $H(z) = z^{-1}$, it is necessary to use two basic cells connected in cascade, as shown in Fig. 2. Here is simultaneously shown, how to realize multiple outputs with different transfer gain constants.

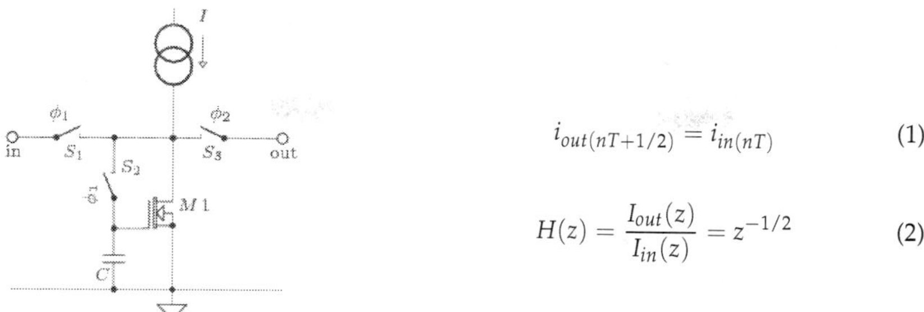

Fig. 1. The basic SI-cell

$$i_{out(nT+1/2)} = i_{in(nT)} \tag{1}$$

$$H(z) = \frac{I_{out}(z)}{I_{in}(z)} = z^{-1/2} \tag{2}$$

Output terminal out 1 pertains to the "pure" memory cell, created by transistors M 1 and M 2 and switches S_1 to S_5. Outputs out 2 and out 3 combine the second basic cell (transistor M 2) together with transistors M 3 and M 4 creating "conventional" current mirrors. Such arrangement allows setting the gain constant $\alpha_{i,\,i=1,2}$ in the form (3) and (4), where W_k, L_k denote the channel width and length of transistor $M\,k,\,_{k=2,3,4}$. Note that ratios W/L can be normalized with respect to the channel parameters of the basic cell transistor - (in our case M 2).

$$H_2(z) = \frac{I_{out\,2}(z)}{I_{in}(z)} = \alpha_1 z^{-1}; \qquad \alpha_1 = \frac{W_3/L_3}{W_2/L_2}, \tag{3}$$

$$H_3(z) = \frac{I_{out\,3}(z)}{I_{in}(z)} = \alpha_2 z^{-1}; \qquad \alpha_2 = \frac{W_4/L_4}{W_2/L_2}. \tag{4}$$

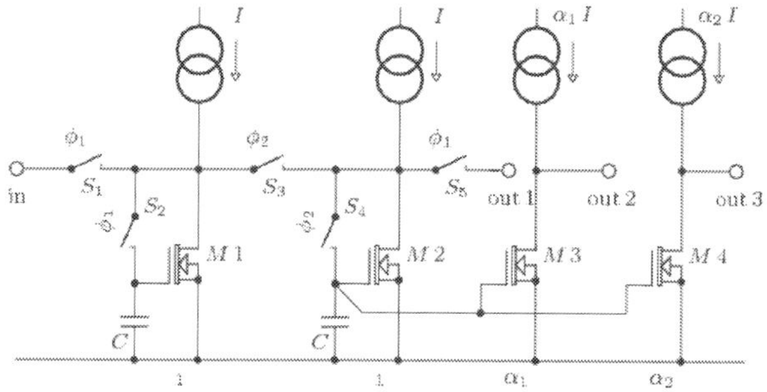

Fig. 2. Multiple-output SI memory cell

Higher-level blocks, as integrator and differentiator, can be derived from the memory cell by simple modification. In the case of integrator the output current samples are added to input, together with input signal. Resulting circuit diagram is shown in Fig. 3. Output signal is obtained under Eq. (5), corresponding to the "standard" backward-difference discrete integration. Corresponding transfer function is defined by Eq. (6).

If the switching phase of the switch S_1 is changed into ϕ_2, we obtain forward difference inverting integrator, whose transfer function is expressed by formula (7).

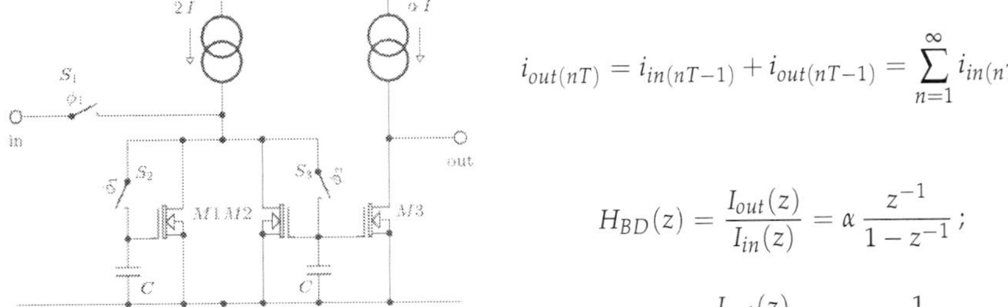

Fig. 3. Non-inverting BD integrator

$$i_{out(nT)} = i_{in(nT-1)} + i_{out(nT-1)} = \sum_{n=1}^{\infty} i_{in(nT)} ; \qquad (5)$$

$$H_{BD}(z) = \frac{I_{out}(z)}{I_{in}(z)} = \alpha \, \frac{z^{-1}}{1 - z^{-1}} ; \qquad (6)$$

$$H_{FD}(z) = \frac{I_{out}(z)}{I_{in}(z)} = -\alpha \, \frac{1}{1 - z^{-1}} . \qquad (7)$$

In contrast to the SC- and continuous-time technique there are no problems with realization of differentiator SI building blocks. A simple example of Si-implementation is shown in Fig. 4. Similarly to an integrator, the differentiator was derived from the digital prototype using equation Eq. (8). Note that the simplified inverting BD differentiator ($\alpha = 1$) can be gained by removing the input current mirror (M1 and M2 transistors).

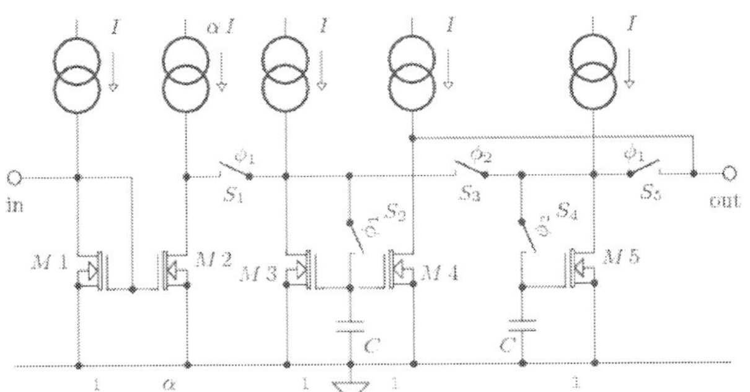

Fig. 4. Non-inverting BD differentiator

$$\frac{\partial i(t)}{\partial t} = \frac{\Delta i(t)}{\Delta t} = \frac{i_{nT} - i_{nT-1}}{T} ; \qquad (8)$$

$$H_{BD}(z) = \frac{I_{out}(z)}{I_{in}(z)} = \alpha \, (1 - z^{-1}) ; \qquad (9)$$

Similarly it is possible to create other SI-building blocks, suitable for current-mode signal processing. It is important to say, that presented schematics correspond to the simplest models of the "real" circuits, without discussion of their real implementation, behavior and further improvements. This is not topic of this chapter. More about SI-circuits and their applications can be found in Toumazou et al. (1993), Toumazou et al. (1996), Mucha (1999), Šubrt (2003), and others.

3. A symbolic analysis of SI circuits

This section describes method of SI circuit analysis based on modified algorithm for switched capacitor circuits, especially for symbolic analysis of idealized circuit. It made it more universal and useful - see Bičák et al. (1999).

The circuit description is based on modified nodal-charge equations - Kurth & Moschytz (1979); Yuan & Opal (2003); making possible to include resistive elements. The simple transformation of charges into currents is the main goal of the developed procedure. This leads to the correct evaluation of nodal voltages in the case of SI circuit. Modified capacitance matrix is possible to use for description of the switched-current (SI) basic cell and complex SI circuit by this way. Let us consider basic configuration of dynamic current-mirror shown in Fig. 5.

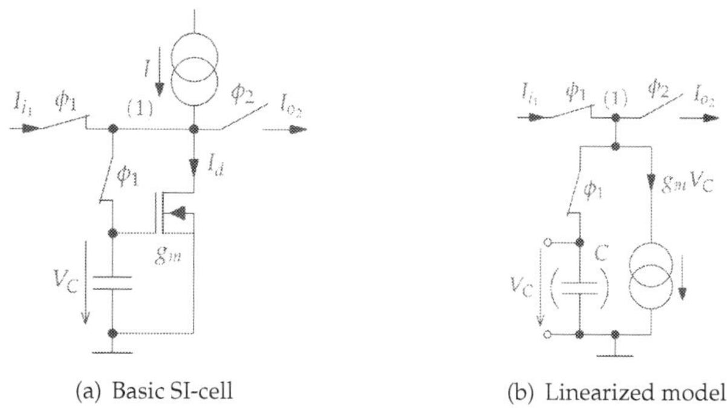

(a) Basic SI-cell (b) Linearized model

Fig. 5. Basic cell of SI circuits and linearized model.

To accomplish the starting conditions of the charge-voltage description, the SI cell is modeled by voltage controlled charge source (instead of current source) with transfer gain g_Q, memory capacitor C and ideal switches. The gain g_Q has the same numeric value as the transistor transconductance g_m, but different unit. Modified model is shown in Fig. 6.

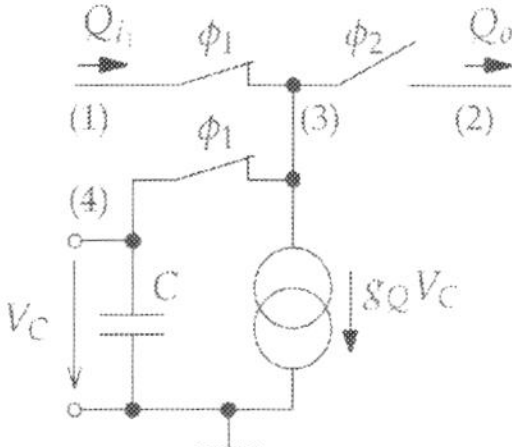

Fig. 6. Model of SI cell used for analysis by charge-voltage equations.

The resultant capacitance matrix of the SI cell model in Fig. 6 can be written in the following form

$$\left[\begin{array}{c} Q_{i_1} \\ \hline Q_{o_2} \\ 0 \end{array} \right] = \left[\begin{array}{c|cc} C + g_Q & 0 & -z^{-1/2}C \\ \hline 0 & 0 & g_Q \\ -z^{-1/2}C & 0 & C \end{array} \right] \times \left[\begin{array}{c} V_{1_1} \\ \hline V_{2_2} \\ U_{4_l} \end{array} \right] \tag{10}$$

The charge transfer from phase ϕ_1 to phase ϕ_2 is than

$$H_Q = \frac{Q_{o_2}}{Q_{i_1}} = -\frac{g_Q\, z^{-1/2}}{g_Q + C(1 - z^{-1})}. \tag{11}$$

The transfer function H_Q contains additional terms, corresponding "parasitic" changes of memory capacitor charge. This effect can be eliminated in idealized circuit description by minimizing capacitance C. When $C \to 0$, the equation (11) limits into the correct known formula (2)

$$H_{id} = \lim_{C \to 0} H = -z^{-1/2} \tag{12}$$

In fact, the described procedure corresponds to the charge $\to$ current transformation in the circuit description (in other words, "charge is divided by time"). In this case, the "starting" description of VCCS by voltage controlled charge source can be turned back ($g_Q \to g_m$)[1] and original nodal voltage-charge description changes into voltage-current equations. Note that presented transformation does not change the numeric value of VCCS gain (transconductance g_m).

It is important to say, the procedure of capacitance zeroing should be performed as the last step of transfer evaluation to avoid the complication in description of phase-to-phase energy transfer. The symbolic or special case of semi-symbolical analysis is necessary with respect to correct simulation result. This fact limits the described method of memory capacitor zeroing. This problem can be solved by special model of the SI cell shown in following figure, Fig. 7.

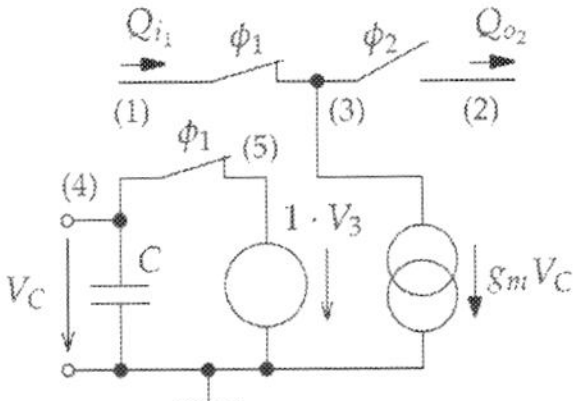

Fig. 7. Model of SI cell with separator.

This circuit can be described by following equations in matrix representation.

$$
\begin{bmatrix} Q_{i_1} \\ 0 \\ Q_{o_2} \\ 0 \\ 0 \end{bmatrix}
=
\left[
\begin{array}{cc|ccc}
0 & g_Q & 0 & 0 & 0 \\
1 & -1 & 0 & 0 & 0 \\
0 & 0 & 0 & g_Q & 0 \\
0 & -z^{1/2}C_1 & 0 & C_1 & 0 \\
0 & 0 & 1 & 0 & -1
\end{array}
\right]
\times
\begin{bmatrix} V_{1_1} \\ V_{4_1} \\ V_{2_2} \\ V_{4_2} \\ U_{5_2} \end{bmatrix}
\tag{13}
$$

The same transfer function as in relation (12) is obtained by computation of Q_{o_2}/Q_{i_1} from this matrix.

This representation is possible to implement directly into the C-matrix for SC circuit description. By this way idealized SI circuit can be analyzed in programs for SC circuit analysis without symbolic formulation of results and without any limit calculation. Larger matrix is the certain disadvantage of the method.

---

[1] The transfer function does not include transconductances in this elementary example.

Direct description of SI cell can be applied in case of special program for idealized SI circuit analysis. Direct matrix representation of SI cell from Fig. 5 for switching in phase ϕ_1 and also in phase ϕ_2 has the following expressions in case of circuit switched in two phases.

$$
\begin{array}{c|c|c}
 & V_{1_1} & V_{1_2} \\
\hline
I_{i_1} & g_m & 0 \\
\hline
I_{i_2} & z^{-1/2}g_m & 0
\end{array}
\ \text{for } \phi_1,
\qquad
\begin{array}{c|c|c}
 & V_{1_1} & V_{1_2} \\
\hline
I_{1_1} & 0 & z^{-1/2}g_m \\
\hline
I_{1_2} & 0 & g_m
\end{array}
\ \text{for } \phi_2,
\tag{14}
$$

where $I_{1_2} = -I_{0_2}$ for circuit switched in phase ϕ_1 and $I_{1_1} = -I_{0_1}$ for circuit switched in phase ϕ_2.

Now the currents are used instead of charges – it is a case of modified node voltages method applied for circuit switched in two phases. In our case the circuit contains only one non-grounded node. It means the matrix has only 2×2 dimension. The memory effect is here described by current source controlled by voltage in phase ϕ_1 and phase ϕ_2 *with non zero transfer (transconductance) from one phase to the other* as can be seen from the above mentioned matrix form.

Presented procedure leads to the simple and easy description of SI structures and their effective analysis in both symbolic and numerical form.

4. Basic SI-biquad structures

This part intends to discuss some aspects of the "digital prototype" approach in sampled-data biquads design.

It is important to say, that many applications of SI technique in sampled-data filter design published from the nineties are mostly based on a two-integrator structure in the case of biquads, or operational simulation of LC-prototype – see e.g. Toumazou et al. (1993). But the principle of SI-circuit operation is rather similar to the digital ones, so there arises possibility to use a "digital prototype" for SI-filter design.

The first and second direct forms of the 2nd-order digital filter were chosen as the prototypes. Firstly, the design using SI memory cells was considered; in this case the final circuit should preserve the dominant features of the prototype. As a generalization of this approach the replacement of the memory cells in the basic structure by a simple BD integrator and differentiator was investigated. The structures obtained were compared in according to their sensitivity properties, an influence of SI building blocks losses and circuit element values spread. The results are demonstrated on the examples of the typical 2nd-order biquad realizations.

As mentioned, the selected prototypes are known as the first and the second direct-form digital filter structures, characterized by common transfer function (15) – see e.g. Antoniou (1979), Mitra (2005).

$$
H(z) = \frac{b_0 + b_1\,z^{-1} + b_2\,z^{-2}}{1 + a_1\,z^{-1} + a_2\,z^{-2}}
\tag{15}
$$

After redrawing, following the SI technique, the block diagrams shown in Figs. 8 and 9 were obtained. Here the symbol CM denotes current copier (multiple-output current mirror), FB means SI building block, for the first time the SI memory cell. The transfer function coefficients are set by current copier gains a_i, b_i, as evident from Fig. 8 and Fig. 9.

With respect to the practical realization aspects, the direct-form 2 structure seems to be more suitable because of simpler input and output current copiers. Multiple outputs of the SI-building blocks do not mean design complications, as is shown in Fig. 2 – see Section 2.

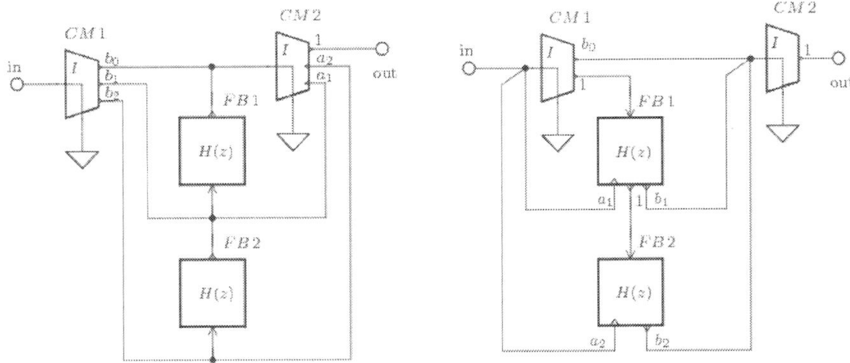

Fig. 8. Case I. SI circuit   Fig. 9. Case II. SI circuit

To obtain a more complex overview about the circuits behavior, the following versions were considered:

1. The SI-FBs are realized by memory cells in compliance with the digital prototype. These are simple in the case of direct form 1, multiple-output under Fig. 2 in the case of direct form 2. The weighted outputs are set using changed W/L output transistor ratios.

2. Memory cells are replaced by non-inverting BD and FD integrators.

3. SI-FBs are realized by BD differentiators under Fig. 4, described by the transfer function $H(z) = \alpha\left(1 - z^{-1}\right)$.

The following evaluative criteria were used for comparing all the considered structures:

-   *Sensitivity properties:* With respect to the discrete-time character of SI circuits, the "equivalent sensitivity" approach has been applied. A more detailed explanation of this approach has been published in Ref. Tichá (2006), and it is shortly indicated in Section 5.

-   *Losses influence:* The important imperfections of SI circuits are caused by parasitic output conductances of SI cells. In the following, these parasitics will be characterized by output conductance g_o or by ratio $x_g = \frac{g_m}{g_o}$, where g_m represents transistor transconductance.

-   *Transistor parameters spread:* With respect to the technological limitations, the limits of spread $\alpha = W/L$ of transistors are crucial. In our considerations the maximum available spread is expected to be in the interval $\alpha_{max}/\alpha_{min} < 50$. In general, the given limit influences the maximum ratio of sampling frequency f_c to ω_{0eq}.

The necessary symbolic analysis were made using MAPLE libraries PraSCan and PraCAn, developed by Bičák & Hospodka (2006), Bičák et al. (1999) for symbolic and numerical analysis of sampled-data circuits.

4.1 Results obtained

Sensitivity evaluation:

At first, let us consider the "original SI networks" under Figs. 8 and 9. The transfer function of both structures corresponds directly to the Eq. (15), and the sensitivity properties can be expressed using procedure described in Sec. 5 in the form (25) and (26), as the functions of parameters a_1, a_2. More suitable for practical design are the sensitivity functions of "continuous-time" $H(s)$ parameters ω_0, Q and sampling period T. In this case the sensitivities can be expressed by (29) and (30).

Evaluated sensitivity graphs of ω_{0eq}- and Q_{eq}-sensitivities on f_c / f_0 ratio in Fig. 10 and Fig. 11 show unsuitable values for higher x_c. This fact limits the use of such biquads to lower values of x_c.

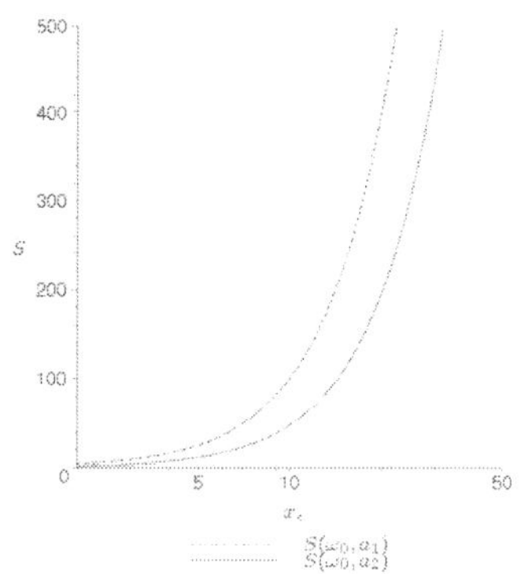

Fig. 10. $S_{a_i}^{\omega_{0eq}} = f(x_c)$

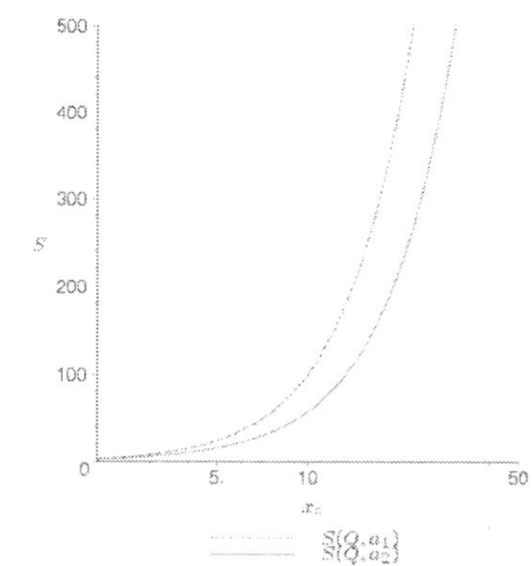

Fig. 11. $S_{a_i}^{Q_{eq}} = f(x_c)$

The modified structures containing integrators or differentiators show better sensitivity properties as is evident from Fig. 12 and Fig. 13. The graphs pertain to the non-inverting BD integrator version of Case I structure; similar behavior was found in versions based on FD integrators, mixed BD-FD integrator combinations or differentiator based circuits.

This behavior can be easily explained, because the introduced integrator- and differentiator-type structures are in fact the special cases of SFG or state-variable based biquad design.

Note that the ω_{0eq} and Q_{eq} sensitivities to the gain constants α_i, $_{i=1,2}$ of integrator- and differentiator-type building blocks are typically 0.5 - 1 and decrease to the limit value $S_{a_i}^{Q_{eq}} = 0.5$ for $x_c \gg 1$. Similar values were obtained in the case of ω_{0eq} sensitivities. Table 1 illustrates the sensitivity properties of the chosen Case I structure versions for starting parameters $f_0 = 2\,\text{kHz}$, $f_c = 48\,\text{kHz}$, $Q = 1/\sqrt{2}$.

Here symbol "M" denotes the "original" structure containing SI memory cells, "BD int" denotes the version using BD integrators and similarly "FD int" denotes the version using FD integrators. Case "FD+BD int" corresponds to the arrangement where FB1 block is implemented as the FD integrator and FB2 block as the BD integrator. The order of FBs is important, a changed arrangement results in increased sensitivities. The last row contains sensitivity values for a BD differentiator based circuit.

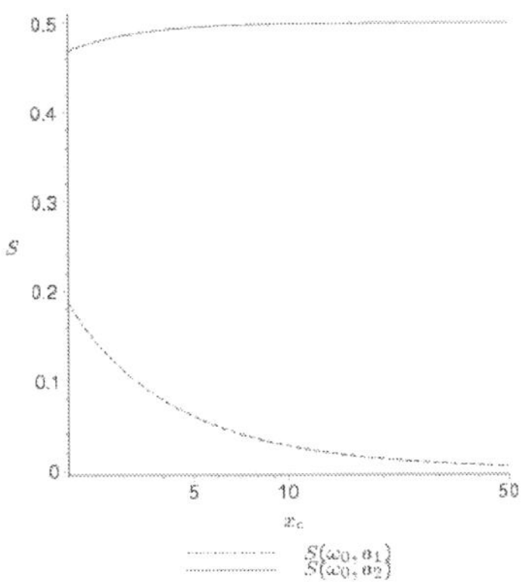

Fig. 12. $S_{a_i}^{\omega_{0eq}} = f(x_c)$

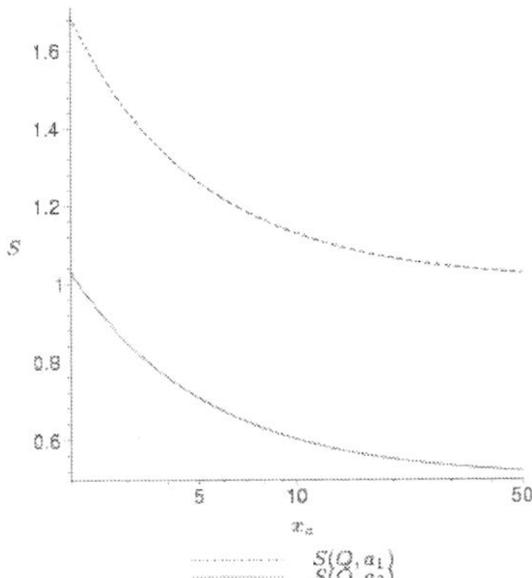

Fig. 13. $S_{a_i}^{Q_{eq}} = f(x_c)$

Type	$S_{a_1}^{\omega_{0eq}}$	$S_{a_2}^{\omega_{0eq}}$	$S_{a_1}^{Q_{eq}}$	$S_{a_2}^{Q_{eq}}$	$S_{\alpha_1}^{Q_{eq}}$	$S_{\alpha_2}^{Q_{eq}}$
M	-14.6	5.97	-14.1	8.42	-	-
BD int	0.109	0.491	-1.29	0.693	-0.601	0.693
FD int	-0.075	0.491	-0.739	0.323	-0.416	0.323
FD+BD int	-0.092	0.508	-0.907	0.491	-0.416	0.491
BD diff	-0.075	-0.416	-0.739	0.416	-0.323	0.416

Table 1. Sensitivity properties

Losses influence:

As mentioned, the finite output conductances of the basic SI cells and current copiers (current mirrors) are crucial in SI circuit design together with the number of blocks in the signal path. With regard to this, it is necessary to distinguish between the Case I and Case II structures. Some simulations showed slightly better behavior of the Case II arrangement. Simultaneously it is important to take into account the finite "on" resistance of switches. Especially differentiator-based circuits are sensitive to switch imperfections.

Table 2 documents typical frequency response errors for the realizations introduced in Table 1. Here the typical ratios $x_g = g_m/g_o = 200$ and r_{on} switches equal to the input resistance of current building blocks were considered.

Transistor parameters spread

This is markedly determined by the designed structure type and f_c/f_0 ratio. For illustration, let us assume the LP biquad designed under the same conditions documented in Table 1 and Table 2.

As is evident from Table 3, the maximum values spread shows the memory cell based version, the max-to-min ratio equals 114.3. The differentiator and integrator based versions are less demanding, the max-to-min ratio was evaluated from 48.5 to 69.9.

Type	$\bar{\varepsilon}$	ε_{max}	$\varepsilon(0)$	$\varepsilon(\omega_0)$
M-Case I	0.0346	0.426	0.426	0.176
M-Case II	0.0274	0.335	0.335	0.142
BD int Case I	0.0136	0.123	0.106	0.0853
BD int Case II	0.0147	0.139	0.126	0.0905
FD int Case I	0.0149	0.127	0.109	0.0915
BD diff Case I	0.0124	0.116	0.109	0.0458

Table 2. Frequency response errors

Note that the last versions have two free parameters α_1, α_2 which can be exploited for design optimization; unfortunately changes to these parameters do not allow any minimization of values spread.

Type	b_0	b_1	b_2	a_1	a_2
M	0.0143	0.285	0.0143	-1.635	0.692
BD int	0.0143	$\dfrac{0.057}{\alpha_1}$	$\dfrac{0.057}{\alpha_1\,\alpha_2}$	$\dfrac{0.365}{\alpha_1}$	$\dfrac{0.057}{\alpha_1\,\alpha_2}$
FD int	0.0206	$\dfrac{0.0824}{\alpha_1}$	$\dfrac{0.0824}{\alpha_1\,\alpha_2}$	$-\dfrac{0.3626}{\alpha_1}$	$\dfrac{0.0824}{\alpha_1\,\alpha_2}$
FD+BD int	0.0206	0	$\dfrac{0.0824}{\alpha_1\,\alpha_2}$	$-\dfrac{0.445}{\alpha_1}$	$\dfrac{0.0824}{\alpha_1\,\alpha_2}$
BD diff	1	$-\dfrac{1}{\alpha_1}$	$-\dfrac{0.25}{\alpha_1\,\alpha_2}$	$\dfrac{4.402}{\alpha}$	$\dfrac{12.139}{\alpha_1\,\alpha_2}$

Table 3. design parameters for $f_0 = 2\,\text{kHz}$

Type	b_0	b_1	b_2	a_1	a_2
M	0.00391	0.00781	0.00391	-1.816	0.831
BD int	0.00391	$\dfrac{0.0156}{\alpha_1}$	$\dfrac{0.0156}{\alpha_1\,\alpha_2}$	$\dfrac{0.184}{\alpha_1}$	$\dfrac{0.0156}{\alpha_1\,\alpha_2}$
FD int	0.0047	$\dfrac{0.0188}{\alpha_1}$	$\dfrac{0.0188}{\alpha_1\,\alpha_2}$	$-\dfrac{0.184}{\alpha_1}$	$\dfrac{0.0156}{\alpha_1\,\alpha_2}$
FD+BD int	0.0047	0	$\dfrac{0.0188}{\alpha_1\,\alpha_2}$	$-\dfrac{0.203}{\alpha_1}$	$\dfrac{0.0188}{\alpha_1\,\alpha_2}$
BD diff	1	$-\dfrac{1}{\alpha_1}$	$-\dfrac{0.25}{\alpha_1\,\alpha_2}$	$\dfrac{9.804}{\alpha}$	$\dfrac{53.21}{\alpha_1\,\alpha_2}$

Table 4. design parameters for $f_0 = 1\,\text{kHz}$

The influence of the f_c/f_0 ratio to the transistor parameters spread is demonstrated in Table 4, showing parameter changes for the lowered $f_0 = 1\,\text{kHz}$ from the previous design.

In this case the max-to-min ratio increases for the memory cell version to 464.4. The best result is obtained for the differentiator based circuit, where the max-to-min ratio equals 212.8. It is evident that such designs are hardly realizable and strongly require lower sampling frequency.

5. Sensitivity approach in discrete-time filters design

The sensitivity approach is a worthwile tool for the optimized design of analog continuous-time and sampled-data filters. Particularly the design of biquadratic sections for cascade realization of higher-order filters is significantly influenced by the sensitivity properties of the considered circuits. Mainly the sensitivities of ω_0- and Q- parameters to the filter elements changes serve as the effective criterion for suitable circuit structure selection and design optimization, because ω_0 and Q uniquely determine the frequency response shape.

The "main" sensitivities of the biquadratic transfer function $H(s)$ (16) are defined by formulas (17), where x_i means active and passive circuit elements. The ω_0 and Q parameters are defined by (18) as the functions of the real and imaginary parts σ_1, ω_1 of the complex-conjugate poles of the 2nd-order biquadratic transfer function (16).

$$H(s) = \frac{k_2\, s^2 + k_1\, s + k_0}{s^2 + \frac{\omega_0}{Q}\, s + \omega_0^2} \tag{16}$$

$$S_{x_i}^{\omega_0} = \frac{\partial \omega_0}{\partial x_i}\, \frac{x_i}{\omega_0}\,; \qquad S_{x_i}^{Q} = \frac{\partial Q}{\partial x_i}\, \frac{x_i}{Q}\,; \tag{17}$$

$$\omega_0 = \sqrt{\sigma_1^2 + \omega_1^2}\,; \qquad Q = \frac{\omega_0}{2\,\sigma_1}\,. \tag{18}$$

Sensitivity concept is less usual in the field of the digital filters, because there is not a direct equivalent of the ω_0 and Q parameters in the s-plane to the similar parameters in z-plane. Nevertheless the relevance of sensitivity usage in digital filter design can be more obvious, if we are aware of the correspondence between rounding errors in "digital area" and tolerances of circuit element values in the "continuous-time" area. Here the sensitivities represent the measure for possible rounding without loss of the accuracy of the filter frequency response. Simultaneously, sensitivities can help to solve problems with the optimum choice of the realization structure with respect to the "non-standard" design conditions, e.g. in design of the digital filters and equalizers for audio signal processing.

To apply sensitivity approach in digital filter design effectively, it is necessary to formularize equivalent sensitivity parameters, transforming z-plane parameters into s-plane and evaluate them like functions of $H(z)$. Such a procedure, described in Tichá (2006), will be presented in the following.

5.1 Equivalent sensitivity evaluation

Let us assume "standard" 2nd-order transfer function $H(z)$ in the form (19). The equivalent parameters ω_0 and Q can be obtained using an appropriate transformation of $H(z)$ into s-plane and comparison to the ordinary form of $H(s)$ under (16)

$$H(z) = \frac{b_0 + b_1\, z^{-1} + b_2\, z^{-2}}{1 - a_1\, z^{-1} - a_2\, z^{-2}}\,; \tag{19}$$

To obtain the generally valid relationship, the $z - s$ transformation should be symbolic. Using inverse bilinear transformation (20) of $H(z)$

$$z = \frac{2 + sT}{2 - sT} \tag{20}$$

we obtain equivalent $H_{eq}(s)$ in the form (21) and after formal rearrangement the final form (22) comparable to (16).

$$H_{eq}(s) = \frac{T^2\,(b_0 - b_1 + b_2)\,s^2 + 4\,T\,(b_0 - b_2)\,s + 4\,(b_0 + b_1 + b_2)}{T^2\,(1 + a_1 - a_2)\,s^2 + 4\,T\,(a_2 + 1)\,s + 4\,(1 - a_1 - a_2)}\; ; \tag{21}$$

$$H_{eq}(s) = \frac{\frac{(b_0 - b_1 + b_2)}{1 + a_1 - a_2}\,s^2 + 4\,\frac{(b_0 - b_2)}{T(1 + a_1 - a_2)}\,s + 4\,\frac{b_0 + b_1 + b_2}{T^2(1 + a_1 - a_2)}}{s^2 + 4\,\frac{(a_2 + 1)}{T(1 + a_1 - a_2)}\,s + 4\,\frac{1 - a_1 - a_2}{T^2(1 + a_1 - a_2)}}\;. \tag{22}$$

A comparison of (22) to (16) gives

$$\omega_{0eq} = \frac{2}{T}\sqrt{\frac{1 - a_1 - a_2}{1 + a_1 - a_2}}\; ; \qquad (23) \qquad\qquad Q_{eq} = \frac{\sqrt{(1 - a_2)^2 - a_1^2}}{2\,(1 + a_2)}\,. \tag{24}$$

Now it is possible to express the equivalent sensitivity of ω_{0eq} and Q_{eq} to the denominator coefficients a_1 and a_2 using formula (17). The symbolic form of the evaluated sensitivities is as follows

$$S_{a_1}^{\omega_0} = -\frac{a_1\,(1 - a_2)}{(1 - a_2)^2 - a_1^2}\; ; \qquad S_{a_1}^{Q} = -\frac{a_1^2}{(1 - a_2)^2 - a_1^2}\; ; \tag{25}$$

$$S_{a_2}^{\omega_0} = \frac{a_1\,a_2}{(1 - a_2)^2 - a_1^2}\; ; \qquad S_{a_2}^{Q} = \frac{a_2\left[a_1^2 - 2\,(1 - a_2)\right]}{(1 + a_2)\left[(1 - a_2)^2 - a_1^2\right]}\,. \tag{26}$$

In some cases it is suitable to express the equivalent sensitivities as the functions of ω_0, Q and T, or $x_c = f_c / \omega_0$. To extend the expressions (25) - (26), it is necessary to transform coefficients a_1, a_2 into s-plane using backward bilinear transformation of $H(z)$ denominator. Doing this, the following expressions were gained:

$$a_1 = \frac{2\,(4 - \omega_0^2\,T^2)\,Q}{2\,\omega_0\,T + 4\,Q + \omega_0^2\,T^2\,Q}\; ; \tag{27}$$

$$a_2 = -\frac{-2\,\omega_0\,T + \omega_0^2\,T^2\,Q + 4\,Q}{2\,\omega_0\,T + 4\,Q + \omega_0^2\,T^2\,Q}\,. \tag{28}$$

Applying (27) and (28) in Eqs. (25) to (26) we obtain the modified sensitivity expressions (29) – (30). The parameter x_c is defined by Eq. (31).

$$S_{a_1e}^{\omega_0} = -\frac{(16\,x_c^4 - 1)}{16\,x_c^2}\; ; \qquad\qquad S_{a_1e}^{Q} = -\frac{(4\,x_c^2 - 1)^2}{16\,x_c^2}\; ; \tag{29}$$

$$S_{a_2e}^{\omega_0} = \frac{x_c^2}{2} - \frac{x_c}{4\,Q} + \frac{1}{16\,x_c\,Q} - \frac{1}{32\,x_c^2}\; ; \qquad S_{a_2e}^{Q} = -\frac{1}{4} + \frac{x_c^2}{2} + \frac{(1 + 4x_c)\,(4Q^2 - 1)}{16\,Q\,x_c} + \frac{1}{32\,x_c^2}\,. \tag{30}$$

$$x_c = \frac{1}{T\,\omega_0} = \frac{f_c}{\omega_0} \tag{31}$$

The formulas obtained are valid directly for the 1st and the 2nd canonic direct form of the digital filters – see Laipert et al. (2000), Antoniou (1979), Mitra (2005) and others. For the other 2nd-order structures it is necessary to express the transfer function $H(z)$ coefficients a_i, b_i, $_{i=0,1,2}$ (19) as the functions of the analyzed structure parameters. The practical use of this will be explained in the following parts.

5.2 Sensitivity properties of the direct canonic forms of digital filters

As mentioned, the sensitivity properties to the parameters of the 1st and the 2nd direct form of the digital 2nd-order filters are straightly specified by above presented formulas, because the coefficients are determined by the multipliers and adders constants of the filter block diagram. The filter general sensitivity properties can be in this case characterized preferably by modified equations (29) and (30) as the functions of equivalent Q-factor and the ratio x_c given by eq. (31). The following figures Fig. 14 and Fig. 15 show the sensitivity $S_{a_{1,2}}^{\omega_{0eq}}$ and $S_{a_{1,2}}^{Q_{eq}}$ as functions of Q_{eq}.

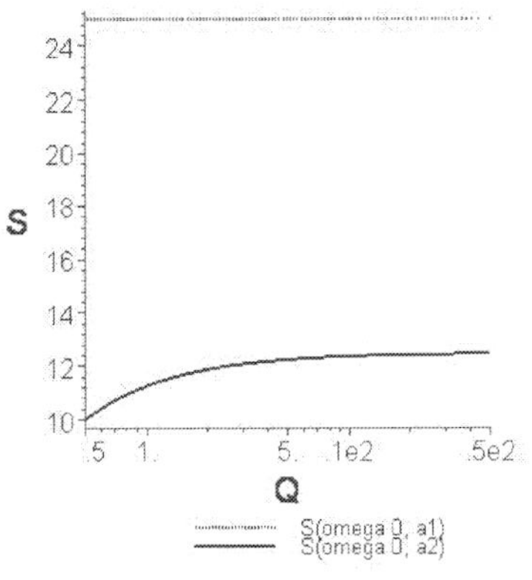

Fig. 14. $S_{a_{1,2}}^{\omega_0} = f(Q)$

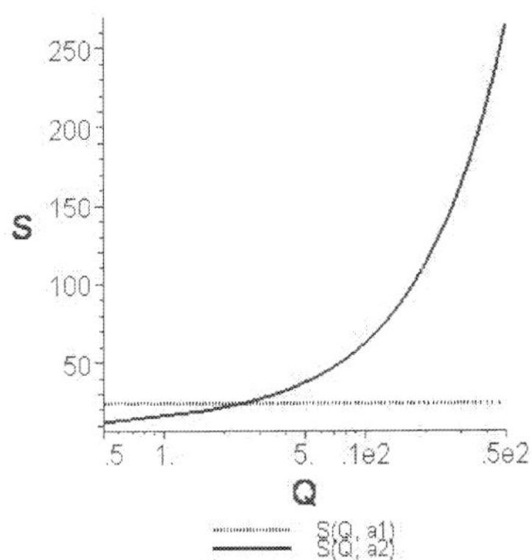

Fig. 15. $S_{a_{1,2}}^{Q} = f(Q)$

As evident, $S_{a_1}^{\omega_{0eq}}$ together with $S_{a_1}^{Q_{eq}}$ do not depend on Q-factor value, in contrast to the $S_{a_2}^{\omega_0}$ sensitivities. Note that sensitivities values are higher in comparison to the similar analogue realizations.

From the practical point-of-view the Figs. 16 and 17 are more important. Here the $S_{a_{1,2}}^{\omega_{0eq}}$ and $S_{a_{1,2}}^{Q_{eq}}$ sensitivities are depicted in dependence of ratio x_c, thus indirectly as the functions of ω_{0eq} and T. These sensitivities are significantly higher than the previous ones and rapidly increase for $x_c \geq 10$. This bears to the known fact, that direct forms of digital filters are less appropriate for such implementations, where the sampling frequency is relative high.

5.3 Digital filters derived from SFG graph

These filters are analogous to the continuous-time 2nd-order filters designed on two-integrator feedback loop. A typical example of such a filter is shown in Fig. 18. Transfer function of this filter given by Eq. (32) was evaluated using modified SYRUP library in the mathematical program MAPLE – see Tichá & Martinek (2007).

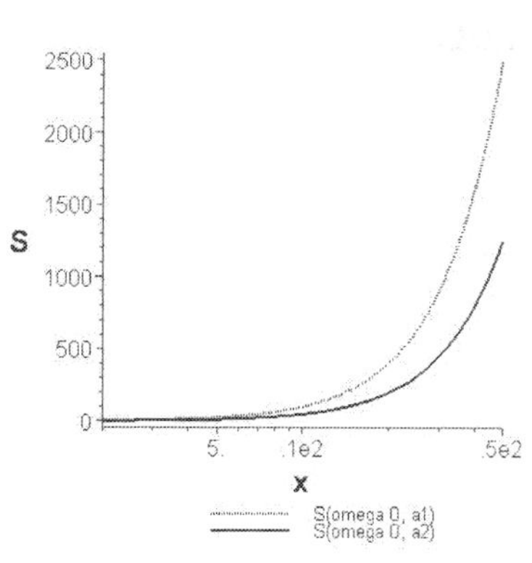

Fig. 16. $S^{\omega_0}_{a_{1,2}} = f(x)$

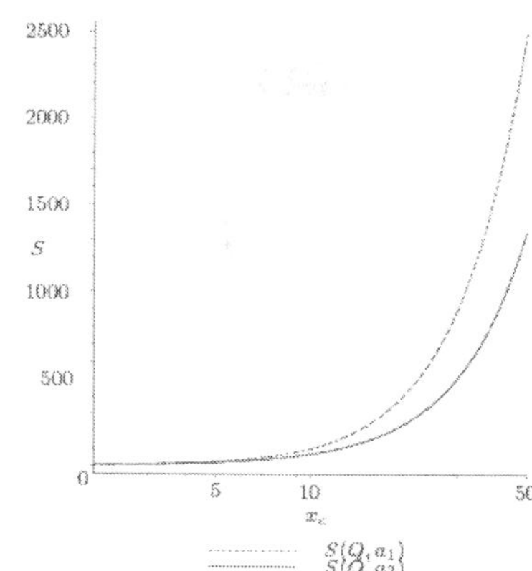

Fig. 17. $S^{Q}_{a_{1,2}} = f(x)$

A sensitivity evaluation was made according to the previous example. The results are as follows:

$$H(z) = \frac{a_5 z^2 + (a_1 - a_5 + a_6)\, z - a_6}{(1 - a_4)\, z^2 - (2 + a_2 - a_4)\, z + 1}\,; \tag{32}$$

$$\omega_{0eq} = \frac{2}{T} \sqrt{-\frac{a_2}{4 + a_2 - 2\,a_4}}\,; \tag{33} \qquad Q_{eq} = \frac{\sqrt{a_2\,(2\,a_4 - a_2 - 4)}}{2\,a_4}\,. \tag{34}$$

The corresponding sensitivities of ω_{0eq} and Q_{eq} to the $H(z)$ denominator coefficients a_i have the form (35) to (38), and the modified sensitivities the form (39) to (42). Note that parameter x_c is defined by Eq. (31)

$$S^{\omega_0}_{a_2} = \frac{2 - a_4}{4 + a_2 - 2\,a_4}\,; \tag{35} \qquad\qquad S^{Q}_{a_2} = \frac{2 + a_2 - a_4}{4 + a_2 - 2\,a_4}\,; \tag{36}$$

$$S^{\omega_0}_{a_4} = \frac{a_4}{4 + a_2 - 2\,a_4}\,; \tag{37} \qquad\qquad S^{Q}_{a_4} = -\frac{4 + a_2 - a_4}{4 + a_2 - 2\,a_4}\,; \tag{38}$$

$$S^{\omega_0}_{a_2 m} = \frac{1}{2} + \frac{1}{8\,x_c^2}\,; \tag{39} \qquad\qquad S^{Q}_{a_2 m} = \frac{1}{2} - \frac{1}{8\,x_c^2}\,; \tag{40}$$

$$S^{\omega_0}_{a_4 m} = -\frac{1}{4\,x_c\,Q}\,; \tag{41} \qquad\qquad S^{Q}_{a_4 m} = -1 + \frac{1}{4\,x_c\,Q}\,. \tag{42}$$

Similarly to the previous example the evaluated sensitivities can be presented as the functions of Q and x_c. The graphical representation of the functions $S^{\omega_0}_{a_i} = f(Q)$ and $S^{Q}_{a_i} = f(Q);\ i=2,3,4$ for given $x_c = 5$ is in Fig. 19. The graphs of functions $S^{\omega_0}_{a_i} = f(x_c)$ and $S^{Q}_{a_i} = f(x_c);\ i=2,4$ for $Q = 2$ are shown in Figs. 20.

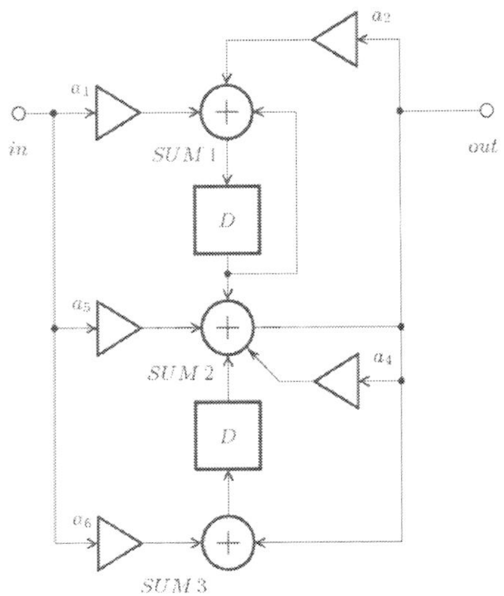

Fig. 18. Digital 2nd-order integrator-based filter

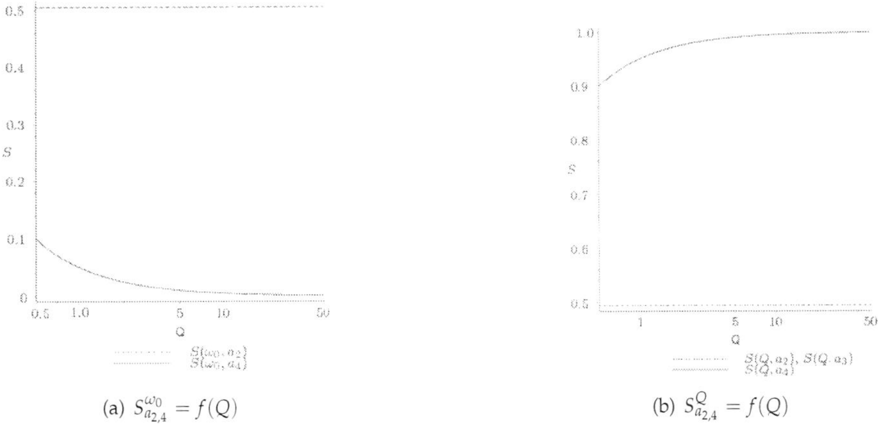

(a) $S_{a_{2,4}}^{\omega_0} = f(Q)$

(b) $S_{a_{2,4}}^{Q} = f(Q)$

Fig. 19. Sensitivities $S_{a_{2,4}}^{\omega_0} = f(Q)$ and $S_{a_{2,4}}^{Q} = f(Q)$ for $x_c = 5$.

In comparison to the direct-form structure all the sensitivities are considerably smaller and do not exceed unit value. It is important to emphasize the sensitivity independence from ratio x_c. It means that such a filter can be implemented successfully under non-standard conditions, where the limited word length or high ratio of ω_0 and f_c lead to the significant frequency response inaccuracy or filter instability.

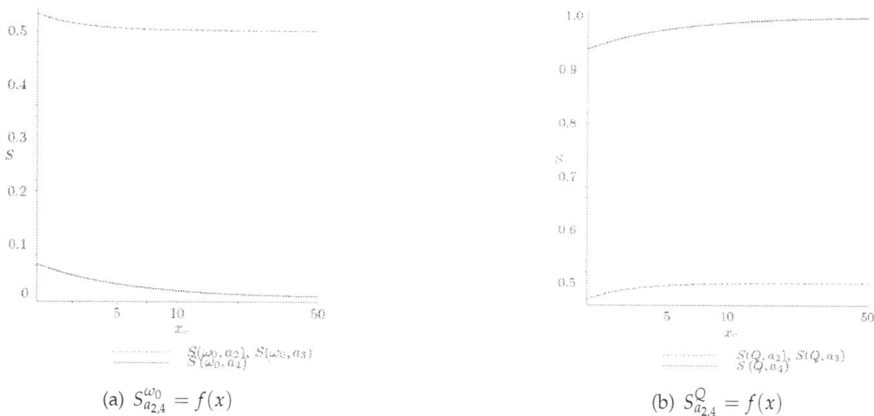

(a) $S_{a_{2,4}}^{\omega_0} = f(x)$

(b) $S_{a_{2,4}}^{Q} = f(x)$

Fig. 20. Sensitivities $S_{a_{2,4}}^{\omega_0} = f(x_c)$ and $S_{a_{2,4}}^{Q} = f(x_c)$ for $Q = 2$.

6. A tool for symbolic analysis of digital filters

Symbolic and semi-symbolic analysis is considered to be an efficient tool for design and optimization of electrical and electronic circuits, not only analogue, but also digital. During
the last period many specialized programs were developed for this purpose, but the most of
them do not allow the direct post-processing of the results obtained. The more prospective
approach is based on the use of mathematical programs oriented to the symbolic mathematics. Here the MAPLE program, especially developed for symbolic computations, seems to be
the most suitable for this purpose. The symbolic analysis of analogue circuit is supported in
MAPLE program by the SYRUP library Riel (2007). The SYRUP represents simple, but very efficient universal tool for circuit analysis, similar to the SPICE program in the circuit numerical
analysis area.
As shown in the following, the SYRUP library can be easily adapted for the digital filters symbolic analysis as well. This assertion results from the fact, that circuit equations describing the
digital filter block diagrams are very similar to the ones describing common analogue circuits.
It leads to the direct use of the modified node-voltage equations method after completing the
basic elements library. In contrast to the commonly used programs for circuit analysis, the
input language of the SYRUP library is very flexible and allows to create models of the digital
filter building block by a simple way.

6.1 The MAPLE-SYRUP library extension
To analyze digital filter block diagrams using SYRUP, it is necessary to complete the basic set
of circuit elements models. The most important "digital" building blocks are the delay element
D and general multiple-input summing element SUM. The first of them is presented in Fig. 21
and the second in Fig. 22. Note that A in the summing element equation means summer
gain; i.e. the multiplication operation can be included into this element. Nevertheless, the
multiplication can be realized independently as well by some of "standard" library elements.

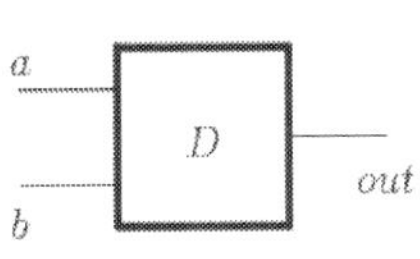

$$Y_{out}(z) = [X_a(z) + X_b(z)]\, z^{-1}$$

```
>   .subckt MEM out a b
>       Vout out 0
(v[a]+v[b])/z

>   .ends
```

Fig. 21. The Delay element model

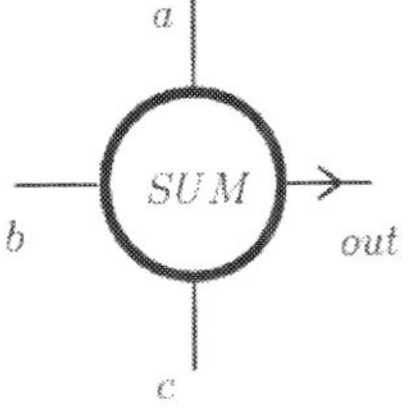

$$Y_{out}(z) = A\,[X_a(z) + X_b(z) + X_c(z)]$$

```
>   .subckt SUM out a b c
>       Vout out 0
A*(v[a]+v[b]+v[c])

>   .ends
```

Fig. 22. The general summer model

All the mentioned blocks can be represented by sub-circuits, based on "voltage" description, as demonstrated by listings in SYRUP language – see Fig. 21 and 22. It is important to say that the multiple-input delay element model can be easily created, and, in this modified form it makes possible significant simplification of the block diagram and its description in the SYRUP input file.

6.2 Post-processing of the results

The MAPLE program environment offers an efficient processing of the symbolic terms including simplification of algebraic expressions, solution of the sets of symbolic or semi-symbolic equations, symbolic differentiation or integration and so forth. This gives facilities for effective post-processing of the symbolic analysis results, especially for the purpose of the analyzed networks optimized design. The following topics can be typically solved:

- *Derivation of the design formulas.*

  The "standard" procedure compares the given numerical transfer function with the symbolic one of the filter designed. It leads to the system of equations for unknown parameters of building blocks (usually multipliers). In the case of the direct form structures the design procedure is the simplest with respect to the canonical character of the solved filter. The general solution of design formulas for the uncanonical structures is not so simple and usually requires any auxiliary tool.

  Design of the IIR filters usually starts from the prewarped continuous-time transfer function $H(s)$, obtained using approximation procedure. Here the necessary $H(s) \rightarrow H(z)$ transformation can be integrated with the designed filter parameters computation, similarly to the design of analogue sampled-data filters. Especially for the 2nd-order partial transfer functions it is easy to derive the direct formulas based on $H(s)$ parameters ω_0 and Q. The use for cascade realization of the higher-order digital filters is evident.

- *Sensitivity properties computations.*

  The relevance of sensitivity computation in digital filter design can be more obvious, if we are aware of the correspondence between rounding errors in "digital area" and tolerances of element values in the "continuous-time area". Therein the sensitivities represent the measure for possible rounding without loss of the accuracy of the filter frequency response.

- *Optimization with respect to the building blocks parameter values spread, dynamics and sensitivity properties.*

  The dynamics optimization is important with respect to the data-overflow. The optimization is based on the partial transfer maxims comparison and their equalization with respect to the "main" transfer maximum. The optimization procedure can be supported by symbolic partial transfers computation and the critical parameter finding. As proved, symbolic analysis is the excellent tool for complex optimization solving all the mentioned criteria.

6.3 Examples

The usage of the extended library is demonstrated on the analysis of some typical examples of digital filters, represented by block diagrams. Note that the obtained transfer functions $H(z)$ can be easily post-processed in MAPLE environment and used for the optimized design of the simulated systems.

The simplest example of symbolic analysis seems to be the 2nd-order digital filter direct form II. structure. The block diagram is shown in Fig. 23 and the SYRUP data file in the Fig. 24.

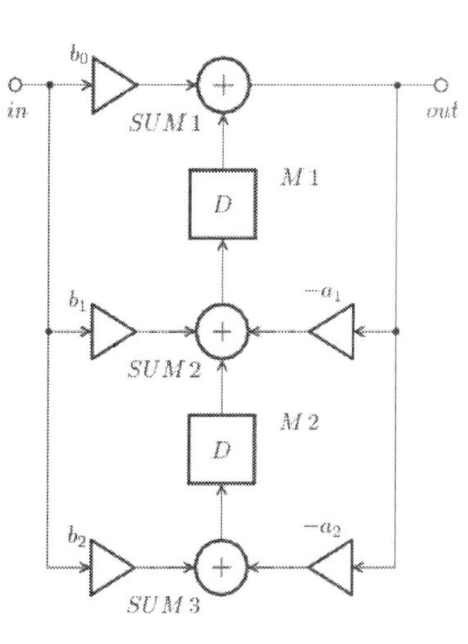

$$HK2 := \frac{b0\,z^2 + b1\,z + b2}{z^2 + a1\,z + a2}$$

Fig. 23. The 2nd-order direct form II.

```
> obvod5:=  "
> Vn    1  0
> XS1   3  1   7  0 SUM(A=1)
> XS2   7  6  11  0 SUM(A=1)
> XM1   5  3   0    MEM
> XM2  10  5   0    MEM
> Ea1   6  0   5  0 -a1
> Ea2  11  0  10  0 -a2
> Eb0   4  0   3  0  b0
> Eb1   8  0   5  0  b1
> XS3   9 12   8  0 SUM(A=1)
> Eb2  12  0  10  0  b2
> XS4   2  4   9  0 SUM(A=1)
> .subckt SUM out a b c
> Vd out 0
A*(v[a]+v[b]+v[c])
> .ends
> .subckt MEM out a b
> Vg out 0 (v[a]+v[b])/z
> .ends
> .end ":
```

Fig. 24. Data-file SYRUP

The presented structure does not require any special procedure for design formulas. On the other hand, it could be interesting to analyze the sensitivity properties.

The obtained expressions are suitable for the estimation of the "starting continuous-time parameters" influence to the digital filter parameters changes. As an example, the following graph in Fig. 25 illustrates the $S^Q_{a_1,a_2}$ sensitivity dependence on the Q-factor, when the ratio $x_c = \frac{f_c}{\omega_0}$ is set to $x_c = 5$. The graph in Fig. 26 presents the $S^Q_{a_1,a_2}$ sensitivities changes for fixed $Q = 2$ and variable x_c. This graph simultaneously explains the realization problems of direct-form structures in the case of relatively high sampling frequencies f_c. Similar results were gained in the case of $S^{\omega_0}_{a_1,a_2}$ sensitivities.

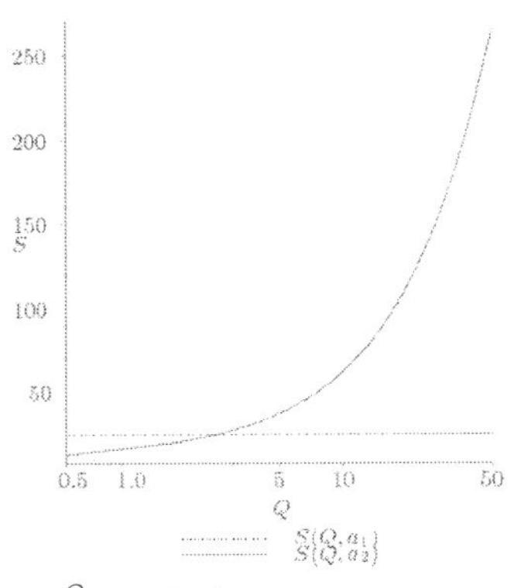

Fig. 25. $S^Q_{a_{1,2}} = f(Q)$

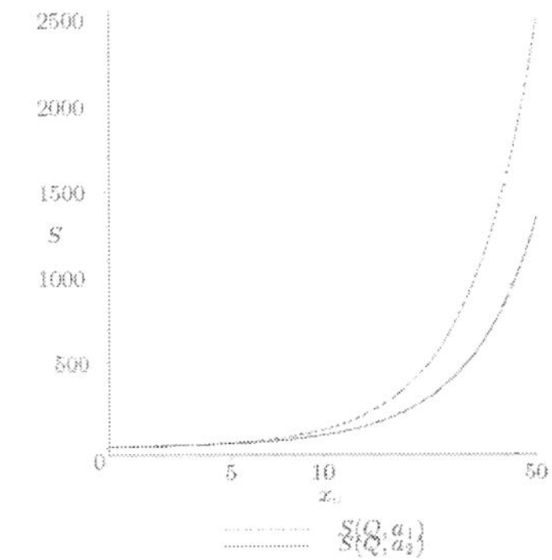

Fig. 26. $S^Q_{a_{1,2}} = f(x)$

Note that the formulas obtained are valid directly for the first and the second canonic direct form of the digital filters – see Mitra (2005), Laipert et al. (2000), Antoniou (1979) and others. For the other 2nd-order structures it is necessary to express the transfer function $H(z)$ coefficients $a_1\ a_2$ as the functions of the analyzed network parameters.

The second example presents the 2nd-order allpass filter from Mitra (2005), based on lattice structure. The block diagram is showed in Fig. 27 and the computed symbolic transfer function in Fig. 28.

The following computations show better sensitivities of the analyzed filter in comparison to the direct-form structure; the symbolic expressions for the $S^Q_{k_1,k_2}$ and $S^{\omega_0}_{k_1,k_2}$ sensitivities were computed in the form

$$S^{\omega_0}_{k_1} = -\frac{k_1}{k_1^2 - 1}; \qquad S^Q_{k_1} = \frac{k_1^2}{k_1^2 - 1}; \tag{43}$$

$$S^{\omega_0}_{k_2} = 0; \qquad S^Q_{k_2} = -\frac{2k_2}{k_2^2 - 1}. \tag{44}$$

The numerical values for $\omega_0 = 2\pi * 1000$, $Q = 2$ and $x = 5$ are $S^Q_{k_1} = -24.50245745$, $S^Q_{k_2} = 10.07523914$ and $S^{\omega_0}_{k_1} = -24.99745744$.

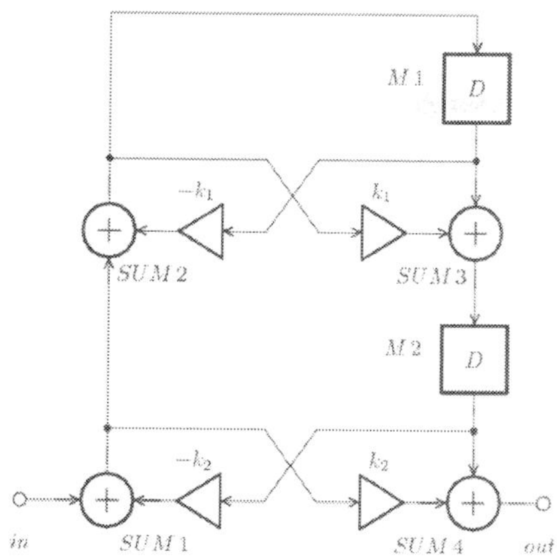

Fig. 27. The 2nd-order all-pass.

```
>   A9:= syrup(obvod9,ac):
>   assign(A9):
>   H9:= collect(v[11]/v[1],
>   z,factor);
```

$$H9 := \frac{k_2\,z^2 + k_1\,(k_2+1)\,z + 1}{z^2 + k_1\,(k_2+1)\,z + k_2}$$

Fig. 28. The all-pass simulation result.

The third example introduces state-space structure from Mitra (2005) whose block diagram is in Fig. 29. This structure contains 9 unknown parameters, which represents 4 freedom degrees in design conditions. Symbolic transfer function is expressed by Eqs.(45)–(47)

$$H_{14} = \frac{NH_{14}}{DH_{14}} \tag{45}$$

where

$$NH_{14} = d\,z^2 + (c_1\,b_1 + c_2\,b_2 - d\,(a_{22}+a_{11}))\,z + d\,\Delta + (-c_1\,a_{22} + c_2\,a_{21})\,b_1 + (c_1\,a_{12} - c_2\,a_{11})\,b_2 \tag{46}$$

$$DH_{14} = z^2 - (a_{22}+a_{11})\,z + \Delta; \qquad \Delta = a_{11}\,a_{22} - a_{12}\,a_{21}. \tag{47}$$

The design conditions can be solved directly in the z-plane, or, after transformation to the s-plane. In this case, the transformed denominator receives the form (48)

$$DH_{14s} = s^2 + \frac{4\,(1-\Delta)\,s}{T\,(1+a_{11}+a_{22}+\Delta)} + \frac{4\,(1-a_{22}+\Delta-a_{11})}{T^2\,(1+a_{11}+a_{22}+\Delta)} \tag{48}$$

A comparison of Eq. (48) to the denominator of the standard form of $H(s)$ (16) allows easily to solve the expressions for ω_{0eq} and Q_{eq} parameters. Free parameters then are chosen with respect to the prescribed optimization criteria.

Similarly the other digital filters or their parts were analyzed as well; e.g. SFG-based 2nd-order sections, published in Tichá (2006), equalizers for audio-signal processing, or a tunable 2nd-order bandpass/bandstop filter structure. All the solved structures were evaluated with the excellent results and MAPLE environment was found as fully acceptable and sufficiently flexible for the required post-processing of the results obtained.

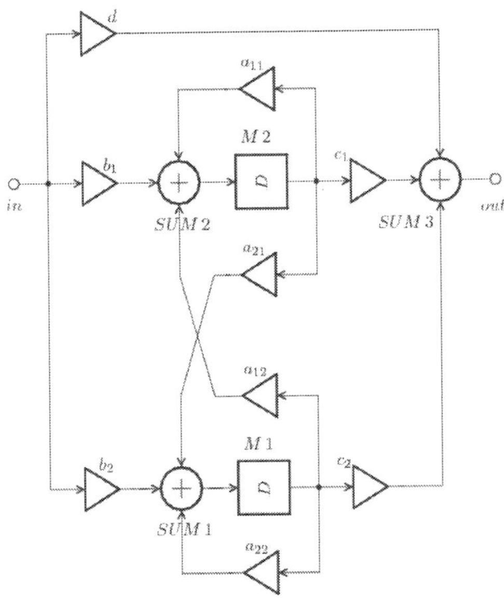

Fig. 29. The general state-space structure.

7. An example of digital filter design

7.1 Introduction

Digital filter design, especially based on cascade connection of the 2nd-order sections usually does not bring problems. But, in the case of non-standard operating conditions, e.g. too high ratio of the sampling-frequency-to-cut-off-filter-frequency, the "standard" direct-form structures fail to satisfy the given requirements. Here the usage of more sophisticated filter sections could be the possible solution. Nevertheless, such structures require more demanding design with respect to the inherency of free design parameters. The two-integrator based sections or state-space biquads introduced in Laipert et al. (2000), Antoniou (1979) or Mitra (2005) should serve as the examples. The design of such sections needs more complex approach, respecting not only the "basic" requirements, but also dynamics, sensitivity, building blocks parameters spread and others.

An efficient design of such filters should be based either on an rigorous mathematical description of the main parameters, or an effective global optimization procedure. This section describes the second way, where the Differential Evolutionary Algorithms were used as the powerful design tool. The reason is in good experience with DE algorithms usage in analog filter optimized design.

The method used is explained on a practical example of state-space 2nd-order IIR section design procedure. The DE algorithms were implemented in MAPLE mathematical program, allowing symbolical computations. Design includes the "basic" computation of the main filter parameters and multi-criteria optimization covering sensitivity properties, dynamics and partial blocks parameter spread. To accelerate necessary computations, filter transfer function, sensitivity expressions and other parameters were preprocessed in symbolic form using

SYRUP library. The symbolic analysis of digital filters using SYRUP was described in Tichá & Martinek (2007), sensitivity computations use the "equivalent sensitivity" approach presented at the last DT Workshop Tichá (2006).

7.2 Design conditions

Let us start by remembering the basic principle of biquad design. It is based on a comparison of a given transfer function $H(z)$ coefficients to the symbolically expressed coefficients of the designed circuit transfer function $H_s(z)$. The comparison leads to the system of design equations for unknown filter component values. Considering "standard" $H(z)$ notation in the form (49)

$$H(z) = \frac{NH(z)}{DH(z)} = \frac{n_2\, z^2 + n_1\, z + n_0}{z^2 + d_1\, z + d_0}\,, \tag{49}$$

$$H_s(z) = (d\, z^2 + (c_1\, b_1 + c_2\, b_2 - d\,(a_{11} + a_{22}))\, z + d\,(a_{11}\, a_{22} - a_{21}\, a_{12}) - c_2\, a_{11}\, b_2$$
$$- c_1\, a_{22}\, b_1 + c_1\, b_2\, a_{12} + c_2\, a_{21}\, b_1) / (z^2 - (a_{11} + a_{22})\, z + a_{11}\, a_{22} - a_{21}\, a_{12}) \tag{50}$$

five equations for unknown filter component parameters are necessary. Provided that the filter structure is canonical, the solution of the design equations system is unique for five multiplier constants. If it be to the contrary, we have some freedom parameters on disposal which usually influence filter sensitivity properties, dynamic behavior and component values spread and can be set independently. They are suitable for the filter design optimization.

As mentioned, the complex design respecting all the additional optimization criteria is hardly solved by rigorous mathematical procedure. An application of the global optimization algorithms, in our case the differential evolutionary algorithm (DEA) was found to be simpler and more efficient way. Its usage is demonstrated on the example of the state-space biquad described in Mitra (2005), whose block diagram is shown in Fig. 29.

Symbolical analysis of the filter block diagram was performed in the previous Section 6 and the resulting transfer function is expressed in the Eqs. (45) - to - (48). It contains 9 unknown component parameters, which represent 4 freedom degrees in design conditions. It means, all the additional optimization criteria can be taken into account.

A "basic" design

is usually solved either directly by comparison of the corresponding coefficients of the given $H(z)$ and the symbolical $H_s(z)$ under (50) in the z-plane, or after $z \Leftrightarrow s$ transformation of the $H_s(z)$ to s-plane, similarly to the sampled-data biquad design procedure. Note that both ways are possible in MAPLE program environment, but the first is preferred with respect to the simpler design equations. In contrast to the mentioned procedures, the application of DE algorithm does not require creation of the design equations.

Sensitivity optimization

is based on equivalent ω_0 and Q sensitivities, discussed in Section 5.

Filter dynamics optimization

serves for equalization of the signal maxims inside filter structure. The critical points are usually inputs or outputs of delay elements and outputs of the summers and multipliers. In the case of the solved state-space biquad the outputs of delay elements D were considered.

Optimization requires an evaluation of partial transfers from filter input to the considered block outputs and their maximum magnitude. As sufficient was found to test partial transfer magnitudes at frequency corresponding to ω_{0eq} and their comparison to the "full" transfer magnitude value.

7.3 Algorithm used

Differential Evolutionary Algorithms applied previously in solution of the analog filter design presented e.g. in Tichá & Martinek (2005) were successfully used in the described tasks as well. To improve computation efficiency, a convergence accelerator using simplex built-in procedure was used. Objective function is critical for the optimum design and it was defined as follows

$$fit = w_e \sum_{i=0}^{5} \delta_i^2 + w_p \frac{m_{max}}{m_{min}} + w_s\,PPs + w_d\,PPd, \tag{51}$$

where δ_i means transfer function coefficient relative errors, PPs represents penalty function for sensitivity optimization defined as

$$PPs = \sum_{i=1}^{4} |S_{m_i}^{\omega_{0eq}}| + \sum_{i=1}^{4} |S_{m_i}^{Q_{eq}}|, \tag{52}$$

and PPd represents dynamics error

$$PPd = \sum_{i=1}^{2} \frac{max|(H(j\omega))|}{max|(H_{Di}(j\omega))|} - 1. \tag{53}$$

Parameters w_e, w_p, w_s and w_d characterize weights of objective function components.

7.4 Results

The described optimized design procedure was tested for more examples of biquadratic functions under different operating conditions. As the first example the band-pass section with equivalent parameters $f_0 = 1\,kHz$, $Q_{eq} = 5$, gain constant $h = 1$ and sampling frequency $f_c = 48\,kHz$ is introduced.

Design was made with respect to the sensitivity and building block parameters minimization, without other limitations. No free parameters were numerically defined.

The design results are:

$a_{11} = 0.9787125$, $a_{12} = -0.0564576$, $a_{21} = 0.290288$, $a_{22} = 0.9787125$, $b_1 = 0.0762136$, $b_2 = -0.1492225$, $c_1 = 0.150311$, $c_2 = -0.0917967$, $d = 0.0136064$.

Parameter values spread $\frac{m_{max}}{m_{min}} = 71.93$ and sensitivity values

$S_{a_{11}}^{\omega_0} = S_{a_{22}}^{\omega_0} = -0.8648$, $S_{a_{12}}^{\omega_0} = S_{a_{21}}^{\omega_0} = 0.4845$ $S_{a_{11}}^{Q} = S_{a_{22}}^{Q} = 36.85$, $S_{a_{12}}^{Q} = S_{a_{21}}^{Q} = 1.126$.

Transfer function coefficient errors were typically $\delta_i \approx 10^{-7}$.

DE algorithm parameters: Number of members in population typically $NP = 90 - 120$, control parameters $CR = 0.75$, $F = 0.8$. The results were obtained after approximately $100 - 200$ generations (iteration cycles).

It is important to say, similar other results were gained as well, with respect to more free parameters.

The second example concerns LP section design with similar parameters to the previous example: $f_0 = 1\,kHz$, $Q_{eq} = 5$, gain constant $h = 1$ and sampling frequency $f_c = 48\,kHz$. Here the dynamics optimization was preferred (of course with respect to the previously defined).

The design results are:
$a_{11} = 0.962724$, $a_{12} = 0.0892054$, $a_{21} = -0.186585$, $a_{22} = 0.994701$, $b_1 = 0.0442087e - 1$, $b_2 = -0.116697$, $c_1 = -0.994701$, $c_2 = -0.517322$, $d = 0.0120655e - 1$.
Parameter values spread $\frac{m_{max}}{m_{min}} = 82.44$ and sensitivity values
$S_{a_{11}}^{\omega_0} = -0.3957$, $S_{a_{22}}^{\omega_0} = -1.349$, $S_{a_{12}}^{\omega_0} = S_{a_{21}}^{\omega_0} = 0.4920$ $S_{a_{11}}^{Q} = 37.31$, $S_{a_{22}}^{Q} = 36.36$, $S_{a_{12}}^{Q} = S_{a_{21}}^{Q} = 1.143$.
Transfer function coefficient errors were similarly to the previous example typically $\delta_i \approx 10^{-7}$. Filter dynamic behavior optimization gives all the partial frequency responses approximately equal with maximum error $\leq 1.8\,\mathrm{dB}$.

8. Conclusions

This chapter introduces some "non-standard" views to the sampled-data and digital filter properties and design. The main goals can be formulated as follows:
As shown, the digital filter direct form prototype can serve for a wider area of implementations. Comparing the implementation using SI memory cells to the modified ones based on simple BD or FD integrators and differentiators, the "exact" implementation shows problems with higher sensitivities and parameter values spread. On the other hand, an influence of SI-blocks parasitics is lower, especially the output conductances g_o cause less frequency shifts and can be respected in design procedure. One possible improvement would be to insert some free parameters into this circuit, e.g. optional gain of the memory cells, but this is a topic for further research.
Sensitivity concept and symbolic analysis are efficient tools for digital filter design, especially when "non-standard" design conditions are required. As shown, the equivalent sensitivity principle allows the appropriate selection of filter structure and, after re-computation, to check the acceptable word-length and ω_{0eq} to f_c ratio.
A new application area of the MAPLE program and its library SYRUP has been introduced. In contrast to the commonly used programs for digital filter design, the presented approach offers wider possibility in filter properties analysis and the evaluated results post-processing. The last section aims at presenting new ways in "complex" design of digital and analog filters using stochastic algorithms. As shown, especially Differential Evolutionary Algorithms are very suitable tool for this purpose and give excellent results in multi-criteria design. Their use in digital filter design presented here is rather demonstrative, more complicated tasks can be successfully solved. The new in this approach is the conjoined application of more design criteria and possibility to prefer such criterion which is more important in particular design. The design procedure is implemented in mathematical program and this allows its easy modification and/or post-processing of the gained results if necessary.

Acknowledgment
This work has been supported by the research program "Research in the Area of the Prospective Information and Navigation Technologies" No. MSM6840770014 of the Czech Technical University in Prague.

9. References

Antoniou, R., (1979) *Digital Filters: Analysis and Design*. McGraw-Hill, New York, 1979.

Bičák, J.; Hospodka, J. & Martinek, P. (2001). Analysis of SI Circuits in MAPLE Program. *Proceedings of ECCTD'01*, Helsinki: Helsinki University of Technology, 2001, vol. 3, pp. 121-124, ISBN 951-22-5572-3.

Bičák, J. & Hospodka, J. (2006) Symbolic Analysis of Periodically Switched Linear Circuits. *SMACDť'06 - Proceedings of the IX. International Workshop on Symbolic Methods and Applications to Circuit Design* [CD-ROM]. Firenze: Universita degli Studi, 2006, vol. 1, ISBN 88-8453-509-3.

Kurth, C. F. & Moschytz, G. S. (1979). Nodal analysis of switched-capacitor networks. *IEEE Transaction on CAS*, Vol. 26, No. 2, February 1979, pp. 93-104.

Laipert, M.; Davídek, V.; Vlček M. (2000) *Analogové a číslicové filtry*. Vydavatelství ČVUT, Praha, 2000.

Martinek P.; Boreš P.; Hospodka J. (2003) *Elektrické filtry* [In Czech], Vydavatelství ČVUT, Praha, 2003, ISBN 80-01-02765-1

Martinek, P. & Tichá, D. (2007) SI-Biquad based on Direct-Form Digital Filters. *Proceedings of 2007 European Conference on Circuit Theory and Design*, Piscataway: IEEE, 2007, vol.1, p.432-435. ISBN 1-4244-1342-7.

Mitra, S. K. (2005) *Digital Signal Processing*. McGraw-Hill, New York, 2005, ISBN 0-07304-837-2.

Mucha, I., (1999) Ultra Low Voltage Class AB Switched Current Memory Cells Based on Floating Gate Transistors. *Analog Integrated Circuits and Signal Processing*, Vol.20, No.1, July 1999, pp. 43-62.

Riel, J. (2007) SYRUP – Symbolic circuit analyzer for MAPLE URL:*http://www.mapleapps.com*, March 2007.

Šubrt, O. (2003) A Versatile Structure of S3I-GGA-casc Switched-Current Memory Cell with Complex Suppression of Memorizing Errors, *Proc. IEEE Conf. ESSCIRC 2003*, Estoril, Portugal, pp. 587-590, 2003 ISBN 0-7803-7996-9.

Tichá, D. (2006) A sensitivity approach in digital filter design. *Proceedings of the Digital Technologies 2006 International Workshop*. University of Žilina, Žilina, Slovak Republic, November 2006.

Tichá, D. & Martinek, P. (2007) MAPLE Program as a Tool for Symbolic Analysis of Digital Filters. *Proceedings of the 17th International Conference Radioelektronika 07*, Brno, Czech Republic, 2007, pp.29-33. ISBN 1-4244-0821-0

Tichá, D. & Martinek, P. (2005) OTA-C Lowpass Design Using Evolutionary Algorithms. *Proc. of 2005 European Conference on Circuit Theory and Design*, University College Cork, Cork, 2005, Vol. 2, s. 197-200. ISBN 0-7803-9066-0

Toumazou, C.; Hughes, J. B. & Battersby, N. C. (1993). *SWITCHED-CURRENTS an analogue technique for digital technology*, Peter Peregrinus Ltd., London 1993, ISBN 0-86341-294-7.

Toumazou, C.; Battersby, N. C.; Porta S. (1996). *Circuits and Systems Tutorials* IEEE Press, Piscataway, 1996, ISBN 0-7803-1170-1.

Yuan, F. & Opal, A. (2003). Computer Methods for Switched Circuits. *IEEE Transactions on CAS I*, Vol. 50, pp. 1013-1024, Aug. 2003.

5

New Design Methods for Two-Dimensional Filters Based on 1D Prototypes and Spectral Transformations

Radu Matei
Technical University "Gh.Asachi" of Iasi
Romania

1. Introduction

The field of two-dimensional filters and their design methods have been approached by many researchers, for more than three decades (Lim, 1990; Lu & Antoniou, 1992). A commonly-used design technique for 2D filters is to start from a specified 1D prototype filter and transform its transfer function using various frequency mappings in order to obtain a 2D filter with a desired frequency response. These are essentially spectral transformations from s to z plane via bilinear or Euler transformations followed by z to (z_1, z_2) mappings, approached in early reference papers (Pendergrass et al., 1976; Hirano & Aggarwal, 1978; Harn & Shenoi, 1986). Generally these spectral transformations conserve stability, so from 1D prototypes various stable recursive 2D filters can be obtained.

There are several classes of filters with orientation-selective frequency response, useful in some image processing tasks, such as edge detection, motion analysis etc. An important class are the steerable filters, synthesized as a linear combination of a set of basis filters (Freeman & Adelson, 1991). Another important category are Gabor filters, with applications in some complex tasks in image processing. A major reference on oriented filters is (Chang & Aggarwal, 1977), where a technique for rotating the frequency response of separable filters is developed. The proposed method considers transfer functions in rational powers of z and realized by input-output signal array interpolations. Anisotropic, in particular elliptically-shaped filters have also been studied extensively and are used in some interesting applications, e.g. in remote sensing for directional smoothing applied to weather images (Lakshmanan, 2004), also in texture segmentation and pattern recognition. Other directionally selective operators are proposed in (Danielsson, 1980).

Another particular class are the wedge filters, named so due to their symmetric wedge-like shape in the frequency plane. They find interesting applications, e.g. in texture classification (Randen & Husoy, 1999). In (Simoncelli & Farid, 1996) the steerable wedge filters were introduced, which are used to analyze local orientation patterns in images.

Linear filter banks of various shapes, combined with pattern recognition techniques have been widely used in image analysis and enhancement, texture segmentation etc. In particular, directional filter banks provide an orientation-selective image decomposition.

The Bamberger directional filter bank (Bamberger & Smith, 1992), is a purely directional decomposition that provides excellent frequency domain selectivity with low computational complexity. This family of filter banks has been successfully used for image denoising, character recognition, image enhancement etc. Diamond filters are currently used as anti-aliasing filters for the conversion between signals sampled on the rectangular sampling grid and the quincunx sampling grid. Some design techniques, mainly for FIR diamond filters were developed (Lim & Low, 1997; Low & Lim, 1998).

Stability of the two-dimensional recursive filters is also an important issue and is more complicated than for 1D filters. For 2D filters, in general, it is quite difficult to take stability constraints into account during the stage of approximation (O'Connor, 1978). For this reason, various techniques were developed to separate the stability from the approximation problem. If the designed filter becomes unstable, some stabilization procedures are needed (Jury, 1977). Unlike 1D filters, in 2D filters the numerator can affect the filter stability and can sometimes stabilize an otherwise unstable filter.

The design methods in the frequency domain described in this chapter are also based on spectral transformations, or frequency transformations, a term more often used in text. Starting from an 1D prototype filter with a desired characteristics, for instance low-pass maximally-flat, selective low-pass or band-pass etc., some specific spectral transformations will be applied in order to obtain the 2D filter with a desired shape. Various types of 2D filters will be approached: directional selective filters, oriented wedge filters, fan filters, diamond-shaped filters etc. All these filters have already found specific applications in image processing. The general case will be approached, when we start from a 1D prototype which is a common digital filter, either maximally-flat or equiripple (Butterworth, Chebyshev, elliptic etc.) given by a transfer function in variable z, which is decomposed into a product of elementary functions of first or second order. In this case the design consists in finding the specific complex frequency transformation from the variable z to the complex plane (z_1, z_2). Once found this mapping, the 2D filter function results directly through substitution. The case of zero-phase 2D filters will be treated as well, since they are very useful in various image filtering applications due to the absence of phase distortions. This method is at the same time simple, efficient and versatile, since once found the adequate frequency transformation, it can be applied to different prototype filters obtaining the 2D filter. The latter inherits the selectivity properties of its 1D counterpart (bandwidth, flatness, transition band etc.). Changing the prototype filter parameters will change the properties of the obtained 2D filter. All the proposed design techniques are mainly analytical but also involve numerical optimization, in particular rational approximations (Padé or Chebyshev-Padé). Since the design starts from a factorized transfer function, the 2D filter function will also result directly factorized, which is a major advantage in its implementation. For each specified shape of the 2D filter, a particular frequency transformation is derived.

Some proposed methods involve the bilinear transform as an intermediate step. Depending on their shape, the designed filters may present non-linearity distortions towards the margins of the frequency plane, due to the frequency warping effect. In order to compensate for these errors, a pre-warping may be applied, which increases the filter order. Other proposed methods avoid from the start the use of bilinear transform and the filter coefficients result through a change of frequency variable and a bivariate Taylor or

Chebyshev expansion of the filter frequency response. Finally the filter transfer function in z_1 and z_2 results directly by identification of the 2D Z transform terms.

An original design method is proposed in section 5 for a class of filters specified by a periodic function expressed in polar coordinates in the frequency plane. The contour plots of their frequency response, resulted as sections with planes parallel with the frequency plane, can be defined as closed curves, described in terms of a variable radius which can be written as a rational and periodic function of the current angle formed with one of the axes. In this class of filters we studied two-lobe filters, selective four-lobe filters with an arbitrary orientation angle, fan filters and diamond filters.

Several related design methods proposed by the author for other types of 2D zero-phase filters, especially with circular and elliptical symmetry were developed in (Matei, 2009, b). In the last section of the chapter, a few applications of the designed wedge filter will be presented through simulation results.

2. 1D Prototype Filters and Spectral Transformations Used in 2D Filter Design

An essential step in designing temporal and spatial filters is the approximation. As mentioned in the above introduction, the proposed design methods for 2D recursive filters are based on 1D prototype filters with imposed specifications. For the 2D filters approached here, we start from 1D digital filters described by a transfer function $H(z)$, resulted from one of the common approximations (Butterworth, Chebyshev, elliptical etc.) and satisfying the desired specifications. Analog prototype filters with transfer functions in variable s can also be used. The choice depends on the 2D filter type, which requires a specific frequency transformation; this must be as simple as possible in order to obtain an efficient, low-order filter. On the other hand we may start from a complex or real-valued filter prototype. In the latter case zero-phase 2D filters will result, which are free of phase distortions.

Let us consider a recursive digital filter of order N with the transfer function:

$$H(z) = \frac{P(z)}{Q(z)} = \sum_{i=0}^{M} p_i \cdot z^i \bigg/ \sum_{j=0}^{N} q_j \cdot z^j \tag{1}$$

We consider this general transfer function with $M = N$ factorized into rational functions of first and second order. An odd order filter $H(z)$ has at least one first order factor:

$$H_1(z) = \left(b_1 z + b_0\right) / \left(z + a_0\right) \tag{2}$$

The transfer function also contains second-order factors referred to as biquad functions:

$$H_2(z) = \left(b_2 z^2 + b_1 z + b_0\right) / \left(z^2 + a_1 z + a_0\right) \tag{3}$$

where in general the second-order polynomials at the numerator and denominator have complex-conjugated roots. The main issue approached in this chapter is to find the transfer function of the desired 2D filter $H_{2D}(z_1, z_2)$ using appropriate frequency transformations of the form: $\omega \rightarrow F(\omega_1, \omega_2)$. The elementary transfer functions (2) and (3) can be put into the form of a complex frequency response:

$$H_1(j\omega) = (b_0 + b_1 \cos\omega + jb_1 \sin\omega)/(a_0 + \cos\omega + j\sin\omega) \tag{4}$$

$$H_2(j\omega) = \frac{b_1 + (b_2 + b_0)\cos\omega + j(b_2 - b_0)\sin\omega}{a_1 + (1 + a_0)\cos\omega + j(1 - a_0)\sin\omega} = \frac{P(\omega)}{Q(\omega)} \tag{5}$$

We notice that the first- and second-order functions have a similar form when expressed as a ratio of complex numbers. Therefore, as shown further, the corresponding 2D transfer functions will be implemented with convolution kernels of the same size. The next step starts from the expressions (4) and (5) of the frequency response and uses of the following accurate rational approximations for sine and cosine on $[-\pi, \pi]$:

$$\cos\omega \cong \frac{1 - 0.435949 \cdot \omega^2 + 0.011319 \cdot \omega^4}{1 + 0.06095 \cdot \omega^2 + 0.0037557 \cdot \omega^4} = \frac{C(\omega)}{Q(\omega)} \tag{6}$$

$$\sin\omega \cong \frac{\omega \cdot (1 - 0.101046 \cdot \omega^2)}{1 + 0.06095 \cdot \omega^2 + 0.0037557 \cdot \omega^4} = \frac{S(\omega)}{Q(\omega)} \tag{7}$$

The above expressions were obtained through a Chebyshev-Padé approximation, found using a symbolic computation software. The advantage of these expressions is that they have the same denominator and can be directly substituted into (4) and (5), yielding a rational expression of the frequency response $H(e^{j\omega})$ of the same order.

In order to design a zero-phase 2D filter, we start from zero-phase prototypes, with real-valued transfer functions. Such a filter may be obtained by finding a rational approximation of the magnitude characteristics of the given prototype. The magnitude $|H(\omega)|$ taken from

$H(z) = H(e^{j\omega})$ of the general form (1) can be approximated by a ratio of polynomials in even

powers of frequency ω, on the range $\omega \in [-\pi, \pi]$. In general this filter will be described by:

$$H_p(\omega) = \sum_{j=0}^{M} b_j \cdot \omega^{2j} \Big/ \sum_{k=0}^{N} a_k \cdot \omega^{2k} \tag{8}$$

where $M \leq N$ and N is the filter order. In (Matei, 2009, b) a different version of approximation was proposed, which using the change of variable $\omega = \arccos x \Leftrightarrow x = \cos\omega$ yields a rational approximation of $|H(\omega)|$ in the variable $\cos\omega$ on the range $\omega \in [-\pi, \pi]$:

$$|H(\omega)| \cong \sum_{n=1}^{N} b_n \cos^n \omega \Big/ \sum_{m=1}^{N} a_m \cos^m \omega \tag{9}$$

This rational trigonometric approximation is particularly useful in designing zero-phase circular or elliptically-shaped filters, approached in (Matei, 2009, b), but less efficient for other 2D filters like directional, wedge-shaped etc.

For instance, considering as 1D prototype a type-2 Chebyshev digital filter with the parameters: order $N = 4$, stopband attenuation $R_s = 40\,\text{dB}$ and passband–edge frequency $\omega_p = 0.5$, where 1.0 is half the sampling frequency, its transfer function in z has the form:

$$H(z) = \left(0.012277 \cdot z^2 - 0.012525 \cdot z + 0.012277\right)\big/\left(z^2 - 1.850147 \cdot z + 0.862316\right) \tag{10}$$

Using a Chebyshev-Padé approximation we can determine the following real-valued zero-phase frequency response which approximates accurately the magnitude of the function (10):

$$\left|H(e^{j\omega})\right| \cong H_{a1}(\omega) = \left(0.9403 - 0.57565 \cdot \omega^2 + 0.0947 \cdot \omega^4\right)\big/\left(1 - 2.067753 \cdot \omega^2 + 4.663147 \cdot \omega^4\right) \tag{11}$$

3. Directional Filters

We propose a design method for a class of 2D oriented low-pass filters which select narrow domains along specified directions in the frequency plane (ω_1, ω_2). Such filters can be used in selecting lines with a given orientation from an input image. Since we envisage to design filters of minimum order, we use IIR filters as prototypes. Here we treat the general case using a complex frequency transformation. Other related methods for directional filter design were discussed in (Matei, 2009, b).

Starting from a real-valued prototype $H(\omega_1)$, a 2D oriented filter is obtained by rotating the axes of the plane (ω_1, ω_2) with an angle φ, as described by the linear transformation:

$$\begin{bmatrix} \omega_1 \\ \omega_2 \end{bmatrix} = \begin{bmatrix} \cos\varphi & \sin\varphi \\ -\sin\varphi & \cos\varphi \end{bmatrix} \cdot \begin{bmatrix} \overline{\omega}_1 \\ \overline{\omega}_2 \end{bmatrix} \tag{12}$$

where ω_1, ω_2 are the original frequency variables and $\overline{\omega}_1, \overline{\omega}_2$ the rotated ones. The filter orientation is specified by an angle φ about ω_1-axis and is defined by the following 1D to 2D spectral transformation of the frequency response $H(\omega_1, \omega_2)$: $\omega \to \omega_1 \cos\varphi + \omega_2 \sin\varphi$. By substitution, we obtain the transfer function of the oriented filter $H_\varphi(\omega_1, \omega_2)$:

$$H_\varphi(\omega_1, \omega_2) = H(\omega_1 \cos\varphi + \omega_2 \sin\varphi) \tag{13}$$

The filter $H_\varphi(\omega_1, \omega_2)$ has the magnitude along the line $\omega_1 \cos\varphi + \omega_2 \sin\varphi = 0$ identical with the prototype $H(\omega)$ and constant along the line $\omega_1 \sin\varphi - \omega_2 \cos\varphi = 0$ (longitudinal axis). Next we will determine a convenient 1D to 2D complex transformation which allows for obtaining an oriented 2D filter from a 1D prototype filter. The special case of zero-phase directional filters was extensively treated in (Matei, 2009, b).

3.1 Design Method for 2D Directional Filters Based on Frequency Transformation

In the following section we will introduce a design method which allows one to obtain a 2D discrete orientation-selective filter. The desired filter will be derived directly from a 1D discrete prototype filter through a complex frequency transformation.

A discrete 1D filter is generally described by a transfer function $H(z)$. The complex variable $z = e^{j\omega} = e^s$ will be mapped into a 2D function $F_\varphi(z_1, z_2)$, where the index φ denotes the dependence upon the orientation angle. Using the frequency transformation (13) which defines the orientation-selective filter with the orientation angle φ, we have successively:

$$e^{j(\omega_1 \cos\varphi - \omega_2 \sin\varphi)} = e^{s_1 \cos\varphi} \cdot e^{s_2 \sin\varphi} = (z_1)^{\cos\varphi} \cdot (z_2)^{\sin\varphi} = f_1(s_1) \cdot f_2(s_2) \tag{14}$$

Therefore the complex frequency transformation is $z \to z_1^{\cos\varphi} \cdot z_2^{\sin\varphi}$. In (Chang & Aggarwal, 1977) the frequency transformation used is $z \to z_1 \cdot z_2^{\beta/\alpha}$, where α and β are integers. The rotation angle is $\varphi = \arctan(\beta/\alpha)$. Using suitable interpolation functions, an interpolated array is generated where signal values are defined on new grid points. The whole scheme requires an input and an output interpolator. For an arbitrary angle, the values of α and β may result inconveniently large, which might complicate the interpolation process.

The proposed design method gives another possible solution and is based on finding appropriate approximations for the two complex functions: $f_1(s_1) = e^{s_1 \cos\varphi}$, $f_2(s_2) = e^{s_2 \sin\varphi}$. These can be developed either in a power series (Taylor) or in a rational function using the Padé or Chebyshev-Padé approximations. We will first use the Padé approximation which has the advantage of yielding analytical expressions for the coefficients. We easily derive the following approximations, as for real variable functions:

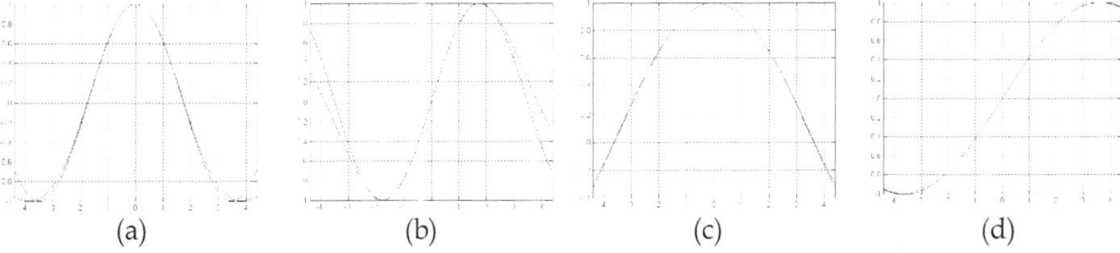

(a)   (b)   (c)   (d)

Fig. 1. Plots of exact functions vs. their approximations: (a) $\cos(\omega_1 \cos\varphi)$; (b) $\sin(\omega_1 \cos\varphi)$; (c) $\cos(\omega_1 \sin\varphi)$; (d) $\sin(\omega_1 \sin\varphi)$

$$f_1(s_1) \cong \left(1 + 0.5\cos\varphi \cdot s_1 + 0.08333\cos^2\varphi \cdot s_1^2\right) / \left(1 - 0.5\cos\varphi \cdot s_1 + 0.08333\cos^2\varphi \cdot s_1^2\right) = f_{a1}(s_1)$$
$$f_2(s_2) \cong \left(1 + 0.5\sin\varphi \cdot s_2 + 0.08333\sin^2\varphi \cdot s_2^2\right) / \left(1 - 0.5\sin\varphi \cdot s_2 + 0.08333\sin^2\varphi \cdot s_2^2\right) = f_{a2}(s_2) \tag{15}$$

Since $f_1(s_1)$ and $f_2(s_2)$ are complex functions ($s_1 = j\omega_1$, $s_2 = j\omega_2$), the above approximations must hold separately for the real and imaginary parts, for instance:

$$\mathrm{Re}\left[f_1(j\omega_1)\right] = \cos(\omega_1 \cos\varphi) \cong \mathrm{Re}\left[f_{a1}(j\omega_1)\right] \qquad \mathrm{Im}\left[f_1(j\omega_1)\right] = \sin(\omega_1 \cos\varphi) \cong \mathrm{Im}\left[f_{a1}(j\omega_1)\right] \tag{16}$$

In Fig.1 we plotted comparatively the real and imaginary parts of the two complex functions $f_1(s_1)$, $f_2(s_2)$ and of their rational approximations $f_{a1}(s_1)$, $f_{a2}(s_2)$ given in (15). We notice that the proposed approximations are very accurate in the range $[-\pi, \pi]$.

As shown in the following section, even using this low-order approximation a very good orientation-selective filter can be obtained. From the functions $f_1(s_1)$ and $f_2(s_2)$ we derive two corresponding discrete functions in the complex variables z_1, z_2. This can be achieved using the bilinear transform, a first-order approximation of the natural logarithm function. The sample interval can be taken $T = 1$ so the bilinear transform is $s = 2(z-1)/(z+1)$. Substituting it into relations (15), we obtain:

$$F_1(z_1) = \frac{(1 - \sin\varphi + 0.4\sin^2\varphi)\cdot z_1^{-1} + (2 - 0.8\sin^2\varphi) + (1 + \sin\varphi + 0.4\sin^2\varphi)\cdot z_1}{(1 + \sin\varphi + 0.4\sin^2\varphi)\cdot z_1^{-1} + (2 - 0.8\sin^2\varphi) + (1 - \sin\varphi + 0.4\sin^2\varphi)\cdot z_1} = \frac{B_1(z_1)}{A_1(z_1)} \qquad (17)$$

$$F_2(z_2) = \frac{(1 - \cos\varphi + 0.4\cos^2\varphi)\cdot z_2^{-1} + (2 - 0.8\cos^2\varphi) + (1 + \cos\varphi + 0.4\cos^2\varphi)\cdot z_2}{(1 + \cos\varphi + 0.4\cos^2\varphi)\cdot z_2^{-1} + (2 - 0.8\cos^2\varphi) + (1 - \cos\varphi + 0.4\cos^2\varphi)\cdot z_2} = \frac{B_2(z_2)}{A_2(z_2)} \qquad (18)$$

We used both negative and positive powers of z_1 and z_2 to put in evidence the coefficients symmetry. The function denoted $F_\varphi(z_1,z_2)$ will thus be the product of the above functions:

$$F_\varphi(z_1,z_2) = F_1(z_1)\cdot F_2(z_2) = B_\varphi(z_1,z_2)/A_\varphi(z_1,z_2) \qquad (19)$$

where $B_\varphi(z_1,z_2) = B_1(z_1)\cdot B_2(z_2)$ and $A_\varphi(z_1,z_2) = A_1(z_1)\cdot A_2(z_2)$.

An important remark here is that the derived frequency transformation is *separable*, as shows relation (19). Separability is a very desirable property of the 2D filter functions. However, the designed 2D oriented filters may not preserve this useful property.

Let $\mathbf{B}_1$, $\mathbf{B}_2$, $\mathbf{A}_1$, $\mathbf{A}_2$ be the coefficient vectors corresponding to $B_1(z_1)$, $B_2(z_2)$, $A_1(z_1)$, $A_2(z_2)$, identified from (17), (18) and $\mathbf{B}_\varphi$, $\mathbf{A}_\varphi$ the 3×3 matrices corresponding to $B_\varphi(z_1,z_2)$, $A_\varphi(z_1,z_2)$. The matrices $\mathbf{B}_\varphi$ and $\mathbf{A}_\varphi$ of size 3×3 result as: $\mathbf{B}_\varphi = \mathbf{B}_1^T \otimes \mathbf{B}_2$, $\mathbf{A}_\varphi = \mathbf{A}_1^T \otimes \mathbf{A}_2$, where the upper index T denotes transposition and the symbol $\otimes$ outer product of vectors. The frequency transformation $z \rightarrow F_\varphi(z_1,z_2)$ can be finally expressed in the matrix form:

$$z \rightarrow F_\varphi(z_1,z_2) = \frac{\left[z_1^{-1}\ \ 1\ \ z_1\right] \times \mathbf{B}_\varphi \times \left[z_2^{-1}\ \ 1\ \ z_2\right]^T}{\left[z_1^{-1}\ \ 1\ \ z_1\right] \times \mathbf{A}_\varphi \times \left[z_2^{-1}\ \ 1\ \ z_2\right]^T} \qquad (20)$$

where $\times$ is matrix/vector product. Throughout the chapter we will use the term *template*, common in the field of cellular neural networks, referring to the coefficient matrices corresponding to the numerator and denominator of a 2D filter transfer function $H(z_1,z_2)$. We will use mainly odd-sized templates (e.g. 3×3, 5×5) which correspond to even order filters and allow for using both positive and negative powers of z_1 and z_2.

Design example:
For an orientation angle $\varphi = \pi/7$ we have $\sin\varphi = 0.43389$, $\cos\varphi = 0.90097$ and we obtain:

$$z \rightarrow F_\varphi(z_1,z_2) = \frac{(0.6414\cdot z_1^{-1} + 1.8494 + 1.5092\cdot z_1)}{(1.5092\cdot z_1^{-1} + 1.8494 + 0.6414\cdot z_1)} \cdot \frac{(0.4237\cdot z_2^{-1} + 1.3506 + 2.2257\cdot z_2)}{(2.2257\cdot z_2^{-1} + 1.3506 + 0.4237\cdot z_2)} = \frac{B_\varphi(z_1,z_2)}{A_\varphi(z_1,z_2)} \qquad (21)$$

The numerator $B_\varphi(z_1, z_2)$ and denominator $A_\varphi(z_1, z_2)$ correspond to the 3×3 templates:

$$B_\varphi = \begin{bmatrix} 0.271787 & 0.783643 & 0.639486 \\ 0.866302 & 2.497802 & 2.038312 \\ 1.427583 & 4.116139 & 3.358945 \end{bmatrix} \qquad A_\varphi = \begin{bmatrix} 3.358945 & 4.116139 & 1.427583 \\ 2.038312 & 2.497802 & 0.866302 \\ 0.639486 & 0.783643 & 0.271787 \end{bmatrix} \qquad (22)$$

It is interesting to remark that matrix B_φ can be obtained from matrix A_φ by flipping successively the rows and columns of the matrix; so the matrix B_φ is the matrix A_φ rotated by 180^0. The matrices have no symmetry, as the transfer function must result complex.

3.2 Oriented Filter Design Using an 1D Prototype

This section presents the design of an oriented filter based on an imposed 1D prototype. Let us consider a second-order digital filter with the transfer function in general form (3). Since we have found in the previous section the complex frequency transformation which leads to a 2D oriented filter from any 1D prototype transfer function in variable z:

$$z \rightarrow F_\varphi(z_1, z_2) = B_\varphi(z_1, z_2) / A_\varphi(z_1, z_2) \qquad (23)$$

we only have to make the above substitution in $H_2(z)$ given in (3) and we obtain the transfer function $H_\varphi(z_1, z_2)$ of the desired oriented filter:

$$H_\varphi(z_1, z_2) = \frac{b_2 B_\varphi^2(z_1, z_2) + b_1 A_\varphi(z_1, z_2) B_\varphi(z_1, z_2) + b_0 A_\varphi^2(z_1, z_2)}{B_\varphi^2(z_1, z_2) + a_1 A_\varphi(z_1, z_2) B_\varphi(z_1, z_2) + a_0 A_\varphi^2(z_1, z_2)} \qquad (24)$$

For a chosen prototype of higher order, we get a similar rational function in powers of $A_\varphi(z_1, z_2)$ and $B_\varphi(z_1, z_2)$. Since the 2D transfer function (24) can be also described in terms of templates B, A corresponding to its numerator and denominator, we have equivalently:

$$B = b_2 \cdot B_\varphi * B_\varphi + b_1 \cdot A_\varphi * B_\varphi + b_0 \cdot A_\varphi * A_\varphi \qquad A = B_\varphi * B_\varphi + a_1 \cdot A_\varphi * B_\varphi + a_0 \cdot A_\varphi * A_\varphi \qquad (25)$$

where $*$ denotes two-dimensional convolution. The templates A and B result of size 5×5. The 2D oriented filter transfer function can be written generally in the matrix form:

$$H_\varphi(z_1, z_2) = \left(Z_1 \times B \times Z_2^T \right) / \left(Z_1 \times A \times Z_2^T \right) \qquad (26)$$

similar to expression (20), where:

$$Z_1 = \begin{bmatrix} z_1^{-2} & z_1^{-1} & 1 & z_1 & z_1^2 \end{bmatrix}, \ Z_2 = \begin{bmatrix} z_2^{-2} & z_2^{-1} & 1 & z_2 & z_2^2 \end{bmatrix} \qquad (27)$$

Generally, the 2D filter described by the templates B and A given in (25) is not strictly separable. However, the numerator and denominator of its transfer function are sums of separable terms. Since matrix convolution and outer product of vectors are commutative operations, using (25) we can express for instance the term:

$$\mathbf{A}_{\varphi} * \mathbf{B}_{\varphi} = \left(\mathbf{A}_1^T \otimes \mathbf{A}_2\right) * \left(\mathbf{B}_1^T \otimes \mathbf{B}_2\right) = \left(\mathbf{A}_1^T * \mathbf{B}_1^T\right) \otimes \left(\mathbf{B}_2 * \mathbf{B}_2\right) = \left(\mathbf{A}_1 * \mathbf{B}_1\right)^T \otimes \left(\mathbf{A}_2 * \mathbf{B}_2\right) \qquad (28)$$

which is the outer product of two 1×5 vectors.

Design example. Next we design an oriented filter with specified parameters. We choose a very selective low-pass second-order digital filter. Let us consider an elliptic digital filter with parameters: pass-band ripple $R_p = 0.1$ dB, stop-band attenuation $R_s = 40$ dB and very low passband-edge frequency $\omega_p = 0.02$ (1.0 is half the sampling frequency). The transfer function in z for this filter is:

$$H_p(z) = \left(0.012277 \cdot z^2 - 0.012525 \cdot z + 0.012277\right) / \left(z^2 - 1.850147 \cdot z + 0.862316\right) \qquad (29)$$

The filter orientation angle is chosen $\varphi = \pi/7$. Following the procedure described above the transfer function $H_\varphi(z_1, z_2)$ results. Fig.2(a) shows the frequency response magnitude. As can be noticed, besides its central portion which looks correct, the filter also features some undesired portions located near the margins of the frequency plane. Also the characteristic tends to be distorted from the longitudinal axis near the frequency plane corners. These errors are due to the approximation errors of the functions $f_1(s_1), f_2(s_2)$ near the ends of the frequency range and the distortions caused by the bilinear transform. In principle, if Padé approximations of higher order are used for $f_1(s_1)$ and $f_2(s_2)$, the errors will be reduced, but the price paid is an increased filter complexity.

The designed filter from Fig.2(a) cannot be used in this form, since it introduces large errors. However, a satisfactory oriented filter can be obtained by applying an additional wide-band low-pass filter which eliminates the distorted portions of the frequency characteristic. Such a "window" filter may be a maximally-flat circular filter, shown in Fig.2(b) and fully designed in (Matei & Matei, 2009). Applying it we get the corrected directional filter whose frequency response and contour plot are given in Fig.2 (c) and (d).

A good oriented filter may be obtained as well using a Chebyshev-Padé approximation of the same order. For comparison, we will design again a filter with $\varphi = \pi/7$. Using MAPLE we get the following approximation for $f_1(s_1) = \exp(s_1 \cos(\pi/7))$ for $\omega \in [-\pi\sqrt{2}, \pi\sqrt{2}]$:

$$f_1(s_1) \cong \left(1.355 \cdot T(0,s_0) + 1.823 \cdot T(1,s_0) + 0.56 \cdot T(2,s_0)\right) / \left(T(0,s_0) - 1.184 \cdot T(1,s_0) + 0.256 \cdot T(2,s_0)\right) \qquad (30)$$

where $T(n,s_0)$ is a Chebyshev polynomial of order n and $s_0 = \left(1/\pi\sqrt{2}\right) \cdot s = 0.22727 \cdot s$. Substituting the expressions of the Chebyshev polynomials into (30), we get immediately:

$$f_1(s_1) \cong \left(1.0714 + 0.55723 \cdot s_1 + 0.77598 \cdot s_1^2\right) / \left(1 - 0.362 \cdot s_1 + 0.035613 \cdot s_1^2\right) \qquad (31)$$

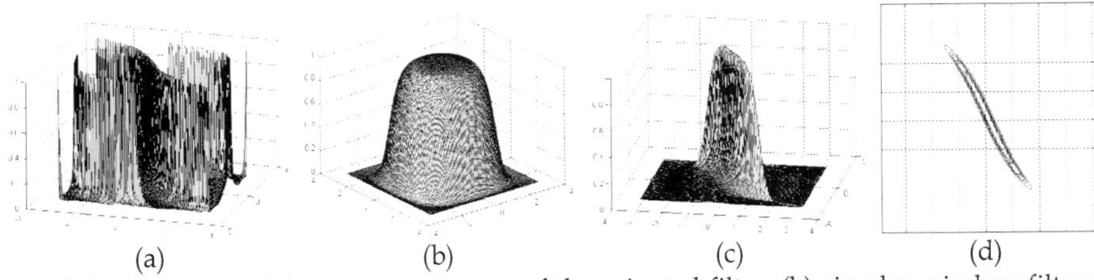

(a)   (b)   (c)   (d)

Fig. 2. (a) Uncorrected frequency response of the oriented filter; (b) circular window filter; (c) corrected filter frequency response; (d) contour plot

As before, in order to obtain a discrete approximation of $f_1(s_1)$, we use the bilinear transform and replace $s_1 = 2(z_1 - 1)/(z_1 + 1)$ in (31); we obtain the rational function:

$$F_1(z_1) = B_1(z_1)/A_1(z_1) = \left(0.1559 \cdot z_1^{-1} + 0.8874 + 1.4555 \cdot z_1\right)\Big/\left(1.0885 \cdot z_1^{-1} + 1 + 0.244 \cdot z_1\right) \quad (32)$$

Similarly we get for $f_2(s_2) = \exp\left(s_2 \sin(\pi/7)\right)$:

$$f_2(s_2) \cong \left(1 + 0.224155 \cdot s_2 + 0.015953 \cdot s_2^2\right)\Big/\left(1 - 0.208336 \cdot s_2 + 0.013297 \cdot s_2^2\right) \quad (33)$$

$$F_2(z_2) = B_2(z_2)/A_2(z_2) = \left(0.3259 \cdot z_2^{-1} + 0.9906 + 0.7994 \cdot z_2\right)\Big/\left(0.7762 \cdot z_2^{-1} + 1 + 0.3361 \cdot z_2\right) \quad (34)$$

We finally obtained the desired separable complex frequency transformation expressed as:

$$z \rightarrow F_\varphi(z_1, z_2) = F_1(z_1) \cdot F_2(z_2) \quad (35)$$

We denote $\mathbf{B}_1$, $\mathbf{B}_2$, $\mathbf{A}_1$, $\mathbf{A}_2$ the coefficient vectors corresponding to the numerators and denominators in (32) and (34). For instance we get from (32): $\mathbf{B}_1 = [0.1559 \quad 0.8874 \quad 1.4555]$. The matrices $\mathbf{B}_\varphi$, $\mathbf{A}_\varphi$ result as shown in section 3.1.

Design example

For comparison we have used the same prototype filter given by (29). The frequency response $H_\varphi(z_1, z_2)$ results using (24); its magnitude from two views is shown in Fig.3(a), (b) and shows less parasitic portions as compared to the filter in Fig.2(a). Applying the same circular window filter, the characteristic is improved, as shown in Fig.3 (c),

The only drawback of the Chebyshev-Padé method is that, unlike Padé, cannot yield literal coefficient expressions in φ as in (17), (18). Therefore, for each specified angle, the complex frequency transform $z \rightarrow F_\varphi(z_1, z_2)$ has to be calculated numerically.

The *stability* properties of this class of 2D IIR filters have still to be investigated. However, according to a theorem (Harn & Shenoi, 1986), if $H(Z)$ is a stable 1D recursive filter and $Z = F_\varphi(z_1, z_2) = F_1(z_1) \cdot F_2(z_2)$, where $F_1(z_1)$ and $F_2(z_2)$ are two stable DST (digital spectral transformation) functions, then $H\left(F_1(z_1) \cdot F_2(z_2)\right)$ is also stable in the (z_1, z_2) plane. The problem reduces to studying the stability of functions $F_1(z_1)$, $F_2(z_2)$ of the form (17), (18).

Here we approached the design of selective filters with a directional frequency response, but the method is more general and can be applied also to other types of prototype filters.

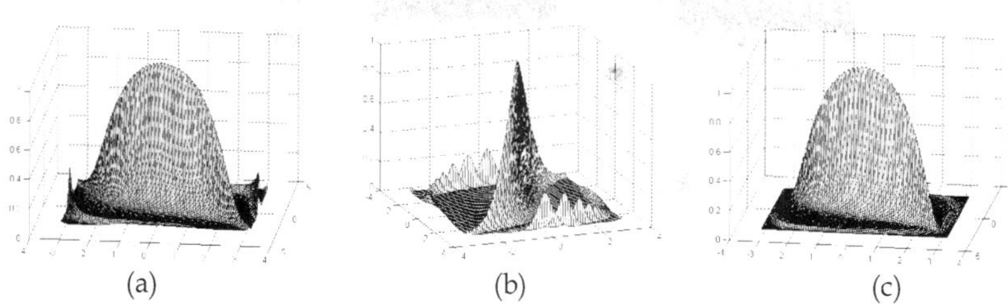

(a)   (b)   (c)

Fig. 3. (a), (b) Original oriented filter magnitude from two angles; (c) Oriented filter magnitude after applying the circular window filter

4. Wedge-Shaped Filters

Here we approach the design of a class of wedge filters in the 2D frequency domain, also treated in (Matei, 2009, a). We consider a general case of a wedge-shaped filter with a given orientation of its longitudinal axis. For design a maximally-flat 1D prototype filter will be used. We approach here only zero-phase filters, often preferred in image filtering due to the absence of phase distortions. Two ideal wedge filters in the frequency plane are shown in Fig.4. The filter in Fig.4 (a) has its frequency response along the axis ω_2. The angle $\sphericalangle AOB = \theta$ will be referred to as aperture angle. In Fig.4 (b) a more general wedge filter is shown, with aperture angle $\sphericalangle BOD = \theta$, oriented along an axis CC', forming an angle $\sphericalangle AOC = \varphi$ with frequency axis $O - \omega_2$.

The Bamberger directional filter bank (Bamberger & Smith, 1992) is an angularly oriented image decomposition that splits the 2D frequency plane into wedge-shape channels with N = 2, 4, 6, and 8 sub-bands (channels). Each sub-band captures spatial detail along a specific orientation. In Fig.5 the frequency band partitions are shown for N = 8.

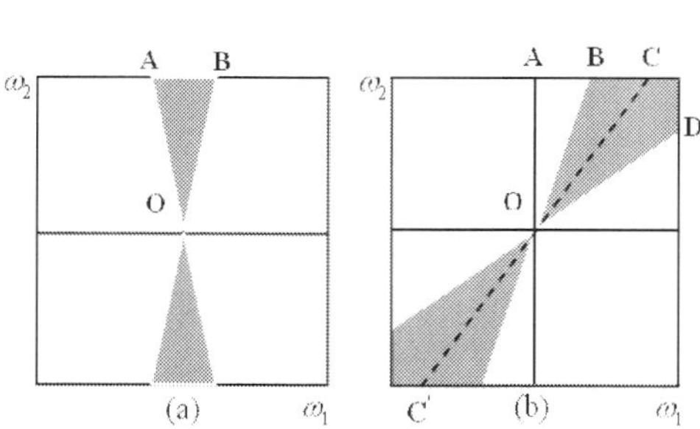

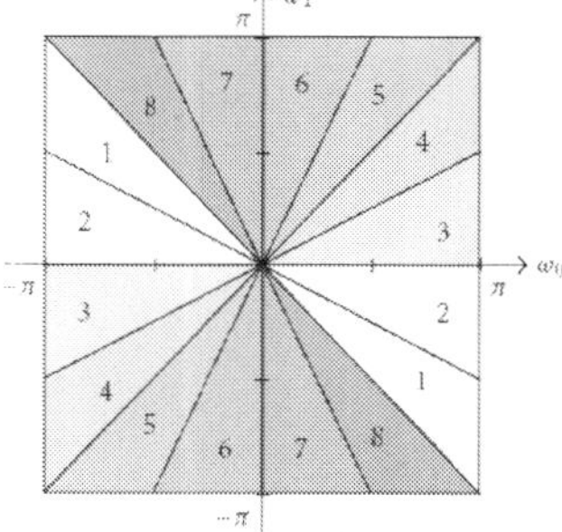

Fig. 4. Ideal wedge filters: (a) along the axis ω_2 ; (b) oriented at an angle φ

Fig. 5. 8-band partitions of the frequency plane

4.1 Wedge Filter Design Using Frequency Transformations

Next we present a design method which leads to 2D zero-phase oriented filters from 1D prototypes. Let us consider a 1D IIR zero-phase low-pass filter frequency response:

$$H_p(\omega) = \left(b_0 + b_1\omega^2 + b_2\omega^4\right)\big/\left(1 + a_1\omega^2 + a_2\omega^4\right) \qquad (36)$$

where usually $b_0 = H_p(0) = 1$, obtained as in section 2, with general expression (8). A wedge filter along frequency axis ω_2 can be obtained using the 1D to 2D frequency transformation:

$$\omega \to f(\omega_1,\omega_2) = a \cdot \omega_1/\omega_2 \quad (\text{for } \omega_2 \neq 0) \qquad (37)$$

We denoted $a = 1/tg(\theta/2)$, where θ is the aperture angle of the wedge filter, as defined in Fig.4. Replacing in (36) ω by the ratio $a\omega_1/\omega_2$, we get the frequency response in ω_1, ω_2:

$$H(\omega_1,\omega_2) = \left(b_0\omega_2^4 + b_1a^2\omega_1^2\omega_2^2 + b_2a^4\omega_1^4\right)\big/\left(\omega_2^4 + a_1a^2\omega_1^2\omega_2^2 + a_2a^4\omega_1^4\right) \qquad (38)$$

At this point we map $H(\omega_1,\omega_2)$ into the complex plane (s_1,s_2), where $s_1 = j\omega_1$, $s_2 = j\omega_2$. Since $\omega_1^2 = -s_1^2$ and $\omega_2^2 = -s_2^2$ we get the function $H_S(s_1,s_2)$:

$$H_S(s_1,s_2) = \left(b_0s_2^4 + b_1a^2s_1^2s_2^2 + b_2a^4s_1^4\right)\big/\left(s_2^4 + a_1a^2s_1^2s_2^2 + a_2a^4s_1^4\right) \qquad (39)$$

A little more difficult task is now to find a mapping of $H_S(s_1,s_2)$ into the complex plane (z_1,z_2). This can be achieved either using the forward or backward Euler approximations, or otherwise the bilinear transform, which gives better accuracy. The bilinear transform for s_1 and s_2 in the complex plane (s_1,s_2) has the form:

$$s_1 = 2(z_1-1)\big/(z_1+1) \qquad s_2 = 2(z_2-1)\big/(z_2+1) \qquad (40)$$

Substituting s_1, s_2 in (39), we find after some algebra a function in z_1, z_2 in matrix form:

$$F(z_1,z_2) = \left(\mathbf{Z}_1 \times \mathbf{B} \times \mathbf{Z}_2^T\right)\big/\left(\mathbf{Z}_1 \times \mathbf{A} \times \mathbf{Z}_2^T\right) \qquad (41)$$

where $\mathbf{Z}_1$ and $\mathbf{Z}_2$ are the vectors given by (27) and $\times$ denotes matrix/vector product. The filter templates $\mathbf{B}$ and $\mathbf{A}$ can be written as a sum of three separable matrices:

$$\begin{aligned}
\mathbf{B} &= b_0 \cdot \mathbf{M}_1^T * \mathbf{M}_2 + b_1a^2 \cdot \mathbf{M}_3^T * \mathbf{M}_3 + b_2a^4 \cdot \mathbf{M}_2^T * \mathbf{M}_1 \\
\mathbf{A} &= \mathbf{M}_1^T * \mathbf{M}_2 + a_1a^2 \cdot \mathbf{M}_3^T * \mathbf{M}_3 + a_2a^4 \cdot \mathbf{M}_2^T * \mathbf{M}_1
\end{aligned} \qquad (42)$$

where $\mathbf{M}_1$, $\mathbf{M}_2$ and $\mathbf{M}_3$ are row vectors: $\mathbf{M}_1 = \begin{bmatrix} 1 & 4 & 6 & 4 & 1 \end{bmatrix}$, $\mathbf{M}_2 = \begin{bmatrix} 1 & -4 & 6 & -4 & 1 \end{bmatrix}$, $\mathbf{M}_3 = \begin{bmatrix} 1 & 0 & -2 & 0 & 1 \end{bmatrix}$ and the operator $*$ denotes outer product of vectors.

In a more general case when the wedge filter axis has an orientation specified by an angle φ (with respect to the axis ω_2), the oriented wedge filter may be obtained by rotating the axes of the plane (ω_1,ω_2) with an angle φ. The rotation is defined by the linear transformation (12). In this case the 1D to 2D frequency transformation can be written as:

$$\omega \rightarrow f_\varphi(\omega_1,\omega_2) = a\left(\omega_1 - \omega_2 \cdot tg\varphi\right)\big/\left(\omega_1 \cdot tg\varphi + \omega_2\right) \tag{43}$$

Using the expression above and the bilinear transform, we finally get a mapping of the form:

$$\omega^2 \rightarrow F(z_1,z_2) = a^2 \cdot \left(\mathbf{z}_1 \times \mathbf{M}_\varphi \times \mathbf{z}_2^T\right)\big/\left(\mathbf{z}_1 \times \mathbf{M}_\varphi^{90^\circ} \times \mathbf{z}_2^T\right) \tag{44}$$

where $\mathbf{z}_1 = \begin{bmatrix} z_1^{-1} & 1 & z_1 \end{bmatrix}$, $\mathbf{z}_2 = \begin{bmatrix} z_2^{-1} & 1 & z_2 \end{bmatrix}$ and $\mathbf{M}_\varphi$ is the 3×3 matrix:

$$\mathbf{M}_\varphi = \begin{bmatrix} (tg\varphi\text{-}1)^2 & 2(tg^2\varphi - 1) & (tg\varphi + 1)^2 \\ -2(tg^2\varphi - 1) & -4(tg^2\varphi + 1) & -2(tg^2\varphi - 1) \\ (tg\varphi + 1)^2 & 2(tg^2\varphi - 1) & (tg\varphi\text{-}1)^2 \end{bmatrix} \tag{45}$$

and $\mathbf{M}_\varphi^{90^\circ}$ is the matrix $\mathbf{M}_\varphi$ rotated by 90°. Applying this frequency transformation directly to the 1D prototype (36), we get the 2D wedge filter transfer function in z_1, z_2 :

$$H_\varphi(z_1,z_2) = \left(\mathbf{Z}_1 \times \mathbf{B}_\varphi \times \mathbf{Z}_2^T\right)\big/\left(\mathbf{Z}_1 \times \mathbf{A}_\varphi \times \mathbf{Z}_2^T\right) \tag{46}$$

where the 5×5 matrices $\mathbf{A}_\varphi$ and $\mathbf{B}_\varphi$ have the expressions:

$$\mathbf{B}_\varphi = b_0(\mathbf{M}_\varphi * \mathbf{M}_\varphi)^{90^\circ} + b_1 a^2(\mathbf{M}_\varphi * \mathbf{M}_\varphi^{90^\circ}) + b_2 a^4(\mathbf{M}_\varphi * \mathbf{M}_\varphi) \tag{47}$$

$$\mathbf{A}_\varphi = (\mathbf{M}_\varphi * \mathbf{M}_\varphi)^{90^\circ} + a_1 a^2(\mathbf{M}_\varphi * \mathbf{M}_\varphi^{90^\circ}) + a_2 a^4(\mathbf{M}_\varphi * \mathbf{M}_\varphi) \tag{48}$$

and Z_1 and Z_2 are the vectors given in (27). Therefore the transfer function $H_\varphi(z_1,z_2)$ in (46) corresponds to a wedge filter with an aperture angle $\theta = 2\cdot arctg(1/a)$ and whose longitudinal axis is tilted about the ω_2 axis in the frequency plane with an angle φ.

Even if this method is straightforward and easy to apply once found the 1D prototype filter, the designed 2D filter will present noticeable distortions towards the limits of the frequency plane as compared to the ideal frequency response (38). This is mainly due to the frequency warping effect introduced by the bilinear transform, expressed by the continuous-time to discrete-time frequency mapping:

$$\omega = (2/T)\cdot arctg\left(\omega_a T/2\right) \tag{49}$$

where ω is the frequency of the discrete-time filter and ω_a the frequency of the continuous-time filter. In order to correct this distortion we next apply a pre-warping, using the inverse of mapping (49). For our purposes we can take $T = 1$ and we substitute $\omega_1 \to 2tg(\omega_1/2)$, $\omega_2 \to 2tg(\omega_2/2)$ in (43). Since these are nonlinear mappings, a polynomial or rational approximation would be more suitable. Using a Chebyshev-Padé approximation we get:

$$tg(\omega/2) \cong \omega \cdot \left(0.5 - 0.008439 \cdot \omega^2\right)\Big/\left(1 - 0.1 \cdot \omega^2\right) = g(\omega) \tag{50}$$

very accurate on a frequency range close to $[-\pi,\pi]$. Using (43) we obtain the frequency transformation which includes frequency pre-warping for ω_1 and ω_2:

$$\omega \to f_{\varphi P}(\omega_1,\omega_2) = a\left(tg(\omega_1/2) - tg(\omega_2/2) \cdot tg\varphi\right)\Big/\left(tg(\omega_1/2) \cdot tg\varphi + tg(\omega_2/2)\right) \tag{51}$$

Substituting in (51) $tg(\omega/2)$ by the rational approximation $g(\omega)$ we get a rational expression in ω_1 and ω_2 for the frequency transformation $\omega \to f_{\varphi P}(\omega_1,\omega_2)$. Then as previously we map $f_{\varphi P}(\omega_1,\omega_2)$ into the complex plane (s_1,s_2) and finally we get using bilinear transform the frequency mapping written again in matrix form: $F : \mathbb{R} \to \mathbb{C}^2$, $\omega \to F(z_1,z_2)$

$$F(z_1,z_2) = \left(\mathbf{Z}_1 \times \mathbf{B}_{P\varphi} \times \mathbf{Z}_2^T\right)\Big/\left(\mathbf{Z}_1 \times \mathbf{A}_{P\varphi} \times \mathbf{Z}_2^T\right) \tag{52}$$

The 4×4 templates corresponding to the numerator and denominator have the form:

$$\mathbf{B}_{p\varphi} = \mathbf{M}_1 - tg\varphi \cdot \mathbf{M}_1^{90^0} \qquad \mathbf{A}_{p\varphi} = tg\varphi \cdot \mathbf{M}_1 + \mathbf{M}_1^{90^0} \tag{53}$$

where $\mathbf{M}_1^{90^0}$ is the matrix $\mathbf{M}_1$ rotated clock-wise by 90^0, numerically given by:

$$\mathbf{M}_1 = \begin{bmatrix} -1 & 1 \\ -1 & 1 \end{bmatrix} * \begin{bmatrix} 0.559283 & 1.081434 & 0.559283 \\ 0.915190 & 1.769619 & 0.915190 \\ 0.559283 & 1.081434 & 0.559283 \end{bmatrix} \tag{54}$$

The elements of $\mathbf{M}_1$ result from combinations of the coefficients occurring in the expression of $g(\omega)$ in (50). Finally we obtain the 1D to 2D frequency transformation in the matrix form:

$$\omega^2 \to F(z_1,z_2) = a^2 \cdot \left(\mathbf{z}_1 \times \mathbf{B} \times \mathbf{z}_2^T\right)\Big/\left(\mathbf{z}_1 \times \mathbf{A} \times \mathbf{z}_2^T\right) \tag{55}$$

where the matrices $\mathbf{B} = \mathbf{B}_{p\varphi} * \mathbf{B}_{p\varphi}$, $\mathbf{A} = \mathbf{A}_{p\varphi} * \mathbf{A}_{p\varphi}$ resulted by convolution are of size 7×7. We can apply this frequency transformation directly to the 1D prototype function (36) and we obtain the 2D wedge filter transfer function in z_1 and z_2:

$$H_{W\varphi}(z_1,z_2) = \left(\mathbf{Z}_1 \times \mathbf{B}_{W\varphi} \times \mathbf{Z}_2^T\right)\Big/\left(\mathbf{Z}_1 \times \mathbf{A}_{W\varphi} \times \mathbf{Z}_2^T\right) \tag{56}$$

where $\mathbf{Z}_1$ and $\mathbf{Z}_2$ are row vectors: $\mathbf{Z}_1 = [z_1^N \quad z_1^{N-1} \quad \ldots \quad z_1 \quad 1]$, $\mathbf{Z}_2 = [z_2^N \quad z_2^{N-1} \quad \ldots \quad z_2 \quad 1]$ with $N = 12$; the 13×13 matrices $\mathbf{A}_{W\varphi}$ and $\mathbf{B}_{W\varphi}$ are:

$$\mathbf{B}_{W\varphi} = b_0(\mathbf{A} * \mathbf{A}) + b_1 a^2(\mathbf{A} * \mathbf{B}) + b_2 a^4(\mathbf{B} * \mathbf{B}) \, , \quad \mathbf{A}_{W\varphi} = \mathbf{A} * \mathbf{A} + a_1 a^2(\mathbf{A} * \mathbf{B}) + a_2 a^4(\mathbf{B} * \mathbf{B}) \tag{57}$$

As an important remark, even if the filter templates result relatively large, this is the price paid for ensuring a good linearity of the filter shape in the frequency plane. The frequency pre-warping has increased the filter order. However, the filter large-size templates result as a convolution of small size matrices (3×3 , 5×5) and can be considered partially separable. At least the numerator of the prototype (36) may have real roots, so it can be factorized, which implies convolution of smaller size matrices. Let us consider the maximally-flat zero-phase 1D IIR prototype filter shown in Fig.6 (a), with the transfer function:

$$H_p(s) = \left(0.887175 + 0.269975 \cdot s^2 + 0.018905 \cdot s^4\right)\Big/\left(1 + 0.600346 \cdot s^2 + 5.332057 \cdot s^4\right) \tag{58}$$

Using this prototype, we designed a wedge filter with an aperture angle $\theta = 0.2\pi$ and orientation angle $\varphi = \pi/5$. For these values we get $a = \text{tg}(\theta/2) = 0.3249$, $\text{tg}\varphi = 0.7265$. The frequency response and contour plot are shown in Fig.6 (b) and (c).

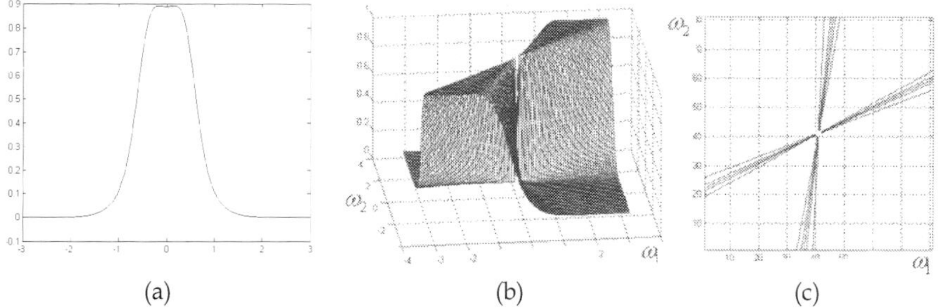

<table>
<tr><td>(a)</td><td>(b)</td><td>(c)</td></tr>
</table>

Fig. 6. Oriented flat-top wedge filter with $\theta = 0.2\pi$ and $\varphi = 0.2\pi$: (a) 1D IIR maximally-flat prototype magnitude; (b) frequency response; (c) contour plot

4.2 Design Method Using Numerical Approximation

The second design method for zero-phase wedge-shaped filters starts again from a zero-phase 1D prototype filter of the general form similar to (36). We will use again the 1D to 2D frequency mapping (43). Since (36) is a rational function of ω^2 , the design method will be based upon finding the discrete approximation of the function

$$F_\varphi(\omega_1,\omega_2) = f_\varphi^2(\omega_1,\omega_2) = a^2\left(\omega_1 - \omega_2 \cdot \text{tg}\varphi\right)^2\Big/\left(\omega_1 \cdot \text{tg}\varphi + \omega_2\right)^2 \tag{59}$$

This approximation will be derived indirectly, using the change of variables: $\omega_1 = \arccos x_1$, $\omega_2 = \arccos x_2$ and the function $F_\varphi(\omega_1, \omega_2)$ will be mapped into a function $G_\varphi(x_1, x_2)$. The next step is to find a two-variable Taylor series expansion of the function $G_\varphi(x_1, x_2)$. Using a symbolic calculation software like MAPLE, we easily determine this series expansion in the variables x_1, x_2. Then we return to the former variables by substituting back $x_1 = \cos\omega_1$, $x_2 = \cos\omega_2$ in $G_\varphi(x_1, x_2)$. Thus we obtain an approximation of $F_\varphi(\omega_1, \omega_2)$ in powers of $\cos\omega_1$, $\cos\omega_2$. Using trigonometric identities, we finally express $F_\varphi(\omega_1, \omega_2)$ as:

$$F_\varphi(\omega_1, \omega_2) \cong \sum_{m=-N}^{N} \sum_{n=-N}^{N} a_{mn} \cdot \cos(m\omega_1 + n\omega_2) \tag{60}$$

where N is chosen to ensure a desired precision (usually $N = 2$). The coefficients a_{mn} depend on the orientation angle φ and they are polynomial expressions in the variable $tg\varphi$. Let us design a wedge filter with the same specifications from section 4.1, i.e. the prototype (58), with the parameters: $a = tg(\theta/2) = 0.3249$, $tg\varphi = 0.7265$. The proposed method yields:

$$F_\varphi(\omega_1, \omega_2) \cong a^2 \cdot [0.195736 - 0.132213 \cdot \cos(\omega_1) + 0.212134 \cdot \cos(\omega_2) - 0.155057 \cdot (\cos(\omega_1 - \omega_2)$$
$$+ \cos(\omega_1 + \omega_2)) - 0.027075 \cdot (\cos(2\omega_1 - \omega_2) + \cos(2\omega_1 + \omega_2)) - 0.042024 \cdot (\cos(\omega_1 - 2\omega_2) \tag{61}$$
$$+ \cos(\omega_1 + 2\omega_2)) + 0.050075\cos(2\omega_1) + 0.124584\cos(2\omega_2) - 0.014742 \cdot (\cos(2\omega_1 - 2\omega_2) + \cos(2\omega_1 + 2\omega_2))]$$

which corresponds to the 5×5 template:

$$W = a^2 \cdot \begin{bmatrix} -0.0073 & -0.0210 & 0.0623 & -0.0210 & -0.0073 \\ -0.0135 & -0.0775 & 0.1060 & -0.0775 & -0.0135 \\ 0.0250 & -0.0661 & 0.1957 & -0.0661 & 0.0250 \\ -0.0135 & -0.0775 & 0.1060 & -0.0775 & -0.0135 \\ -0.0073 & -0.0210 & 0.0623 & -0.0210 & -0.0073 \end{bmatrix} \tag{62}$$

found after identifying coefficients of the 2D $\mathbf{Z}$ transform corresponding to (61). Once obtained the 1D to 2D frequency mapping of the form: $\omega^2 \rightarrow F_\varphi(\omega_1, \omega_2)$ given by the expression (61), the next design step is straightforward and consists simply in substituting in $H_p(\omega)$ from (36) ω^2 with $F_\varphi(\omega_1, \omega_2)$. The templates $\mathbf{B}$ and $\mathbf{A}$ of the wedge filter result according to the numerator and denominator of $H_p(\omega)$ as:

$$\mathbf{B} = b_0 \cdot \mathbf{E} + b_1 \cdot \mathbf{W_b} + b_2 \cdot \mathbf{W} * \mathbf{W} \qquad \mathbf{A} = \mathbf{E} + a_1 \cdot \mathbf{W_b} + a_2 \cdot \mathbf{W} * \mathbf{W} \tag{63}$$

where $*$ stands for matrix convolution and $\mathbf{E}$ is a 9×9 matrix with zero elements and the central element 1. The 9×9 matrix $\mathbf{W_b}$ is obtained by bordering the 5×5 matrix $\mathbf{W}$ with zeros in order to be summed with matrices $\mathbf{E}$ and $\mathbf{W} * \mathbf{W}$.

An advantage of the second design method is that it avoids the use of the bilinear transform, which is known to introduce distortions unless a frequency pre-warping is applied, as in the previous section. The pre-warping increases the filter complexity, as shown. As a general remark, the second design approach is somewhat simpler than the first but requires the use of bivariate Taylor series expansion for a given orientation angle φ.

4.3 Fan Filters Design

Although there exist design methods for FIR or IIR fan filters (Kayran & King, 1983), they can be derived as well using the proposed method. We consider two types of fan filters specified in the plane (ω_1, ω_2) as in Fig.7 (a), (b). The filter in Fig.7 (a) can be described ideally as:

$$H_F(\omega_1, \omega_2) = \begin{cases} 1, & |\omega_2| \leq |\omega_1| \\ 0, & \text{otherwise} \end{cases} \tag{64}$$

This fan filter is a particular case of a wedge filter with the aperture angle $\theta = \pi/2$ and orientation $\varphi = 0$, therefore $a = 1$ and $\mathrm{tg}\varphi = 0$; the frequency transformation (43) reduces to the simple expression $\omega \rightarrow f_\varphi(\omega_1, \omega_2) = \omega_1/\omega_2$. In this particular case the template $\mathbf{W}$ results:

$$\mathbf{W} = \begin{bmatrix} 0.0072 & -0.0413 & 0.1038 & -0.0413 & 0.0072 \\ 0.0134 & -0.1056 & 0.1746 & -0.1056 & 0.0134 \\ 0.0281 & -0.1474 & 0.2975 & -0.1474 & 0.0281 \\ 0.0134 & -0.1056 & 0.1746 & -0.1056 & 0.0134 \\ 0.0072 & -0.0413 & 0.1038 & -0.0413 & 0.0072 \end{bmatrix} \tag{65}$$

The frequency response of a fan filter of this type, using the above specifications and the prototype given in (58), is shown in Fig.7 (c). We notice that it preserves the 1D prototype maximally-flat characteristics in the pass-band.

For the second fan filter type in Fig.7 (b) we have the parameters: $\theta = \pi/2$ and $\varphi = \pi/4$, therefore $a = 1$ and $\mathrm{tg}\theta = 1$; in this case the frequency transformation (43) simplifies to:

$$\omega \rightarrow f_\varphi(\omega_1, \omega_2) = (\omega_1 - \omega_2)/(\omega_1 + \omega_2) \tag{66}$$

In this particular case the template $\mathbf{W}$ results as:

$$\mathbf{W} = \begin{bmatrix} -0.0071 & -0.0126 & 0.0383 & -0.0126 & -0.0071 \\ -0.0126 & -0.0681 & 0.0131 & -0.0681 & -0.0126 \\ 0.0383 & 0.0131 & 0.0760 & 0.0131 & 0.0383 \\ -0.0126 & -0.0681 & 0.0131 & -0.0681 & -0.0126 \\ -0.0071 & -0.0126 & 0.0383 & -0.0126 & -0.0071 \end{bmatrix} \tag{67}$$

The filter templates result again using relations (63).

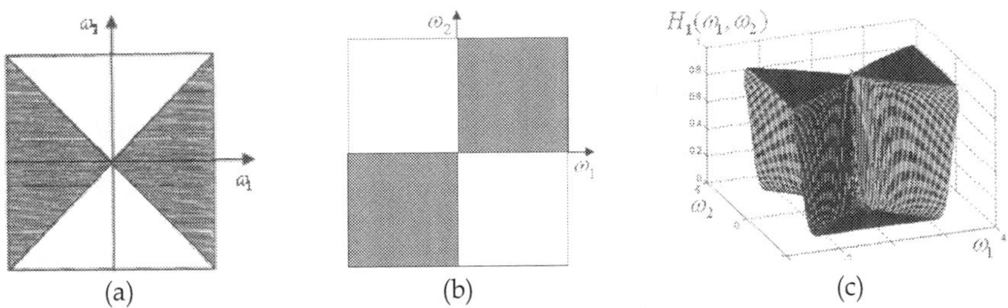

(a)   (b)   (c)

Fig. 7. (a), (b) Two versions of ideal fan filters; (c) fan filter frequency response

5. 2D Filters Designed in Polar Coordinates

We will approach next a particular class of 2D filters, namely filters whose frequency response is symmetric about the origin and has at the same time an angular periodicity. The contour plots of their frequency response, resulted as sections with planes parallel with the frequency plane, can be defined as closed curves which can be described in terms of a variable radius which is a periodic function of the current angle formed with one of the axes. Therefore it can be described in polar coordinates by $\rho = \rho(\varphi)$ where φ is the angle formed by the radius OP with ω_1-axis, as shown in Fig.8 (a) for a four-lobe filter. Therefore $\rho(\varphi)$ is a periodic function of the angle φ in the range $\varphi \in [0, 2\pi]$.

The proposed design method is based on a zero-phase prototype whose real-valued transfer function can be expressed as a ratio of polynomials in even powers of the frequency ω:

$$H_p(\omega) = \sum_{j=0}^{M} b_j \cdot \omega^{2j} \Big/ \sum_{k=0}^{N} a_k \cdot \omega^{2k} \tag{68}$$

where $M \leq N$ and N is the filter order. This function may be obtained using a rational approximation of a prototype filter magnitude (e.g. Chebyshev, elliptic). The proposed design method for this class of 2D filters is based on a frequency transformation of the form:

$$F : \mathbb{R} \to \mathbb{C}^2, \quad \omega^2 \to F(z_1, z_2) \tag{69}$$

The frequency transformation (69) maps the real frequency axis ω onto the complex plane (z_1, z_2) and will be defined by a frequency mapping of the form:

$$F_1 : \mathbb{R} \to \mathbb{R}^2, \quad \omega^2 \to F_1(\omega_1, \omega_2) = (\omega_1^2 + \omega_2^2)/\rho(\omega_1, \omega_2) \tag{70}$$

$\rho(\omega_1, \omega_2)$ plays the role of a radial compressing function and is initially determined in the angle variable φ as $\rho(\varphi)$. In the frequency plane (ω_1, ω_2) we have:

$$\cos \varphi = \omega_1 \Big/ \sqrt{\omega_1^2 + \omega_2^2} \tag{71}$$

If the radial function $\rho(\varphi)$ can be expressed in the variable $\cos\varphi$, using (71) we obtain by substitution the function $\rho(\omega_1,\omega_2)$. We will express the function $\rho(\varphi)$ as a polynomial or a ratio of polynomials in the variable $\cos\varphi$. For instance, the four-lobe filter with contour plot given in Fig.8 (a) corresponds to a function:

$$\rho(\varphi) = a + b\cos 4\varphi = a + b - 8b\cos^2\varphi + 8b\cos^4\varphi \tag{72}$$

plotted in Fig.8 (b) for $\varphi \in [0, 2\pi]$. As 1D prototype we consider a type-2 Chebyshev digital filter with the parameters: order $N = 4$, stopband attenuation $R_s = 40\,\text{dB}$ and passband-edge frequency $\omega_p = 0.5$ (1.0 is half the sampling frequency). The transfer function in z is:

$$H_p(z) = \left(0.012277 \cdot z^2 - 0.012525 \cdot z + 0.012277\right)\Big/\left(z^2 - 1.850147 \cdot z + 0.862316\right) \tag{73}$$

Its magnitude for $\omega \in [-\pi, \pi]$ is shown in Fig.8 (c). Using the Chebyshev-Padé method and a symbolic computation software, we determine the real-valued transfer function which accurately approximates the magnitude of the digital filter function $H_p(z)$:

$$H_{a1}(s) = \left(0.9403 + 0.5756 \cdot s^2 + 0.0947 \cdot s^4\right)\Big/\left(1 + 2.067753 \cdot s^2 + 4.66314 \cdot s^4\right) \tag{74}$$

This method can be applied for any prototype like (73). More generally, the 2D filter in polar coordinates can be rotated in the frequency plane with a specified angle φ_0 about one of the frequency axes, e.g. $O - \omega_2$. For instance, in the case of a four-lobe filter, two opposite lobes are oriented along a direction at an angle φ_0, and the other two at $\varphi_0 + \pi/2$, as in Fig.9 (d). It can be shown that the cosine of the current angle φ with initial phase φ_0 can be expressed:

$$\cos^2(\varphi + \varphi_0) = \left(\cos^2\varphi_0 \cdot \omega_1^2 + \sin^2\varphi_0 \cdot \omega_2^2 + 0.5\sin 2\varphi_0 \cdot \omega_1\omega_2\right)\Big/\left(\omega_1^2 + \omega_2^2\right) \tag{75}$$

A filter with $\varphi_0 \neq 0$ is designed in subsection 5.2. For filters with an even number of lobes, as shown further, the radial function $\rho(\varphi)$ is expressed in even powers of $\cos\varphi$ or $\cos(\varphi + \varphi_0)$.

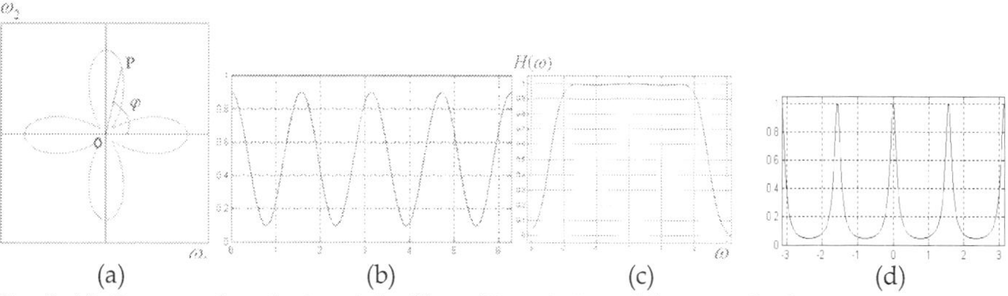

(a)   (b)   (c)   (d)

Fig. 8. (a) Contour plot of a four-lobe filter; (b) variation of the periodic function $\rho(\varphi)$; (c) maximally-flat low-pass prototype; (d) very selective radial function

Next we approach the design of several types of recursive zero-phase 2D filters belonging to this class, namely two-lobe and four-lobe filters, fan filters and diamond-shaped filters. The transformation $\omega^2 \rightarrow F(z_1, z_2)$ and the filter frequency response is calculated in each case.

5.1 Two-Lobe Filter

A very simple 2D filter belonging to this class is one given by a function $\rho(\varphi)$ of the form:

$$\rho(\varphi) = a + b\cos 2\varphi = a - b + 2b\cos^2 \varphi \tag{76}$$

Using (70), (71) and (76) we get the frequency transformation:

$$\omega^2 \rightarrow F_1(\omega_1, \omega_2) = \left(\omega_1^2 + \omega_2^2\right)^2 \Big/ \left((a+b)\cdot \omega_1^2 + (a-b)\cdot \omega_2^2\right) \tag{77}$$

Since $\omega_1^2 = -s_1^2$ and $\omega_2^2 = -s_2^2$ we get the function $F_1(s_1, s_2)$ in the complex plane (s_1, s_2):

$$F_1(s_1, s_2) = -\left(s_1^2 + s_2^2\right)^2 \Big/ \left((a+b)\cdot s_1^2 + (a-b)\cdot s_2^2\right) \tag{78}$$

Finally we derive a transfer function of the 2D filter $H(z_1, z_2)$ in the complex plane (z_1, z_2). This can be achieved if we find a discrete counterpart $R(z_1, z_2)$ of the function $\rho(\omega_1, \omega_2)$. A possible method is to express the function $\rho(\omega_1, \omega_2)$ in the complex plane (s_1, s_2) and then find the appropriate mapping to (z_1, z_2) using the bilinear transform for the variables s_1, s_2. Using (40) in (78), we find the frequency transformation in z_1, z_2 in matrix form:

$$\omega^2 \rightarrow F(z_1, z_2) = B(z_1, z_2)/A(z_1, z_2) = \left(\mathbf{Z}_1 \times \mathbf{B} \times \mathbf{Z}_2^\mathsf{T}\right)\Big/\left(\mathbf{Z}_1 \times \mathbf{A} \times \mathbf{Z}_2^\mathsf{T}\right) \tag{79}$$

with $\mathbf{Z}_1$, $\mathbf{Z}_2$ given in (27). The templates $\mathbf{B}$, $\mathbf{A}$ giving the coefficients of $B(z_1, z_2)$, $A(z_1, z_2)$ result as convolutions of 3×3 matrices: $\mathbf{B} = 8 \cdot \mathbf{B_1} * \mathbf{B_1}$, $\mathbf{A} = \mathbf{A_1} * \mathbf{A_2}$, where:

$$\mathbf{B_1} = \begin{bmatrix} 1 & 0 & 1 \\ 0 & -4 & 0 \\ 1 & 0 & 1 \end{bmatrix}; \quad \mathbf{A_1} = \begin{bmatrix} a & 2b & a \\ -2b & -4a & -2b \\ a & 2b & a \end{bmatrix}; \quad \mathbf{A_2} = \begin{bmatrix} 1 & 2 & 1 \\ 2 & 4 & 2 \\ 1 & 2 & 1 \end{bmatrix} \tag{80}$$

The parameters a and b from (76) are chosen imposing the minimum and maximum values of $\rho(\varphi)$, $m = a - b$ and $M = a + b$. For instance with $m = 0.04$, $M = 4$ we get $a = 2.02$, $b = 1.98$. We next use the maximally-flat filter prototype (74). We substitute the mapping (79) into the general prototype (36) and get the desired 2D transfer function:

$$H(z_1, z_2) = \frac{b_2 B^2(z_1, z_2) + b_1 A(z_1, z_2)B(z_1, z_2) + b_0 A^2(z_1, z_2)}{a_2 B^2(z_1, z_2) + a_1 A(z_1, z_2)B(z_1, z_2) + A^2(z_1, z_2)} = B_f(z_1, z_2)/A_f(z_1, z_2) \tag{81}$$

where the coefficients b_0, b_1, b_2, a_1, a_2 may take the values in (74). Since function (81) can be described by the templates $\mathbf{B}_f$, $\mathbf{A}_f$ corresponding to $B_f(z_1, z_2)$, $A_f(z_1, z_2)$, we have:

$$\mathbf{B}_f = b_2 \cdot \mathbf{B} * \mathbf{B} + b_1 \cdot \mathbf{A} * \mathbf{B} + b_0 \cdot \mathbf{A} * \mathbf{A} \qquad\qquad \mathbf{A}_f = a_2 \cdot \mathbf{B} * \mathbf{B} + a_1 \cdot \mathbf{A} * \mathbf{B} + \mathbf{A} * \mathbf{A} \qquad (82)$$

where $*$ denotes matrix convolution. For our filter, the templates $\mathbf{B}_f$ and $\mathbf{A}_f$ result of size 9×9. In Fig.9 (a) the two-lobe filter frequency response is shown.

5.2 Very Selective Four-Lobe Filter

The design of a very selective four-lobe filter in polar coordinates was presented in (Matei, 2009, b) and is briefly reconsidered as follows. Let us consider the radial function:

$$H_r(\varphi) = 1/\left(p \cdot \tilde{B}(\varphi) - p + 1\right) \qquad (83)$$

where $\tilde{B}(\varphi)$ is a periodic function; let $\tilde{B}(\varphi) = \cos(4\varphi)$. We use this function to design a 2D filter with four narrow lobes in the frequency plane. Using trigonometric identities, we get:

$$H_r(\varphi) = 1/\left(1 + 8p \cdot (\cos\varphi)^2 - 8p \cdot (\cos\varphi)^4\right) \qquad (84)$$

plotted for $\varphi \in [-\pi, \pi]$ in Fig.8 (d). This periodic function has the period $\Phi = \pi/4$ and the shape of a "comb" filter. In order to control the shape of this function, we introduce another parameter k, such that the radial function $\rho(\varphi)$ becomes $\rho(\varphi) = k \cdot H_r(\varphi)$. We get using (70):

$$\omega^2 \rightarrow F(\omega_1, \omega_2) = \left(\omega_1^4 + (2 + 8p)\omega_1^2\omega_2^2 + \omega_2^4\right)/\left(k(\omega_1^2 + \omega_2^2)\right) \qquad (85)$$

$$F_2(s_1, s_2) = -\left(s_1^4 + (2 + 8p)s_1^2 s_2^2 + s_2^4\right)/\left(k(s_1^2 + s_2^2)\right) \qquad (86)$$

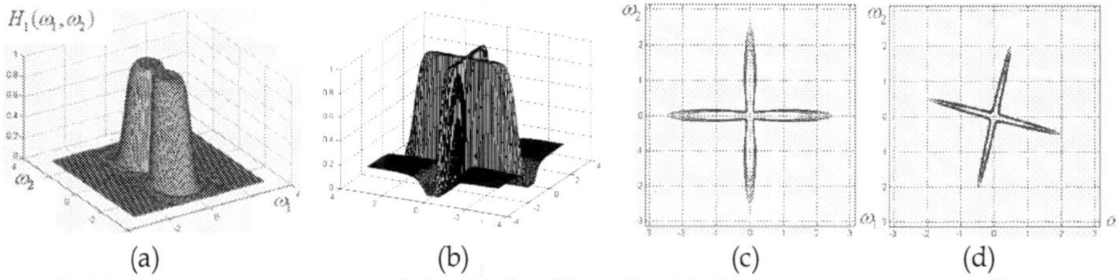

(a)   (b)   (c)   (d)

Fig. 9. (a) Frequency response of the 2-lobe filter; (b), (c) frequency response and contour plot for a narrow 4-lobe filter; (d) contour plot of a rotated 4-lobe filter

As in the previous example we find the transformation of the same form (79), where $\mathbf{Z}_1$ and $\mathbf{Z}_2$ are the vectors given by (27), and $\mathbf{B}$, $\mathbf{A}$ are the 5×5 matrices :

$$\mathbf{B} = 8 \cdot \begin{bmatrix} -1-2p & 0 & 4p-2 & 0 & -1-2p \\ 0 & 8 & 0 & 8 & 0 \\ 4p-2 & 0 & -8p-20 & 0 & 4p-2 \\ 0 & 8 & 0 & 8 & 0 \\ -1-2p & 0 & 4p-2 & 0 & -1-2p \end{bmatrix} \quad \mathbf{A} = k \cdot \begin{bmatrix} 1 & 0 & 1 \\ 0 & -4 & 0 \\ 1 & 0 & 1 \end{bmatrix} * \begin{bmatrix} 1 & 2 & 1 \\ 2 & 4 & 2 \\ 1 & 2 & 1 \end{bmatrix} = k \cdot \mathbf{A}_1 * \mathbf{A}_2 \quad (87)$$

Using the prototype (74) we get a transfer function $H(z_1,z_2)$ similar to (81) and the templates result from (82). The designed filter has the frequency response and contour plot as in Fig. 9 (b), (c). We remark that the filter is very selective simultaneously along both axes.

The same procedure can be applied to design a four-lobe filter with a specified inclination angle. Using the double bilinear transform (40), the expression (75) for $\cos^2(\varphi+\varphi_0)$ corresponds to the following frequency transformation in the complex variables z_1, z_2 :

$$\cos^2(\varphi+\varphi_0) \rightarrow F(z_1,z_2) = B(z_1,z_2)/A(z_1,z_2) = \left(\mathbf{Z}_1 \times \mathbf{B}_\mathbf{C} \times \mathbf{Z}_2^\mathsf{T} \right) / \left(\mathbf{Z}_1 \times \mathbf{A}_\mathbf{C} \times \mathbf{Z}_2^\mathsf{T} \right) \quad (88)$$

where $\mathbf{A}_\mathbf{C} = 2 \cdot \mathbf{A}_1$ with $\mathbf{A}_1$ given in (87) and

$$\mathbf{B}_\mathbf{C} = \begin{bmatrix} 1+0.5\sin(2\varphi_0) & -2\cos(2\varphi_0) & 1-0.5\sin(2\varphi_0) \\ 2\cos(2\varphi_0) & -4 & 2\cos(2\varphi_0) \\ 1-0.5\sin(2\varphi_0) & -2\cos(2\varphi_0) & 1+0.5\sin(2\varphi_0) \end{bmatrix} \quad (89)$$

The radial compression function for this filter will be $\rho(\varphi) = k / \left(1 + 8p \cdot (\cos\varphi)^2 - 8p \cdot (\cos\varphi)^4 \right)$ corresponding to the following pair of 5×5 matrices:

$$\mathbf{B}_\rho = k \cdot \mathbf{A}_\mathbf{C} * \mathbf{A}_\mathbf{C} \qquad \mathbf{A}_\rho = \mathbf{A}_\mathbf{C} * \mathbf{A}_\mathbf{C} + 8p \cdot \mathbf{B}_\mathbf{C} * \mathbf{A}_\mathbf{C} - 8p \cdot \mathbf{B}_\mathbf{C} * \mathbf{B}_\mathbf{C} \quad (90)$$

The final frequency transformation is given by (79), where $\mathbf{B} = -4 \cdot \mathbf{A}_\rho$, $\mathbf{A} = k \cdot \mathbf{A}_\mathbf{C} * \mathbf{A}_2$ and $\mathbf{A}_2$ results from (87).

5.3 Fan Filter Design in Polar Coordinates

Besides the design method based on wedge filters addressed in subsection 4.3, fan filters can also be designed in polar coordinates. Let us consider the symmetric fan-type filter specified in the plane (ω_1,ω_2) as in Fig.7 (a), given in the ideal case by relation (64).

The fan filter contour can be exactly described as:

$$\rho(\varphi) = \begin{cases} \pi/\cos\varphi & \text{for } \varphi \in [-\pi/4, \pi/4] \cup [3\pi/4, 5\pi/4] \\ 0 & \text{otherwise} \end{cases} \tag{91}$$

Using a change of variable and a Chebyshev-Padé approximation, we obtain the following approximation $\rho_a(\varphi)$ of $\rho(\varphi)$ for $\varphi \in [-\pi/2, \pi/2]$:

$$\rho_a(\varphi) \cong 0.1424 \cdot \left(\cos^4\varphi - 0.106111\cos^2\varphi - 0.01047\right) / \left(\cos^4\varphi - 1.401727\cos^2\varphi + 0.544317\right) \tag{92}$$

As before, we looked for an expression in $\cos^2\varphi$ in order to substitute the relation (71). We get an expression for $\rho(\omega_1, \omega_2)$, then we write it in the plane (s_1, s_2) and finally find a frequency transformation similar to (79). The templates $\mathbf{B}$ and $\mathbf{A}$ result of size 5×5, and $\mathbf{A}$ can be decomposed as a convolution of 3×3 templates: $\mathbf{A} = \mathbf{A_1} * \mathbf{A_1}$ where $\mathbf{A_1}$ is given in (87). The frequency response of the fan filter preserves the 1D prototype maximally-flat characteristics in the pass-band.

5.4 Diamond-Shaped Filters Design in Polar Coordinates

In this section a new analytical design method for diamond-shaped filters is described, using the above-discussed approach in polar coordinates (Matei, 2010).

As a first step, we determine analytically the mapping which transforms a circle of given radius, in the frequency plane, into a square, having its vertices on the same circle. We refer to the geometrical construction in Fig.10 (a). In the frequency plane (ω_1, ω_2) spanned by the axes $O\omega_1$, $O\omega_2$, we consider the circle of radius R. The default value will be $R = \pi$.

Let us take an arbitrary point P_1 situated on the first side of the square $(A_1 A_2)$, and let φ be the angle between the segment OP_1 and the axis $O\omega_1$; φ_0 is the angle between OA_1 and axis $O\omega_1$, where A_1 is the first vertex of the square. In the triangle $P_1 O A_1$ we have the angles: $\sphericalangle OA_1P_1 = \pi/4$; $\sphericalangle P_1OA_1 = \varphi - \varphi_0$; $\sphericalangle OP_1A_1 = 3\pi/4 - \varphi + \varphi_0$. Applying the sine theorem in the triangle P_1OA_1, we find the measure of segment OP_1 as a function of R and φ:

$$OP_1 = R \cdot \sin(OA_1P_1) / \sin(OP_1A_1) = \left(R\sqrt{2}/2\right) / \cos(\varphi - \varphi_0 - \pi/4) \tag{93}$$

Thus we found the measure of OP_1 as a function of the current angle. However, (93) is valid only in the range: $\varphi \in \left[\varphi_0 + 2n\pi/4, \varphi_0 + 2(n+1)\pi/4\right]$. For a standard diamond filter $\varphi_0 = 0$, $R = 1$ and in the first quadrant of the frequency plane $\rho(\varphi) = 1/\sqrt{2}\cos(\varphi - \pi/4)$. To express the value OP_n for an arbitrary angle φ, when point P_n is located on any side of the square, including the vertices, we find a periodic function $\rho(\varphi)$ of the current angle φ. This function has the period $\Phi = \pi/2$ and is plotted in Fig.10 (b). A convenient way to obtain a closed-form periodic approximation of this function is by using a rational approximation (e.g. Chebyshev-Padé). We look for such an approximation of the function $\rho(\varphi) = 1/\cos\varphi$ for a phase $\varphi \in [-\pi/4, \pi/4]$, in powers of the variable $\cos 4\varphi$, which is a periodic function with period $\pi/2$. Thus, the rational function will actually approximate the function $\rho(\varphi)$ over the entire range $[0, 2\pi]$. Since $\rho(\varphi)$ is not differentiable in the points $\varphi = -\pi, -\pi/2, 0, \pi/2$ (corresponding to square vertices), as can be noticed in Fig.10 (b), we consider the function $\rho_1(\varphi)$ on the range $\varphi \in [-\pi/4, \pi/4]$, which is differentiable everywhere within this interval; we obtain:

$$\rho(\varphi) = 1/\cos\varphi \cong \left(1 + 0.087481 \cdot \varphi^2\right) / \left(1 - 0.413 \cdot \varphi^2\right) \tag{94}$$

Now we use the variable change $x = \cos(4\varphi)$ getting the intermediate function in variable x:

$$\rho_i(x) = \left(1.082679 + 1.189232 \cdot x + 0.202714 \cdot x^2\right) / \left(1 + 1.202559 \cdot x + 0.271879 \cdot x^2\right) \tag{95}$$

Returning to the initial variable $\varphi = 0.25 \cdot \arccos x$, by substituting back $x = \cos(4\varphi)$, we obtain a rational approximation in powers of $\cos(4\varphi)$. In this expression we must replace φ by $\varphi - \pi/4$, to get the final approximation for the function $\rho(\varphi)$:

$$\rho_1(\varphi) = \frac{1.04234 - 1.046915 \cdot \cos(4\varphi) + 0.089227 \cdot \cos(8\varphi)}{1 - 1.058647 \cdot \cos(4\varphi) + 0.119671 \cdot \cos(8\varphi)} \cong \rho(\varphi) \tag{96}$$

$\rho_1(\varphi)$ is plotted in Fig.10 (c) and is an accurate approximation of the original function $\rho(\varphi)$. Using trigonometric identities, this becomes a rational expression in $(\cos\varphi)^{2n}$ with $n = 1...4$.

$$\rho(x) = 0.7456 \cdot \frac{(x + 0.347)(x + 0.0156)(x - 1.0156)(x - 1.347)}{(x + 0.2342)(x + 0.0136)(x - 1.0136)(x - 1.2342)} \tag{97}$$

where by x we denoted here $(\cos\varphi)^2$. At this point, substituting $x = (\cos\varphi)^2 = \omega_1^2 / (\omega_1^2 + \omega_2^2)$ we finally reach an expression of the radial function $\rho(\varphi)$ of the frequency variables ω_1 and ω_2, i.e. $\rho(\omega_1, \omega_2)$.

Next a more general design method for a diamond shaped filter is proposed. It starts from a digital filter prototype, with transfer function $H(z)$ of order N. We discuss the common case when the numerator and denominator of $H(z)$ are polynomials in z of equal degrees. Let us consider a transfer function $H(z)$ of even order N, factorized into second order functions (biquads), with the general form (3) and the frequency response (5), defined in section 2.

In the case of diamond filters, the frequency mapping defined in (70) is modified, becoming:

$$F_1 : \mathbb{R} \to \mathbb{R}^2, \quad \omega \to F_1(\omega_1, \omega_2) = \sqrt{\omega_1^2 + \omega_2^2} / \rho(\omega_1, \omega_2) \tag{98}$$

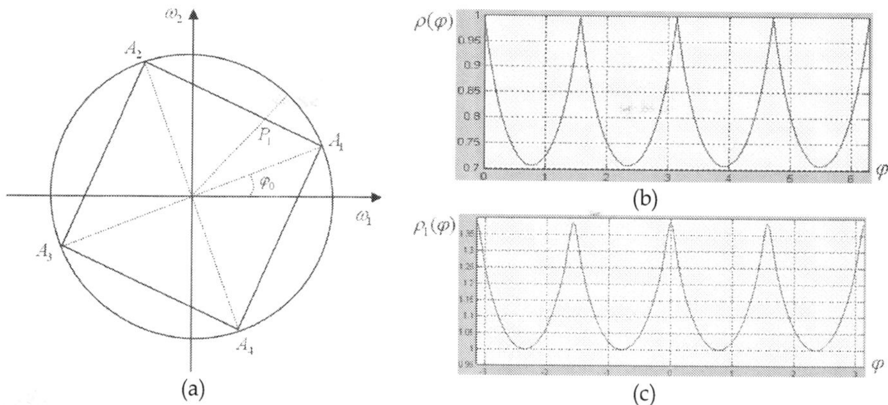

(a) (b) (c)

Fig. 10. (a) Square inscribed in the circle of radius R in the frequency plane, with an initial phase φ_0; (b) periodic function $\rho(\varphi)$; (b) its periodic approximation $\rho_1(\varphi)$

The expression (96), using trigonometric identities, can be written in powers of $(\cos\varphi)^2$; then, according to (71) we have $(\cos\varphi)^2 = \omega_1^2 / (\omega_1^2 + \omega_2^2)$ and by substitution we obtain an expression of the radial function $\rho(\varphi)$ in the two frequency variables ω_1 and ω_2, denoted $\rho(\omega_1,\omega_2)$. Finally we get an expression of the real frequency transformation of the general form (98). The next step is to find numerically approximations of the functions:

$$C(\omega_1,\omega_2) = \cos\left(\sqrt{\omega_1^2 + \omega_2^2}\big/\rho(\omega_1,\omega_2)\right), \; S(\omega_1,\omega_2) = \sin\left(\sqrt{\omega_1^2 + \omega_2^2}\big/\rho(\omega_1,\omega_2)\right) \qquad (99)$$

We will approximate the above functions using a trigonometric series of the general form:

$$F(\omega_1,\omega_2) \cong \sum_{m=-N}^{N} \sum_{n=-N}^{N} a_{mn} \cos(m\omega_1 + n\omega_2) \qquad (100)$$

where N is imposed by the required precision. This approximation is derived indirectly, using again the change of variables: $\omega_1 = \arccos x_1$, $\omega_2 = \arccos x_2$. Thus we obtain from $C(\omega_1,\omega_2)$ and $S(\omega_1,\omega_2)$ the functions $C_x(x_1,x_2)$ and $S_x(x_1,x_2)$ with rather complicated expressions. However, using a symbolic calculation software, we can derive immediately the bivariate Taylor series expansion in x_1 and x_2, of the general form:

$$F_x(x_1,x_2) \cong \sum_{k=-N}^{N} \sum_{l=-N}^{N} b_{kl} \cdot x_1^k x_2^l \qquad (101)$$

Finally by substituting back in (101) $x_1 = \cos\omega_1$ and $x_2 = \cos\omega_2$ we return to the former variables and applying again trigonometric identities we obtain the desired expansions of the form (100). For instance with $N = 2$ the expansions for $C(\omega_1,\omega_2)$ and $S(\omega_1,\omega_2)$ are:

$$
\begin{aligned}
C(\omega_1,\omega_2) &\cong -0.419822 + 0.517714 \cdot (\cos\omega_1 + \cos\omega_2) + 0.177207 \cdot (\cos(\omega_1+\omega_2) + \cos(\omega_1-\omega_2)) \\
&-0.054476 \cdot (\cos(\omega_1+2\omega_2) + \cos(\omega_1-2\omega_2) + \cos(2\omega_1+\omega_2) + \cos(2\omega_1-\omega_2)) \\
&+0.094109 \cdot (\cos 2\omega_1 + \cos 2\omega_2) - 0.008439 \cdot (\cos(2\omega_1+2\omega_2) + \cos(2\omega_1-2\omega_2))
\end{aligned}
\tag{102}
$$

$$
\begin{aligned}
S(\omega_1,\omega_2) &\cong 0.552617 + 0.393861 \cdot (\cos\omega_1 + \cos\omega_2) - 0.233406 \cdot (\cos(\omega_1+\omega_2) + \cos(\omega_1-\omega_2)) \\
&-0.041057 \cdot (\cos(\omega_1+2\omega_2) + \cos(\omega_1-2\omega_2) + \cos(2\omega_1+\omega_2) + \cos(2\omega_1-\omega_2)) \\
&-0.1238 \cdot (\cos 2\omega_1 + \cos 2\omega_2) + 0.009519 \cdot (\cos(2\omega_1+2\omega_2) + \cos(2\omega_1-2\omega_2))
\end{aligned}
\tag{103}
$$

Next, expressing each cosine term as a function of the complex variables $z_1 = e^{j\omega_1}$, $z_2 = e^{j\omega_2}$:

$\cos(m\omega_1 + n\omega_2) = 0.5\left(z_1^m z_2^n + z_1^{-m} z_2^{-n}\right)$, we get according to (99) the real functions $C_Z(z_1,z_2)$, $S_Z(z_1,z_2)$. Through the real frequency transformation (98) we finally reached the mappings:

$$
\cos\omega \to C_Z(z_1,z_2) \qquad \sin\omega \to S_Z(z_1,z_2)
\tag{104}
$$

Taking into account the expression (5), the 1D biquad function $H_2(z)$ given in (3) is mapped into the following 2D function $H_{2D}(z_1,z_2)$ in the variables z_1 and z_2 :

$$
H_{2D}(z_1,z_2) = B(z_1,z_2)/A(z_1,z_2) = \frac{b_1 + (b_0 + b_2) \cdot C_Z(z_1,z_2) + j \cdot (b_2 - b_0) \cdot S_Z(z_1,z_2)}{a_1 + (1 + a_0) \cdot C_Z(z_1,z_2) + j \cdot (1 - a_0) \cdot S_Z(z_1,z_2)}
\tag{105}
$$

We remark that the obtained 2D filter function has complex coefficients if it is expressed in the 2D **Z** transform. The real functions $C_Z(z_1,z_2)$, $S_Z(z_1,z_2)$ can further be written as:

$$
C_Z(z_1,z_2) = \mathbf{Z}_1 \times \mathbf{C} \times \mathbf{Z}_2^T \qquad S_Z(z_1,z_2) = \mathbf{Z}_1 \times \mathbf{S} \times \mathbf{Z}_2^T
\tag{106}
$$

where the vectors $\mathbf{Z}_1$, $\mathbf{Z}_2$ are again given in (27) and $\mathbf{C}$, $\mathbf{S}$ are matrices of size 5×5 which have as elements the coefficients identified from the expressions (102) and (103) of $C(\omega_1,\omega_2)$ and $S(\omega_1,\omega_2)$. For instance the matrix $\mathbf{C}$ results as:

$$
\mathbf{C} = \begin{bmatrix}
0.0471 & -0.0272 & -0.0042 & -0.0272 & 0.0471 \\
-0.0272 & 0.0886 & 0.2588 & 0.0886 & -0.0272 \\
-0.0042 & 0.2588 & -0.4198 & 0.2588 & -0.0042 \\
-0.0272 & 0.0886 & 0.2588 & 0.0886 & -0.0272 \\
0.0471 & -0.0272 & -0.0042 & -0.0272 & 0.0471
\end{bmatrix}
\tag{107}
$$

where the elements were limited to 4 decimals. The matrices $\mathbf{C}$ and $\mathbf{S}$ have horizontal and vertical symmetry. Since the element values decrease rapidly towards margins, the size

5×5 for the templates $\mathbf{C}$ and $\mathbf{S}$ is sufficient to ensure the accuracy of the numerical approximation, and higher order terms can be ignored with a negligible error. Taking into account relations (105) and (106), we finally express the complex matrices $\mathbf{B}$ and $\mathbf{A}$ that correspond to the numerator and denominator of $H_{2D}(z_1,z_2)$, i.e. $\mathbf{B}(z_1,z_2)$ and $\mathbf{A}(z_1,z_2)$:

$$\mathbf{B} = b_1 \cdot \mathbf{E} + (b_0 + b_2) \cdot \mathbf{C} + j(b_2 - b_0) \cdot \mathbf{S} \qquad \mathbf{A} = a_1 \cdot \mathbf{E} + (1 + a_0) \cdot \mathbf{C} + j(1 - a_0) \cdot \mathbf{S} \qquad (108)$$

By $\mathbf{E}$ we denoted the 5×5 zero matrix with the central element of value 1. The mapping of the biquad function $H_b(z)$ to $H_{2D}(z_1,z_2)$ can be written as:

$$H_b(z) \rightarrow H_{2D}(z_1,z_2) = \left(\mathbf{Z}_1 \times \mathbf{B} \times \mathbf{Z}_2^T\right)\Big/\left(\mathbf{Z}_1 \times \mathbf{A} \times \mathbf{Z}_2^T\right) \qquad (109)$$

The filter templates result complex due to the fact that $C(\omega_1,\omega_2)$ and $S(\omega_1,\omega_2)$ have even parity in ω_1 and ω_2 and thus can be developed in a trigonometric series of $\cos(m\omega_1 + n\omega_2)$.
Design example. Let us consider the elliptic low-pass prototype filter function

$$H(z) = \frac{0.1539 \cdot z^4 + 0.482 \cdot z^3 + 0.6734 \cdot z^2 + 0.482 \cdot z + 0.1539}{z^4 + 0.155 \cdot z^3 + 0.7649 \cdot z^2 - 0.0376 \cdot z + 0.079} \qquad (110)$$

of order $N = 4$, $R_p = 0.7$ dB passband ripple, a minimum stop-band attenuation $R_S = 40$ dB, pass-band edge frequency $\omega_S = 0.5$, having a maximally-flat frequency response magnitude, with a relatively steep descent (Fig.11(a)). We design a diamond shaped filter starting from this prototype. $H(z)$ can be factorized as follows:

$$H(z) = 0.1539 \cdot \frac{(z^2 + 1.2884z + 1)}{(z^2 + 0.2554z + 0.6732)} \cdot \frac{(z^2 + 1.8425z + 1)}{(z^2 - 0.1004z + 0.1173)} \qquad (111)$$

For the first biquad from (111), we identify the coefficients of the general form (3): $b_2 = 1$, $b_1 = 1.2884$, $b_0 = 1$, $a_1 = 0.2554$, $a_0 = 0.6732$. Since $b_0 = b_2$, the matrix $\mathbf{B}$ from (108) results real (the imaginary part is cancelled), while matrix $\mathbf{A}$ results complex:

$$\mathbf{B}_1 = 1.2884 \cdot \mathbf{E} + 2 \cdot \mathbf{C} \qquad \mathbf{A}_1 = 0.2554 \cdot \mathbf{E} + 1.6732 \cdot \mathbf{C} + 0.3268j \cdot \mathbf{S} \qquad (112)$$

For the second biquad from (111) we get as well:

$$\mathbf{B}_2 = 1.8425 \cdot \mathbf{E} + 2 \cdot \mathbf{C} \qquad \mathbf{A}_2 = -0.1004 \cdot \mathbf{E} + 1.1173 \cdot \mathbf{C} + 0.8827j \cdot \mathbf{S} \qquad (113)$$

The final filter templates $\mathbf{B}$, $\mathbf{A}$ result as convolutions of the templates for the two biquads:

$$\mathbf{B} = 0.1359 \cdot \mathbf{B}_1 * \mathbf{B}_2 \qquad \mathbf{A} = \mathbf{A}_1 * \mathbf{A}_2 \qquad (114)$$

The coefficient in front of $H(z)$ from (111) was included in $\mathbf{B}$.

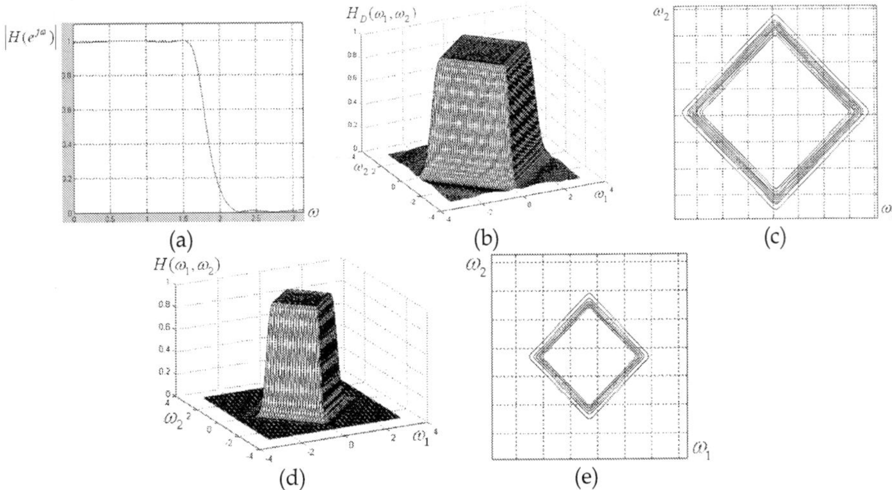

Fig. 11. (a) Magnitude of the elliptic low-pass prototype filter; frequency responses (b), (d) and contour plots (c), (e) for two diamond filters

6. Applications and Simulation Results

All the filters discussed in this chapter have interesting applications in image processing. For the directional filters designed in section 3 some examples are given in (Matei & Matei, 2009) and for zero-phase directional filters in (Matei, 2009, b).

The wedge filter can be used in image filtering to select from a given image the lines with a specified orientation. The spectrum of a straight line is oriented in the plane (ω_1, ω_2) at an angle of $\pi/2$ with respect to the line direction. The binary test image in Fig.12 (a) contains straight lines with different lengths and orientations and is filtered with a maximally-flat wedge filter with aperture $\theta = \pi/6$ and orientation $\varphi = \pi/5$, designed using the method from sub-section 4.1. In the filtered image (Fig.12 (b)) only the lines which have the spectrum oriented more or less along the filter characteristic, remain practically unchanged, while all the other lines appear more or less blurred, due to directional low-pass filtering. The directional resolution depends on the filter angular selectivity given by θ. In the second example shown in Fig.12 (c) we consider a real grayscale image representing a straw texture. The straws have random directions and choosing different filter orientations we can select the ones with roughly the same orientation and filter out the rest. The aperture angle was $\theta = \pi/5$ and three different orientations were used ($\varphi = \pi/6$, $\varphi = \pi/3$, $\varphi = 2\pi/3$), obtaining the filtered images (d), (e), (f). These simple examples illustrate the wedge filter capabilities.

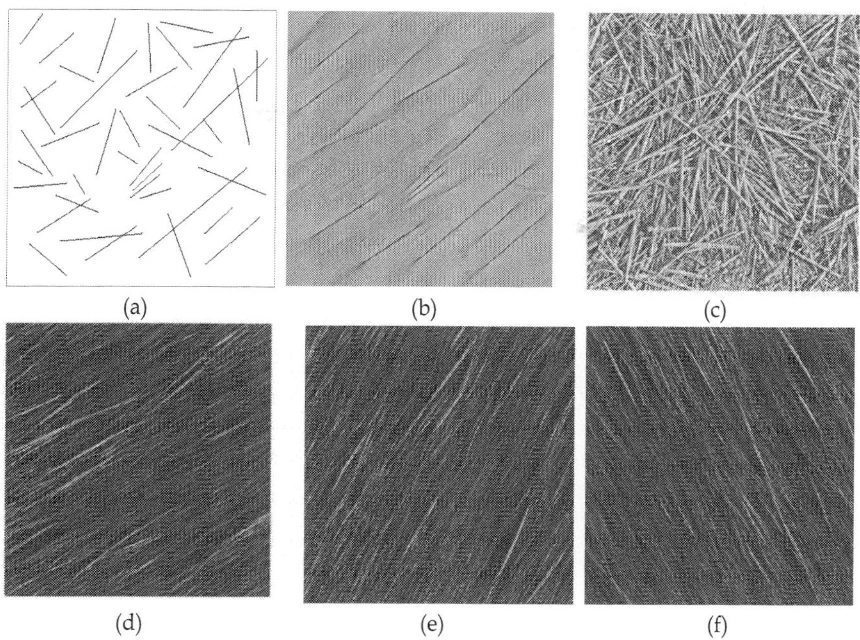

Fig. 12. (a) Binary test image; (b) wedge filter output ($\theta = \pi/6$, $\varphi = \pi/5$); (c) grayscale straw texture image; (d), (e), (f) filtering results using $\theta = \pi/5$ and $\varphi = \pi/6$, $\varphi = \pi/3$, $\varphi = 2\pi/3$

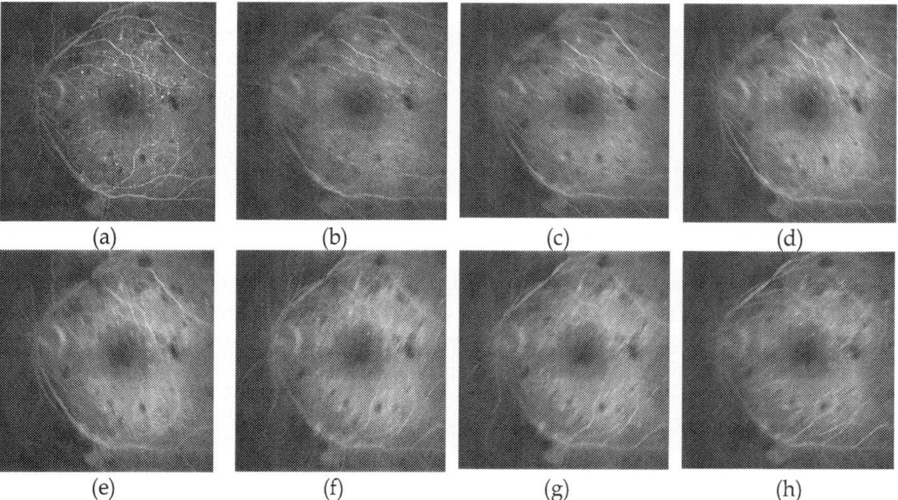

Fig. 13. (a) Retina angiography; (b)-(h) images resulted as output of the filter bank channels

Applying the design method for wedge filters with arbitrary aperture and orientation, it is easy to obtain the components of the Bamberger-type filter bank with 8 bands (Fig.5). It is sufficient to design only two adjacent component filters of the bank (bands 5 and 6), the others resulting from symmetry. This filter bank was applied in filtering a typical medical image. The most currently used vascular imaging technique is X-ray angiography, mainly in diagnosing cardio-vascular pathologies, but also in assessing diabetic retinopathy, a severe complication seriously impairing vision. Clinicians usually search in angiograms relevant features like number and position of vessels (arteries, capillaries).

A filter bank like the one presented above may be used in analyzing angiography images by detecting vessels with a given orientation. Let us consider the retina angiogram in Fig.13 (a), featuring some pathological elements indicating a diabetic retinopathy. This image is applied to the designed 8-band wedge filter bank. Fig.13 (b)-(h) show the directionally filtered images. The vessels whose spectrum overlaps more or less with the filter characteristic remain visible, while the others are blurred, an effect of the low-pass filtering.

7. Conclusion

The design methods presented in this chapter are mainly analytical but include as well some numerical optimization techniques. The 2D filters result from specified 1D prototypes with a desired characteristic, usually low-pass and maximally-flat or very selective. Then for each type of 2D filter, a particular spectral transformation is derived. Thus the 2D filter results from its factorized prototype function by a simple substitution. Only recursive filters were approached, since we envisaged obtaining efficient, low-order filters. The designed filters are versatile in the sense that prototype parameters (band-width, selectivity) can be adjusted and the 2D filter will inherit these properties. An advantage of the analytical approach over the completely numerical optimization techniques is the possibility to control the 2D filter parameters by adjusting the prototype. Several types of 2D filters were approached. A novelty is the analytical design method in polar coordinates, which can yield selective two-directional and even multi-directional filters, and also fan and diamond filters. In polar coordinates more general filters with a specified rotation angle can be synthesized.

Another is the design of zero-phase 2D filters from prototypes with real transfer functions, derived by approximating the magnitude of a common IIR filter. Stability of the designed filters is also an important problem and will be studied in detail in future work on this topic. In principle the spectral transformations used preserve the stability of the 1D prototype. The derived 2D filter could become unstable only if the numerical approximations introduce large errors. In this case the precision of approximation has to be increased by considering higher order terms, which would increase in turn the filter complexity; however, this is the price paid for obtaining efficient and stable 2D filters. Further research will focus on an efficient implementation of the designed filters and also on their applications in real-life image processing.

Acknowledgment

This work was supported by the National University Research Council under Grant PN2 – ID_310 "Algorithms and parallel architectures for signal acquisition, compression and processing".

8. References

Bamberger, R.H. & Smith, M. A filter bank for the directional decomposition of images: theory and design, *IEEE Trans. Signal Processing*, Vol. 40(4), Apr. 1992, pp.882-893

Chang, H. & Aggarwal, J. (1977). Design of two-dimensional recursive filters by interpolation. *IEEE Trans. Circuits Systems*, vol. CAS-24, pp.281-291, June 1977

Danielsson, P.E. (1980). Rotation-Invariant Linear Operators with Directional Response. *Proceedings of 5th International Conf. on Pattern Recognition*, Miami, USA, Dec. 1980

Freeman, W.T. & Adelson, E.H. (1991). The design and use of steerable filters. *IEEE Trans. on Pattern Analysis and Machine Intelligence*, Vol.13 (9), Sept. 1991, pp.891-906

Harn, L. & Shenoi, B. (1986). Design of stable two-dimensional IIR filters using digital spectral transformations. *IEEE Trans. Circ. Systems*, CAS-33, May 1986, pp. 483-490

Hirano, K. & Aggarwal, J.K. (1978). Design of two-dimensional recursive digital filters. *IEEE Trans. Circuits Systems*, CAS-25, Dec. 1978, pp.1066-1076

Jury, E.I.; Kolavennu, V.R. & Anderson, B.D. (1977). Stabilization of certain two-dimensional recursive digital filters. *Proceedings of the IEEE*, vol. 65, no. 6, 1977, pp. 887–892

Kayran, A. & King, R. (1983). Design of recursive and nonrecursive fan filters with complex transformations, *IEEE Trans. on Circuits and Systems*, CAS-30(12), 1983, pp.849-857

Lakshmanan, V. (2004). A separable filter for directional smoothing. *IEEE Geoscience and Remote Sensing Letters*, July 2004, Vol.1, pp.192-195

Lim, J.S. (1990). *Two-Dimensional Signal and Image Processing*. Prentice-Hall 1990

Lim, Y.C. & Low, S.H. (1997). The synthesis of sharp diamond-shaped filters using the frequency response masking approach. *Proc. of IEEE Int. Conf. on Acoustics, Speech & Signal Processing, ICASSP-97*, pp.2181-2184, Munich, Germany, Apr. 21-24, 1997

Low, S.H. & Lim, Y. C. (1998). A new approach to design sharp diamond-shaped filters. *Signal Processing*, Vol. 67 (1), May 1998, pp. 35-48, ISSN:0165-1684

Lu, W.S. & Antoniou, A. (1992). *Two-Dimensional Digital Filters*, CRC Press, 1992

Matei, R. & Matei, D. (2009). Orientation-selective 2D recursive filter design based on frequency transformations, *Proceedings of IEEE Region 8 EUROCON 2009 Conference*, pp. 1320-1327, ISBN 978-1-4244-3861-7, St. Petersburg, Russia, May 18-23, 2009

Matei, R. (2009, a). Design Method for Wedge-Shaped Filters, *Proceedings of the International Conference on Signal Processing and Multimedia Applications SIGMAP 2009*, pp. 19-23, ISBN 978-989-674-005-4, Milano, Italy, July 7-10, 2009

Matei, R. (2009, b). New Model and Applications of Cellular Neural Networks in Image Processing, In: "Advanced Technologies", Kankesu Jayanthakumaran (Ed.), pp. 471-501, IN-TECH Vienna, 2009, ISBN: 978-953-307-009-4

Matei, R. (2010). A New Design Method for IIR Diamond-Shaped Filters, *Proceedings of the 18th European Signal Processing Conference EUSIPCO 2010*, pp. 65-69, ISSN 2076-1465, Aalborg, Denmark, Aug. 23-27, 2010

O'Connor, B.T. & Huang, T.S. (1978). Stability of general two-dimensional recursive digital filters," *IEEE Trans. Acoustics, Speech & Signal Processing*, vol.26 (6), 1978, pp.550–560

Pendergrass, N.; Mitra, S.K. & Jury, E.I. (1976). Spectral transformations for two-dimensional digital filters. *IEEE Transactions Circuits & Systems*, vol. CAS-23, Jan. 1976, pp. 26-35

Randen, R. & Husoy, J.H. (1999). Filtering for texture classification: a comparative study. *IEEE Trans. Pattern Analysis and Machine Intelligence*, Vol.21(4), Apr.1999, pp.291-310

Simoncelli, E.P. & Farid, H. (1996). Steerable wedge filters for local orientation analysis. *IEEE Trans.on Image Processing*, Vol. 5 (9), Sep 1996, pp.1377-1382, ISSN: 1057-7149

6

Integration of digital filters and measurements

Jan Peter Hessling
Measurement Technology, SP Technical Research Institute of Sweden

1. Introduction

Digital filters (Hamming, 1998; Chen, 2001) are versatile, practical and effective. They can be used in most computerized applications of modern technology and science. Nearly every person in technologically developed regions daily encounter digital filters in cars, dvd-recorders, computers, telecommunication systems etc. Usually, digital filters are designed and optimized by signal processing experts for standardized tasks in specific systems. Extensive work may result in advanced and complex filters. This is motivated by massive duplication. The marginal production cost for a filter is practically zero and the development cost per unit is negligible. The advantages of using digital instead of analogue filters are often profound. Not only are the costs negligible, their flexibility makes it possible to achieve superior results. Even unstable operations can be realized by means of reversed filtering. The limitations of digital filters are mainly mathematical, rather than physical as for analogue filters.

Dynamic measurements condense observations into quantitative representations (Hessling, 2010a). Dynamic methods for improving, interpreting and assessing the quality of measurements are relatively scarce. These methods can be formulated in terms of ideal prototype systems acting on physical signals to produce the desired information. A dynamic calibration procedure is usually required to find the model from which such prototypes are determined. Ideal prototypes are approximated and optimized into realizable prototypes which can be cast into digital filters by means of sampling. These filters differ from most common filters of today. They are dedicated filters with a high level of adaptation and flexibility, designed to improve or simplify the evaluation of a wide range of measurements for many different purposes. The common denominator of all filters is that they are intended to provide a supporting link of standardized dynamic analysis between the 'raw' measurements and an inexperienced destined user. The digital filters and the measurement devices are preferably seamlessly integrated in the final application, which most often already has a computer program for administrating the measurement.

The motivation for making any measurement is to extract information. The desired information is rarely identical to measured signals. Measured signals need to be processed or analyzed. Signals may be corrected. To determine how wrong the result might be, the uncertainty needs to be estimated. The measurement system may be one part of a complex dynamic system, for instance, an accelerometer attached to a vibrating vehicle. Sometimes transformations between various points in space, or electrical quantities etc. are required. We might be interested in the consequences of measured signals. The impact of interest is often quantified in scalar measures or *features* like peak loads in crash testing, average power in electrical systems, or accumulated risk of injury.

The analysis is based on how dynamic systems are modeled with differential equations, rather than any specific system which can be electrical, mechanical, etc. To illustrate the design, or *synthesis* and application of digital filters, mechanical systems will be used. There are two reasons for this choice: Mechanical systems are widely understood and digital filters have not yet been utilized in this field to any significant extent. The applications will be split into two categories, analysis of measured signals (section 3) and feature extraction (section 4). For analyzing measured signals the same mechanical transducer system as well as triangular input signal will be used. This example represents the simplest possible non-trivial dynamic measurement system, which is good for illustration of principles rather than details. Two examples of feature extraction are given, the analysis of road humps (section 4.1) and the determination of road surface roughness, or texture (section 4.2). Both examples relate to traffic and the structure of road surface, and both address potential health risks. The geometric scales differ: A speed limiting road hump is a 3-20 m long intentionally modified part of the road. The texture relates to unevenness of 5-50 mm wavelength. The road hump profile is translated to a time-dependent excitation signal of a bandwidth varying with the speed of passage. The surface texture example illustrates that digital filters are not limited to the time domain but work perfectly well also for space domain analysis.

The digital filters will be expressed on a standard linear-in-response finite/infinite impulse response (FIR/IIR) form for direct implementation. It will be indicated how any filter may be transferred to a state-space form for generalization into a Kalman filter (Simon, 2006).

2. Synthesis of digital filters from prototypes

2.1 General framework

The real world of observable physical quantities are almost exclusively continuous in time as well as amplitude. The world of information we are interested in may contain anything we can imagine. The link between the two is the world of computers which is discrete in time as well as amplitude. Our interest may be expressed in *prototype systems*. These hybrid systems are not generally physical, but are formulated as if they would. The prototypes for dynamic correction in section 3.2 and the sensitivity systems in section 3.3.1 are two examples. The prototypes will specify the desired filter operation completely. No conventional filter specification in terms of pass-band, stop-band and allowed ripple etc. will be used. Prototypes are widely used in filter synthesis. The concept is here further generalized to describe virtually anything we might be interested in.

The major part of this chapter will be devoted to derivation of *realizable* dynamic prototype systems *continuous in time* (CT). These prototypes are sampled to convert them into systems *discrete in time* (DT), for direct interpretation as digital filters. The translation of *any* continuous formulation to a discrete formulation will be denoted *sampling*. The terminology is here generalized to reflect symmetries: Signals, systems as well as statistical information may be sampled. The methods of sampling are rather different though. Sampling of signals is unique. Sampling of systems necessarily adds distortion and there is a multitude of different well-known methods. *Random sampling* of statistical information is practiced in Monte Carlo simulations (Metropolis, 1949; Rubenstein & Kroese, 2007) but there are other recent and more effective methods of *deterministic sampling* (Julier & Uhlmann, 2004).

Sampling is here lifted to a more abstract level since statistical information is neither physical, nor directly observable. Statistical dynamic models may be sampled twice: The statistical information is first sampled to obtain a finite set of CT prototype systems. Each prototype system is then sampled to find a corresponding digital filter. Sampling of CT systems will always render systematic model errors. These will be called *discretization time errors* (DTE) (Hessling, 2008a). The DTE is different for different input signals and may thus be visualized in various ways, depending on the chosen measure of signal error. If the DTE is given as a function of system bandwidth, the *utilization* of a mapping expresses how much of the maximum (DTE=0) bandwidth that may be used for acceptable DTE. The theoretical limit is set by the sampling rate $f_S = T_S^{-1}$ which results in a maximum bandwidth given by the Nyquist frequency $f_N = f_S/2$. For many prototypes though there may be other lower bandwidth limits, for instance the limit of unacceptable noise amplification. *Reversed* or backward digital filtering is an allowed luxury for analyzing measurements. It simplifies many tasks like stabilization and elimination of phase distortion tremendously and will be used extensively. Reversed filtering is implemented in three steps: 1. The beginning and the end of the signal are exchanged to 'reverse direction'. 2. Forward filtering 3. Repetition of step 1. *Symmetric* forward and reverse filtering (Gustafsson, 1996) is in its simplest form (Hamming, 1998) implemented as repeated filtering in both directions. The fall-off rate as well as the attenuation at the nominal cross-over frequency is doubled compared to forward filtering. The total phase response vanishes identically (at all frequencies).
The methods for sampling of prototype systems fall into two categories, numerical sampling and *mapping* techniques. Numerical sampling minimizes the discrepancy between characterizations of the CT prototype and the sampled DT model (Elster et. al., 2007). The characterizations may be given in any representation, for instance in the time or frequency domain. The deviation is often quantified with a weighted least square error (Bjork, 1996). Splitting system identification of CT models (Pintelon & Schoukens, 2001) and numeral sampling into successive steps of analysis is strongly discouraged: The two operations are comparable and better optimized jointly, as is conventional (Ljung, 1999). Mapping techniques are based on universal relations between CT and DT models and it is simple to switch sampling rate. Robustness and simplicity are paid with a minor reduction of accuracy due to lack of optimality of the mapping rule. The accuracy is determined by the calculated DTE, and controlled by the selection of mapping. A brief recapitulation of some mappings and their properties are given in the next section.

2.2 Mappings for sampling of prototypes
A common class of mappings samples the response of the CT prototype system to an input signal of particular interest. The calculated CT response is sampled like any signal to yield a DT system which does not distort, or is *invariant* with respect to the selected input signal. The *impulse invariance* method (IMP) (Chen, 2001) samples the impulse response $h(t)$. The calculation is facilitated by expansion in residues r_k and poles p_k,

$$H(s) = \frac{\prod_k (s - z_k)}{\prod_k (s - p_k)} = \sum_k \frac{r_k}{s - p_k} \quad \Rightarrow \quad h(t) = \sum_k r_k \exp(p_k t). \tag{1}$$

Sampling with sampling time interval $T_S = f_S^{-1}$ results in the DT impulse response g_n and transfer function $G(z)$,

$$g_n = h(nT_S) = \sum_k r_k \exp(np_k T_S) \quad \Rightarrow \quad G(z) = T_S \sum_n g_n z^{-n} = \sum_k \frac{r_k T_S z}{z - \exp(p_k T_S)}. \tag{2}$$

The IMP method requires a decaying frequency response $H(i\omega) \approx 0, \omega > \pi f_S$ to avoid aliasing. Thus it can only be used if the number of poles of the CT prototype exceeds its number of zeros. The static amplification is *not* preserved, see Fig. 1 (left). Poles of the CT system are mapped to poles of the sampled DT system with an exponential mapping $p_k \to \exp(p_k T_S)$. The zeros of the two systems have no simple relation, not even their number is preserved. If instead also zeros are mapped like the poles of the IMP method, the exponential pole-zero mapping (EXP) results (Chen, 2001; Hessling, 2008a),

$$q_k \to \exp(q_k T_S), \quad q_k = z_k, p_k. \tag{3}$$

This simple mapping preserves the static amplification, the numbers of poles and zeros as well as the stability properties. The high frequency amplification is bounded. Its major drawback is a fairly low utilization. The mapping is transparent as the underlying CT model in the s-plane can be discerned in the z-plane. This will be the default mapping.

'Functional' mappings are described by substitution rules $s = M(z)$. The DT transfer function $G(z)$ is found from the CT transfer function $H(s)$ as $G(z) = H(M(z))$. It is important to compensate for the time delays τ_G, τ_H of the DT and CT systems, respectively. The delays should conform to the measure of the DTE. If the DTE ΔH is expressed in the frequency domain, $\Delta H = \exp(i\omega\tau_G)G(\exp(i\omega T_S)) - \exp(i\omega\tau_H)H(i\omega)$. The standard bi-linear mapping (BIL) (Chen, 2001) is a functional mapping,

$$s = \frac{2(z-1)}{T_S(z+1)}. \tag{4}$$

The BIL mapping unfortunately introduces singularities at the Nyquist frequency $(z = -1)$. It also results in a non-linear mapping of the frequency axis called *frequency warping* (Chen, 2001).

Since $s = M(z)$ is the differential operator and z the translation operator, the mapping function is nothing else than a discrete time approximation of a simple derivative expressed in translations. The symmetric difference quotient approximation $\partial_t f(t) \approx [f(t + T_S) - f(t - T_S)]/2T_S$ directly renders the mapping $s = (z - z^{-1})/2T_S$. A novel n-th order symmetric approximation is obtained by expanding in symmetric difference quotients of various integer steps k,

$$M^{(n)}(z) = \sum_{k=1}^{n} c_k^{(n)} \frac{z^k - z^{-k}}{2kT_S}. \tag{5}$$

The coefficients $c_k^{(n)}$ may be found by minimizing the DTE over the whole frequency axis up to the Nyquist frequency using linear regression for the approximation,

$$1 \approx \sum_{k=1}^{n} c_k^{(n)} \frac{\sin(kx)}{kx}, \quad x \in [0, \pi]. \tag{6}$$

A low-frequency approximation is found by expanding the sine-function and matching as many powers as allowed by the order n. This yields a whole sequence of difference quotient mappings $DQ(n)$. The DTE decreases rapidly with n, but the number of poles and zeros increases with a factor of $2n$.

The choice of method for sampling prototypes is in practice influenced by many aspects. It should be stressed that the DTE seldom is the only relevant issue. The discussion of various mappings for sampling of prototype systems is concluded with an illustration of the DTE (Fig. 1), for the example model described in section 3.1.1.

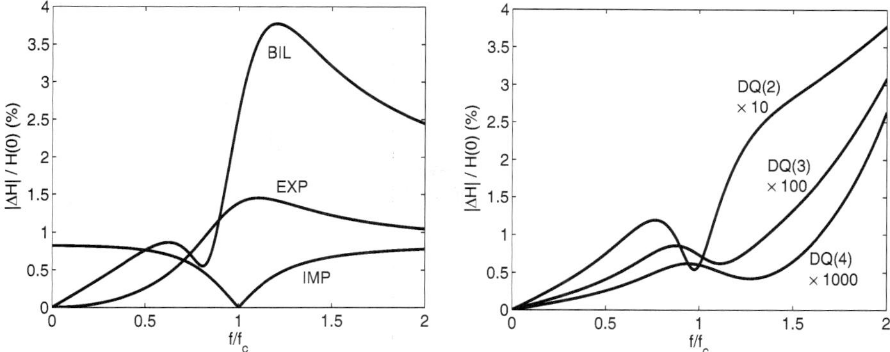

Fig. 1. The normalized DTE for the transducer model (Eq. 11) and various mappings (notation is given in the text). The mappings $DQ(n)$ are rescaled for comparison (right).

2.3 State space formulation for Kalman filter

Kalman filters are popular tools for optimal estimation of signals in noisy measurements (Simon, 2006). Conventional digital filters are closely related to Kalman filtering. In this section it will be briefly indicated how any digital filter can be converted into the formulation used for Kalman filters.

Kalman filters utilize DT state-space equations, which are equivalent to transfer functions. State-space equations exist for both CT and DT and are not uniquely specified by the system. Their main feature is linearity in the differential ∂_t (CT) or displacement operator Δ (DT). State-space equations are convenient for analyzing large and complex multiple-input multiple-output systems, like finding the response of vehicles (section 4.1.2), using linear algebra. Sampling of CT state-space equations can be made by transformation to transfer functions, sample (section 2.2) and transform to DT state-space equations.

A state-space formulation contains two equations, a dynamic state-space equation and a static measurement equation. The state-space equation is the 'engine' that drives the system in response to its input. The measurement equation describes how our quantity of interest is related to the state-space variables and the input. This separation makes it possible to use virtually any set of [state-space] variables. They may be physical quantities but often are not. The key aspect of all sets of variables is that they split the model into several equations linear in the differential ∂_t (CT) or displacement Δ (DT) operator. In CT,

$$\begin{aligned} \partial_t u &= Au + Bx \\ y &= Cu + Dx \end{aligned} \tag{7}$$

The input x, the output y and the state-space variables u are all column vectors. Applying the La-place transform, the transfer function is obtained by matrix inversion,

$$H(s) = \frac{Y(s)}{X(s)} = \left[C(s-A)^{-1} B + D \right] = \sum_{k=0}^{m} b_k s^k \Bigg/ \sum_{k=0}^{n} a_k s^k . \tag{8}$$

This transformation from any linear state-space formulation to the corresponding transfer function non-linear in s is unique. The set of canonical state-space variables is one of many choices of transformation in the opposite direction. This choice must however be extended to allow for prototypes with $m > n-1$ (subscripts indicate sizes of sub-matrices),

$$\begin{aligned} U_1(s) &= s^m X(s) \Bigg/ \sum_{k=0}^{n} a_k s^k & A &= \begin{pmatrix} 0_{(1\times(m-n+1))} & -a_{n-1}/a_n & -a_{n-2}/a_n & \cdots & -a_0/a_n \\ & \mathrm{diag}(1)_{(m\times m)} & & & 0_{(m\times 1)} \end{pmatrix} \\ U_k(s) &= \begin{cases} \dfrac{1}{s} U_{k-1}(s), \\ k = 2,3,\ldots m+1 \end{cases} \Rightarrow \begin{aligned} B &= \begin{pmatrix} 1 & 0 & \cdots & 0 \end{pmatrix}^T \\ C &= \begin{pmatrix} b_m & b_{m-1} & \cdots & b_0 \end{pmatrix} \\ D &= 0 \end{aligned} \end{aligned} \tag{9}$$

The transformations are similar for DT, essentially let $\partial_t \to \Delta$ and $s \to z$. The noise enters as process noise (w) in state variables as well as measurement noise (v) in the measured quantity. The process noise effectively corresponds to the uncertainty of our model (section 3.3), but is expressed differently. Depending on the state variables it may be difficult to assign a reasonable model of process noise in any other way than studying the result. The measurement noise is physical and observable and therefore much easier to estimate. Adding noise in the DT state-space model we finally arrive at the Kalman filter equations,

$$\begin{aligned} \Delta u &= Au + Bx + w \\ y &= Cu + Dx + v \end{aligned}, \quad \Delta u_k = u_{k+1} . \tag{10}$$

3. Applications related to calibration

The result of a dynamic calibration of a measurement system is difficult to use directly (Hessling, 2010a). The performance of the system depends strongly on the variation of the signal and has to be calculated for *every* measured signal. Parts of this calculation can be formulated as digital filtering of measured signals. The time-invariant unique filters are then synthesized from the calibration result. The filter coefficients *represent* the calibration result. Digital filters are already used in some measurement systems. The novel aspect here is to use digital filtering as a method to formulate the calibration result for every measured signal. Digital filters will here be used for dynamic correction (section 3.2) and for estimating the model uncertainty of this correction (section 3.3).

The measured signal results from the specific combination of input signal and measurement system. The statistical dynamic model of the measurement system will be assumed time-invariant and linear-in-response, but non-linear-in-parameters. The variable performance is due to the time-dependence of the signal and not the system. Of primary interest is to correct the measured signal to resemble the physical input of the measurement system as much as possible. That is an inverse problem, as it requires the construction of a prototype for the inverse system. The uncertainty of the model is transferred to uncertainty of this prototype of correction. When applying the correction filter, the uncertainty of the corrected signal increases further due to measurement noise. Thus there are two principal sources of uncertainty for corrected signals, model uncertainty and noise. For the addressed linear-in-response systems the measurement noise and the measured signal propagate identically through the correction filter. Propagation of measurement noise will not be addressed here as it only relates to the correction filter and is elementary (Hessling, 2009). The model uncertainty propagates very differently – a perturbation of a dynamic model leads to a non-trivial perturbation of the corrected signal.

3.1 Example of measurement

3.1.1 Measurement system

The model of a measurement may be determined from calibration and/or from first principles. First principles often suggest structures of the model while the values of the parameters are deduced from experimental calibration data by means of system identification (Ljung, 1999; Pintelon & Schoukens, 2001). To focus on synthesis of digital filters rather than modeling, a strongly simplified model will be used. Mechanical sensors for measuring acceleration, pressure, force and torque are often made of a strain-gauge element attached to a flexible sensor material. The mechanical construction is well described by two masses separated by a damped spring (Crosswy & Kalb, 1970). This results in a simple resonance at frequency f_C with relative damping ζ. Usually the damping is moderate $(\zeta < 1)$ (Moghisi & Squire, 1980) giving a complex-conjugated pole pair (p, p^*) in the s-plane,

$$H(s) = \frac{K|p|^2}{(s-p)(s-p^*)} = \frac{r_1}{s-p} + \frac{r_2}{s-p^*}, \qquad \begin{aligned} p &= 2\pi f_C\left(-\zeta \pm i\sqrt{1-\zeta^2}\right) = p_R + ip_I \\ r_k &= i(-1)^k K|p|^2 / 2\,\mathrm{Im}(p) \end{aligned} \qquad (11)$$

The mean $\langle \cdot \rangle$ and the covariance matrix for the parameters are given in Table 1. The complex-valued frequency response is given by $H(i\omega)$. The first parameterization is made in K and the roots, or poles (p) of the denominator polynomial, rather than its coefficients. This factorization makes the models less non-linear-in-parameters. The high sensitivity to variations in coefficients would make the estimation of measurement uncertainty (section 3.3) more difficult. These problems increase rapidly with the order of the model. The second parameterization is made in residues (r) and poles. All models are linear in residues. Exploring different parameterizations is strongly encouraged as that may improve and simplify the analysis significantly. Since the input as well as output signal of the measurement system is real-valued, poles and zeros are either real, or complex-conjugated in pairs. This physical constraint must be fully respected in all steps of the analysis. The simple transducer model has only one complex-conjugated pole pair but that is sufficient for illustrating the various methods. The general case with an arbitrary number of poles and zeros is discussed in recent publications (Hessling, 2008a; 2009).

$$
\begin{pmatrix} \langle K \rangle \\ \langle f_C \rangle \\ \langle \varsigma \rangle \end{pmatrix} = \begin{pmatrix} 1.00 \\ 50.0\,\text{kHz} \\ 0.300 \end{pmatrix}, \quad \text{cov}(K, p_R, p_I) = 10^{-4} \begin{pmatrix} 0.50^2 & 0 & 0 \\ 0 & 1.00^2 & 1.20^2 \\ 0 & 1.20^2 & 2.00^2 \end{pmatrix}, \quad \begin{aligned} \text{S/N} &= 50\text{dB} \\ f_S &= 20 f_C \end{aligned}
$$

Table 1. Mean values and covariance matrix of the parameters of the dynamic model (Eq. 11), signal-to-noise ratio S/N at zero frequency, and chosen sampling rate f_S.

3.1.2 Input and output signal

The performance of the measurement system is different for different physical input signals. For illustration it is sufficient to study only one input signal. In order to obtain visible effects, its bandwidth is chosen high. Its regularity or differentiability should also be low as that implies a high sensitivity to the proposed filtering. The triangular pulse in Fig. 2 fulfills these requirements. The distortion is due to both amplitude and phase imperfections of the frequency response of the system within its bandwidth, as well as a limited bandwidth.

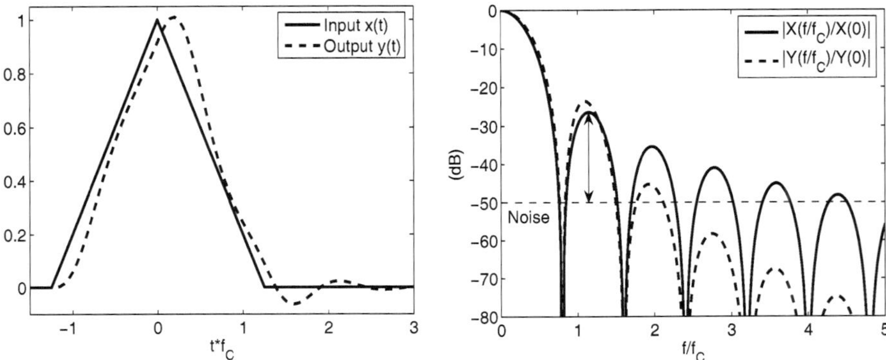

Fig. 2. Input and output signal of the measurement system (left) and magnitudes of their spectra (right). The arrow (right) indicates the signal-to-noise ratio (S/N) of the input signal.

3.2 Dynamic correction

Correction of measured signals using knowledge of the measurement system (Pintelon et. al., 1990; Hessling, 2010a) is practiced in many fields of science and engineering. Surprisingly, dynamic correction is not yet generally offered in the context of calibrations, despite that static corrections in principle are required (ISO GUM, 1993). Dynamic correction will here refer to reduction of all kinds of dynamic imperfections of the measurement. The digital correction filter essentially propagates measured signals backwards through a mathematical model of the system to their physical origin. Backwards propagation can be viewed as either an inverse or reversed propagation. Not surprisingly, reversed filtering is sometimes useful when realizing correction filters (Hessling, 2008a).

Correction requires an estimate of the inverse model of the measurement. In the time domain, it is a fairly complex operation to find the inverse differential equation. For a model parameterized in poles and zeros of a transfer function it is trivial. The inverse is then found by exchanging poles and zeros. A pole (zero) of the measurement system is then eliminated or *annihilated* with its 'conjugate' zero (pole) of the correction filter.

A generic and unavoidable problem for all methods of dynamic correction is due to the finite bandwidth of the measurement system. The bandwidth of the system and the level of measurement noise set a definite limit to which extent any signal may be corrected. The high frequency amplification of the inverse system is virtually without bound. Therefore, some kind of low-pass 'noise' filters must always be included in a correction. These reduce the total gain and hence the level of noise to a predefined acceptable level. Incidentally, if the sampling rate is low enough, the bandwidth set by the Nyquist frequency may be sufficient to limit the gain of the correction filter. The noise filter is preferably chosen 'optimal' to balance measurement error and noise in the most relevant way. To determine the degree of optimality requires a measure of the error, or the deviation between the corrected signal and the input signal of the measurement system. The time delay and the dynamic error are usually distinguished as different causes for deviations between signals (study Fig. 2, left). A unique definition of the time delay is therefore also required (Hessling, 2006). Since the error is different for different measured signals, so is also the optimal correction.

When dynamic correction fails it is usually either due to neglect of noise amplification, or insufficient model quality. On one hand, the required model quality may be underestimated. A model with almost perfect match of only the amplitude $|H(i\omega)|$ of the frequency response may result in a 'correction' which *increases* the error! The phase $\arg H(i\omega)$ is equally important as the magnitude (Ekstrom, 1972; Hessling, 2006): A correction applied with the wrong sign doubles instead of eliminates the error. On the other hand, the required model quality should not be overestimated. As long as the error is mainly due to bandwidth limitations, the model quality within the band is irrelevant. The best strategy is then to optimize the noise filter or regularization technique to be able to dig up the last piece of high frequency information from the measured signal (Hale & Dienstfrey, 2010).

The proposed pragmatic design (Hessling, 2008a) inspired by Wiener de-convolution (Wiener, 1949) will here be applied for determining the noise filter. To develop the method further, the noise filter will be determined for the actual input signal (Fig. 2). The correction filter is then not only *applied* to but also uniquely *synthesized* for every measured signal. The proposed optimal noise filter has a cross-over frequency f_N determined from the frequency where the system amplification has decayed to the inverse of the signal-to-noise ratio (S/N). The S/N-ratio oscillates for the triangular input signal. To find the desired cross-over it is thus necessary to estimate the envelope of the S/N-ratio, as shown in Fig. 3 (left) below. A property of the noise filter which is equally important as the cross-over is the asymptotic fall-off rate in the frequency domain (Hessling, 2006). The proposed noise filter is suggested to be applied symmetrically in both directions of time to cancel its phase. In that case, the fall-off rate of the noise filter and the measurement system should be the same. The fall-off rates of the correction filter with the noise filter applied twice and the measurement system are then the same. For the transducer, the noise filter should be of second order. Other details of the amplitude fall-off were ignored, as they are beyond reach for optimal correction in practice.

The prototype for correction was constructed by annihilating the poles of the model (Eq. 11) with zeros. This CT prototype was then sampled to DT using the simple exponential mapping (section 2.2). The poles and zeros of the correction filter are shown in Fig. 5 (top left). The impulse response (Fig. 5, bottom left) of the correction filter is non-causal since time-reversed noise filtering was adopted. The correction was carried out by filtering the output signal of the measurement system to find the corrected signal x_C in Fig. 3 (right).

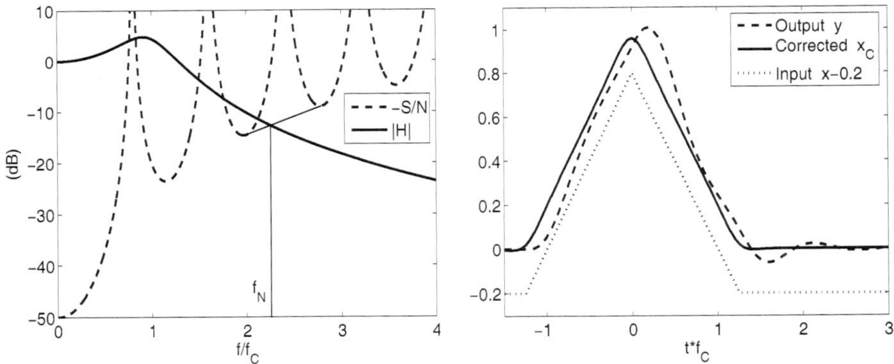

Fig. 3. Left: Signal to noise ratio (S/N) for the input signal (Fig. 2) and amplification $|H|$ of the measurement system, for determining the cut-off frequency f_N of the noise filter. Right: The output and the corrected output. The input signal is indicated (displaced for clarity).

3.3 Measurement uncertainty

The primary indicator of measurement quality is measurement uncertainty. It is usually expressed as a confidence interval for the measurement result. How to find the confidence interval from a probability density function (pdf) of the uncertain parameters that influence the quantity of interest is suggested in the Guide to the Expression of Uncertainty (ISO GUM, 1993). It is formulated for static measurements with a time-independent measurement equation. The dynamic measurements of interest here is beyond its original scope. Nevertheless, the guide is based on a standard perturbation analysis of first order which may be generalized to dynamic conditions. The instantaneous analysis is then translated into filtering operations. The uncertainty of the parameters of the dynamic model and the measurement noise contribute to the dynamic measurement uncertainty. Only propagation of model uncertainty will be discussed here.

The linearity of a measurement system is a common source of misunderstanding. Any dynamic system h may be linear-in-response (LR), or linear-in-parameters (LP). LR does *not* imply that the output signal is proportional to the input signal. Instead it means that the response to a sum of signals y_1, y_2 equals the sum of the responses of the signals, or $h(\alpha y_1 + \beta y_2, q) = \alpha \cdot h(y_1, q) + \beta \cdot h(y_2, q)$, for all α, β. Analogously, a model LP would imply that $h(y, \alpha q_1 + \beta q_2) = \alpha \cdot h(y, q_1) + \beta \cdot h(y, q_2)$. A model h equal to a sum of LP models h_k, $h = \sum h_k$, would then *not* be classified LP. Nevertheless, such models are normally considered LP as they are linear expansions. Therefore, any model that can be expressed as a sum of LP models will be considered LP.

To be a useful measurement system we normally require high linearity in response. Conventional linear digital filtering requires LR. A lot of effort is therefore made by manufacturers to fulfill this expectation and by calibrating parties to verify it. LR is a physical property of the system completely beyond control for the user, as well as the calibrator. In contrast, LP is determined by the model, which is partly *chosen* with the parameterization. It is for instance possible to exchange non-linearity in zeros with linearity in residues (section 3.1.1).

The non-linear propagation of measurement uncertainty by means of linear digital filtering in section 3.3.2 refers to measurement systems non-linear-in-parameters but linear-in-response. The presented method is an alternative to the non-degenerate unscented method (Hessling et. al., 2010b). At present there is no other published or established and consistent method used in calibrations for this type of non-linear propagation of measurement uncertainty, beyond inefficient Monte-Carlo simulations. For linear propagation of dynamic measurement uncertainty with digital filters, there is only one original publication (Hessling, 2009). In this reference, a complete description of estimation of measurement uncertainty is given.

3.3.1 Linear propagation using sensitivities

The established calculation of uncertainty (ISO GUM, 1993) follows the standard procedure of first order perturbation analysis adopted in most fields of science and engineering. Consistent application of the guide is strictly limited to linearization of the model equation (Hessling et. al., 2010b). Here, the analysis translates into linearization of the transfer function or impulse response in uncertain parameters. The derivation will closely follow a recent presentation (Hessling, 2010a). For correction of the mechanical transducer,

$$\delta H^{-1}(s) \approx \delta K \frac{\partial H^{-1}}{\partial K} + \delta p \frac{\partial H^{-1}}{\partial p} + \delta p^* \frac{\partial H^{-1}}{\partial p^*}. \tag{12}$$

The pole pair p, p^* of the original measurement system (section 3.1.1) is here a pair of zeros of the CT prototype H^{-1} of correction (section 3.2). The variations $\delta p, \delta p^*$ are completely correlated. Rather than modeling this correlation it is simpler to change variables. Evaluating the derivatives (Hessling, 2009),

$$\delta H^{-1}H(s) \approx E_K \frac{\delta K}{K} + E_p^{(22)}(s)\rho_1 + E_p^{(12)}(s)\rho_2,$$

$$E_K = -1, \quad E_p^{(m2)}(s) = \frac{2\left(-s/|p|\right)^m}{\left(p/|p| - s/|p|\right)\left(|p|/p - s/|p|\right)}, \quad \rho_n = \frac{\delta p}{|p|} \bullet \left(\frac{p}{|p|}\right)^n. \tag{13}$$

If the dynamic sensitivity systems $E_K, E_p^{(22)}(s), E_p^{(12)}(s)$ operate on the corrected signal $x_C(t)$ it will result in three time-dependent sensitivity signals $\xi_K(t), \xi_p^{(22)}(t), \xi_p^{(12)}(t)$ describing the sensitivity to the stochastic quantities $\delta K/K, \rho_1, \rho_2$. The latter quantities are written as vector scalar products or projections in the complex s-plane between the relative fluctuation $\rho \equiv \delta p/|p|$ and powers of the normalized pole vector $p/|p|$, as illustrated in Fig. 4.

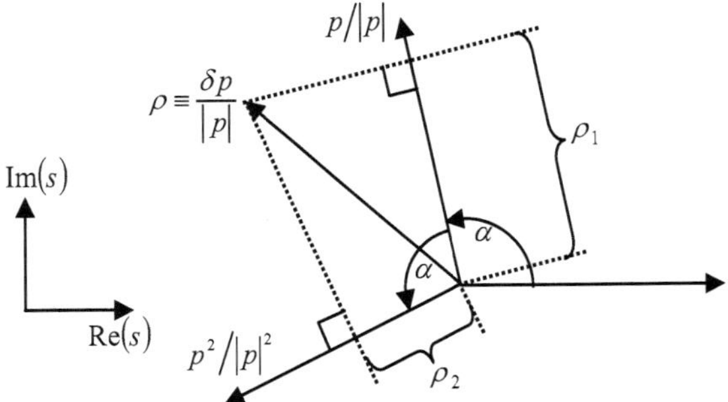

Fig. 4. Illustration of the relative variation ρ and associated projections ρ_1, ρ_2 in the s-plane.

If the sensitivity signals $\xi_K(t), \xi_p^{(22)}(t), \xi_p^{(12)}(t)$ are organized in rows of a $3 \times m$ matrix ξ, the variation of the correction will be given by $\chi = \xi^T \varphi, \varphi \equiv [\delta K/K \quad \rho_1 \quad \rho_2]^T$. The auto-correlation function of the signal χ resulting from the uncertainty of the model is found by squaring and calculating the statistical expectation $\langle \cdot \rangle$ over the variations of the parameters,

$$\langle \chi \chi^T \rangle = \xi^T \langle \varphi \varphi^T \rangle \xi = \xi^T \operatorname{cov}(K, \rho_1, \rho_2)\xi. \tag{14}$$

The matrix $\langle \varphi \varphi^T \rangle$ of expectation values of squared parameter variations is usually referred to as the covariance matrix $\operatorname{cov}(K, \rho_1, \rho_2)$. In Table 1 it was given in the parameters $K, \mathrm{Re}(p), \mathrm{Im}(p)$. In Table 2 it is translated to parameters K, ρ_1, ρ_2 with a linear but non-unitary transformation $T\left(TT^T \neq 1\right)$ (Hessling, 2009),

$$\mathrm{cov}(K,\rho_1,\rho_2)=T\,\mathrm{cov}(K,\mathrm{Re}(p),\mathrm{Im}(p))T^{T}=10^{-4}\begin{pmatrix}0.50^2 & 0 & 0\\ 0 & 1.70^2 & -1.68^2\\ 0 & -1.68^2 & 1.83^2\end{pmatrix}$$

$$\begin{pmatrix}K\\ \rho_1\\ \rho_2\end{pmatrix}=T\begin{pmatrix}K\\ p_R\\ p_I\end{pmatrix},\quad T=\begin{pmatrix}1 & 0 & 0\\ 0 & p_R/|p| & p_I/|p|\\ 0 & p_R^2/|p|^2-p_I^2/|p|^2 & 2p_Ip_R/|p|^2\end{pmatrix},\quad \begin{aligned}p_R &\equiv \mathrm{Re}(p)\\ p_I &\equiv \mathrm{Im}(p)\end{aligned}$$

Table 2. Covariance matrix for the static amplification and the two projections, (K,ρ_1,ρ_2), and transformation matrix T. The covariance $\mathrm{cov}(K,\mathrm{Re}(p),\mathrm{Im}(p))$ is given in Table 1.

The measurement uncertainty is given by the *half*-width x_P of the confidence interval of the measurement. This width can be calculated as the standard deviation at each time instant, multiplied by an estimated coverage factor k_P (ISO GUM, 1993). This coverage factor is difficult to determine accurately for dynamic measurements, since the type of distribution varies with time. The standard deviation is obtained as the square root of the variance, i.e. the square root of the auto-correlation for zero lag,

$$u = k_P \cdot \sqrt{\mathrm{diag}(\langle \chi\chi^T\rangle)} = k_P \cdot \sqrt{\mathrm{diag}(\xi^T\,\mathrm{cov}(K,\rho_1,\rho_2)\xi)}. \tag{15}$$

The sensitivity signals ξ can be calculated with digital filtering. *Sensitivity filters* are found by sampling the CT sensitivity systems $E_K, E_p^{(22)}(s), E_p^{(12)}(s)$. The noise filter is a necessity rather than a part of the actual correction and gives rise to a systematic error. The uncertainty of the noise filtering is thus the same as the uncertainty of this systematic error. That is of no interest without an accurate estimate of the systematic error. Estimating this error is very difficult since much of the required information is unconditionally lost in the measurement due to bandwidth limitations. No method has been presented other than a very rough universal conservative estimate (Hessling, 2006). The uncertainty of the error is much less than the accuracy of this estimate and therefore completely irrelevant.
The gain of the sensitivity filters is bounded at all frequencies and no additional noise filters are required. The sensitivity filters differ from the correction filter in numerous ways: As the complexity of the model increases, the types of sensitivity filter remain but their number increases. There are only three types of sensitivity filters, one for real-valued and the same pair for complex-valued poles and zeros. For the transducer, the correction filter and the two sensitivity filters were sampled with the same exponential mapping (section 2.2). The resulting impulse responses and z-plane plots of all filters are shown in Fig. 5.
Filtering the corrected signal with the sensitivity filters $E_K, E_p^{(22)}(z), E_p^{(12)}(z)$ resulted in the sensitivities $\xi_K(t), \xi_p^{(22)}(t), \xi_p^{(12)}(t)$ in Fig. 6 (left). The time-dependent half-width of the confidence interval for the correction in Fig. 6 (right) was then found from Eq. 15, using the covariance matrix in Table 2 and $k_P = 2$ for an assumed normal distributed correction.

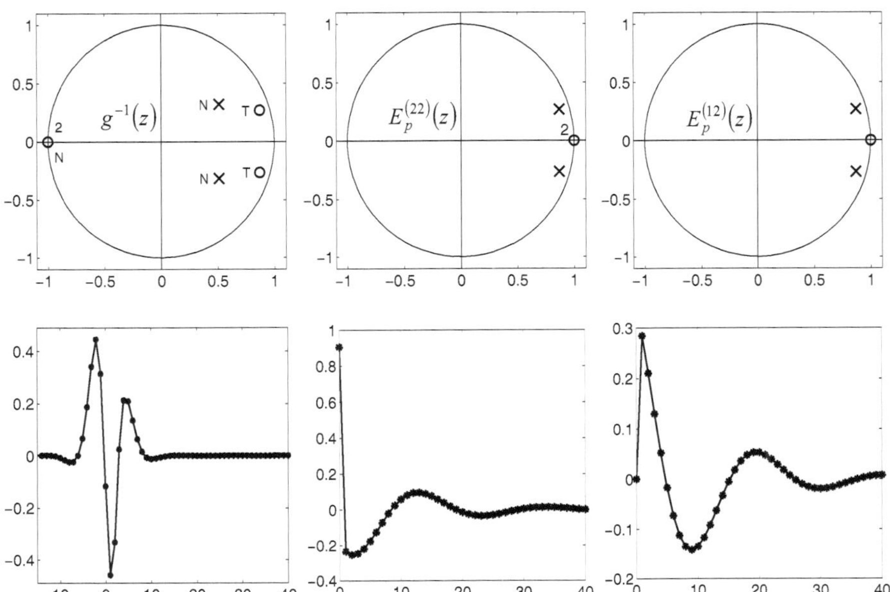

Fig. 5. Poles (x) and zeros (o) (top) and impulse responses (bottom) of the correction $g^{-1}(z)$ (left) and digital sensitivity filters $E_p^{(22)}(z)$ (middle) and $E_p^{(12)}(z)$ (right) for the two projections ρ_1 and ρ_2, respectively.

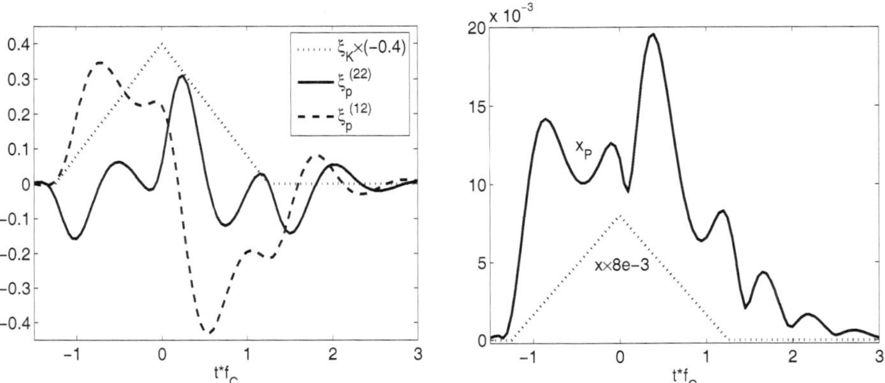

Fig. 6. Left: Sensitivity signals ξ for the amplification K and the two pole projections ρ_1, ρ_2, obtained by digital filtering of the corrected output shown in Fig. 3 (right). Right: Resulting confidence interval half-width x_P. For comparison, the rescaled input signal is shown (dotted).

3.3.2 Non-linear propagation utilizing unscented binary sampling

The uncertainty of the correction can be estimated by simulating a representative set or ensemble of different corrections of the same measured signal. The probability density function (pdf) of the parameters is then sampled to form a *finite* number of 'typical' sets of parameters: The multivariate pdf $f(\{q_k\})$ for all parameters $\{q_k\}$ is substituted with an ensemble of m sets of n samples $\{\hat{q}_k^{(v)}\}$, where $v = 1,2,...m$ denotes the different members of the ensemble and $k = 1,2...n$ the different parameters of the model. To be most relevant, these sets should preserve as many statistical moments as possible. Expressed in deviations $\delta\hat{q}_k^{(v)} \equiv \hat{q}_k^{(v)} - \langle\hat{q}_k^{(v)}\rangle$ from the first moment,

$$
\begin{aligned}
0 = \langle\delta q_i\rangle &= \int \delta q_i f(\{q_k\}) dq_1 dq_2 \cdots dq_n &\hat{=}\; \frac{1}{m}\sum_{v=1}^{m} \delta\hat{q}_i^{(v)} \\
\langle\delta q_i \delta q_j\rangle &= \int \delta q_i \delta q_j f(\{q_k\}) dq_1 dq_2 \cdots dq_n &\hat{=}\; \frac{1}{m}\sum_{v=1}^{m} \delta\hat{q}_i^{(v)}\delta\hat{q}_j^{(v)} \\
\langle\delta q_i \delta q_j \delta q_k\rangle &= \cdots &\hat{=}\; \frac{1}{m}\sum_{v=1}^{m} \delta\hat{q}_i^{(v)}\delta\hat{q}_j^{(v)}\delta\hat{q}_k^{(v)} \\
\vdots\;\; &= \cdots &\hat{=}\; \cdots
\end{aligned}
\tag{16}
$$

The *sampling of the pdf* is indicated by $\hat{=}$. In contrast to signals and systems, pdfs are not physical and not observable. That makes sampling of pdfs even less evident than sampling of systems (section 2.2). Only a few of many possible methods have so far been proposed. Perhaps the most common way to generate an ensemble $\{\delta\hat{q}_k^{(v)}\}$ is to employ random generators with the same statistical properties as the pdf to be sampled. With a sufficiently large ensemble, typically $m \sim 10^6$, all relevant moments of pdfs of *independent* parameters may be accurately represented. This random sampling technique is the well known Monte Carlo (MC) simulation method (Metropolis, 1949; Rubenstein, 2007). It has been extensively used for many decades in virtually all fields of science where statistical models are used. The efficiency of MC is low: Its outstanding simplicity of application is paid with an equally outstanding excess of numerical simulations. It thus relies heavily upon technological achievements in computing and synthesis of good random generators. Modeling of dependent parameters provides a challenge though. With a linear change of variables, ensembles with any second moment or covariance may be generated from independent generators. It is generally difficult to include any higher order moment in the MC method in any other way than directly construct random generators with relevant dependences. Another constraint is that the models must not be numerically demanding as the number of simulations is just as large as the size of the ensemble (m). For dynamic measurements this is an essential limitation since every realized measurement requires a full dynamic simulation of a differential equation over the entire time epoch. For a calibration service the limitation is even stronger as the computers for evaluation belongs to the customer and not the calibrator. A fairly low computing power must therefore be allowed. There are thus many reasons to search for more effective sampling strategies.

An alternative to random sampling is to construct the set $\{\delta\hat{q}_k^{(v)}\}$ from the given statistical moments (Eq. 16) with a *deterministic* method. The first versions of this type of *unscented* sampling techniques appeared around 15 years ago and was proposed by Simon Julier and Jeffrey Uhlmann (Julier, 1995) for use in Kalman filters (Julier, 2004). The name unscented means without smell or bias and refers to the fact that *no* approximation of the deterministic model is made. The number of realizations is much lower and the efficiency correspondingly higher for unscented than for random sampling. The unavoidable cost is a lower statistical accuracy as fewer moments are correctly described. The realized vectors of parameters $\{\hat{q}_1^{(v)} \quad \hat{q}_2^{(v)} \quad \cdots \quad \hat{q}_n^{(v)}\}$ were called *sigma-points* since they were constructed to correctly reproduce the second moments. The required *minimum* number of such points, or samples depends on how many moments one wants to correctly describe. The *actual* number of samples is often larger and depends on the sampling strategy. There is no general approach for deterministic sampling of pdf corresponding to the use of random generators for random sampling. The class of unscented sampling techniques is very large. It is all up to your creativity to find a method which reproduce as many moments as possible with an acceptable number of sigma-points. For correct reproduction of the first and second moment, the simplex set of sigma-points (Julier, 2004, App. III) utilizes the minimum number of $n+1$ samples while the standard unscented Kalman filter use $2n$ samples (Simon, 2006). The minimum number of samples is given by the number of degrees-of-freedom (NDOF). For the first and second moment, $NDOF = 1+n$. The sampling method that will be presented here is close to the standard UKF, apart from a few important differences:

- The amplification of the standard deviation with $\sqrt{n} > 1$ in the standard UKF (see below) is strongly undesirable since parameters may be sampled outside their region of possible variation, which is prohibited. For instance, poles must remain in the left hand side of the s-plane to preserve stability. The factor $\sqrt{n}$ may violate such critical physical constraints.
- The confidence interval of the measurement is of primary interest in calibrations, rather than the covariance as in the UKF. For non-linear propagation of uncertainty it is crucial to expand the sampled parameters to the desired confidence level, and not the result of the simulation. Expanded sigma-points will be denoted *lambda-points*. This expansion makes the first aspect even more critical.

The standard UKF samples sigma-points by calculating a square root of the covariance matrix. A square root is easily found if the covariance matrix first is transformed to become diagonal. To simplify notation, let $q = \begin{bmatrix} q_1 & q_2 & \cdots & q_n \end{bmatrix}^T$. It is a widely practiced standard method (Matlab, m-function 'eig') to determine a unitary transformation U, which makes the covariance matrix diagonal,

$$\text{cov}(U\delta q) = U \text{cov}(q) U^T = \text{diag}\begin{pmatrix} \sigma_1^2 & \sigma_2^2 & \cdots & \sigma_n^2 \end{pmatrix}, \quad UU^T = U^T U = 1. \tag{17}$$

The first moments (Eq. 16) will vanish if the lambda-points $\hat{q}^{(v)} \rightarrow \lambda^{(v,s)}$ are sampled symmetrically around the mean $\langle q \rangle$. Expressing the sampled variations $\delta\hat{q}^{(v)}$ in the diagonal basis and expanding with coverage factors $k_P^{(v)}$,

$$\lambda^{(v,s)} = \langle q \rangle + s \cdot k_P^{(v)} U^T \delta\hat{q}^{(v)}, \quad v = 1,2...m/2, \quad s = \pm. \tag{18}$$

The column vectors $\delta\hat{q}^{(v)}$ of variations are for convenience collected into columns of a matrix Δ. The condition to reproduce the second moment in Eq. 16 then reads,

$$\text{diag}\!\left(\sigma_1^2 \quad \sigma_2^2 \quad \cdots \quad \sigma_n^2\right) = \frac{2}{m}\Delta\Delta^T . \tag{19}$$

Clearly, $\Delta = \sqrt{m/2}\cdot\text{diag}\!\left(\sigma_1 \quad \sigma_2 \quad \cdots \quad \sigma_n\right)$ $(m=2n)$ is a valid but as will be discussed, not a unique solution. Except for the unitary transformation, that corresponds to the standard UKF (Simon, 2006, chapter 14.2). The factor $\sqrt{m/2}$ may result in prohibited lambda-points and appeared as a consequence of normalization. This square root is by no means unique: *Any* 'half'-unitary[1] transformation $\widetilde{\Delta} \equiv \Delta V, VV^T = 1$ yields an equally acceptable square root matrix since $\widetilde{\Delta}\widetilde{\Delta}^T \equiv \Delta VV^T\Delta^T = \Delta\Delta^T$. This degree of freedom will be utilized to eliminate the factor $\sqrt{m/2}$. Note that $VV^T = 1$ does not imply that V must be a square matrix, or $m=2n$. To arrive at an arbitrary covariance matrix though, the rank of V must be at least the same as for $\text{cov}(U\delta q)$, or $m \geq 2n$. Since the 'excitation' of the different parameters is controlled by the matrix V it will be called the *excitation matrix*. The lambda-points are given by,

$$\lambda^{(v,s)} = \langle q\rangle + s\cdot k_P^{(v)} U^T \sqrt{U\,\text{cov}(q)U^T}\,U\,\Psi^{(v)}, \quad \Psi = \left(\Psi^{(1)} \quad \Psi^{(2)} \quad \cdots \quad \Psi^{(m/2)}\right) \equiv \sqrt{m/2}\,U^T V . \tag{20}$$

Here, $\Psi^{(v)}$ is column v of the scaled excitation matrix, expressed in the original basis of correlated coordinates q. The main purpose of applying the unitary transformation or rotation U as well as using the excitation matrix V is to find physically allowed lambda-points in a simple way.

After the pdf has been sampled into lambda-points (λ), the confidence interval $\left[x_C(t)-x_P(t), x_C(t)+x_P(t)\right]$ of the corrected signal $\hat{x}(t)$ is evaluated as,

$$\begin{aligned}
x_C(t) &= \langle\hat{x}(\lambda,t)\rangle_\lambda, \quad \hat{x}(\lambda,t) = y(t)*g^{-1}(\lambda,t), \quad \langle f\rangle_\lambda \equiv \frac{1}{m}\sum_{v=1}^{m} f\!\left(\lambda^{(v)}\right)\\
x_P(t) &= \sqrt{\left\langle\left[\hat{x}(\lambda,t)-x_C(t)\right]^2\right\rangle_\lambda}
\end{aligned} \tag{21}$$

The impulse response of the digital correction filter is here denoted $g^{-1}(\lambda,t)$ and y is the measured signal, while the filtering operation is described by the convolution $*$ (section 3.2). The auto-correlation function of the measurement may be similarly obtained from the associated sigma-points (let $k_P^{(v)} \to 1$ and $\lambda \to \sigma$ in Eqs. 20-21),

$$\langle\delta x(t)\delta x(t-\tau)\rangle = \left\langle\left[\hat{x}(\sigma,t)-x_C(t)\right]\cdot\left[\hat{x}(\sigma,t-\tau)-x_C(t-\tau)\right]\right\rangle_\sigma . \tag{22}$$

---

[1] The matrix is not unitary since that also requires $V^T V = 1$.

As a matter of fact, it is simple to evaluate all statistical moments of the correction,

$$\left\langle \delta x(t_1) \delta x(t_2) \cdots \delta x(t_r) \right\rangle = \left\langle \prod_{k=1}^{r} \left[\hat{x}(\sigma, t_k) - x_C(t_k) \right] \right\rangle_\sigma . \tag{23}$$

Consistency however, requires at least as many moments of the sampled parameters to agree with the underlying pdf (Eq. 16). It is no coincidence that for propagating the covariance of the parameters to the correction, the mean and the covariance of the sampled parameters were correctly described. Thus, to propagate higher order moments the sampling strategy needs to be further improved.

The factor $\sqrt{m/2}$ may be extinguished by exciting all uncertain parameters, i.e. filling all entries of V with elements of unit magnitude, but with different signs chosen to obtain orthogonal rows. This will lead to $m = 2^n$ lambda-points instead of $m = 2n$. Since the lambda-points will represent all binary combinations, this sampling algorithm will be called the method of *unscented binary sampling* (Hessling, 2010c). All lambda-points will be allowed since the scaling factor $\sqrt{m/2}$ will disappear with the normalization of V. The *combined* excitation of several parameters may nevertheless not be statistically allowed. This subtlety is not applicable within the current second moment approximation of sampling and can be ignored. The rapid increase in the number of lambda-points for large n is indeed a high price to pay. For dynamic measurements this is worth paying for as prohibited lambda-points may even result in unstable and/or un-physical simulations! In practice, the number of parameters is usually rather low. It may also be possible to remove a significant number of samples. The only requirements are that the rank of V is sufficient $(m \geq 2n)$, and that the half-unitary condition $\left(VV^T = 1 \right)$ can be met.

For the mechanical transducer, there are three uncertain parameters, the amplification and the real and imaginary parts of the pole pair ($\lambda = K, \mathrm{Re}(p), \mathrm{Im}(p)$). The full binary excitation matrix is for three parameters given by,

$$V = \frac{1}{2} \begin{pmatrix} 1 & -1 & 1 & -1 \\ 1 & 1 & -1 & -1 \\ 1 & 1 & 1 & 1 \end{pmatrix} . \tag{24}$$

Unscented binary sampling thus resulted in $m = 2^3 = 8$ 'binary' lambda-points, or digital correction filters illustrated in Fig. 7 (top left). Applying these filters to the measured signal yielded eight corrected signals, see Fig. 7 (top right). The statistical evaluation at every instant of time (Eq. 21) resulted in the confidence interval of the correction displayed in Fig. 7 (bottom). The coverage factors were assumed to be equal and represent normal distributed parameters $(k_P = 2)$.

The simplicity of unscented propagation is striking. The uncertainty of correction is found by filtering measured signals with a 'typical' set of correction filter(-s). An already implemented dynamic correction (Bruel&Kjaer, 2006) can thus easily be parallelized to also find its time-dependent uncertainty, which is unique for every measured signal.

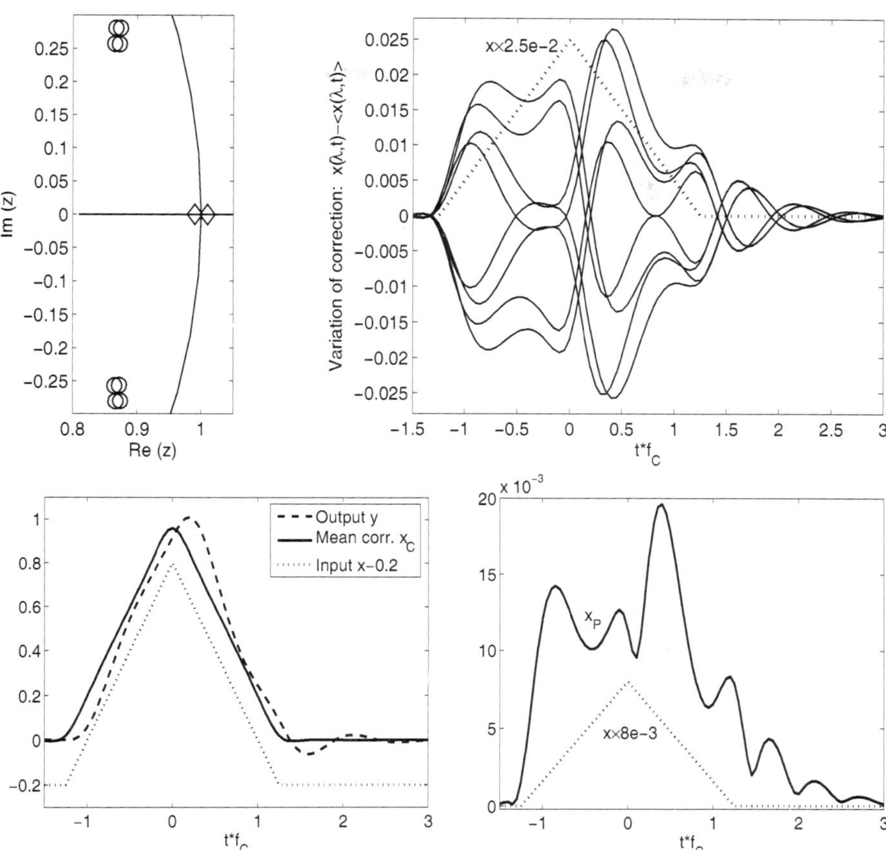

Fig. 7. Top left: Poles and zeros of the eight sampled digital correction filters, excluding the fixed noise filter. The static gains $(\diamond)$ are displayed on the real z-axis (close to $z = 1$). Top right: The variation of all corrections from their mean. Bottom: Center x_C (left) and half-width x_P (right) of the confidence interval for the correction. The (rescaled/displaced) input signal of the measurement system is shown (dotted) for comparison.

3.3.3 Comparison of methods

The two proposed methods in sections 3.3.1 and 3.3.2 for estimating the model uncertainty are equivalent and may be compared. The correct confidence interval is not known but can be estimated by means of computationally expensive random sampling or Monte Carlo simulations (Rubenstein, 2007). The lambda-points are then substituted with a much larger ensemble generated by random sampling. The errors of the estimated confidence interval of the correction were found to be different for the two methods, see Fig. 8.

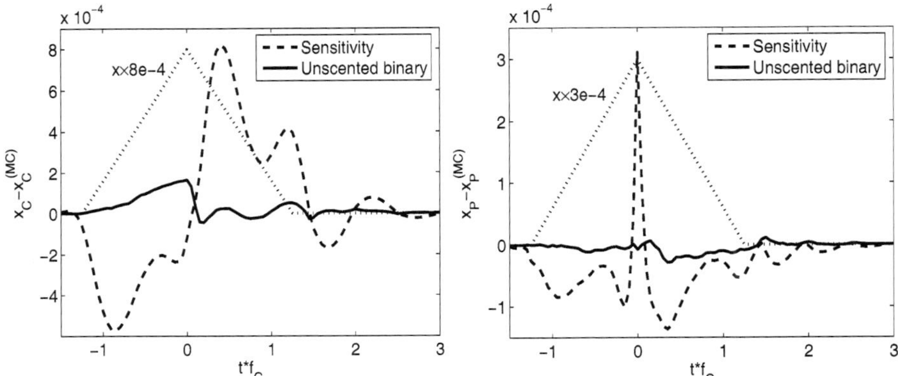

Fig. 8. The errors of the center x_C (left) and the half-width x_P (right) of the confidence interval of the correction, for the sensitivity analysis (section 3.3.1) and the method of unscented binary sampling (section 3.3.2). The errors are estimated with random sampling of 10^6 correction filters. For comparison, the rescaled input signal is shown (dotted).

The center (Fig. 8, left) as well as the width (Fig. 8, right) is best determined with the unscented binary method, in agreement with the performance of extended (based on sensitivity) and unscented Kalman filters (Julier, 2004). The errors of the sensitivity analysis are small which indicate minor non-linear effects. The half-width of the confidence interval, or measurement uncertainty changes much less $(\leq 3e-4)$ due to non-linear effects, than the center $(\leq 8e-4)$ of the interval. That is typical for non-linear propagation of uncertainty. Hence it is inconsistent to include non-linear contributions in the estimate of the measurement uncertainty but not in the estimate of the mean correction (Hessling, 2010b). The unscented method might be superior in performance but its simplicity is perhaps a greater advantage. The calculation of time-dependent sensitivities is also a source for making mistakes.

The unitary transformation U was here chosen (Eq. 17) to *easily* find *time-invariant* lambda-points, rather than to be optimal. An optimized choice is made in the unscented non-degenerate method (Hessling, 2010b). The *time-varying* lambda-points are then sampled in the direction of the time-dependent gradient (in the parameter space).

The estimation of mean correction and estimation of uncertainty with sensitivities were made with different methods. With unscented sampling these operations are synthesized jointly as different statistical moments. The symmetry implies that the analysis can be extended to higher moments to more accurately include parametric dependencies. However, that would require a sampling method which takes more moments into account (Eq. 16), as well as much more information of the stochastic dynamic model than is usually available.

4. Feature extraction

There are many examples of extracting dynamic information from measurements which qualify as 'feature extraction' and can be partly or completely realized with digital filters. A crucial aspect is to have a complete and robust specification of the feature to be extracted. The two selected examples here are related to the safety of traffic, road hump analysis and determination of road texture.

4.1 Road humps

Maintaining speed limits in the traffic is a global problem. Radar measurements of the speed and supervision by policemen are commonly used to enforce speed limits. A popular passive control measure is the 'sleeping policeman' or road hump (Engwall, 1979). Vehicles are intentionally excited in excess when passing the hump which is a modified usually elevated short (~3-20m) section of the road. Below the speed limit, road humps should provide a safe and comfortable passage, but also be gentle to the vehicle. Above the speed limit, the discomfort should increase rapidly to enforce a distinct speed reduction. With respect to the human reaction, there are two important features of all road humps, one positive and one negative: their efficiency and the risk of injury. The efficiency is central for any particular hump design (Hessling & Zhu, 2008c). The risk of injury is normally low for single passages, but for multiple daily passages it may be substantial. Especially for professional drivers of taxis and buses in towns with many road humps this may be a problem. What has been in focus and will be addressed here is the potential damage of the human lumbar spine.

The vibration pulses generated by vehicles travelling over rough surfaces such as road humps are believed to cause fatigue stresses in the lumbar spine. Modeling of the load on the human body is rather complex and is described in a recent international standard for evaluating the human exposure to whole-body vibrations (ISO 2631-5, 2004). It is based on non-linear digital filtering followed by statistical evaluation. The adverse health effects of prolonged exposure are condensed into an 'R'-dose. This dose is the feature to extract from every complex set of road hump passages. A typical driver uses different vehicles, follows different time tables and drive on different roads, from the first to the last working day. The dose is normalized to unity which is the threshold for a 'significant' risk of injury. The calculation of the dose consists of counting peak amplitudes and weighing with exponent six. This weighing models the accumulated fatigue stress of the lumbar spine.

The standard for whole body vibration (ISO 2631-5, 2004) addresses the propagation of vibrations from the seat pad of the driver seat to the spinal cord. The road hump problem is more complex. Geometric road hump profiles are translated into an excitation signal in time via the variable speed of the vehicles. For a fixed hump, the bandwidth of the road height signal increases with the speed – that is the fundamental principle of road humps. The vehicles may also be drastically different with respect to size as well as construction. For instance, the center-of-gravity is far away from the driver in buses but not in cars. This affects the response substantially (Hessling & Zhu, 2008c). The seats may also be different. Preferably, the vehicle as well as the seat response may be simulated with digital filters, just like the human response. The analysis of a particular road hump passage is then made with several digital filters, as shown in Fig. 9 below. The human lumbar spine filter and the vehicle filters are non-trivial and will be discussed below.

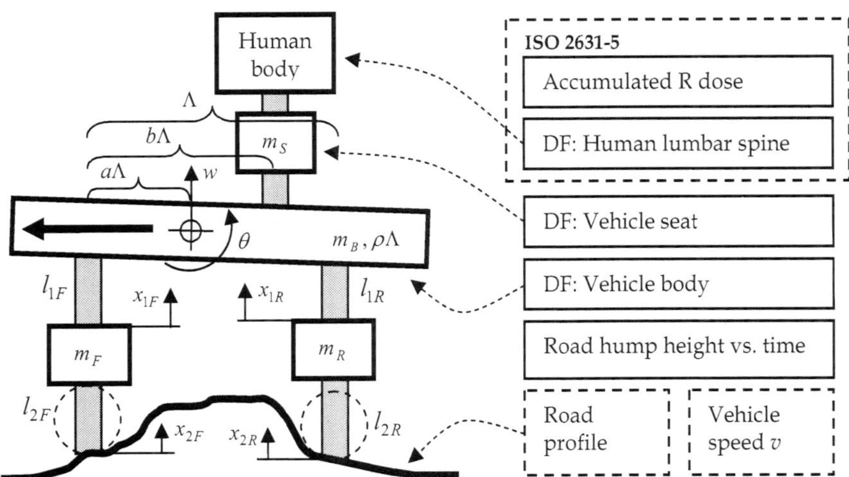

Fig. 9. The road hump response from the road, via the vehicle (moves to the left), to the human lumbar spine (left), is simulated with multiple digital filtering (DF) (right).

4.1.1 Human lumbar spine filter

In the horizontal directions, the response of the lumbar spine is modeled with a linear second order resonant system with one degree of freedom, similar to the transducer in section 3.1.1. In the vertical direction, advanced non-linear filtering is applied. The predominant vertical motion will be discussed here. All details of the evaluation of the lumbar spine response are included in the standard (ISO 2631-5, 2004). Aspects of particular interest in the context of digital filtering will be highlighted here. The (output) vertical lumbar spine acceleration $y(k)$ at time sample $t_k = kT_S$ is calculated with a *recurrent neural network* (RNN) model from the (input) seat acceleration $x(k)$ as,

$$y(k) = \sum_{j=1}^{7} W_j u_j(k) + W_8$$

$$u_j(k) = \tanh\left[\sum_{i=1}^{4} w_{ji} y(k-i) + \sum_{i=5}^{12} w_{ji} x(k-i+4) + w_{j13}\right]$$

(25a-b)

The constants w_{ji}, W_j are given in the standard, where also the derivation of this RNN is discussed (annex C). The RNN is a non-linear IIR filter. The output is a linear combination of neurons $u_j(k)$ (Eq. 25b). If the neurons are viewed as input signals, the model is static and linear as only neurons at the same time instant (k) as the output are weighted (Eq. 25a). Disregarding this weighing of neurons and considering $x(k)$ as input and $y(k)$ as output, the second sum in Eq. 25b corresponds to a FIR-filter while the first sum describes the recursion or feed-back of an IIR-filter. The tanh function provides the non-linearity which is individually tuned for each neuron by adjusting the constants $w_{j13} \in [-0.96, 1.03]$.

The small amplitude dynamic response of the lumbar spine can be understood by a linear approximation of the filter. If each neuron u_j is linearized around w_{j13},

$$\sum_{i=0}^{4} a_i y(k-i) = \sum_{i=0}^{8} b_i x(k-i)$$

$$a = \begin{bmatrix} 1 & -\alpha_1 & -\alpha_2 & -\alpha_3 & -\alpha_4 \end{bmatrix}, \quad \alpha_i \equiv \sum_{j=1}^{7} W_j \left[1 - \tanh^2\left(w_{j13}\right) \right] w_{ji}$$
$$b = \begin{bmatrix} 0 & \alpha_5 & \alpha_6 & \cdots & \alpha_{12} \end{bmatrix}$$

(26)

The poles, zeros and the magnitude of the frequency response of this filter are shown in Fig. 10. The amplitude response is almost flat $\left(-1.5\,\text{dB/octave}, 10\,\text{Hz} \leq f \leq 20\,\text{Hz}\right)$ above the peak at $4.7\,\text{Hz}$ generated by nearly cancelation of a pole and a zero pair.

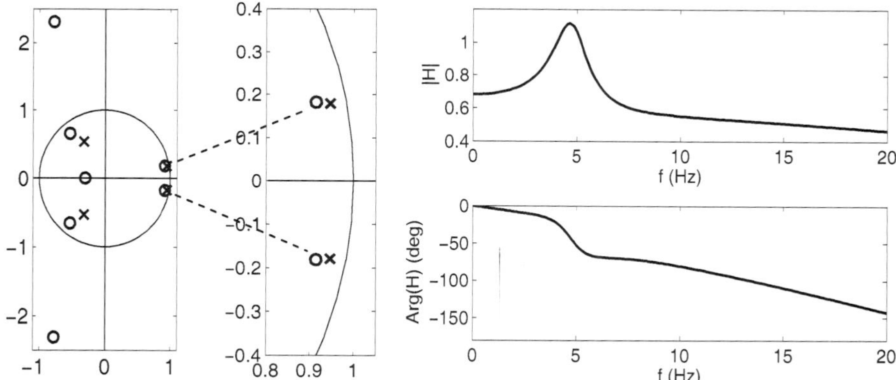

Fig. 10. All poles and zeros (left), the almost cancelling pole and zero pairs (middle) and the frequency response (right) of the linearized human lumbar spine filter.

The degree of non-linearity is different for different neurons, since their weights w_{j13} are different (Eq. 25). The onset of non-linear behavior in each neuron can be found by quadratic expansion, $\tanh(a_0 + w) \approx \tanh(w) + a_0 \partial \tanh(w) + a_0^2/2 \cdot \partial^2 \tanh(w)$, for a constant input acceleration a_0. The largest ratio between the quadratic and linear term is given by,

$$\max_j \left[\frac{a_0 \partial^2 \tanh\left(w_{j13}\right)}{2 \cdot \partial \tanh\left(w_{j13}\right)} \right] = a_0 \cdot \max_j \left[\left(H(0) \cdot \sum_{i=1}^{4} w_{ji} + \sum_{i=5}^{12} w_{ji} \right) \tanh\left(w_{j13}\right) \right] \approx 0.02 \cdot a_0. \quad (27)$$

A significant non-linearity $(\leq 20\%)$ is expected for $a_0 \geq 10\,\text{m/s}^2$. Indeed, that is confirmed by the simulations in Fig. 11. The response of the lumbar spine filter is linear for accelerations $a \leq 1\,\text{m/s}^2$ and static for pulse widths $\tau \gg 1/f_C = 0.2s$.

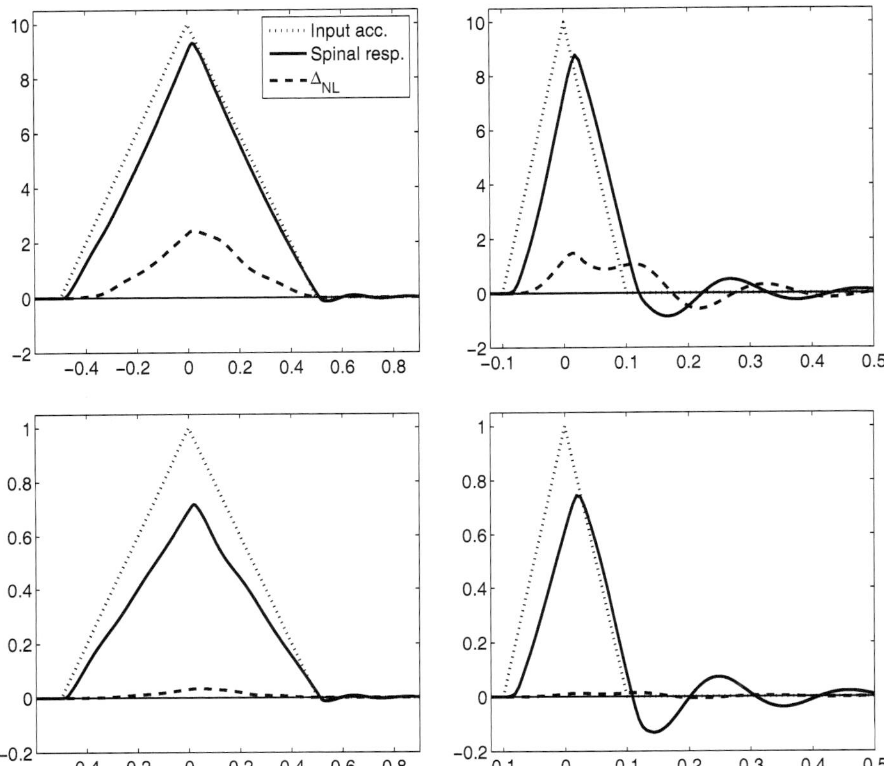

Fig. 11. Lumbar spine response and its difference to linearized response Δ_{NL}, for various pulse acceleration amplitudes A and widths T: $A = 10\,\mathrm{m/s^2}$ (top), $A = 1\,\mathrm{m/s^2}$ (bottom), $T = 1\,\mathrm{s}$ (left), and $T = 0.2\,\mathrm{s}$ (right). The units are $\mathrm{m/s^2}$ (vertical) and s (horizontal).

4.1.2 Vehicle filters

A vehicle is a dynamic system which responds to the road hump signal, similarly to how a measurement system responds to its input signal. A vehicle is a composed mechanical system. It may be approximated with a lumped linear system with solid masses (m) and spring $(l = k)$ and damping elements $(l = c)$ (Hessling et. al., 2008c), similarly to a recent model of material testing machines (Hessling, 2008b). A two axes vehicle is modeled in Fig. 9 (left). The front (x_{2F}) and rear (x_{2R}) coordinates are the two related input signals describing height, $x_{2R}(t) = x_{2F}(t - \Lambda/v)$, where Λ is the distance between the axes and v is the speed. The translation w and scaled rotation $\Lambda\theta$ of the vehicle are the two outputs. The transfer function is thus a 2×2 matrix. The topology of the model can be expressed by a symmetric matrix,

$$L = \begin{pmatrix} -l_{1F}-l_{1R} & al_{1F}-(1-a)l_{1R} & l_{1F} & l_{1R} \\ al_{1F}-(1-a)l_{1R} & -a^2l_{1F}+(1-a)^2l_{1R} & -al_{1F} & (1-a)l_{1R} \\ l_{1F} & -al_{1F} & -l_{1F}-l_{2F} & 0 \\ l_{1R} & (1-a)l_{1R} & 0 & -l_{1R}-l_{2R} \end{pmatrix}. \tag{28}$$

When used for the spring (damping) constants $l_n = k_n$ $(l_n = c_n)$, the matrix will be denoted K (C). The dynamic equations are given by Newton's force and torque laws,

$$\sum_n f_{kn} = m_k \partial_t^2 x_k, \quad \sum_n \frac{\mu_n}{\Lambda} = \rho^2 m_B \partial_t^2 (\Lambda\theta), \tag{29}$$

where ∂_t is the time-derivative while f_{kn} and μ_n represent the n-th force and torque, respectively, and $\rho\Lambda$ is the radius of gyration. For a contraction Δx, the spring force is $f = -k\Delta x$ and the damping force $f = -c\partial_t\Delta x$. The topology matrix in Eq. 28 results from Eq. 29 with a specific choice of state-space variables $u \equiv (u_1 \quad u_2 \quad \cdots \quad u_8)^T$,

$$\begin{aligned} (u_1 \quad u_2 \quad u_3 \quad u_4) &\equiv (w \quad \Lambda\theta \quad x_{1F} \quad x_{1R}) \\ u_{k+d} &\equiv \partial_t u_k, \quad k=1,2,3,4 \end{aligned}. \tag{30}$$

The state-space equation will be given in the topology matrix $L \to K,C$,

$$\begin{aligned} \begin{pmatrix} 1 & 0 \\ 0 & \hat{M} \end{pmatrix} \partial_t u &= \begin{pmatrix} 0 & 1 \\ K & C \end{pmatrix} u + E \begin{pmatrix} x_{2F} \\ x_{2R} \end{pmatrix} \\ \hat{M} &= \mathrm{diag}(M \quad \rho^2 m_B \quad m_F \quad m_R) \\ E &= \begin{pmatrix} 0 & \cdots & 0 & k_{2F}+c_{2F}\partial_t & 0 \\ 0 & \cdots & 0 & 0 & k_{2R}+c_{2R}\partial_t \end{pmatrix}^T \end{aligned}. \tag{31}$$

The measurement equation relates the seat coordinate (Fig. 9) to the state-space variables,

$$y = (1 \quad (b-a) \quad 0 \quad \cdots \quad 0)u \equiv Pu. \tag{32}$$

The transfer function from the road hump signal, or front wheel coordinate $x_{2F}(t)$ is found by applying the La-place transform to the state-space equation (Eq. 31) as in section 2.3,

$$H(s) = P\left[s - \begin{pmatrix} 0 & 1 \\ \hat{M}^{-1}K & \hat{M}^{-1}C \end{pmatrix}\right]^{-1} E(s) \begin{pmatrix} 1 \\ e^{\left(\frac{s\Lambda}{v}\right)} \end{pmatrix}. \tag{33}$$

The vehicle system $H(s)$ can be sampled as described in section 2.2 to find a digital *vehicle filter*. Alternatively, this filter can be found by calibrating the vehicle and analyzing its response (Zhu et. al., 2009). A bank of such digital vehicle filters can be used to represent the relevant traffic. The road height signals are determined by the road height profile and the speed of the vehicle. These signals are then filtered with vehicle filters to find the response of various vehicles, and with the lumbar spine filter in section 4.1.1 to find the human response. In this way, the health risk of road humps can be evaluated with digital filtering.

4.2 Road surface texture

The texture of roads is a critical feature. It affects the friction between the road surface and the tire. Slippery roads in rain are often a consequence of lack of texture of the road and/or the tire. If a road has been found to have insufficient texture, it must be modified to avoid accidents. Since it is very costly to rebuild roads, the pass and fail criteria are crucial. The surface texture is determined in two steps. The road surface is first measured and densely sampled, often with a *profilograph*. It is a vehicle equipped with a height measuring system. The vehicle motion is determined with inertial navigation and the distance between its height and the road is measured with a laser. The difference signal describes the road surface. The surface height map is then condensed into a feature called mean profile depth (MPD), according to an international standard (ISO 13473-1, 1997). Unfortunately, the evaluation lacks robustness. Independent evaluations may result in different values of the MPD. Hence, the method needs to be improved. The current evaluation is first described and commented in section 4.2.1. An improved method based on digital filtering will then be proposed in section 4.2.2. Digitals filters are robust as they specify the calculation completely. Fixing the sampling rate, the proposed filter coefficients can be directly stated in a revised standard, similarly to the specification of the lumbar spine filter (ISO 2631-5, 2004).

4.2.1 Mean profile depth (MPD)

The standard for characterization of road/pavement texture (ISO 13473-1, 1997) follows the steps in Fig. 12 to evaluate road height variations with wavelengths in the range of $5-50\,\text{mm}$, corresponding to a frequency band $20-200\,\text{m}^{-1}$. Inverse distance is a frequency equivalent to inverse time.

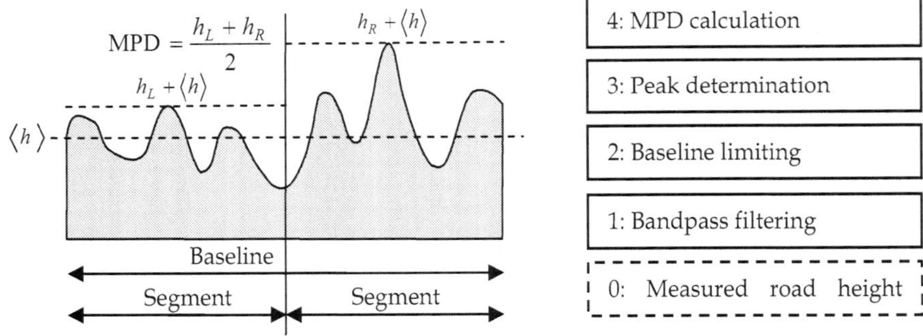

Fig. 12. The mean profile depth (MPD) (left) is according to the standard (ISO 13473-1, 1997) determined in four steps (right), using a measured map of heights h (Step 0).

The road height profile (step 0) must be sampled with a horizontal resolution of at least $1\,\text{mm}$. That is plausible considering the shortest wavelength of interest $(5\,\text{mm})$. The bandpass-filtering (step 1) is not further specified than the $-3\,\text{dB}$ cross-over frequencies $[10, 400]\,\text{m}^{-1}$ and minimal slopes $[6, 12]\,\text{dB/octave}$. The upper cross-over frequency is on the borderline of being consistent with the sampling rate – the utilization is as high as $400/500 = 80\%$. The specification of *minimal* slope may be understood from the widespread concept of ideal 'square' filter response in the frequency domain. It cannot be understood from considerations in the space domain: A too abrupt cut-off in the frequency domain must result in oscillations in the space domain. Further, in the space domain the phase distortion is important. No requirement on the phase response of the band-pass filter is however made. Baseline limiting (step 2) consists of dividing the measured surface profile into consecutive baseline intervals of 100 ± 10 mm length. The peaks in the two adjacent segments of equal length (50 mm) are then detected (step 3). The MPD is finally determined as the average of these peaks, measured relative to the mean height (step 4).

Dividing the profile into baselines and detecting isolated peaks in this way may be common but is definitely not robust. The result is sensitive to translations of the dividing points of adjacent baselines, as well as changes in the position of the peaks. Any peak occurring only once in each segment will be counted in full but together with a larger peak, it will be completely neglected. These deficiencies will result in noisy MPD-signals.

4.2.2 Modified MPD (MMPD)

Many aspects of the current standard can be improved without major deviations from the intentions of the standard. The degree of agreement between the modified mpd (MMPD) to be proposed and the current MPD will *not* be a measure of quality. Rather, the quality is to be found in fulfillment of the intentions of the current standard (ISO 13473-1, 1997) and desired properties such as low sensitivity to irrelevant disturbances, repeatability in independent evaluations and simplicity of implementation.

The band-pass filtering in step 1 (Fig. 12) describes the selection of relevant information. The filter needs to be specified in more detail to improve the repeatability as well as reducing the distortion. A simple method to eliminate phase distortion is to use symmetric forward and reversed digital filtering (section 2.1). The fall-off rate can be chosen as low as possible by using a first-order filter. The suggestion is to use a standard digital Butterworth filter of first order with cross-over frequencies $[6.5, 434]\,\mathrm{m}^{-1}$, and apply it in both directions of space. A sampling rate $f_S = 1000\,\mathrm{m}^{-1}$ complies with the required resolution and gives a numerically acceptable utilization. That will result in a fall-off rate of $[12,12]\,\mathrm{dB/octave}$ and zero phase response. This filter fulfills all requirements of the current standard.

The MPD calculation requires major adjustments to become robust. The division into disjoint baselines (step 2, Fig. 12) is preferably substituted with overlapping baselines. Calculating the average height $\langle h \rangle$ will then directly correspond to digital filtering of the road profile with an averaging FIR-filter with equal coefficients $b_k = 1/100, k = 1,2,\ldots 100$. Averaging filters belong to the class of smoothing filters and are well-known to be anything but perfect (Hamming, 1998). They have an oscillating frequency response, an undesirable finite amplification at the Nyquist frequency f_N, as well as an unwanted finite slope at zero frequency. Applying an averaging filter is equivalent of piecewise linear regression with a constant. A better alternative is to use a polynomial. Such *polynomial smoothing FIR-filters* (includes the averaging filter) have linear phase (symmetric coefficients). Polynomial filters have the same deficiency of finite amplification at f_N. This undesired response may be removed by adjusting the identical first and last coefficients. Treating them as a free parameter they may be adjusted for zero gain of the filter at f_N. That will improve the high frequency attenuation considerably, see Fig. 13 (right). The unavoidable change in bandwidth may be compensated by adjusting the length of the filter. These filters will be called *modified polynomial filters*. The regularity or differentiability at zero frequency increases with the order of the polynomial: An n-th order polynomial filter has $n-1$ vanishing derivatives at zero frequency. Thus, they resemble the Butterworth 'max-flat' design (Hamming, 1998). The modified polynomial FIR filter is thus comparable to the IIR Butterworth filter, see Fig. 13 (left). Avoiding recursion requires many more coefficients – filters like the polynomial filters could be obtained by truncated sampling of the infinite impulse response of Butterworth filters. This truncation introduces oscillations as shown in Fig. 13 (right).

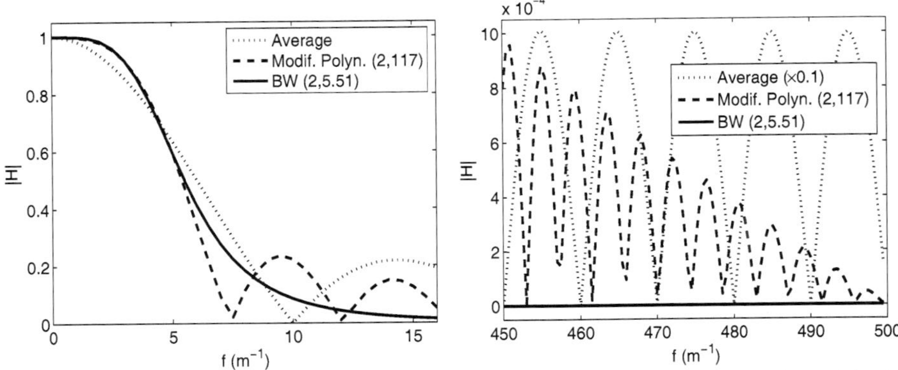

Fig. 13. Magnitude of frequency response of smoothing filters, in the low (left) and high (right) frequency range: the averaging filter(right: ×0.1) , the modified square polynomial 117-tap FIR filter, and the proposed second order Butterworth filter (BW) with cross-over frequency $5.5\,\mathrm{m}^{-1}$.

The smoother roll-off of the recursive Butterworth filter results in a more robust analysis of noisy measurements. Its low number of filter coefficients is also preferable in a standard document. The complexity of implementation is low as well as the risk of making errors. The order of filtering is not critical for the remaining steps of the analysis and can be increased. The phase distortion may once again be eliminated with symmetric forward and reverse filtering (section 2.1). The effective order will then double to four.

The peaks detected in step 3 (Fig. 12) are closely related to percentiles determined from cumulative probability distributions. Percentiles are for instance used in calibrations (ISO GUM, 1993). The n-th percentile $P_n(\{x\})$ is the value exceeding precisely n per cent of all samples $\{x\}$. Statistical moments (section 3.3.2) are superior to high percentiles in robustness as they utilize weighing over *all* samples. The ratios of percentiles and the standard deviation are called coverage factors (section 3.3). A robust measure of peaks is found by combining a short-range standard deviation and a long-range percentile. The number of samples in every baseline is far too low for evaluation of percentiles. Each set of 100 consecutive recordings of the road depth in each baseline may be considered as samples drawn from a unique pdf. The widths of different pdfs belonging to different baselines are likely different. The coverage factors or the types of these pdfs are likely much less different. A plausible assumption is that the coverage factors for different baselines are nearly equal and can be estimated using *all* samples. This global coverage factor is as robust as possible. The mean of the two peaks in Fig. 12 are rather well described by the $99-$th percentile. The calculation of the standard deviation is robust enough to be calculated for each baseline. The smoothing filter used to calculate the mean baseline depth $\langle h \rangle$ can also be used to evaluate the mean baseline square deviation $\left\langle \left(h - \langle h \rangle \right)^2 \right\rangle = \left\langle h^2 \right\rangle - \langle h \rangle^2$, or squared standard deviation. The smoothing filter is effectively a rather sharp anti-alias filter. The MPD signal may therefore be directly down-sampled to be consistent with the baseline resolution. This concludes the derivation of the method for determining the *modified MPD* (MMPD):

1. The measured road profile is sampled with $f_S = 1000\,\text{m}^{-1}$. Otherwise, linear down-sampling is applied.

2. The road profile is filtered in both directions of time with a digital band-pass Butterworth filter of order one with cross-over frequencies $f_C = [6.5,434]\,\text{m}^{-1}$. Filter coefficients[2]: $b = [0.8119 \quad 0 \quad -0.8119]$, $a = [1.000 \quad -0.3099 \quad -0.6237]$.

3. The running mean and variance of the depth are evaluated with the same smoothing filter. The digital Butterworth filter is of order two, has a cross-over frequency $f_C = 5.5\,\text{m}^{-1}$, and is applied in both directions of time. The band-pass filtered road profile h and its square h^2 are filtered to give $\langle h \rangle_S$ and $\left\langle h^2 \right\rangle_S$, respectively. Filter coefficients: $b = 10^{-3} \times [0.2921 \quad 0.5842 \quad 0.2921]$, $a = [1.000 \quad -1.9511 \quad 0.9522]$.

4. The $99-$th percentile of the road depth, $P_{99}\left(h - \langle h \rangle_A \right)$, where $\langle \cdot \rangle_A$ denotes *average* over *all* samples, will be called *GPD – Global Profile Depth*. It is a measure of the mean MMPD. The global coverage factor is given by, $k_P = \text{GPD} \Big/ \sqrt{\left\langle h^2 \right\rangle_A - \langle h \rangle_A^2}$.

5. The mean profile depth is given by, $\text{MMPD} = \text{GPD} \times \sqrt{\left\langle h^2 \right\rangle_S - \langle h \rangle_S^2} \Big/ \sqrt{\left\langle h^2 \right\rangle_A - \langle h \rangle_A^2}$.

6. Finally, the MMPD is down-sampled to $f_S = 20\,\text{m}^{-1}$.

An example of calculated MMPD is shown in Fig. 14. The generated road profile was an uncorrelated normally distributed variation of depth with standard deviation equal to one. The smoothing filter of the MMPD is compared to the average filter suggested by the current standard. Clearly, the robustness improved considerably – the noise of the calculated mean profile depth disappeared.

---

[2] Defined according to a common convention (Matlab): Numerator $b = [b_0 \quad b_1 \quad \cdots]$ and denominator $a = [a_0 \quad a_1 \quad \cdots]$, where the indices denote the lag in samples.

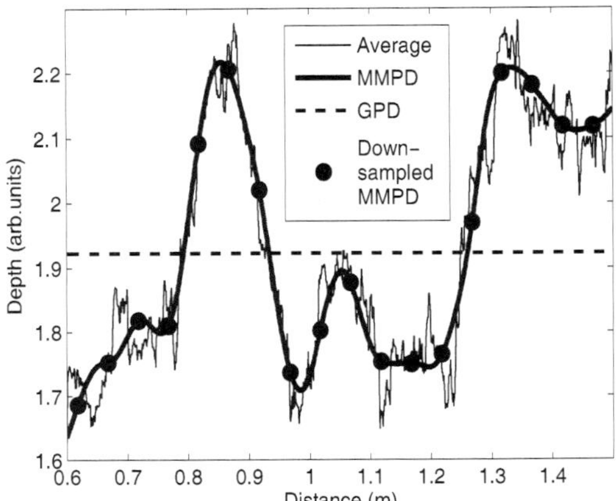

Fig. 14. The proposed smoothing of the MMPD compared to the average smoothing of the present MPD, for an uncorrelated normally distributed road profile.

5. Conclusions

A multitude of different digital filters for exploring and refining measurements have been discussed: single correction filters or ensembles of correction filters, sensitivity filters, lumbar spine filter, banks of vehicle filters, and road texture filters. The analyses they realize differ substantially. All digital filters were designed or synthesized in three steps: dynamic model – prototype – digital filter. The identification of models was not considered as a part of the synthesis of digital filters and was omitted. The model describes the physical system and the prototype what we are interested in. The major part of the chapter focused on the construction of prototypes from models. The prototypes were sampled into digital filters. A brief survey of some well established sampling techniques was given. In the examples, prototypes were sampled with the exponential pole-zero mapping.

The discussed filters fell into one of two categories: 1. Analysis of measured signals utilizing calibration information of the measurement system. 2. Extraction of any feature of interest that is related to a measured signal. Digital filters devised to correct and analyze measured signals are preferably considered as a part of an improved measurement system. The extracted feature could be a constant like an accumulated dose describing the risk of injury, or a spatially varying measure of road texture. A feature is justified by its broad acceptance and they are therefore often defined in standard documents. A feature which is not robust is questionable and may lose its importance. Low robustness originates from the definition of the feature and/or its incomplete specification. In this context digital filters are ideal, as they completely describe how the extraction is made with a finite set of numerical numbers. Many operations are difficult to realize in real time, like zero-phase filtering and stabilization. These become trivial with reversed filtering, as was illustrated repeatedly.

The only example of non-linear digital filtering, the human lumbar spine filter, was analyzed but not synthesized. It is strongly desired that measurement systems are as linear-in-response as possible. Correction of the non-linear response of measurement systems with non-linear digital filters is virgin territory. It requires non-linear model identification, which needs to be further developed to reach the 'off-the-shelf' status of linear identification methods. The sampling techniques for linear systems can to some extent probably be inherited to sampling of non-linear prototypes.

A challenge for the future is to find novel and unique applications where digital filters really make a difference to how measurements are processed into valuable results. Digital filters are dynamic time-invariant systems with feedback. That sets their potential but also their limitations. Sampling is separate from construction of prototypes. Even though sampling of systems always introduces errors, it seldom limits the performance of digital filters. Normally, it is the quality of the underlying model that is crucial. A digital filter can never perform better than the model from which its prototype is constructed.

Differential equations in time are ubiquitous and are used in perhaps the majority of all physical and technological models, but rarely for calibrating measurement systems. For all such models, digital filters are potential candidates for modeling, refining results and extracting information. Digital filters supporting measurements and synthesized by a third-party (neither manufacturers, nor users) are still in their infancy. It is truly amazing how useful such digital filters often turn out to be in various applications.

6. References

Björk, A. (1996). *Numerical methods for least squares problems*, Siam, ISBN-13: 978-0-898713-60-2 / ISBN-10: 0-89871-360-9, Philadelphia

Bruel&Kjaer (2006). Magazine No. 2 / 2006, pp. 4-5; http://www.bksv.com/products/pulseanalyzerplatform/pulsehardware/ reqxresponseequalisation.aspx

Chen, C. (2001). *Digital Signal Processing*, Oxford University Press, ISBN 0-19-513638-1, New York

Crosswy, F.L. & Kalb, H.T. (1970). Dynamic Force Measurement Techniques, *Instruments and Control Systems*, Febr. 1970, pp. 81-83

Ekstrom, M.P. (1972). Baseband distortion equalization in the transmission of pulse information, *IEEE Trans. Instrum. Meas.* Vol. 21, No. 4, pp. 510-5

Elster, C.; Link, A. & Bruns, T. (2007). Analysis of dynamic measurements and determination of time-dependent measurement uncertainty using a second-order model, *Meas. Sci. Technol.* Vol. 18, pp. 3682-3687

Engwall, B. (1979). Device to prevent vehicles from passing a temporarily speed-reduced part of a road with high speed, United States Patent 4135839

Gustafsson, F. (1996). Determining the initial states in forward-backward filtering, *IEEE Trans. Sign. Proc.*, Vol. 44, No. 4, pp. 988-992

Hale, P.D. & Dienstfrey, A. (2010). Waveform metrology and a quantitative study of regularized deconvolution, *Instrum. Meas. Technol. Conf. Proc. 2010, I2MTC '10, IEEE*, Austin, Texas

Hamming, R.W. (1998). *Digital filters*, Dover/Lucent Technologies, ISBN 0-486-65088-X, New York

Hessling, J.P. (2006). A novel method of estimating dynamic measurement errors, *Meas. Sci. Technol.* Vol. 17, pp. 2740-2750

Hessling, J.P. (2008a). A novel method of dynamic correction in the time domain, *Meas. Sci. Technol.* Vol. 19, pp. 075101 (10p)

Hessling, J.P. (2008b). Dynamic calibration of uni-axial material testing machines, *Mech. Sys. Sign. Proc.*, Vol. 22, 451-66

Hessling, J.P. & Zhu, P.Y. (2008c). Analysis of Vehicle Rotation during Passage over Speed Control Road Humps, *ICICTA 2008, International Conference on Intelligent Computation Technology and Automation*, Changsha, China, Oct. 20-22, 2008.

Hessling, J.P. (2009). A novel method of evaluating dynamic measurement uncertainty utilizing digital filters, *Meas. Sci. Technol.* Vol. 20, pp. 055106 (11p)

Hessling, J.P. (2010a). *Metrology for non-stationary dynamic measurements, Advances in Measurement Systems*, Milind Kr Sharma (Ed.), ISBN: 978-953-307-061-2, INTECH, Available from: http://sciyo.com/articles/show/title/metrology-for-non-stationary-dynamic-measurements

Hessling, J.P.; Svensson, T. & Stenarsson, J. (2010b). Non-degenerate unscented propagation of measurement uncertainty, submitted for publication

Hessling, J.P. (2010c). Unscented binary propagation of uncertainty, in preparation

ISO 2631-5 (2004). *Evaluation of the Human Exposure to Whole-Body Vibration*, The International Organization for Standardization, Geneva

ISO 13473-1 (1997). *Characterization of pavement texture by use of surface profiles – Part 1: Determination of Mean Profile Depth*, The International Organization for Standardization, Geneva

ISO GUM (1993). *Guide to the Expression of Uncertainty in Measurement*, 1st edition, International Standard Organization, ISBN 92-67-10188-9, Geneva

Julier, S.; Uhlmann, J. & Durrant-Whyte, H. (1995). A new approach for filtering non-linear systems, *American Control Conference*, pp. 1628-1632

Julier, S. & Uhlmann, J.K. (2004). Unscented Filtering and Nonlinear Estimation, *Proc. IEEE*, Vol. 92, No. 3, (March 2004) pp. 401-422

Ljung, L. (1999). *System Identification: Theory for the User*, 2nd Ed, Prentice Hall, ISBN 0-13-656695-2, Upper Saddle River, New Jersey

Matlab with System Identification, Signal Processing Toolbox and Simulink, The Mathworks, Inc.

Metropolis, N. & Ulam, S. (1949). The Monte Carlo Method, *Journal of the American Statistical Association*, Vol. 44, No. 247,pp 335-341

Moghisi, M. & Squire, P.T. (1980). An absolute impulsive method for the calibration of force transducers, *J. Phys. E.: Sci. Instrum.* Vol. 13, pp. 1090-2

Pintelon, R. & Schoukens, J. (2001). *System Identification: A Frequency Domain Approach*, IEEE Press, ISBN 0-7803-6000-1, Piscataway, New Jersey

Pintelon, R.; Rolain, Y.; Vandeen Bossche, M. & Schoukens, J. (1990). Toward an Ideal Data Acquisition Channel, *IEEE Trans. Instrum. Meas.* Vol. 39, pp. 116-120

Rubenstein, R.Y. & Kroese, D.P. (2007). Simulation and the Monte Carlo Method (2nd Ed.) John Wiley & Sons ISBN 9780470177938

Simon, D. (2006). *Optimal State Estimation: Kalman, H_∞ and non-linear approaches*, Wiley, ISBN-13 978-0-471-70858-2, New Jersey

Wiener, N. (1949). *Extrapolation, Interpolation, and Smoothing of Stationary Time Series*, Wiley, ISBN 0-262-73005-7, New York; http://en.wikipedia.org/wiki/Wiener_deconvolution

Zhu, P.Y.; Hessling, J.P. & Wan, R. (2009). Dynamic Calibration of a bus, *Proceedings of XIX IMEKO World Congress*, Lisbon, Portugal Sept., 2009

7

Low-sensitivity design of allpass based fractional delay digital filters

G. Stoyanov[1] , K. Nikolova[1] and M. Kawamata[2]
[1]Technical University of Sofia, Bulgaria
[2]Tohoku University, Sendai, Japan

1. Introduction

Conventional linear digital circuits are providing usually a delay response that is equal to an integer number of sampling intervals (as in linear-phase FIR (finite-impulse-response) realizations) or is changing uncontrollably with the frequency (for all IIR (infinite-impulse-response) digital filters). It appeared, however, that we might often need a circuit with a delay response that is a fraction of the sampling interval and is fixed or variable (or only adjustable). Design and implementation of such circuits with given and properly controlled fractional delay (FD) is the hottest digital filters topic in the last ten years. These circuits are invaluable in many telecommunications applications, like time adjustment and precise jitter elimination in digital receivers, echo cancellation, phase-array antenna systems, trans-multiplexers, sample-rate converter and software radio. They are needed in speech synthesis and processing, image interpolation, sigma-delta modulators, time-delay estimation, in some biomedical applications and for modeling of musical instruments. Most of these applications are overviewed in (Laakso et al., 1996) and (Valimaki & Laakso, 2001).

1.1 FIR fractional delay filters

The design of fixed FIR FD filters (FDF) is well developed and quite a mature field, because it is relatively easy to formulate the design problem and to obtain an optimal solution. Many methods, so far, have been advanced and most of them are well summarized in (Laakso et al., 1996) and (Valimaki & Laakso, 2001). They include a least squared (LS) integral error design, often combined with properly selected window functions or other methods for smoothing the filter transition band; weighted LS (WLS) integral error approximation of the frequency response (Laakso et al., 1996); maximally-flat FD design based on Lagrange interpolation (very popular and widely used, but with several drawbacks (Deng & Nakagawa, 2004); (Deng, 2009a)); minimax design, achieving lower than LS and Lagrange filters maximal error (Valimaki & Laakso, 2001); splines-based FDF design (Laakso et al., 1996). Most of these methods are used to design also variable FD (VFD) FIR filters. There are many other VFD FIR filters design methods like a constrained minimax optimization method (Vesma & Saramaki, 2000), a singular value decomposition method (Deng & Nakagawa, 2004), a Taylor series expansion method (Johanson & Lovenborg, 2003), and the WLS design (Tseng, 2004); (Huang et al., 2009). Recently a new method (Tseng & Lee, 2009) and a new criterion (Shyu et al., 2010) for design of such filters have been proposed. Most of the VFD FIR filters are using the Farrow structure (Farrow, 1988), its modifications (Yli-Kaakinen & Saramaki, 2006) or transformations (Deng, 2009a). In (Deng, 2010a) several new hybrid structures with reduced complexity have been developed. Common disadvantages of all the FIR FDFs are their higher complexity (higher order transfer function (TF) and too many multipliers and delays), very high overall delay and not constant for all frequencies magnitude response, varying additionally when the delay is tuned.

1.2 General IIR fractional delay filters

Recently, several methods for design and implementation of general IIR variable FDFs have been proposed. The method in (Zhao & Kwan, 2007) is based on a two-steps procedure, where in the first step a set of fixed delay general IIR filters are designed by minimizing a quadratic objective function defined by integrated error criterion; in the second step the TF coefficients of the fixed delay filters are represented as polynomials and are fitted for any given FD. The method in (Tsui et al., 2007) is based on a new model reduction technique and is applicable to IIR TFs that are decomposable to sub-filters with a common denominator (which will stay fixed when the filter is tuned), realized then as Farrow structures. These methods are further generalized and expanded to FIR, allpass, Hilbert transformers and other devices in (Kwan & Jiang, 2009); (Pei et al., 2010). Both methods are achieving an impressive FD variability, but at a price of too higher TF order (30 or 55 in (Zhao & Kwan, 2007)) and calculation of too many multiplier coefficients (for example 426 in (Zhao & Kwan, 2007)), to be practical. The interest in general IIR VFD realizations, will grow, however, because they may offer a lower overall group delay time compared to the allpass realizations (Kwan & Jiang, 2009) and also could be used for a simultaneous magnitude and phase approximation.

1.3 Allpass-based fractional delay filters

There are IIR FDFs (fixed and variable), avoiding all the disadvantages of the FIR and of the general IIR FDFs, and they are based on allpass structures. The main advantage of the allpass-based FDF is that their magnitude is unity for all frequencies and it remains unity when the FD is tuned. The TF order of these filters is low and so are the circuit complexity and the total delay time compared to those of the FIR realizations. Many methods for design of allpass based FDF have been described in (Laakso et al., 1996) and (Valimaki & Laakso, 2001) and many more new methods (mainly for variable FDFs) have been proposed after that.

One group in (Laakso et al., 1996) and (Valimaki & Laakso, 2001) consists of several WLS methods. Recently (Tseng, 2002) a new iterative WLS method was developed, but it was shown (Deng, 2006) that very often it is not converging. A new noniterative approach solving the minimization problem by using a matrix equation and thus avoiding the convergence problems was advanced in (Deng, 2006). Both methods are rigorously proven and are producing very impressive results (very low frequency response error), but as with the general IIR methods, the TF order is very high (35 for example), each of the multiplier coefficients is represented by polynomial of 5th or 6th order (making thus the total number of the coefficients higher than 200). Then 100 sets of coefficients are calculated to cover the frequency range from 0 to 0.9π, and another 30 sets are calculated to cover the range of FD from -0.5 to 0.5. And, if the required FD is not coinciding with some of these 30 sets, new coefficients are calculated using a polynomial interpolation. The method in (Deng, 2006) was further generalized in (Deng, 2009b) throughout an optimization of the range of the variable part of the delay-time, a usage of different order subfilters (canceling thus the application of the matrix approach), and a reformulation of the WLS design. As a result, the complexity of the final structure was additionally reduced (to only 158 filter coefficients, compared to 210 and 175 for the example with the three methods), making this the best in the group. The structure complexity and the computational load, however, are still very high and we consider this approach to realize allpass-based VFDFs quite unpractical and not permitting a real time tuning.

Another group of design methods encompasses all the minimax approaches to allpass FDFs design in terms of minimal phase error, phase-delay or group-delay error (Laakso et al., 1996). An improved optimization method was proposed in (Yli-Kaakinen & Saramaki, 2004) to overcome the problems with the convergence when designing VFDFs. It is based on a gradual increase of the filter order and optimization in minimax sense to obtain optimal values for the adjustable parameters. This method is addressing the famous "gathering structure" (Makundi et al., 2001), widely used for realization of allpass-based VFDFs. Recently another method, approximately formulating the minimax design as a linear programming problem, solved noniteratively or iteratively, was advanced (Deng, 2010b). These methods are efficient and the results are impressive, but the design procedures, including complicated optimizations, are quite difficult to be applied in an engineering design.

The third and most popular group of methods is the maximally-flat design of allpass FDFs based on Thiran approximation (Thiran, 1971), giving a closed-form solution for the TF coefficients. The Thiran-based design of VFDF is somehow connected to the gathering structure, which permits very easy real-time tuning by recalculating and reprogramming a single coefficient value. This structure was criticized recently for its long critical path and big difference between the coefficient values (requiring longer wordlength) and an improved structure was proposed in (Cho et al., 2007). Another way to use Thiran approximation but to avoid usage of gathering structure to realize VFDF (and thus to avoid the division operation in the recalculation of the coefficients) was proposed in (Hacıhabiboğlu et al., 2007) and it is called "root displacement interpolation (RDI) method" (See Sect. 6.1). The resulting structure, however, is quite complicated, the range of tuning is narrow and the tuning error is quite high.

All general IIR and allpass-based VFD filters are having a common drawback, consisting of considerable transients appearing every time when the filter is tuned. Suppression of these transients is a difficult problem, several methods to solve it are discussed in (Valimaki & Laakso, 1998); (Valimaki & Laakso, 2001); (Makundi et al., 2002) and (Hacıhabiboğlu et al., 2007), but publications on this topic are very few and a lot more remains to be done.

The main aim of the present chapter is to investigate and compare the existing and to develop new methods of design, realization and tuning of allpass-based FDFs and to increase the accuracy throughout minimization of their sensitivities. It will permit more efficient multiplierless realizations, shorter wordlength and lower power consumption. The design procedures should be straightforward, without iterative and complicated optimization steps, in order to be easily used by practicing engineers and the structures have to be with the lowest possible TF order and complexity, in order to be easily tuned in real time.

2. Low-Sensitivity Design Principles

It is clear from the above considerations that allpass based FDFs (with fixed and variable FD) are most appropriate for almost all practical applications, providing lower order TF, low complexity and low total delay-time realizations, permitting an easy real-time FD tuning.

We select to use the Thiran approximation procedure (Thiran, 1971) for designing allpass based FD digital filters with maximally flat group delay response. This procedure gives an easy way to express the TF coefficients a_k as a function of the desired fractional delay parameter value D:

$$a_k = (-1)^k \binom{N}{k} \prod_{n=0}^{N} \frac{D-N+n}{D-N+k+n}, \; for \; k=0,1,2...N,$$ (1)

for every allpass TF of N-th order

$$H_{AP}(z) = \frac{a_N + a_{N-1}z^{-1} + ... + a_1 z^{N-1} + a_0 z^{-N}}{a_0 + a_1 z^{-1} + a_2 z^{-2} + ... + a_N z^{-N}} = \frac{B(z)}{A(z)}.$$ (2)

In the literature very often this allpass TF is realized as a direct form ($2N + 1$ multipliers and N delays are needed for the realization) or a lattice structure ($2N$ multipliers and N delays), which are by far non-canonic with respect to the multipliers number (a canonic allpass structure of N-th order should contain only N multipliers) and the direct structure is also very sensitive to the changes of the coefficient values. The strategy to achieve our aim is based on our approach, described in (Stoyanov et al., 2007) and using (when possible) a cascade realization of the allpass TF. It is well known that a cascade realization of the allpass TF will decrease considerably the overall sensitivity and will open the way for further sensitivity reduction. To achieve this we propose, after decomposing the allpass TF to first- and second-order terms, to minimize the sensitivities of the individual first- and second-order allpass sections, realizing each real pole or couple of complex-conjugate poles. This minimization may consist of a careful selection of proper sections (there are too many allpass sections already known) according to the position of the poles in the z-plane or of development of new allpass sections when there is no low sensitivity realizations readily available for given pole positions. These sections should be with canonic structures with respect to the number of the multipliers and the delay elements. The new low-sensitivity sections could be developed using the coefficient conversion method, proposed by Nishihara (Nishihara, 1984) or some other known methods.

We choose to use the classical (normalized) sensitivity of the phase response $\theta(\omega)$ to the changes of the multiplier coefficients m_k

$$S_{m_k}^{\theta(\omega)} = \frac{\partial \theta(\omega)}{\partial m_k} \frac{m_k}{\theta(\omega)}.$$ (3)

For evaluation of the sensitivity to the changes of all the multiplier coefficients, neccessary as a figure of merit in a case of sensitivity minimization or as a measure when different realizations are compared, we can use the worst-case sensitivity

$$WS_m^{\theta(\omega)} = \sum_{k=1}^{N} \left| S_{m_k}^{\theta(\omega)} \right|$$

(4)

or the so called Schoeffler (statistical) sensitivity, employing squared addends in (4). Both sensitivities are easily calculated for every given section topology by using the package PANDA (Sugino & Nishihara, 1990).

Very convenient tool to evaluate the sensitivity of second-order sections when realizing poles in different areas within the unit-circle is the pole-density for given multiplier coefficients wordlength, but there are some problems in calculating this density of sections obtained throughout a coefficient conversion.

Decreasing the sensitivity (throughout a proper design) would reduce the error of the fixed FD filter realizations in a limited wordlength environment especially when a fixed-point arithmetic is used. In a case of variable FD filters it will improve additionally the accuracy of tuning, as lower sensitivity means more possible values of the FD for given multiplier coefficients wordlength. Instead of higher accuracy, the low sensitivity could be used to decrease the power consumption and the computational load by using a shorter wordlength and this is of a prime importance when realizing different portable devices.

Many low-sensitivity filter (and allpass) sections have been developed through the years, but mainly to improve the performance of different narrowband and very selective amplitude filters, having their TF poles usually situated in the area near unity in the z-plane. These sections might not be useful to realize low-sensitivity phase and FD filters because their TF poles could be located in some other areas of the unit-circle. Because of that, our consideration starts with a study of the typical pole positions of the TFs obtained using the Thiran approximation.

3. FD Allpass Transfer Functions Poles Loci Investigations

The sensitivities of the realizations are strongly depending on the position of their TF poles in the z-plane, so it is important to know how the poles of the allpass-based FD filters are situated there.

3.1 Real poles behavior

The possible FD TF real poles are positioned differently depending on N and D as follows:

1. Odd order FD TF and $N-1 < D < N$ - the real pole is negative. When the FD parameter values are increasing from $N-1$ to N, the possible pole positions are moving from $z = -1$ to the area near $z = 0$ (as case 1 in Fig. 1).

2. Odd order FD TF and $D > N$ - the real pole is positive and increasing D to infinity moves the pole from the area near $z = 0$ to the area near $z = 1$ (as case 2 in Fig. 1).

3. Even order FD TF and $N-1 < D < N$ - there are one negative and one positive real poles as shown in the Fig. 1 for sixth order FD TF. When the FD is increasing from $N-1$ to N, these two poles are moving as in the above mentioned cases 1 and 2.

3.2 Complex-conjugate poles behavior

The complex-conjugate poles behavior falls into two categories regarding the range of the FD parameter values.

1. $N-1 < D < N$ – the complex-conjugate poles pairs are situated around the area $z = 0$ and can be either with positive or negative real part depending of a given FD parameter value as can be seen from Fig. 1.

2. $D > N$ – the behavior of the poles is more dynamic. The complex-conjugate poles are positioned mainly in the right half of the unit circle and only the higher order TFs have poles in the left half, as illustrated in Fig. 1. The dashed line with number 3 shows the poles movement when increasing the FD parameter values to infinity.

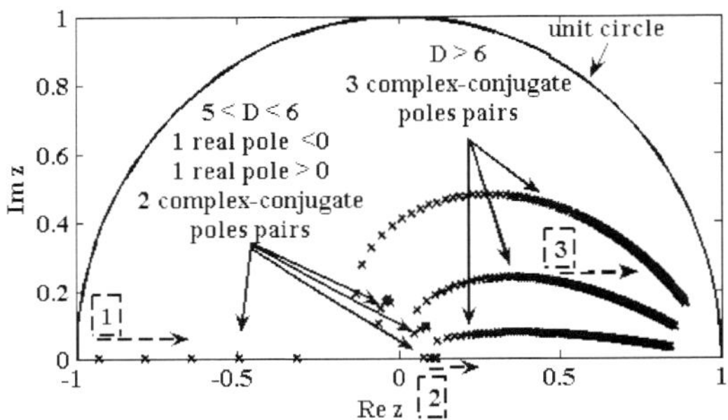

Fig. 1. Possible poles position of real poles (for odd-order TF) and of all the poles of sixth order allpass FD TF.

4. Allpass Sections Sensitivities Study

4.1 First order allpass sections

It follows from Fig. 1 that if a cascade realization of the FD allpass filters would be used, as the possible real pole positions are scattered all around the real axes, first-order allpass sections with low sensitivities for all these positions will be needed. About 20 such sections, including several newly developed, have been investigated and compared in (Stoyanov & Clausert, 1994) and it was shown that several low-sensitivity sections for every real pole-position could be found. We select to use four of them, shown in Fig. 2, namely the ST1 section, providing low-sensitivity for poles near $z=1$, MH1 and SC, having low sensitivity for poles near $z=0$ and SV section for poles near $z=-1$. Their TFs are:

$$H_{ST1}(z) = \frac{-(1-a)+z^{-1}}{1-(1-a)z^{-1}};$$

(5)

$$H_{MH1}(z) = \frac{-b+z^{-1}}{1-bz^{-1}};$$

(6)

$$H_{SC}(z) = \frac{-b-z^{-1}}{1+bz^{-1}};$$

(7)

$$H_{SV}(z) = \frac{1-c+z^{-1}}{1+(1-c)z^{-1}}. \tag{8}$$

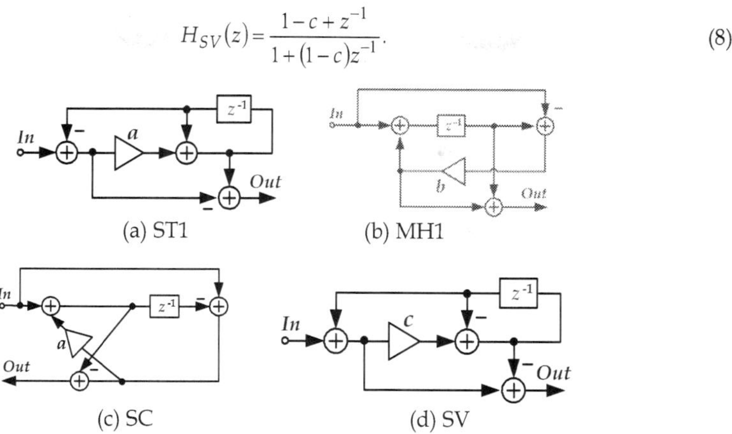

Fig. 2. Different first-order allpass sections.

The closed form solutions for their TF coefficients for given FD parameter D are:

$$a_{ST1} = \frac{2}{D+1}; \quad b_{MH1} = \frac{D-1}{D+1}; \tag{9}$$

$$b_{SC} = -\frac{D-1}{D+1}; \quad c_{SV} = \frac{2D}{D+1}. \tag{10}$$

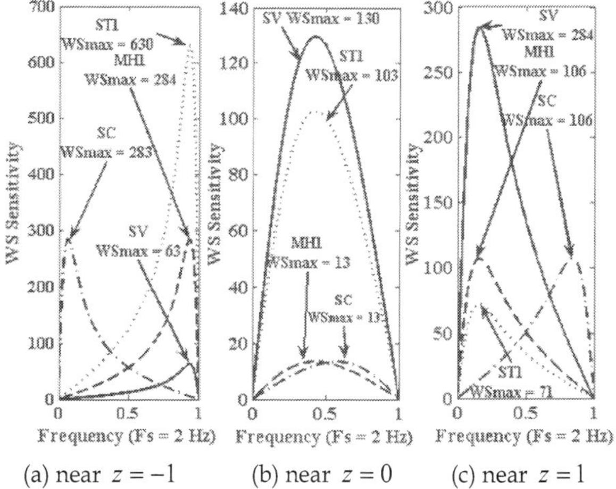

Fig. 3. Worst-case phase-sensitivities of first order allpass sections for different pole-positions.

In Fig. 3 the worst-case phase-response-sensitivities of these four sections are given for realizations with different TF pole positions. It is clearly seen that there exists a proper choice of sections for every possible pole position and the difference between the maximal values of the sensitivities may reach 10 times.

4.2 Second order allpass sections

There are a great number of second order allpass sections in the literature and we need some preliminary selection among them before starting deeper study. The complex-conjugate poles are positioned mainly in the right half of the unit circle and only rarely (for higher TFs order) in the left half, as illustrated in Fig. 1. Our extensive investigations show that the study, the classification and the selection of second order allpass sections will be eased if those complex-conjugate poles are grouped into 11 zones as shown in Fig. 4 for the upper half of the unit circle. The poles positions of tenth order allpass based FD filter, for example, for values of D in the range $N<D<50$ will scatter as shown in Fig. 4, but for $N<D<N+1$ (the most typical case) they all will concentrate only in zones 1, 2, 5, 6. This is valid also for TFs of any order. Thus, we will need most often second-order allpass sections with minimized sensitivities for complex-conjugate poles pairs positioned in these zones in order to obtain low-sensitivity FD realization and better FD time accuracy. These zones are not typical for conventional selective filters, whose poles are situated usually near $z = 1$, so we selected initially the most popular sections, having canonic structures and known with low sensitivities. They are the Gray-Markel section (GM2), the Mitra and Hirano sections (MH2A and MH2B), the Kwan sections (KW2A and KW2B) and the low sensitivity section ST2A, shown in Fig. 5 and developed or discussed (together with many other sections with similar sensitivities) in (Topalov & Stoyanov, 1991); (Stoyanov & Nishihara, 1995); (Stoyanov & Kawamata, 1998); (Stoyanov & Kawamata, 2003); (Stoyanov et al., 2005) and in the references there-in. These sections are realizing the following TFs:

$$H_{GM2}(z) = \frac{-a_1 - a_2(1-a_1)z^{-1} + z^{-2}}{1 - a_2(1-a_1)z^{-1} - a_1 z^{-2}} ; \tag{11}$$

$$H_{MH2A}(z) = \frac{b_1 b_2 - b_1 z^{-1} + z^{-2}}{1 - b_1 z^{-1} + b_1 b_2 z^{-2}} ; \tag{12}$$

$$H_{MH2B}(z) = \frac{b_2 - b_1 z^{-1} + z^{-2}}{1 - b_1 z^{-1} + b_2 z^{-2}} ; \tag{13}$$

$$H_{KW2A}(z) = \frac{1 + a_1 - a_2 - (a_1 + a_2)z^{-1} + z^{-2}}{1 - (a_1 + a_2)z^{-1} + (1 + a_1 - a_2)z^{-2}} ; \tag{14}$$

$$H_{KW2B}(z) = \frac{d_1 + d_2 - 1 - (d_1 - d_2)z^{-1} + z^{-2}}{1 - (d_1 - d_2)z^{-1} + (d_1 + d_2 - 1)z^{-2}} ; \tag{15}$$

$$H_{ST2A}(z) = \frac{1 - 2b - 2(1-b)(1-2a)z^{-1} + z^{-2}}{1 - 2(1-b)(1-2a)z^{-1} + (1-2b)z^{-2}} . \tag{16}$$

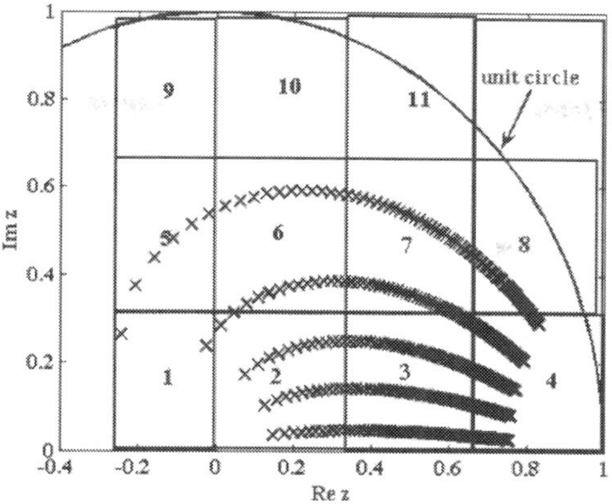

Fig. 4. Zoning of the z-plane for allpass FD TFs pole positions.

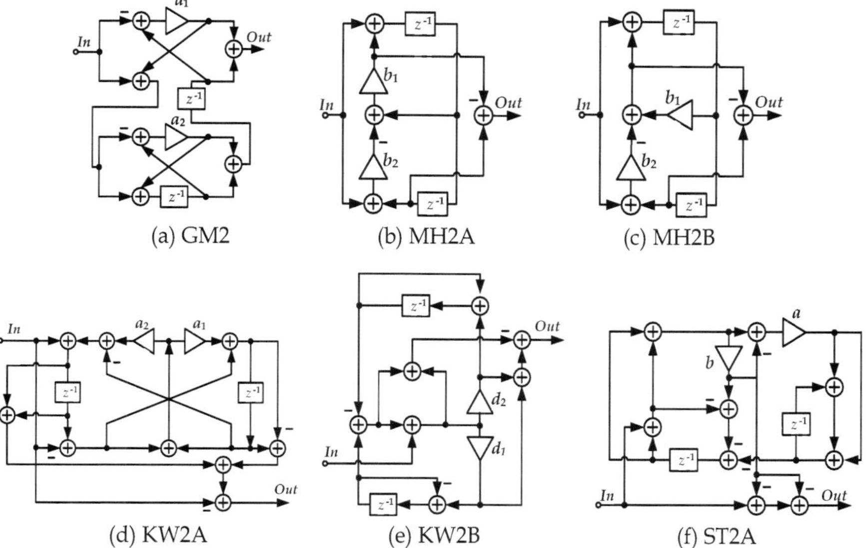

Fig. 5. Different popular canonic second-order allpass sections.

It appeared, however, that all these sections, developed for selective filters applications, are not having enough low sensitivities for poles in zones 1, 2, 5, 6, as shown in Fig. 7, where especially wrong choice is ST2A. We have developed in (Ivanova & Stoyanov, 2007); (Nikolova et al., 2009) a new section, shown in Fig. 6 (we shall call it IS-section) and with minimized sensitivity for the TF poles situated exactly in zone 2. Its transfer function is

$$H_{IS}(z) = \frac{b + (-a - 2b + ab)z^{-1} + z^{-2}}{1 + (-a - 2b + ab)z^{-1} + bz^{-2}}, \tag{17}$$

it is canonic with respect to the number of the multipliers and the delays, its round-off noises are constant and very low and it is structurally lossless and structurally bounded real.

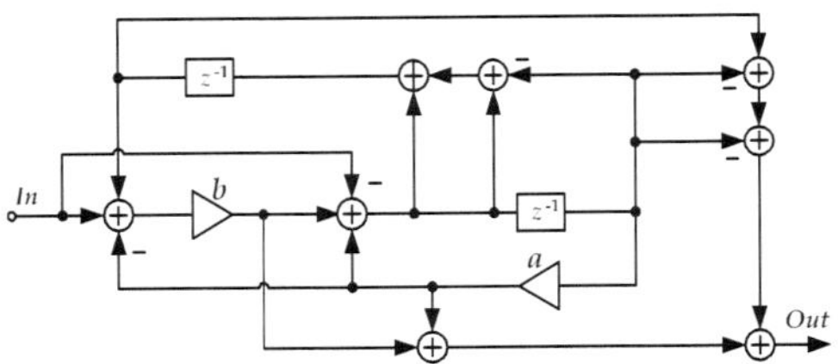

Fig. 6. IS allpass section, suitable for FD filter realizations with TF poles in zone 2.

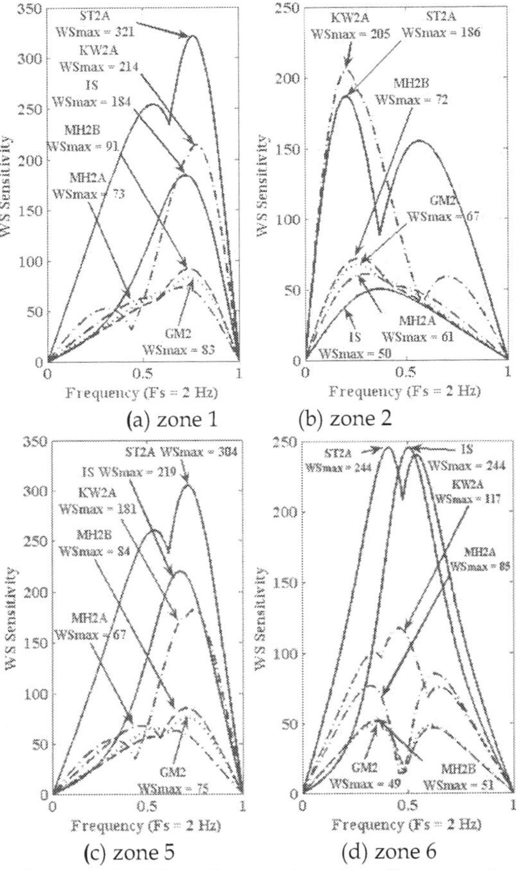

Fig. 7. Worst-case phase-sensitivities of second order allpass sections for TF poles in different zones.

The phase sensitivities of the new allpass section together with these of the other second-order allpass sections were investigated for complex-conjugate pole pairs in zones 1, 2, 5 and 6. The results for the worst-case phase sensitivities are given in Fig. 7. It is obvious that the worst case phase sensitivity of the IS section is the lowest for small values of the FD parameter D ($D \approx N$) which correspond to TF poles situated in zone 2. The other allpass sections suitable for realizations of small values of FD are GM2 and MH2B (zone 6) and GM2 and MH2A (zone 1 and zone 5). KW2A, KW2B and ST2A (and the other numerous known sections) generally cannot be recommended and have to be investigated in every specific case. The TF coefficients as function of D are given in Tables 1–3.

IS		GM2	
a	b	a_1	a_2
$\dfrac{D-2}{D}$	$\dfrac{(D-1)(D-2)}{(D+1)(D+2)}$	$-\dfrac{(D-1)(D-2)}{(D+1)(D+2)}$	$\dfrac{(D-2)(D+2)}{(D^2+2)}$

Table 1. IS and GM2 FD transfer function coefficients.

MH2A		MH2B	
b_1	b_2	b_1	b_2
$2\dfrac{(D-2)}{(D+1)}$	$\dfrac{(D-1)}{2(D+2)}$	$2\dfrac{(D-2)}{(D+1)}$	$\dfrac{(D-1)(D-2)}{(D+1)(D+2)}$

Table 2. MH2A and MH2B FD transfer function coefficients.

KW2A		KW2B	
a_1	a_2	d_1	d_2
$\dfrac{(D^2-3D-4)}{(D+1)(D+2)}$	$\dfrac{(D^2+3D-4)}{(D+1)(D+2)}$	$2\dfrac{(D-1)}{(D+2)}$	$\dfrac{6}{(D+1)(D+2)}$

Table 3. KW2A and KW2B FD transfer function coefficients.

5. Low-Sensitivity Design of fixed FD Filters

Having in mind the principles of high-accuracy design from Sect. 2 and taking into account the results obtained here-above, we propose the following design procedure:

1. Apply the Thiran approximation to obtain an allpass TF with order N ensuring a phase-delay error within given limits over the required frequency range. Broadening excessively this range will increase considerably the order N.

2. Decompose the TF to first and second-order terms and check in which zones the poles of these terms are situated.

3. Select or develop new first and second-order allpass sections providing lowest sensitivities for each real or couple of complex-conjugate poles.

4. For poles in some zones, as seen in Figs. 3 and 7, several allpass sections are equally good possible candidates. In such case compose several sets of allpass sections and investigate the overall sensitivity of each set to select the one with the lowest sensitivity.

This procedure was applied to obtain an FD allpass structure realizing D=11.2. The 11th order TF has five pairs of complex-conjugate poles (two pairs in zone 1 and three – in zone 2) and one real pole, as shown in Fig. 8. The most recommendable (from what follows from Figs. 3 and 7) set of allpass sections is suggested in the same figure, but the other possible four sets have also been considered. The worst-case phase sensitivities of the realizations, corresponding to all the five sets, are shown in Fig. 9.

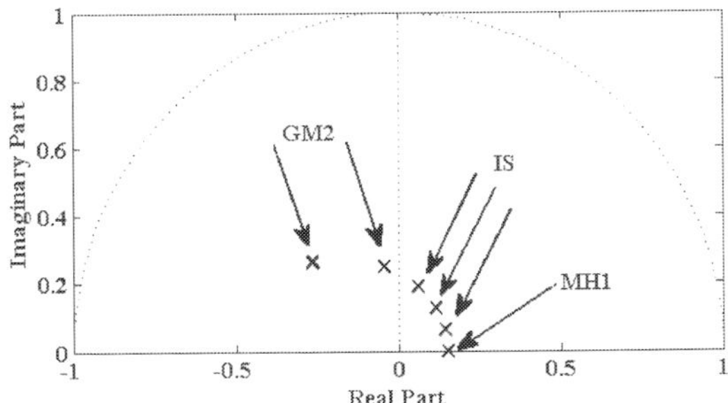

Fig. 8. Pole-position plot of 11-th order allpass FD filter realizing $D = 11.2$.

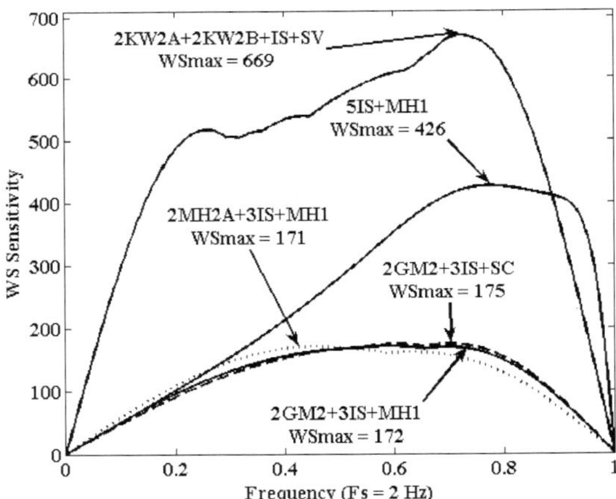

Fig. 9. Worst-case phase-sensitivities of different sets of sections realizing an 11-th order allpass-based FD TF with $D = 11.2$.

It is seen from Fig. 9 that the method is working properly and two of the sets are by far worst than the other three. It is amazing that for this specific example there are three sets of allpass sections that are having very similar overall worst-case sensitivity and the final choice has to be made after considering other details, like total number of adders, range of values of multiplier coefficients and deterioration of the delay response after the coefficients quantization.

The reduction of the overall sensitivity permits a considerable shortening of the coefficients wordlength followed by more efficient multiplierless implementation. We have applied this approach in (Ivanova et al., 2005) and after deriving closed form expressions for the coefficients of the allpass sections given in Sect. 4, we have obtained multiplierless realizations with no more than three adders per coefficient. A further improvement of the multiplierless design was achieved in (Stoyanov et al., 2009) by applying a genetic algorithm to optimize the values of the coefficients within the set of possible values limited by the quantization.

6. Low-Sensitivity Design and Implementation of Variable FD Filters

6.1 Design procedure

The calculation of the coefficients obtained by Thiran approximation (1) include too many division operations that are making difficult tuning of such circuit in real time. In (Makundi et al., 2001) the coefficients (1) have been presented as:

$$\hat{a}_k = (-1)^k \binom{N}{k} \frac{\prod_{n=0}^{k-1}(d+n)}{\prod_{n=1}^{k}(d+N+n)} \prod_{n=1}^{N}(d+N+n) =$$
$$= (-1)^k \binom{N}{k} \prod_{n=0}^{k-1}(d+n) \prod_{n=k+1\leq N}^{N}(d+N+n) = \sum_{l=1}^{N}\hat{e}_{lk}d^l, \ for \ k=1,2...N, \tag{18}$$

where d is the fractional part of the phase-delay and $d = D - N$.
Then, the allpass TF (2) was given in the form

$$H_{AP}(z) = \frac{g(d)[\hat{a}_N + ... + \hat{a}_1 z^{-(N-1)}] + z^{-N}}{1 + g(d)[\hat{a}_1 z^{-1} + ... + \hat{a}_N z^{-N}]}, \tag{19}$$

and the coefficient $g(d)$ was approximated using the truncated Maclaurin series as

$$g(d) = \frac{1}{\prod_{n=1}^{N}(d+N+n)} =$$
$$\cong \frac{N!}{(2N)!}\prod_{n=1}^{N}\left[1 + \sum_{k=1}^{I}(-1)^k\left(\frac{d}{N+n}\right)^k\right] \cong \sum_{i=0}^{I}g_i d^i, \tag{20}$$

where I is the order of the approximating polynomial. The structure obtained through this method is called "gathering structure". Even though very famous, this structure has many drawbacks:

    (a) it contains a great number of multipliers and adders leading to long critical paths;

    (b) as any direct structure it has higher sensitivity;

    (c) for higher TF order N there is a big difference between the smallest and the biggest coefficient (about 10^2 for $N = 2$, $I = 2$; about 10^3 for $N = 2$, $I = 3$ and 10^5 for $N = 3$, $I = 3$), requiring very large wordlength.

To avoid them, the following representation was proposed in (Cho et al., 2007):

$$a_k = \sum_{i=0}^{I} g_i d^i \cdot \sum_{l=1}^{N} \hat{e}_{lk} d^l = \sum_{m=1}^{I+N} \left[\sum_{l=1}^{m} g_{m-l} \hat{e}_{lk} \right] d^m =$$

$$\cong \sum_{m=1}^{P} \left[\sum_{l=1}^{m} g_{m-l} \hat{e}_{lk} \right] d^m = \sum_{m=1}^{P} \left[\sum_{n=1}^{N} c_{mn} \right] d^m ,$$

(21)

where P is the order of the approximating polynomial and it is in the range $N \leq P \leq N + I$. We shall call the variable structure obtained by using (21) "Cho-Parhi-structure". It has less multipliers and shorter critical path, compared to gathering structure, and similar values of the coefficients c_{mn} (21).

We found in (Nikolova & Stoyanov, 2008) that it is possible to obtain even more efficient variable realizations by expressing each transfer function coefficients a_k (2) as a Taylor series expansion with respect to d and then to truncating after the linear, quadratic or cubic term (T = 1, 2, 3) depending on the desired accuracy. To achieve the tuning in real time we propose the following design procedure:

1. Select of the allpass TF order corresponding to given requirements (desired fractional delay value d and/or the bandwidth with maximally flat phase delay response).

2. Obtain an allpass FD filter using Thiran approximation.

3. Taylor series expansion of each TF coefficient and truncation after the linear (when only adjustment of the phase delay is required), quadratic or cubic term (if tuning over larger range of values of the phase delay is required).

4. Realize all the multiplier coefficients as composite multipliers (see Figs. 10, 11).

The proposed design procedure is simple to use and the obtained structures have no critical path. The method can be applied for an arbitrary TF order but in the cases of first and second order TFs it allows to implement structures different from direct form and to minimize the sensitivity of the realizations. For the low-sensitivity structure IS (Fig. 6), for example, the coefficients are expressed by d as

$$a = \frac{d}{d+2} ; \quad b = \frac{d(d+1)}{(d+3)(d+4)} .$$

(22)

After expanding (22) to Taylor series and truncating after the quadratic or the cubic term, we get correspondingly:

$$a = \frac{1}{2} d - \frac{1}{4} d^2 ; \quad b = \frac{1}{12} d + \frac{5}{144} d^2 ;$$

(23)

$$a = \frac{1}{2} d - \frac{1}{4} d^2 + \frac{1}{8} d^3 ; \quad b = \frac{1}{12} d + \frac{5}{144} d^2 - \frac{47}{1728} d^3 .$$

(24)

All these coefficients have homogenous structure, they do not include division operation and can be realized as composite multipliers containing fixed and variable multipliers. The composite multiplier realizations for second and third order Taylor approximation of a are shown in Fig. 10 and Fig. 11.

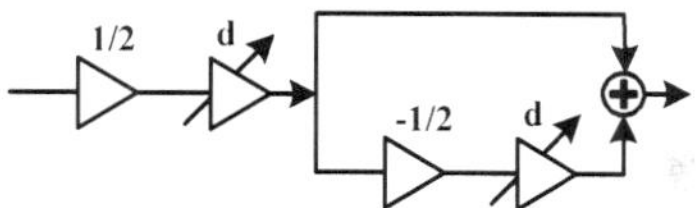

Fig. 10. Composite variable multiplier realization of a (23) after a second order Taylor approximation.

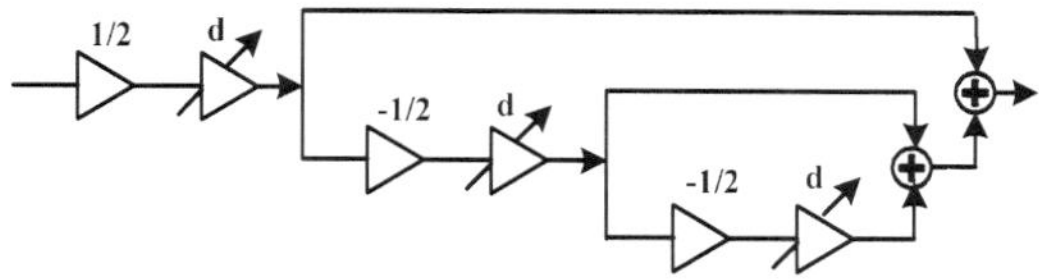

Fig. 11. Composite variable multiplier realization of a (24) after a third order Taylor approximation.

It is worth mentioning that some of the fixed multiplier coefficients values, obtained after the Taylor series expansions (23), (24), are machine representable (they have values $\pm 2^{\pm i}$) and will be realized by using only shifts and adds. In fact, in Fig. 10 and 11 all fixed multipliers are of this type and thus the complexity of the composite multipliers is kept very low. The RDI-method (Hacıhabiboğlu et al., 2007), is using two N^{th} order allpass FD TFs approximating different FD values D_1 and D_2 to obtain a new allpass FD filter with phase delay time D_i such that $D_1 < D_i < D_2$. The denominator of (2) (the denominators of the two initial allpass transfer functions) is represented as (Hacıhabiboğlu et al., 2007):

$$A_i(z) = \begin{cases} \left[1 - r_i z^{-1}\right] \times \prod_{k=1}^{(N-1)/2}\left[1 - c_{i,k}^2 z^{-2}\right], & N \ odd \\[2em] \prod_{k=1}^{N-1}\left[1 - c_{i,k}^2 z^{-2}\right], & N \ even \end{cases} \tag{25}$$

where $\left\{c_{i,k}, c_{i,k}^*\right\}$ is k-th complex-conjugate pole pair and r_i is the real pole of the filter with TF $H_i(z)$ (2). The complex-conjugate poles (for real pole is the same procedure) are sorted with respect to their angles and are paired according to their angular proximity. The interpolated complex poles are calculated from the paired poles as

$$c_{\text{int},k} = [1-\rho]c_{1,k} + \rho c_{2,k}, \tag{26}$$

where ρ is a constant between 0 and 1. This can be realized using only adders and multipliers, as shown in (Hacıhabiboğlu et al., 2007), and the phase-delay time D_i can be tuned within the range $D_1 < D_i < D_2$ by trimming only the constant ρ. This method is not connected to any particular realization of the initial allpass filters of order N, so the sensitivity cannot be an object of consideration in this case. Two disadvantages are readily seen, however: quite complicated circuitry (two allpass filters plus four additional multipliers) and narrow range of tuning of D with growing error of tuning in the middle of this range.

6.2 Accuracy investigations

To compare the accuracy of the first three methods, considered in Sect. 6.1, we have designed and investigated realizations and tuning in the range $1.5 < D < 2.5$ (i.e. $d = \pm 0.5$) of second order allpass FD filters. For the polynomial approximation of the TF coefficients truncation after the third order term was used, i.e. $I = 3$ (20), $P = 3$ (21) and $T = 3$ (for

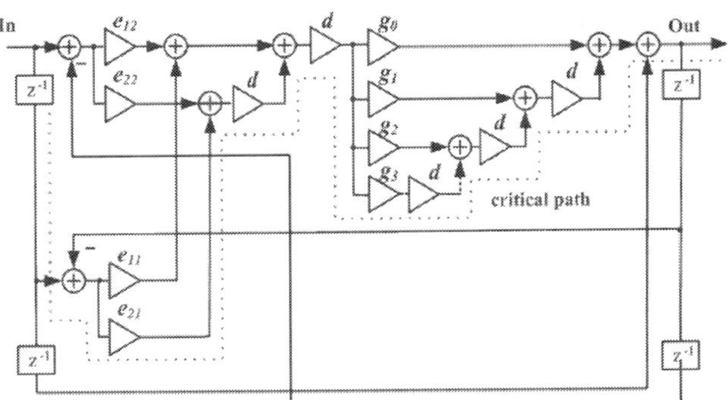

Fig. 12. Gathering structure realizing a second-order variable FD allpass filter (with $I = 3$).

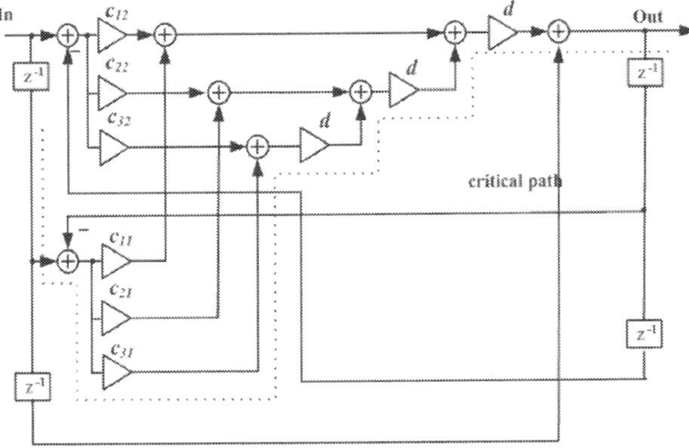

Fig. 13. Cho-Parhi structure realizing a second-order variable FD allpass filter ($P = 3$).

our method) circuit-diagrams so obtained are given in Figs. 12, 13 and 14. For our method, the IS-section (Fig. 6) with composite multipliers was used. The values of the coefficients of the three realizations are given in Table 4, Table 5, and Eq. (24), correspondingly.

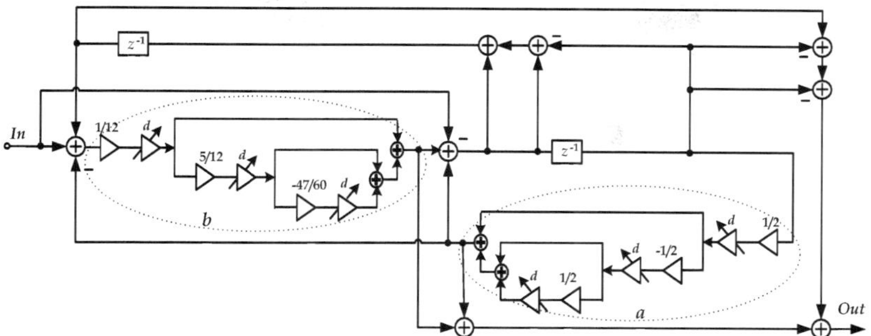

Fig. 14. IS structure realizing a second-order variable FD allpass filter with $T = 3$.

$\hat{a}_k$		$g(d)$
$\hat{e}_{11} = -8$	$\hat{e}_{12} = 1$	$g_0 = 0.083333$
$\hat{e}_{21} = -2$	$\hat{e}_{22} = 1$	$g_1 = -0.048611$
		$g_2 = 0.021412$
		$g_3 = -0.0084394$

Table 4. TF coefficients of gathering structure.

$c_{11} = -0.666667$	$c_{21} = 0.222222$	$c_{31} = -0.074074$
$c_{12} = 0.083333$	$c_{22} = 0.034722$	$c_{32} = -0.027199$

Table 5. TF coefficients of Cho-Parhi–structure.

In Fig. 15 the worst-case phase sensitivities of the three realizations for several values of the fractional part d of the phase-delay time are given. It is seen that our approach and the Cho-Parhi method are decreasing considerably the sensitivity, compared to that of the gathering structure, for $d = \pm 0.5$ (our structure is behaving better than that of Cho-Parhi for positive values of d and it is opposite for the negative values). For small values of d our structure is the best, but generally the IS and the Cho-Parhi structures are having similar sensitivities. The possible explanation for this is that the Cho-Parhi approach, when reducing the range of values of the multiplier coefficients, compared to those of the gathering structure, is decreasing the largest values. It is well known, that when the values of the multiplier coefficients are decreased, the sensitivities to these coefficients are decreased too.

In Table 6 the complexities of the three variable realizations are compared. The Cho-Parhi– and the IS- variable structures are having an equal number of multipliers (three of the multiplier coefficients in IS are machine representable and will be realized by using only adds and shifts), but the IS-structure has only two delays, it is not having a critical path and it will be shown in the Experiments that it is behaving better in a limited wordlength environment.

The RDI-method is not considered here, as it is not connected to some specific realization. Its accuracy is investigated in the Experiments (Sect. 7).

	Variable IS structure	Gathering structure	Cho-Parhi structure
	$T = 3$	$I = 3$	$P = 3$
Multipliers	12 (9)	13	9
Adders	14	9	8
Delay elements	2	4	4

Table 6. Comparison of the complexity of the structures.

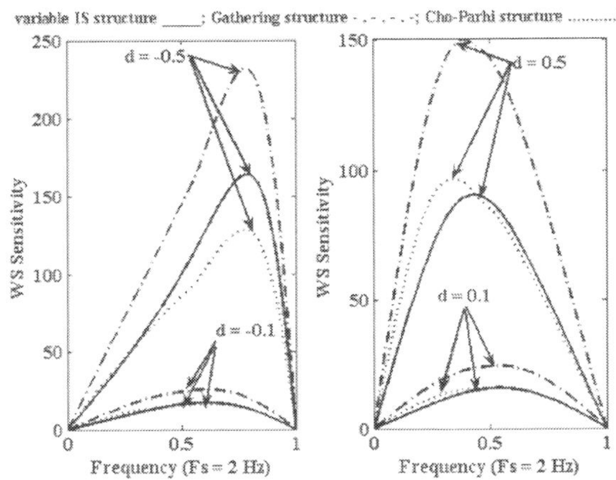

Fig. 15. Worst-case phase-sensitivities of second-order allpass based FD filter ($I = 3, P = 3$, $T = 3$).

7. Experiments

In order to verify the proposed low-sensitivity design procedure and to investigate how the FD time accuracy is maintained after coefficient quantization, we have designed and simulated all the five realizations considered in Sect. 5 (11th order TF realizing D=11.2). The phase delay responses of the quantized TFs are given in Fig. 16 (without these of 2GM2+3IS+SC, almost fully coinciding with 2GM2+3IS+MH1, as it might be anticipated from Fig. 7). The higher overall sensitivity of the 2KW2A+2KW2B+IS+SV-structure (WS$_{max}$=669 in Fig. 9) is the reason for its poor performance in a limited wordlength environment – the phase delay error for low frequencies is considerable even after a mild quantization down to 4 bits in CSD code (11.235 instead of 11.2 in Fig. 16a) and this response is almost totally destroyed for 2 bits wordlength. For the best structure (2MH2A+3IS+MH1) this error is almost negligible – 11.195 instead of 11.2 (Fig. 16d) and is quite acceptable even for wordlength of only 2 bit. The other sets from Sect. 5 are behaving as it could be predicted from Fig. 7. The main conclusion from these experiments is that our approach is working very successfully and is ensuring a considerable improvement of the accuracy in a limited wordlength environment.

In order to observe and compare the tuning accuracy of the three methods and variable structures from Sect. 6 (gathering structure, Cho-Parhi-structure and IS-structure), we have designed three second order allpass FD filters with third order TF-coefficients approximation ($I=3$, $P=3$, $T=3$) and a given fractional delay parameter value $d=0.3$. The results after the coefficient quantization are given in Fig. 17. Because of the lower sensitivity of the IS structure the tuning accuracy is higher than that of the gathering structure and Cho-Parhi structure even when the TF coefficients are quantized to 2 significant bits (in CSD code). The deviations from the desired phase delay (0.3 samples) of variable IS FD filter near DC for 4, 3 and 2 bits are correspondingly smaller than 10^{-5}, -0.002 and -0.0179, while these of the gathering structure are -0.0029, -0.009 and -0.041 and of the Cho-Parhi-structure – -0.0018, -0.0086 and -0.041.

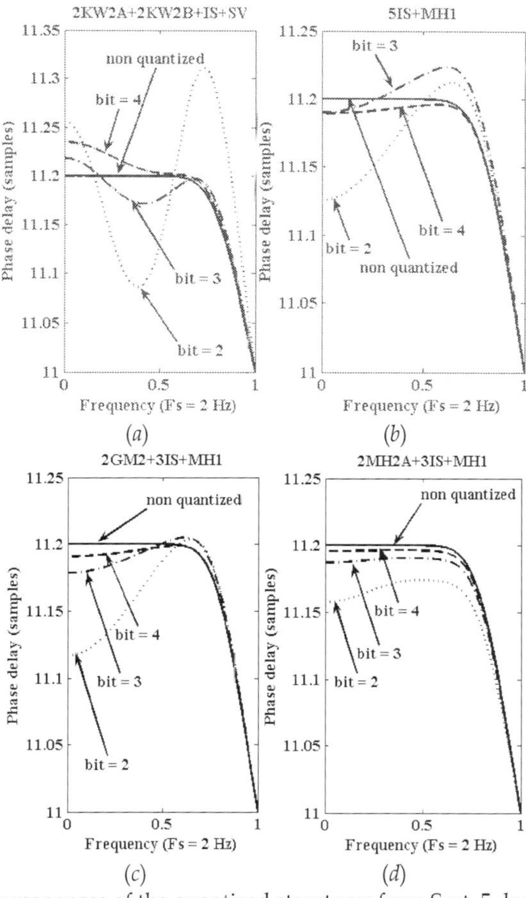

Fig. 16. Phase delay responses of the quantized structures from Sect. 5 designed for $D=11.2$.

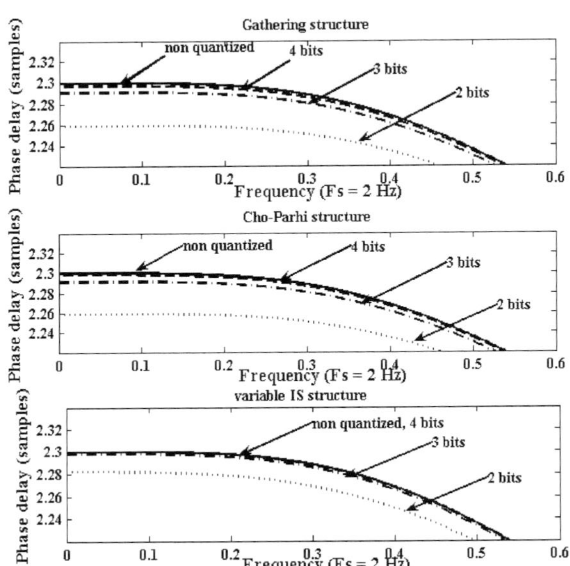

Fig. 17. Wordlength dependence of the accuracy of tuning of the phase delay of second order allpass FD filters realized as gathering-, Cho-Parhi- and IS-structures for $d = 0.3$ in a case of $I = 3$, $P = 3$, $T = 3$.

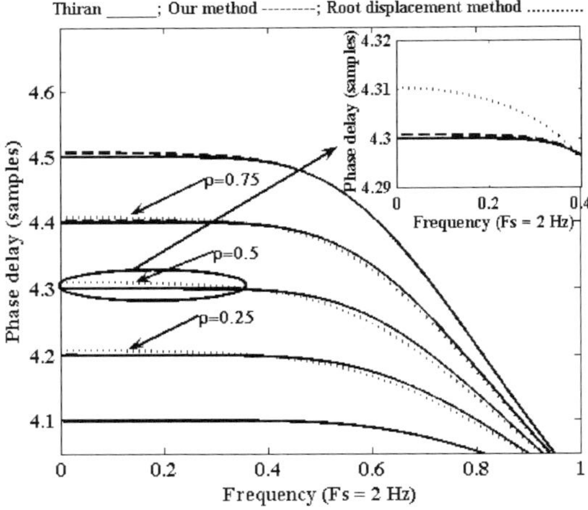

Fig. 18. Tuning accuracy comparison of the root-displacement method and our method for 4th order allpass FD filters for different values of D.

As the RDI-method is not connected to a specific structure, we have compared its accuracy to our method by simulating the tuning of the FD from 4.1 to 4.5 of the TFs with $N = 4$. For our method a direct-form structure was used and the coefficients have been approximated by third-order Taylor polynomials. It is seen from Fig. 18 that the phase-delay of the RDI TF is having a higher error compared to that of our method and is losing its maximally-flat behavior for all intermediate values of D (note that for $D = 4.5$ there is no tuning in the case of RDI-method and thus no error will appear). It was found, additionally, that there is no direct connection between the desired value of the phase-delay D and the value of the tuning factor ρ (26) and this uncertainty in tuning cannot be avoided.

8. Conclusions and Future Work

In this chapter, a new approach to achieve a high accuracy of implementation and tuning of fixed and variable allpass-based fractional delay filters through sensitivity minimizations have been proposed. The method is based on a phase-sensitivity minimization of each individual first- and second-order allpass section in the filter cascade realization. It was shown that the poles of the FD TFs are taking positions not typical for the conventional filters. Then, after studying the possible combinations of real and complex-conjugate poles for different values of the FD parameter D and of the TF order N, it was proposed to divide the unit-circle to 11 zones and it was shown that FD TF poles (obtained using Thiran approximation) of most practical cases are located only in four of them and very often – in only one (zone 2). The behavior of the most popular allpass sections when having poles in these zones was investigated and it was shown that the proper selection of the sections is very important when trying to minimize the overall sensitivity. A new second-order allpass section, providing low sensitivity for zone 2 (and thus very suitable for high accuracy FD realizations) was developed by the authors. This section was turned also to tunable and high tuning accuracy was achieved. A new approach to obtain tunable allpass FD filters was developed and it was compared with the other known methods. It was shown also that the low sensitivity so achieved permits a very short coefficient wordlength, i.e. efficient multiplierless implementations, higher processing speed and lower power consumption.

The proposed approach to design low-sensitivity allpass-based FD filters could be easily applied to further improve the performance of different allpass-based FD filters, obtained using most of the design methods overviewed in Sect. 1.3. provided that the allpass TFs of the filters and sub-filters in these realizations are clearly identifiable.

It is well known that all IIR digital filters are producing different types of parasitic noises, especially when a fixed-point arithmetic is employed. These noises have not been investigated in the present chapter. It is also well known, however, that low sensitivity and low noises usually go together and as only allpass sections with very low sensitivities are considered here and they are selected and used in frequency ranges and TF pole-positions zones where they would exhibit their lowest sensitivities, it might be expected that they will have very low level of the noises. These noises are expected to be low also because of the specific pole-positions of the FD filters – their TF poles are usually situated in the central part of the unit circle (as shown in Sect. 3.2), while noises are dangerously growing when the poles are approaching the unit-circle (typical for highly selective amplitude filters). All this should be verified, however, and it would be done in the future work.

Next problem that should be addressed in the future is that of the transients, typical for all recursive realizations and affecting especially strongly all tunable IIR structures. These transients may compromise the proper work of the system for quite considerable time-intervals, following the moments of trimming of some multipliers, and more efficient than the presently known methods to decrease these effects should be developed and investigated.

Acknowledgments

This work was supported by the Bulgarian National Science Fund under Grant No DO-02-135/15.12.08 and by the Technical University of Sofia under Grant No 102NI065-7/2010 of the University Research Fund.

9. References

Cho, K.; Park, J.; Kim, B.; Chung, J. & Parhi, K. (2007). "Design of a sample-rate converter from CD to DAT using fractional delay allpass filter", *IEEE Trans. Circuits Syst. II, Exp. Briefs*, vol. 54, No. 1, pp. 19-23, Jan. 2007.

Deng, T. & Nakagawa, Y. (2004). "SVD–based design and new structures for variable fractional-delay digital filters", *IEEE Trans. Signal Processing*, vol. 52, No. 9, pp. 2513–2527, Sept. 2004.

Deng, T. (2006). "Noniterative WLS design of allpass variable fractional-delay digital filters", *IEEE Trans. Circuits Syst. I, Regular Papers*, vol. 53, No. 2, pp. 358-371, Feb. 2006.

Deng, T. (2009a). "Robust structure transformation for causal Lagrange-type variable fractional-delay filters", *IEEE Trans. Circuits Syst. I, Regular Papers*, vol. 56, No. 8, pp. 1681-1688, Aug. 2009.

Deng, T. (2009b). "Generalized WLS method for designing allpass variable fractional-delay digital filters", *IEEE Trans. Circuits Syst. I, Regular Papers*, vol. 56, No. 10, pp. 2207-2220, Oct. 2009.

Deng, T. (2010a). "Hybrid structures for low-complexity variable fractional-delay FIR filters", *IEEE Trans. Circuits Syst. I, Regular Papers*, vol. 57, No. 4, pp. 897-910, Apr. 2010.

Deng, T. (2010b). "Minimax design of low-complexity allpass variable fractional-delay digital filters", *IEEE Trans. Circuits Syst. I, Regular Papers*, vol. 57, No. 8, pp. 2075-2086, Aug. 2010.

Farrow, C. W. (1988). "A continuous variable digital delay element", *Proc. ISCAS'1988*, Espoo, Finland, pp. 2641-2645, June 1988.

Hacıhabiboğlu, H.; Günel, B. & Kondoz, A. (2007). "Analysis of root displacement interpolation method for tunable allpass fractional-delay filters", *IEEE Trans. on Signal Processing*, vol. 55, No. 10, pp. 4896–4906, Oct. 2007.

Huang, Y.; Pei, S. & Shyu, J. (2009). "WLS design of variable fractional-delay FIR filters using coefficient relationship", *IEEE Trans. Circuits Syst. II, Exp. Briefs*, vol. 56, No. 3, pp. 220-224, March 2009.

Ivanova, K.; Anzova, V. & Stoyanov, G. (2005). "Cascaded multiplierless realizations of low sensitivities allpass based fractional delay filters", *Proc. 7th Intern. Conf. TELSIKS'2005*, Nish, Serbia, vol. 1, pp. 451-460, Sept. 28–30, 2005.

Ivanova, K. & Stoyanov, G. (2007). "A new low sensitivity second order allpass section suitable for fractional delay filter realizations", *Proc. 8th Intern. Conf. TELSIKS'2007*, Nish, Serbia, vol. 1, pp. 317-320, Sept. 26–28, 2007.

Johanson, H. & Lovenborg, P. (2003). "On the design of adjustable fractional delay FIR filters", *IEEE Trans. Circuits Syst. II*, vol. 50, pp. 164-169, Apr. 2003.

Kwan, H. & Jiang, A. (2009). "FIR, allpass, and IIR fractional delay digital filter design", *IEEE Trans. Circuits Syst. I, Regular Papers*, vol. 56, No. 9, pp. 2064-2074, Sep. 2009.

Laakso, T.; Valimaki, V.; Karjalainen, M. & Laine, U. (1996). Splitting the unit delay – tools for fractional delay design. *IEEE Signal Process. Mag.*, vol. 13, No. 1, pp. 30–60, Jan. 1996.

Makundi, M.; Laakso, T. & Välimäki, V. (2001). "Efficient tunable IIR and allpass filter structures", *Elect. Lett.*, vol. 37, no. 6, pp. 344–345, 2001.

Makundi, M.; Laakso, T. & Liu, Y. (2002). "Asynchronous implementation of transient suppression in tunable IIR filters", *Proc. 14th Intern. Conference DSP'2002*, Santorini, Greece, vol. 2, pp. 815–818, July 01-03, 2002.

Nikolova, K. & Stoyanov, G. (2008). "A new method of design of variable fractional delay digital allpass filters", *Proc. 43th Intern. Conference ICEST'2008*, Nish, Serbia, vol. 1, pp. 75– 8, June 25-27, 2008.

Nikolova, K.; Stoyanov, G. & Kawamata, M. (2009). "Low-sensitivity design and implementation of allpass based fractional delay digital filters", *Proc. European Conf. on Circuit Theory and Design (ECCTD'09)*, Antalya, Turkey, pp. 603-606, Aug. 23-27, 2009.

Nishihara, A. (1984). "Low-sensitivity second-order digital filters - analysis and design in terms of frequency sensitivity", *Trans. IECE of Japan*, vol. E 67, No 8, pp. 433-439, Aug. 1984.

Pei, S.; Wang, P. & Lin, C. (2010). "Design of fractional delay filter, differintegrator, fractional Hilbert transformer, and differentiator in time domain with Peano kernel", *IEEE Trans. Circuits Syst. I, Regular Papers*, vol. 57, No. 2, pp. 391-404, Feb. 2010.

Shyu, J.; Pei, S.; Cheng, C.; Huang, Y. & Lin, S. (2010). "A new criterion for the design of variable fractional-delay FIR digital filters", *IEEE Trans. Circuits Syst. I, Regular Papers*, vol. 57, No. 2, pp. 368-377, Feb. 2010.

Stoyanov, G. & Clausert H. (1994). "A comparative study of first order digital allpass structures", *Frequenz*, vol. 48, No. 9/10, pp. 221–226, Sept./Oct. 1994.

Stoyanov, G. & Nishihara, A. (1995). "Very low sensitivity design of digital IIR filters using parallel and cascade-parallel connections of allpass sections", *Bulletin of INCOCSAT*, Tokyo Institute of Technology, vol. 1, pp. 55–64, March 1995.

Stoyanov, G. & Kawamata, M. (1998). "Improved tuning accuracy design of parallel-allpass-structures-based variable digital filters", *Proc. ISCAS'1998*, Monterey, California, vol. 5, pp. V-379–V-382, May 1998.

Stoyanov, G. & Kawamata, M. (2003). "Variable biquadratic digital filter section with simultaneous tuning of the pole and zero frequencies by a single parameter", *Proc. ISCAS'2003*, Bangkok, Thailand, vol. 3, pp. III-566–III-569, May 2003.

Stoyanov, G.; Uzunov, I. & Kawamata, M. (2005). "High tuning accuracy design of variable IIR filters as a cascade of identical sub-filters", *Proc. ISCAS'2005*, Kobe, Japan, pp. 3729–3732, May 23-26, 2005.

Stoyanov, G.; Nikolova, Z.; Ivanova, K. & Anzova, V. (2007). "Design and realization of efficient IIR digital filter structures based on sensitivity minimizations", *Proc. 8th Intern. Conf. TELSIKS'2007*, Nish, Serbia, vol.1, pp. 299–308, Sept. 26-28, 2007.

Stoyanov, G.; Nikolova, K. & Markova, V. (2009). "High-accuracy design and realization of fixed and variable allpass-based fractional delay digital filters", *Proc. TELSIKS'2009*, Nish, Serbia, vol.1, pp. 167-176, Oct. 07-09, 2009.

Sugino, N. & Nishihara, A. (1990). "Frequency-domain simulator of digital networks from the structural description", *Trans. IECE of Japan*, vol. E 73, No.11, pp. 1804-1806, Nov. 1990.

Thiran, J.-P. (1971). "Recursive digital filter with maximally flat group delay", *IEEE Trans. Circuit Theory*, vol. 18, No. 6, pp. 659–664, Nov. 1971.

Topalov, I. & Stoyanov, G. (1991). "A systematic approach to the design of low-sensitivity limit-cycle-free universal bilinear and biquadratic digital filter sections", *Proc. 10th European Conf. on Circuit Theory and Design (ECCTD'91)*, Copenhagen, Denmark, vol. 1, pp. 213-222, Sept. 02-06, 1991.

Tseng, C. (2002). "Design of 1-D and 2-D variable fractional delay allpass filters using weighted least-squares method", *IEEE Trans. Circuits Syst. I, Fundam. Theory Appls*, vol. 49, No. 10, pp. 1413-1422, Oct. 2002.

Tseng, C. (2004). "Design of variable fractional delay FIR filters using symmetry", *Proc. ISCAS'2004*, Vancouver, Canada, vol. 3, pp. 477-480, May 2004.

Tseng, C. & Lee, S. (2009). "Closed-form design of variable fractional delay filters using discrete Fourier transform", *Proc. EUSIPCO'2009*, Glasgow, Scotland, vol. 3, pp. 426-430, Aug. 24-28, 2009.

Tsui, K.; Chan, S. & Kwan, H. (2007). "A new method for designing causal stable IIR variable fractional delay filters", *IEEE Trans. Circuits Syst. II, Exp. Briefs*, vol. 54, No. 11, pp. 999-1003, Nov. 2007.

Valimaki, V. & Laakso, T. (1998). "Suppression of transient in variable recursive digital filters with a novel and efficient cancellation method", *IEEE Trans. Signal Processing*, vol. 46, No. 12, pp. 3408–3414, Dec. 1998.

Valimaki, V. & Laakso, T. (2001). Fractional delay filters – design and applications, In *Nonuniform Sampling: Theory and Applications*, Marvasti, F. (Ed.), (pp. 835-895), Kluwer/Plenum, New York, 2001.

Vesma, J. & Saramaki, T. (2000). "Design and properties of polynomial-based fractional-delay filters", *Proc. ISCAS'2000*, Geneva, Switzerland, vol. 1, pp. 104-107, May 2000.

Yli-Kaakinen, J. & Saramaki, T. (2004). "An algorithm for the optimization of adjustable fractional-delay allpass filters", *Proc. ISCAS'2004*, Vancouver, Canada, vol. 3, pp. 153-155, May 2004.

Yli-Kaakinen, J. & Saramaki, T. (2006). "Multiplication-free polynomial-based FIR filters with an adjustable fractional delay", *Circuits, Syst. Sign. Proc.*, vol. 25, No. 2, pp. 265-294, 2006.

Zhao, H. & Kwan, H. (2007). "Design of 1-D stable variable fractional delay IIR filters", *IEEE Trans. Circuits Syst. II, Exp. Briefs*, vol. 54, No. 1, pp. 86-90, Jan. 2007.

8

Integrated Design of IIR Variable Fractional Delay Digital Filters with Variable and Fixed Denominators

Hon Keung Kwan and Aimin Jiang
Department of Electrical and Computer Engineering
University of Windsor, Windsor, ON N9B 3P4
Canada

1. Introduction

In this chapter, the following abbreviations are used: Variable-denominator IIR VFD filters as VdIIR VFD filters. Fixed-denominator IIR VFD filters as FdIIR VFD filters. Allpass VFD filters as AP VFD filters. FIR VFD filters the same as FIR VFD filters. Symbol t is used to represent fractional delay (instead of the symbol d normally used to denote the operation of differentiation). Five frequently referenced design methods are abbreviated for ease of reference in Sections 5-8 as: (Zhao & Kwan, 2007) as (ZK); (Kwan & Jiang, 2009a) as (KJ); (Tsui et al., 2007) as (TCK); (Lee et al., 2008) as (LCR); and (Lu & Deng, 1999) as (LD).

Variable fractional delay (VFD) digital filters have various applications in signal processing and communications (Laakso et al., 1996). So far, finite impulse response (FIR) VFD digital filters have been studied and a number of design methods (Deng, 2001; Deng & Lian, 2006; Kwan & Jiang, 2009a, 2009b; Lu & Deng, 1999; Tseng, 2002a; Zhao & Yu, 2006) have been advanced. Since the frequency response of an FIR VFD filter is a linear function of its polynomial coefficients, an optimal design can be obtained by numerical procedures (Kwan & Jiang, 2009a, 2009b; Tseng, 2002a; Zhao & Yu, 2006) or in closed forms (Deng, 2001; Deng & Lian, 2006; Lu & Deng, 1999). In contrast to FIR VFD filter design, allpass (AP) VFD filter design faces additional challenges due to the existence of a denominator. Since allpass VFD filters have fullband unity magnitude responses, the problem of designing an allpass VFD filter is to minimize the approximation error of phase or group delay response between an allpass VFD filter to be designed and the ideal one. A number of algorithms (Lee, et al., 2008; Tseng, 2002a, 2002b) have been proposed based on this strategy. Another property of allpass VFD filters which has been exploited in (Kwan & Jiang, 2009a; Deng, 2006) is the mirror symmetric relation between the numerator and the denominator. Such algorithms (Kwan & Jiang, 2009a; Deng, 2006) minimize the approximation error in terms of frequency responses of the denominator. The resulting problem is nonconvex, which is either simplified and solved (Kwan & Jiang, 2009a) as a quadratic programming (QP) problem with positive-realness-based stability constraints, or solved (Deng, 2006) in closed-form.

Results obtained in (Kwan & Jiang, 2009a, 2009b; 2007) indicate that general infinite impulse response (IIR) digital filters exhibit lower mean group delay (compared to allpass digital filters) and wider band characteristics (compared to allpass and FIR digital filters) in VFD filter design. In general, general IIR VFD filter design methods (Kwan et al., 2006; Kwan & Jiang, 2007, 2009a, 2009b; Tsui et al., 2007; Zhao & Kwan, 2005, 2007; Zhao et al., 2006) can be classified as two-stage approach and semi-integrated approach. Under the two-stage approach (Kwan et al., 2006; Kwan & Jiang, 2007, 2009a, 2009b; Zhao & Kwan, 2005, 2007; Zhao et al., 2006), a set of stable IIR digital filters with sampled fractional delays (FDs) are designed first, and then the polynomial coefficients are determined by fitting the obtained IIR FD filter coefficients in the least-squares (LS) sense. Under the semi-integrated approach (Tsui et al., 2007), direct optimization is carried out on the polynomial coefficients of each filter coefficient of the numerator. In (Kwan et al., 2006; Kwan & Jiang, 2007; Zhao & Kwan, 2005, 2007; Zhao et al., 2006), both the numerator and denominator coefficients are variable. In (Kwan & Jiang, 2009a, 2009b; Tsui et al., 2007), only the numerator coefficients are variable. In (Kwan & Jiang, 2007), both variable and fixed denominators are considered.

In this chapter, sequential and gradient-based methods are applied to design IIR VFD filters with variable and fixed denominators, but unlike (Kwan & Jiang, 2007), these methods are integrated design methods. Second-order cone programming (SOCP) is used to formulate the problem in the sequential design method, and in the initial design of the gradient-based design method. An advantage of using the SOCP formulation of the problem is that both linear and (convex) quadratic constraints can be readily incorporated. On the other hand, unlike the design algorithm of (Tsui et al., 2007), which models the denominator and optimizes the numerator separately, the proposed methods optimize them simultaneously during the design procedures. As described in this chapter, the sequential and especially the gradient-based design methods could achieve some improved results as compared to (a) our previous designs presented in (Zhao & Kwan, 2007) for variable-denominator IIR VFD filters, in (Kwan & Jiang, 2009a) and (Tsui et al., 2007) for fixed-denominator IIR VFD filters, and in (Kwan & Jiang, 2009a) for allpass and FIR VFD filters; and (b) the allpass (Lee et al., 2008) and the FIR (Lu & Deng, 1999) VFD filters of other researchers. A preliminary version of the sequential design method can be found in (Jiang & Kwan, 2009b). The chapter is organized as follows: In Section 2, the weighted least-squares (WLS) design problem is formulated. A sequential design method is introduced in Section 3. Then, a gradient-based design method is introduced in Section 4. Four sets of filter examples are presented in Section 5 and their design performances using the proposed and a number of other methods are analyzed in Section 6. Section 7 gives a summary of the chapter. Finally, conclusions are made in Section 8.

2. Problem formulation

Let the ideal frequency response of a VFD digital filter be defined as

$$H_d(\omega,t) = e^{-j(D+t)\omega}, \quad \omega \in [0, \alpha\pi] \tag{1}$$

where $0 < \alpha < 1$, D denotes a mean group delay, and t denotes a variable fractional delay within the range of $[-0.5, 0.5]$. The transfer function of an IIR VFD filter can be expressed as

$$H(z,t) = \frac{P(z,t)}{Q(z,t)} = \frac{\sum_{n=0}^{N} p_n(t)z^{-n}}{1 + \sum_{m=1}^{M} q_m(t)z^{-m}} = \frac{\varphi_1^T(z)\,p(t)}{1 + \varphi_2^T(z)\,q(t)} \tag{2}$$

where

$$\varphi_1(z) = \begin{bmatrix} 1 & z^{-1} & \cdots & z^{-N} \end{bmatrix}^T \tag{3}$$

$$\varphi_2(z) = \begin{bmatrix} z^{-1} & z^{-2} & \cdots & z^{-M} \end{bmatrix}^T \tag{4}$$

$$p(t) = \begin{bmatrix} p_0(t) & p_1(t) & \cdots & p_N(t) \end{bmatrix}^T \tag{5}$$

$$q(t) = \begin{bmatrix} q_1(t) & q_2(t) & \cdots & q_M(t) \end{bmatrix}^T \tag{6}$$

In (2)-(6), the superscript T denotes the transposition of a vector (or matrix). Each of the numerator coefficients $p_n(t)$ for $n = 0, 1, \ldots, N$ (or the denominator coefficients $q_m(t)$ for $m = 1, 2, \ldots, M$) can be expressed as an order K_1 (or K_2) polynomial of the fractional delay t as

$$p_n(t) = \sum_{k=0}^{K_1} a_{n,k} t^k = a_n^T v_1(t) \tag{7}$$

$$q_m(t) = \sum_{k=0}^{K_2} b_{m,k} t^k = b_m^T v_2(t) \tag{8}$$

where

$$v_1(t) = \begin{bmatrix} 1 & t & \cdots & t^{K_1} \end{bmatrix}^T \tag{9}$$

$$v_2(t) = \begin{bmatrix} 1 & t & \cdots & t^{K_2} \end{bmatrix}^T \tag{10}$$

$$a_n = \begin{bmatrix} a_{n,0} & a_{n,1} & \cdots & a_{n,K_1} \end{bmatrix}^T \tag{11}$$

$$b_m = \begin{bmatrix} b_{m,0} & b_{m,1} & \cdots & b_{m,K_2} \end{bmatrix}^T \tag{12}$$

All the polynomial coefficients $a_{n,k}$ and $b_{m,k}$ are assumed to be real values. By stacking all a_n for $n = 0$ to N together, the numerator coefficient vector a can be defined as

$$a = \begin{bmatrix} a_0^T & a_1^T & \cdots & a_N^T \end{bmatrix}^T \tag{13}$$

Similarly, the denominator coefficient vector b can be defined as

$$b = \begin{bmatrix} b_1^T & b_2^T & \cdots & b_M^T \end{bmatrix}^T \tag{14}$$

Then, $P(z,t)$ and $Q(z,t)$ in (2) can be written as

$$P(z,t) = a^T u_1(z,t) \tag{15}$$

$$Q(z,t) = 1 + b^T u_2(z,t) \tag{16}$$

where

$$u_1(z,t) = \begin{bmatrix} v_1^T(t) & z^{-1}v_1^T(t) & \cdots & z^{-N}v_1^T(t) \end{bmatrix}^T \tag{17}$$

$$u_2(z,t) = \begin{bmatrix} z^{-1}v_2^T(t) & z^{-2}v_2^T(t) & \cdots & z^{-M}v_2^T(t) \end{bmatrix}^T \tag{18}$$

Given a nonnegative weighting function $W(\omega,t)$, the WLS design problem can be expressed as

$$\min_{x} \quad J(x) = \int_0^{\alpha\pi} \int_{-0.5}^{0.5} W(\omega,t)|e(\omega,t)|^2 \, dt d\omega \tag{19}$$

where $x = [a^T, b^T]^T$, and the complex approximation error $e(\omega,t)$ is defined as

$$e(\omega,t) = H(e^{j\omega},t) - H_d(\omega,t) \tag{20}$$

For the general IIR VFD filter design problem expressed in (19), there is an implicit stability requirement on the denominator $Q(z,t)$, that is, all the roots of $Q(z,t)$ for $\forall t \in [-0.5, 0.5]$ should lie inside the unit circle on the z-plane. The derivations shown under Sections 2-4 are formulated for VdIIR VFD filters which are applicable to FdIIR VFD filters by setting $K_2 = 0$. For $K_2 = 0$, $q_m(t) = q_m$ for $m = 1$ to M; hence, $q(t) = q = [q_1 \, q_2 \, \ldots \, q_M]^T$ and $Q(z,t) = Q(z)$.

3. Sequential design of IIR VFD digital filters

The nonlinear nature of the general problem defined by (19)-(20) can be simplified using the Levy's method (Levy, 1959), solved iteratively using Sanathanan and Koerner algorithm (Sanathanan & Koerner, 1963), and formulated as an iterative design problem for stable IIR digital filters by (Lu et al., 1998). In this section, the sequential design procedure for IIR VFD filters developed from (Lu et al., 1998) will be described first. Then, linear inequality constraints are introduced to guarantee the stability of a designed IIR VFD filter.

3.1 Sequential design procedure

The sequential design procedure starts from a specified initial point $x^{(0)}$. At the lth iteration ($l = 1, 2, \ldots$), the integrand of the cost function in (19) is reformulated as

$$
\begin{aligned}
W^{(l-1)}&(\omega,t)\left|P^{(l)}(e^{j\omega},t)-H_d(\omega,t)Q^{(l)}(e^{j\omega},t)\right|^2 \\
&= W^{(l-1)}(\omega,t)\left|x^{(l)T}u(\omega,t)-e^{-j(D+t)\omega}\right|^2 \\
&= W^{(l-1)}(\omega,t)x^{(l)T}\operatorname{Re}\{U(\omega,t)\}x^{(l)} \\
&\quad -2W^{(l-1)}(\omega,t)x^{(l)T}\operatorname{Re}\{u(\omega,t)e^{j(D+t)\omega}\} \\
&\quad +W^{(l-1)}(\omega,t)
\end{aligned}
\tag{21}
$$

where

$$
W^{(l-1)}(\omega,t) = \frac{W(\omega,t)}{\left|Q^{(l-1)}(e^{j\omega},t)\right|^2}
\tag{22}
$$

$$
u(\omega,t) = \begin{bmatrix} u_1(e^{j\omega},t) \\ -e^{-j(D+t)\omega}u_2(e^{j\omega},t) \end{bmatrix}
\tag{23}
$$

$$
\begin{aligned}
U(\omega,t) &= u(\omega,t)u^H(\omega,t) \\
&= \begin{bmatrix} u_1(e^{j\omega},t)u_1^H(e^{j\omega},t) & -e^{j(D+t)\omega}u_1(e^{j\omega},t)u_2^H(e^{j\omega},t) \\ -e^{-j(D+t)\omega}u_2(e^{j\omega},t)u_1^H(e^{j\omega},t) & u_2(e^{j\omega},t)u_2^H(e^{j\omega},t) \end{bmatrix}
\end{aligned}
\tag{24}
$$

In (21), $\operatorname{Re}\{\cdot\}$ denotes the real part of a complex variable. In (24), the superscript H represents the conjugate transpose of a complex-valued vector or matrix. Using (21), the cost function of (19) can be expressed in the following quadratic form

$$
J^{(l)}(x^{(l)}) = x^{(l)T}G^{(l-1)}x^{(l)} - 2x^{(l)T}g^{(l-1)} + c^{(l-1)}
\tag{25}
$$

where

$$\boldsymbol{G}^{(l-1)} = \int_0^{\alpha\pi} \int_{-0.5}^{0.5} W^{(l-1)}(\omega,t)\,\mathrm{Re}\left\{\boldsymbol{U}(\omega,t)\right\} dt\,d\omega \tag{26}$$

$$\boldsymbol{g}^{(l-1)} = \int_0^{\alpha\pi} \int_{-0.5}^{0.5} W^{(l-1)}(\omega,t)\,\mathrm{Re}\left\{\boldsymbol{u}(\omega,t)e^{j(D+t)\omega}\right\} dt\,d\omega \tag{27}$$

$$c^{(l-1)} = \int_0^{\alpha\pi} \int_{-0.5}^{0.5} W^{(l-1)}(\omega,t)\,dt\,d\omega \tag{28}$$

Note that the matrix $\boldsymbol{G}^{(l-1)}$ is symmetric and positive semidefinite (PSD). Therefore, only the upper (or lower) triangular part of $\boldsymbol{G}^{(l-1)}$ needs to be computed. In practice, the integrals in (26)-(28) can be replaced by finite summations of grid points taken from $[0,\ \alpha\pi] \times [-0.5, 0.5]$. In practice, minimization of (25) is a straight-forward task. However, if linear or nonlinear constraints (such as the linear stability constraints (34) or (35) introduced later in Section 3.2) are required to be incorporated, (25) can be reformulated as (29) by introducing an auxiliary variable $\varepsilon^{(l)}$. Consequently, at the lth iteration, the WLS design problem can be cast as the following SOCP problem

$$\min \varepsilon^{(l)} \tag{29}$$

$$\mathrm{s.t.}\ \left\|\overline{\boldsymbol{G}}^{(l-1)}\boldsymbol{x}^{(l)}\right\|^2 \le 2\boldsymbol{x}^{(l)T}\boldsymbol{g}^{(l-1)} + \varepsilon^{(l)} \tag{29a}$$

where $\overline{\boldsymbol{G}}^{(l-1)} = [\boldsymbol{G}^{(l-1)}]^{1/2}$, and $\|.\|$ denotes the Euclidean norm of a vector. In (29), the decision variables are $\boldsymbol{x}^{(l)}$ and $\varepsilon^{(l)}$. The constraint (29a) is a hyperbolic constraint, which can be further transformed into a second-order cone (SOC) constraint.

To guarantee the stability of a design obtained by (29), either the stability constraints (34) or (35) are to be incorporated into (29). Also, to improve the numerical robustness of the sequential design procedure, the filter coefficients $\boldsymbol{x}^{(l)}$ are updated using the iteration scheme (Jiang & Kwan, 2009a; Lu et al., 1998; Lu, 1999; Tsang, 2004; Tsang & Lee, 2002) as

$$\boldsymbol{x}^{(l)} = \lambda\Psi(\boldsymbol{x}^{(l-1)}) + (1-\lambda)\boldsymbol{x}^{(l-1)} \tag{30}$$

where $0 < \lambda < 1$ is a relaxation constant, and Ψ represents the mathematical operation of mapping a $\boldsymbol{x}^{(l-1)}$ to a solution $\boldsymbol{x}^{(l)}$ by (29). Our design experience indicates that generally λ can be chosen within the range [0.1, 0.5]. A larger λ could cause numerical instability. Stability guarantee and robustness improvement serve different purposes and do not affect each other.

The sequential design procedure continues until the following condition is satisfied

$$\frac{J(\boldsymbol{x}^{(l-1)}) - J(\boldsymbol{x}^{(l)})}{J(\boldsymbol{x}^{(l-1)})} \le \mu \tag{31}$$

where μ is a specified positive small tolerance and $J(x)$ is the cost function defined in (19). The stopping criterion (31) means that the sequential design procedure is to be terminated as the WLS error cannot be further reduced in a meaningful manner. It should be emphasized that if $[J(x^{(l-1)})-J(x^{(l)})]/J(x^{(l-1)}) < 0$, we have $J(x^{(l-1)}) < J(x^{(l)})$, which means the performance of the current design is worse than that of the previous design, the filter coefficients obtained at the previous iteration through (30) should be restored and adopted as the final design.

3.2 Stability consideration

The IIR VFD filter designed by the sequential design procedure presented in Section 3.1 cannot definitely guarantee the stability of obtained IIR VFD filters. Therefore, stability constraints have to be incorporated. For ease of explanation, a stability constraint based on the positive realness is first introduced for designing IIR VFD filters with the fixed denominator. Then, the stability constraint can be readily extended to the case of designing IIR VFD filters with the variable denominator.

A sufficient condition for the stability of designed IIR digital filters has been introduced in (Dumitrescu & Niemistö, 2004), which is stated as: If $Q^{(l-1)}(z)$ is a Schur polynomial, i.e., all the roots of $Q^{(l-1)}(z)$ lie inside the unit circle, and the transfer function $R^{(l)}(z) = Q^{(l)}(z)/Q^{(l-1)}(z)$ is strictly positive real (SPR), i.e.,

$$\mathrm{Re}\left\{R^{(l)}(e^{j\omega})\right\} > 0, \quad \forall \omega \in [0,\pi] \tag{32}$$

then all the convex combination of $Q^{(l-1)}(z)$ and $Q^{(l)}(z)$, i.e., $Q_\gamma^{(l)}(z) = (1-\gamma)Q^{(l-1)}(z)+\gamma Q^{(l)}(z)$ for $\forall \gamma \in [0, 1]$, is a Schur polynomial. According to this condition, a stability domain with an interior point $q^{(l-1)}$ can be defined as $D_s = \{q^{(l)} \mid R^{(l)}(z) \text{ is SPR}\}$. Note that the condition that $R^{(l)}(z)$ is SPR is equivalent to requiring that

$$R^{(l)}(z)+R^{(l)}(z^{-1})$$
$$=\frac{Q^{(l)}(z)Q^{(l-1)}(z^{-1})+Q^{(l-1)}(z)Q^{(l)}(z^{-1})}{Q^{(l-1)}(z)Q^{(l-1)}(z^{-1})} \tag{33}$$

is real and positive on the unit circle. Since the denominator of (33) is always positive on the unit circle, it follows that the symmetric numerator polynomial of (33) must be positive on the unit circle for $\forall \omega \in [0, \pi]$, which can be cast as a linear matrix inequality (LMI) constraint independent of frequency ω (Dumitrescu & Niemistö, 2004). Here, the stability constraint $R^{(l)}(e^{j\omega})+R^{(l)}(e^{-j\omega}) > 0$ can be expressed in the form of linear inequality constraints as

$$\mathrm{Re}\left\{Q^{(l-1)}(e^{-j\omega_i})\varphi_2^T(e^{j\omega_i})\right\}q^{(l)} \geq v - \mathrm{Re}\left\{Q^{(l-1)}(e^{j\omega_i})\right\}$$
$$\omega_i \in [0,\pi], i = 1,\cdots,I \tag{34}$$

where v is a specified small positive number. If variable denominator is utilized in $H(z,t)$, the term $q^{(l)T}\varphi_2(e^{j\omega})$ in (34) should be replaced by $b^{(l)T}u_2(e^{j\omega},t)$. Thereby, (34) can be expressed as

$$\mathrm{Re}\left\{Q^{(l-1)}(e^{-j\omega_i},t_j)\boldsymbol{u}_2^T(e^{j\omega_i},t_j)\right\}\boldsymbol{b}^{(l)} \geq v - \mathrm{Re}\left\{Q^{(l-1)}(e^{j\omega_i},t_j)\right\}$$

$$\omega_i \in [0,\pi], i = 1,\cdots,I; \quad t_j \in [-0.5,0.5], \, j = 1,\cdots,J \tag{35}$$

4. Gradient-based design of IIR VFD digital filters

In this section, a gradient-based design method for IIR VFD digital filters is presented. An initial design is first obtained by solving a SOCP problem, and a local search procedure is then applied to refine the design.

4.1 Initial design using SOCP

IIR VFD filter design using optimization is a non-convex problem and there could be many local minima on its error performance surface. Also, a large IIR VFD filter design problem involves many variables $(N+1)(K_1+1)+M(K_2+1)$. In order to obtain a good initial design that would lead to a satisfactory final design, consider the following initial design problem derived from (19) by applying the Levy's method (Levy, 1959) on $e(w,t)$ to obtain $e(w,t)Q(e^{jw},t)$ as

$$\min_{x} \; J_1(\boldsymbol{x}) = \int_0^{\alpha\pi} \int_{-0.5}^{0.5} W(\omega,t)\left|e(\omega,t)Q(e^{j\omega},t)\right|^2 dt d\omega$$

$$= \boldsymbol{x}^T \boldsymbol{G}\boldsymbol{x} - 2\boldsymbol{x}^T\boldsymbol{g} + c \tag{36}$$

where G, g, and c can be readily obtained by replacing the weighting function $W^{(l-1)}(\omega, t)$ of (22) in (26)-(28) by $W(\omega, t)$ of (19). Similar to (25)-(29), the design problem (36) can be transformed into the following SOCP problem as

$$\min \varepsilon \tag{37}$$

$$\mathrm{s.t.} \; \left\|\bar{\boldsymbol{G}}\boldsymbol{x}\right\|^2 \leq 2\boldsymbol{x}^T\boldsymbol{g} + \varepsilon \tag{37a}$$

where the matrix $\bar{\boldsymbol{G}} = G^{1/2}$.

4.2 Stability consideration

In order to guarantee the stability of a designed IIR VFD filter, stability constraints should be incorporated in (37). The linear stability constraints (34) or (35) can be directly incorporated into the design problem (37). Besides (34) or (35), the following strategy can also be employed to ensure the stability. It is known that by suppressing $\left\|q(t)\right\|^2$, the poles can be forced to move towards the origin in the z-plane (Zhao & Kwan, 2007). To do so, a regularization term defined in (38) below is introduced as

$$J_2(\boldsymbol{x}) = \int_{-0.5}^{0.5} \left\|q(t)\right\|^2 dt = \sum_{m=1}^{M} \boldsymbol{b}_m^T V_2 \boldsymbol{b}_m = \boldsymbol{b}^T V \boldsymbol{b} \tag{38}$$

where

$$V_2 = \int_{-0.5}^{0.5} v_2(t) v_2^T(t)\, dt \tag{39}$$

$$V = \begin{bmatrix} V_2 & & & \\ & V_2 & & \\ & & \ddots & \\ & & & V_2 \end{bmatrix} \tag{40}$$

By combining $J_2(x)$ with the cost function $J_1(x)$ of (36) through a regularization coefficient β, the design problem (36) is then formulated as

$$\min_{x} \quad J_1(x) + \beta J_2(x) \tag{41}$$
$$= x^T \hat{G} x - 2 x^T g + c$$

where

$$\hat{G} = G + \begin{bmatrix} \mathbf{0}_{(N+1)(K_1+1)\times(N+1)(K_1+1)} & \mathbf{0}_{(N+1)(K_1+1)\times M(K_2+1)} \\ \mathbf{0}_{M(K_2+1)\times(N+1)(K_1+1)} & \beta V \end{bmatrix} \tag{42}$$

In (42), $\mathbf{0}_{m\times n}$ represents a zero matrix of size m-by-n. The design problem (41) can then be formulated as a SOCP problem similar to (37) as

$$\min \hat{\varepsilon} \tag{43}$$

$$\text{s.t.} \quad \left\| \tilde{G} x \right\|^2 \leq 2 x^T g + \hat{\varepsilon} \tag{43a}$$

where $\tilde{G} = \hat{G}^{1/2}$.

4.3 Local search

Although both the design problem (37) subject to stability constraints (34) or (35) and the design problem (43) are convex and can be efficiently solved, the obtained design in either case may not be a truly (locally) optimal design in the WLS sense, since the cost function $J_1(x)$ of (36) is not equivalent to the original one in (19). Therefore, a local search should be performed to locate the local optimum near the initial design (obtained by solving (37) with appropriate stability constraints (34) or (35) or by solving (43)). Here, a general-purpose gradient-based optimization algorithm (e.g., quasi-Newton) is employed to achieve a local optimal design. Normally, such an algorithm requires a designer to provide subroutines to calculate the function value and the gradient at a given point. Thus, the formulas to calculate the gradients of $J(x)$ defined in (19) can be derived as

$$\nabla_a J(x) = \nabla_a \left[\int_0^{\alpha\pi} \int_{-0.5}^{0.5} W(\omega,t) |e(\omega,t)|^2 \, dt d\omega \right]$$

$$= 2 \int_0^{\alpha\pi} \int_{-0.5}^{0.5} W(\omega,t) \operatorname{Re} \left\{ \frac{e^*(\omega,t)}{Q(e^{j\omega},t)} u_1(e^{j\omega},t) \right\} dt d\omega \qquad (44)$$

$$\nabla_b J(x) = \nabla_b \left[\int_0^{\alpha\pi} \int_{-0.5}^{0.5} W(\omega,t) |e(\omega,t)|^2 \, dt d\omega \right]$$

$$= -2 \int_0^{\alpha\pi} \int_{-0.5}^{0.5} W(\omega,t) \operatorname{Re} \left\{ \frac{e^*(\omega,t) H(e^{j\omega},t)}{Q(e^{j\omega},t)} u_2(e^{j\omega},t) \right\} dt d\omega \qquad (45)$$

In (44)-(45), the subscript $*$ denotes complex conjugate operation. It is noted that if an initial design is stable, the IIR filter obtained by the local search is stable. It is because if any of the poles moves close to the unit circle, it will create a large approximation error; and in case the situation that a pole and a zero nearly cancel or cancel each other emerges, the error performance will degrade due to a reduced filter order. Since a gradient-based algorithm can only find local minima around an initial design, if pole-zero cancellation does not appear in an initial design, pole-zero cancellation is not likely to appear in the subsequent local search using a gradient-based algorithm. Furthermore, the step size of a gradient-based algorithm can be automatically adjusted to guarantee that the obtained filter in each iteration stays inside the stable domain. The above scheme works well in all our designs. In the designs, the optimization command 'fminunc' in MATLAB was adopted to perform the local search. The stability of a designed VdIIR VFD filter is ensured if its maximum pole radius is within the unity circle at each of the fractional delay values obtained from a dense grid of fractional delay $t \in [-0.5, 0.5]$. On the other hand, the stability of a designed FdIIR VFD filter can simply be checked by ensuring its maximum pole radius is within the unity circle.

5. Design specifications

In this section, four sets of filter examples are presented to demonstrate the effectiveness of the sequential and gradient-based design methods. For a fair comparison, at each of the four specified cutoff frequencies, all the three types (IIR, allpass, and FIR) of VFD filters are specified to have the same number of variable coefficients, i.e., $(N+1)(K_1+1)+M(K_2+1) = M_{AP}(K_1+1) = (L_{FIR}+1)(K_1+1)$, where M_{AP} and L_{FIR} denote, respectively, the filter order of an allpass VFD filter and the filter order of an FIR VFD filter. To achieve a good IIR VFD filter design based on a general IIR digital filter, the denominator order needs not be as high as the numerator order. Therefore, in each of the IIR VFD filter designs, the denominator order M is chosen to be 6 which is smaller than the corresponding numerator order N. The filter specifications of the IIR VFD filters with variable and fixed denominators are summarized in Table 1 whereas the design specifications of allpass and FIR VFD filters are summarized in Table 2.

a	(K_1, K_2)	(N, M, D)
0.9625	$(5, 5)$	$(49, 6, 25)$, $(49, 6, 28)$, $(49, 6, 31)$
	$(5, 0)$	$(54, 6, 27)$, $(54, 6, 30)$, $(54, 6, 33)$
0.9500	$(5, 5)$	$(46, 6, 23)$, $(46, 6, 26)$, $(46, 6\ 29)$
	$(5, 0)$	$(51, 6, 26)$, $(51, 6, 29)$, $(51, 6\ 32)$
0.9250	$(5, 5)$	$(41, 6, 21)$, $(41, 6, 24)$, $(41, 6, 27)$
	$(5, 0)$	$(46, 6, 23)$, $(46, 6, 26)$, $(46, 6, 29)$
0.9000	$(5, 5)$	$(36, 6, 18)$, $(36, 6, 21)$, $(36, 6, 24)$
	$(5, 0)$	$(41, 6, 21)$, $(41, 6, 24)$, $(41, 6, 27)$

Table 1. IIR VFD filter specifications (Keys: α: Normalized passband; K_1 (K_2): Numerator (Denominator) coefficient polynomial order; N (M): Numerator (Denominator) order; D: IIR mean group delay)

a	K_1	(M_{AP}, D_{AP})	(L_{FIR}, D_{FIR})
0.9625	5	$(56, 56)$	$(55, 28)$
0.9500	5	$(53, 53)$	$(52, 26)$
0.9250	5	$(48, 48)$	$(47, 24)$
0.9000	5	$(43, 43)$	$(42, 21)$

Table 2. Allpass and FIR VFD filter specifications (Keys: α: Normalized passband; K_1: Coefficient polynomial order; M_{AP}: Allpass order; D_{AP}: Allpass mean group delay; L_{FIR}: FIR order; D_{FIR}: FIR mean group delay)

The respective mean group delay is somehow related to (a) the numerator and denominator orders, N and M, for an IIR VFD filter; (b) the filter order M_{AP} of an allpass VFD filter; and (c) the filter order L_{FIR} of an FIR VFD filter. In Tables 1 and 2, the respective mean group delay is chosen as: (a) D = the round up value of $(N+M)/2$ for an IIR VFD filter; (b) D_{AP} = the filter order M_{AP} for an allpass VFD filter; and (c) D_{FIR} = the round up value of $L_{FIR}/2$ for an FIR VFD filter. The choice of mean group delay values $D = \lceil (N+M)/2 \rceil$ and $\lceil (N+M)/2 \rceil \pm 3$ shown in Table 1 for all the IIR VFD filter design methods allows a comparison of their relative performances in order to determine the best design method upon which its best mean group delay value that yields a minimum e_{rms} can be determined by simulations to be described in Section 6.2. The design results obtained by the proposed designs are compared with those of the IIR VFD filters with variable denominators designed by (ZK), the IIR VFD filters with fixed denominators designed by (KJ) and (TCK), the allpass VFD filters designed by (KJ) and (LCR), and the FIR VFD filters designed by (KJ) and (LD). For fair comparisons, the weighting function $W(\omega,t)$ in (19) and (36) is always set equal to 1 for $\forall \omega \in [0, a\pi]$ and $\forall t \in [-0.5, 0.5]$. The relaxation constant λ used in (30) and the tolerance μ used in the stopping criterion (31) are chosen as 0.5 and 10^{-4}, respectively. The stability constraints (35) are imposed on 21×21 discrete points evenly distributed over the domain $[0, \pi] \times [-0.5, 0.5]$. For $K_2 = 0$, the stability constraints (34) are imposed on 21 frequency points, which are equally spaced over the range $[0, \pi]$. The parameter v in (34) and (35) are chosen as 10^{-3}. The optimal value of β used in (46) is 10^{-10} (except for VdIIR VFD filters at $\alpha = 0.9625$, $\beta = 10^{-9}$; and for

FdIIR VFD filters at $\alpha = 0.9$, $\beta = 0$). At each iteration, the SOCP problems in (29), (37) and (43) are solved using *SeDuMi* (Sturm, 1999) under MATLAB environment.

6. Performance analysis

6.1 Error measurements and stability check

To evaluate the performances of each designed VFD filter, the maximum absolute error e_{max}, and the normalized root-mean-squared (RMS) error e_{rms} of its (a) frequency responses, (b) magnitude responses, and (c) fractional group delay responses are adopted and they are defined, respectively, by

$$e_{max} = \max\left\{\left|e(\omega,t)\right|, \ \omega \in [0,\alpha\pi], t \in [-0.5, 0.5]\right\} \tag{46}$$

$$e_{rms} = \left[\frac{\int_0^{\alpha\pi} \int_{-0.5}^{0.5} \left|e(\omega,t)\right|^2 dtd\omega}{\int_0^{\alpha\pi} \int_{-0.5}^{0.5} \left|H_d(\omega,t)\right|^2 dtd\omega}\right]^{1/2} \tag{47}$$

$$e_{max,1} = \max\left\{\left|e_{MAG}(\omega,t)\right|, \ \omega \in [0,\alpha\pi], t \in [-0.5, 0.5]\right\} \tag{48}$$

$$e_{rms,1} = \left[\frac{\int_0^{\alpha\pi} \int_{-0.5}^{0.5} \left|e_{MAG}(\omega,t)\right|^2 dtd\omega}{\int_0^{\alpha\pi} \int_{-0.5}^{0.5} \left|H_d(\omega,t)\right|^2 dtd\omega}\right]^{1/2} \tag{49}$$

$$e_{max,2} = \max\left\{\left|e_{FGD}(\omega,t)\right|, \ \omega \in [0,\alpha\pi], t \in [-0.5, 0.5]\right\} \tag{50}$$

$$e_{rms,2} = \left[\frac{\int_0^{\alpha\pi} \int_{-0.5}^{0.5} \left|e_{FGD}(\omega,t)\right|^2 dtd\omega}{\int_0^{\alpha\pi} \int_{-0.5}^{0.5} t^2 dtd\omega}\right]^{1/2} \tag{51}$$

where

$$e_{MAG}(\omega,t) = \left|H(e^{j\omega},t)\right| - \left|H_d(\omega,t)\right| \tag{52}$$

$$e_{FGD}(\omega,t) = \tau(\omega,t) - t \tag{53}$$

In (53), $\tau(\omega,t)$ denotes the actual fractional group delay of a designed VFD filter. Since the design problem is formulated in the WLS sense (see (19)), so the e_{rms} of the frequency responses is the most appropriate criterion for comparisons among different design methods. In case two designs have the same e_{rms}, other error measurements shall be compared. For each of the designed VdIIR VFD filters and AP VFD filters, a uniform grid consisting of 1001 discrete fractional delay values t were used to ensure all these 1001 VFD filters are stable. By checking individual maximum pole radius to be within the unity circle, each of the designed VFD filters has been verified to be stable.

6.2 IIR VFD filter performances

Based on the design specifications of Table 1, the error performances of the designed IIR VFD filters are summarized in Tables 3-4. The keywords adopted in Tables 3-4 are defined as follows: The "Sequential design" refers to the minimization problem defined by (29) subject to (a) stability inequality constraints (35) for VdIIR VFD filter design; and (b) stability inequality constraints (34) for FdIIR VFD filter design. The "Gradient-based design with (35)" refers to the minimization problem defined by (37) subject to stability inequality constraints (35) for an initial VdIIR VFD filter design, and followed by a local search. The "Gradient-based design with (34)" refers to the minimization problem defined by (37) subject to stability inequality constraints (34) for an initial FdIIR VFD filter design, and followed by a local search. The "Gradient-based design with (43)" refers to the minimization problem defined by (43) for an initial VdIIR or FdIIR VFD filter design, and followed by a local search. Within each of the four sets of designs, the relative e_{rms} (in frequency responses) performances are ranked from top to bottom as shown in Tables 3-4. The top performer of each IIR VFD design method in Tables 3-4 is listed in Table 5.

As shown in Table 5, the e_{rms} performances among the VdIIR VFD filters can be summarized as follows: The top performers for $0.95 \leq \alpha \leq 0.9625$ are the gradient-based designs with (35). The top performers for $0.9 \leq \alpha \leq 0.925$ are the gradient-based designs with (43). The bottom performer is the two-stage design of (ZK). The performance of the sequential designs (29) ranks at the middle between the designs of (ZK) and the gradient-based designs with (35) and with (43). As also shown in Table 5, the e_{rms} performances among the FdIIR VFD filters can be summarized as follows: The top performers for $0.925 \leq \alpha \leq 0.9625$ are the gradient-based designs with (43) but has an average performance for $\alpha = 0.9$. The top performer for $\alpha = 0.9$ is the gradient-based design with (34) which has close but lower performances than those of the gradient-based designs with (43) for $0.925 \leq \alpha \leq 0.95$. The bottom performer for $0.925 \leq \alpha \leq 0.9625$ is (TCK) but it ranks second among all the FdIIR VFD designs for $\alpha = 0.9$. Between (KJ) and the sequential design (29), the former ranks higher than those of the sequential designs (29) for $0.95 \leq \alpha \leq 0.9625$ but vice versa for $0.9 \leq \alpha \leq 0.925$. Comparing (KJ) and (TCK), the former yields better performances for $0.925 \leq \alpha \leq 0.9625$ but vice versa for $\alpha = 0.9$.

a	N	D	A	R	Freq. Responses		Mag. Responses		FGD Responses	
					e_{max} (dB)	e_{rms}	$e_{max,1}$(dB)	$e_{rms,1}$	$e_{max,2}$	$e_{rms,2}$
α_1	49	25	(29)	9	-35.490	1.892e-3	-37.360	1.289e-3	1.763	2.754e-1
			(35)	3	-50.347	3.683e-4	-50.402	2.923e-4	3.970e-1	6.042e-2
			(43)	4	-46.317	4.790e-4	-46.373	3.607e-4	5.621e-1	7.708e-2
			(ZK)	12	-11.622	2.766e-2	-12.295	2.402e-2	1.972	4.208e-1
		28	(29)	8	-40.026	1.403e-3	-40.664	1.036e-3	1.160	1.823e-1
			(35)	2	-50.808	3.444e-4	-51.710	2.318e-4	4.850e-1	7.108e-2
			(43)	5	-45.817	4.981e-4	-48.255	3.327e-4	6.545e-1	9.443e-2
			(ZK)	11	-12.042	2.623e-2	-13.067	2.268e-2	1.892	4.291e-1
		31	(29)	7	-42.041	8.851e-4	-42.698	6.840e-4	9.504e-1	1.431e-1
			(35)	1	-52.436	2.890e-4	-53.731	1.833e-4	4.442e-1	6.963e-2
			(43)	6	-45.492	5.203e-4	-46.819	3.439e-4	6.152e-1	1.034e-1
			(ZK)	10	-12.674	2.460e-2	-13.590	2.110e-2	1.797	4.203e-1
α_2	46	23	(29)	9	-43.309	8.175e-4	-46.118	5.256e-4	6.791e-1	1.095e-1
			(35)	5	-57.964	1.563e-4	-57.970	1.230e-4	1.561e-1	2.346e-2
			(43)	6	-55.398	2.194e-4	-56.439	1.629e-4	2.370e-1	3.347e-2
			(ZK)	10	-17.857	1.511e-2	-18.471	1.328e-2	1.097	2.441e-1
		26	(29)	8	-48.237	4.151e-4	-50.465	2.946e-4	3.830e-1	6.093e-2
			(35)	3	-59.298	1.354e-4	-60.759	9.100e-5	1.680e-1	2.487e-2
			(43)	4	-59.500	1.442e-4	-59.567	1.025e-4	1.855e-1	2.446e-2
			(ZK)	11	-17.735	1.531e-2	-18.573	1.340e-2	1.021	2.346e-1
		29	(29)	7	-48.984	3.667e-4	-49.148	2.845e-4	3.047e-1	4.843e-2
			(35)	1	-60.500	1.171e-4	-63.434	7.782e-5	1.400e-1	2.453e-2
			(43)	2	-59.982	1.310e-4	-60.924	9.276e-5	1.434e-1	2.400e-2
			(ZK)	12	-11.036	2.871e-2	-12.351	2.526e-2	1.702	3.513e-1
α_3	41	21	(29)	9	-57.865	1.108e-4	-61.693	6.780e-5	1.306e-1	1.993e-2
			(35)	5	-62.965	5.007e-5	-63.189	3.882e-5	5.270e-2	7.486e-3
			(43)	6	-64.763	6.303e-5	-67.058	4.233e-5	7.008e-2	1.016e-2
			(ZK)	10	-18.100	1.752e-2	-18.330	1.493e-2	4.667e-1	1.575e-1
		24	(29)	7	-60.523	8.940e-5	-60.973	6.550e-5	9.716e-2	1.449e-2
			(35)	4	-66.111	4.390e-5	-67.968	3.004e-5	5.477e-2	8.191e-3
			(43)	3	-69.381	3.348e-5	-70.084	2.327e-5	4.344e-2	6.336e-3
			(ZK)	11	-15.405	1.998e-2	-15.883	1.767e-2	6.691e-1	1.745e-1
		27	(29)	8	-59.811	9.295e-5	-59.859	7.225e-5	7.450e-2	1.322e-2
			(35)	2	-67.930	3.255e-5	-72.267	2.048e-5	4.415e-2	7.135e-3
			(43)	1	-75.807	1.269e-5	-78.312	8.311e-6	2.229e-2	2.984e-3
			(ZK)	12	-13.440	2.520e-2	-14.190	2.242e-2	1.020	2.197e-1

a	N	D	A	R	e_{max}	e_{rms}	$e_{max,1}$(dB)	$e_{rms,1}$	$e_{max,2}$	$e_{rms,2}$
α_4	36	18	(29)	7	-70.872	3.336e-5	-74.955	2.250e-5	2.631e-2	4.264e-3
			(35)	9	-71.177	3.592e-5	-71.466	2.760e-5	2.270e-2	3.510e-3
			(43)	4	-71.255	2.661e-5	-73.122	1.942e-5	2.182e-2	3.217e-3
			(ZK)	11	-20.667	1.381e-2	-20.070	1.113e-2	2.332e-1	1.109e-1
		21	(29)	6	-71.817	3.311e-5	-73.389	2.411e-5	2.564e-2	3.895e-3
			(35)	5	-72.620	2.730e-5	-73.472	1.881e-5	2.110e-2	3.541e-3
			(43)	2	-79.979	7.880e-6	-83.184	5.360e-6	8.086e-3	1.170e-3
			(ZK)	10	-21.880	1.139e-2	-22.079	9.317e-3	2.680e-1	1.033e-1
		24	(29)	8	-71.882	3.488e-5	-72.448	2.545e-5	1.982e-2	3.541e-3
			(35)	3	-75.763	2.294e-5	-77.805	1.494e-5	2.183e-2	3.434e-3
			(43)	1	-83.278	6.257e-6	-85.250	4.068e-6	8.721e-3	1.314e-3
			(ZK)	12	-14.311	2.847e-2	-14.477	2.483e-2	5.477e-1	1.958e-1

Table 3. Performances of VdIIR VFD filters (Keys: α_1= 0.9625, α_2= 0.95, α_3= 0.925, α_4= 0.9; A: Design method; (29): Sequential design; (35): Gradient-based design with (35); (43): Gradient-based design with (43); (ZK): (Zhao & Kwan, 2007); R: Rank; FGD: Fractional group delay)

a	N	D	A	R	Freq. Responses		Mag. Responses		FGD Responses	
					e_{max}	e_{rms}	$e_{max,1}$(dB)	$e_{rms,1}$	$e_{max,2}$	$e_{rms,2}$
α_1	54	27	(29)	12	-38.000	1.426e-3	-40.368	9.325e-4	1.556	2.398e-1
			(34)	6	-51.464	2.796e-4	-52.628	2.229e-4	3.141e-1	4.812e-2
			(43)	5	-49.821	2.791e-4	-49.826	2.345e-4	2.523e-1	4.390e-2
			(KJ)	9	-39.632	5.615e-4	-39.696	4.623e-4	8.980e-1	1.365e-1
			(TCK)	15	-30.303	2.429e-3	-31.218	1.974e-3	3.359	5.846e-1
		30	(29)	11	-42.034	9.887e-4	-43.963	7.094e-4	1.014	1.559e-1
			(34)	4	-50.852	2.683e-4	-53.605	1.810e-4	3.932e-1	6.088e-2
			(43)	3	-49.940	2.663e-4	-51.336	1.906e-4	3.675e-1	5.526e-2
			(KJ)	7	-40.645	5.044e-4	-41.407	3.952e-4	1.010	1.446e-1
			(TCK)	14	-31.333	2.206e-3	-34.075	1.415e-3	3.364	6.026e-1
		33	(29)	10	-43.634	6.475e-4	-45.398	4.989e-4	8.047e-1	1.196e-1
			(34)	2	-50.271	2.647e-4	-54.681	1.649e-4	4.254e-1	6.933e-2
			(43)	1	-58.117	1.360e-4	-59.459	1.055e-4	1.553e-1	2.391e-2
			(KJ)	8	-40.973	5.101e-4	-42.615	3.681e-4	1.143	1.668e-1
			(TCK)	13	-33.233	1.793e-3	-38.764	8.176e-4	2.853	5.160e-1
α_2	51	26	(29)	12	-46.106	4.757e-4	-49.348	3.021e-4	4.745e-1	7.514e-2
			(34)	9	-56.847	1.423e-4	-59.984	1.015e-4	1.334e-1	2.122e-2
			(43)	3	-60.282	1.172e-4	-62.605	9.084e-5	8.234e-2	1.344e-2
			(KJ)	5	-55.680	1.241e-4	-58.979	8.890e-5	2.465e-1	3.491e-2
			(TCK)	15	-38.816	8.603e-4	-38.917	7.661e-4	1.178	1.856e-1

			(29)	11	-49.943	2.895e-4	-52.464	2.166e-4	2.821e-1	4.396e-2
			(34)	8	-55.870	1.386e-4	-63.233	8.848e-5	1.524e-1	2.632e-2
		29	(43)	2	-60.166	1.051e-4	-64.946	7.397e-5	8.715e-2	1.359e-2
			(KJ)	4	-56.758	1.193e-4	-59.001	8.726e-5	1.691e-1	2.528e-2
			(TCK)	14	-40.109	8.059e-4	-42.311	5.295e-4	1.314	2.294e-1
			(29)	10	-51.166	2.425e-4	-52.046	1.934e-4	2.142e-1	3.369e-2
			(34)	7	-55.703	1.382e-4	-61.363	9.540e-5	1.556e-1	2.623e-2
		32	(43)	1	-58.723	1.018e-4	-65.813	7.060e-5	1.013e-1	1.683e-2
			(KJ)	6	-55.965	1.287e-4	-55.998	9.835e-5	1.528e-1	2.498e-2
			(TCK)	13	-41.867	6.935e-4	-48.144	3.326e-4	1.023	1.822e-1
			(29)	12	-56.063	1.152e-4	-60.966	7.670e-5	1.237e-1	1.812e-2
			(34)	3	-59.700	7.518e-5	-67.140	5.471e-5	4.434e-2	6.868e-3
		23	(43)	4	-61.491	7.567e-5	-66.350	5.607e-5	3.709e-2	5.591e-3
			(KJ)	10	-58.608	9.039e-5	-62.759	6.328e-5	8.504e-2	1.145e-2
			(TCK)	13	-55.650	1.372e-4	-56.367	1.175e-4	1.242e-1	1.750e-2
			(29)	7	-60.462	8.640e-5	-64.213	6.376e-5	6.447e-2	9.586e-3
			(34)	6	-59.137	8.352e-5	-66.130	5.871e-5	6.708e-2	9.784e-3
α_3	46	26	(43)	2	-61.693	7.237e-5	-68.770	5.183e-5	3.782e-2	5.498e-3
			(KJ)	9	-61.008	8.814e-5	-63.846	6.359e-5	5.162e-2	7.425e-3
			(TCK)	14	-54.098	1.536e-4	-55.608	1.325e-4	2.001e-1	2.945e-2
			(29)	5	-61.122	8.273e-5	-64.300	6.255e-5	5.129e-2	7.660e-3
			(34)	11	-58.753	9.176e-5	-65.279	6.558e-5	7.955e-2	1.131e-2
		29	(43)	1	-60.702	7.065e-5	-69.047	5.209e-5	3.796e-2	5.501e-3
			(KJ)	8	-62.337	8.694e-5	-64.720	6.295e-5	4.210e-2	6.087e-3
			(TCK)	15	-54.170	1.639e-4	-57.739	8.782e-5	2.696e-1	4.845e-2
			(29)	8	-63.290	6.478e-5	-68.632	4.749e-5	2.587e-2	3.957e-3
			(34)	1	-62.541	5.875e-5	-71.768	4.111e-5	2.003e-2	3.037e-3
		21	(43)	5	-64.151	6.078e-5	-71.767	4.448e-5	1.876e-2	2.673e-3
			(KJ)	11	-66.316	7.136e-5	-70.722	5.197e-5	7.839e-3	1.202e-3
			(TCK)	2	-64.839	5.948e-5	-71.691	4.386e-5	2.400e-2	3.768e-3
			(29)	6	-63.812	6.103e-5	-69.829	4.557e-5	1.439e-2	2.480e-3
			(34)	3	-61.956	5.978e-5	-70.458	4.250e-5	2.073e-2	3.177e-3
α_4	41	24	(43)	4	-63.959	6.049e-5	-69.984	4.491e-5	1.615e-2	2.565e-3
			(KJ)	12	-65.803	7.137e-5	-70.716	5.194e-5	1.140e-2	1.686e-3
			(TCK)	14	-63.694	8.469e-5	-64.780	5.867e-5	6.538e-2	1.150e-2
		27	(29)	7	-64.154	6.237e-5	-69.549	4.676e-5	1.283e-2	2.222e-3
			(34)	9	-62.223	6.748e-5	-66.374	4.933e-5	1.815e-2	3.434e-3

		(43)	10	-62.973	7.050e-5	-65.414	5.395e-5	1.670e-2	3.412e-3
		(KJ)	13	-66.208	7.147e-5	-70.498	5.203e-5	1.101e-2	1.632e-3
		(TCK)	15	-58.427	1.680e-4	-58.631	1.203e-4	7.196e-2	1.499e-2

Table 4. Performances of FdIIR VFD filters (Keys: α_1= 0.9625, α_2= 0.95, α_3= 0.925, α_4= 0.9; A: Design method; (29): Sequential design; (34): Gradient-based design with (34); (43): Gradient-based design with (43); (KJ): (Kwan & Jiang, 2009a); (TCK): (Tsui et al., 2007); R: Rank; FGD: Fractional group delay)

α		VdIIR				FdIIR				
		(29)	(35)	(43)	(ZK)	(29)	(34)	(43)	(KJ)	(TCK)
α_1	e_{rms}	8.851e-4	2.890e-4	4.790e-4	2.460e-2	6.475e-4	2.647e-4	1.360e-4	5.044e-4	1.793e-3
	R	3	1	2	4	4	2	1	3	5
α_2	e_{rms}	3.667e-4	1.171e-4	1.310e-4	1.511e-2	2.425e-4	1.382e-4	1.018e-4	1.193e-4	6.935e-4
	R	3	1	2	4	4	3	1	2	5
α_3	e_{rms}	8.940e-5	3.255e-5	1.269e-5	1.752e-2	8.273e-5	7.518e-5	7.065e-5	8.694e-5	1.372e-4
	R	3	2	1	4	3	2	1	4	5
α_4	e_{rms}	3.311e-5	2.294e-5	6.257e-6	1.139e-2	6.103e-5	5.875e-5	6.049e-5	7.136e-5	5.948e-5
	R	3	2	1	4	4	1	3	5	2

Table 5. Top-performed (e_{rms}) VFD filters from Tables 3-4 (Keys: α_1= 0.9625, α_2= 0.95, α_3= 0.925, α_4= 0.9; (ZK): (Zhao & Kwan, 2007); (KJ): (Kwan & Jiang, 2009a); (TCK): (Tsui et al., 2007); R: Rank)

6.3 Allpass and FIR VFD filter performances

The error performances of the AP VFD filters designed by (KJ) and (LCR) and the FIR VFD filters designed by (KJ) and (LD) are summarized in Table 6. In general, the two AP VFD filters achieve e_{rms} improvements over the two FIR VFD filters (except for (LD) at α = 0.9625). The top e_{rms} performances of the AP VFD filters are (KJ) for $0.925 \leq \alpha \leq 0.9625$ and (LCR) for α = 0.9.

6.4 Optimal gradient-based designs with (43)

It can be observed in Tables 3-4 that the error performances of VdIIR and FdIIR VFD filters at any specified cutoff frequency is a function of the mean group delay value D. To investigate this property further, consider the case of the gradient-based design with (43) in Table 5 in which it ranks top among VdIIR VFD filters for $0.9 \leq \alpha \leq 0.925$ and ranks top among FdIIR VFD filters for $0.925 \leq \alpha \leq 0.9625$. For each of the four cutoff frequencies, the error performances of the gradient-based designs with (43) for VdIIR and FdIIR VFD filters versus mean group delay D (at a step size of 3) are, respectively, summarized in Tables 7-8 and their corresponding e_{rms} values versus D are plotted in Figs. 1-8. From Tables 7-8, their mean group delay values D that yield minimum e_{rms} values are summarized in Table 9. For comparisons, the e_{rms} performances of the AP and FIR VFD filters from Table 6 are also listed under Table 9. The magnitude responses and group delay responses of the widest band designs at $\alpha = 0.9625$ obtained by the VdIIR and FdIIR VFD filters shown in Table 9 are plotted in Figs. 9-12.

a	OD	A/F	Freq. Responses		Mag. Responses		FGD Responses	
			e_{max} (dB)	e_{rms}	$e_{max,1}$ (dB)	$e_{rms,1}$	$e_{max,2}$	$e_{rms,2}$
a_1	56, 56	A(KJ)	-40.677	3.246e-4	N.A.	N.A.	1.980	1.717e-1
		A(LCR)	-24.604	9.309e-3	N.A.	N.A.	5.920e-1	1.374e-1
	55, 28	F(KJ)	2.798	8.242e-1	-24.807	3.048e-3	2.117	1.761
		F(LD)	-31.994	3.573e-3	-31.997	2.933e-3	1.548	3.248e-1
a_2	53, 53	A(KJ)	-61.643	5.626e-5	N.A.	N.A.	4.437e-1	3.779e-2
		A(LCR)	-55.710	2.258e-4	N.A.	N.A.	8.224e-2	2.181e-2
	52, 26	F(KJ)	-32.726	1.493e-3	-32.770	1.216e-3	8.027e-1	1.633e-1
		F(LD)	-38.421	1.552e-3	-38.432	1.229e-3	6.470e-1	1.459e-1
a_3	48, 48	A(KJ)	-70.691	1.264e-5	N.A.	N.A.	2.011e-2	1.745e-3
		A(LCR)	-73.920	1.265e-5	N.A.	N.A.	2.991e-3	9.069e-4
	47, 24	F(KJ)	2.474	7.957e-1	-42.609	3.731e-4	7.122e-1	1.732
		F(LD)	-50.268	3.654e-4	-50.411	2.917e-4	1.802e-1	3.536e-2
a_4	43, 43	A(KJ)	-80.513	4.987e-6	N.A.	N.A.	5.892e-3	5.193e-4
		A(LCR)	-84.237	4.119e-6	N.A.	N.A.	3.870e-4	1.044e-4
	42, 21	F(KJ)	-53.561	1.310e-4	-53.810	1.027e-4	7.986e-2	1.609e-2
		F(LD)	-59.247	1.354e-4	-59.572	1.015e-4	5.479e-2	1.223e-2

Table 6. Performances of allpass and FIR VFD filters (Keys: $\alpha_1 = 0.9625$, $\alpha_2 = 0.95$, $\alpha_3 = 0.925$, $\alpha_4 = 0.9$; OD: Filter order and mean group delay (M_{AP}, D_{AP}) or (L_{FIR}, D_{FIR}); A: Allpass design, F: FIR design; (KJ): (Kwan & Jiang, 2009a); (LCR): (Lee et al., 2008); (LD): (Lu & Deng, 1999); FGD: Fractional group delay)

The relationship between numerator and denominator orders, and optimal mean group delay of a VdIIR or FdIIR VFD filter is a subject of interest. Table 10 summarizes such relationships among those VdIIR and FdIIR VDF filters listed in Table 9. It can be observed from Table 10 that as α changes from $0.9 \le \alpha \le 0.9625$, the ratio $D/(N+M)$ changes from 0.64 to 0.67 for VdIIR VFD filters, and changes from 0.57 to 0.55 for FdIIR VFD filters. Also, as seen from Figs. 1-8, for the higher wideband side with $\alpha = 0.9625$ and 0.95, there is a mean group delay value that yields a minimum e_{rms} value; but for the lower wideband side with $\alpha = 0.925$ and 0.9, each of the mean group delay curves shows that e_{rms} becomes lower much earlier at smaller D before reaching its minimum e_{rms} value. In other words, the mean group delay requirement is lower for lower wideband cutoff frequencies. From Table 10, in general, the VdIIR VFD filters require slightly higher optimal mean group delay values D than those of the corresponding FdIIR VFD filters.

a	N	D	R	Freq. Responses		Mag. Responses		FGD Responses	
				e_{max} (dB)	e_{rms}	$e_{max,1}$ (dB)	$e_{rms,1}$	$e_{max,2}$	$e_{rms,2}$
a_1	49	25	6	-46.317	4.790e-4	-46.373	3.607e-4	5.621e-1	7.708e-2
		28	7	-45.817	4.981e-4	-48.255	3.327e-4	6.545e-1	9.443e-2
		31	8	-45.492	5.203e-4	-46.819	3.439e-4	6.152e-1	1.034e-1
		34	3	-55.689	1.709e-4	-56.650	1.203e-4	3.135e-1	4.301e-2
		37	1	-56.746	1.157e-4	-56.792	8.227e-5	2.371e-1	3.090e-2
		40	2	-54.753	1.333e-4	-55.272	8.621e-5	2.725e-1	3.913e-2
		43	4	-52.061	1.811e-4	-54.511	1.181e-4	3.634e-1	5.468e-2
		46	5	-48.664	2.877e-4	-48.979	2.016e-4	3.676e-1	6.420e-2
a_2	46	23	7	-55.398	2.194e-4	-56.439	1.629e-4	2.370e-1	3.347e-2
		26	6	-59.500	1.442e-4	-59.567	1.025e-4	1.855e-1	2.446e-2
		29	5	-59.982	1.310e-4	-60.924	9.276e-5	1.434e-1	2.400e-2
		32	2	-63.424	6.157e-5	-66.513	4.168e-5	1.025e-1	1.451e-2
		35	1	-64.515	5.514e-5	-67.411	3.558e-5	1.019e-1	1.364e-2
		38	3	-62.722	6.798e-5	-63.918	4.290e-5	1.184e-1	1.767e-2
		41	4	-57.588	9.448e-5	-57.757	7.247e-5	1.200e-1	1.731e-2
		44	8	-48.195	2.999e-4	-52.186	2.194e-4	5.620e-1	5.862e-2
a_3	41	18	8	-49.959	3.716e-4	-50.563	2.537e-4	2.966e-1	4.916e-2
		21	6	-64.763	6.303e-5	-67.058	4.233e-5	7.008e-2	1.016e-2
		24	5	-69.381	3.348e-5	-70.084	2.327e-5	4.344e-2	6.336e-3
		27	2	-75.807	1.269e-5	-78.312	8.311e-6	2.229e-2	2.984e-3
		30	1	-75.789	1.082e-5	-80.087	6.474e-6	2.048e-2	3.090e-3
		33	3	-71.425	1.823e-5	-71.675	1.433e-5	2.420e-2	3.420e-3
		36	4	-67.853	2.618e-5	-69.170	1.809e-5	3.759e-2	5.315e-3
		39	7	-59.463	7.159e-5	-61.018	5.770e-5	1.011e-1	1.101e-2
a_4	36	12	8	-54.423	3.608e-4	-54.631	2.655e-4	2.113e-1	3.317e-2
		15	7	-62.453	1.158e-4	-64.365	8.504e-5	7.312e-2	1.147e-2
		18	6	-71.255	2.661e-5	-73.122	1.942e-5	2.182e-2	3.217e-3
		21	3	-79.979	7.880e-6	-83.184	5.360e-6	8.086e-3	1.170e-3
		24	2	-83.278	6.257e-6	-85.250	4.068e-6	8.721e-3	1.314e-3
		27	1	-81.501	5.606e-6	-82.356	4.315e-6	6.449e-3	9.108e-4
		30	4	-76.734	8.225e-6	-82.492	5.195e-6	1.332e-2	1.626e-3
		33	5	-68.507	2.048e-5	-73.101	1.519e-5	2.204e-2	3.328e-3

Table 7. Performances of gradient-based design (43) of VdIIR VFD filters versus mean group delay (Keys: α_1= 0.9625, α_2= 0.95, α_3= 0.925, α_4= 0.9; R: Rank; FGD: Fractional group delay)

a	N	D	R	Freq. Responses		Mag. Responses		FGD Responses	
				e_{max} (dB)	e_{rms}	$e_{max.1}$ (dB)	$e_{rms.1}$	$e_{max.2}$	$e_{rms.2}$
a_1	54	24	9	-47.551	4.030e-4	-48.815	3.254e-4	3.946e-1	6.066e-2
		27	8	-49.821	2.791e-4	-49.826	2.345e-4	2.523e-1	4.390e-2
		30	7	-49.940	2.663e-4	-51.336	1.906e-4	3.675e-1	5.526e-2
		33	1	-58.117	1.360e-4	-59.459	1.055e-4	1.553e-1	2.391e-2
		36	2	-54.776	1.581e-4	-56.752	1.100e-4	2.200e-1	3.225e-2
		39	3	-53.351	1.695e-4	-58.289	1.097e-4	3.108e-1	4.832e-2
		42	4	-52.767	1.852e-4	-57.168	1.246e-4	3.521e-1	5.312e-2
		45	5	-51.723	2.027e-4	-54.003	1.500e-4	3.394e-1	4.971e-2
		48	6	-50.532	2.165e-4	-53.051	1.745e-4	3.007e-1	4.414e-2
a_2	51	23	7	-57.352	1.585e-4	-57.948	1.258e-4	1.085e-1	1.823e-2
		26	4	-60.282	1.172e-4	-62.605	9.084e-5	8.234e-2	1.344e-2
		29	2	-60.166	1.051e-4	-64.946	7.397e-5	8.715e-2	1.359e-2
		32	1	-58.723	1.018e-4	-65.813	7.060e-5	1.013e-1	1.683e-2
		35	3	-56.737	1.073e-4	-63.980	7.180e-5	1.307e-1	1.956e-2
		38	5	-56.078	1.210e-4	-60.347	8.811e-5	1.470e-1	2.142e-2
		41	6	-57.176	1.354e-4	-58.376	1.015e-4	1.199e-1	1.825e-2
		44	8	-54.520	1.590e-4	-57.346	1.155e-4	1.488e-1	2.299e-2
		47	9	-51.036	2.173e-4	-58.471	1.441e-4	3.066e-1	5.044e-2
a_3	46	17	9	-54.883	1.565e-4	-56.964	1.190e-4	1.131e-1	1.781e-2
		20	8	-60.232	7.723e-5	-65.677	5.865e-5	3.142e-2	5.028e-3
		23	5	-61.491	7.567e-5	-66.350	5.607e-5	3.709e-2	5.591e-3
		26	2	-61.693	7.237e-5	-68.770	5.183e-5	3.782e-2	5.498e-3
		29	1	-60.702	7.065e-5	-69.047	5.209e-5	3.796e-2	5.501e-3
		32	3	-62.120	7.440e-5	-66.268	5.689e-5	2.962e-2	4.939e-3
		35	4	-60.883	7.454e-5	-66.131	5.552e-5	4.267e-2	6.465e-3
		38	7	-59.235	7.703e-5	-67.887	5.477e-5	6.825e-2	1.023e-2
		41	6	-58.976	7.603e-5	-66.870	5.497e-5	6.936e-2	1.007e-2
a_4	41	12	9	-55.792	1.883e-4	-58.359	1.342e-4	1.093e-1	1.991e-2
		15	8	-62.408	7.731e-5	-65.923	5.838e-5	3.030e-2	5.618e-3
		18	2	-63.307	5.875e-5	-71.407	4.177e-5	1.061e-2	1.921e-3
		21	5	-64.151	6.078e-5	-71.767	4.448e-5	1.876e-2	2.673e-3
		24	4	-63.959	6.049e-5	-69.984	4.491e-5	1.615e-2	2.565e-3
		27	1	-63.586	5.820e-5	-70.713	4.244e-5	9.738e-3	1.712e-3
		30	3	-61.756	5.975e-5	-70.908	4.170e-5	2.336e-2	3.916e-3
		33	6	-62.236	6.151e-5	-70.075	4.376e-5	3.241e-2	4.699e-3
		36	7	-61.444	6.189e-5	-68.939	4.454e-5	2.113e-2	3.729e-3

Table 8. Performances of gradient-based design (43) of FdIIR VFD filters versus mean group delay (Keys: α_1= 0.9625, α_2= 0.95, α_3= 0.925, α_4= 0.9; R: Rank; FGD: Fractional group delay)

α		VdIIR	FdIIR	AP		FIR	
		(43)	(43)	(KJ)	(LCR)	(KJ)	(LD)
α_1	D	37	33	56	56	28	28
	e_{rms}	1.157e-4	1.360e-4	3.246e-4	9.309e-3	8.242e-1	3.573e-3
α_2	D	35	32	53	53	26	26
	e_{rms}	5.514e-5	1.018e-4	5.626e-5	2.258e-4	1.493e-3	1.552e-3
α_3	D	30	29	48	48	24	24
	e_{rms}	1.082e-5	7.065e-5	1.264e-5	1.265e-5	7.957e-1	3.654e-4
α_4	D	27	27	43	43	21	21
	e_{rms}	5.606e-6	5.820e-5	4.987e-6	4.119e-6	1.310e-4	1.354e-4

Table 9. Performances (e_{rms}) of VFD filters selected from Tables 6-8 (Keys: α_1= 0.9625, α_2= 0.95, α_3= 0.925, α_4= 0.9; (KJ): (Kwan & Jiang, 2009a); (LCR): (Lee et al., 2008); (LD): (Lu & Deng, 1999))

	α	D	N	M	$N+M$	$D/(N+M)$
VdIIR	α_1	37	49	6	55	0.6727
	α_2	35	46	6	52	0.6731
	α_3	30	41	6	47	0.6383
	α_4	27	36	6	42	0.6429
FdIIR	α_1	33	54	6	60	0.5500
	α_2	32	51	6	57	0.5614
	α_3	29	46	6	52	0.5577
	α_4	27	41	6	47	0.5745

Table 10. D/(N+M) for IIR VFD filters (Keys: α_1= 0.9625, α_2= 0.95, α_3= 0.925, α_4= 0.9)

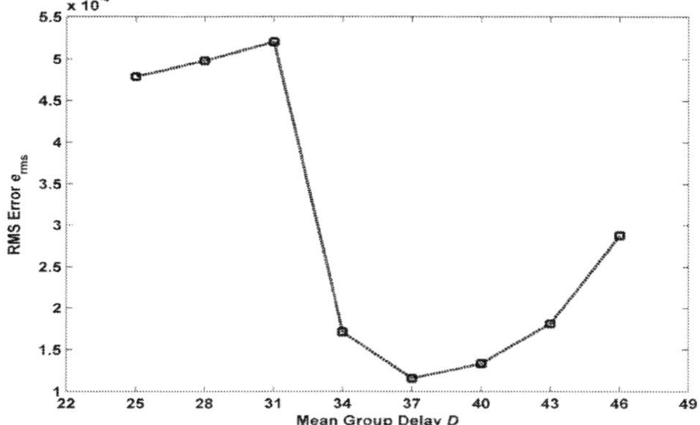

Fig. 1. e_{rms} versus mean group delay D (VdIIR VFD filter, a = 0.9625, N = 49, M = 6)

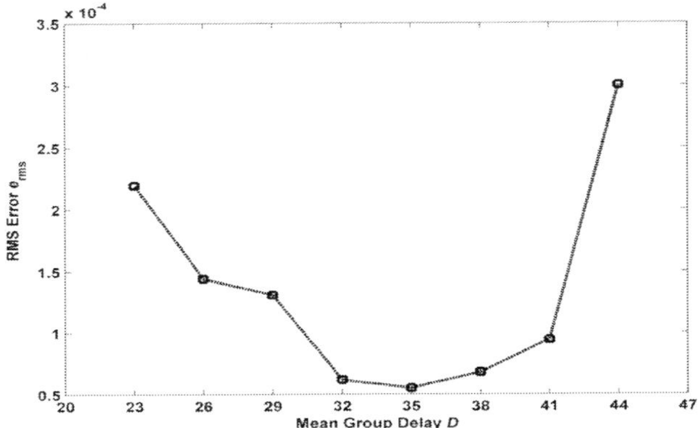

Fig. 2. e_{rms} versus mean group delay D (VdIIR VFD filter, $a = 0.95$, $N = 46$, $M = 6$)

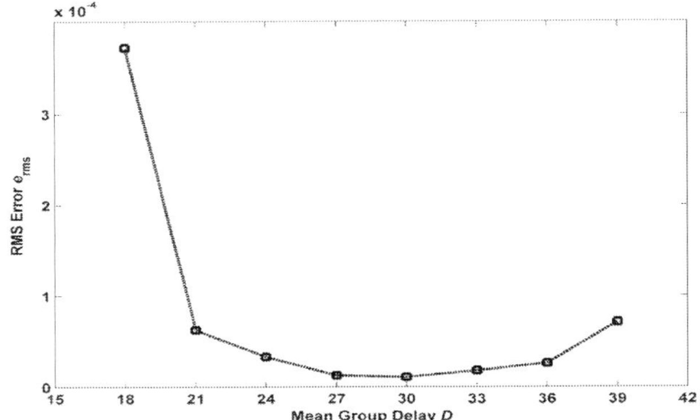

Fig. 3. e_{rms} versus mean group delay D (VdIIR VFD filter, $a = 0.925$, $N = 41$, $M = 6$)

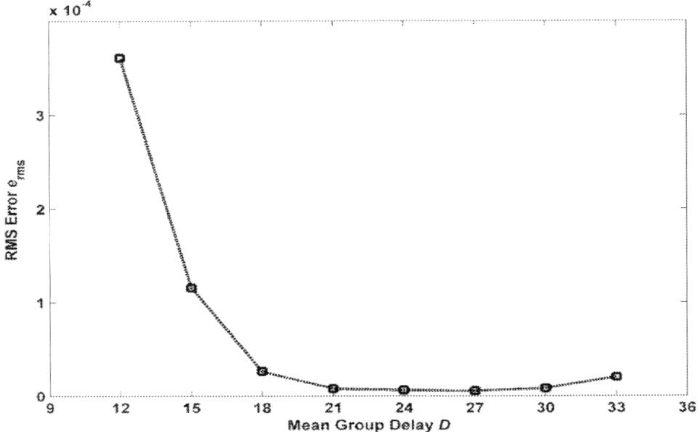

Fig. 4. e_{rms} versus mean group delay D (VdIIR VFD filter, $a = 0.90$, $N = 36$, $M = 6$)

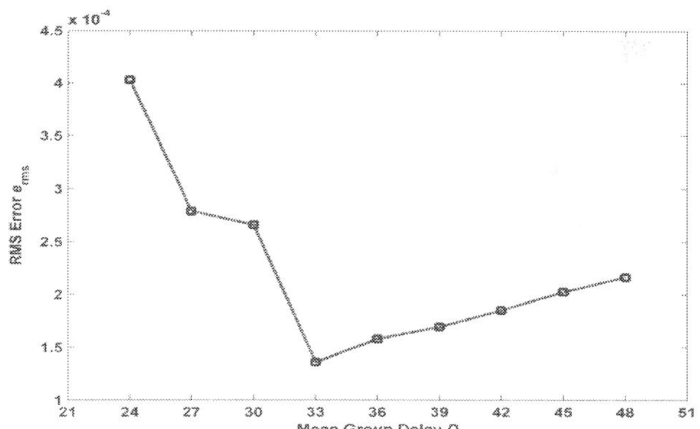

Fig. 5. e_{rms} versus mean group delay D (FdIIR VFD filter, $a = 0.9625$, $N = 54$, $M = 6$)

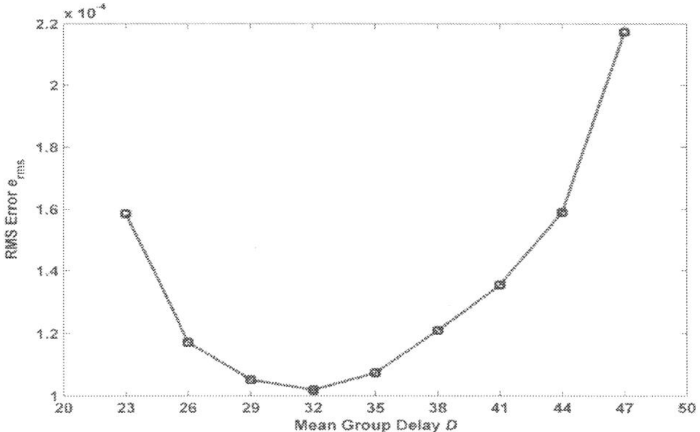

Fig. 6. e_{rms} versus mean group delay D (FdIIR VFD filter, $a = 0.95$, $N = 51$, $M = 6$)

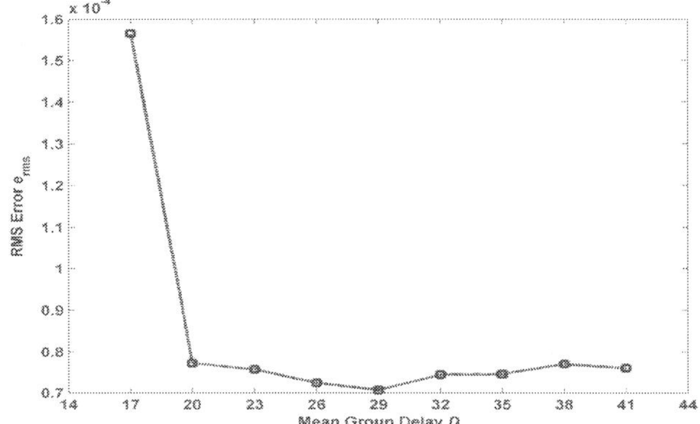

Fig. 7. e_{rms} versus mean group delay D (FdIIR VFD filter, $a = 0.925$, $N = 46$, $M = 6$)

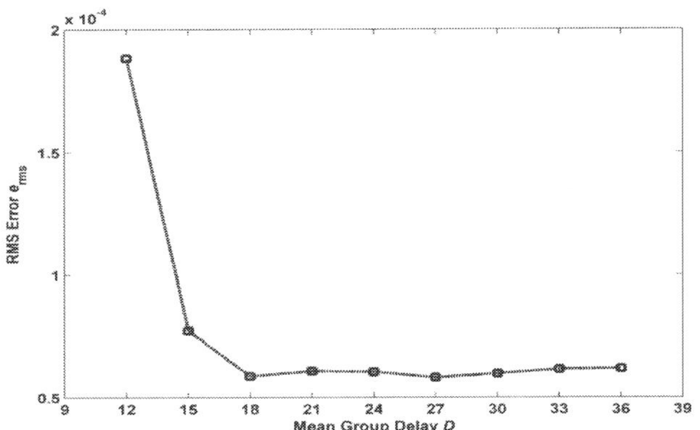

Fig. 8. e_{rms} versus mean group delay D (FdIIR VFD filter, $a = 0.90$, $N = 41$, $M = 6$)

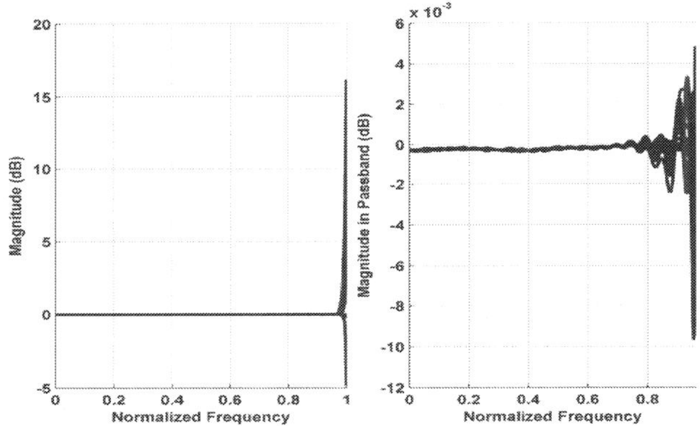

Fig. 9. Magnitude responses of VdIIR VFD filter obtained by gradient-based design method with (43) ($a = 0.9625$, $N = 49$, $M = 6$, $D = 37$)

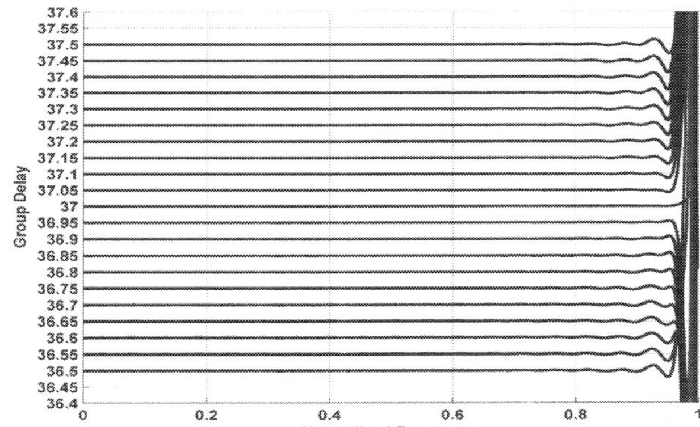

Fig. 10. Group delay responses of VdIIR VFD filter obtained by gradient-based design method with (43) ($a = 0.9625$, $N = 49$, $M = 6$, $D = 37$)

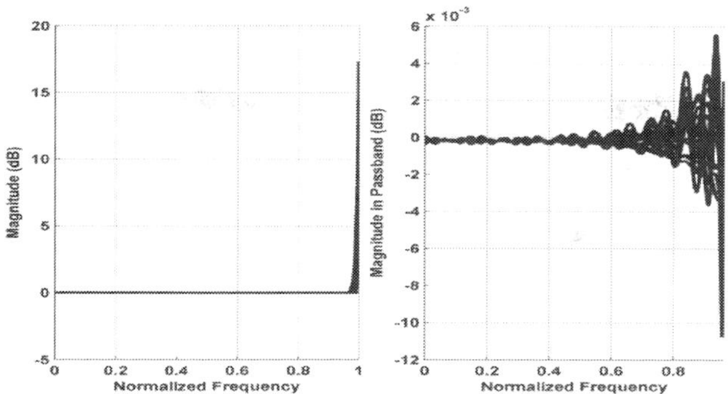

Fig. 11. Magnitude responses of FdIIR VFD filter obtained by gradient-based design method with (43) ($a = 0.9625$, $N = 54$, $M = 6$, $D = 33$)

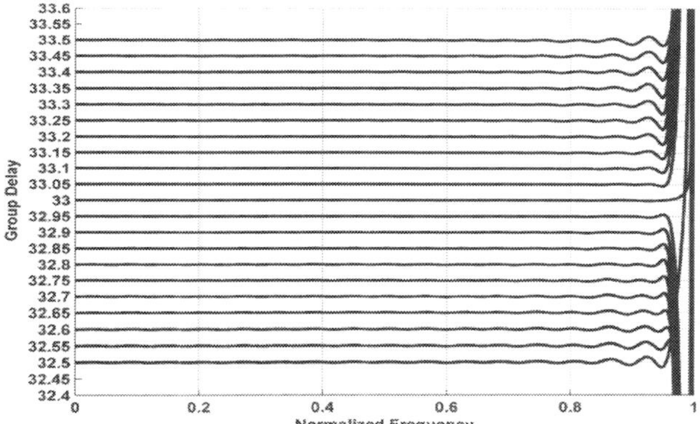

Fig. 12. Group delay responses of FdIIR VFD filter obtained by gradient-based design method with (43) ($a = 0.9625$, $N = 54$, $M = 6$, $D = 33$)

6.5 Overall IIR, allpass, and FIR VFD filter performances

To facilitate explanation in this sub-section, (29), (34), (35), (43) denote different proposed VdIIR and FdIIR VFD design methods explained at the beginning of Section 6.2 and listed on Tables 3-5 and 9. Using the same number of distinct variable coefficients at each of the four specified wideband cutoff frequencies, design results indicate that: (a) When compared to the corresponding FIR VFD filters (KJ; LD) shown in Table 6: As seen from Table 5, all the design methods (except (ZK)) for VdIIR and FdIIR VFD filters could achieve improved e_{rms} performances. (b) When compared to the corresponding AP VFD filters (KJ; LCR) shown in Table 6, the following VdIIR VFD filters could achieve improved e_{rms} performances: (i) (29) over (LCR) for $\alpha = 0.9625$ (see Table 5); (ii) (35) over (KJ; LCR) for $\alpha = 0.9625$ and over (LCR) for $\alpha = 0.95$ (see Table 5); and (iii) (43) over (KJ; LCR) for $0.925 \leq \alpha \leq 0.9625$ (see Table 9). (c) When compared to the corresponding AP VFD filters (KJ; LCR) shown in Table 6, the following FdIIR VFD filters could achieve improved e_{rms} performances: (i) (29) over (LCR) for $\alpha = 0.9625$ (see Table 5); (ii) (34) over (KJ; LCR) for $\alpha = 0.9625$ and over (LCR) for $\alpha = 0.95$

(see Table 5); (iii) (43) over (KJ; LCR) for $\alpha = 0.9625$ and over (LCR) for $\alpha = 0.95$ (see Table 9); (iv) (KJ) over (LCR) for $0.95 \leq \alpha \leq 0.9625$ (see Table 5); and (v) (TCK) over (LCR) for $\alpha = 0.9625$ (see Table 5).

Due to the mirror symmetric coefficient relation in an allpass VFD filter and for stability reason, it is a common practice to select its mean group delay to be the same as its filter order. Based on Table 10, as a decreases from 0.9625 to 0.9, the reductions in mean group delay values of (a) VdIIR VFD filters versus AP VFD filters range approximately from 1.5 to 1.6 times; and (b) FdIIR VFD filters versus AP VFD filters are higher and range approximately from 1.7 to 1.6 times.

The maximum pole radius versus fractional delay t of the four VdIIR VFD filters as listed in Table 9 and the four AP VFD filters designed by (KJ) and (LCR) are plotted with 1001 points, respectively, in Figs. 13-15. Figs. 13-15 indicate that all the three types of variable-denominator designs are stable; and the maximum pole radius at any t reduces as the passband cutoff frequency is lowered. As a general trend, it can be observed from the results that the error performances of each type of the VdIIR VFD filters, the FdIIR VFD filters, the AP VFD filters, and the FIR VFD filters improves along with a reduction in filter order with decreasing passband cutoff frequency $a\pi$.

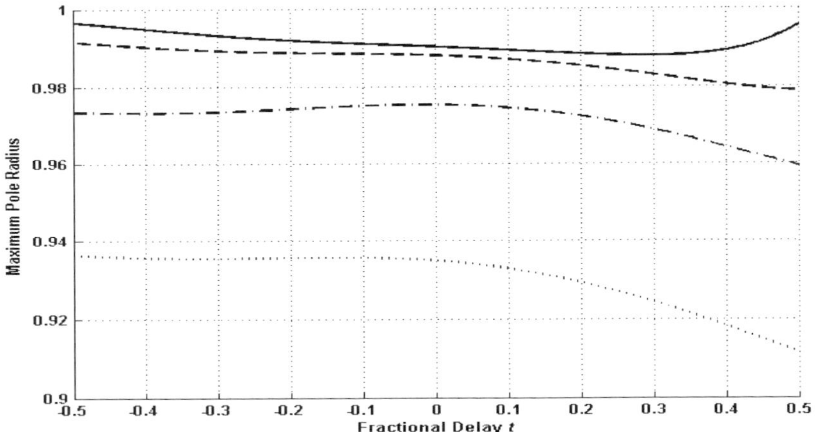

Fig. 13. Maximum pole radius of VdIIR VFD filter obtained by gradient-based design method with (43) versus fractional delay t (Solid: $a = 0.9625$, $N = 49$, $M = 6$, $D = 37$; Dashed: $a = 0.95$, $N = 46$, $M = 6$, $D = 35$; Dash-dot: $a = 0.925$, $N = 41$, $M = 6$, $D = 30$; Dotted: $a = 0.90$, $N = 36$, $M = 6$, $D = 27$)

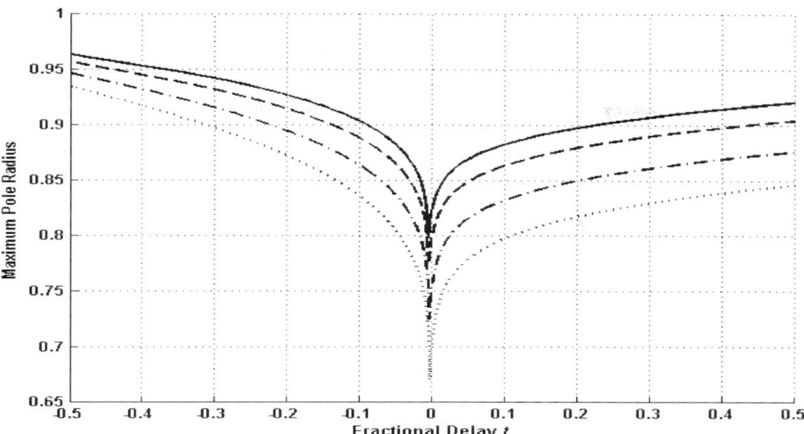

Fig. 14. Maximum pole radius of allpass VFD filter designed by (Kwan & Jiang, 2009a) versus fractional delay t (Solid: $a = 0.9625$, $M_{AP} = D_{AP} = 56$; Dashed: $a = 0.95$, $M_{AP} = D_{AP} = 53$; Dash-dot: $a = 0.925$, $M_{AP} = D_{AP} = 48$; Dotted: $a = 0.90$, $M_{AP} = D_{AP} = 43$)

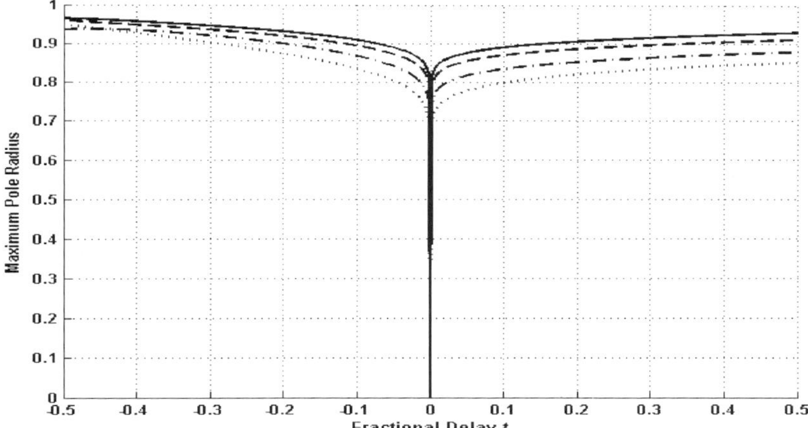

Fig. 15. Maximum pole radius of allpass VFD filter designed by (Lee et al., 2008) versus fractional delay t (Solid: $a = 0.9625$, $M_{AP} = D_{AP} = 56$; Dashed: $a = 0.95$, $M_{AP} = D_{AP} = 53$; Dash-dot: $a = 0.925$, $M_{AP} = D_{AP} = 48$; Dotted: $a = 0.90$, $M_{AP} = D_{AP} = 43$)

7. Summary

This chapter introduces an integrated design of IIR variable fractional delay (VFD) digital filters with variable and fixed denominators. Both sequential and gradient-based design approaches in the weighted least-squares (WLS) sense are adopted. The results obtained are compared to other design methods for IIR, allpass, and FIR VFD filters. In the sequential design method, the Levy's method is adopted along with an iterative reweighting technique to transform the original nonconvex approximation error into a (convex) quadratic form. The design problem (at each iteration) can be further cast as a second-order cone programming (SOCP) problem. The stability of such a designed IIR VFD filter can be ensured by imposing a set of linear stability constraints derived from a sufficient condition in terms of the positive realness. In the gradient-based design method, a simple SOCP problem is first formulated using the Levy's method. The design is then refined through a local search starting from the initial design obtained. The stability of the initial filter can be ensured by the linear positive-realness based stability constraints or with the use of a regularization term aimed to suppress the energy of the denominator coefficients. Four sets of wideband filter examples are adopted with performances analyzed to illustrate the performances of the proposed design methods.

8. Conclusions

In this chapter, an integrated sequential design method and an integrated gradient-based design method for IIR VFD filters with variable-denominator and fixed-denominator have been presented. In contrast to the previous two-stage design methods, by merging the polynomial coefficient fitting into each respective integrated design, the approximation error caused by a separate polynomial coefficient fitting stage is eliminated. Also, instead of modeling denominator and optimizing numerator in separate steps, each of the sequential and gradient-based design methods jointly optimizes the numerator and denominator coefficients. Consequently, during the design procedure any change on any numerator or denominator coefficient can be utilized to optimize all the numerator and denominator coefficients in the subsequent design procedure. This facilitates the search of a better design in the coefficient vector space. The results of four sets of wideband filter examples designed using the proposed design methods, the VdIIR VFD (ZK) and the FdIIR VFD (KJ; TCK) design methods, and a number of AP VFD (KJ; LCR) and FIR VFD (KJ; LD) design methods indicate that IIR VFD filters could achieve some e_{rms} improvements over the other two types of VFD filters along with reduced mean group delays when compared to AP VFD filters. In particular, e_{rms} improvements can be observed in (a) the proposed gradient-based VdIIR design (with (43)) for wider band designs with $0.925 \leq \alpha \leq 0.9625$; and (b) the proposed gradient-based FdIIR design (with (43)) for the widest band design with $\alpha = 0.9625$. For narrower band designs such as $\alpha = 0.9$, e_{rms} improvements become obvious in the AP VFD designs (KJ; TCK). In term of design complexity, the FIR VFD designs (KJ; LD) remain to be the simplest. Finally, it should be emphasized that the error performances of a VFD filter design depend not only on the type (IIR, AP, and FIR) of VFD filters, but also depend on the effectiveness of its design method.

9. References

Brandenstein, H. & Unbehauen, R. (1998). Least-squares approximation of FIR by IIR digital filters. *IEEE Transactions on Signal Processing*, Vol. 46, No. 1, (January 1998), pp. 21-30, ISSN 1053-587X.
Brandenstein, H. & Unbehauen, R. (2001). Weighted least-squares approximation of FIR by IIR digital filters. *IEEE Transactions on Signal Processing*, Vol. 49, No. 3, (March 2001), pp. 558-568, ISSN 1053-587X.

Deng, T.-B. (2001). Discretization-free design of variable fractional-delay FIR filters. *IEEE Transactions on Circuits and Systems II*, Vol. 48, No. 6, (June 2001), pp. 637–644, ISSN 1057-7130.

Deng, T.-B. (2006). Noniterative WLS design of allpass variable fractional-delay digital filters. *IEEE Transactions on Circuits and Systems I*, Vol. 53, No. 2, (February 2006), pp. 358–371, ISSN 1549-8328.

Deng, T.-B. & Lian, Y. (2006). Weighted-least-squares design of variable fractional-delay FIR filters using coefficient symmetry. *IEEE Transactions on Signal Processing*, Vol. 54, No. 8, (August 2006), pp. 3023-3038, ISSN 1053-587X.

Dumitrescu, B. & Niemistö, R. (2004). Multistage IIR filter design using convex stability domains defined by positive realness. *IEEE Transactions on Signal Processing*, Vol. 52, No. 4, (April 2004), pp. 962-974, ISSN 1053-587X.

Jiang, A. & Kwan, H. K. (2009a). IIR digital filter design with novel stability criterion based on argument principle. *IEEE Transactions on Circuits and Systems I*, Vol. 56, No. 3, (March 2009), pp. 583-593, ISSN 1549-8328.

Jiang, A. & Kwan, H. K. (2009b). Iterative design of IIR variable fractional delay digital filters, *Proceedings IEEE International Conference on Electro/Information Technology*, pp. 163–166, Print ISBN 978-1-4244-3354-4, Windsor, ON, Canada, June 7–9, 2009.

Kwan, H. K., Jiang, A., & Zhao, H. (2006). IIR variable fractional delay digital filter design, *Proceedings of TENCON*, PO5.27, TEN-863, pp. 1-4, ISBN 1-4244-0549-1/Print ISBN 1-4244-0548-3, Hong Kong, November 14-17, 2006.

Kwan, H. K. & Jiang, A. (2007). Design of IIR variable fractional delay digital filters, *Proceedings of IEEE International Symposium on Circuits and Systems*, pp. 2714-2717, Print ISBN 1-4244-0920-9, New Orleans, May 27-30, 2007.

Kwan, H. K. & Jiang, A. (2009a). FIR, allpass, and IIR variable fractional delay digital filter design. *IEEE Transactions on Circuits and Systems I*, Vol. 56, No. 9, (September 2009), pp. 2064-2074, ISSN 1549-8328.

Kwan, H. K. & Jiang, A. (2009b). Low-order fixed denominator IIR VFD filter design, *Proceedings of IEEE International Symposium on Circuits and Systems*, pp. 481-484, Print ISBN 978-1-4244-3827-3, Taipei, Taiwan, May 24-27, 2009.

Laakso, T. I., Valimaki, V., Karjalainen, M., & Laine, U. K. (1996). Splitting the unit delay. *IEEE Signal Processing Magazine*, Vol. 13, No. 1, (January 1996), pp. 30-60, ISSN 1053-5888.

Lee, W. R., Caccetta, L., & Rehbock, V. (2008). Optimal design of all-pass variable fractional-delay digital filters. *IEEE Transactions on Circuits and Systems I*, Vol. 55, No. 5, (June 2008), pp. 1248–1256, ISSN 1549-8328.

Levy, E. C. (1959). Complex curve fitting. *IRE Transactions on Automatic Control*, Vol. AC-4, (May 1959), pp. 37-43, ISSN 0096-199X.

Lu, W.-S., Pei, S.-C., & Tseng, C.-C. (1998). A weighted least-squares method for the design of stable 1-D and 2-D IIR digital filters. *IEEE Transactions on Signal Processing*, Vol. 46, No. 1, (January 1998), pp. 1–10, ISSN 1053-587X.

Lu, W.-S. & Deng, T.-B. (1999). An improved weighted least-squares design for variable fractional delay FIR filters. *IEEE Transactions on Circuits and Systems II*, Vol. 46, No. 8, (August 1999), pp. 1035–1040, ISSN 1057-7130.

Lu, W.-S. (1999). Design of stable IIR digital filters with equiripple passbands and peak-constrained least-squares stopbands. *IEEE Transactions on Circuits and Systems II*, Vol. 46, No. 11, (November 1999), pp. 1421-1426, ISSN 1057-7130.

Sanathanan, C. K. & Koerner, J. (1963). Transfer function synthesis as a ratio of two complex polynomials. *IEEE Transactions on Automatic Control*, Vol. AC-8, No. 1, (January 1963), pp. 56-58, ISSN 0018-9286.

Sturm, J. F. (1999). Using SeDuMi 1.02, a MATLAB toolbox for optimization over symmetric cones. *Optimization Methods and Software*, Vol. 11-12, 1999, pp. 625-653, Print ISSN 1055-6788/Online ISSN 1029-4937.

Tseng, C.-C. & Lee, S.-L. (2002). Minimax design of stable IIR digital filter with prescribed magnitude and phase responses. *IEEE Transactions on Circuits and Systems I*, Vol. 49, No. 4, (April 2002), pp. 547-551, ISSN 1549-8328.

Tseng, C.-C. (2002a). Eigenfilter approach for the design of variable fractional delay FIR and all-pass filters. *IEE Proceedings - Visual, Image, Signal Processing*, Vol. 149, No. 5, (October 2002), pp. 297-303, ISSN 1350-245X.

Tseng, C.-C. (2002b). Design of 1-D and 2-D variable fractional delay allpass filters using weighted least-squares method. *IEEE Transactions on Circuits and Systems I*, Vol. 49, No. 10, (October 2002), pp. 1413–1422, ISSN 1549-8328.

Tseng, C.-C. (2004). Design of stable IIR digital filter based on least p-power error criterion. *IEEE Transactions on Circuits and Systems I*, Vol. 51, No. 9, (September 2004), pp. 1879-1888, ISSN 1549-8328.

Tsui, K. M., Chan, S. C., & Kwan, H. K. (2007). A new method for designing causal stable IIR variable fractional delay digital filters. *IEEE Transactions on Circuits and Systems II*, Vol. 54, No. 11, (November 2007), pp. 999–1003, ISSN 1057-7130.

Zhao, H. & Kwan, H. K. (2005). Design of 1-D stable variable fractional delay IIR filters, *Proceedings of International Symposium on Intelligent Signal Processing and Communication Systems*, pp. 517-520, ISBN 978-0-7803-9266-3, Hong Kong, December 13-16, 2005.

Zhao, H. & Yu, J. (2006). A simple and efficient design of variable fractional delay FIR filters. *IEEE Transactions on Circuits and Systems II*, Vol. 53, No. 2, (February 2006), pp. 157–160, ISSN 1057-7130.

Zhao, H., Kwan, H. K., Wan, L., & Nie, L. (2006). Design of 1-D stable variable fractional delay IIR filters using finite impulse response fitting, *Proceedings of International Conference on Communications, Circuits and Systems*, pp. 201-205, ISBN 978-0-7803-9584-8, Guilin, China, June 25-28, 2006.

Zhao, H. & Kwan, H. K. (2007). Design of 1-D stable variable fractional delay IIR filters. *IEEE Transactions on Circuits and Systems II*, Vol. 54, No. 1, (January 2007), pp. 86–90, ISSN 1057-7130.

9

Complex Coefficient IIR Digital Filters

Zlatka Nikolova, Georgi Stoyanov, Georgi Iliev and Vladimir Poulkov
Technical University of Sofia
Bulgaria

1. Complex Coefficient IIR Digital Filters – Basic Theory

1.1 Introduction

Interest in complex signal processing goes back quite some time: in 1960 Helstrom (Helstrom, 1960) and Woodward (Woodward, 1960) used the complex envelope presentation to solve problems with signal detection, as did Bello (Bello, 1963), who used it to describe time-invariant linear channels. A number of publications at that time also considered complex signal processing but on a purely theoretical basis. The concept of digital filters with complex coefficients, which will be also referred to as *complex filters*, was developed by Crystal and Ehrman (Crystal & Ehrman, 1968). This work in fact marks the beginning of interest in complex filters and is one of the most often-cited publications. It demonstrated the increased effectiveness of complex signal processing compared to real signal processing and focused the attention of researchers on that new area of science. This area subsequently progressed well, especially in telecommunications, where the complex representation of signals is very useful as it allows the simple interpretation and realization of quite complicated processing tasks, such as modulation, sampling and quantization.

Digital filters with complex coefficients have attracted great interest, owing to their advantages when processing both real and complex signals. As they have both real and imaginary inputs and outputs, the signals they process have to be likewise separated into real and imaginary parts in order to be represented as complex signals. Complex filters have been of theoretical interest for a long time but have only been the subject of intensive experimental investigation over the past two decades, thanks to the rapid development of technology. They have many areas of application, one of the most important being modern telecommunications, which very often uses narrowband signals which are complex in nature (Martin, 2003). Digital complex filters are used to generate SSB (Single Side Band) narrowband signals, typically employed in many wireless telecommunication devices, e.g. SSB transmitters and receivers, complex $\Delta\Sigma$-modulators, trans-multiplexors, radio-receivers, mobile terminals etc. These devices employ processes such as complex modulation, filtering, mixing, speech analysis and synthesis, and adaptive filtering. Complex filtering is also preferred when DFT (Discrete Fourier Transform) is carried out, as it is a linear combination of complex components. This type of processing is required for high-speed wireless standards. Many of the research problems associated with complex digital filtering have been successfully solved but scientific and technological advances challenge researchers with new problems or require new and better solutions to existing problems.

In this chapter we examine IIR (Infinite Impulse Response) digital filters only. They are more difficult to synthesize but are more efficient and selective than FIR (Finite Impulse Response) filters. In general, the choice between FIR and IIR digital filters affects both the filter design process and the implementation of the filter. FIR filters are sufficient for most filtering applications, due to their two main advantages: an exact linear phase response and permanent stability.

1.2 Complex Signals and Complex Filters – an Overview

A complex signal is usually depicted by:

$$X(t) = A\left[\cos\left(\theta_c t\right) + j\sin\left(\theta_c t\right)\right] = Ae^{j\theta_c t} = X_R(t) + jX_I(t) \tag{1}$$

where "R" and "I" indicate real and imaginary components. The spectrum of the complex signal $X(t)$ is in the positive frequency θ_C, while that of the real one $X_R(t)$ is in the frequencies θ_C and $-\theta_C$.

There are two well-known approaches to the complex representation of the signals – by inphase and quadrature components, and using the concept of analytical representation. These approaches differ in the way the imaginary part of the complex signal is formed. The first approach can be regarded as a low-frequency envelope modulation using a complex carrier signal. In the frequency domain this means linear translation of the spectrum by a step of θ_C. Thus, a narrowband signal with the frequency of θ_C can be represented as an envelope (the real part of the complex signal – $X_R(t)$), multiplied by a complex exponent $e^{j\theta_C t}$, named cissoid (Crystal & Ehrman, 1968) or complexoid (Martin, 2003) (Fig. 1).

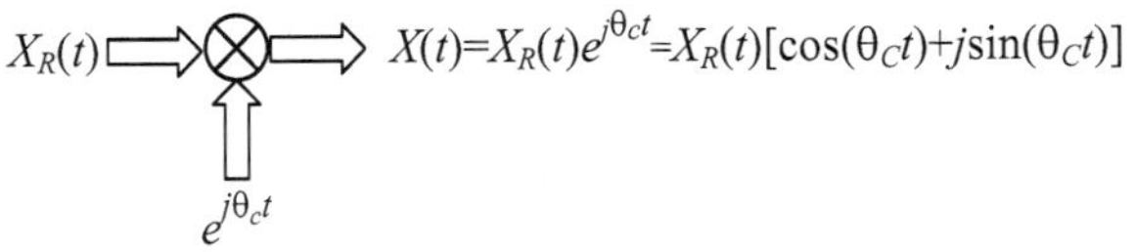

$$X_R(t) \Longrightarrow \bigotimes \Longrightarrow X(t){=}X_R(t)e^{j\theta_c t}{=}X_R(t)[\cos(\theta_C t){+}j\sin(\theta_C t)]$$

$$e^{j\theta_c t}$$

Fig. 1. Complex representation of a narrowband signal.

Analytical representation is the second basic approach to displaying complex signals. The negative frequency components are simply reduced to zero and a complex signal named *analytic* is formed. The real signal and its Hilbert transform are respectively the real and imaginary parts of the analytic signal, which occupies half of the real signal frequency band while its real and imaginary components have the same amplitude and 90° phase-shift. Analytic signals are, for example, the multiplexed OFDM (Orthogonal Frequency Division Multiplexing) symbols in wireless communication systems.

Complex signals are easily processed by complex circuits, in which complex coefficient digital filters play a special role. In contrast to real coefficient filters, their magnitude responses are not symmetric with respect to the zero frequency. A bandpass (BP) complex filter, which is arithmetically symmetric with regards to its central frequency, can be derived by linear translation with a step θ of the magnitude response of a real lowpass (LP) filter (Crystal & Ehrman, 1968). This is equivalent to applying the substitution:

$$z^{-1} \rightarrow z^{-1}e^{j\theta} = z^{-1}(\cos\theta + j\sin\theta) \tag{2}$$

to the real transfer function (also called real-prototype transfer function) thus obtaining the analytical expression of the complex transfer function:

$$H_{Real}(z)\xrightarrow{\;z^{-1}=z^{-1}(\cos\theta + j\sin\theta)\;} H_{Complex}(z) = H_R(z) + jH_I(z). \tag{3}$$

$H_{Complex}(z)$ is a transfer function with complex coefficients and with the same order of N as the real prototype $H_{Real}(z)$, while its real and imaginary parts $H_R(z)$ and $H_I(z)$ are of doubled order $2N$ real coefficient transfer functions. When $H_{Real}(z)$ is an LP transfer function then $H_R(z)$ and $H_I(z)$ are of BP type. For a highpass (HP) real prototype transfer function we get $H_R(z)$ and $H_I(z)$, respectively of BP and bandstop (BS) types.

The substitution (2) is also termed "pole rotation" because it rotates the poles of the real transfer function to an angle of θ both clockwise and anti-clockwise, simultaneously doubling their number (Fig. 2).

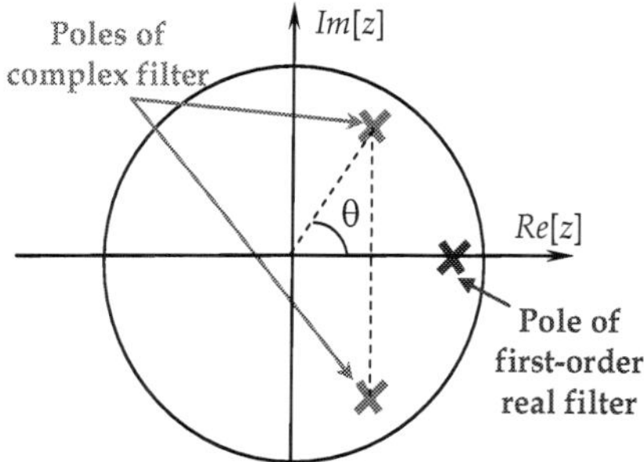

Fig. 2. Pole rotation of a first-order real transfer function after applying the substitution (2).

Starting with:

$$Y(z) = H_{Complex}(z)X(z) \tag{4}$$

and supposing that the quantities in (4) are complex, they can be represented by their real and imaginary parts:

$$Y(z) = Y_R(z) + jY_I(z); \quad X(z) = X_R(z) + jX_I(z); \quad H_{Complex}(z) = H_R(z) + jH_I(z). \tag{5}$$

Then the equation (4) becomes:

$$\begin{aligned} Y(z) &= [H_R(z) + jH_I(z)][X_R(z) + jX_I(z)] = \\ &= [H_R(z)X_R(z) - H_I(z)X_I(z)] + j[H_I(z)X_R(z) + H_R(z)X_I(z)], \end{aligned} \tag{6}$$

and its real and imaginary parts respectively are:

$$Y_R(z) = H_R(z)X_R(z) - H_I(z)X_I(z); \qquad Y_I(z) = H_I(z)X_R(z) + H_R(z)X_I(z).$$ (7)

According to the equations (7), the block-diagram of a complex filter will be as shown in Fig. 3.

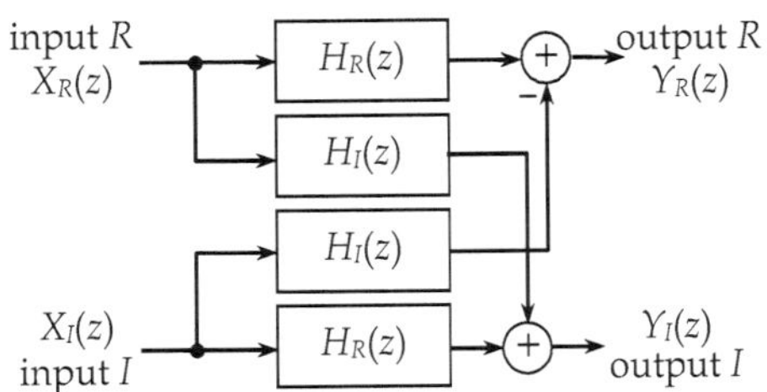

Fig. 3. Block-diagram of a complex filter.

The synthesis of a complex filter is an important procedure because its sensitivity is influenced by the derived realization. A non-canonic complex filter realization will be obtained if $H_R(z)$ and $H_I(z)$ are synthesised individually.

The process of synthesising the complex filter can be better understood by examining a particular filter realization – a real LP first-order filter section (Fig. 4a) with transfer function:

$$H_{Real}^{LP}(z) = \frac{1 + z^{-1}}{1 - a_1 z^{-1}}.$$ (8)

The complex transfer function obtained after the substitution (2) is applied to the real transfer function (8) is:

$$H_{Real}^{LP}(z) = \frac{1 + z^{-1}}{1 - a_1 z^{-1}} \xrightarrow{z^{-1} = z^{-1}(\cos\theta + j\sin\theta)} H_{Complex}(z) = \frac{1 + \cos\theta z^{-1} + j\sin\theta z^{-1}}{1 - a_1 \cos\theta z^{-1} - ja_1 \sin\theta z^{-1}}.$$ (9)

The separation of its real and imaginary parts produces:

$$H_{Complex}(z) = H_R(z) + jH_I(z) = \frac{1 + (1 - a_1)\cos\theta z^{-1} + a_1 \sin\theta z^{-2}}{1 + 2a_1 \cos\theta z^{-1} + a_1^2 z^{-2}} + j\frac{(1 + a_1)\sin\theta z^{-1}}{1 + 2a_1 \cos\theta z^{-1} + a_1^2 z^{-2}}.$$ (10)

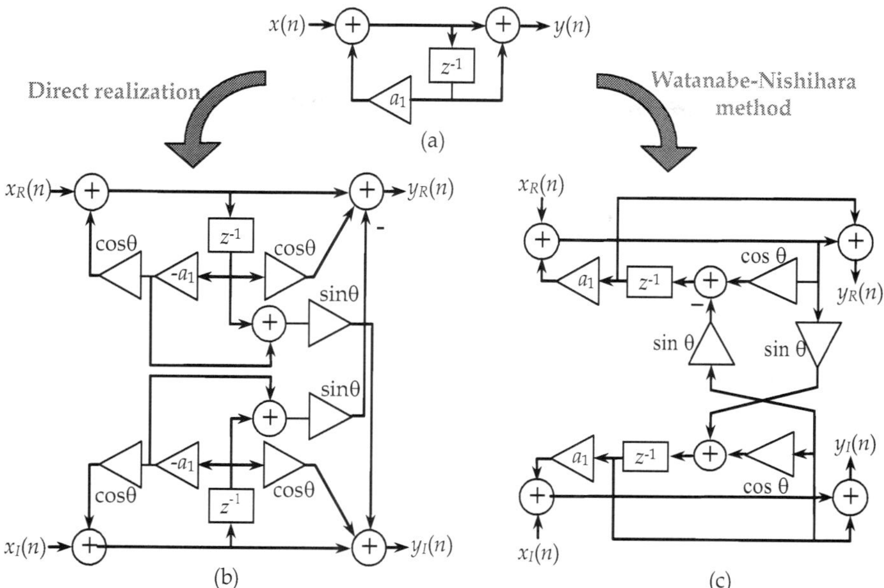

Fig. 4. Realization of (a) real LP first-order filter section; (b) direct-form complex BP filter section; (c) complex BP filter (Watanabe-Nishihara method).

The difference equation corresponding to the transfer function (9) is:

$$y_R(n) + jy_I(n) = [x_R(n) + \cos\theta x_R(n-1) - \sin\theta x_I(n-1) - a_1\cos\theta y_R(n-1) + a_1\sin\theta y_I(n-1)] +$$
$$+ j[x_I(n) + \cos\theta x_I(n-1) + \sin\theta x_R(n-1) - a_1\cos\theta y_I(n-1) - a_1\sin\theta y_R(n-1)] \qquad (11)$$

Direct realization of (11) leads to the structure depicted in Fig. 4b. Obviously the realization is canonic only with respect to the delays. The direct realization of complex filters is studied in some publications (Sim, 1987) although the sensitivity is not minimized.

One of the best methods for the realization of complex structures is offered by Watanabe and Nishihara (Watanabe & Nishihara, 1991). The structure of the real prototype is doubled, for the real input and output as well as for the imaginary input and output (Fig. 5). Bearing in mind that processed signals are complex, after applying the complex transformation (2) the signals after each delay unit are described as:

$$B_R = z^{-1}(A_R\cos\theta - A_I\sin\theta); \qquad B_I = z^{-1}(A_R\sin\theta + A_I\cos\theta). \qquad (12)$$

Applying the Watanabe-Nishihara method to the real LP first-order filter section in Fig. 4a, the complex filter shown in Fig. 4c is derived.

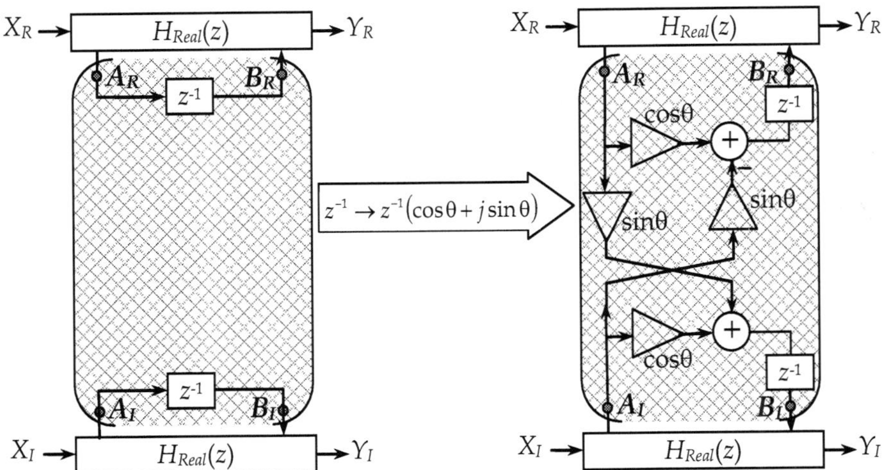

Fig. 5. Complex structure realized by Watanabe and Nishihara method.

The Watanabe-Nishihara method is universally applicable to any real structure, the complex structure obtained being canonic with respect to the multipliers and delay units if the sin- and cosin-multipliers are not counted. Moreover, the number of identical circuit transformations performed and the number of multipliers in the real filter-prototype are the same.

A special class of filters, named *orthogonal complex filters*, is derived (Sim, 1987) (Watanabe & Nishihara, 1991) (Nie et al., 1993), when θ is exactly equal to π/2 in the complex transformation (2):

$$z^{-1} = z^{-1}\left(\cos\frac{\pi}{2} + j\sin\frac{\pi}{2}\right) \text{ or } z = -jz .\tag{13}$$

These filters are used for narrowband signal processing. Obtained after the orthogonal transformation (13) is applied, the orthogonal complex transfer function $H(-jz)$ has alternately-changing coefficients, i.e. real and imaginary. The magnitude response of an orthogonal complex filter is symmetric with respect to the central frequency ω_c, which is exactly 1/4 of the real filter's sampling frequency ω_s.

1.3 Sensitivity Considerations

Digital filters are prone to problems from two main sources of error. The first is known as *transfer function sensitivity with respect to coefficients* and refers to the quantization of multiplier coefficients, which changes the transfer function carried out by the filter. The second source of error is *roundoff noise* due to finite arithmetical operations, which degrades the signal-to-noise ratio (SNR) at the digital filter output. These errors have been extensively discussed in the literature.

In this chapter normalized (classical or Bode) sensitivity is used to estimate how the changes of a given multiplier coefficient α influence the magnitude response of the structure:

$$S_\alpha^{|H(j\omega)|} = \frac{\partial |H(j\omega)|}{\partial \alpha} \frac{\alpha}{|H(j\omega)|} . \tag{14}$$

The overall sensitivity to all multiplier coefficients is evaluated using the worst-case sensitivity

$$WS_{\alpha_i}^{H(e^{j\omega})} = \sum_i \left| S_{\alpha_i}^{H(e^{j\omega})} \right| , \tag{15}$$

or the Schoefler sensitivity (SS), defined as WS but with quadratic addends (Proakis & Manolakis, 2006):

$$SS_{\alpha_i}^{H(e^{j\omega})} = \sum_i \left| S_{\alpha_i}^{H(e^{j\omega})} \right|^2 . \tag{16}$$

Minimization of sensitivity is a well-studied problem but the method that is most widely used by researchers is *sensitivity minimization by coefficient conversion*. In this chapter we use Nishihara's coefficient conversion approach (Nishihara, 1980).

The sensitivity of magnitude, phase response, group-delay etc. is a function of frequency. This has to be taken into account when different digital structures are compared to each other because the sensitivity may differ in the different frequency bands. An indirect criterion for the sensitivity of a transfer function in a particular frequency band is the pole-location density in the corresponding area of the unit circle for a given word-length.

Frequency-dependent sensitivities allow different digital filter realizations to be compared to each other in a wide frequency range. For this reason, magnitude sensitivity function (14) and worst-case sensitivity (15) will mainly be considered in this work.

2. Orthogonal Complex IIR Digital Filters – Synthesis and Sensitivity Investigations

2.1 Introductory Considerations

The synthesis of orthogonal complex low-sensitivity canonic first- and second-order digital filter sections allows an efficient orthogonal cascade filter to be achieved. Such a filter can be developed using the method of approximation and design given in (Stoyanov et al., 1997). The procedure is simple in the case of arithmetically symmetric BP/BS specifications and consists of the following steps:

1. Shift the specifications along the frequency axis until the zero frequency becomes central for them.

2. Apply any possible LP or HP (for BS specifications) approximation, which produces the transfer function in a factored form.

3. Select or develop low-sensitivity canonic first- and second-order LP/HP filter sections.

4. Apply the circuit transform (13) $z^{-1} \rightarrow -jz^{-1}$ to obtain the orthogonal sections, which are used to form the desired orthogonal complex BP/BS cascade realization.

The procedure becomes a lot more difficult in the case of non-symmetric specifications. There are, however, methods of solving the problems but at the price of quite complicated mathematics and transformations (Takahashi et. al., 1992) (Martin, 2005).

The last two steps in the above-described procedure are discussed here. Some low-sensitivity canonic first- and second-order orthogonal complex BP/BS digital filter sections are developed and their low sensitivities are experimentally demonstrated.

The Watanabe-Nishihara method (Watanabe & Nishihara, 1991) is selected to develop new sections. According to this method, it is expected that the sensitivity properties of the proto-type circuit will be inherited by the orthogonal circuit obtained after the transformation. Starting from that expectation, we apply the following strategy: first select or develop very low-sensitivity LP/HP prototypes for a given pole-position and then apply the orthogonal circuit transformation to derive the orthogonal complex BP/BS digital filter sections.

The selection of LP/HP first- and second-order real prototype-sections requires the following criteria to be met:
- The circuits must have canonic structures;
- The magnitude response must be unity for DC (in the case of LP transfer functions), likewise for fs/2 (in the case of HP transfer functions), thus providing zero magnitude sensitivity;
- The sensitivity must be minimized;
- Prototype sections must be free of limit cycles

2.2 Low-Sensitivity Orthogonal Complex IIR First- Order Filter Sections

In order to derive a narrowband orthogonal complex BP filter, a narrowband LP real filter-prototype must be used. When the orthogonal substitution is applied to an HP real prototype, the orthogonal complex filter will have both BP and BS outputs. The most advantageous approach is to employ a universal real digital filter section, which simultaneously realizes both LP and HP transfer functions.

After a comprehensive search, we selected the best two universal first-order real filter-prototype structures that meet the above-listed requirements. They are: MHNS-section (Mitra et al., 1990-a) and a low-sensitivity LS1b-structure (Fig. 6a) (Topalov & Stoyanov, 1990).

When the Watanabe-Nishihara orthogonal circuit transformation is applied to the real filter-prototypes, the orthogonal complex LS1b (Fig. 6b) and MHNS filter structures are obtained (Stoyanov et al., 1996).

After the orthogonal circuit transform (13) is applied to the LP real transfer function (18) $H_{LS1b}^{LP}(z)$ the resulting orthogonal complex transfer function $H_{LS1b-LP}(-jz)$ has complex coefficients, which are alternating real and imaginary numbers. Being a complex transfer function, it can be represented by its real and imaginary parts, which are of double order and are real coefficients:

$$H_{LS1b-LP}(-jz) = H_{LS1b-LP}^{R}(z) + jH_{LS1b-LP}^{I}(z).$$

(17)

Because the real prototype section is universal, i.e. has simultaneous LP and HP outputs, the orthogonal structure has two inputs – real and imaginary, and four outputs – two real ($R1$ and $R2$) and two imaginary ($I1$ and $I2$). Thus there are eight realized transfer functions, in the form of four pairs: the two parts of each pair are identical to each other and also equal to the real and imaginary parts of the LP- and HP-based orthogonal transfer functions - (20)÷(23). Only (22) is of BS type, the rest are BP. The central frequency of an orthogonal filter ω_C is constant and is a quarter of the sampling frequency ω_s.

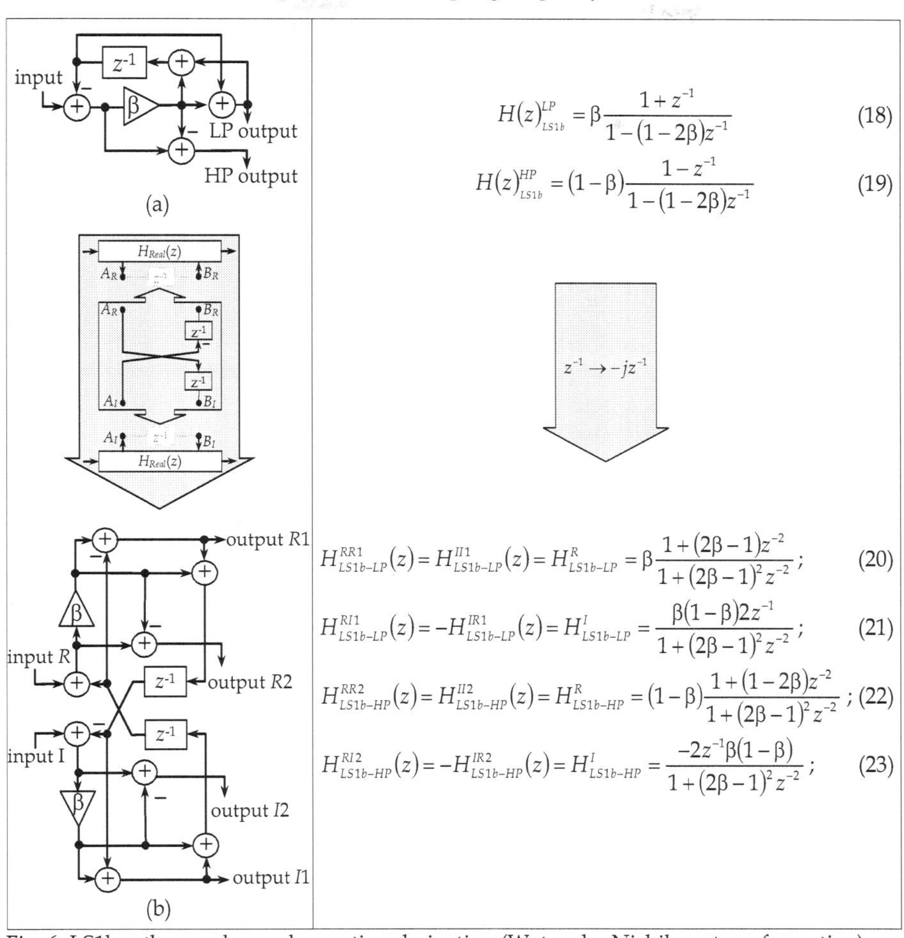

$$H(z)^{LP}_{LS1b} = \beta\frac{1+z^{-1}}{1-(1-2\beta)z^{-1}} \qquad (18)$$

$$H(z)^{HP}_{LS1b} = (1-\beta)\frac{1-z^{-1}}{1-(1-2\beta)z^{-1}} \qquad (19)$$

$$z^{-1} \rightarrow -jz^{-1}$$

$$H^{RR1}_{LS1b-LP}(z) = H^{II1}_{LS1b-LP}(z) = H^{R}_{LS1b-LP} = \beta\frac{1+(2\beta-1)z^{-2}}{1+(2\beta-1)^2 z^{-2}} \; ; \qquad (20)$$

$$H^{RI1}_{LS1b-LP}(z) = -H^{IR1}_{LS1b-LP}(z) = H^{I}_{LS1b-LP} = \frac{\beta(1-\beta)2z^{-1}}{1+(2\beta-1)^2 z^{-2}} \; ; \qquad (21)$$

$$H^{RR2}_{LS1b-HP}(z) = H^{II2}_{LS1b-HP}(z) = H^{R}_{LS1b-HP} = (1-\beta)\frac{1+(1-2\beta)z^{-2}}{1+(2\beta-1)^2 z^{-2}} \; ; \qquad (22)$$

$$H^{RI2}_{LS1b-HP}(z) = -H^{IR2}_{LS1b-HP}(z) = H^{I}_{LS1b-HP} = \frac{-2z^{-1}\beta(1-\beta)}{1+(2\beta-1)^2 z^{-2}} \; ; \qquad (23)$$

Fig. 6. LS1b orthogonal complex section derivation (Watanabe-Nishihara transformation).

The same approach, when applied to the MHNS real filter-prototype section, produces the orthogonal complex MHNS structure (Stoyanov et al., 1996).

Fig. 7a depicts the worst-case gain-sensitivities for the same pole positions in LS1b and MHNS universal real filter-prototypes. It is apparent that the LS1b real section shows around a hundred times lower sensitivity than the MHNS real structure in almost the entire frequency range – from 0 to $\omega_s/2$. The LS1b-section realizes unity gain on both its outputs, it is canonic with respect to the multipliers and exhibits very low sensitivity in the important applications of narrowband LP and wideband HP filters.

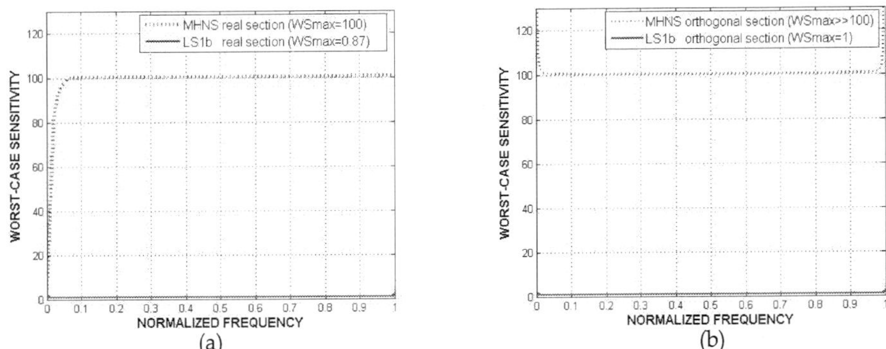

Fig. 7. Worst-case sensitivities for the LS1b and MHNS filters (a) real –prototypes (LP outputs); (b) orthogonal structures for real input – real output BP transfer functions.

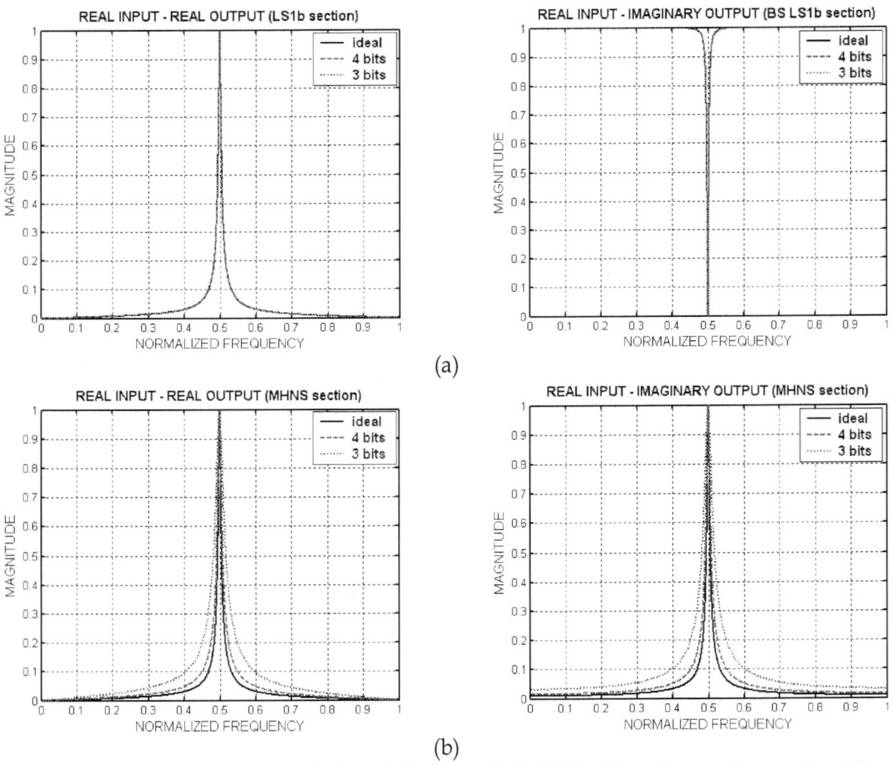

Fig. 8. Magnitude responses of the LS1b (a) and MHNS (b) orthogonal complex filter sections for different word-lengths.

For the same poles (α=0.99 and β=0.005), the worst-case sensitivity is also investigated for the orthogonal complex structures. In Fig. 7b graphical results for the BP transfer functions $H^R_{LS1b-LP}(z)$ and $H^R_{MHNS-LP}(z)$ are presented. The sensitivity of the LP LS1b-based orthogonal section is approximately a hundred times lower over the whole frequency range. Hence, in terms of sensitivity, the orthogonal structures have the same behaviour pattern as their real filter-prototypes.

Some experimental results of the magnitude responses following the quantization of α and β multipliers are shown in Fig. 8. Canonic Sign-Digit Code (CSDC) is used, together with fixed point arithmetic. Narrowband BP and BS orthogonal complex filters are investigated for poles close to the unit circle ($p_{1,2}=\pm j0.99$). The magnitude response of the LS1b orthogonal complex filter does not deteriorate but coincides with the ideal when the word-length is 4, or even 3, bits (Fig. 8a). The MHNS orthogonal structure (Fig. 8b) is more sensitive, and its magnitude response changes significantly, for both 3-bit and 4-bit word-lengths. The pass-band expands while the attenuation in the stop-bands decreases. Hence, the low-sensitivity structure LS1b is a better choice for applications involving analytic signal processing.

2.3. Low-Sensitivity Orthogonal Complex Second-Order IIR Filter Sections

In the odd-order cascade filter structures there is one first-order section, the rest being second-order. These sections may have higher sensitivity than the first-order sections and can be more seriously affected by parasitic effects - the limit cycles and quantization noises can completely disrupt the filtering process. This is why the second-order filter sections are better investigated and a large number of sections already exists.

A very low-sensitivity second-order orthogonal complex filter section, named LS2, is derived and comparatively investigated (Stoyanov et. al., 1997), (Stoyanov et al., 1996). This structure, obtained after the Watanabe-Nishihara circuit transformation is applied to the LS2 real filter-prototype (Fig. 9a), is shown in Fig. 9b. All the transfer functions of the LS2 orthogonal section are of BP type except for (28), which are BS.

The orthogonal complex LS2 filter section is compared with two other often-studied second-order orthogonal complex sections: DF-section (Direct Form) (Eswaran et al., 1991) and MN-section (Minimum Norm) (Nie et al., 1993). Both real filter-prototypes and orthogonal complex filters are investigated, when realizing the same poles of the transfer function, in (Stoyanov et. al., 1997), (Stoyanov et al., 1996).

In Fig. 10a the worst-case gain-sensitivities for the real prototypes are depicted. The results convincingly show that the sensitivity of the LS2 real filter section is thousands of times lower than the sensitivity of the other two real sections. The LS2 section is canonic with respect to the multipliers but a higher number of adders is the price for its very low sensitivity.

In Fig. 10b the worst-case gain-sensitivities of the BP transfer functions when real input and real output are used for the three orthogonal structures are shown. It is clearly seen that the LS2 orthogonal section has a tenfold lower sensitivity compared to the MN and DF orthogonal structures, while using more than three times fewer multipliers. The same results were also obtained for the other transfer functions (Stoyanov et. al., 1997).

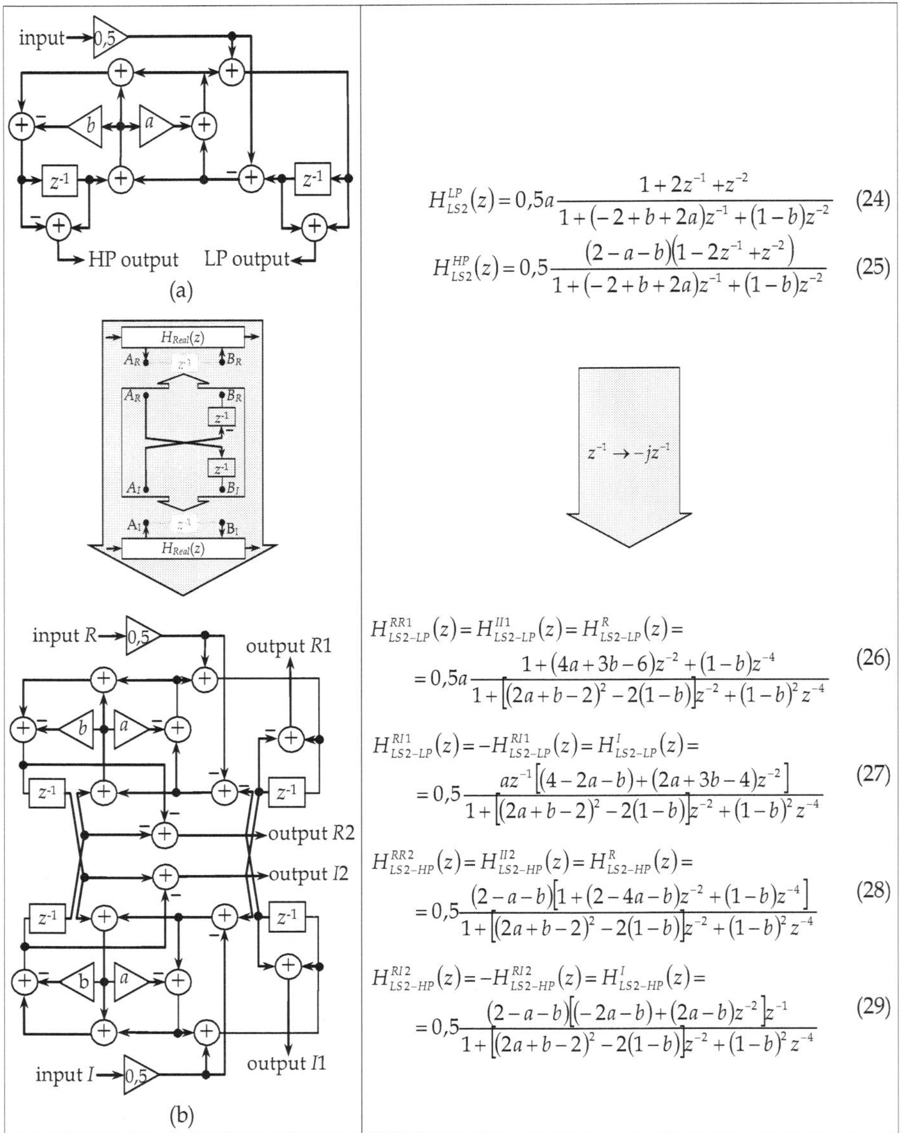

$$H_{LS2}^{LP}(z) = 0{,}5a\,\frac{1 + 2z^{-1} + z^{-2}}{1 + (-2 + b + 2a)z^{-1} + (1 - b)z^{-2}} \qquad (24)$$

$$H_{LS2}^{HP}(z) = 0{,}5\,\frac{(2 - a - b)(1 - 2z^{-1} + z^{-2})}{1 + (-2 + b + 2a)z^{-1} + (1 - b)z^{-2}} \qquad (25)$$

$$z^{-1} \rightarrow -jz^{-1}$$

$$H_{LS2-LP}^{RR1}(z) = H_{LS2-LP}^{II1}(z) = H_{LS2-LP}^{R}(z) =$$
$$= 0{,}5a\,\frac{1 + (4a + 3b - 6)z^{-2} + (1 - b)z^{-4}}{1 + \left[(2a + b - 2)^2 - 2(1 - b)\right]z^{-2} + (1 - b)^2 z^{-4}} \qquad (26)$$

$$H_{LS2-LP}^{RI1}(z) = -H_{LS2-LP}^{RI1}(z) = H_{LS2-LP}^{I}(z) =$$
$$= 0{,}5\,\frac{az^{-1}\left[(4 - 2a - b) + (2a + 3b - 4)z^{-2}\right]}{1 + \left[(2a + b - 2)^2 - 2(1 - b)\right]z^{-2} + (1 - b)^2 z^{-4}} \qquad (27)$$

$$H_{LS2-HP}^{RR2}(z) = H_{LS2-HP}^{II2}(z) = H_{LS2-HP}^{R}(z) =$$
$$= 0{,}5\,\frac{(2 - a - b)\left[1 + (2 - 4a - b)z^{-2} + (1 - b)z^{-4}\right]}{1 + \left[(2a + b - 2)^2 - 2(1 - b)\right]z^{-2} + (1 - b)^2 z^{-4}} \qquad (28)$$

$$H_{LS2-HP}^{RI2}(z) = -H_{LS2-HP}^{RI2}(z) = H_{LS2-HP}^{I}(z) =$$
$$= 0{,}5\,\frac{(2 - a - b)\left[(-2a - b) + (2a - b)z^{-2}\right]z^{-1}}{1 + \left[(2a + b - 2)^2 - 2(1 - b)\right]z^{-2} + (1 - b)^2 z^{-4}} \qquad (29)$$

Fig. 9. Orthogonal complex LS2 second-order filter section derivation.

It is clear from Fig. 10a and 10b that the orthogonal structures inherit the sensitivity of their real filter-prototypes and that the shapes of the worst-case sensitivity curves are transferred from the prototypes to the orthogonal structures, becoming symmetric around the frequency $\omega_s/4$.

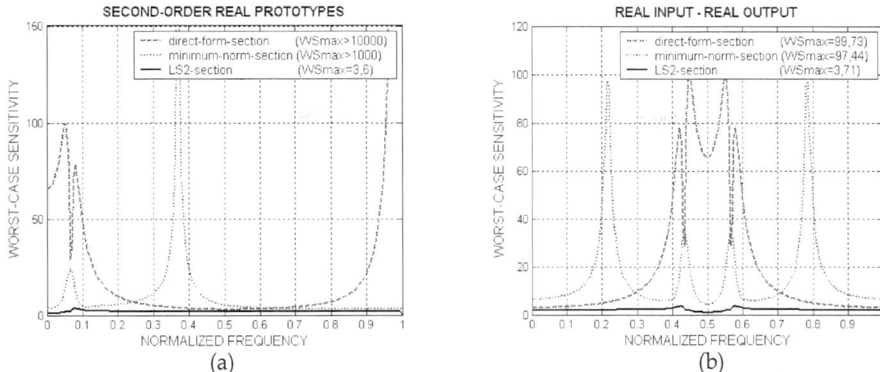

Fig. 10. Worst-case sensitivities for the DF, MN and LS2 filters (a) real –prototypes (LP outputs); (b) orthogonal structures for real input – real output BP transfer functions.

The effect of the coefficient quantization on the magnitude responses is experimentally investigated and some of the results for the three orthogonal structures are shown in Fig. 11.

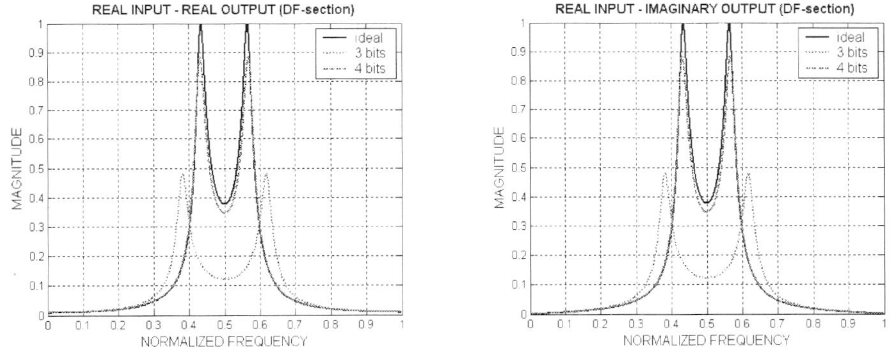

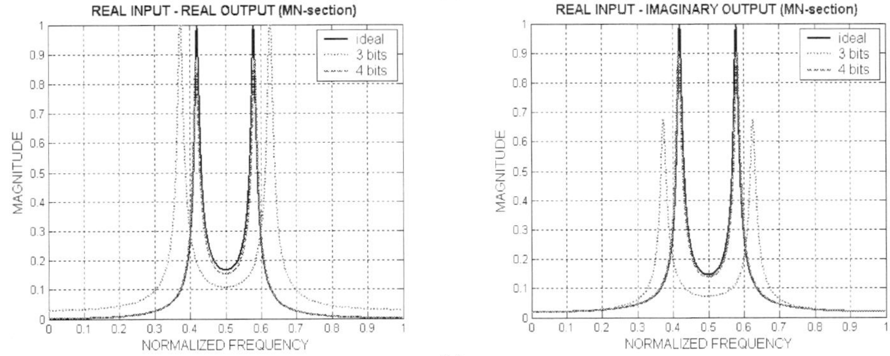

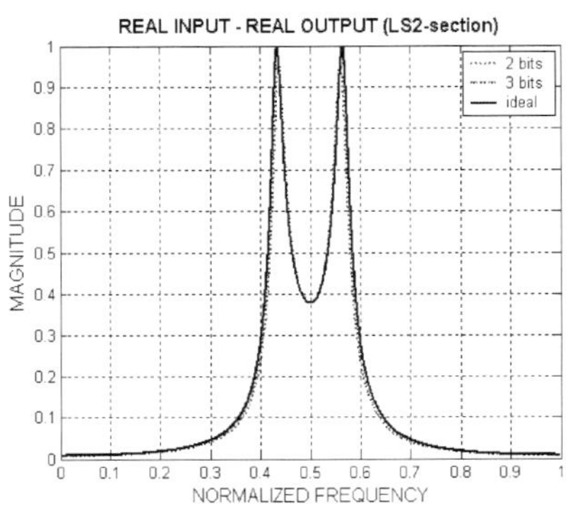

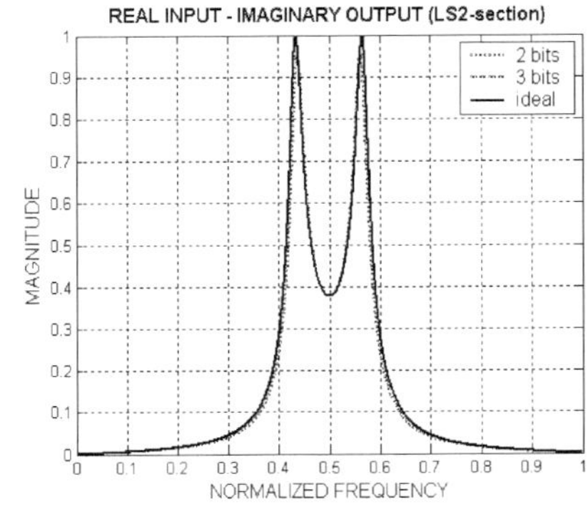

(c)

Fig. 11. Magnitude responses of the second-order orthogonal filter sections for different word-lengths (a) DF; (b) MN; (c) LS2.

It can be seen that the LS2 orthogonal structure has a magnitude response almost coinciding with the ideal one, even when the word-length is reduced to only 3 bits (Fig. 11c), whilst the DF-structure magnitude response is considerably changed when the word-length is 4 bits and deteriorates completely when the quantization is 3 bits (Fig. 11a). Similar behaviour is observed also in the MN-orthogonal filter section (Fig. 11b).

The low-sensitivity orthogonal complex first- and second-order sections presented in this section can be used as building blocks for a higher order cascade digital filter design. Their low sensitivities also ensure the low sensitivity of the cascade filter structure. Low sensitivity reduces the effect of the possible mismatch between the real and imaginary channels of the complex filter, which may have a crucial effect on the circuit performance.

Low-sensitivity orthogonal sections are very useful in analytic signal processing applications, permitting a considerable reduction in both the complexity and cost of the equipment.

3. Variable Complex IIR Digital Filters

3.1 Overview

Variable digital filters (VDF) with independently tunable central frequency ω_c and bandwidth (BW) are needed for many applications such as digital audio and video processing, medical electronics, radar systems, wireless communications etc. An overview of all the main approaches to the designed structures of FIR and IIR digital filters is set out in (Stoyanov & Kawamata, 1997).

Complex coefficient VDFs provide additional advantages in processing both real and complex signals, which are frequently encountered in telecommunications.

Real and complex VDFs are usually designed by employing the all-pass Constantinides transformations, consisting of the replacement of all delay elements in the LP filter-prototype with different all-pass sections. However, when the prototype is of IIR type it is difficult to avoid producing delay-free loops. The best-known method partly solving the problem is that of Mitra, Nevuvo and Roivainen (MNR-method) (Mitra et al., 1990-b), based on parallel all-pass real or complex structures and employing truncated Taylor series expansions of the filter coefficients to calculate them after the all-pass transformations. The method is good for real digital filters but in the case of complex filters there are two series truncations and, as a result, a tuning of the BW without degradation of the magnitude characteristics is possible only over a very narrow frequency band. The other main disadvantage of the method is the high stop-band sensitivity, which causes additional degradation of the filter characteristics. There is yet another approach (Murakoshi et al., 1994), based on a circuit transformation proposed in (Watanabe & Nishihara, 1991), which is able to turn any real circuit into a complex one. Using some new transformations, variable complex BP/BS filters with tunable BW, but with one cut-off frequency remaining fixed, are obtained. The variable BP filter in (Murakoshi et al., 1994) employs too many elements and there are limitations in respect of the BW and requirements for fixing one of the pass-band edges.

This section examines a method of designing complex variable filters with independently tunable central frequency and BW, which has a wider range of tuning of the BW and lower stop-band sensitivity than those in (Mitra et al., 1990-b) and reduced complexity and higher freedom of tuning compared to those in (Murakoshi et al., 1994).

3.2 Variable Complex Filter Design Procedure Outline

For any given specifications or more general requirements for the desired complex BP or BS filter, the design procedure consists of the following steps (Stoyanov & Nikolova, 1999):

1. Shift the given BP or BS arithmetically symmetric magnitude specifications along the frequency axes until the zero frequency coincides with the central frequency ω_c of the specifications, thus turning them into LP or HP type.

2. Apply any possible approximation - classical or more general. As a result an LP or HP real coefficient transfer function is obtained.

3. Factor the transfer function to second-order (and possibly one first-order) terms and design the corresponding LP/HP first and second-order filter sections. For each section apply the Constantinides LP to LP spectral transformation:

$$z^{-1} \rightarrow \frac{z^{-1}-\beta}{1-\beta z^{-1}} = T(z) . \tag{30}$$

This produces a composite multiplier coefficient $\hat{\beta}$ that is a function of β and makes the BW variable.

4. Expand the composite multipliers $\hat{\beta}$ into Taylor series and take only the linear terms, thereby ensuring that the BW variable real LP / HP digital filters will not contain delay-free loops.

5. Using complex transformation (2) $z^{-1} \rightarrow z^{-1}e^{j\theta} = z^{-1}(\cos\theta + j\sin\theta)$ or the circuit transformation (Watanabe & Nishihara, 1991) applied to the designed real filter sections, obtain the complex coefficient structures with variable central frequency ω_c changed independently of θ.

The proposed design procedure produces no delay-free loops, even if only one Taylor series truncation is used. The method permits the design of BP/BS filters of any even order and any possible approximation can be applied. It is also free from BW limitations and from the requirement to fix some of the pass-band edge frequencies encountered in some other design methods.

3.3 High Tuning Accuracy Variable Complex Digital Filters Sections

The Constantinides LP to LP spectral transformation (30), applied on LS1b universal section's LP (18) and HP (19) real transfer functions, transforms them into BW-variable real transfer functions:

$$\hat{H}(z)_{LS1b}^{LP} = \hat{\beta}\frac{1+z^{-1}}{1-\left(1-2\hat{\beta}\right)z^{-1}} ; \qquad \hat{H}(z)_{LS1b}^{HP} = \left(1-\hat{\beta}\right)\frac{1-z^{-1}}{1-\left(1-2\hat{\beta}\right)z^{-1}} . \tag{31}$$

The composite multiplier $\hat{\beta}$ (Fig. 12) is expanded into a Taylor series and only the linear terms are taken:

$$\hat{\beta} = \beta + \gamma c_1 , \text{ where } c_1 = 2\beta(\beta - 1). \tag{32}$$

The BW can be tuned to some extent by changing γ ($\gamma < 0$ - wider BW; $\gamma > 0$ - narrower BW).

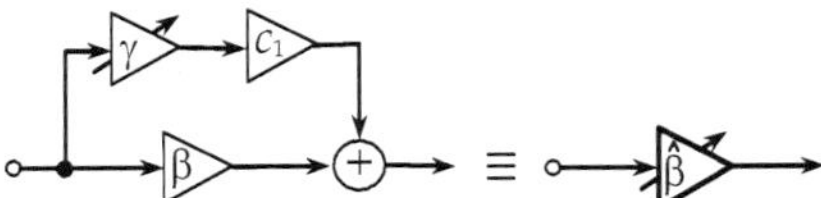

Fig. 12. Composite multiplier $\hat{\beta}$ tuning the BW.

The complex transformation (2) is applied on BW-variable real LP and HP transfer functions (31), thus obtaining the complex coefficient transfer functions, variable in regard to the central frequency ω_c, tuned by changing θ. For the variable complex LS1b digital filter structure (Fig. 13) the variable transfer functions are:

$$\hat{H}_{LS1b-LP}^{RR1}(z) = \hat{H}_{LS1b-LP}^{II1}(z) = \hat{\beta}\frac{1+2\hat{\beta}\cos\theta z^{-1} + \left(2\hat{\beta}-1\right)z^{-2}}{1+2\left(2\hat{\beta}-1\right)\cos\theta z^{-1} + \left(2\hat{\beta}-1\right)^2 z^{-2}} ; \tag{33}$$

$$\hat{H}_{LS1b-LP}^{RI1}(z) = -\hat{H}_{LS1b-LP}^{IR1}(z) = \hat{\beta}\frac{2\left(1-\hat{\beta}\right)\sin\theta z^{-1}}{1+2\left(2\hat{\beta}-1\right)\cos\theta z^{-1} + \left(2\hat{\beta}-1\right)^2 z^{-2}} ; \tag{34}$$

$$\hat{H}_{LS1b-HP}^{RR2}(z) = \hat{H}_{LS1b-HP}^{II2}(z) = \left(1-\hat{\beta}\right)\frac{1-2\left(1-\hat{\beta}\right)\cos\theta z^{-1} + \left(1-2\hat{\beta}\right)z^{-2}}{1+2\left(2\hat{\beta}-1\right)\cos\theta z^{-1} + \left(2\hat{\beta}-1\right)^2 z^{-2}} ; \tag{35}$$

$$\hat{H}_{LS1b-HP}^{RI2}(z) = -\hat{H}_{LS1b-HP}^{IR2}(z) = \left(1-\hat{\beta}\right)\frac{-2\hat{\beta}\sin\theta z^{-1}}{1+2\left(2\hat{\beta}-1\right)\cos\theta z^{-1} + \left(2\hat{\beta}-1\right)^2 z^{-2}} . \tag{36}$$

All of these are of BP type except (35), which are of BS type. The variable complex LS1b digital filter performance is verified by extensive simulations. Fig. 14 shows how the central frequency ω_c of narrowband ($\beta = 0.98$) variable complex BP (33) and BS (35) transfer functions are tuned by changing θ. It is obvious that ω_c can be tuned without any limitations over the entire frequency range.

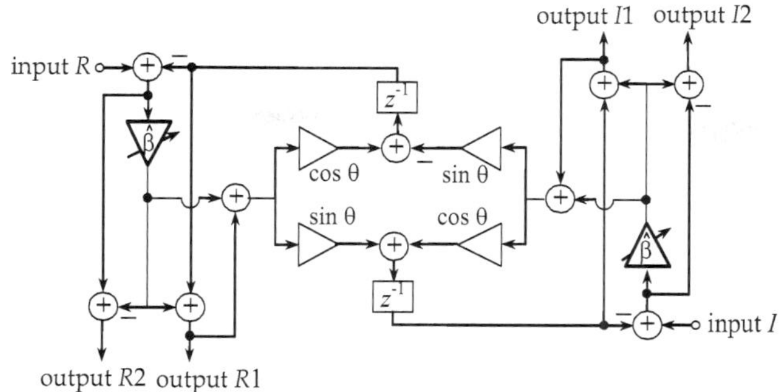

Fig. 13. Variable complex LS1b digital filter structure.

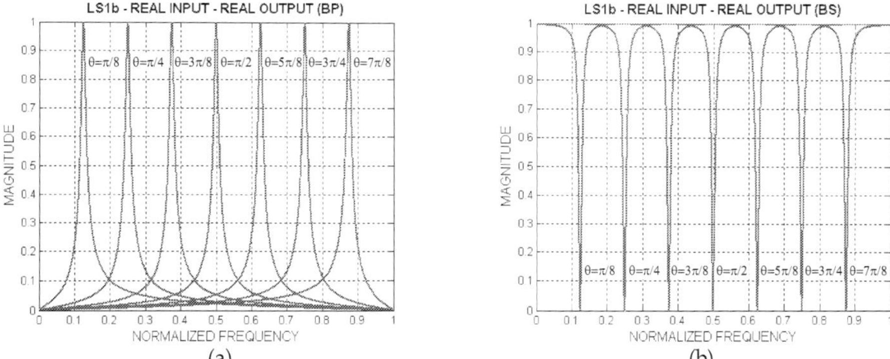

(a)   (b)

Fig. 14. Magnitude responses of variable BP (a) and BS (b) variable complex LS1b section for different values of θ and fixed γ=0.

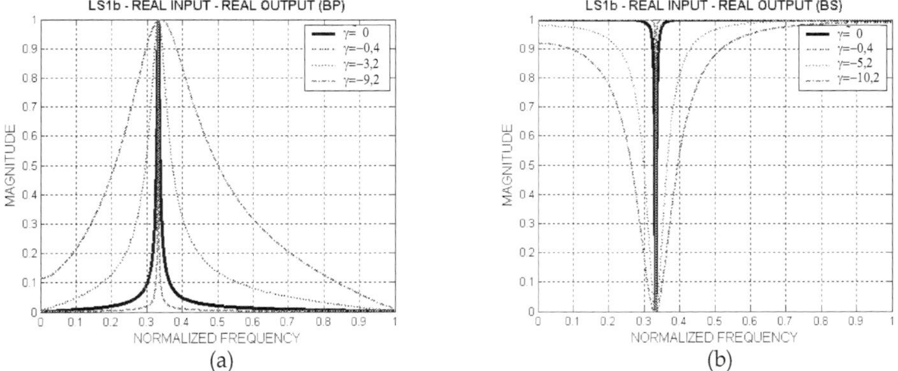

(a)   (b)

Fig. 15. Magnitude responses of variable BP (a) and BS (b) variable complex LS1b section for different values of γ and fixed θ=π/3.

In Fig. 15 the tuning of the BW of the same LS1b by changing γ is demonstrated.

In Fig. 16 the behaviour of the complex LS1b and MHNS variable digital filters in a limited wordlength is compared. It is clear that the characteristics of the MHNS-based complex filter are changed considerably after the multiplier coefficients' truncation to 4 or 3 bits while those of the LS1b-based complex filter remain practically unchanged. This is due to the very low sensitivity inherited from the LS1b prototype.

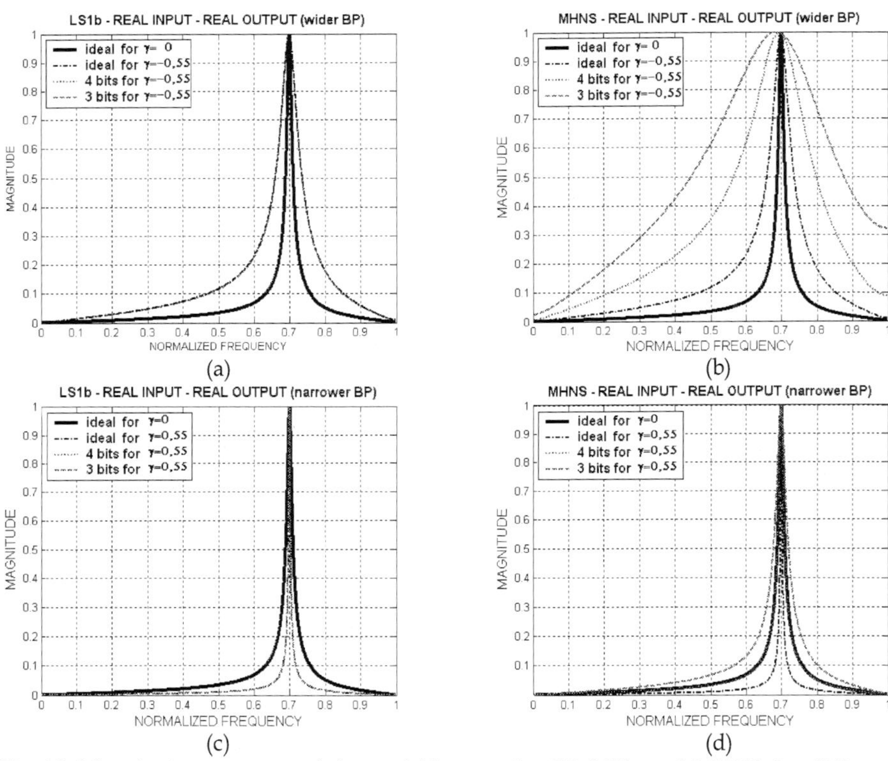

Fig. 16. Magnitude responses of the variable complex BP LS1b and MHNS for different coefficients word-length and BW tuned ($\theta=7\pi/10$).

The improved design method proposed in this section is also applicable to real second-order filter sections – the LS2 (Fig. 9a) and DF (Eswaran et al., 1991). The variable complex LS2 structure is shown in Fig. 17 and the transfer functions that it realizes are:

$$\hat{H}^{RR1}_{LS2-H4}(z) = \hat{H}^{II1}_{LS2-H4}(z) =$$

$$= \frac{\hat{a}}{2}\frac{1+\left[(2\hat{a}+\hat{b})A\right]z^{-1}+\left[2(2\hat{a}+\hat{b}-2)+(2-\hat{b})(A^2-C^2)\right]z^{-2}+\left[(2\hat{a}-\hat{b})A\right]z^{-3}+(1-\hat{b})z^{-4}}{D(z)} \qquad (37)$$

$$\hat{H}^{RI1}_{LS2-HЧ}(z) = -\hat{H}^{IR1}_{LS2-HЧ}(z) = \frac{\hat{a}}{2}\frac{\left(4-2\hat{a}-\hat{b}\right)Cz^{-1} + 2\hat{b}ACz^{-2} + \left(2\hat{a}+3\hat{b}-4\right)Cz^{-3}}{D(z)} \tag{38}$$

$$\hat{H}^{RR2}_{LS2-BЧ}(z) = \hat{H}^{II2}_{LS2-BЧ}(z) =$$
$$= B\frac{1 + \left[\left(2\hat{a}+\hat{b}-4\right)A\right]z^{-1} + \left[-2\left(2\hat{a}+\hat{b}-2\right)+\left(2-\hat{b}\right)\left(A^2-C^2\right)\right]z^{-2} + \left[\left(2\hat{a}+3\hat{b}-4\right)A\right]z^{-3} + \left(1-\hat{b}\right)z^{-4}}{D(z)} \tag{39}$$

$$\hat{H}^{RI2}_{LS2-BЧ}(z) = -\hat{H}^{IR2}_{LS2-BЧ}(z) = B\frac{\left(-2\hat{a}-\hat{b}\right)Cz^{-1} + 2\hat{b}ACz^{-2} + \left(2\hat{a}-\hat{b}\right)Cz^{-3}}{D(z)} \tag{40}$$

where $A=\cos\theta$, $C=\sin\theta$, $B = 0{,}5\left(2-\hat{a}-\hat{b}\right)$, and

$$D(z) = 1 + 2\left(2\hat{a}+\hat{b}-2\right)Az^{-1} + \left[\left(2\hat{a}+\hat{b}-2\right)^2 + 2\left(1-\hat{b}\right)\left(A^2-C^2\right)\right]z^{-2} + 2\left(1-\hat{b}\right)\left(2\hat{a}+\hat{b}-2\right)Az^{-3} + \left(1-\hat{b}\right)^2 z^{-4}.$$

Composite multipliers $\hat{a}$ and $\hat{b}$ have analytical expressions, analogous to (32). The coefficient θ changes the central frequency ω_c, while the BW is changed by γ (the composite multipliers $\hat{a}$ and $\hat{b}$ are functions of γ).

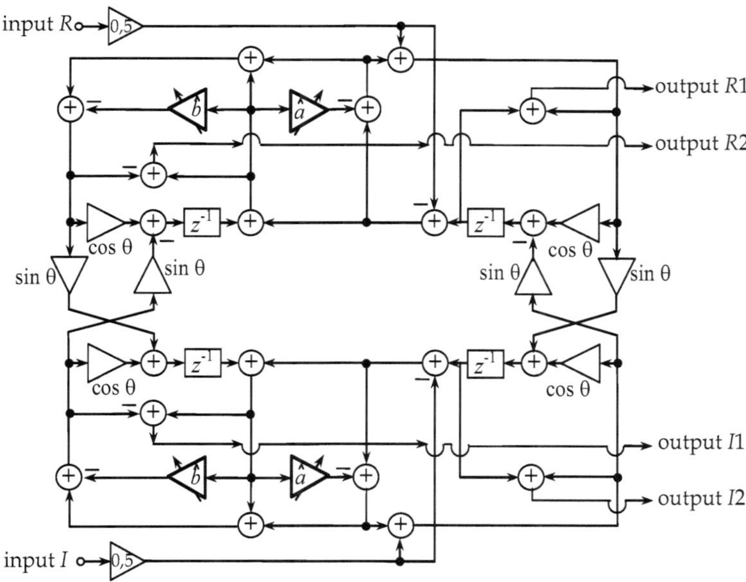

Fig. 17. Variable complex second-order LS2 digital filter section.

Fig. 18 and Fig. 19 show experimental results in regard to the tuning abilities of the BP (37) and BS (39) transfer functions.

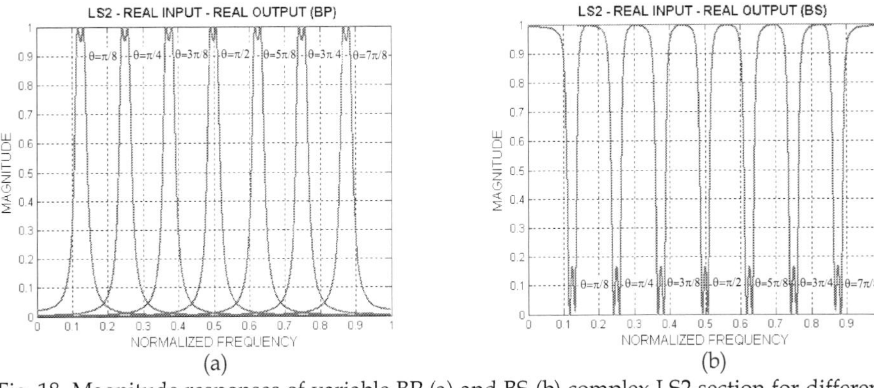

Fig. 18. Magnitude responses of variable BP (a) and BS (b) complex LS2 section for different values of θ (central frequency tuning) and fixed γ=0.

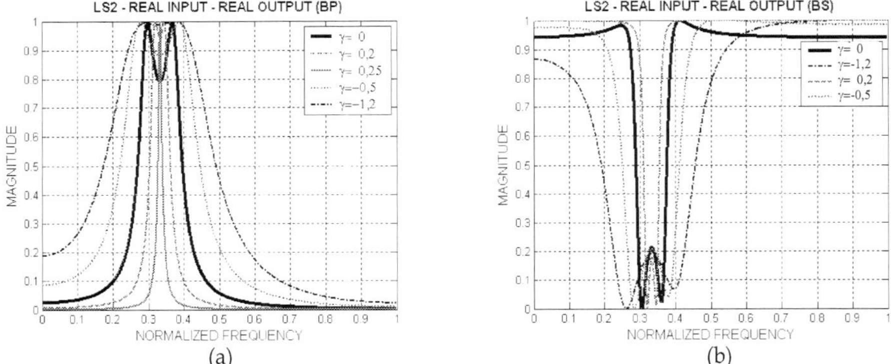

Fig. 19. Magnitude responses of variable BP (a) and BS (b) complex LS2 section for different values of γ (BW tuning) and fixed θ=π/3.

Variable complex LS2 and DF digital filter structures are compared for different word-lengths of the coefficients and the experimental results are depicted in Fig. 20.

The graphics in Fig. 20 show that the low-sensitivity LS2 variable complex section is undoubtedly superior to the DF section when the coefficients are quantized.

The variable complex DF filter does not preserve the magnitude shape either when the BW is made wider or when it is narrower. In addition, the DF-attenuation in the pass-band increases two-fold for a word-length of 3 bits (Fig. 20b,d) whilst in the LS2 structure it remains unchanged throughout the whole frequency range.

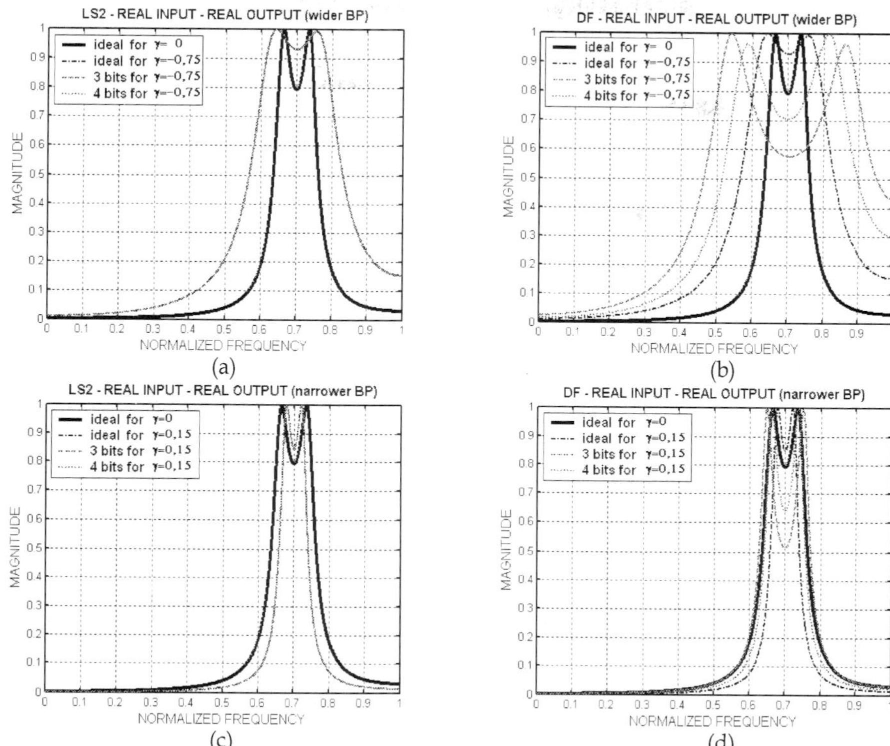

Fig. 20. Magnitude responses of the variable complex BP LS2 and DF for different coefficients word-length and BW tuned ($\theta=7\pi/10$).

3.4 Design Example and Experiments

To demonstrate the advantages of the proposed improved method for designing variable complex filters, a design example will be displayed (Stoyanov & Nikolova, 1999). Two eighth-order variable complex filters will be compared to each other – an LS2-based cascade structure and an MNR-method-based all-pass structure (Mitra et. al., 1990-b).

The required specification is as follows: a variable complex BP filter with pass-band tuned from 0.04 to 0.16 (nominal value 0.1), intermediate band 0.06, R_p = 2 dB, R_s = 40 dB and central frequency ω_c tuned over the entire frequency range $0 \div 1$. Following the procedure given in section 3.2, and using a Chebyshev approximation, a fourth-order LP transfer function is obtained. It is presented as a cascade realization consisting of two second-order terms. Worst-case sensitivities of the LP second-order LS2-based and parallel all-pass structure are examined and the results are depicted in Fig. 21. It is obvious that the LS2-section has about 50 times lower sensitivity in the pass-band than the all-pass structure. On the other hand, in the stop-band the parallel all-pass structure shows lower sensitivity.

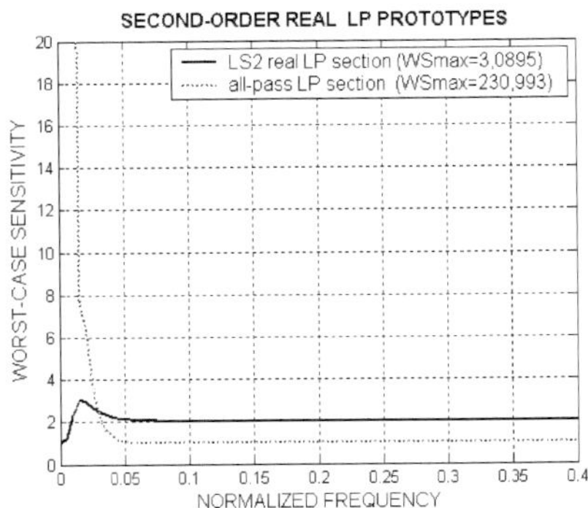

Fig. 21. Worst-case sensitivity of second-order LS2 and all-pass real digital filter sections.

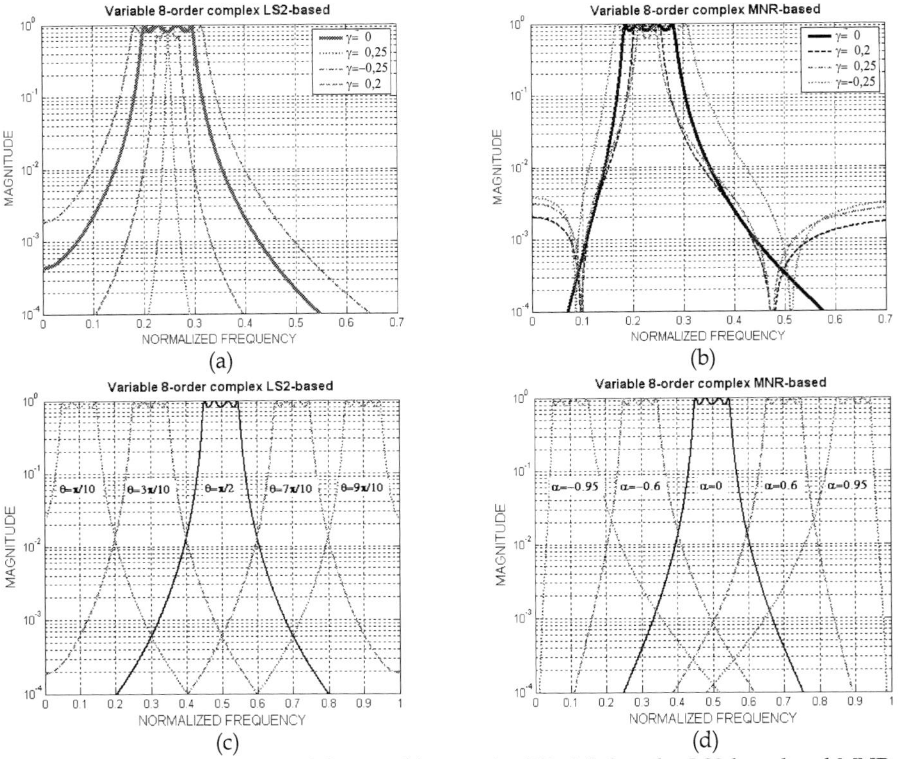

Fig. 22. Magnitude responses of the variable complex BP eighth-order LS2-based and MNR-based filters – BW tuning (a,b – for $\theta=\pi/4$) and central frequency tuning (c,d – for $\gamma=0$).

Then, a variable complex filter using two sections identical to the one in Fig. 17 is designed and the eighth-order BP filter thus obtained is simulated. The results for the BW tuning are shown in Fig. 22a, while those for central frequency tuning are in Fig. 22c. Next, a complex all-pass sections based variable filter, following the MNR-method, was designed and the results from the simulation for the BW and central frequency tuning are shown in Fig. 22b and Fig. 22d respectively. It can be seen that, while the BW of the LS2 filter is tuned without problem over a frequency range much wider than required, the MNR filter turns from a Chebyshev into a kind of elliptic when tuned. The possibilities of tuning in a narrowing direction are very limited (tuning after $\gamma>0.2$ is actually impossible) and the shape of the magnitude varies strongly during the tuning process. As far as the central frequency tuning is concerned, no problems were observed for either filter - as is apparent from Fig. 22c, d. The behaviour of both filters in a limited word-length environment is also investigated and some results are shown in Fig. 23.

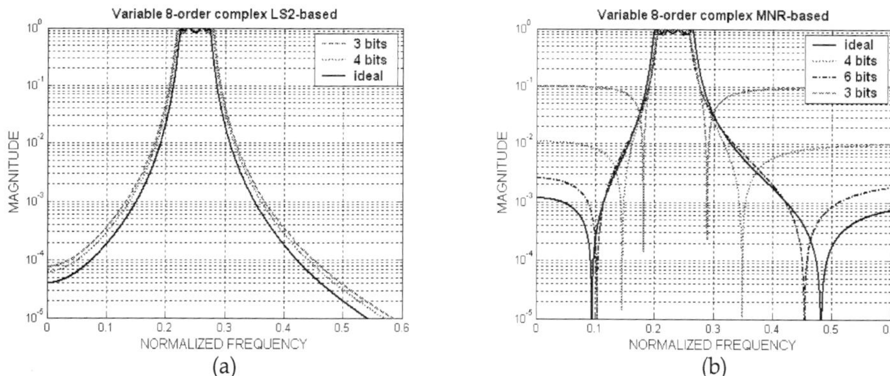

Fig. 23. Magnitude responses of the variable complex BP eighth-order LS2-based (a) and MNR-based (b) filters for different coefficients word-length ($\gamma=0.15$; $\theta=\pi/4$).

While the LS2-based filter behaves well with 3-bits word-length, the magnitude response of the MNR-filter is strongly degraded even with 6-bit words, due to the higher sensitivity of the LP-prototype (Fig. 21) and the double usage of Taylor series truncation. Despite the lower sensitivity of the real all-pass structure in the stop-band (Fig. 21), the magnitude response of the obtained MNR-variable complex filter is completely degraded even for stop-band frequencies (Fig. 23b and Fig. 23b). The explanation lies in the imperfection of the MNR-method with respect to the variable complex filter design.

The complex coefficient variable BP and BS filters designed using the improved method examined in this section have a BW and central frequency which can be independently tuned with high accuracy. The possible BW tuning range is wider compared to that of the other known methods. The filter sections used have lower sensitivity and thus are less susceptible to the inaccuracies due to series truncations. The accuracy of tuning is higher and it is possible to use coefficients with a shorter word-length, thereby decreasing the power consumption and the volume of computations for both the filtering and updating of the coefficients. Similar results are obtained for other efficient IIR digital filter structures based on sensitivity minimization design, such as efficient multiplierless realizations and fractional-delay filters (Stoyanov et al., 2007).

4. Adaptive Complex Systems

4.1 Outline and Applications

FIR digital filter structures are usually preferred as the building blocks in adaptive systems, including complex ones, due to their absolute stability; however the use of IIR filters is increasing, owing to their definite advantages. A number of IIR adaptive complex filters were put forward as possible solutions to the problems typically encountered in many telecommunications applications dealing with the detection, tracking and suppression / elimination of complex signals embedded in noise. Wideband wireless communication systems are very sensitive to narrowband interference (NBI), which can even prevent the system operating (Giorgetti et al., 2005). For NBI suppression in quadrature phase shift keying (QPSK) spread-spectrum communication systems, an adaptive complex notch filter is used (Jiang et al., 2002).

Discrete multi-tone (DMT) modulation systems, such as DMT VDSL, are very sensitive to radio-frequency interference (RFI) and RFI-suppression has been discussed in many works, such as (Starr et al., 2003) (Yaohui et al., 2001). OFDM is the other leading technology for many broadband communication systems, such as MB-OFDM ultra wideband systems (UWB). As a result of NBI, signal-to-interference ratio (SIR) dropping can seriously degrade the characteristics of these systems (Carlemalm et al., 2004).

The problem of interference is encountered in various kinds of broadband telecommunications systems but the methods for interference suppression proposed so far can be broadly categorized into two approaches. The first concerns various frequency excision methods, whilst the second relates to so-called cancellation techniques. These techniques aim to eliminate or reduce interference in the received signal by the use of adaptive notch filtering-based methods or NBI identification (Baccareli et al., 2002).

This section deals with adaptive complex filtering as a noise-cancellation method associated with analytic signals and complex NBI suppression. An adaptive complex system is developed, based on the very low-sensitivity variable complex filters studied in section 3. The quality of adaptive filtering is influenced by two major factors – the efficiency and convergence of the adaptive algorithm, and the properties of the adaptive structure. Most research studies barely consider the details of adaptive filter realizations and their properties, although a lot has been done to improve the adaptive algorithms. The efficiency of adaptive complex filter sections and their beneficial properties considerably influence the adaptive process.

4.2 Adaptive Complex Systems Design

In Fig. 24 a block-diagram of an adaptive complex system is shown (Iliev et al., 2004).

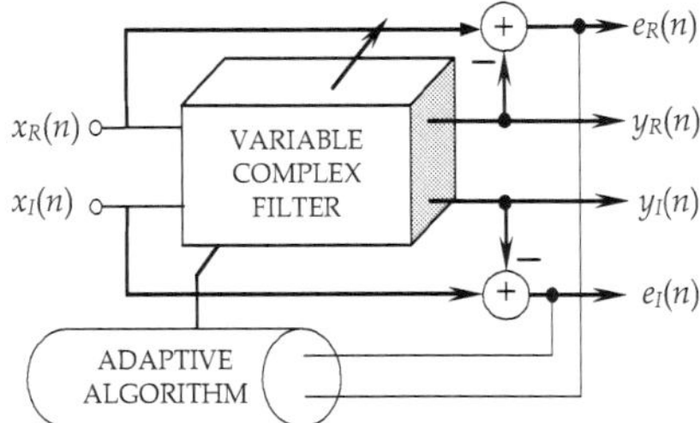

Fig. 24. Block-diagram of a BP/BS adaptive complex filter section.

The adaptive complex system design starts with a description of input-output equations. The BP/BS variable complex LS1b-based filter is considered and its BP real output is as follows:

$$y_R(n) = y_{R1}(n) + y_{R2}(n) , \tag{41}$$

where

$$\begin{aligned} y_{R1}(n) &= -2(2\beta-1)\cos\theta(n)y_{R1}(n-1) - (2\beta-1)^2 y_{R1}(n-2) + \\ &+ 2\beta x_R(n) + 4\beta^2\cos\theta(n)x_R(n-1) + 2\beta(2\beta-1)x_R(n-2) \end{aligned} ; \tag{42}$$

$$\begin{aligned} y_{R2}(n) &= -2(2\beta-1)\cos\theta(n)y_{R2}(n-1) - (2\beta-1)^2 y_{R2}(n-2) - \\ &- 4\beta(1-\beta)\sin\theta(n)x_I(n-1). \end{aligned} \tag{43}$$

The imaginary output is given by the following equation:

$$y_I(n) = y_{I1}(n) + y_{I2}(n) , \tag{44}$$

where

$$\begin{aligned} y_{I1}(n) &= -2(2\beta-1)\cos\theta(n)y_{I1}(n-1) - (2\beta-1)^2 y_{I1}(n-2) + \\ &+ 4\beta(1-\beta)\sin\theta(n)x_R(n-1) \end{aligned} ; \tag{45}$$

$$\begin{aligned} y_{I2}(n) &= -2(2\beta-1)\cos\theta(n)y_{I2}(n-1) - (2\beta-1)^2 y_{I2}(n-2) + \\ &+ 2\beta x_I(n) + 4\beta^2\cos\theta(n)x_I(n-1) + 2\beta(2\beta-1)x_I(n-2). \end{aligned} \tag{46}$$

For the BS variable complex LS1b filter there is a real output:

$$e_R(n) = x_R(n) - y_R(n) , \tag{47}$$

and an imaginary output:

$$e_I(n) = x_I(n) - y_I(n) . \tag{48}$$

The cost-function is the power of BS filter output signal:

$$[e(n)e^*(n)] , \tag{49}$$

where

$$e(n) = e_R(n) + je_I(n) . \tag{50}$$

At this stage an adaptive algorithm should be applied and the Least Mean Squares (LMS) algorithm is chosen since it combines low computational complexity and relatively fast adaptation rate. The LMS algorithm updates the filter coefficient responsible for the central frequency as follows:

$$\theta(n+1) = \theta(n) + \mu\,\mathrm{Re}[e(n)\dot{y}^*(n)] , \tag{51}$$

where μ is the step-size controlling the speed of convergence, (*) denotes complex-conjugate, $y'(n)$ is a derivative of $y(n) = y_R(n) + jy_I(n)$ with respect to the coefficient that is the subject of adaptation:

$$y'_R(n) = 2(2\beta - 1)\sin\theta(n)y_{R1}(n-1) - 4\beta^2\sin\theta(n)x_R(n-1) + \\ + 2(2\beta - 1)\sin\theta(n)y_{R2}(n-1) - 4\beta(1-\beta)\cos\theta(n)x_I(n-1)$$ (52)

and

$$y'_I(n) = 2(2\beta - 1)\sin\theta(n)y_{I1}(n-1) + 4\beta(1-\beta)\cos\theta(n)x_R(n-1) + \\ + 2(2\beta - 1)\sin\theta(n)y_{I2}(n-1) - 4\beta^2\sin\theta(n)x_I(n-1).$$ (53)

The adaptive process for the BP/BS variable complex second-order LS2-based filter can be similarly defined (Iliev et al., 2006).
In order to ensure the stability of the adaptive algorithm, the range of the step size μ should be set according to (Douglas, 1999):

$$0 < \mu < \frac{P}{N\sigma^2}.$$ (54)

In this case N is the filter order, σ^2 is the power of the signal $y'(n)$ and P is a constant which depends on the statistical characteristics of the input signal. In most practical situations P is approximately equal to 0.1.

4.3 Adaptive Complex Filtering Investigations

The good performance of low-sensitivity complex filters in finite word-length environments and their low coefficient sensitivities significantly improve the quality of the adaptive filtering process and this will be experimentally confirmed. The narrowband low-sensitivity adaptive complex filters are examined for elimination / enhancement of narrowband complex signals. By changing the transformation factor θ, the central frequency ω_c of the complex filter can be tuned over the entire frequency range adaptively. The accuracy of tuning is very high and it is possible to use coefficients with shorter word-length, thus decreasing the power consumption for both the adaptive filtering and the updating of the coefficients. The convergence of the adaptive algorithm for the developed low-sensitivity variable complex filters is investigated experimentally and the efficiency of the adaptation is demonstrated.
The experiments are conducted in three basic set-ups. First, we test the convergence speed of the adaptive complex filter sections with respect to different values of step size μ. In Fig. 25 the learning curves of this adaptation are shown. The input signal is a mixture of white noise and complex (analytic) sinusoid with frequency $f = 0.25$. It can be observed that as the step-size increases a higher speed of adaptation is achieved. It obvious that the adaptive complex filter based on LS2 reaches steady state in the case of $\mu=0.005$ after about 100 iterations (Fig. 25b), which is considerably less than the number of iterations needed for the filter based on LS1b (approximately 2000, Fig. 25a).

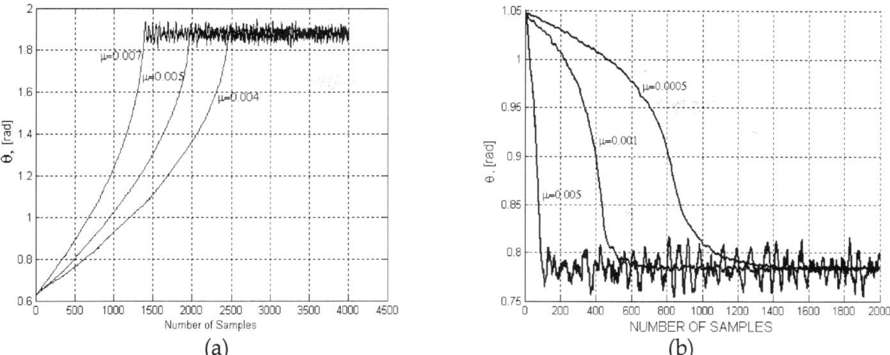

Fig. 25. Trajectories of the coefficient θ for different step size μ for the (a) LS1b-based; (b) LS2-based complex filter section.

In Fig. 26 results for different filter BW are presented. It is clear that narrowing the filter BW slows the process of convergence. It should be mentioned that if some other (non low-sensitivity) adaptive complex sections were to be used, the coefficient β could not take values smaller than -0.1 without destroying the magnitude shape. Thus a faster convergence of the adaptive filtering can be obtained because of the wider BW. Comparing LS1b and LS2 realizations it can be concluded that, for the same BW, the LS2 filter converges 5 times faster.

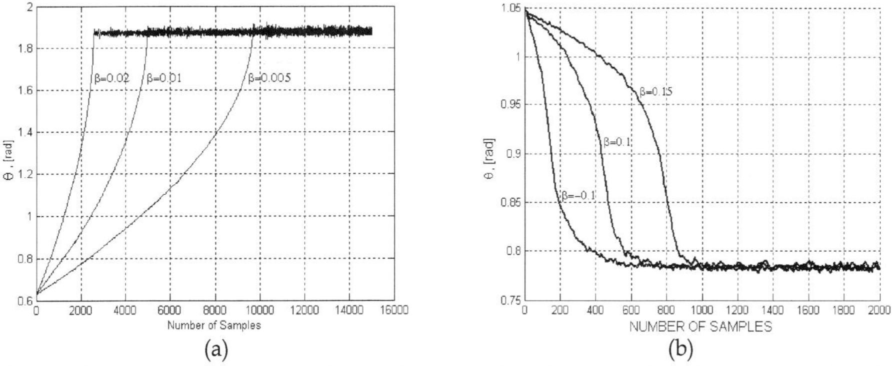

Fig. 26. Trajectories of the coefficient θ for different BW β for the (a) LS1b-based; (b) LS2-based complex filter section.

Finally, Fig. 27 shows the behaviour of LS1b and LS2 filters for a wide range of frequencies. In all cases the low-sensitivity filter structures converge to the proper frequency value.

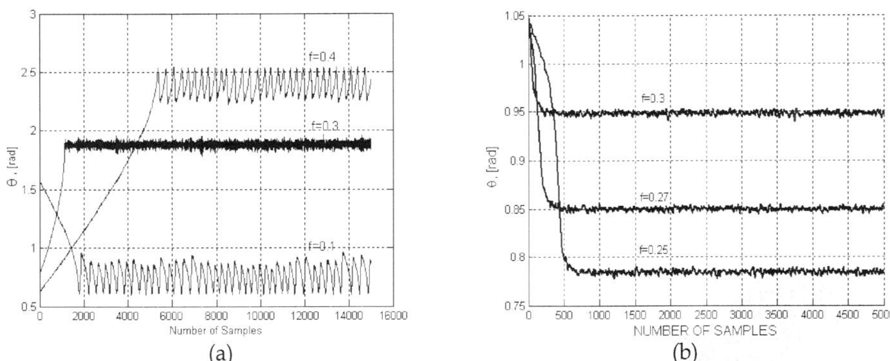

Fig. 27. Trajectories of the coefficient θ for different frequency f for the (a) LS1b-based; (b) LS2-based complex filter section.

4.4 Adaptive Complex Filters Applications

The first- and second-order low-sensitivity adaptive complex filter sections examined in this section are suitable for both independent use and as building blocks for the higher order cascade or parallel realizations needed in many telecommunications applications.

Adaptive complex narrowband filtering is used for noise cancellation in an OFDM transmission scheme and shows that better SNR and bit-error rate (BER) performance can be achieved (Iliev et al., 2006). Another application of low-sensitivity narrowband adaptive complex filtering is NBI cancellation in MB-OFDM systems (Nikolova et al., 2006), multi-inputs multi-outputs (MIMO) OFDM systems (Iliev et al., 2009), and DMT VDSL systems (Ovtcharov et al., 2009-a). An advantage of the proposed scheme is that the adaptive complex system is universal, realizing BP and BS outputs simultaneously. Besides being suppressed, the NBI can also be monitored and the adaptive complex system can be deactivated when the interference disappears or is reduced to an acceptable level. In (Iliev et al., 2010) a method is proposed for NBI suppression in MIMO MB-OFDM UWB communication systems, using adaptive complex narrowband filtering based on the LS1b variable complex section. A comparative study shows that the NBI method is an optimal solution that offers a trade-off between outstanding NBI suppression efficiency and computational complexity. Various problems with OFDM systems and their possible solutions are summarized in (Nikolova et al., 2009); adaptive complex filtering is one of the most efficient methods for noise suppression in these systems (Nikolova et al., 2010). Adaptive complex filtering is an accurate and robust approach for RFI suppression in UWB communication systems (Ovtcharov et al., 2009-b) and GDSL MIMO systems (Poulkov et al., 2009).

5. Conclusions

Complex coefficient digital filters are used in many DSP applications relating to complex signal representations. Orthogonal signals occur often in different telecommunications applications and can be effectively processed by a special class of complex filters, the so-called orthogonal complex filters. A method for designing these filters is examined in this chapter and first- and second-order IIR orthogonal complex sections are synthesized. They can be used as filter sections for designing cascade structures and also as single filter structures. The derived orthogonal sections are canonic very low-sensitivity structures which permit the use of a very short coefficient word-length, leading to higher accuracy, lower power consumption and simple implementation.

An improved method for designing variable complex filters is proposed. It is possible to use any classical or more general approximation, producing transfer function of any even order. The structures avoid delay-free loops and have a canonical number of elements. The variable complex filters designed with the improved method have central frequency and BW that are tuned independently and very accurately over a wide frequency range. Very narrowband BP/BS structures can be developed, such as the low-sensitivity LS1b and LS2 variable complex sections. Compared to other often-used methods they show higher freedom of tuning, reduced complexity and lower stop-band sensitivity.

A BP/BS adaptive complex system is developed based on the derived narrowband LS1b and LS2 variable complex filters, and the simple but efficient LMS adaptive algorithm. Both low-sensitivity adaptive complex sections are examined for suppression/enhancement of narrowband complex signals. They demonstrate excellent abilities and are appropriate to be applied in a number of telecommunications systems where the problem of eliminating complex noise, RFI or NBI exists.

Acknowledgment

This work was supported by the Bulgarian National Science Fund – Grant No. ДО-02-135/2008 "Research on Cross Layer Optimization of Telecommunication Resource Allocation" and by the Technical University of Sofia (Bulgaria) Research Funding, Grant No. 102НИ065-07 "Computer System Development for Design, Investigation and Optimization of Selective Communication Circuits".

6. References

Baccareli, E.; Baggi, M. & Tagilione, L. (2002). A novel approach to in-band interference mitigation in ultra wide band radio systems. *IEEE Conf. on Ultra Wide Band Systems and Technologies*, pp. 297-301, 7 Aug. 2002.

Bello, P. A. (1963). Characterization of randomly time-variant linear channels, *IEEE Trans. on Commun. Syst.*, vol. CS-11, pp. 360-393, Dec. 1963.

Carlemalm, C.; Poor, H. V. & Logothetis, A. (2004). Suppression of multiple narrowband interferers in a spread-spectrum communication system. *IEEE Journal Select. Areas Commun.*, vol. 3, No.5, pp. 1431-1436, 2004.

Crystal, T. & Ehrman, L. (1968). The design and applications of digital filters with complex coefficients, *IEEE Trans. on Audio and Electroacoustics*, vol. 16, Issue: 3, pp. 315-320, Sept. 1968.

Douglas, S. (1999). Adaptive filtering, in *Digital signal processing handbook*, D. Williams & V. Madisetti, Eds., Boca Raton: CRC Press LLC, pp. 451-619, 1999.

Eswaran, C.; Manivannan, K. & Antoniou, A. (1991). An alternative sensitivity measure for designing low-sensitivity digital biquads, *IEEE Trans. on Circuits Syst.*, vol. CAS-38, No.2, pp. 218 - 221, Feb. 1991.

Giorgetti, A.; Chiani, M. & Win, M. Z. (2005). The effect of narrowband interference on wideband wireless communication systems. *IEEE Trans. on Commun.*, vol. 53, No. 12, pp. 2139-2149, 2005.

Helstrom, C. W. (1960). *Statistical theory of signal detection*, Pergamon, New York, 1960.

Iliev, G.; Nikolova, Z.; Poulkov, V. & Ovtcharov, M. (2010). Narrowband interference suppression for MIMO MB-OFDM UWB communication systems, *Intern. Journal on Advances in Telecommunications (IARIA Journals)*, ISSN: 1942-2601, vol. 3, No. 1&2, pp. 1-8, 2010.

Iliev, G.; Nikolova, Z.; Poulkov, V. & Stoyanov, G. (2006). Noise cancellation in OFDM systems using adaptive complex narrowband IIR filtering, *IEEE Intern. Conf. on Communications (ICC-2006)*, Istanbul, Turkey, pp. 2859 – 2863, 11-15 June 2006.

Iliev, G.; Nikolova, Z.; Stoyanov, G. & Egiazarian, K. (2004). Efficient design of adaptive complex narrowband IIR filters, *Proc. of XII European Signal Proc. Conf. (EUSIPCO'04)*, pp. 1597-1600, Vienna, Austria, 6-10 Sept. 2004.

Iliev, G.; Ovtcharov, M.; Poulkov, V. & Nikolova, Z. (2009). Narrowband interference suppression for MIMO OFDM systems using adaptive filter banks, *The 5th Intern. Wireless Communications and Mobile Computing Conf. (IWCMC 2009) MIMO Systems Symp.*, pp. 874–877, Leipzig, Germany, 21-24 June 2009.

Jiang, H.; Nishimura, S. & Hinamoto, T. (2002). Steady-state analysis of complex adaptive IIR notch filter and its application to QPSK communication systems. *IEICE Trans. Fundamentals*, vol. E85-A, No. 5, pp. 1088-1095, May 2002.

Martin, K. (2003). Complex signal processing is not – complex, *Proc. of the 29th European Conf. on Solid-State Circuits (ESSCIRC'03)*, pp. 3-14, Estoril, Portugal, 16-18 Sept. 2003.

Martin, K. (2005). Approximation of complex IIR bandpass filters without arithmetic symmetry, *IEEE Trans. on Circuits Syst. I: Regular Papers*, vol. 52, No. 4, pp. 794 – 803, Apr. 2005.

Mitra, S. K.; Hirano, S.; Nishimura & Sugahara, K. (1990). Design of digital bandpass/bandstop filters with independent tuning characteristics, *Frequenz*, vol. 44, No. 3-4, pp. 117- 121, 1990.

Mitra, S. K.; Neuvo, Y. & Roivainen, H. (1990). Design of recursive digital filters with variable characteristics, *Intern. Journal of Circuit Theory and Appl.*, vol. 18, No. 2, pp. 107-119, 1990.

Murakoshi, N.; Nishihara, A. & Watanabe, E. (1994). Synthesis of variable filters with complex coefficients, *Electronics and Commun. in Japan*, Part 3, vol. 77, No. 5, pp. 46-57, 1994.

Nie, H.; Raghuramireddy, D. & Unbehauen, R. (1993). Normalized minimum norm digital filter structure: a basic building block for processing real and complex sequences, *IEEE Trans. on Circuits Syst.-II: Analog and Digital Signal Proc.*, vol.40, No.7, pp. 449 - 451, July 1993.

Nikolova Z.; Iliev, G.; Ovtcharov, M. & Poulkov, V. (2009). Narrowband interference suppression in wireless OFDM systems, *African Journal of Information and Communication Technology*, vol. 5, No. 1, pp. 30-42, March 2009.

Nikolova, Z.; Poulkov, V.; Iliev, G. & Egiazarian, K. (2010). New adaptive complex IIR filters and their application in OFDM systems, *Journal of Signal, Image and Video Proc., Springer*, vol. 4, No. 2, pp. 197-207, June, 2010, ISSN: 1863-1703.

Nikolova, Z.; Poulkov, V.; Iliev, G. & Stoyanov, G. (2006). Narrowband interference cancellation in multiband OFDM systems, *3rd Cost 289 Workshop "Enabling Technologies for B3G Systems"*, pp. 45-49, Aveiro, Portugal, 12-13 July 2006.

Nishihara, A. (1980). Realization of low-sensitivity digital filters with minimal number of multipliers, *Proc. of 14th Asilomar Conf. on Cir., Syst. and Computers*, Pacific Globe, California, USA, pp. 219-223, Nov.1980.

Ovtcharov, M.; Poulkov, V.; Iliev, G. & Nikolova, Z. (2009), Radio frequency interference suppression in DMT VDSL systems, *"E+E"*, ISSN:0861-4717, pp. 42 - 49, 9-10/2009.

Ovtcharov, M.; Poulkov, V.; Iliev, G. & Nikolova, Z. (2009). Narrowband interference suppression for IEEE UWB channels, *The Fourth Intern. Conf. on Digital Telecommunications (ICDT 2009)*, pp. 43–47, Colmar, France, July 20-25, 2009.

Poulkov, V.; Ovtcharov, M.; Iliev, G. & Nikolova, Z. (2009). Radio frequency interference mitigation in GDSL MIMO systems by the use of an adaptive complex narrowband filter bank, *Intern. Conf. on Telecomm. in Modern Satellite, Cable and Broadcasting Services - TELSIKS-2009*, pp. 77 – 80, Nish, Serbia, 7-9 Oct. 2009.

Proakis, J. G. & Manolakis, D. K. (2006). *Digital signal processing*, Prentice Hall; 4th edition, ISBN-10: 0131873741.

Sim, P. K. (1987). SSB generation using complex digital filters, *IASTED Intern. Symp. on Signal Proc. and its Appl. (ISSPA'87)*, Brisbane, Australia, pp. 206 - 211, 24-28 Aug. 1987.

Starr, T.; Sorbara, M.; Cioffi, J. & Silverman, P. (2003). *DSL advances*, Prentice Hall, 2003.

Stoyanov, G. & Kawamata, M. (1997). Variable digital filters. *Journal of Signal Proc.*, vol. 1, No. 4, pp. 275- 290, July 1997.

Stoyanov, G.; Kawamata, M. & Valkova, Z. (1996) Very low-sensitivity complex coefficients bandpass filter sections, *Technical reports of IEICE. Sc. Meeting on Digital Signal Proc.*, Tokyo, Japan, vol. 96, No. 424, pp. 39-45, 13 Dec. 1996.

Stoyanov, G.; Kawamata, M. & Valkova, Z. (1997). New first and second-order very low-senitivity bandpass/bandstop complex digital filter sections, *Proc. IEEE Region 10th Annual Conf. "TENCON'97"*, Brisbane, Australia, vol.1, pp.61-64, 2-4 Dec. 1997.

Stoyanov, G. & Nikolova, Z. (1999). Improved method of design of complex coefficients variable IIR digital filters, *TELECOM'99*, Varna, Bulgaria, vol. 2, pp. 40-46, 26-28 Oct. 1999.

Stoyanov, G.; Nikolova, Z.; Ivanova, K. & Anzova, V. (2007). Design and realization of efficient IIR digital filter structures based on sensitivity minimizations, *Intern. Conf. on Telecomm. in Modern Satellite, Cable and Broadcasting Services - TELSIKS-2007*, vol.1, pp. 299 – 308, Nish, Serbia, 26 - 28 Sept. 2007.

Takahashi, A.; Nagai, N. & Miki, N. (1992). Complex digital filters with asymmetrical characteristics, *Proc. of IEEE Intern. Symp. on Circuits and Syst. (ISCAS'92)*, vol. 5, pp. 2421 - 2424, San Diego, USA, June 1992.

Topalov, I. & Stoyanov, G. (1990). Low-sensitivity universal first-order digital filter sections without limit cycles, *Electronics Letters*, vol. 26, No.1, pp. 25-26, January 1990.

Watanabe, E. & Nishihara, A. (1991). A synthesis of a class of complex digital filters based on circuit transformation, *IEICE Trans. Fundamentals*, vol. E74, No.11, pp. 3622-3624, Nov. 1991.

Woodward, P. M. (1960). *Probability and information theory with application to radar*, Pergamon, New York, 1960.

Yaohui, L.; Laakso, T. I. & Diniz, P. S. R. (2001). Adaptive RFI cancellation in VDSL systems. *European Conf. on Circuit Theory and Design (ECCTD'01)*, Espoo, Finland, pp. III-217-III-220, 28-31 Aug. 2001.

10

Low-Complexity and High-Speed Constant Multiplications for Digital Filters Using Carry-Save Arithmetic

Oscar Gustafsson and Lars Wanhammar
Linköping University
Sweden

1. Introduction

In many digital filter implementations the filter coefficients are known beforehand. Based on this fact, the problem of constant multiplications, replacing general multipliers with shifts and adders[1], has been an active research topic for a few decades. Much work has been done on finding algorithms and filter coefficients where the filter coefficients can be represented using few signed-power-of-two (SPT) terms (Lim, 1990; Yli-Kaakinen & Saramäki, 2007). Furthermore, there has been work on realizing constant multipliers using few adders (Dempster & Macleod, 1994; Gustafsson et al., 2006; Thong & Nicolici, 2009). Additionally, mainly motivated by transposed direct form FIR filters, as shown in Fig. 1, several algorithms have been proposed for utilizing redundancies when a single data is multiplied with several constant coefficients, known as multiple constant multiplication (Aksoy et al., 2010; Dempster & Macleod, 1995; Gustafsson, 2007; Hartley, 1996; Potkonjak et al., 1996; Voronenko & Püschel, 2007).

Most of this previous work has considered carry-propagation adders (CPAs), i.e., adders with two inputs and one output, as shown in Fig. 2. Even though there has been many different techniques proposed to accelerate the carry-propagation, these typically lead to an increased area and power consumption. For high-speed implementations, an alternative is to use carry-save adders (CSAs). These adders do not propagate the carry, but instead have two outputs, one for the sum and one for the carry. Furthermore, as no carries are propagated, the adder can use the carry-input as a third input. A carry-save adder is illustrated in Fig. 3.

The mapping between CPAs and CSAs is not consistent (Gustafsson, 2008). Hence, there is a need to solve the CSA constant multiplications using specialized algorithms. The inconsistency is illustrated in Fig. 4, where a multiple constant multiplication for the coefficients 3, 11,

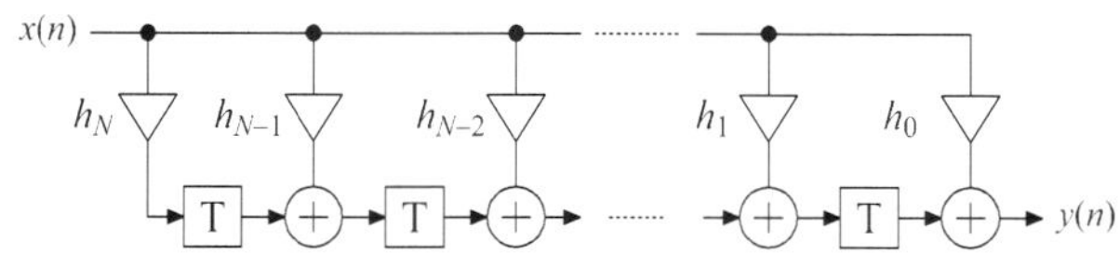

Fig. 1. Transposed direct form FIR filter.

---

[1] Adders refers to both adders and subtractors.

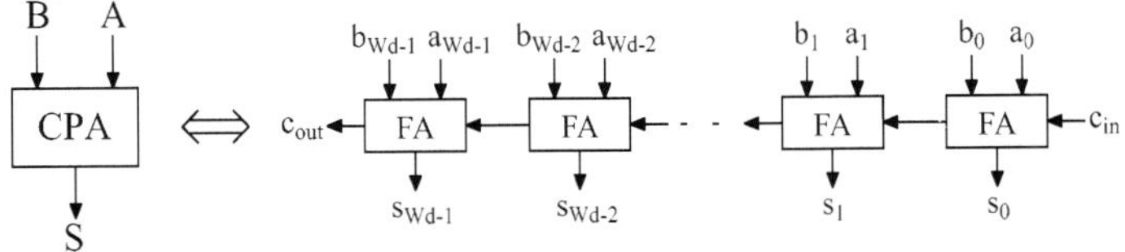

Fig. 2. Carry-propagation adder.

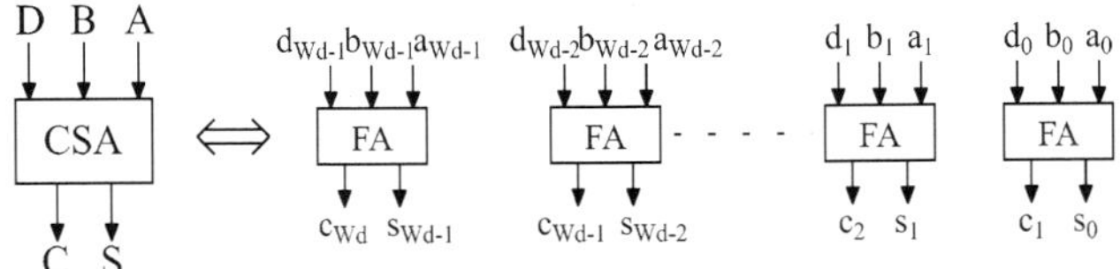

Fig. 3. Carry-save adder.

and 27 is shown. In Fig. 4, $<< n$ denotes a left-shift by n, i.e., a multiplication by 2^n. The CPA solution in Fig. 4(a) is optimal in terms of adders. However, when the three CPAs are mapped to CSAs, as shown in Fig. 4(b) it is clear that a CPA can result in zero, one, or two CSAs. The different cases are summarized in Table 1.

In this chapter we consider the realization of constant multiplications using CSAs. Primarily, we will consider the case where the input is in non-redundant format, typically two's complement, and the output is in carry-save format. In most application one would eventually convert the carry-save format back to non-redundant form using a CPA. However, it should be noted that it is possible to use CSAs throughout the application and that stability can be retained in wave digital filters (Kleine & Noll, 1987). As such we also consider single constant multiplication with carry-save input. In general, it is possible to use algorithms for CPAs as one CPA results in two CSAs when both inputs are in carry-save format, see Table 1. However, the number of cascaded adders does not follow directly, as the CSAs can be arranged in different structures. The work presented in this chapter originates from (Gustafsson et al., 2004; 2001; Gustafsson & Wanhammar, 2007). Related work has later on been presented in (Aksoy & Güneş, 2008; Hosangadi et al., 2006; Jaccottet et al., 2010).

2. Carry-Save Arithmetic

A carry-save adder as that in Fig. 3 can add three two's complement numbers and produce the result as two two's complement numbers, where the sum of the two outputs is the sum of the three inputs. The weights of the carry-bits are one higher than those of the sum-bits. This leads to two things: the least significant carry-bit is always zero and the MSB of the sum and

CPA input 1	CPA input 2	Number of CSAs
multiplier input	multiplier input	0
multiplier input	adder output	1
adder output	adder output	2

Table 1. Possible cases of mapping a CPA to CSA.

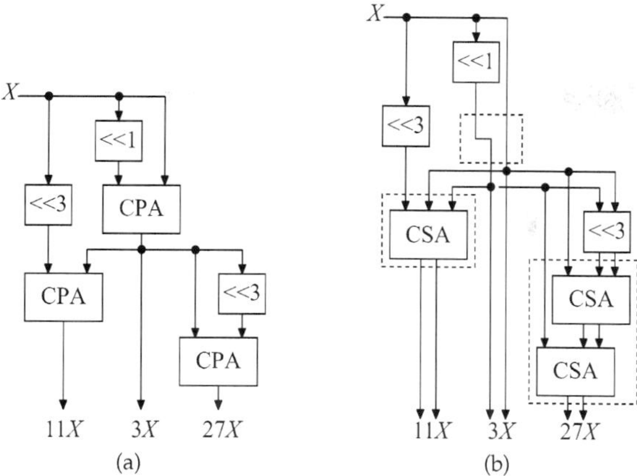

Fig. 4. Multiple constant multiplication for $\{3, 11, 27\}$. (a) Optimal CPA solution. (b) Mapped CSA solution.

carry have different weights. The latter causes problems when adding these in later stages as all two's complement vectors should have the same length for addition to work.

2.1 Subtraction in carry-save arithmetic

To subtract a two's complement number using CPAs, the standard way is to negate the number to be subtracted and add a one to the carry-input of the least significant full adder, indicated by c_{in} in Fig. 2. However, for a carry-save adder there is no such "free" input. Instead one can utilize the least significant carry-bit and set that to one in case of a subtraction. This clearly only works if one of the three inputs should be subtracted. For cases where two inputs should be subtracted it is often possible to change the sign of the output such that the initially positive term is now subtracted. This will be further illustrated in the example in Section 3.2.

2.2 Handling of sign-bits in carry-save arithmetic

Consider the addition of the three numbers 0, 0.5, and -0.5 in two's complement representation with a CSA as shown in Fig. 3. The inputs, $\{A, B, D\}$, and outputs, $\{C, S\}$ are

$$
\begin{array}{c|c|c}
A & 0.0 & 0.0_{10} \\
B & 0.1 & 0.5_{10} \\
D & 1.1 & -0.5_{10} \\
\hline
C & 01. & \\
S & 1.0 & \\
\end{array}
$$

Now, as the result, 0, is within the valid range of the number representation used we can without any problems remove the leading carry bit and obtain the result in a carry save representation as $C = 1.0, S = 1.0$. Adding these gives the expected result $C + S = 0.0 = 0_{10}$, after removing the carry out of the carry propagation addition. However, now shift the results right one position to obtain $C = 1.10, S = 1.10$. If we add these vectors we get $C + S = 1.00 = -1_{10}$.

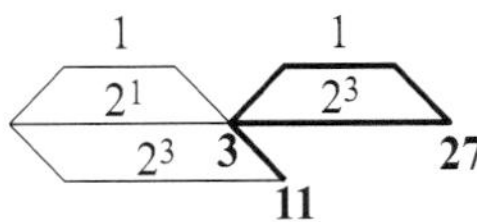

Fig. 5. Graph representation of the shift-and-add network in Fig. 4(b). The graph is directed from left to right.

Obviously, we can not straightforwardly shift the carry and the sum vector after a carry-save addition, despite the fact that they are both in two's complement representation and the shifted result for each vector separately is correct.

Shifting of carry-save data is crucial in the realization of CSA-based constant multiplication, and, hence, a shiftable representation is required.

In (Noll, 1991) this erroneous behavior was named *carry overflow*. A solution for a single CSA was proposed as replacing the most significant carry and sum bits with

$$c_0' = c_{out} \tag{1}$$
$$s_0' = s_0 \oplus c_0 \oplus c_{out} \tag{2}$$

where c_0' and s_0' are the corrected sign-bits. For the simple example above we would obtain the corrected vectors $C = 0.0, S = 0.0$ which clearly can be shifted arbitrarily and still resulting in a correct sum.

For the general case that we have two vectors C and S and want to truncate them to a given number of bits the sign-bits can be computed as

$$c_i' = c_i \oplus c_{i+1} \oplus s_{i+1} \tag{3}$$
$$s_i' = s_i \oplus c_{i+1} \oplus s_{i+1} \tag{4}$$

Hence, it is possible to add an arbitrary number of words using only one guard bit and obtain a valid two's complement representation with correct sign-bits that can be shifted arbitrarily, given that we know that the final result is within the given range.

An alternative technique is of course to sign-extend the sum-output. However, this would lead to an increasing wordlength compared to the corresponding non-redundant wordlength. Furthermore, that approach can not be used in recursive algorithms.

3. Carry-Save Arithmetic Constant Multipliers with Non-Redundant Input

It is in many cased practical to represent the shift-and-add networks as graphs, where the edges corresponds to shifts and the vertices corresponds to additions. Typically, the sign of the operation is represented on the edges. As an example, the network in Fig. 4(b) has a graph-representation as in Fig. 5, where the thin lines correspond to data in non-redundant format, while the bold lines corresponds to data in carry-save format. Each node has a value, called a *fundamental*, which is the ratio between the output of the adder and the input, i.e., the multiplier coefficient. The fundamentals are indicated with a bold font. The adder graphs are directed. However, for clarity, the arrows are neglected.

It is possible to define graphs corresponding to all possible interconnections of N adders. They have the following properties (Gustafsson & Wanhammar, 2007):

- Each edge can either be in non-redundant or in carry-save representation.

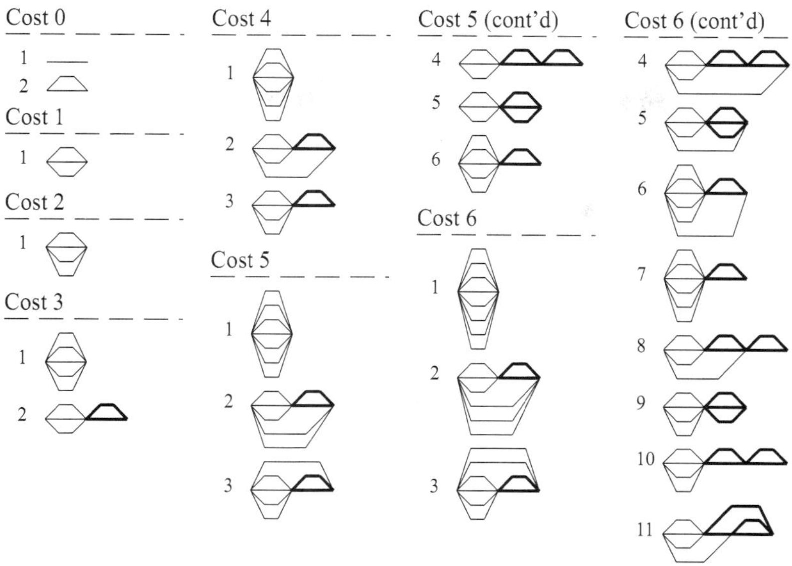

Fig. 6. Possible carry-save adder graphs with non-redundant input generating different coefficient sets for 0 to 6 carry-save adders. The graphs are directed from left to right.

- The cost of a vertex is the number of incoming edges corresponding to non-redundant words plus two times the number of incoming edges corresponding to carry-save words minus two.

- The output edge(s) of a vertex is in carry-save representation, except for the initial vertex.

All possible combinations of edge values for the given graphs can be searched and the minimum-adder solution can easily be found. In Fig. 6 all possible graphs generating different sets of coefficients using up to six carry-save adders is shown. As in Fig. 5 the thin lines represent data in a non-redundant format, while the bold lines represent carry-save format. Note that cost-0 graph 1 has a non-redundant output. The first graphs for each nonzero cost corresponds to the CSD multiplier. Hence, this case is always covered by the proposed approach.

It is worth noting that when four or more carry-save adders are required in a vertex it is possible to re-arrange the adders into, e.g., a Wallace tree (Wallace, 1964). This will reduce the adder depth of the multiplier.

3.1 Results

Exhaustive searches have been performed for multipliers containing up to six adders. This has been done by searching all different combinations of possible shifts and signs for all graphs up to six adders and saving the minimum number of adders in a table. The result is that all integer numbers between 1 and 2^k for wordlength k up to 19 can be obtained using six adders. The maximum number of adders required for a given wordlength is shown in Fig. 7 for both CSD multipliers and the proposed approach.

Number of adders	Graph number	Maximum nonzero digits	Minimum adder depth
0	1	1	0
	2	2	0
1	1	3	1
2	1	4	2
3	1	5	3
	2	6	3
4	1	6	3
	2	7	4
	3	8	4
5	1	7	4
	2	8	4
	3	9	5
	4	12	5
	5	9	4
	6	10	5
6	1	8	4
	2	9	4
	3	10	5
	4	13	6
	5	10	5
	6	11	6
	7	12	5
	8	14	6
	9	12	5
	10	16	6
	11	11	5

Table 2. Maximum number of nonzero digits and minimum adder depth for the CSA multiplier graphs in Fig. 6 with non-redundant input data.

The average number of adders required for a given wordlength is shown in Fig. 8. It is clear that savings only occurs when the coefficient wordlength is larger than nine bits. Figure 9 shows the average savings using the proposed approach. For 19 coefficient bits the savings are just over 10%.

The maximum number of nonzero digits and minimum depth for each graph is shown in Table 2. It can be seen that the graph 1 for each nonzero cost, the CSD multiplier graph, has the smallest adder depth, but also the lowest number of maximum nonzero digits. Furthermore, the graph with the highest number of maximum nonzero digits also is one of the multipliers with the largest depth. Based on the observations in Fig. 6 and Table 2 we can conclude that the maximum number of non-zero digits for $K > 0$ carry-save adders is

$$3 \cdot 2^{\frac{K-1}{2}} \tag{5}$$

for odd K and

$$2^{\frac{K+1}{2}} \tag{6}$$

for even K.

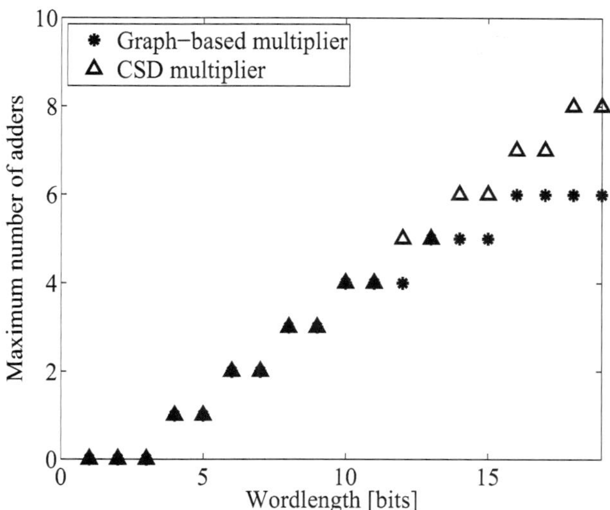

Fig. 7. Maximum number of CSAs as a function of coefficient wordlength for CSD multipliers and proposed optimal multipliers.

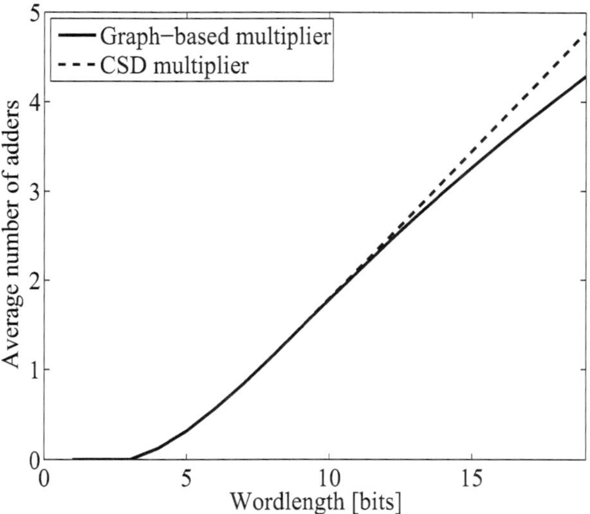

Fig. 8. Average number of CSAs as a function of coefficient wordlength for CSD multipliers and proposed optimal multipliers.

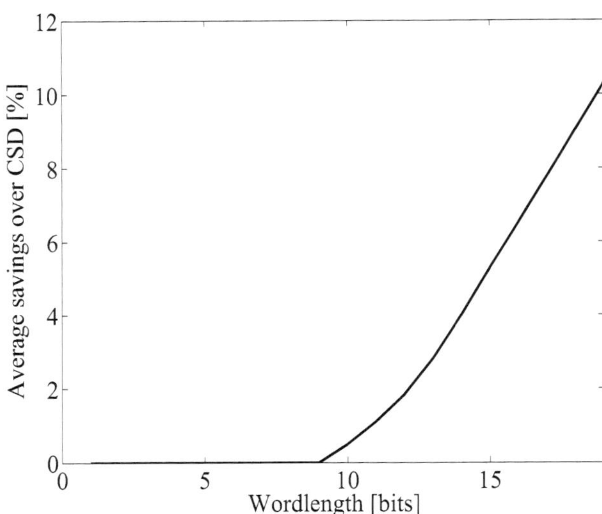

Fig. 9. Average percentage savings of CSAs for the proposed optimal multipliers over CSD multipliers as a function of coefficient wordlength.

3.2 Example

Consider the coefficient $693 = (10\bar{1}0\bar{1}0\bar{1}0101)_{\mathrm{CSD}}$. To implement a multiplication with 693 using a CSD multiplier requires four CSAs. However, using graph-based multiplier 2 of cost 3 in Fig. 6 only three CSAs are required. The resulting graph and implementation is shown in Fig. 10, where $<< n$ denotes a left-shift of n bits.

For the example it can be noted that the first fundamental is -11 instead of 11 to avoid two negative input terms[2]. This is compensated for in the second adder stage.

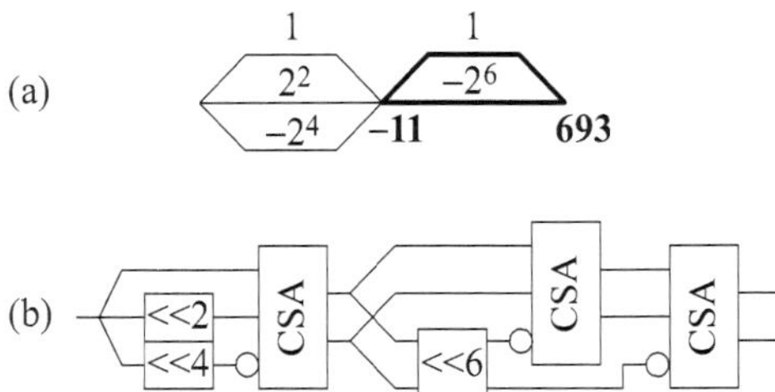

Fig. 10. Optimal CSA-based multiplication with 693: (a) graph representation directed form left to right and (b) structure.

---

[2] In this particular case it could also have been possible to use the representation $11 = 1 + 2 + 8$ to avoid subtractions.

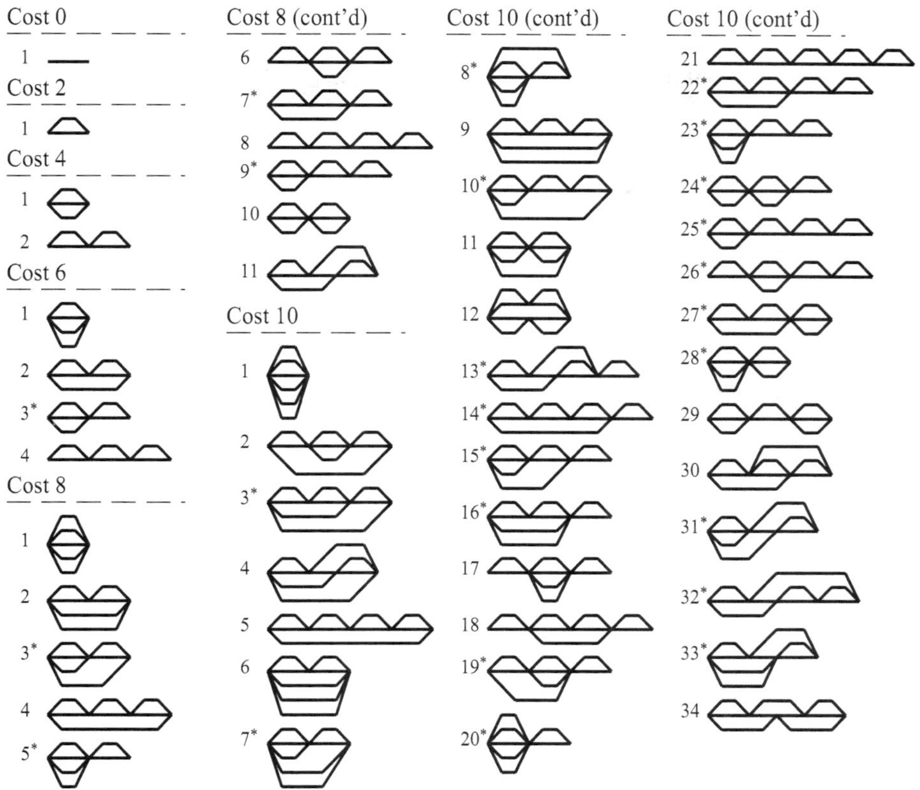

Fig. 11. Possible carry-save adder graphs with carry-save input generating different coefficient sets for 0 to 10 carry-save adders. The graphs are directed from left to right.

4. Carry-Save Arithmetic Constant Multipliers with Carry-Save Representation Input

When the input data is in carry-save representation it is possible to use the same graphs as in (Gustafsson et al., 2006). Now all words are in carry-save representation, and, hence, the number of carry-save adders is two times the number of incoming edges minus two. The possible graphs with up to ten adders are shown in Fig. 11.

4.1 Results

The possible savings in number of adders are similar to those in (Gustafsson et al., 2006) and the average number of adders is shown in Fig. 12. The average savings of the graph-based multipliers over CSD multipliers are shown in Fig. 13. Here, it can be seen that the average savings are about 25% for 19-bits coefficients. Also, the maximum number of CSAs required is reduced from 18 CSAs for a worst-case 19-bit CSD multiplier to 10 CSAs for a graph-based multiplier.

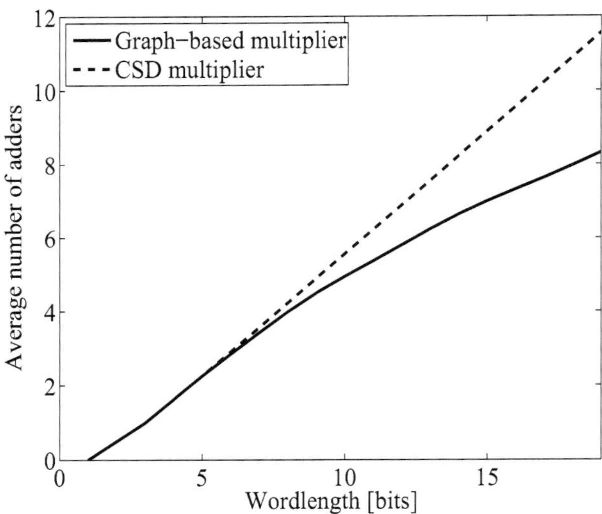

Fig. 12. Average number of CSAs as a function of coefficient wordlength for CSD multipliers and proposed optimal multipliers with carry-save input.

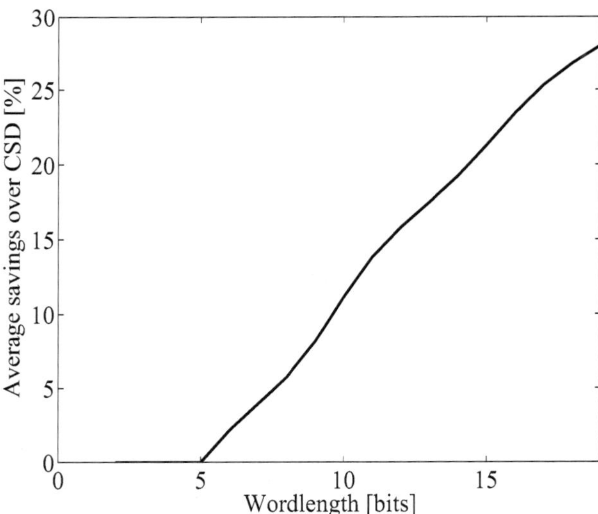

Fig. 13. Average percentage savings of CSAs for the proposed optimal multipliers over CSD multipliers as a function of coefficient wordlength with carry-save input.

The adder depth for the CSA-based graphs can not be easily computed based on results from the CPA-based graphs. The maximum number of nonzero digits and minimum depth for each graph is shown in Table 3. Using a similar reasoning as in (Gustafsson et al., 2006) we get that the maximum number of nonzero digits for a coefficient realized with K carry-save adders is (K is always even)

$$2^{K/2} \tag{7}$$

5. Multiple Constant Multiplication

For the case where several coefficients are multiplied with the same input a different approach can be used. Here, it is beneficial to be able to share partial results among the different coefficients to be able to reduce the total number of adders. It can be noted that the minimum number of adders per coefficient is simply one. Ideally, one would just need one extra adder for each unique[3] result. This is clearly the case for transposed direct form FIR filters, where the additions between the delay elements in Fig. 1, called *structural additions*, can be replaced by subtractions for negative coefficients. It may be beneficial to use CSA-based structural adders to obtain a high-speed implementation (Jain et al., 1991).

5.1 Proposed Algorithm

The proposed algorithm can be divided into an optimal part and a suboptimal part. The optimal part of the algorithm is described as:

1. The algorithm only considers positive odd fundamentals. Hence, negative fundamentals should be negated and even fundamentals should be divided by a suitable power of two to obtain an odd fundamental.

2. The fundamental one and fundamentals on the form $2^n \pm 1$ are removed as no CSAs are required to obtain these fundamentals. The remaining fundamentals form a set of unrealized fundamentals.

3. From the set of unrealized fundamentals add to the realized fundamental set all fundamentals, if any, that can be realized using one CSA, i.e., fundamentals on the form $2^m \pm 2^n \pm 1$, where $m > n > 1$.

4. Form all possible combinations of the fundamentals in the realized set times a power of two and a power of two, i.e., fundamentals on the form $2^m a \pm 1$ and $|a \pm 2^m|$, where a is an already realized fundamental. If any of these fundamentals are found in the unrealized set, move these to the realized set. If any fundamental has been realized and there are unrealized fundamentals remaining go to 4.

Each fundamental, added in steps 3 and 4, costs one adder. If all fundamentals are realized after this stage, the realization is known to be optimal in terms of adders. If not, at least two adders must be used to obtain one of the remaining fundamentals.

There are three different ways to obtain new fundamentals using two adders: fundamentals that requires two adders to be realized on its own, adding two powers of two to a power of two of an already realized fundamental, and a combination of two already realized fundamentals. As the two first ways realizes yet another fundamental, these two have preference over the combination of realized fundamentals. When two adders are required it is no longer certain that the solution is optimal. The possibly suboptimal part of the algorithm is described as:

---

[3] As shifts are free and sign often can be compensated for at some other part of the algorithm, all coefficients are normalized to be odd and positive.

Number of adders	Graph number	Maximum nonzero digits	Minimum adder depth
2	1	2	2
4	1	3	3
	2	4	4
6	1	4	4
	2	5	5
	3	6	5
	4	8	6
8	1	5	5
	2	6	6
	3	7	6
	4	9	7
	5	8	6
	6	12	7
	7	10	7
	8	16	8
	9	12	7
	10	9	6
	11	8	7
10	1	6	5
	2	13	8
	3	11	8
	4	9	8
	5	17	9
	6	7	7
	7	8	7
	8	9	7
	9	10	8
	10	13	8
	11	10	7
	12	8	6
	13	16	9
	14	18	9
	15	14	8
	16	12	8
	17	16	8
	18	20	9
	19	12	8
	20	10	7
	21	32	10
	22	20	9
	23	16	8
	24	18	8
	25	24	9
	26	24	8
	27	15	8
	28	12	7
	29	18	8
	30	12	8
	31	11	8
	32	14	9
	33	10	8
	34	13	9

Table 3. Maximum number of nonzero digits and minimum adder depth for the CSA multiplier graphs in Fig. 11 with carry-save input data.

5. From the set of unrealized fundamentals find all fundamentals that can be realized using two CSAs, i.e., fundamentals on the form $2^m \pm 2^n \pm 2^p \pm 1$, where $m > n > p > 1$. These fundamental can be derived from one and up to ten different fundamentals of cost-1. Find the cost-1 fundamental that is common to most unrealized fundamentals and add that fundamental to the realized set. Also move all fundamentals that can be realized from that cost-1 fundamental to the realized set. If there are more than one cost-1 fundamental that can realize the maximal number of fundamentals chose the minimum one. If there are unrealized fundamentals remaining and any fundamental was added go to 4.

6. If there are unrealized fundamentals remaining, form the set of all fundamentals that can be realized from one previously realized fundamental and two powers of two, i.e., on the form $|a \pm 2^m \pm 2^n|$ or $|2^m a \pm 2^n \pm 1|$. If any fundamental in the unrealized set is present in the generated set, move one of the fundamentals to the generated set. One intermediate fundamental is also generated, select the one (out of two) with the lowest magnitude to add to the set of realized fundamentals. If there are unrealized fundamentals remaining and any fundamental was added go to 4.

7. If there are unrealized fundamentals remaining, form a set of combinations of previously realized fundamentals times a power of two, i.e., on the form $|2^m a \pm b|$. If any fundamental in the unrealized set is present in the generated set, move one of the fundamentals to the generated set. If there are unrealized fundamentals remaining and any fundamental was added go to 4.

8. If there are unrealized fundamentals remaining, it is necessary to add a complete coefficient to the realized fundamental set. Complete coefficients with minimum number of adders can be generated using the work described in Section 3. Select the coefficient with the smallest sum of all its fundamentals (Dempster & Macleod, 1995). If there are there are unrealized fundamentals remaining go to 4.

5.2 Results

We compare our algorithm with the RAGn algorithm (Dempster & Macleod, 1995), where the resulting multiplier block is transformed to CSAs. Furthermore, we compare it to a modified version of the algorithm in (Pasko et al., 1999). In the original algorithm all subexpressions down to two bits were identified. As subexpressions with two bits are not useful when using CSAs, the algorithm is modified so that it only identifies subexpressions with at least three bits.

For sets of 25 coefficient with varying number of coefficient bits the average number of adders are shown in Fig. 14. For comparison the results using carry-propagation adders and the RAGn algorithm is included. Figure 14 shows that the proposed algorithm is better than both the modified algorithm from (Pasko et al., 1999) and design using CPAs. However, if only the actual number of adders is considered the CPA approach is better for nine coefficient bits and above. This is due to the greater flexibility in using intermediate fundamentals for CPAs.

The average number of adders for different sized coefficient sets with 12-bits coefficients is shown in Fig. 15. Again, the proposed algorithm is better compared to other algorithms. The multiplier block based on CPAs requires fewer adders for all sizes of the coefficient set with 12-bits coefficients.

It is clear that when CSAs are required the proposed algorithm is better than both the modified algorithm from (Pasko et al., 1999), which is based on subexpression sharing, and using the RAGn algorithm for CPAs. However, it is also clear that if only the number of adders, i.e., the

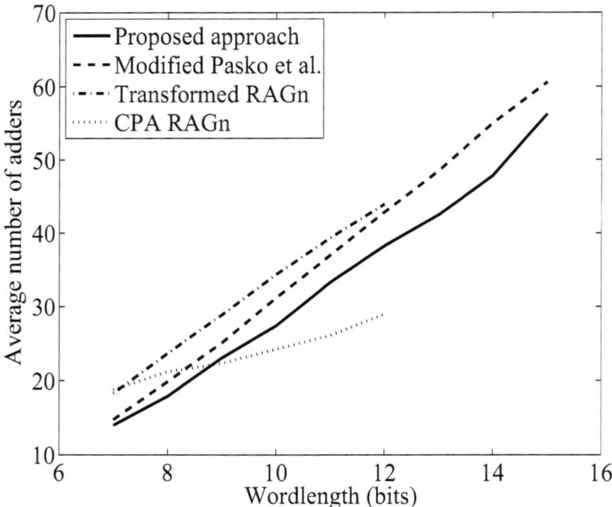

Fig. 14. Average number of adders for sets of 25 random coefficients.

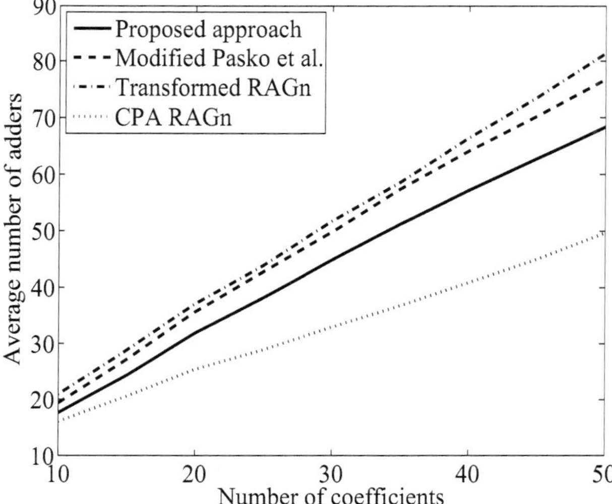

Fig. 15. Average number of adders for sets with 12-bits coefficients.

chip area, is of interest the RAGn algorithm with CPAs is the best choice. It should be noted that for the CSA multiplier block each coefficient requires a CPA to convert the carry-save representation to a non-redundant form, unless the redundant representation is used in later processing such as when carry-save structural adders are used.

6. Conclusions

Carry-save adders are useful to obtain high-speed implementation as carry-propagation can be avoided. However, when designing constant multipliers special care must be taken where the properties of the CSAs are considered. In this chapter we described the optimal design of single constant multipliers for coefficients with up to 19 bits wordlength. Both the cases with non-redundant representation as well as carry-save representation of the input was considered.

An algorithm for the multiple constant multiplication problem, suitable for transposed direct form FIR filters using carry-save representation of intermediate results but non-redundant input, was also presented.

For the non-redundant input cases, the results show that the number of CSAs is higher than the corresponding number of CPAs. Hence, from a complexity point of view, CPAs are advantageous. As such, the proposed techniques are useful when a high-speed realization is required.

7. References

Aksoy, L. & Güneş, E. O. (2008). Area optimization algorithms in high-speed digital FIR filter synthesis, *Proc. Symp. Integrated Circuits System Design*, pp. 64–69.

Aksoy, L., Güneş, E. O. & Flores, P. (2010). Search algorithms for the multiple constant multiplications problem: Exact and approximate, *Microprocessors and Microsystems* **34**(5): 151–162.

Dempster, A. G. & Macleod, M. D. (1994). Constant integer multiplication using minimum adders, *IEE Proc. Circuits Devices Systems*, Vol. 141, pp. 407–413.

Dempster, A. G. & Macleod, M. D. (1995). Use of minimum-adder multiplier blocks in FIR digital filters, *IEEE Trans. Circuits and Systems II: Analog and Digital Signal Processing* **42**(9): 569–577.

Gustafsson, O. (2007). Lower bounds for constant multiplication problems, *IEEE Transactions on Circuits and Systems II: Express Briefs* **54**(11): 974–978.

Gustafsson, O. (2008). Comments on 'A 70 MHz Multiplierless FIR Hilbert Transformer in 0.35 μm Standard CMOS Library', *IEICE Trans. Fundamentals* **91**(3): 899–900.

Gustafsson, O., Dempster, A. G., Johansson, K., Macleod, M. D. & Wanhammar, L. (2006). Simplified design of constant coefficient multipliers, *Circuits Systems Signal Processing* **25**(2): 225–251.

Gustafsson, O., Dempster, A. G. & Wanhammar, L. (2004). Multiplier blocks using carry-save adders, *Proc. IEEE Int. Symp. Circuits Systems*, Vol. 2, pp. 473–476.

Gustafsson, O., Ohlsson, H. & Wanhammar, L. (2001). Minimum-adder integer multipliers using carry-save adders, *Proc. IEEE Int. Symp. Circuits Systems*, pp. 709–712.

Gustafsson, O. & Wanhammar, L. (2007). Low-complexity constant multiplication using carry-save arithmetic for high-speed digital filters, *Proc. Int. Symp. Image and Signal Processing and Analysis*, pp. 212–217.

Hartley, R. I. (1996). Subexpression sharing in filters using canonic signed digit multipliers, *IEEE Trans. Circuits Systems II: Analog and Digital Signal Processing* **43**(10): 677–688.

Hosangadi, A., Fallah, F. & Kastner, R. (2006). Optimizing high speed arithmetic circuits using three-term extraction, *Proc. Conf. Design Automation Test in Europe*, pp. 1294–1299.

Jaccottet, D., Costa, E., Aksoy, L., Flores, P. & Monteiro, J. (2010). Design of low-complexity and high-speed digital finite impulse response filters, *Proc. IEEE/IFIP Int. Conf. VLSI System-on-Chip*, pp. 292–297.

Jain, R., Yang, P. & Yoshino, T. (1991). FIRGEN: A computer-aided design system for high performance FIR filter integrated circuits, *IEEE Trans. Signal Processing* **39**(7): 1655–1668.

Kleine, U. & Noll, T. (1987). On the forced response stability of wave digital filters using carry-save arithmetic, *AEU, Archiv für Elektronik und Übertragungstechnik* **41**(6): 321–324.

Lim, Y. C. (1990). Design of discrete-coefficient-value linear phase FIR filters with optimum normalized peak ripple magnitude, *IEEE Trans. Circuits Systems* **37**(12): 1480–1486.

Noll, T. (1991). Carry-save architectures for high-speed digital signal processing, *J. VLSI Signal Processing* **3**(1): 121–140.

Pasko, R., Schaumont, P., Derudder, V., Vernalde, S. & Durackova, D. (1999). A new algorithm for elimination of common subexpressions, *IEEE Trans. Computer-Aided Design Integrated Circuits Systems* **18**(1): 58–68.

Potkonjak, M., Srivastava, M. B. & Chandrakasan, A. P. (1996). Multiple constant multiplications: efficient and versatile framework and algorithms for exploring common subexpression elimination, *IEEE Trans. Computer-Aided Design Integrated Circuits Systems* **15**(2): 151–165.

Thong, J. & Nicolici, N. (2009). Time-efficient single constant multiplication based on overlapping digit patterns, *IEEE Trans. VLSI Systems* **17**(9): 1353–1357.

Voronenko, Y. & Püschel, M. (2007). Multiplierless multiple constant multiplication, *ACM Trans. Algorithms* **3**.
URL: *http://doi.acm.org/10.1145/1240233.1240234*

Wallace, C. (1964). A suggestion for a fast multiplier, *IEEE Trans. Electronic Computers* (1): 14–17.

Yli-Kaakinen, J. & Saramäki, T. (2007). A systematic algorithm for the design of lattice wave digital filters with short-coefficient wordlength, *IEEE Trans. Circuits Systems I: Regular Papers* **54**(8): 1838–1851.

11

A Systematic Algorithm for the Synthesis of Multiplierless Lattice Wave Digital Filters

Juha Yli-Kaakinen and Tapio Saramäki
Tampere University of Technology
Finland

1. Introduction

Among the best structures for implementing recursive digital filters are lattice wave digital (LWD) filters (parallel connections of all-pass filters). They are characterized by many attractive properties, such as a reasonably low coefficient sensitivity, a low roundoff noise level, and the absence of parasitic oscillations. This book chapter describes an efficient algorithm for the design of multiplierless LWD filters in the following three cases. In the first case, the overall filter is constructed as a cascade of low-order LWD filters. As a consequence, the number of bits required for both the data and coefficient representations are significantly reduced compared with the conventional direct-form LWD filter. In the second case, approximately linear-phase LWD filters are constructed as a single block because it has been observed that in this case the use of a cascade of several filter blocks does not provide any benefits over the direct-form LWD filter design. The third case concentrates on the design of special recursive single-stage and multistage Nth-band decimators and interpolators providing the sampling rate conversion by the factor of N. For this filter class, the decimation and interpolation filter in the single-stage design (the kth decimation and interpolation filter in the multistage design, where N is factorizable as a product of K integers as $N = N_1 N_2 \cdots N_K$) is characterized by the fact that it can be decomposed into parallel connection of N (N_k) polyphase components that are obtainable from cascades of first-order all-pass filters by substituting for each unit delay N (N_k) unit delays.

The coefficient optimization is performed using the following three steps. First, an initial infinite-precision filter is designed such that it exceeds the given criteria in order to provide some tolerance for coefficient quantization. Second, a nonlinear optimization algorithm is used for determining a parameter space of the infinite-precision coefficients including the feasible space where the filter meets the given criteria. The third step involves finding the filter parameters in this space so that the resulting filter meets the given criteria with the simplest coefficient representation forms. The proposed algorithm guarantees that the optimum finite-precision solution can be found for the multiplierless coefficient representation forms. Filters of this kind are very attractive in very large-scale integration implementations because the realization of these filters does not require the use of very costly general multiplier elements. Several examples are included to illustrate the benefits of the proposed synthesis scheme as well as the resulting filters.

2. Lattice Wave Digital Filters

One of the best structures for implementing recursive digital filters are the lattice wave digital (LWD) filters (Fettweis, 1986; Fettweis *et al.*, 1974; Gazsi, 1985; Wanhammar, 1998) that are related to certain analog prototype networks. The number of multipliers required in the implementation is directly the filter order, unlike in some other implementation forms, such as in the canonical direct-form realizations requiring approximately twice the number of multipliers.

An LWD filter consists of a parallel connection of all-pass filters. These all-pass subfilters can be realized by using first- and second-order sections as basic building blocks. The resulting filter structures are highly modular, thereby making them suitable for very large-scale integration (VLSI) implementations (Milić & Lutovac, 1999; Saramäki & Ritoniemi, 1993). All-pass subfilters are also the basic building blocks of recursive half-band filters (Ansari & Liu, 1983; Gazsi, 1985), Hilbert transformers (Brophy & Salazar, 1975; Regalia, 1993; Saramäki & Renfors, 1995), filters approximately providing an arbitrary linear-phase phase response or an arbitrary phase delay in the given passband (Saramäki & Renfors, 1995), several efficient recursive filter-bank classes (Bregović, 2003; Saramäki & Bregović, 2002; Vollmer & Kopmann, 2002), and recursive Nth-band filters (Renfors & Saramäki, 1987; Taxén, 1981) that have been found to be very efficient in sampling rate conversion applications. It is also possible to design LWD filters to have an approximately linear phase in the passband (Jaworski & Saramäki, 1994; Jones *et al.*, 1991; Renfors & Saramäki, 1986; Surma-aho, 1997; Surma-aho & Saramäki, 1999). Such designs are suitable in applications where linear-phase finite-impulse response (FIR) filters would have an excessive signal delay, that is, in applications demanding narrow transition bandwidth. This is due to the fact that the order of linear-phase FIR filters is roughly inversely proportional to the transition bandwidth (Herrmann *et al.*, 1973; Saramäki, 1993). In addition, those approximately linear-phase LWD filters proposed in (Surma-aho, 1997; Surma-aho & Saramäki, 1999) are superior over their linear-phase FIR equivalents, in terms of the required number of multipliers, adders, and delay elements, in narrow-band cases, where linear-phase FIR filters have inherently a high filter order.

This section revises the transfer functions of the filter classes under consideration in this contribution. These filter classes consist of cascades of low-order LWD filters, approximately linear-phase LWD filters, and recursive Nth-band decimators and interpolators.

2.1 Cascade Connection of LWD Filters

When considering the parallel connection of two all-pass filters, it is well-known that the coefficient sensitivity is very low in the passband provided that the all-pass filter structures are constructed such that their transfer functions remain all-pass in spite of coefficient quantization (Regalia *et al.*, 1988). However, the stopband sensitivity is not as good. In most cases, it has turned out that the required coefficient wordlength is roughly proportional to the required stopband attenuation (Renfors & Saramäki, 1986). Therefore, the coefficient wordlength requirements can be reduced if the filter is realized using subfilters with lower stopband attenuations, e.g., in cascade or, more generally, as a tapped cascaded interconnection of identical subfilters (Saramäki & Renfors, 1987).

An approach to designing recursive filters using a cascade of different LWD filters has been proposed in (Saramäki & Yli-Kaakinen, 2002; Yli-Kaakinen, 2002; Yli-Kaakinen & Saramäki, 1999b). The main advantage of this approach is that the poles of the cascaded LWD filters are further away from the unit circle compared with the direct LWD filters. This means that the number of data bits and the number of bits required for the coefficient representations can be significantly reduced. By properly determining the number of filter stages to be cascaded as well as their orders, all the coefficient values can be optimized to be representable as a few powers of two. This makes the proposed filter structure very attractive for VLSI implementations as under these circumstances all the coefficient values can be simply implemented using hardwired logic consisting of only shift operations as well as additions and/or subtractions, instead of using very costly general multiplier elements.

The transfer function of a cascade connection of LWD filters is given by

$$H(z) = \prod_{k=1}^{K} H_k(z), \quad \text{where} \quad H_k(z) = \frac{1}{2}\left[A_0^{(k)}(z) + A_1^{(k)}(z)\right]. \tag{1}$$

Here, the $A_0^{(k)}(z)$'s and $A_1^{(k)}(z)$'s are the transfer functions of stable all-pass filters of orders $M_0^{(k)}$ and $M_1^{(k)}$, respectively. An implementation of the above transfer function is depicted in Fig. 1. In the sequel, the main emphasis is laid on synthesizing low-pass filters even though high-pass, band-pass, and band-stop filters can be designed in a similar manner as will be described in some detail in the sequel. In the low-pass case, $M_0^{(k)} = M_1^{(k)} - 1$ or $M_0^{(k)} = M_1^{(k)} + 1$, so that $M_0^{(k)} + M_1^{(k)}$, the overall order of $H_k(z)$, is odd. If the $A_0^{(k)}(z)$'s and $A_1^{(k)}(z)$'s are implemented as a cascade of first- and second-order wave digital all-pass structures and $M_0^{(k)}$ and $M_1^{(k)}$ are assumed to be odd and even, respectively, then the $A_0^{(k)}(z)$'s and $A_1^{(k)}(z)$'s are expressible in terms of the adaptor coefficients as follows [see, e.g., (Gazsi, 1985)]:

$$A_0^{(k)}(z) = \frac{-\gamma_0^{(k)} + z^{-1}}{1 - \gamma_0^{(k)} z^{-1}} \prod_{\ell=1}^{L_0^{(k)}} \frac{-\gamma_{2\ell-1}^{(k)} + \gamma_{2\ell}^{(k)}\left(\gamma_{2\ell-1}^{(k)} - 1\right) z^{-1} + z^{-2}}{1 + \gamma_{2\ell}^{(k)}\left(\gamma_{2\ell-1}^{(k)} - 1\right) z^{-1} - \gamma_{2\ell-1}^{(k)} z^{-2}} \quad \text{with} \quad L_0^{(k)} = \frac{M_0^{(k)} - 1}{2} \tag{2a}$$

and

$$A_1^{(k)}(z) = \prod_{\ell=L_0^{(k)}+1}^{L_0^{(k)}+L_1^{(k)}} \frac{-\gamma_{2\ell-1}^{(k)} + \gamma_{2\ell}^{(k)}\left(\gamma_{2\ell-1}^{(k)} - 1\right) z^{-1} + z^{-2}}{1 + \gamma_{2\ell}^{(k)}\left(\gamma_{2\ell-1}^{(k)} - 1\right) z^{-1} - \gamma_{2\ell-1}^{(k)} z^{-2}} \quad \text{with} \quad L_1^{(k)} = \frac{M_1^{(k)}}{2}. \tag{2b}$$

If $A_0^{(k)}(z)$ possesses a real pole at $z = r_0^{(k)}$ and $L_0^{(k)}$ complex-conjugate pole pairs at $z = r_\ell^{(k)} \exp(\pm j\theta_\ell^{(k)})$ for $\ell = 1, 2, \ldots, L_0^{(k)}$ and $A_1^{(k)}(z)$ possesses $L_1^{(k)}$ complex-conjugate pole pairs at $z = r_\ell^{(k)} \exp(\pm j\theta_\ell^{(k)})$ for $\ell = L_0^{(k)} + 1, L_0^{(k)} + 2, \ldots, L_0^{(k)} + L_1^{(k)}$, then

$$\gamma_0^{(k)} = r_0^{(k)}, \tag{3a}$$

whereas

$$\gamma_{2\ell-1}^{(k)} = -\left(r_\ell^{(k)}\right)^2 \quad \text{and} \quad \gamma_{2\ell}^{(k)} = \frac{2r_\ell^{(k)} \cos\left(\theta_\ell^{(k)}\right)}{1 + \left(r_\ell^{(k)}\right)^2} \quad \text{for} \quad \ell = 1, 2, \ldots, L_0^{(k)} + L_1^{(k)}. \tag{3b}$$

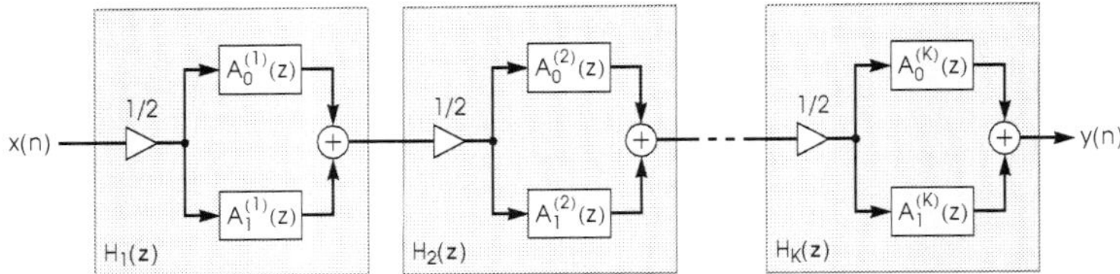

Fig. 1. Filter structure for a cascade connection of LWD filters. The detailed implementation of the kth transfer function $H_k(z)$ as a parallel connection of $A_0^{(k)}(z)$ and the $A_1^{(k)}(z)$ is shown in Fig. 2.

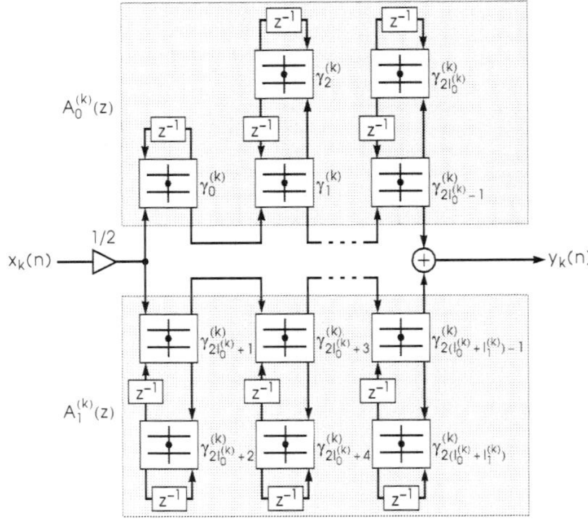

Fig. 2. Implementation of the kth transfer function in Fig. 1 as a parallel connection of two all-pass filter transfer functions. $A_0^{(k)}(z)$ and $A_1^{(k)}(z)$ are stable all-pass filter transfer functions consisting of a cascade of first- and second-order wave digital all-pass sections. These first- and second-order wave digital all-pass sections are constructed based on the use of two-port adaptor structures to be described in Section 3.

Figure 2 shows the realization for a low-pass sub-filter transfer function $H_k(z)$, where the first- and second-order sections of (2a) and (2b) are implemented as a cascade of first- and second-order wave-digital all-pass structures, out of which the best ones for the main purposes of this book chapter will be considered in detail in Section 3.

In the high-pass case, the corresponding transfer function is obtained by simply changing the sign of $A_0^{(k)}(z)$ or $A_1^{(k)}(z)$ in (1) (Gazsi, 1985). In the band-stop case, $M_0^{(k)}$ and $M_1^{(k)}$ are two times an odd integer and an even integer, respectively, and $M_0^{(k)} = M_1^{(k)} - 2$ or $M_0^{(k)} = M_1^{(k)} + 2$. The corresponding band-pass design can be generated by changing the sign of $A_0^{(k)}(z)$ or $A_1^{(k)}(z)$. The main difference of the band-pass and band-stop filter designs in comparison with the low-pass and high-pass filter designs is thus that the first-order section is absent.

2.2 Approximately Linear-Phase LWD Filters

One of the most difficult problems in digital filter synthesis is the simultaneous optimization of the phase and magnitude responses of recursive digital filters. This is because the phase of recursive filters is inherently nonlinear and, therefore, the frequency selectivity and phase linearity are conflicting requirements. The most straightforward approach to arrive at a recursive filter having simultaneously a selective magnitude response and an approximately linear-phase response in the passband region is to generate the filter in two steps. First, a filter with the desired magnitude response is designed. Then, the phase response of this filter is made approximately linear in the passband by cascading it with an all-pass phase equalizer (Deczky, 1972; Rabiner & Gold, 1975). The main drawback in this approach is that the phase response of the frequency-selective filter is usually very nonlinear and, therefore, a very high-order phase equalizer is needed in order to make the phase response of the overall filter approximately linear.

It has turned out (Földvári-Orosz et al., 1991; Jaworski & Saramäki, 1994; Jones et al., 1991; Lawson & Wicks, 1992; Leeb, 1991; Surma-aho, 1997; Surma-aho & Saramäki, 1999) to be more beneficial to implement an approximately linear-phase recursive filter directly without using a separate phase equalizer. In the design techniques described in (Földvári-Orosz et al., 1991; Jaworski & Saramäki, 1994; Jones et al., 1991; Lawson & Wicks, 1992; Leeb, 1991; Surma-aho, 1997; Surma-aho & Saramäki, 1999), it has been observed that in order to simultaneously achieve a selective magnitude response and an approximately linear-phase performance in the passband, it is required that some zeros of the filter be located outside the unit circle.

For approximately linear-phase LWD filters, it has been discovered in (Saramäki & Yli-Kaakinen, 2002) that the use of a cascade of several filter blocks does not provide any benefits in the VLSI implementations. Therefore, the transfer function for the approximately linear-phase LWD filters is given by (1) with $K = 1$, that is, $H(z)$ is expressible as

$$H(z) = \frac{1}{2}\left[A_0^{(1)}(z) + A_1^{(1)}(z)\right],\qquad(4)$$

where $A_0^{(1)}(z)$ and $A_1^{(1)}(z)$ are given by (2a) and (2b), respectively.

2.3 Recursive Nth-Band Decimators and Interpolators

The best structures for implementing decimation and interpolation filters in cases where the phase linearity is not important, are the so-called recursive Nth-band filters (Renfors & Saramäki, 1987; Saramäki & Renfors, 1998; Yli-Kaakinen et al., 1999).[1] These recursive Nth-band filters when used alone for decimation by the factor of N suffer, due to their properties, from the drawback that, after specifying the passband edge to be $\omega_p = \alpha\pi/N$ with $\alpha < 1$, only aliasing into the passband region $[0, \omega_p]$ can be fully avoided, but aliasing into the transition band $[\omega_p, \pi/N]$ occurs. In the interpolation case, this causes the corresponding imaging effects. If these effects can be tolerated and a linear-phase performance is not required, then these recursive polyphase filters require the lowest computational complexities among the known decimators and interpolators. From a computational point of view, it is very advantageous to use multistage decimators and interpolators whenever possible, instead of using a single-stage realization. The design of recursive Nth-band filters and their use for decimation

---

[1] It is also possible to design recursive Nth-band filters to have an approximately linear-phase response in the passband (Ansari & Liu, 1983; Renfors & Saramäki, 1987). These filters require significantly higher computational complexities than the corresponding nonlinear-phase Nth-band filters, but they compare favorably with conventional linear-phase FIR filters.

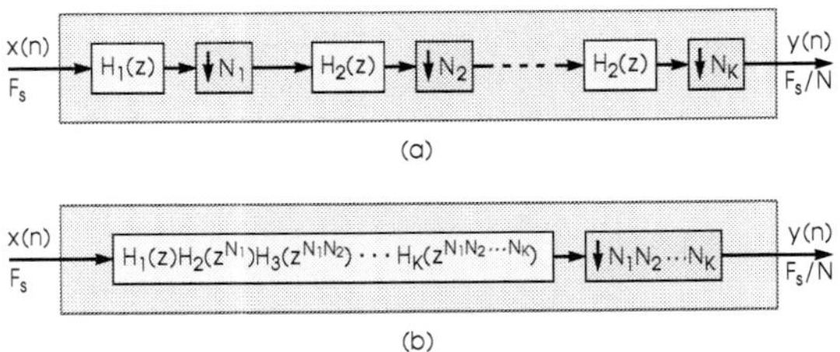

(a)

(b)

Fig. 3. (a) A general implementation form for an N-to-1 decimator. (b) Its single-stage equivalent.

and interpolation has been discussed in detail in (Renfors & Saramäki, 1987). In this article, it has also been described how to get around the above-mentioned drawbacks by using an additional LWD filter at the output of the overall decimator or at the input of the overall interpolator.

Due to the duality between decimators and interpolators, the discussion in this book chapter will concentrate on the design of decimators. If the sampling rate conversion ratio can be factored into the product

$$N = \prod_{k=1}^{K} N_k, \tag{5}$$

where $N_1, N_2, \ldots, N_K$ are integers, then the overall decimation by the factor of N can be implemented using K stages as shown in Fig. 3(a) (Renfors & Saramäki, 1987). In order to considerably clarify the analysis and determination of the roles of the sub-blocks of Fig. 3(a) in simultaneously providing the desired decimation by the overall factor of N, it is advantageous to replace the implementation of Fig. 3(a) by its its single-stage equivalent of Fig. 3(b). In this equivalent, only one filter with transfer function

$$H(z) = \prod_{k=1}^{K} H_k(z^{\tilde{N}_k}), \quad \text{where} \quad \tilde{N}_1 = 1 \quad \text{and} \quad \tilde{N}_r = \prod_{k=1}^{r-1} N_k \quad \text{for } r = 2, 3, \ldots, K \tag{6}$$

is involved followed by decimation by a factor of N. The magnitude response of the above overall filter is thus

$$|H(e^{j\omega})| = \prod_{k=1}^{K} H_k(e^{j\tilde{N}_k\omega}). \tag{7}$$

When the transfer functions $H_k(z)$ for $k = 1, 2, \ldots, K$ in Fig. 3(a) are implemented with the aid of the K recursive (nonlinear-phase) N_kth-band filters, where N_k is the decimation factor after the kth subfilter, the transfer function in the single-stage equivalent of Fig. 3(b) is used as a basic transfer function when synthesizing Nth-band decimators. For this purpose, this transfer function is expressed as

$$H(z) = \prod_{k=1}^{K} H_k(z^{\tilde{N}_k}), \quad \text{where} \quad H_k(z) = \frac{1}{N_k} \sum_{n=0}^{N_k-1} z^{-n} A_n^{(k)}(z^{N_k}). \tag{8a}$$

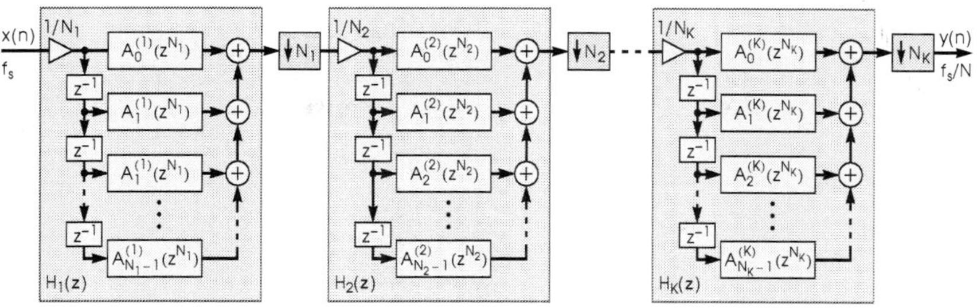

Fig. 4. Filter structure for multistage recursive Nth-band decimators. The $A_n^{(k)}(z)$'s are the transfer functions of stable all-pass filters consisting of a cascade of first-order wave-digital all-pass sections.

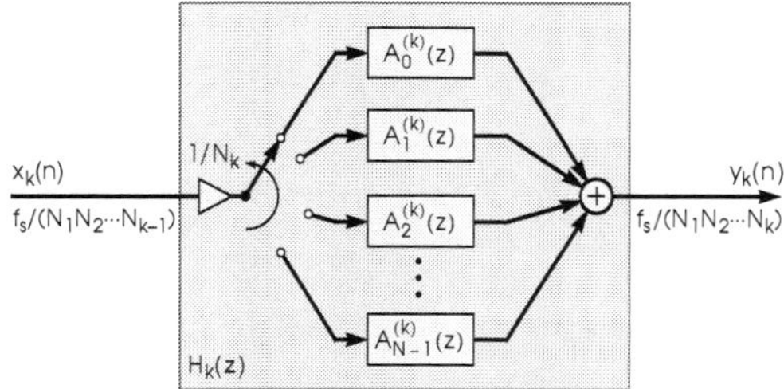

Fig. 5. Commutative structure for the kth stage in Fig. 4.

Here, the transfer functions $A_n^{(k)}(z)$ are the following cascades of first-order stable all-pass transfer functions:

$$A_n^{(k)}(z) = \prod_{\ell=\widetilde{L}_n^{(k)}+1}^{\widetilde{L}_n^{(k)}+L_n^{(k)}} \frac{-\gamma_\ell^{(k)} + z^{-1}}{1 - \gamma_\ell^{(k)} z^{-1}} \quad \text{for } n = 0, 1, \ldots, N_k - 1 \text{ and for } k = 1, 2, \ldots, K, \qquad (8b)$$

where

$$\widetilde{L}_0 = 0 \quad \text{and} \quad \widetilde{L}_n^{(k)} = \sum_{r=0}^{n-1} L_r^{(k)} \quad \text{for } n = 0, 1, \ldots, N_k - 1. \qquad (8c)$$

Hence, each $A_n^{(k)}$ for $n = 0, 1, \ldots, N_k - 1$ and for $k = 1, 2, \ldots, K$ possesses $L_n^{(k)}$ real poles at $z = r_\ell^{(k)} = \gamma_\ell^{(k)}$ for $\ell = \widetilde{L}_n^{(k)} + 1, \widetilde{L}_n^{(k)} + 2, \ldots, \widetilde{L}_n^{(k)} + L_n^{(k)}$.

The transfer function of (8a), (8b), and (8c) corresponds to the decimation structure of Fig. 4. From the practical implementation point of view, this structure becomes very attractive if the kth transfer function followed by decimation by the factor of N_k is replaced by the highly efficient commutative structure of Fig. 5 (Crochiere & Rabiner, 1983). The advantages of this structure are that the delay line is not needed and the branch filters $A_n^{(k)}(z^{N_k})$'s are implemented as $A_n^{(k)}(z)$'s at the lower sampling rate. This reduces by the factor of N_k both the number of multiplications per input sample and the delay terms required for implementing the branch filters.

3. Coefficient Representation under Consideration

This contribution concentrates on the coefficient quantization in fixed-point arithmetic. In many implementations, it is attractive to carry out the multiplication of a data sample by a filter coefficient value using a sequence of shifts and adds and/or substracts. For such a purpose, it is desirable to express the coefficient values in the form

$$\sum_{r=1}^{R} a_r 2^{-P_r}, \tag{9}$$

where each of the a_r's is either 1 or -1 and the P_r's are non-negative integers in the increasing order.

The goal in optimization problems stated in Section 4 is to minimize the implementation cost by finding all the coefficient values in such a way that, first, R, the number of powers of two, is made as small as possible and, then, P_R, the number of fractional bits, is made as small as possible.

A reasonable estimate for the implementation cost of the filter is the number of adders and/or subtracters required to implement all the adaptor coefficients. When using this estimate, the overall silicon area and the power consumption required by the full-custom VLSI implementation of the filter is roughly minimized (Ohlsson et al., 2001; Wanhammar, 1998).

It should be pointed out that, in addition to adders and/or subtracters needed for the adaptor coefficients, several structural adders are also required for implementing the wave-digital all-pass sections. These first- and second-order wave-digital all-pass sections are constructed based on the use of two-port adaptor structures and delays as depicted in Fig 2. For LWD filters, there exists a great variety of adaptor structures according to the realization possibilities of the analog reference filters (Fettweis, 1986; Fettweis et al., 1974; Gazsi, 1985). The actual multipliers to be implemented and the number of structural adders required to implement the two-port adaptor structures depends on the selected adaptor type.

Figure 6 shows particular symmetric two-port adaptor structures that lead to the optimal scaling for a sinusoidal excitation according to the discussion in (Gazsi, 1985). However, it has been shown, based a further study performed in (Renfors & Zigouris, 1988), that in some cases for the second-order wave-digital all-pass sections, the additional scaling factors c and $1/c$ are required at the input and the output of the second adaptor, respectively, in order to achieve the optimal scaling. In order to keep the resulting second-order sections still all-pass, c must be a (positive or negative) power of two. Due to this fact, the above improved scaling has no effect on the overall procedure and the results achieved in this contribution.

The selection among the four optional structures of Fig. 6 depends on the value of the multiplier γ such that the structures of Figs. 6(a), 6(b), 6(c), and 6(d) are chosen for $\frac{1}{2} < \gamma < 1$, $0 < \gamma \leq \frac{1}{2}$, $-\frac{1}{2} \leq \gamma < 0$, and $-1 < \gamma < -\frac{1}{2}$, respectively. In these cases, the value of α, the actual multiplier to be implemented, depends on the value of γ as follows:

$$\alpha = \begin{cases} 1 - \gamma & \text{for} \quad \frac{1}{2} < \gamma < 1 \\ \gamma & \text{for} \quad 0 < \gamma \leq \frac{1}{2} \\ -\gamma & \text{for} \quad -\frac{1}{2} \leq \gamma < 0 \\ 1 + \gamma & \text{for} \quad -1 < \gamma < -\frac{1}{2}. \end{cases} \tag{10}$$

Consequently, the value of α is always positive and less than or equal to half. Therefore, when the absolute value of γ is greater than half, the number of adders required for implementing the corresponding α coefficient decreases by one.

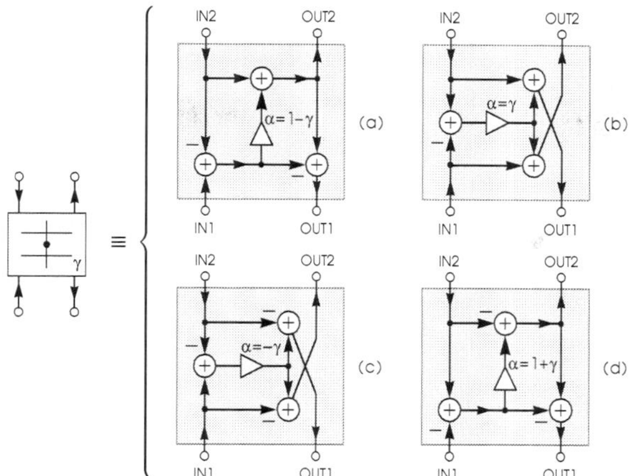

Fig. 6. Efficient two-port adaptor structures yielding optimal scaling for a sinusoidal excitation (Gazsi, 1985).

4. Optimization Problems for the Filter Classes under Consideration

This chapter summarizes the optimization problems for all the three filter classes under consideration in this book chapter. For each filter class, the specifications, the adjustable parameter vector, and the optimization problem will be described.

Before stating the optimization problem for each of the above-mentioned three filter classes, the transfer function for each filter class is denoted in the same manner by $H(\Phi, z)$, where Φ is the adjustable parameter vector containing the adjustable parameters which depend on the filter class at hand in a manner to be described later on. Similarly, the magnitude criteria are stated in the common manner as follows. Given Ω_p and Ω_s, the passband and stopband regions, respectively, as well as δ_p and δ_s, the passband and stopband ripples, respectively, the magnitude specifications for the filter are stated as follows:

$$1 - \delta_p \leq |H(\Phi, e^{j\omega})| \leq 1 \quad \text{for } \omega \in \Omega_p \tag{11a}$$

$$|H(\Phi, e^{j\omega})| \leq \delta_s \quad \text{for } \omega \in \Omega_s. \tag{11b}$$

It is worth pointing out that these specifications are typical of most recursive filters built using all-pass filters as building blocks as, in these most cases, the filter structure constrains the maximum of the magnitude response to be unity. Alternatively, the above criteria are expressible as

$$|E(\Phi, \omega)| \leq 1 \quad \text{for } \omega \in \Omega_p \cup \Omega_s \tag{12a}$$

$$E(\Phi, \omega) \leq 0 \quad \text{for } \omega \in \Omega_p, \tag{12b}$$

where

$$E(\Phi, \omega) = W(\omega)[|H(\Phi, e^{j\omega})| - D(\omega)] \tag{12c}$$

with

$$D(\omega) = \begin{cases} 1 & \text{for } \omega \in \Omega_p \\ 0 & \text{for } \omega \in \Omega_s \end{cases} \quad \text{and} \quad W(\omega) = \begin{cases} 1/\delta_p & \text{for } \omega \in \Omega_p \\ 1/\delta_s & \text{for } \omega \in \Omega_s. \end{cases} \tag{12d}$$

As the third option for later use, the above magnitude criteria are stated as

$$0 \leq 20 \log_{10}|H(\Phi, e^{j\omega})| \leq -A_p \quad \text{for } \omega \in \Omega_p \tag{13a}$$

$$20 \log_{10}|H(\Phi, e^{j\omega})| \leq -A_s \quad \text{for } \omega \in \Omega_s, \tag{13b}$$

where

$$A_p = -20 \log_{10}(1 - \delta_p) \quad \text{and} \quad A_s = -20 \log_{10}(\delta_s) \tag{13c}$$

are the admissible positive passband variation and stopband attenuation, respectively. These criteria will be mainly used in connection of Examples of Section 6 for specifying the magnitude criteria for the three filter classes under consideration.

The target in all of the following optimization problems is to find the quantized values of the adaptor coefficients corresponding to the parameter values included in Φ such that, first, the coefficient values are expressible in the form of (9) and, second, the number of adders and subtracters required to implement all the adaptor coefficient is minimized.

4.1 Cascade Connection of LWD Filters

According to the construction of the overall transfer function for these filters in Subsection 2.1 by means of (1), (2a), (2b), (3a), and (3b), the optimization problem is stated in the low-pass case as follows: Find K, the number of sub-stages, $M_0^{(k)}$ and $M_1^{(k)}$ for $k = 1, 2, \ldots, K$, the orders of the all-pass subfilters, as well as the adjustable parameter vector as given by

$$\begin{aligned}
\Phi = \Big[& r_0^{(1)}, r_1^{(1)}, \ldots, r_{L_0^{(1)}+L_1^{(1)}}^{(1)}, \theta_1^{(1)}, \theta_2^{(1)}, \ldots, \theta_{L_0^{(1)}+L_1^{(1)}}^{(1)}, \\
& r_0^{(2)}, r_1^{(2)}, \ldots, r_{L_0^{(2)}+L_1^{(2)}}^{(2)}, \theta_1^{(2)}, \theta_2^{(2)}, \ldots, \theta_{L_0^{(2)}+L_1^{(2)}}^{(2)}, \ldots, \\
& r_0^{(K)}, r_1^{(K)}, \ldots, r_{L_0^{(K)}+L_1^{(K)}}^{(K)}, \theta_1^{(K)}, \theta_2^{(K)}, \ldots, \theta_{L_0^{(K)}+L_1^{(K)}}^{(K)} \Big],
\end{aligned} \tag{14}$$

in such a way that the criteria given by (12a)–(12d) are met and the above-mentioned target for the coefficient implementations is achieved.

4.2 Approximately Linear-Phase LWD Filters

In the sequel, when synthesizing approximately linear-phase low-pass LWD filters, in addition to the magnitude criteria of (12a)–(12d), the phase requirements are stated as follows (Surma-aho & Saramäki, 1999):

$$|\arg H(\Phi, e^{j\omega}) - \tau\omega| \leq \Delta \quad \text{for } \omega \in \Omega_p. \tag{15}$$

Here, $\arg H(\Phi, e^{j\omega})$ denotes the unwrapped phase response of the filter, whereas τ is the value minimizing the maximum absolute value of $\arg H(\Phi, e^{j\omega}) - \tau\omega$ on the passband region Ω_p and Δ is the upper limit for this maximum. Since only a single LWD filter is under optimization, the adjustable vector reduces to

$$\Phi = \Big[r_0^{(1)}, r_1^{(1)}, \ldots, r_{L_0^{(1)}+L_1^{(1)}}^{(1)}, \theta_1^{(1)}, \theta_2^{(1)}, \ldots, \theta_{L_0^{(1)}+L_1^{(1)}}^{(1)} \Big]. \tag{16}$$

In this case, the optimization problem is the following: Find $M_0^{(1)}$ and $M_1^{(1)}$, the orders of the all-pass subfilters, as well as the adjustable parameter vector Φ, as given by (16), in such a way that in addition to meeting the magnitude criteria of (12a)–(12d), the phase specifications of (15) are satisfied and the above-mentioned target for the coefficient implementations is achieved.

4.3 Recursive Nth-Band Decimators and Interpolators

If the desired sampling rate conversion factor is N, then the passband region of the decimation filter is selected as $\Omega_p = [0, \omega_p]$ where $\omega_p < \pi/N$. The selection of the stopband region Ω_s depends on whether or not aliasing is allowed into the transition band $[\omega_p, \pi/N]$ of the filter. Due to the properties of recursive Nth-band filters, their stopband region for the above-specified passband region is inherently restricted to be (Renfors & Saramäki, 1987)

$$\Omega_s = \bigcup_{r=1}^{\lfloor N/2 \rfloor} \left[r\frac{2\pi}{N} - \omega_p, \min\left(r\frac{2\pi}{N} + \omega_p, \pi\right) \right]. \tag{17}$$

This region has the following properties. First, for $N > 3$, Ω_s is a multiband stopband region that consist of $\lfloor N/2 \rfloor$ bands such that the first $\lfloor N/2 \rfloor - 1$ bands are $[r2\pi/N - \omega_p, r2\pi/N + \omega_p]$ for $r = 1, 2, \ldots, \lfloor N/2 \rfloor - 1$ and the last band is $[\pi - \omega_p, \pi]$ and $[(N-1)2\pi/N - \omega_p, (N-1)\pi/N + \omega_p]$ for N even and odd, respectively (As a typical example, see Fig. 19 in Subsection 6.3 showing the magnitude response for a finite-precision eighth-band ($N = 8$) design.). Second, for $N = 2$ and $N = 3$, $\Omega_s = [\pi - \omega_p, \pi]$ and $\Omega_s = [2\pi/3 - \omega_p, 2\pi/3 + \omega_p]$, respectively. Therefore, first, the lower edge of the first stopband region is located at $\omega = 2\pi/N - \omega_p$ and, second, Ω_s has for $N > 2$, in addition to the transition band of width $2(\pi/N - \omega_p)$, don't care bands of the same width around $\omega_r = (2r+1)\pi/N$ for $r = 1, 2, \ldots, \lfloor (N+1)/2 \rfloor - 1$. The above stopband region guarantees that the aliasing is fully avoidable into the passband region. If this control is desired to extend onto $[0, \pi/N]$, then an additional LWD filter can be implemented after the overall decimation (Renfors & Saramäki, 1987).

This book chapter concentrates on the design of those single-stage and multistage recursive Nth-band decimators, where this additional LWD filter is excluded. For this purpose, the following second main characteristics of the recursive Nth-band filters is utilized. If the maximum magnitude value of the filter on Ω_s is δ_s, then it is guaranteed that in the minimum magnitude value on the passband region $[0, \omega_p]$ is larger than or equal $\sqrt{1 - (N-1)(\delta_s)^2}$ (Renfors & Saramäki, 1987). This implies that for any practical stopband attenuation on Ω_s, the passband variation becomes negligible. Consequently, the design of recursive Nth-band decimator can concentrate on the stopband region Ω_s only. Therefore, the criteria of (11) can be reduced into the following form:

$$E(\Phi, \omega) = |H(\Phi, e^{j\omega})| \leq \delta_s \quad \text{for } \omega \in \Omega_s, \tag{18}$$

where Ω_s is given by (17).

According to the construction of the overall transfer function in the single-stage equivalent in Subsection 2.3 by means of (5), (6), (8a), (8b), and (8c), the optimization problem is stated as follows: Find K, the number of sub-stages, $N_1, N_2, \ldots, N_K$, the decimation factors of the sub-stages, the $L_n^{(k)}$'s, the orders of the branch filters, as well as the adjustable parameter vector as given by

$$
\Phi = \Big[r_1^{(1)}, r_2^{(1)}, \ldots, r_{L_0^{(1)}+L_1^{(1)}+\cdots+L_{N_1-1}^{(1)}}^{(1)},
$$
$$
r_1^{(2)}, r_2^{(2)}, \ldots, r_{L_0^{(2)}+L_1^{(2)}+\cdots+L_{N_2-1}^{(2)}}^{(2)}, \ldots, \tag{19}
$$
$$
r_1^{(K)}, r_2^{(K)}, \ldots, r_{L_0^{(K)}+L_1^{(K)}+\cdots+L_{N_K-1}^{(K)}}^{(K)} \Big],
$$

in such a way that criteria given by (18) are met and the above-mentioned target for the coefficient implementations is achieved.

5. Filter Optimization

The solutions to the three optimization problems stated in the previous section can be found in a similar manner by using the following three steps. In the first step, a filter with infinite-precision coefficients is determined in such a way that it exceeds the given frequency-domain criteria in order to provide some tolerance for coefficient quantization. Then, in the second step, the smallest and largest values are determined for each adjustable parameter by reoptimizing the remaining unknowns in the parameter vector in such a manner that the given specifications are met. This enables one to find the parameter space of the infinite-precision coefficients including the feasible space where the filter meets the specifications. Finally, the third step involves finding the filter parameters in this space so that the resulting filter meets the given criteria with the simplest coefficient representation forms. This strategy is general but particularly efficient for LWD filters due to the fact that for these filters only the denominator coefficients of the all-pass sections have to be quantized.

The proposed quantization scheme provides significant advantages over those based on the use of other existing techniques. First of all, it is always guaranteed that the optimum solution can be found to the above three optimization problems. Second, the computational workload to arrive at the optimum finite-precision solution is in most cases significantly smaller than in other existing techniques.

5.1 Generating the Initial Infinite-Precision Solution

In many cases, finding a good initial solution is not trivial as it implies a good understanding and characterization of the problem. Furthermore, for each problem at hand the way of generating the start-up solution is very different. If there is a systematic approach for finding an initial solution being close to the optimum one, then the above-described three-step procedure gives in most cases more quickly a solution that is better than those obtained, e.g., by using simulated annealing or genetic algorithms.

5.1.1 Cascade connection of LWD filters

The design of an initial conventional LWD filter for further optimization can be carried out by, first, using an appropriate classical analog-filter approximation and, then, converting the resulting continuous-time transfer function into a desired discrete-time transfer function (Antoniou, 1993; Rabiner & Gold, 1975; Schüßler, 2010). Another approach for designing an initial filter is to use explicit formulas developed directly for digital filters in (Gazsi, 1985). It is well known that the odd-order elliptic filter is the most selective low-pass or high-pass filter being implementable as a parallel connection of two all-pass filters [see, e.g., (Gazsi, 1985)]. For

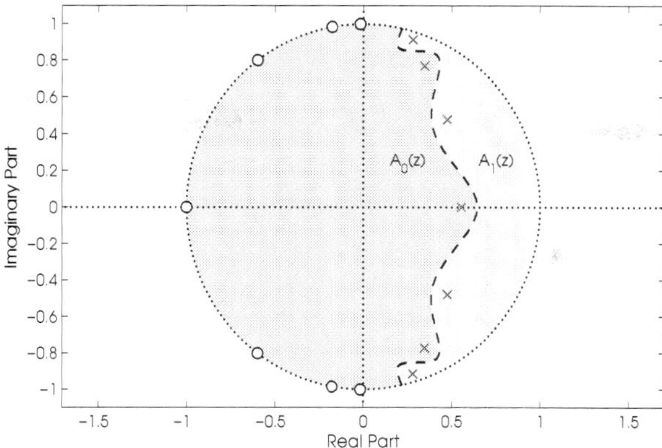

Fig. 7. Alternating distribution for the poles of a prototype filter among the two all-pass filters $A_0(z)$ and $A_1(z)$ for a seventh-order low-pass filter with $\omega_p = 0.4\pi$, $\omega_s = 0.5\pi$, $A_p = 0.2$ dB ($\delta_p = 0.0228$), and $A_s = 60$ dB ($\delta_s = 10^{-3}$).

conventional low-pass, high-pass, band-pass and, band-stop criteria, the order of an elliptic filter meeting the given specifications can be estimated using the well-known approximation formulas (Antoniou, 1993; Rabiner & Gold, 1975; Schüßler, 2010).

Since the real pole and the complex-conjugate pole pairs of the all-pass filters for low-pass and high-pass designs have the real zero and complex-conjugate zero pairs in conjugate reciprocal positions (Antoniou, 1993; Schüßler, 2010), the poles of the designed filter unambiguously determine the all-pass filters. After knowing the poles of the filter, the problem is to implement the overall transfer function in such a way that the poles are properly shared between the two all-pass sections $A_0(z)$ and $A_1(z)$. If the poles are distributed in the low-pass case in a regular manner, then $A_0(z)$ can be selected to realize the real pole, the second innermost complex-conjugate pole pair, the fourth innermost complex-conjugate pole pair and so on, whereas $A_1(z)$ realizes the remaining poles (Gazsi, 1985). For a very complicated pole distribution, the procedure described in (Saramäki, 1985) can be used for sharing the poles between $A_0(z)$ and $A_1(z)$. The alternating distribution of the poles among the two all-pass filters for a seventh-order elliptic prototype filter is illustrated in Fig. 7.

The above discussion applies directly to a single LWD filter. For the cascades of low-order LWD filters, in turn, it has turned out to be advantageous in most cases to select all the $A_0^{(k)}(z)$'s and the $A_1^{(k)}(z)$'s to be of the same order, respectively. In this case, the starting point filter for further optimization can be determined by using several identical copies of the same subfilter. For K identical copies of the same subfilter, the passband and stopband ripples for this subfilter should be approximately equal to δ_p/K and $\sqrt[K]{\delta_s}$, respectively. There is clearly a trade-off between K, the number of subfilters, and the order of the subfilter; the higher is the value of K, the lower is the order of the subfilter. However, since the subfilter order is restricted to be an odd integer, there are only a few practical combinations for the subfilter order and K. It is not necessary for the subfilter being an odd-order elliptic filter to exactly meet the ripple requirements. This is due to the fact that further optimization makes the subfilters different and simultaneously improves the overall filter performance.

5.1.2 Approximately linear-phase LWD filters

For these low-pass LWD filters, there exist no closed-form solution for satisfying both the magnitude criteria of (12a)–(12d) and the phase criteria of (15). Therefore, these filters have to be designed using optimization techniques. An efficient systematic algorithm for designing an initial solution for these filters has been proposed in (Surma-aho, 1997; Surma-aho & Saramäki, 1999). This design scheme consists of two basic steps. The first step involves finding in a simple straightforward manner a good suboptimal solution that determines Φ so that Δ in (15) has a reasonably small value subject to the magnitude specifications. In the second step, this solution is then used as an initial filter for further optimization carried out with the aid of a constrained optimization for minimizing the value of Δ in (15) subject to the magnitude criteria.

5.1.3 Recursive Nth-band decimators and interpolators

The initial infinite-precision solutions for the recursive Nth-band filter in both the single-stage and multistage implementations can be properly synthesized by utilizing the synthesis schemes described in (Renfors & Saramäki, 1987). The design of single-stage filters relies on the properties of these filters and enables one to significantly reduce the number of the original unknowns. Furthermore, the remaining unknowns can be found by means of an efficient Remez-type algorithm. As a result, solutions being very close to the optimized solutions can be achieved in a very fast and reliable manner in comparison with other existing very time-consuming optimization techniques, which are based on optimizing the original unknowns and do not necessarily guarantee the arrival at the optimized solution.

The multistage design, in turn, counts on the fact that each stage, as has been observed in (Renfors & Saramäki, 1987), has its own predetermined frequency range to take care of in order to provide the desired magnitude response for the overall design. Based on this fact, the simultaneous design of the sub-stages can be conveniently performed by iteratively determining them such that they provide for the overall filter as high attenuation as possible in their predetermined frequency ranges. This iteration is continued until the successive overall solutions become practically the same. What is left is to determine the minimum filter orders to meet the given specifications.

5.2 Optimization of Infinite-Precision Filters

The optimization algorithm is based on the following observation. Finding the smallest and largest values for each adjustable parameter by reoptimizing the remaining unknowns in the parameter vector so that the given criteria are still met enables one to determine a parameter space including the feasible space where the filter specifications are satisfied. After figuring out this space, all that is needed is to check whether in this space there exist the desired discrete values for the given coefficient representation form.

5.2.1 Cascade connection of LWD filters

For cascaded LWD filters, the parameter space of the infinite-precision coefficients can be determined as follows. For each complex-conjugate pole pair, the smallest and largest values for both the radius and the angle are determined so that by reoptimizing the locations of the remaining poles the given overall magnitude criteria of (12a)–(12d) can still be met. For the real pole, the smallest and largest values for the radius are found in the same manner. The above procedure gives for the upper-half-plane pole of each complex-conjugate pole pair $r_\ell^{(k)} \exp(\pm j\theta_\ell^{(k)})$ for $\ell = 1, 2, \ldots, L_0^{(k)} + L_1^{(k)}$ and for $k = 1, 2, \ldots, K$, the region $R \exp(j\Theta)$ where

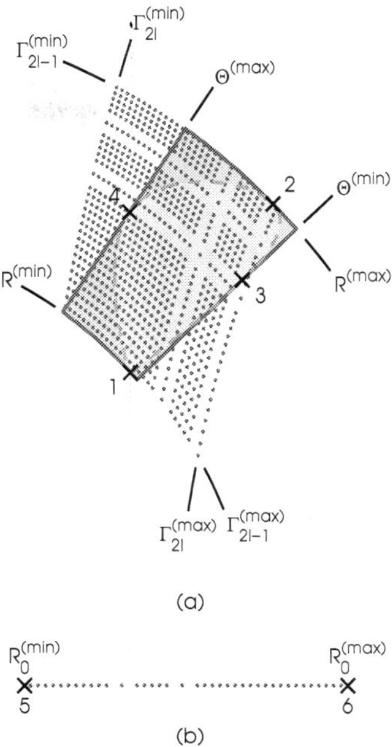

Fig. 8. Typical search spaces for the poles when three powers of two with seven fractional bits ($R = 3$ and $P_R = 7$) are used for the adaptor coefficients. (a) Upper-half-plane pole for the complex-conjugate pole pair. (b) Real pole.

$R^{(\min)} \leq R \leq R^{(\max)}$ and $\Theta^{(\min)} \leq \Theta \leq \Theta^{(\max)}$, as illustrated in Fig. 8(a). The crosses numbered by 1, 2, 3, and 4 correspond, respectively, to the points where the smallest radius $R^{(\min)}$, the largest radius $R^{(\max)}$, the smallest angle $\Theta^{(\min)}$, and the largest angle $\Theta^{(\max)}$ are reached. Inside this region, there is the feasible region, given by the dashed line in Fig. 8(a), where the pole can be located such that by relocating the remaining poles the given overall criteria are still met by using an infinite-precision arithmetic. For each real pole $r_0^{(k)}$ for $k = 1, 2, \ldots, K$, there exists the corresponding region $R_0^{(\min)} \leq R \leq R_0^{(\max)}$ that is simultaneously the feasible region. In Fig. 8(b), the crosses numbered by 5 and 6 indicate $R_0^{(\min)}$ and $R_0^{(\max)}$, respectively.

For the complex-conjugate pole pairs, the larger region is used because it can be found very quickly by applying only four times the algorithm to be described next. For the real pole, there is a need to use this algorithm only twice. Hence, in order to find the above-mentioned regions for all the poles of the low-pass transfer function, as given by (1), (2a), (2b), (3a), and (3b), there are for each of the K sub-stages $2 + 4(L_0^{(k)} + L_1^{(k)})$ problems of the following form: Find the adjustable parameter vector Φ to minimize ψ subject to the conditions of (12a)–(12d). For these problems, ψ is $r_0^{(k)}$ and $-r_0^{(k)}$ for the real pole, whereas for the complex-conjugate pole pairs, ψ is selected to be $r_\ell^{(k)}$, $-r_\ell^{(k)}$, $\theta_\ell^{(k)}$, and $-\theta_\ell^{(k)}$ for $\ell = 1, 2, \ldots, L_0^{(k)} + L_1^{(k)}$.

In order to guarantee the stability of the resulting filters and to prevent the poles from changing their ordering, e.g., to inhibit the outermost complex-conjugate pole pair from becoming the second outermost complex-conjugate pole pair when minimizing its radius, the following additional constraints:

$$-1 \leq r_0^{(1)} \leq r_0^{(2)} \leq \cdots \leq r_0^{(K)} < 1 \tag{20a}$$

and

$$0 \leq r_1^{(1)} \leq r_1^{(2)} \leq \cdots \leq r_1^{(K)} \leq r_{L_0^{(1)}+1}^{(1)} \leq r_{L_0^{(2)}+1}^{(2)} \leq \cdots \leq r_{L_0^{(K)}+1}^{(K)}$$

$$\leq r_2^{(1)} \leq r_2^{(2)} \leq \cdots \leq r_2^{(K)} \leq r_{L_0^{(1)}+2}^{(1)} \leq r_{L_0^{(2)}+2}^{(2)} \leq \cdots \leq r_{L_0^{(K)}+2}^{(K)} \leq \cdots$$

$$\leq r_{L_0^{(1)}}^{(1)} \leq r_{L_0^{(2)}}^{(2)} \leq \cdots \leq r_{L_0^{(K)}}^{(K)} \leq r_{L_0^{(1)}+L_1^{(1)}}^{(1)} \leq r_{L_0^{(2)}+L_1^{(2)}}^{(2)} \leq \cdots \leq r_{L_0^{(K)}+L_1^{(K)}}^{(K)} < 1 \tag{20b}$$

are required.[2]

For later use, $\Phi_1^{(k)}$ and $\Phi_2^{(k)}$ denote the solutions with minimized $r_0^{(k)}$ and $-r_0^{(k)}$ (maximized $r_0^{(k)}$), whereas

$$\Phi_{2+\ell}^{(k)}, \quad \Phi_{2+(L_0^{(k)}+L_1^{(k)})+\ell}^{(k)}, \quad \Phi_{2+2(L_0^{(k)}+L_1^{(k)})+\ell}^{(k)}, \quad \text{and} \quad \Phi_{2+3(L_0^{(k)}+L_1^{(k)})+\ell}^{(k)}$$

for $\ell = 1, 2, \ldots, L_0^{(k)} + L_1^{(k)}$ denote the solutions with the minimized $r_\ell^{(k)}$, the minimized $-r_\ell^{(k)}$ (maximized $r_\ell^{(k)}$), the minimized $\Theta_\ell^{(k)}$, and the minimized $-\Theta_\ell^{(k)}$ (maximized $\Theta_\ell^{(k)}$), respectively.

To solve these problems, the passband and stopband regions in the magnitude criteria of (12a)–(12d) are discretized into the frequency points $\omega_i \in \Omega_p$ for $i = 1, 2, \ldots, \Xi_p$ and $\omega_i \in \Omega_s$ for $i = \Xi_p + 1, \Xi_p + 2, \ldots, \Xi_p + \Xi_s$, which gives rise to the following discretized criteria:

$$|E(\Phi, \omega_i)| - 1 \leq 0 \quad \text{for} \quad i = 1, 2, \ldots, \Xi_p + \Xi_s \tag{21a}$$

and

$$E(\Phi, \omega_i) \leq 0 \quad \text{for} \quad i = 1, 2, \ldots, \Xi_p. \tag{21b}$$

The resulting discrete minimization problems are to find Φ to minimize ψ subject to the constraints of (20a) and (20b) and the constraints of (21a) and (21b). Here, ψ is one of the above-mentioned $2 + 4(L_0^{(k)} + L_1^{(k)})$ problems for each of the K sub-stages, that is, the total number

---

[2] In these constraints, it is assumed that the following two facts are valid. First, the transfer function, as given by (1), (2a), (2b), (3a), and (3b), is either a low-pass or high-pass filter design. Second, the orders of K subfilters, as given by $2(L_0^{(k)} + L_1^{(k)}) + 1$ for $k = 1, 2, \ldots, K$ are the same, denoted by $2\tilde{L} + 1$ so that each stage has $\tilde{L}$ complex-conjugate pole-pairs. Under these assumptions, (20a) means that the radius of the real pole for the $(k+1)$th stage is larger than that for the kth stage for $k = 1, 2, \ldots, K - 1$. According to (20b), the same is true when considering the radii of the innermost complex-conjugate pole pairs included in the K sub-stages. Furthermore, this fact is valid up to the $\tilde{L}$th innermost pole pairs (that are simultaneously the outmost pole pairs) in these sub-stages. In addition, (20b) implies that the radius of the second innermost complex-conjugate pole pair in the first stage is larger than the radius of the innermost complex-conjugate pole pair in the last stage and the same constraint is true up to the $\tilde{L}$th innermost pole pairs.

of problems is

$$\sum_{k=1}^{K} \left[2 + 4(L_0^{(k)} + L_1^{(k)}) \right].$$

The above-mentioned problems can be conveniently solved by using the second algorithm of Dutta and Vidyasagar (Dutta & Vidyasagar, 1977) or the function **fmincon** from the optimization toolbox provided by MathWorks, Inc. (Coleman *et al.*, 1999). For more detail, see (Saramäki & Yli-Kaakinen, 2002; Yli-Kaakinen, 2002; Yli-Kaakinen & Saramäki, 2007).

For transfer functions, as given by (1), (2a), (2b), (3a), and (3b), the key goal is to quantize the adaptor coefficients $\gamma_\ell^{(k)}$ for $\ell = 0, 1, \ldots, 2(L_0^{(k)} + L_1^{(k)})$ and for $k = 1, 2, \ldots, K$ to achieve the optimization target stated in Section 4. It can be shown that the larger region including the feasible region, where LWD filter meets the given criteria, can be determined, by means of the above solutions $\Phi_p^{(k)}$ for $p = 1, 2, \ldots, 2 + 4(L_0^{(k)} + L_1^{(k)})$ and for $k = 1, 2, \ldots, K$, by specifying the minimum and maximum values of $\gamma_\ell^{(k)}$ for $\ell = 0, 1, \ldots, 2(L_0^{(k)} + L_1^{(k)})$ and for $k = 1, 2, \ldots, K$ as follows:

$$\gamma_\ell^{(k)(\min)} = \min_{p=1,2,\ldots,2+4(L_0^{(k)}+L_1^{(k)})} \{\gamma_{\ell,p}^{(k)}\} \quad \text{and} \quad \gamma_\ell^{(k)(\max)} = \max_{p=1,2,\ldots,2+4(L_0^{(k)}+L_1^{(k)})} \{\gamma_{\ell,p}^{(k)}\}, \quad (22)$$

where $\gamma_{\ell,p}^{(k)}$ denotes the value of $\gamma_\ell^{(k)}$ determined according to the pth solution, $\Phi_p^{(k)}$, of the above-mentioned optimization problems.

As shown in Fig. 8(a), the search space determined in the above manner by the adaptor coefficient values for the complex-conjugate pole pairs is significantly larger than the corresponding original space found in terms of the radius and the angle for the pole pair under consideration. When concentrating in the sequel on determining desired finite-precision values for the adaptor coefficients, the use of the smaller search space will be utilized in a manner to be described later on in Subsection 5.3.4.

5.2.2 Approximately linear-phase LWD Filters

When determining the smallest and largest radius of the real pole and the smallest and largest values of the radius and the angle for each of the complex-conjugate pole pairs for the approximately linear-phase LWD filters, there are two main differences compared to the cascaded LWD filters. First, the overall filter is constructed as a single stage, that is, $K = 1$. Therefore, the constraints of (20a) and (20b) reduce, in the low-pass case, to the constraints that all the radii are less than unity and the complex-conjugate pole pairs are ordered in terms of their radii such that their ordering remains intact. Second, in addition to the above-mentioned constraints on the radii of the poles and the magnitude-response constraints of (21a) and (21b), the following phase-response constraints:

$$\left| \arg H(\Phi, e^{j\omega_i}) - \tau\omega_i \right| - \Delta \leq 0 \quad \text{for } i = 1, 2, \ldots, \Xi_p \tag{23}$$

should be included. These constraints are obtained from the original phase response constraint, as given by (15) in Subsection 4.2, by dicretizing the passband region into the frequency points $\omega_i \in \Omega_p$ for $i = 1, 2, \ldots, \Xi_p$ in a manner similar to that performed earlier for the magnitude criteria.

5.2.3 Recursive Nth-band decimators and interpolators

For recursive Nth-band decimators and interpolators, there are also two differences compared to the cascaded LWD filters when determining the parameter space of the infinite-precision coefficients. First, the transfer functions, as given by (8a), (8b), and (8c), have only real poles and, therefore, the number of problems reduces to $2\sum_{n=0}^{N_k-1} L_n^{(k)}$ for each of the K sub-stages. For these problems, ψ is $r_\ell^{(k)}$ and $-r_\ell^{(k)}$ for $\ell = 1, 2, \ldots, L_0^{(k)} + L_1^{(k)} + \cdots + L_{N_k-1}^{(k)}$ and for $k = 1, 2, \ldots, K$. In this case,

$$\Phi_\ell^{(k)} \quad \text{and} \quad \Phi_{L_0^{(k)}+L_1^{(k)}+\cdots+L_{N_k-1}^{(k)}+\ell}^{(k)}$$

for $\ell = 1, 2, \ldots, L_0^{(k)} + L_1^{(k)} + \cdots + L_{N_k-1}^{(k)}$ denote the solutions with minimized $r_\ell^{(k)}$ and $-r_\ell^{(k)}$ (maximized $r_\ell^{(k)}$), respectively. The above procedure gives for each real pole $r_\ell^{(k)}$ for $\ell = 1, 2, \ldots, L_0^{(k)} + L_1^{(k)} + \cdots + L_{N_k-1}^{(k)}$ and for $k = 1, 2, \ldots, K$, the region $r_\ell^{(k)(\min)} \leq r_\ell^{(k)} \leq r_\ell^{(k)(\max)}$ that is directly the feasible region, where the pole can be located such that by relocating the remaining poles the given overall criteria are still met by using the infinite-precision arithmetic. Second, the constraints of (20a) and (20b) for the radii of the real poles and for the complex-conjugate pole pairs are replaced by the following constraints for radii of the real poles:

$$-1 \leq r_1^{(k)} \leq r_{L_0^{(k)}+1}^{(k)} \leq \cdots \leq r_{L_0^{(k)}+L_1^{(k)}+\cdots+L_{N_1-2}^{(k)}+1}^{(k)}$$
$$\leq r_2^{(k)} \leq r_{L_0^{(k)}+2}^{(k)} \leq \cdots \leq r_{L_0^{(k)}+L_1^{(k)}+\cdots+L_{N_1-2}^{(k)}+2}^{(k)} \leq \cdots \leq$$
$$\leq r_{L_0^{(k)}}^{(k)} \leq r_{L_0^{(k)}+L_1^{(k)}}^{(k)} \leq \cdots \leq r_{L_0^{(k)}+L_1^{(k)}+\cdots+L_{N_1-1}^{(k)}}^{(k)} \leq 0, \tag{24}$$

for $k = 1, 2 \ldots, K$.[3]

---

[3] In this constraint, each of the K sub-stages is considered independently of each other due to their own predetermined frequency-response shaping responsibilities in providing the desired overall magnitude response (Renfors & Saramäki, 1987) in contrast to the cascaded LWD filters, where all the filter stages generate as joint effort the overall response in the same passband and stopband regions. For the kth stage for $k = 1, 2, \ldots, K$, the above constraint simply means the following four experimentally observed facts. First, all the poles are located on the negative real axis. Second, if the overall number of adjustable poles in the kth stage is $T_1 N_k + T_2$, where N_k is the decimation factor after this stage and T_1 and T_2 are integers, then the nth all-pass filter transfer function $A_n^{(k)}(z)$, which is involved in generating the kth stage in the single-stage equivalent in Section 2.3 according to (8a), (8b), and (8c), contains $T_1 + 1$ and T_1 adjustable real pole locations for $n = 0, 1, \ldots, T_2 - 1$ and for $n = T_2, T_2 + 1, \ldots, N_k - 1$, respectively. Third, when considering the radii of the outermost poles in the above-mentioned all-pass filter transfer functions for $n = 0, 1, \ldots, T_2 - 1$, the radius of the nth transfer function is less than that of $(n + 1)$th transfer function. Fourth, if $T_1 > 1$ and it is assumed that the outermost real pole is absent for $n = T_2, T_2 + 1, \ldots, N_k - 1$, then the following two additional facts are true. First, the above-mentioned third fact is true starting from the second outermost real poles up to the innermost real pole for $n = 0, 1, \ldots, N_k - 1$. Second, if the location of the pole of the last transfer function is more innermost than that of first transfer function, then its radius is smaller.

5.3 Optimization of Finite-Precision Filters

It has been experimentally proved that the above-defined parameter space for each of three filter types under consideration forms a space including the feasible space where the filter specifications are satisfied. After finding this larger space, all that is needed is to check whether in this space there exist combinations of the discrete pole positions with which the given overall criteria are met.

5.3.1 Cascade connection of LWD filters

For cascade connections of low-order LWD filters, this search can be conveniently accomplished by first finding the sets of powers-of-two numbers $\Gamma_\ell^{(k)}$ for $\ell = 0, 1, \ldots, 2(L_0^{(k)} + L_1^{(k)})$ and for $k = 1, 2, \ldots, K$ between the smallest and largest values of each adaptor coefficient, that is, by determining

$$\left\{ \Gamma_\ell^{(k)} \in \text{POT}_{(R,P_R)} \mid \gamma_\ell^{(k)(\min)} \leq \Gamma_\ell \leq \gamma_\ell^{(k)(\max)} \right\}. \tag{25}$$

for $\ell = 0, 1, \ldots, 2(L_0^{(k)} + L_1^{(k)})$ and for $k = 1, 2, \ldots, K$. Here, $\text{POT}_{(R,P_R)}$ denotes the space of the powers-of-two numbers for R, the given maximum number of power-of-two terms, and P_R, the maximum number of fractional bits [cf. (9)]. Denote by $S_\ell^{(k)}$ the number of powers-of-two values between $\gamma_\ell^{(k)(\min)}$ and $\gamma_\ell^{(k)(\max)}$. Furthermore, denote by $\Gamma_\ell^{(k)(s)}$ for $s = 1, 2, \ldots, S_\ell^{(k)}$ the sth existing discrete value between these smallest and largest values.

The magnitude response is then evaluated for each combination of the $\Gamma_\ell^{(k)(s)}$ for $\ell = 0, 1, \ldots, 2(L_0^{(k)} + L_1^{(k)})$ and $s = 1, 2, \ldots, S_\ell^{(k)}$ to check whether the filter meets the given specifications. Hence, the number of discrete coefficient value combinations to be considered is

$$\prod_{k=1}^{K} \prod_{\ell=0}^{2(L_0^{(k)}+L_1^{(k)})} S_\ell^{(k)}. \tag{26}$$

5.3.2 Approximately linear-phase LWD Filters

For approximately linear-phase LWD filters, the phase response is evaluated for all the solutions satisfying the magnitude specifications to make sure that the finite-wordlength filter meets the given overall criteria, that is, also the phase criteria of (23).

5.3.3 Recursive Nth-band decimators and interpolators

For multistage decimators and interpolators, this finite-precision search can be performed independently for each filter stage as in the single-stage equivalent described in Subsection 2.3, all the filter stages have, according to the discussion in (Renfors & Saramäki, 1987), their own roles in providing the given attenuation in the predetermined stopband regions. This considerably reduces the overall optimization time. Furthermore, having only real poles in the overall implementation significantly reduces the overall finite-precision optimization time.

5.3.4 Finite wordlength considerations

The proper values for R and P_R are selected to be the smallest values for which there exist the discrete coefficient values between the smallest and largest values for the adaptor coefficients. If no solution satisfying the prescribed criteria are found for the predetermined discrete coefficient representation form, then another less stringent coefficient representation has to be tried, that is, the wordlength or the maximum number of power-of-two terms is gradually increased and the search is restarted until one or more desired finite-precision filters meeting the given specifications are found.

It should be pointed out that for certain given wordlengths, there are typically several solutions meeting the magnitude specifications. Therefore, it is advisable to find first all the solutions satisfying the given criteria and then to choose among which the one with the best attenuation characteristics or the minimum number of adders and/or subtracters required to implement all the multipliers for the given wordlength.

In Fig. 8, the dots indicate the allowable locations for both the upper-half-plane complex-conjugate pole and a real pole when three power-of-two terms with seven fractional bits are used for the adaptor coefficient representations ($R = 3$ and $P_R = 7$). Note that these distributions are highly irregular for a few power-of-two terms due to the desired coefficient representation form. However, as can be seen from this figure, there are, particularly for the innermost complex-conjugate pole, regions where the angle of the pole corresponding to finite-precision values of γ_{2l-1} and γ_{2l} is smaller than $\Theta^{(min)}$ or larger than $\Theta^{(max)}$. For this reason, it is advisable to check whether the angle of the discrete pole is in the prescribed region in order to avoid the vain evaluation of the corresponding magnitude response. In addition, it is beneficial, in order to speed up the search, to check whether the filter meets the given magnitude specifications in two steps. First, the magnitude response is evaluated at band edges, that is, in the low-pass case at $\omega = \omega_p$ and at $\omega = \omega_s$. Second, only if the magnitude response at these points stays within the given specifications, the remaining frequency points are evaluated. This is because the worst-case deviations in both the passband(s) and stopband(s) of the resulting finite-precision filter occur most likely at the band edges.

6. Numerical Examples

This section shows, by means of examples, the applicability of the overall synthesis scheme described in the previous section for solving three optimization problems stated in Section 4. More examples can be found in (Yli-Kaakinen, 1998; 2002; Yli-Kaakinen & Saramäki, 1999a;b; 2000; 2005; 2007).

6.1 Example 1

This example is included to illustrate the performance of the proposed overall synthesis scheme for designing cascade connections of low-order LWD filters as well as to show the superiority of these cascaded filters over direct LWD filters in finite wordlength implementations.

It is desired to design a low-pass filter with the passband and stopband edges at $\omega_p = 0.1\pi$ and at $\omega_s = 0.2\pi$, respectively. The maximum allowable passband ripple is $A_p = 0.5$ dB ($\delta_p = 0.0559$) and the minimum stopband attenuation is at least $A_s = 100$ dB ($\delta_s = 10^{-5}$), respectively.

When the three-stage quantization scheme described in Section 5 is applied to $K = 4$, that is, the overall transfer function is a cascade of four LWD filters of the same order, the initial infinite-precision start-up solution for further optimization described in Subsection 5.1.1 (the first main step of Section 5) can be determined by using four identical copies of a third-order elliptic filter with the passband ripple of $\delta_p/4 = 0.0143$ and the stopband ripple of $\sqrt[4]{\delta_s} = 0.0562$. The minimum odd order of an elliptic filter to meet the given magnitude criteria is three. For this third-order initial elliptic subfilter just meeting the given passband criteria, the minimum stopband attenuation is 25.75 dB ($\delta_s = 0.05158$). The radius of the real pole as well

$A_0^{(1,2,3,4)}(z)$	$A_1^{(1,2,3,4)}(z)$	
$r_0^{(1,2,3,4)} = 0.714\,855$	$r_1^{(1,2,3,4)} = 0.893\,594$	$\theta_1^{(1,2,3,4)} = 0.118\,835\pi$

Table 1. Initial pole locations for the cascade of four LWD filters in Example 1.

as the radius and positive angle of the complex-conjugate pole pair for these initial subfilters are given in Table 1. This initial filter already meets the given magnitude specifications and can, therefore, be used itself without further optimization for accomplishing the second main step of Section 5 that is described for these cascaded LWD filters in Subsection 5.2.1.

The smallest and largest values of the adaptor coefficients after the infinite-precision optimization of this subsection are included in Table 2. In addition, this table gives the smallest and largest values of the adaptor coefficients quantized at the third main step of Section 5 that is described for these filters in Section 5.3.1 to the three power-of-two terms and five fractional bits ($R = 3$ and $P_R = 5$).[4] The number of admissible discrete values $S_\ell^{(k)}$ between $\gamma_\ell^{(k)(\min)}$ and $\gamma_\ell^{(k)(\min)}$ for $\ell = 0, 1, 2$ and for $k = 1, 2, 3, 4$ are also summarized in this table. In this case, the overall number of combinations to be evaluated is approximately $134 \cdot 10^6$ [cf. (26)]. The CPU time required by a Fortran 95 program to evaluate all these finite-precision coefficient combinations on a 1.4-GHz Pentium-M with $\Xi_p = \Xi_s = 30$ [cf. (21a) and (21b)] was approximately 400 seconds.

The search space after the infinite-precision optimization is depicted in Fig. 9. In this figure, the circles indicate the allowable locations for the poles inside the search space for the above-mentioned adaptor coefficient representation form, whereas the largest, the second largest, the third largest, and the smallest search spaces correspond to the kth sub-stage for $k = 1$, $k = 2$, $k = 3$, and $k = 4$, respectively.

The specifications are met by the adaptor coefficients given in Table 3. A total of only six adders and/or subtracters are required to implement all the adaptor coefficients when the adaptors shown in Fig. 6 are used. Note that two sub-stages are identical. For this coefficient representation form, there are 17 finite-precision solutions meeting the specifications among which the one with the minimum implementation cost is selected. In Figure 9, the crosses denote the pole locations of this optimal solution. Figure 10 shows for this design the magnitude responses of the four sub-stages as well as that of the overall filter. In addition, the passband details of the magnitude response for the overall filter is included in this figure. The pole-zero plot for the overall design is depicted in Fig. 11.

For $K = 1$, in turn, that is, for the single-stage design, the given criteria are met by the ninth-order filter with adaptor coefficients given in Table 4. In this case, four power-of-two terms with nine fractional bits ($R = 4$ and $P_R = 9$) are required by the adaptor coefficients to still meet the magnitude criteria. The magnitude responses and the pole-zero plot for this direct LWD design are depicted in Figs. 12 and 13, respectively.

The above cascade of four low-order LWD filter sections is very attractive for VLSI implementations because the use of a costly multiplier element can be replaced by a harwired logic. If the adaptors of Fig. 6 are utilized, then this harwired logic requires at most two power-of-two

---

[4] In this case, three power-of-two terms and four fractional bits ($R = 3$ and $P_R = 4$) is the shortest wordlength for which there exist at least one discrete value between the smallest and largest values of each adaptor coefficient. However, for this coefficient wordlength, there is no solution satisfying the given specifications.

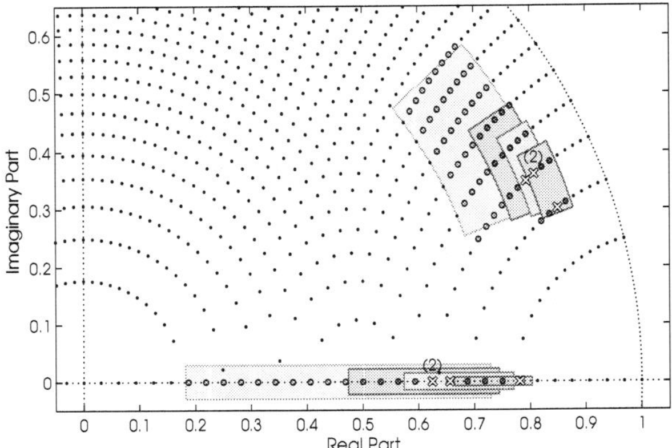

Fig. 9. Search spaces for the cascade of four LWD filters in Example 1 in the $R = 3$ and $P_R = 5$ case.

k	ℓ	$\gamma_\ell^{(k)(\min)}(z)$	$\gamma_\ell^{(k)(\max)}(z)$	$\Gamma_\ell^{(k)(1)}(z)$	$\Gamma_\ell^{(k)(S_\ell^{(k)})}(z)$	$S_\ell^{(k)}$
	0	0.182392	0.729620	$2^{-2} - 2^{-4}$	$1 - 2^{-2} - 2^{-5}$	18
1	1	-0.802832	-0.531560	$-1 + 2^{-2} - 2^{-5}$	$-2^{-1} - 2^{-4}$	8
	2	0.739326	0.931286	$1 - 2^{-2}$	$1 - 2^{-3} + 2^{-5}$	6
	0	0.473568	0.745019	2^{-1}	$1 - 2^{-2} - 2^{-5}$	8
2	1	-0.817631	-0.666228	$-1 + 2^{-2} - 2^{-4}$	$-1 + 2^{-2} + 2^{-4}$	5
	2	0.835625	0.934313	$1 - 2^{-3} - 2^{-5}$	$1 - 2^{-3} + 2^{-5}$	3
	0	0.573298	0.770266	$2^{-1} + 2^{-3} - 2^{-5}$	$1 - 2^{-2}$	6
3	1	-0.834543	-0.726433	$-1 + 2^{-2} - 2^{-4}$	$-1 + 2^{-2}$	3
	2	0.863579	0.937735	$1 - 2^{-3}$	$1 - 2^{-4}$	3
	0	0.663425	0.802724	$1 - 2^{-2} - 2^{-4}$	$1 - 2^{-2} + 2^{-5}$	4
4	1	-0.861770	-0.757413	$-1 + 2^{-3} + 2^{-5}$	$-1 + 2^{-2} - 2^{-5}$	3
	2	0.887134	0.942355	$1 - 2^{-3} + 2^{-5}$	$1 - 2^{-4}$	2

Table 2. The smallest and largest values for both the infinite-precision and finite-precision coefficients in Example 1.

terms, instead of $R = 3$ terms, containing only $P_R = 5$ fractional for implementing all the α values in these adaptors.

In comparison, the direct LWD design requires for some coefficient values $R = 4$ power-of-two terms and $P_R = 9$ fractional bits. The price paid for this significantly reduced complexity in implementing the adaptor coefficient values in the cascaded implementation is a slight increase (from nine to twelve) in the overall filter order compared to the direct LWD filter.

Another remarkable advantage of the proposed cascaded filter in comparison with the direct LWD filter is that the radius of the outermost complex-conjugate pole pair is significantly

$A_0^{(k)}(z)$		$A_1^{(k)}(z)$	
$\gamma_0^{(1,2)} = 2^{-1} + 2^{-3}$	$\gamma_1^{(1,2)} = -1 + 2^{-2} - 2^{-5}$	$\gamma_2^{(1,2)} = 1 - 2^{-3} + 2^{-5}$	
$\gamma_0^{(3)} = 2^{-1} + 2^{-3} + 2^{-5}$	$\gamma_1^{(3)} = -1 + 2^{-2}$	$\gamma_2^{(3)} = 1 - 2^{-3} + 2^{-5}$	
$\gamma_0^{(4)} = 1 - 2^{-2} + 2^{-5}$	$\gamma_1^{(4)} = -1 + 2^{-2} - 2^{-4}$	$\gamma_2^{(4)} = 1 - 2^{-4}$	

Table 3. Optimized finite-precision adaptor coefficients for the cascade of four LWD filters in Example 1.

$A_0^{(0)}(z)$	$A_1^{(1)}(z)$
$\gamma_0^{(1)} = 1 - 2^{-3} + 2^{-6}$	
$\gamma_1^{(1)} = -1 + 2^{-3} + 2^{-6} + 2^{-9}$	$\gamma_5^{(1)} = -1 + 2^{-2} - 2^{-4} + 2^{-9}$
$\gamma_2^{(1)} = 1 - 2^{-5}$	$\gamma_6^{(1)} = 1 - 2^{-6} + 2^{-9}$
$\gamma_3^{(1)} = -1 + 2^{-5} - 2^{-7} - 2^{-9}$	$\gamma_7^{(1)} = -1 + 2^{-4} + 2^{-6}$
$\gamma_4^{(1)} = 1 - 2^{-4} - 2^{-8}$	$\gamma_8^{(1)} = 1 - 2^{-4} + 2^{-6} - 2^{-8}$

Table 4. Optimized finite-precision adaptor coefficients for the direct LWD filter in Example 1.

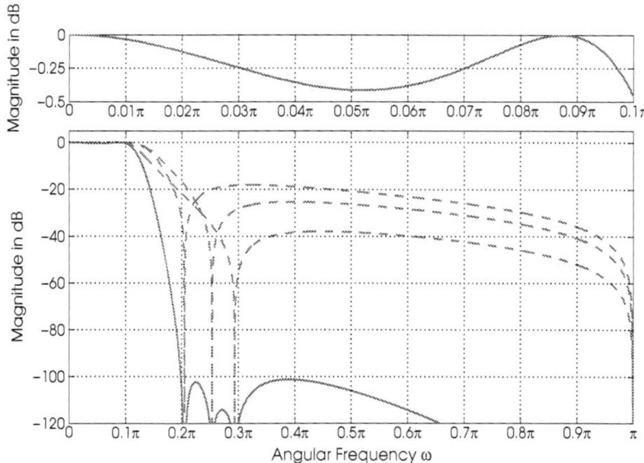

Fig. 10. Some magnitude responses for the cascade of four optimized finite-precision LWD filters in Example 1. The solid and dashed lines show the responses for the overall filter and the subfilters, respectively. Two subfilters are identical (the dashed line with the lowest attenuation).

smaller. For $K = 1$ and $K = 4$, these values are 0.98920 and 0.90138, respectively. When using the adaptors shown in Fig. 6, the output noise gains are 31.9 dB and 21.8 dB for $K = 1$ and $K = 4$, respectively. This means that for $K = 4$ roughly two fewer bits are required for the data representation to arrive at approximately the same output noise level as with the corresponding direct LWD filter.

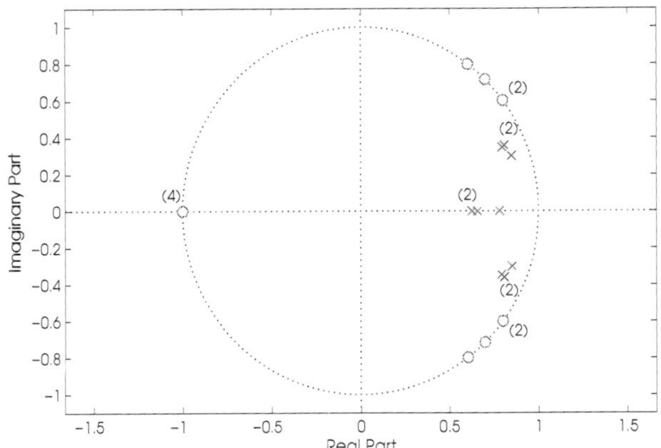

Fig. 11. Pole-zero plot for the cascade of four optimized finite-precision LWD filters in Example 1.

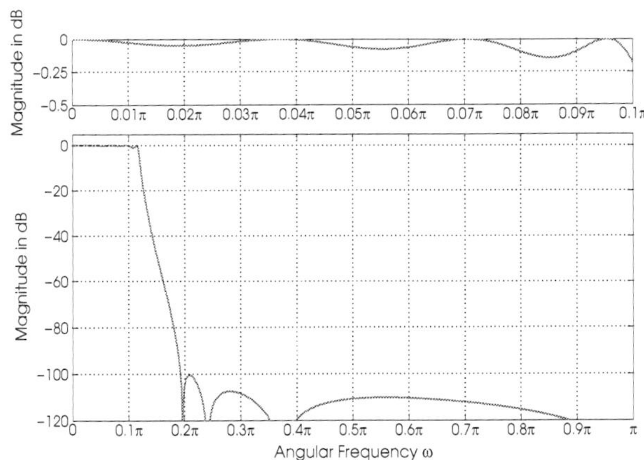

Fig. 12. Some magnitude responses for the optimized finite-precision direct LWD filter in Example 1.

6.2 Example 2

This example is included to illustrate the performance of the proposed overall synthesis scheme for designing approximately linear-phase finite-precision LWD filters as well as to compare these filters with their linear-phase FIR filter equivalents.

It is desired to design a low-pass filter with passband and stopband edges at $\omega_p = 0.05\pi$ and at $\omega_s = 0.1\pi$, respectively. The maximum allowable passband ripple is $A_p = 0.2$ dB ($\delta_p = 0.0228$) and the stopband attenuation is $A_s = 60$ dB ($\delta_s = 10^{-3}$). The maximum allowable phase deviation in the passband from the average slope, in turn, is $\Delta = 0.5$ degrees. In this case, an excellent phase performance is obtained by using a ninth-order LWD filter.

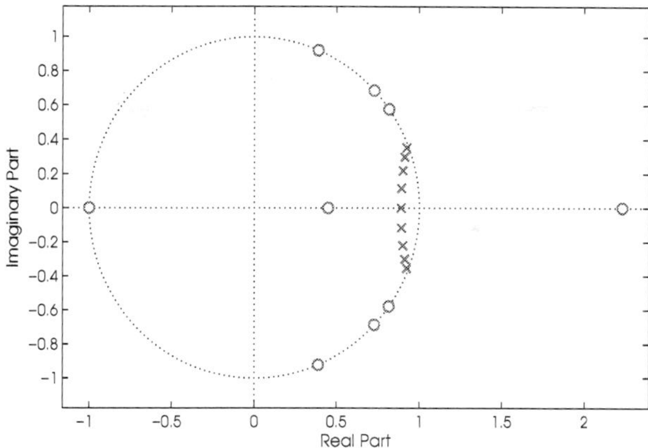

Fig. 13. Pole-zero plot for the optimized finite-precision direct LWD filter in Example 1.

$A_0^{(1)}(z)$	$A_1^{(1)}(z)$
$\gamma_0^{(1)} = 1 - 2^{-4}$	
$\gamma_1^{(1)} = -1 + 2^{-5} - 2^{-7}$	$\gamma_5^{(1)} = -1 + 2^{-4} + 2^{-7} + 2^{-9}$
$\gamma_2^{(1)} = 1 - 2^{-5} + 2^{-7}$	$\gamma_6^{(1)} = 1 - 2^{-6} - 2^{-9} + 2^{-11}$
$\gamma_3^{(1)} = -1 + 2^{-3} - 2^{-6} + 2^{-10}$	$\gamma_7^{(1)} = -1 + 2^{-3} - 2^{-8}$
$\gamma_4^{(1)} = 1 - 2^{-7} - 2^{-10}$	$\gamma_8^{(1)} = 1 - 2^{-8}$

Table 5. Optimized finite-precision adaptor coefficients for the approximately linear-phase LWD filter in Example 2.

The filter specifications are met if the adaptor coefficient are represented using four power-of-two terms with eleven fractional bits ($R = 4$ and $P_R = 11$) as given in Table 5. A total of ten adders and/or subtracters are required to implement all the adaptor coefficients when the adaptors shown in Fig. 6 are utilized. The magnitude and phase characteristics of the resulting filter are depicted in Fig. 14, whereas Fig. 15 gives the pole-zero plot.

The minimum order of a linear-phase FIR filter to meet the same magnitude specifications is 107, requiring 107 delay elements and 54 multipliers when exploiting coefficient symmetry. The delay of the linear-phase FIR equivalent is 53.5 samples, whereas for the proposed recursive filter the delay is only 40.9 samples.

6.3 Example 3

This example is included to illustrate the performance of the proposed overall design algorithm for synthesizing recursive Nth-band decimators. It is desired to design an eighth-band ($N = 8$) filter with the passband edge at $\omega_p = 0.0785\pi = 0.628\pi/8$. The minimum stopband attenuation is at least $A_s = 60$ dB ($\delta_s = 10^{-3}$). In this case, the stopband region, as given by (17), is $\Omega_s = [0.1715\pi, 0.3285\pi] \cup [0.4215\pi, 0.5785\pi] \cup [0.6715\pi, 0.8285\pi] \cup [0.9215\pi, \pi]$, that is, the aliasing into to the transition band $[0.0785\pi, 0.125\pi]$ is allowed from the bands $[0.3285\pi, 0.4215\pi]$, $[0.5785\pi, 0.6715\pi]$, and $[0.8285\pi, 0.9215\pi]$.

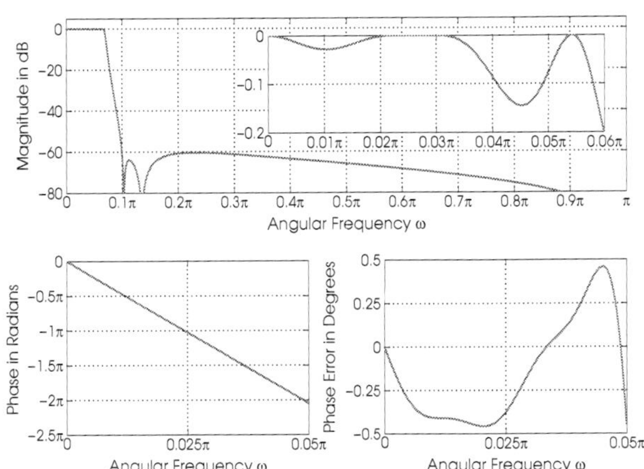

Fig. 14. Magnitude and phase responses for the optimized finite-precision approximately linear-phase LWD filter in Example 2.

For the three-stage design, the only option to factor the sampling rate conversion ratio is $N_1 = N_2 = N_3 = 2$. This factorization gives, according to the discussion of Subsection 2.3, rise to a single-stage equivalent with the transfer function of the form $H(z) = H_1(z)H_2(z^2)H_3(z^4)$ where $H_1(z)$, $H_2(z)$, and $H_3(z)$ are half-band LWD filters. According to the design scheme described in (Renfors & Saramäki, 1987), the desired 60-dB stopband attenuation is achieved by simultaneously determining these three subfilters such that $H_3(z^4)$, $H_2(z^2)$, and $H_1(z)$ primarily take care of providing this attenuation on $[0.1715\pi, 0.3285\pi] \cup [0.6715\pi, 0.8285\pi]$, $[0.4215\pi, 0.5785\pi]$, and $[0.9215\pi, \pi]$, respectively. The resulting minimum orders of $H_1(z)$, $H_2(z)$, and $H_3(z)$ to simultaneously meet the given specifications become 3, 5, and 7, respectively. When following the notations of Subsection 2.3, the orders $L_0^{(k)}$ and $L_1^{(k)}$ of the branch transfer functions $A_0^{(k)}(z)$ and $A_1^{(k)}(z)$ of $H_k(z)$ for $k = 1, 2, 3$ become $L_0^{(1)} = 1$ and $L_1^{(1)} = 0$; $L_0^{(2)} = L_0^{(2)} = 1$; and $L_0^{(3)} = 2$ and $L_1^{(3)} = 1$; respectively.
The initial adaptor coefficient values for $H_3(z^4)$ are $\gamma_1^{(3)} = -0.085\,523$, $\gamma_2^{(3)} = -0.718\,273$, and $\gamma_3^{(3)} = -0.326\,452$, for $H_2(z^2)$, $\gamma_1^{(2)} = -0.116\,797$ and $\gamma_2^{(2)} = -0.548\,630$, and for $H_1(z)$, $\gamma_1^{(1)} = -0.338\,473$. The stopband attenuations provided by these initial sub-stages $H_3(z^4)$, $H_2(z^2)$, and $H_1(z)$ in the stopband regions they primarily concentrate on are 73.21 dB, 83.97 dB, and 66.45 dB, respectively. The smallest and largest values for the adaptor coefficients of the sub-stages $H_3(z^4)$, $H_2(z^2)$, and $H_1(z)$ after applying the infinite-precision optimization of Subsection 5.2 are given in Table 6.
For this overall filter, the maximum number of power-of-two terms required to implement all the adaptor coefficients is four ($R = 4$), whereas eight fractional bits ($P_R = 8$) are required to meet the magnitude specifications. For this coefficient representation form, the number of discrete coefficient values between the smallest and largest values for the coefficients of $H_3(z^3)$ is 14, 21, and 33, that is, the number of coefficient combinations for the last stage is $14 \cdot 21 \cdot 33 = 9702$. The number of discrete coefficient values between the smallest and largest values for the coefficients of $H_2(z^2)$ are 19 and 33, that is, the number of coefficient

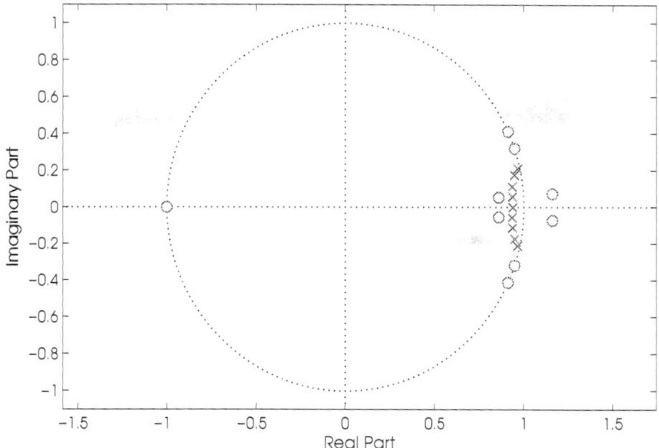

Fig. 15. Pole-zero plot for the optimized finite-precision approximately linear- phase LWD filter in Example 2.

$H_3(z^4)$	$A_0^{(3)}(z^4)$	$\gamma_1^{(3)(\min)} = -0.111\,647$		$\gamma_1^{(3)(\max)} = -0.057\,811$	
		$\gamma_2^{(3)(\min)} = -0.771\,093$		$\gamma_2^{(3)(\max)} = -0.681\,117$	
	$A_1^{(3)}(z^4)$	$\gamma_3^{(3)(\min)} = -0.395\,188$		$\gamma_3^{(3)(\max)} = -0.268\,425$	
$H_2(z^2)$	$A_0^{(2)}(z^2)$	$\gamma_1^{(2)(\min)} = -0.156\,770$		$\gamma_1^{(2)(\max)} = -0.082\,365$	
	$A_1^{(2)}(z^2)$	$\gamma_2^{(2)(\min)} = -0.618\,978$		$\gamma_2^{(2)(\max)} = -0.489\,915$	
$H_1(z)$	$A_0^{(1)}(z)$	$\gamma_1^{(1)(\min)} = -0.341\,785$		$\gamma_1^{(1)(\max)} = -0.336\,582$	

Table 6. The smallest and largest infinite-precision coefficient values for the subfilters $H_3(z^4)$, $H_2(z^2)$, and $H_1(z)$ in Example 3.

$H_3(z^4)$	$A_0^{(3)}(z^4)$	$\gamma_1^{(3)} = -0.078\,125\,00 = -2^{-4} - 2^{-6}$
		$\gamma_2^{(3)} = -0.710\,937\,50 = -1 + 2^{-2} + 2^{-5} + 2^{-7}$
	$A_1^{(3)}(z^4)$	$\gamma_3^{(3)} = -0.312\,500\,00 = -2^{-2} - 2^{-4}$
$H_2(z^2)$	$A_0^{(2)}(z^2)$	$\gamma_1^{(2)} = -0.125\,000\,00 = -2^{-3}$
	$A_1^{(2)}(z^2)$	$\gamma_2^{(2)} = -0.562\,500\,00 = -2^{-1} - 2^{-4}$
$H_1(z)$	$A_0^{(1)}(z)$	$\gamma_1^{(1)} = -0.339\,843\,75 = -2^{-1} + 2^{-3} + 2^{-5} + 2^{-8}$

Table 7. Optimized finite-precision coefficient values for the three-stage eighth-band filter in Example 3.

combinations for the second stage is 627. For the first stage with transfer function $H_1(z)$, there exists only one discrete coefficient value between the smallest and largest values of the single coefficient. The CPU time required when using a Fortran 95 program on a 1.4 GHz Pentium-

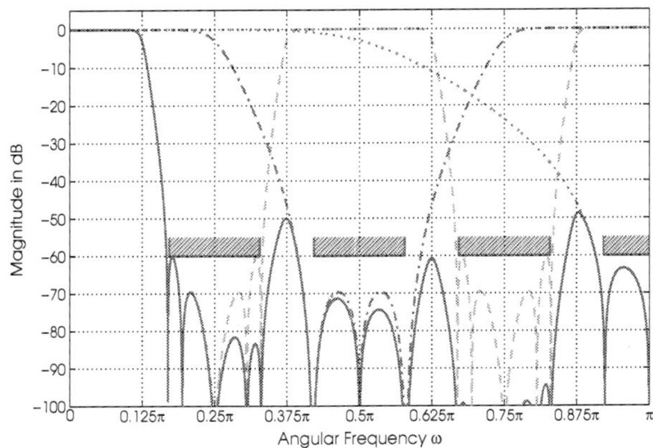

Fig. 16. Magnitude responses for the optimized finite-precision three-stage eighth-band decimator in Example 3. The solid line gives the magnitude response for the single-stage equivalent $H_1(z)H_2(z^2)H_3(z^4)$, whereas the dotted, dot-dashed, and dashed lines give the responses for $H_1(z)$, $H_2(z^2)$, and $H_3(z^4)$, respectively.

$$A_0^{(1)}(z) \quad \gamma_1^{(1)} = -0.01953125 = -2^{-6} - 2^{-8} \qquad \gamma_2^{(1)} = -0.53125000 = -2^{-1} - 2^{-5}$$
$$A_1^{(1)}(z) \quad \gamma_1^{(1)} = -0.04687500 = -2^{-4} + 2^{-6} \qquad \gamma_2^{(1)} = -0.62500000 = -2^{-1} - 2^{-3}$$
$$A_2^{(1)}(z) \quad \gamma_1^{(1)} = -0.07812500 = -2^{-4} - 2^{-6} \qquad \gamma_2^{(1)} = -0.71875000 = -1 + 2^{-2} + 2^{-5}$$
$$A_3^{(1)}(z) \quad \gamma_1^{(1)} = -0.12109375 = -2^{-3} + 2^{-8} \qquad \gamma_2^{(1)} = -0.80859375 = -1 + 2^{-2} - 2^{-4} + 2^{-8}$$
$$A_4^{(1)}(z) \quad \gamma_1^{(1)} = -0.17968750 = -2^{-2} + 2^{-4} + 2^{-7} \quad \gamma_2^{(1)} = -0.87890625 = -1 + 2^{-3} - 2^{-8}$$
$$A_5^{(1)}(z) \quad \gamma_1^{(1)} = -0.24218750 = -2^{-2} + 2^{-7} \qquad \gamma_2^{(1)} = -0.94921875 = -1 + 2^{-4} - 2^{-6} + 2^{-8}$$
$$A_6^{(1)}(z) \quad \gamma_1^{(1)} = -0.32031250 = -2^{-2} - 2^{-4} - 2^{-7}$$
$$A_7^{(1)}(z) \quad \gamma_1^{(1)} = -0.43359375 = -2^{-1} + 2^{-4} + 2^{-8}$$

Table 8. Optimized finite-precision adaptor coefficients for the single-stage eighth-band decimator in Example 3.

M to evaluate all these combinations with $\Xi_s = 100$ stopband grid points was less than one second.

The number of adders and/or subtracters required to implement all the adaptor coefficients is seven when the adaptors shown in Fig. 6 are utilized. The optimized finite-precision coefficients values are given in Table 7, whereas the magnitude responses for the sub-stages as well as for the single-stage equivalent are depicted in Fig. 16. The pole-zero plot for this equivalent is, in turn, shown in Fig. 17. The passband variation and the minimum stopband attenuation for the optimized finite-precision overall filter are $A_p = -4.278 \cdot 10^{-6}$ dB and $A_s = 60.21$ dB, respectively. An efficient implementation of the optimized eight-band decimator is depicted in Fig. 18

For the single-stage design, that is, for a direct eighth-band filter, the minimum orders $L_n^{(1)}$ of the eight all-pass branch filters $A_n^{(1)}(z)$ for $n = 0, 1, \ldots, 7$ to meet the given specifications are $L_n^{(1)} = 2$ for $n = 0, 1, \ldots, 5$ and $L_6^{(1)} = L_7^{(1)} = 1$ so that the minimum number of multipli-

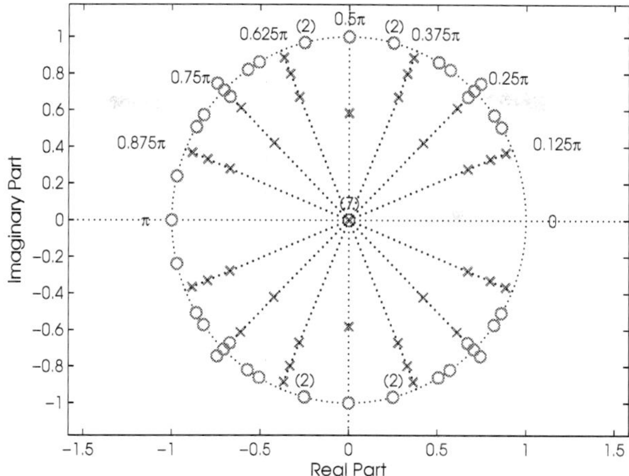

Fig. 17. Pole-zero plot for the optimized finite-precision three-stage eighth-band decimator in Example 3.

ers in the overall implementation is 14. The stopband attenuation of this initial filter is 60.84 dB. Again, the specifications are met by $R = 4$ and $P_R = 8$ even though the allowable margin for the coefficient quantization is only 0.84 dB. The specifications are met by the adaptor coefficients given in Table 8. In this case, the number of adders and/or subtracters required to implement all the coefficients is 17 when the adaptors shown in Fig. 6 are utilized. The passband variation and the minimum stopband attenuation for this optimized finite-precision single-stage decimation filter are $A_p = 1.584 \cdot 10^{-5}$ dB and $A_s = 60.18$ dB, respectively. The magnitude response and the pole-zero plot for this decimation filter are depicted in Figs. 19 and 20, respectively.

7. Conclusions

A systematic three-step algorithm has been developed for designing lattice wave digital (LWD) filters with short coefficient wordlength. The filter classes under consideration have been cascades of low-order LWD filters, approximately linear-phase LWD filters, and recursive Nth-band decimators and interpolators. The transfer functions, filter specifications, and optimization problems have been stated for each filter class under consideration. Then, the proposed three-step algorithm has been adapted for solving these optimization problems. The goal has been to find all the coefficient values such that the overall implementation does not require general multipliers. It has been shown that significant savings in the implementation cost are achieved by using the proposed technique. The efficiency and the robustness of the proposed algorithm has been demonstrated by means of several examples.

8. References

Ansari, R. & Liu, B. (1983). Efficient sampling rate alteration using recursive IIR digital filters, *IEEE Trans. Acoust., Speech, Signal Processing* **ASSP-31**: 1366–1373.

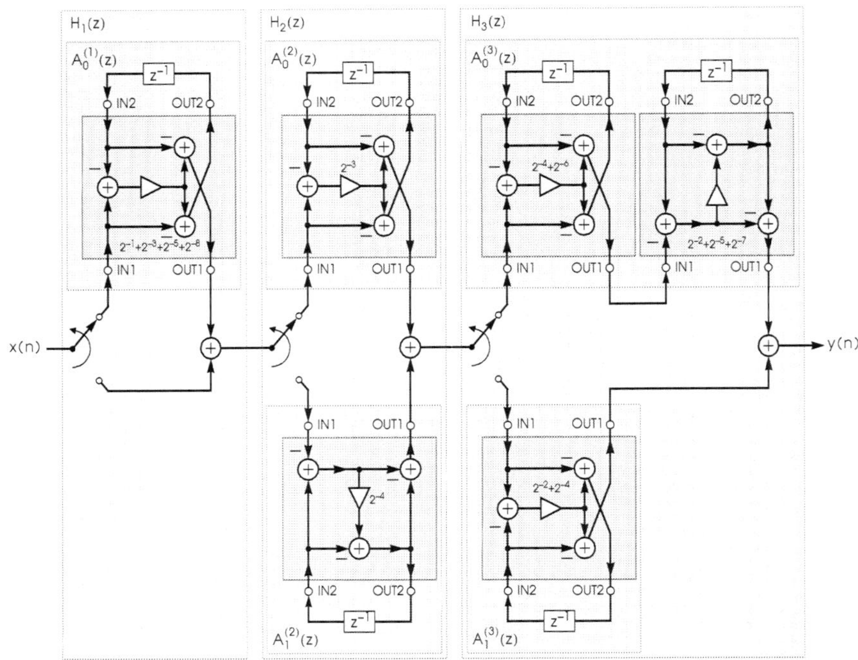

Fig. 18. An efficient implementation for the optimized finite-precision three-stage eighth-band decimator in Example 3.

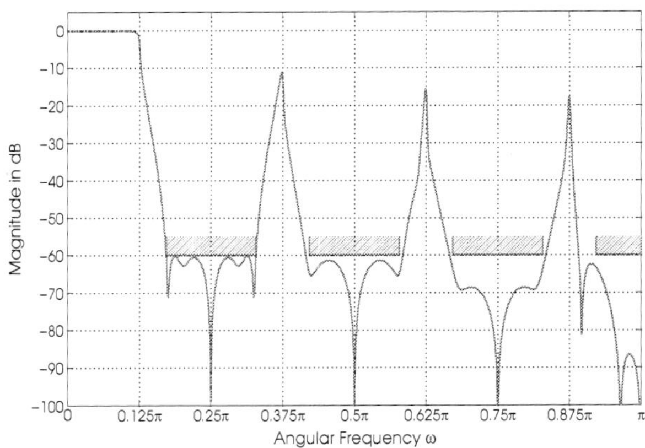

Fig. 19. Magnitude response for the optimized finite-precision single-stage eighth-band decimator in Example 3.

Antoniou, A. (1993). *Digital Filters: Analysis, Design, and Applications*, 2nd edn, McGraw-Hill.

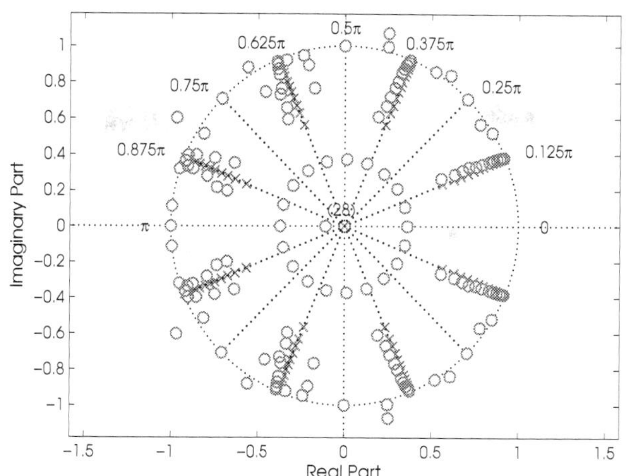

Fig. 20. Pole-zero plot for the optimized finite-precision single-stage eighth-band decimator in Example 3.

Bregović, R. (2003). *Optimal design of perfect-reconstruction and nearly perfect-reconstruction multirate filter banks*, Dr. Tech. dissertation, Dept. of Inform. Tech., Tampere Univ. of Tech, Finland, Tampere, Finland.

Brophy, F. J. & Salazar, A. C. (1975). Two design techniques for digital phase network, *Bell System Technical J.* **54**: 767–781.

Coleman, T., Branch, M. A. & Grace, A. (1999). *Optimization Toolbox User's Guide*, The MathWorks, Inc. Version 2.

Crochiere, R. E. & Rabiner, L. R. (1983). *Multirate Digital Signal Processing*, NJ: Prentice-Hall, Englewood Cliffs.

Deczky, A. G. (1972). Synthesis of recursive digital filters using the minimum-p error criterion, *IEEE Trans. Audio Electroacoust.* **AU-20**: 257–263.

Dutta, S. R. K. & Vidyasagar, M. (1977). New algorithms for constrained minimax optimization, *Math. Program.* **13**: 140–155.

Fettweis, A. (1986). Wave digital filters: Theory and practice, *Proc. IEEE* **74**: 270–327.

Fettweis, A., Levin, H. & Sedlmeyer, A. (1974). Wave digital lattice filters, *Int. J. Circuit Theory Appl.* **2**(2): 203–211.

Földvári-Orosz, J., Henk, T. & Simonyi, E. (1991). Simultaneous amplitude and phase approximation for lumped and sampled filters, *Int. J. Circuit Theory Appl.* **19**: 77–100.

Gazsi, L. (1985). Explicit formulas for lattice wave digital filters, *IEEE Trans. Circuits Syst.* **CAS-32**(1): 68–88.

Herrmann, O., Rabiner, L. R. & Chan, D. S. (1973). Practical design rules for optimum finite impulse response lowpass digital filters, *Bell Syst. Tech. J.* **52**(6): 769–799.

Jaworski, B. & Saramäki, T. (1994). Linear phase IIR filters composed of two parallel allpass sections, *Proc. IEEE Int. Symp. Circuits Syst.*, London, England, pp. 537–540.

Jones, A., Lawson, S. & Wicks, T. (1991). Design of cascaded allpass structures with magnitude and delay constraint using simulated annealing and quasi-Newton methods, *Proc. IEEE Int. Symp. Circuits Syst.*, Vol. 5, Singapore, pp. 2439–2442.

Lawson, S. & Wicks, T. (1992). Design of efficient digital filters satisfying arbitrary loss and delay specifications, *Proc. Inst. Elect. Eng., Pt. G* **139**: 611–620.

Leeb, F. (1991). Lattice wave digital filters with simultaneous conditions on amplitude and phase, *Proc. IEEE Int. Conf. Acoustics, Speech, and Signal Processing*, Toronto, Canada, pp. 1645–1648.

Milić, L. D. & Lutovac, M. D. (1999). Design of multiplierless elliptic IIR filters with a small quantization error, *IEEE Trans. Signal Processing* **47**: 469–479.

Ohlsson, H., Gustafsson, O. & Wanhammar, L. (2001). Arithmetic transformations for increased maximal sample rate of bit-parallel bireciprocal lattice wave digital filters, *Proc. IEEE Int. Symp. Circuits Syst.*, Sydney, Australia.

Rabiner, L. & Gold, B. (1975). *Theory and Application of Digital Signal Processing*, Englewood Cliffs, NJ: Prentice-Hall.

Regalia, P. A. (1993). Special filter design, *in* S. K. Mitra & J. F. Kaiser (eds), *Handbook for Digital Signal Processing*, John Wiley and Sons, New York, chapter 13, pp. 907–980.

Regalia, P. A., Mitra, S. K. & Vaidyanathan, P. P. (1988). The digital all-pass filter: A versatile signal processing building block, *Proc. IEEE* **76**(1): 19–37.

Renfors, M. & Saramäki, T. (1986). A class of approximately linear phase digital filters composed of allpass subfilters, *Proc. IEEE Int. Symp. Circuits Syst.*, San Jose, CA, pp. 678–681.

Renfors, M. & Saramäki, T. (1987). Recursive Nth-band digital filters — Part I: Design and properties; Part II: Design of multistage decimators and interpolators, *IEEE Trans. Circuits Syst.* **CAS-34**(1): 24–51.

Renfors, M. & Zigouris, E. (1988). Signal processor implementation of digital all-pass filters, *IEEE Trans. Acoust., Speech, Signal Processing* **36**: 714–729.

Saramäki, T. (1985). On the design of digital filters as a sum of two all-pass filters, *IEEE Trans. Circuits Syst.* **CAS-32**(11): 1191–1193.

Saramäki, T. (1993). Finite impulse response filter design, *in* S. K. Mitra & J. F. Kaiser (eds), *Handbook for Digital Signal Processing*, New York: John Wiley and Sons, chapter 4, pp. 155–277.

Saramäki, T. & Bregović, R. (2002). Multirate systems and filter banks, *in* G. Jovanovic-Dolecek (ed.), *Multirate Systems: Design & Applications*, Hershey: Idea Group Publishing, chapter II, pp. 27–85.

Saramäki, T. & Renfors, M. (1987). A novel approach for the design of IIR filters as a tapped cascaded interconnection of identical allpass subfilters, *Proc. IEEE Int. Symp. Circuits Syst.*, Philadelphia, PA, pp. 629–632.

Saramäki, T. & Renfors, M. (1995). A Remez-type algorithm for designing digital filters composed of all-pass sections based on phase approximations, *Proc. 38th Midwest Symp. Circuits Syst.*, Rio de Janeiro, Brazil, pp. 571–575.

Saramäki, T. & Renfors, M. (1998). Nth-band filter design, *Proc. IX European Signal Processing Conf.*, Island of Rhodes, Greece, pp. 1943–1947.

Saramäki, T. & Ritoniemi, T. (1993). Optimization of digital filter structures for VLSI implementation, *Automatica* **34**: 111–116.

Saramäki, T. & Yli-Kaakinen, J. (2002). Design of digital filters and filter banks by optimization: Applications, *Technical Report No. 15*, Tampere International Center for Signal Processing. 119 pages.

Schüßler, H. (2010). *Digitale Signalverarbeitung 2*, Springer-Verlag, Berlin.

Surma-aho, K. (1997). *Design of approximately linear-phase recursive filters*, Master's thesis, Dept. of Electr. Eng., Tampere Univ. of Tech., Finland.

Surma-aho, K. & Saramäki, T. (1999). A systematic technique for designing approximately linear phase recursive digital filters, *IEEE Trans. Circuits Syst. II* **46**(7): 956–962.

Taxén, L. (1981). Polyphase filter banks using wave digital filters, *IEEE Trans. Acoust., Speech, Signal Processing* **ASSP-29**: 423–428.

Vollmer, M. & Kopmann, H. (2002). A novel approach to an IIR digital filter bank with approximately linear phase, *Proc. IEEE Int. Symp. Circuits Syst.*, Vol. II, Scottsdale, Arizona, pp. 512–515.

Wanhammar, L. (1998). *DSP Integrated Circuits*, New York: Academic.

Yli-Kaakinen, J. (1998). *Optimization of recursive digital filters for practical implementation*, Dipl. Eng. thesis, Dept. of Elect. Eng., Tampere Univ. of Tech., Finland.

Yli-Kaakinen, J. (2002). *Optimization of digital filters for practical implementations*, Dr. Tech. dissertation, Dept. of Inform. Tech., Tampere Univ. of Tech., Finland.

Yli-Kaakinen, J., Kupiainen, T., Hu, M., Uusikartano, R. & Renfors, M. (1999). Multirate digital filter design for a PAL TV modulator, *IEEE Trans. Consumer Electron.* **45**(3): 970–974.

Yli-Kaakinen, J. & Saramäki, T. (1999a). Design of very low-sensitivity and low-noise recursive filters using a cascade of low-order lattice wave digital filters, *IEEE Trans. Circuits Syst. II* **46**(7): 906–914.

Yli-Kaakinen, J. & Saramäki, T. (1999b). An efficient algorithm for the design of lattice wave digital filters with short coefficient wordlength, *Proc. IEEE Int. Symp. Circuits Syst.*, Vol. III, Orlando, FL, pp. 443–448.

Yli-Kaakinen, J. & Saramäki, T. (2000). An algorithm for the design of multiplierless approximately linear-phase lattice wave digital filters, *Proc. IEEE Int. Symp. Circuits Syst.*, Vol. 2, Geneva, Switzerland, pp. 77–80.

Yli-Kaakinen, J. & Saramäki, T. (2005). A systematic algorithm for designing multiplierless computationally efficient recursive decimators and interpolators, *Proc. 2005 IEEE Int. Symp. Image and Signal Process. Analysis*, Zagreb, Croatia, pp. 167–172.

Yli-Kaakinen, J. & Saramäki, T. (2007). A systematic algorithm for the desing of lattice wave digital filters with short-coefficient wordlength, *IEEE Trans. Circuits Syst. I* **54**(8): 1838–1851.